HARVARD STUDIES IN BUSINESS HISTORY

1. JOHN JACOB ASTOR, BUSINESS MAN
BY KENNETH WIGGINS PORTER

2. JAY COOKE, PRIVATE BANKER
BY HENRIETTA M. LARSON

3. THE JACKSONS AND THE LEES: TWO GENERATIONS OF MASSACHUSETTS MERCHANTS, 1765–1844
BY KENNETH WIGGINS PORTER

4. THE MASSACHUSETTS–FIRST NATIONAL BANK OF BOSTON, 1784–1934
BY N. S. B. GRAS

5. THE HISTORY OF AN ADVERTISING AGENCY: N. W. AYER & SON AT WORK, 1869–1949
REVISED EDITION, BY RALPH M. HOWER

6. MARKETING LIFE INSURANCE: ITS HISTORY IN AMERICA
BY *J.* OWEN STALSON

7. HISTORY OF MACY'S OF NEW YORK, 1858–1919: CHAPTERS IN THE EVOLUTION OF THE DEPARTMENT STORE
BY RALPH M. HOWER

8. THE WHITESMITHS OF TAUNTON: A HISTORY OF REED & BARTON, 1824–1943
BY GEORGE SWEET GIBB

9. DEVELOPMENT OF TWO BANK GROUPS IN THE CENTRAL NORTHWEST: A STUDY IN BANK POLICY AND ORGANIZATION
BY CHARLES STERLING POPPLE

10. THE HOUSE OF HANCOCK: BUSINESS IN BOSTON, 1724–1775
BY W. T. BAXTER

11. TIMING A CENTURY: HISTORY OF THE WALTHAM WATCH COMPANY
BY C. W. MOORE

12. GUIDE TO BUSINESS HISTORY: MATERIALS FOR THE STUDY OF AMERICAN BUSINESS HISTORY AND SUGGESTIONS FOR THEIR USE
BY HENRIETTA M. LARSON

13. PEPPERELL'S PROGRESS: HISTORY OF A COTTON TEXTILE COMPANY, 1844–1945
BY EVELYN H. KNOWLTON

14. THE HOUSE OF BARING IN AMERICAN TRADE AND FINANCE: ENGLISH MERCHANT BANKERS AT WORK, 1763–1861
BY RALPH W. HIDY

15. THE WHITIN MACHINE WORKS SINCE 1831: A TEXTILE MACHINERY COMPANY IN AN INDUSTRIAL VILLAGE
BY THOMAS R. NAVIN

16. THE SACO–LOWELL SHOPS: TEXTILE MACHINERY BUILDING IN NEW ENGLAND, 1813–1949
BY GEORGE SWEET GIBB

HARVARD STUDIES IN BUSINESS HISTORY
XVI

EDITED BY N. S. B. GRAS
STRAUS PROFESSOR OF BUSINESS HISTORY
AND HENRIETTA M. LARSON
ASSOCIATE PROFESSOR OF BUSINESS HISTORY

GRADUATE SCHOOL OF BUSINESS ADMINISTRATION
GEORGE F. BAKER FOUNDATION
HARVARD UNIVERSITY

Distributed in Great Britain by

GEOFFREY CUMBERLEGE

OXFORD UNIVERSITY PRESS

LONDON

The York Mills, Saco, Maine, about 1839

THE SACO-LOWELL SHOPS

TEXTILE MACHINERY BUILDING IN NEW ENGLAND

1813–1949

by

GEORGE SWEET GIBB

Formerly Instructor in Business History
Graduate School of Business Administration
Harvard University
At present Senior Associate in Research
Business History Foundation, Inc.

HARVARD UNIVERSITY PRESS

CAMBRIDGE · MASSACHUSETTS

1950

PRINTED IN THE UNITED STATES OF AMERICA

To

RUTH

CONTENTS

PART II

THE ADVENTUROUS MIDDLE YEARS

SACO-LOWELL'S PARENT SHOPS FROM 1845 TO 1912

PART III

THE SACO-LOWELL SHOPS, 1912–1948

APPENDICES

ILLUSTRATIONS

TABLES

CHARTS

EDITORS' INTRODUCTION

The company's original plan for a history was to have the research done in its own advertising department and then have the material molded into a connected story presumably by someone within the concern. The work was actually begun, but by 1944 it was clear that it would never be completed on this basis. Accordingly, we at the Harvard School of Business were asked to undertake the task as soon as we could find a competent research man. The invitation could not be accepted until we learned whether there were records in sufficient quantity and of the right quality and whether there were older employees who could provide the leads and explanations. After visits to the Boston office, the Biddeford plant, and elsewhere, it was decided in October, 1944, that we could assume the responsibility. For several months the interviewing continued so that we should not miss the irreplaceable evidence of the older executives and workmen.

The end of the war brought Mr. George S. Gibb back to renewed opportunities for research in business history. His *Whitesmiths of Taunton* had demonstrated his insight into business problems and human nature as well as his capacity to record his findings in simple and revealing words. Saco-Lowell records and an over-all opportunity provided him with a new challenge. During a period of forty-one months he was largely engaged in the research and writing, for thirty-six months as instructor at the Harvard School of Business and for nearly five months as senior associate in research in the Business History Foundation in New York.

During the whole period of research and writing, the author has enjoyed the sympathetic coöperation of Mr. David F. Edwards, the president of the Saco-Lowell Shops, who has never questioned our insistence upon full information and complete freedom in stating facts and formulating conclusions. Mr. Edwards has shown the insight of the business man that he is and the scholar that he has never ceased to be.

An original hope was that at last in this history the author could dig deeply into operations so as to recapture the story of workers and machines, discipline, and the division of labor. In truth, however, the author has found enough difficulty in holding together the threads of organization and administrative policy. Had there been only one plant and had the records of internal operation been adequate, the story might have been different. As it is, some of the inside situations and operations could be set forth in the final chapter dealing with the most recent period.

Always there looms the question of what to emphasize in a history. There are *many* choices in recording crowded events in the long history of a business unit. If one has but little inside information, he will devote many pages to the general history of the times. If one has little knowledge of business problems and techniques, he will deal with the economic history of the period. But, in the writing of a business history much of the external world may well be left to the intelligent reader, and the major contributions must lie in the details of the principal story at hand. The interest of the social sciences would dictate the accumulation of materials which would go into the history of the industry (textile machinery in this case), business history in general, and ultimately social history. To popularize is to pad. The Harvard Studies in Business History have had the long-time contributions in mind without losing sight of readability. Mr. Gibb has followed the spirit of the Series, which indeed he has helped to create.

We wonder how significant it is that the burning questions of the economic historical past have so dimly flickered in the realities of business history. Think of those pressing problems of the tariff and coinage of silver that have loomed so large in political discussion and polemic strife, and yet seemingly cut so small a figure in the real life and work of the American people. Does this mean that the past has not been realistic or that we are now in later days missing something of importance?

In the long story of the manufacture of textile machinery in New England (1813–1949), we see through the eyes of the author many developments, problems, and solutions. We observe the flow of capital and management from mercantile capitalism to industrial capitalism. We see the rise of petty capitalists into the position of industrial capitalists or into the status of superintendents and foremen within an industrial capitalistic concern. We learn how Boston business men set up and managed manufactories in surrounding industrial satellites such as Waltham, Lowell, Newton, and Biddeford. We discover how effectively Americans have imitated English manufacturers and ultimately equaled or surpassed their performance. We note how continuous has been the improvement in mechanical operation, either through invention or through engineering refinement. Perhaps we are not surprised to observe how in the course of development there have been shifts from specialization to diversification and then back again, sometimes the only apparent merit being the challenge that lies in change. How disastrously keen the competition became in the first phase of industrial capitalism is clearly set forth. How this competition led to merger and reduction in the number of units with a probable increase in efficiency is also observed.

And, then, we learn from the author how, in spite of all efforts, disaster was threatened and rescue came from the outside — from State Street — in the form of financial capitalism through the combined efforts of Boston commercial banks, investment bankers, and their legal aides. How once more a single individual leader to whom were given both trust and support pulled a strong and steady oar and brought the leaky craft into the harbor. How the genius of an organization, often threatened with disaster, could rise again without government aid. How an unconscious tradition of coöperation of earnest management and skilled labor could overcome almost insuperable difficulties, the evidence indicating that neither capital nor labor was predatory during the long stretch of a hundred and thirty-six years. How clearly is illustrated the residual position of invested capital, which on the whole has been less rewarded than either the workers or the consumers. How obscure and still important a business can be, in peace and in war, when it does not cater directly to the people in producing consumers' goods. How a business unit can struggle on in an old region against the odds of high taxes, uncoöperative labor unions, and increasing distance from the developing market for machinery in the South. How a lack of financial strength can force a concern to improve its product so as to gain headway, or even to survive, in the face of great competition. How a single business unit can remain in the shadow of national capitalism and social democracy in peace, though not in war, without being greatly influenced.

This history has resulted from the coöperation of business and education. The Saco-Lowell Shops has financed the research, writing, and publication in large part. The Business History Foundation has assisted in the writing to the extent of allowing the author much free time in finishing the composition of the text and appendices. The Business Historical Society has financed the presentation and distribution of copies to its members; and in all these processes the work has been underwritten by the Harvard Graduate School of Business Administration.

N. S. B. Gras
Henrietta M. Larson

May 28, 1949

AUTHOR'S PREFACE

I SHOULD LIKE to make plain at the outset what the Saco-Lowell history is and what it is not. The pages which follow are intended as a study in business administration as it evolved in a group of related companies over a span of one hundred and thirty-six years. No reader (and I am thinking particularly of those who know the company well) should approach this book in the belief that it is, or could possibly hope to be, more than an outline of Saco-Lowell's history.

My greatest task over the past three years of compilation and writing has been to decide what to include and what to pass by. In certain areas, of course, the decision was not mine to make, for whole segments of Saco-Lowell history have been consigned to the fire. The process of record destruction in the present company and in parent organizations of earlier years has been carried out with remarkable thoroughness. This destruction obviously has been a by-product of extensive and frequent corporate changes, including the abandonment of entire plants and the attendant "house-cleaning" which so often paralyzes subsequent efforts to re-create the past from corporate records. The process of record destruction has certainly not been carried out with the historian's needs in mind, but neither, I believe, has it been undertaken with the deliberate intention of thwarting him. As to the historical material which has survived, my judgment is that what I have included constitutes the heart of the story and the most important information of all that has been unearthed. I do not ask the reader to agree with my judgment, but I should like him to know that selective judgment has been applied.

The preparation of this history took place amidst circumstances which probably have been unique in the field of business history, and which would not soon be repeated. At about the same time that the Saco-Lowell project was conceived, the Whitin Machine Works also authorized a history. The two projects, involving the two competing companies which at present constitute a substantial part of the preparatory textile machinery industry, were actually launched within a few weeks of each other, and proceeded together to completion in adjacent offices and under common editorial guidance. Mr. Thomas R. Navin, compiler and author of the Whitin study, and I have worked independently in our own record collections and have reached our separate conclusions. This simultaneous double effort in one relatively narrow field has unquestionably resulted in a higher degree of coverage and accuracy than would otherwise have been possible; and the two books, considered together, give a fair industry picture — something which is not always possible in a single history of a single company. Moreover, the difference in the two companies proved to be so profound that the histories are quite unlike in treatment, and the reader will find less duplication in content than he might reasonably anticipate. The two volumes supplement rather than overlap one another. Mr. Navin's friendship and coöperation and the unusual opportunity for three years of close association with one devoted to a task almost identical to my own have been of inestimable value in the preparation of the Saco-Lowell history.

There has been another unique aspect to the compilation of this history. I should like to point out the contributions made to this book by Saco-Lowell's president, Mr. David F. Edwards. Business historians will, I think, agree with my statement that impartiality and intellectual honesty are not always encountered in the successful business man at the zenith of his career — at least, these qualities can easily, if unconsciously, be submerged when he comments on his own company. Successful industrialists have been known to become scholars after retirement, but the experience of finding a scholarly mind actively functioning behind an executive desk is by no means a usual one. I found my chapters being subjected to penetrating criticism by Mr. Edwards, not only as to facts presented (the only area in which many executives are capable of assisting an author), but also at every conceivable editorial level. He has corrected my spelling and challenged my theories. My notes covering many hours of conversation with Mr. Edwards range from the most minute operational details to the broadest analyses of company, industry, national, and international trends. Some of my most severe criticisms of company administration have been derived from information or leads furnished by him. His objectivity and frankness at first startled me, and I now confess with considerable embarrassment that initial incredulity drove me to check and recheck his observations against other sources of information. His ready acquiescence and prompt assistance in enabling me to contact men who, as both he and I knew, would criticize his administration severely and often unfairly is but one example of that objectivity. The danger in all this, which I readily confess, is that in profiting by Mr. Edwards' unusual contributions I might have become dulled in perception and partial in spirit. I can only say that this danger has been constantly in my mind throughout the preparation of this work and that I have done my best to be as objective as Mr. Edwards himself has been in our many talks. The reader can best judge after he has examined the final two chapters of this book.

I can scarcely hope to thank individually all those in the Saco-Lowell Shops who helped and encouraged me. Every person with whom I came in contact was coöperative and interested. The research task was thereby made not only profitable in results achieved, but a very real personal pleasure as well. Many persons in the Boston office and at the Biddeford plant have been not just informants but friends. I hope that I shall be forgiven on the grounds of professional honesty for having occasionally criticized the business policies and management of those who have helped me most, and for employing knowledge imparted by them to support conclusions which in some instances, I feel sure, they would deny or wish left unstated.

I have been assisted by a very great number of persons outside the company — librarians, bankers, manufacturers, lawyers, local historians, and residents of Biddeford, Saco, Portland, Newton, and Lowell. Without such help that area of the history which lies outside the record books would have been difficult to penetrate, and the last three chapters, in particular, could scarcely have been written. The names of these people would mean nothing to the reader of this book; to me they stand for the ultimate in generous assistance and stimulating interest.

Any volume in the Harvard Studies in Business History is, by definition, the culmination of a group effort. I can add little to what authors of preceding works in the Series have repeatedly said about the experience of working under Professor N. S. B. Gras and with the Business History group at the Harvard School of Business. Professor Gras nurses these volumes to life by a quite indefinable process of inspiration. Those who have worked under him will at once recognize what I mean to say, but there is little I can tell the reader who is personally unacquainted with Professor Gras as a scholar, administrator, and friend.

Dr. Henrietta M. Larson, co-editor of the Harvard Studies in Business History, has been most generous in allowing me time from other tasks to complete the Saco-Lowell manuscript, and association with her has been prolific of stimulating ideas. Mrs. Elsie Hight Bishop prepared the index for this book, and her keen eye and sharp pencil bridged the forbidding gap between manuscript and printed page. Her task has been an unusually difficult one, and the reader will find that it has been well done. I have had the benefit of research assistance from Mrs. Martha Starr and Miss Elva Tooker. Mrs. Evelyn H. Knowlton cleared certain difficult avenues of research through her work on the history of the Pepperell Manufacturing Company, and speeded my efforts by many weeks. I have been more than fortunate, too, in receiving the advice of Miss Josepha M. Perry in many matters relating to form and content of the book. Miss Helen F. Ballou and Mr. Richmond Fletcher Bingham spent much time in the preparation of charts and illustrations, and Mrs. Whitman C. Kearns completed the final typing of the manuscript. Beyond the specific and indispensable assistance of these persons, the interest and understanding of those with whom I have worked and lived over the past three years has played a major part in the writing of this history.

I cannot seem to phrase the final acknowledgment with any degree of adequacy. Ruth, my wife, worked beside me faithfully and cheerfully. She made the project her interest because it was mine, and she gave up many things for me and for my work. In her memory and because of her very great devotion, I should like to have this book recognized for what it is — as our book, rather than mine alone.

George Sweet Gibb

Part One

THE FORMATIVE YEARS, 1813–1853

CHAPTER I

ORIGINS OF THE THREE PARENT COMPANIES 1813–1825

Over the course of a century, machines have molded civilization into new patterns. Much is known of the users and the products of those machines; little about the men who made them. The history of the Saco-Lowell Shops is a story of machine-builders — an important segment in an almost completely neglected chapter of American history.

Saco-Lowell has its origins in the early years of the nineteenth century when the small manufacturer of the countryside, oblivious to his bright destiny, tinkered hopefully with new mechanical ideas. This was the start of the American Industrial Revolution, in which Saco-Lowell's beginnings are entwined and which the textile-machinery builders did much to speed.

In the once thriving seaports, however, there was uneasiness and confusion. In Boston, business failures echoed ominously among the countinghouses on Long Wharf. Merchants still in the prime of life abruptly withdrew to their gardens, and some devoted their days of premature retirement to castigating the new age which they could neither understand nor tolerate. There was dissension in high places. In aristocratic mercantile circles the strong bonds of kinship were often strained as some men went the new way and others held steadfast to the old. Few could see it clearly, but an economic system was crumbling, and in its accelerating decay was threatening a whole social order. Saco-Lowell's parent companies were part and parcel of this upheaval — experiments in an experimental age, launched by merchant capital, managed by merchants who hoped to find in the untried field of manufactures a medium for creating new wealth and perpetuating old dynasties. These companies were clearly an answer to an economic challenge.

There are three beginnings of equal significance in Saco-Lowell's history — three principal companies came together to form the organization which, since 1912, has been known as the Saco-Lowell Shops. The three parent companies were organized at Waltham, Massachusetts, in 1813; at Newton, Massachusetts, in 1814; and at Saco, Maine, in 1825. The founding aim of each was to produce, not machines, but cloth. Each, nevertheless, sired an independent textile-machine shop. From the Boston Manufacturing Company at Waltham came the Lowell Machine Shop. From the Elliot Manufacturing Company at Newton came the Pettee Machine Works. From the Saco Manufacturing Company came the Saco Water Power Machine Shop. These three textile-machine shops originated some time after the first American efforts to produce textile machinery; but, while the pioneer firms gradually disappeared, these three shops grew and prospered and came, at one point, to dominate the industry. Leadership was sought, achieved, shared, thrown away, and recaptured with the changing fortunes of business; but at no point do the three companies play an insignificant part in the history of the textile machinery industry. That industry itself lies like a shadow behind the looms and spindles that clothe the world, dimly perceived, its outlines hitherto barely traced and scarcely traceable, but tremendously important in terms of industrial progress and invention. To that progress Saco-Lowell has contributed much, commencing with those stirring days in old Boston when Francis Cabot Lowell was designing not just a power loom, but a whole new manufacturing technique for the textile industry and the country.

1. 1813: The Waltham Venture

There were several cogent reasons for the departure of Francis Cabot Lowell and his family to England in the year 1810. Both he and his wife were sickly, and at that time it was to England that sickly Bostonians of means were beginning to go for rest and cure. That country was also sought by some as a haven of intellectual relief, and Lowell was determined to round out the education of his three boys in an atmosphere not alien to his class and interests. These reasons were reinforced by the remarkable confusion in mercantile affairs of the day. To a man of Lowell's training, disposition, and position a prolonged foreign excursion at this time could scarcely have been without commercial motive.

Francis Lowell had grown up in a commercial environment, into which he fitted with ease and success. His paternal forebears were clerics, but his mother was a Cabot. Francis followed the paternal line to Harvard and a law degree. From there he followed the maternal line to the countinghouse. His youth was an active one, though his body was frail. He marched with the Independent Cadets under Major T. H. Perkins, and he touched off an irreverent bonfire in Harvard Yard, for which he was "rusticated" to Bridgewater and placed under the watchful eye of a local clergyman for the remainder of his college career. In this suburban setting Lowell's scholastic abilities matured. His reverend caretaker in due course confessed that the youth who came to him an incendiary departed a scholar, with a happy genius in mathematics and a flair for calculating projecting eclipses.[1]

Lowell entered commercial life soon after 1793, in a prosperous era of trade and with the best of family connections. His initial ventures were made in partnership with his mother's brother, William Cabot. Trips to France, Canada, and throughout the seaboard States followed in natural course, for cosmopolitan knowledge paid cash premiums. Other trade alliances were formed: with importer Nathan Appleton; with his brother-in-law, Patrick Tracy Jackson; with Uriah Cutting, Boston merchant and promoter of public improvements. Letters from Jackson addressed "Dear Frank" reveal contacts with the India trade after 1802. In 1804 the powerful mercantile firm of J. and T. H. Perkins thought it expedient to seek Lowell's good will, noting that he was "extensively concerned in a distillery."[2] In 1805 Lowell and Cutting financed the extension of Broad Street, and built warehouses there. In 1807 the same associates became prominent among the "Proprietors of India Wharf," building the wharf itself and India Street. Somewhat later Lowell, in partnership with three Jackson brothers, was tapping the Canton trade and preparing to export flour to Spain. But now ill health and an apprehension induced by capricious politics indicated that a break with the past was imminent.

Trade had been prosperous for Lowell, the Cabots, the Jacksons, the Lees, the Appletons, and others of this highly integrated Boston and Salem merchant group. Francis Cabot Lowell himself, though only thirty-five years of age, had amassed a comfortable fortune by 1810. But that trade — with England, the Continent, India, Canton, and the Indies — had staggered at times. After 1807 the Non-Intercourse and Embargo Acts restricted and at times prohibited the movement of vessels. To Lowell and his associates the thought of a war with England which would further hamstring commerce was abhorrent. Political events in Washington were a cause of prolonged consternation among Boston Federalists. Seven long years of trade restriction and suppression by a "villainous government" administered by "republican vagabonds" provoked one crusty merchant to voice the despair of his class in his cry, "Spare Massachusetts and I care not what happens to the other States!" [3]

It would have been surprising indeed if Lowell by 1810 had not foreseen the end of immediate profits in foreign trade. It may well have been, however, that he saw more than this. Subsequent events indicate that Lowell sensed opportunity — that he, almost alone among his fellow Boston merchants, knew what was soon to come and what now must be done. The thriving example was there; the pound and thrust of the water wheel had already been acclaimed in places other than Boston as the heart-beat of American civilization.

By 1810, American mercantile capital had already been invested in the manufacture of yarn by water power. As early as 1786, attempts were being made to introduce the new English inventions of Sir Richard Arkwright and others into Massachusetts. Francis Lowell's own uncles, John, Andrew, and George Cabot, had set up a cotton factory in Beverly. This venture was boldly conceived, but not even a State land grant coupled with the sale of lottery tickets could lighten the increasing debt, or least of all make up for want of skill in the construction and use of the machinery. This and contemporary experiments were premature. Technical knowledge was inadequate. Much of the experimental effort was expended on introducing and improving the jenny. This machine was best adapted to manual operation, and did not possess the potentialities for large-scale production inherent in the water-driven Arkwright spinning frame.

It remained for Samuel Slater, financed by Providence merchants and assisted by native mechanics, to set up the first successful and profitable spinning factory in America. When Slater started his Arkwright machines in the old fulling mill at Pawtucket bridge in 1790, he provided an impelling stimulus to the industrialization of the country. It was principally from his mills that knowledge of textile machinery spread throughout the country. Slater-trained men left Pawtucket and started mills of their own, or built machinery for the few enterprising capitalists who sought to imitate Slater. There were also occasional fresh infusions of technical knowledge from England. The years of trade restriction and embargo bemoaned by the mercantile capitalists and the acts of government labeled in Boston as "tricks to amuse the mob" were hailed with more enthusiasm by manufacturers in the Blackstone Valley.[4] The "cotton factory fever" began to rage. By 1810 there were almost three hundred mills in operation in the country, and the peak had not been reached.[5]

This progress was but a faint, delayed echo of events across the water. England was half a century ahead of her former colonies in the manufacture of textile machinery. Long before Americans fired a shot in the cause of Independence, English inventors had established the principles of preparing cotton fiber on fine-toothed revolving cylinders and drawing it out between rollers into yarn. By 1785 the great cycle of invention which gave England her water-driven carding, roving, spinning, and weaving machinery was completed. England maintained jealous guard over her supremacy, and Samuel Slater was forced to don a farmer's disguise to slip past British customs officials when he sought to migrate to America with his important machine knowledge. This act of Slater's in 1789 was unquestionably one of the most lucrative individual smuggling feats in history, but Slater came too early to bring all the treasure with him. He left the power loom behind.

History says only that Lowell sailed for England for personal reasons of health. Beyond this it can be said, but without proof, that Lowell probably was already interested in cotton manufacture. By 1810 the power loom was in widespread use in England. In America, yarn from three hundred spinning mills was piling up at the feet of the thousands of hand-loom weavers. The fly shuttle had speeded and cheapened hand weaving, but the textile trades in

America were still out of joint. This fact was recognized in America before 1810 and reflected in the several abortive efforts to produce a successful power loom. It is scarcely conceivable that a man of Lowell's wide interests, knowledge, and alertness could have lived unaware amidst opportunity. To believe this is to deprive Lowell of credit for the exquisite timing of the English visit, and to label as an innocuous pleasure journey what may well have been a brilliant and dangerous business gamble.

Upon his arrival in England Lowell was almost immediately impressed by the thriving state of the textile industry there, and by the comparative perfection of English tools and machines. He traveled from one manufacturing center to another, questioning, observing, and accumulating impressions. The eagerness of his inquiries was concealed by an air of casual interest, for access to the English mills was achieved only by delicate diplomacy and was a privilege not lightly to be abused. Trade secrecy in general was a serious barrier. The power looms, unpopular symbols of a trend held dangerous to the masses, were particularly well shielded by their various proprietors. Lowell's position as a notable Boston merchant traveling for his health opened many doors which would have been bolted in the face of an American suspected of mechanical taint. When Nathan Appleton, a fellow Boston merchant, visited Lowell in Edinburgh, some time in 1811, the decision had already been made. Lowell told Appleton that he contemplated establishing a cotton manufactory in America.[6] Appleton promised his support.

The ensuing year was spent by Lowell in guarded endeavors to pry loose from the wary English every possible technical secret. With a confidence based more on his keen practical instincts than on his equally keen Massachusetts patriotism, Lowell returned home in 1812 predicting that abundant water power, native mechanical skill, and the general intelligence of the working people would enable America to compete with superior English experience and lower English labor costs.

The founding of the Boston Manufacturing Company, effected amidst war and financial insecurity, was a venture of more than passing boldness. This was in accord with Francis Cabot Lowell's character and background; it was made possible by the strength of

Francis Cabot Lowell
Founder of the Boston Manufacturing Company

Paul Moody

First Superintendent of the Boston Manufacturing Company

the clan. Lowell possessed that forceful, driving energy and utter disregard for self so often found in a fragile body. He also possessed the administrative talents and experience of the upper merchant class. He was accustomed to commanding coöperation in the launching of speculative ventures, for this had been his life prior to 1810. It was this combination of qualifications which enabled Lowell, without precision tools, without patterns or machines, with not much more than a mental picture of what he must build, to raise the capital for the new venture.

His Cabot uncles refused their coöperation, for they were practical men with bitter personal experience in cotton manufacture. The Cabots not only refused to subscribe, but their predictions of certain failure may well have hampered Lowell's efforts to raise capital in other quarters. Patrick Tracy Jackson was enthusiastic, however; he not only assumed the management of the company, but contributed $20,000 of capital. Jackson's two brothers contributed $15,000 more. Two other brothers-in-law, Benjamin Gorham and Warren Dutton, signed for a total of $5,000. Israel Thorndike, a Salem millionaire, undismayed by his earlier participation with the Cabots in the unsuccessful Beverly Cotton Factory, contributed $10,000; his son subscribed for $10,000 more. Two other merchants, John Gore and James Lloyd, took $15,000 of stock between them, and Uriah Cutting contributed $5,000. Nathan Appleton was asked to contribute $10,000. His response indicated a lesser degree of enthusiasm than he had shown in Edinburgh: "I told them that, theoretically, I thought the business ought to succeed, but all which I had seen of its practical operation was unfavorable. . . ." With this response Appleton limited his subscription to $5,000.

These men were gambling. Their optimism was based on three factors — the current prosperity of the textile industry, the ability of Francis Lowell to produce a loom, and the personal integrity and managerial ability of Lowell and P. T. Jackson. Lowell himself contributed $15,000 to bring the subscription total to $100,000. The act of incorporation was approved by the Commonwealth of Massachusetts on February 23, 1813, and the subscription list was completed by September of that year.

Nothing in Francis Lowell's experience suggests that he had had any mechanical training before 1813. His talents in applied mathematics were great and he was astute in the countinghouse. The presence of these aptitudes does not preclude the existence of mechanical ability, but ability was an imperfect substitute for experience. Lowell commenced experimenting on his loom in a Broad Street loft, probably late in 1812. In his initial efforts he appears occasionally to have been assisted by Jackson, who also possessed mechanical ability. The joint efforts of the two merchants were sufficient to produce a loom model, but the basic need of the venture was for practical mechanics — men who could translate Lowell's mathematical calculations and his models into workable machinery. Without such assistance the success of the loom experiment would have been dubious, and Lowell's enlarged plan for spinning as well as weaving would have been impossible. While an unsettled mercantile economy provided capital and management for the Waltham enterprise, the rapid and exceptionally vigorous growth of native mechanical skill provided the tools which helped to transform Lowell's experiments and ideas into a practical business venture. The small forges and artisans' shops of the countryside proved to be fully as potent a force in Saco-Lowell origins as were the countinghouses of Boston.

The fact that Samuel Slater, in 1790, and Francis Lowell, in 1813, could find skilled native workmen to assist them is attributable to the training of many generations of farmer-mechanics in the workshops of colonial New England. The manufacturing enterprises which existed in the heart of America's eighteenth-century mercantile-agricultural economy were numerous and diversified, and the many skills of American craftsmen were full of portent for future industrial development. Varied and dextrous mechanical abilities were all but universal, and it is a fact of great significance that large segments of the population had long been accustomed to working with their hands.[7] In organization the factories of the early nineteenth century were a distinct departure from the colonial workshops, but the Industrial Revolution in its infancy produced surprisingly few basic technical skills not already familiar to American mechanics. In the experimental decade which followed 1800 there was little of the precision and there were few of the power tools which later were to come. Superb skill was displayed in the use of hand tools, but machine tolerances of 1/32 of an inch were the best that toolmakers strove for.[8] By 1813, workers in iron were being called mechanics as well as blacksmiths, but few mechanics and even fewer blacksmiths could aspire to the title of machinist. There were few mechanical engineers and no industrial scientists, for the union of scientific theory with workbench skills was too new to have borne fruit. The competent mechanic at that time was the man who could hang a water wheel and rig the shafting with that precise balance of forces which transferred clumsy wood and iron into harnessed power, and who could work a true plane surface with tools which he had made himself. The mechanic of 1813 was at once a carpenter, a millwright, and a toolmaker. Yet America, in 1813, had machine tools of a kind, and men who could use them to build intricate machines. Even if, as a Massachusetts manufacturer of the time said, these machines were slightly constructed and had to be nursed with all the attention required by rickety children, the very existence of these machines was prophetic.[9] If the gulf which separated English and American achievements in machine-building was wide, America needed only the stimulus of men like Slater and Lowell to give fresh motion and new direction to the tremendous forces of existing native genius.

Slater had required assistance to put his machines together. George S. White, his biographer, says, "it appears, that at the commencement of the business, Mr. Slater was under the necessity of hiring mechanics, or workmen, in iron and wood, of the then common trades of the country, and teaching them the trade of building machinery."[10] Thirteen years later Francis Cabot Lowell, however, had a double advantage. He had at his disposal mechanics who possessed not only their basic skills in the "then common trades" but also a practical knowledge of textile machinery as it then existed. Paul Moody was such a mechanic, and even though he was Lowell's second choice he immediately proved to be as powerful and significant a figure in the Boston Manufacturing Company as Francis Lowell himself.

The first choice was Jacob Perkins of Amesbury. The position which he was offered in the Boston Manufacturing Company was that of superintendent. The selection of an able man for that post was of crucial importance, for it carried with it responsibility for assisting Lowell to perfect his power loom, for getting all the machinery started, and for directing the technical operation of a type of factory that was without precedent in America. Perkins was one of America's outstanding manufacturing inventors, and unquestionably he had the technical qualifications necessary to make an excellent superintendent. Perkins, however, had ambitious plans of his own and he declined Lowell's offer. He recommended Moody, with whose abilities he was well acquainted.[11]

Paul Moody was one of the many village mechanics of the time. Most of these men were brawny sons of countryside yeomanry, who learned metal-working and practical hydraulics in the forges and fulling mills of their fathers. In contrast to these, Moody came of an educated family, prominent in Newbury and Byfield Parish affairs. Paul did not follow his six brothers through Dummer Academy. At the age of twelve he started to earn his living with his hands, and in the northern Massachusetts district of his birth there was ample opportunity for such employment. In 1795 he was a hand weaver in the Newbury shop of the Scholfield brothers, whose pioneering work in woolen-textile machinery was comparable to that of Slater in cotton. Moody then entered the nail factory of Jacob Perkins and moved with it to Amesbury in 1801. These associations with the Scholfields and the gifted Perkins must have been of exceptional value to the young man, and he advanced steadily as his experience accumulated. Some time before 1812 Moody was employed by the firm of Kendrick & Worthen, who were building carding machines in Amesbury. Moody set up these machines in several places in Maine and New Hampshire.[12] In 1812 he became associated with Ezra Worthen and two others in the construction of a factory to manufacture satinets. The call from Waltham came in October of 1813, when Moody was thirty-four years old and already a successful man by his own efforts. From this time and for the year to follow, the success or failure of the Boston Manufacturing Company was to rest less with the promoters, administrators, and mechanical theorists than in the skillful hands of Paul Moody, the practical mechanic.

Moody's ultimate objective, as defined by the charter of the company, was to turn out finished cloth. In the fall of 1813, however, that objective seemed remote in comparison with the immediate necessities. The slow synthesis of men, tools, and materials and the vital task of constructing a practical loom from Lowell's model began. Following the usual pattern of the day, when mills built most of their own machinery, a machine shop was immediately set up at Waltham. This shop, in 1814, became the heart of the new enterprise. Moody's task, however, was easier in 1814 than it would have been earlier, for by this time it was possible to purchase ready-made at least a part of the necessary machinery and tools and to copy most of the rest. Invention actually played a lesser part in setting up the Boston Manufacturing Company than did imitation and the incorporation of already existing machinery. By the late summer of 1814 the construction of the mill was nearly finished, and some of the spinning machinery was ready to run. The stockholders, however, were uneasy.

Well over a year had passed since the company had been chartered, and as yet the first loom was not ready to be put into operation. The war prosperity had reached a peak, and in the southern States there was severe financial difficulty. Cotton prices were down. Manufacturers were beginning to ponder the possible effects of peace and the return of British competition on their tenuous ventures. Lowell's experiments had been conducted in strict secrecy — only Jackson had ever seen the model — and had so far afforded scant encouragement to the stockholders. To Nathan Appleton's impatient inquiries Lowell had only replied that he would be given notice when the loom was completed. By November of 1813 the model and two looms had been constructed at a cost of $534.69.[13] These must have been imperfect, for a year later Lowell and Moody were still experimenting. Jackson's multiple duties as agent and treasurer of the new company could scarcely have left him time to participate in the continuing experiments at the machine shop. Some assistance was received from outside the company, for others had also put their hands to the same problem. In 1796 Amos Whittemore, of Cambridge, had invented a self-acting loom for duck.[14] In 1809 a Thomas Mussey, of Exeter, New Hampshire, was making "water looms,"[15] and in 1812 Thomas Williams set up a power loom in a

Rhode Island mill.[16] How much, if anything, Lowell owed to the efforts of such men is not known. Records of the company show two interesting purchases, however: in March, 1814, a loom was bought from E. Stowell for $100 and in December another from J. Stimpson for $200.[17] The Stimpson loom contained valuable temple improvements, and both were probably purchased with the idea of incorporating their more promising features into the Lowell loom.

In the autumn of 1814 Lowell was at last able to open the long-closed doors to Nathan Appleton, who wrote of that eventful occasion, "I well recollect the state of admiration and satisfaction with which we sat by the hour, watching the beautiful movement of this new and wonderful machine, destined as it evidently was, to change the character of all textile industry." [18]

This invention, if indeed it could be called that, was the generating spark which brought the first and largest of Saco-Lowell's parent companies to life. Those same conditions which prompted Francis Cabot Lowell to experiment with the power loom also inspired the formation of Saco-Lowell's second parent company—a venture contemporary with and not far removed from the new factory at Waltham.

2. 1814: Newton Snuff and Cotton

In Newton, Massachusetts, as in nearby Waltham, it was the effort of a cotton manufactory to construct its own machinery which in time created a great machine shop. The Elliot Manufacturing Company, like the Boston Manufacturing Company, achieved initial success by the happy alliance of merchant capital with native mechanical ingenuity.

Above the dam of the Boston Manufacturing Company on the Charles River at Waltham lay other manufacturing sites. In several places this usually placid and swamp-bound river made quick descents between rocky banks. These natural constrictions were first utilized by the Indians, who had constructed fish and eel weirs there, and later by the early colonists, who bought out the Indian rights and built grist, saw, and fulling mills. At Newton Upper Falls, lying on a U-shaped bend of the Charles River six miles west of Boston, the water fell perpendicularly 20 feet, and then descended 35 feet in the course of the next half-mile. Before the Revolution a community of less than half a dozen families supported itself comfortably here on the produce of small but rich hillside fields, and on the seasonal abundance of fish in the river and of waterfowl in the bottomlands. The river was harnessed to serve the limited requirements of local millers, sawyers, blacksmiths, and fullers, but it was not until 1778 that this excellent water privilege began to be developed intensively and that non-resident capital became invested here.

Simon Elliot was a wealthy Boston merchant specializing in tobacco. Little is known of him except that he was successful. In 1760 his house on King Street was consumed in the Great Fire, and he built a mansion on fashionable Federal Street. He later became the proprietor of four stores — three on Butler's Row and one on State Street.[19] In 1778, exactly a hundred years after the first use of water at Newton Upper Falls for manufacturing purposes, Elliot purchased a tract of land there and the privilege "of drawing water from the stream out of Charles River to carry any kind of Mills."[20] In 1782 he constructed a snuff mill on this privilege and in the next twelve years added three more snuff mills, a grist mill, and a nail factory. These ventures all appear to have been small, for the population at the Upper Falls village did not expand greatly with the increase in manufacturing activity. Nevertheless, Elliot left an estate valued, in 1794, at close to 15,000 pounds. His son, known to Boston society as "the General" — a tribute both to his bearing and to his activities in the State Militia — inherited position as well as fortune, and strengthened both position and fortune by his own efforts.

General Elliot maintained the family control over the Newton mills, and eventually built a house near them which served to facilitate frequent family excursions to "The Falls." He was also associated with the famous merchant Thomas Handasyd Perkins and his partners in the slave trade. His business connections were strengthened by the ties of kinship and a strong social bond. Thomas Perkins married General Elliot's daughter, after which the Federal Street home became a gathering place for the Elliot-Perkins clan. This family connection was comparable and contemporary with the alliance of Francis Cabot Lowell and the Jacksons, and was to have somewhat similar results. The marriage added manufacturing interests to Perkins' extensive mercantile investments, for he came into possession of one half of the Elliot mills and privileges at the Upper Falls.

Thomas H. Perkins belonged to a different business group from that of Francis Cabot Lowell, but Perkins and Lowell grew up almost together in Boston and had much in common. Perkins, like Lowell, built up a mercantile fortune and saw it threatened by the political and military troubles of the 1807–14 period. Like Lowell (possibly inspired by Lowell's example) Perkins sensed a bright future in textile manufacturing and proceeded to back his predictions with capital. In November of 1814, a month after the completion of the mill at Waltham, Thomas Perkins and his brother James purchased from General Elliot for $20,000 a substantial additional interest in the properties at Newton Upper Falls.[21] It is at this point that we begin to sense fundamental differences in the business policies of Thomas H. Perkins and Francis Cabot Lowell.

Perkins was a promoter only. He had none of Lowell's technical aptitude, and neither was he disposed to devote himself exclusively to the promotion and management of a manufacturing enterprise. Perkins continued to be primarily interested in his mercantile enterprises, and his connection with manufactures came to be that of an investor. Perkins had only capital to contribute to his manufacturing venture, while Lowell provided not only capital but a vital new technological improvement. There is no evidence that the Newton company was predicated upon anything more than utilization of unimproved textile machinery of the prevailing types.

Early in 1814 that machinery was producing profit for many mills, but the end was in sight. War had served as a highly effective tariff on foreign cloth. Peace, arriving late in the year, ended immunity from competition and speedily revealed the inferiority of the American system of cotton manufacture to that of the English. The absence of a protective tariff after the arrival of peace left the American textile industry in a naked position, and hopes were not high for quick legislative relief. Many mills closed down as English cloth flooded the American market. Drastic improvements in machinery and techniques were required if the other mills were to remain in operation. Lowell had anticipated this basic need — Perkins had not.

Spindles began to turn at Waltham. The plans for a mill at Newton Upper Falls were postponed indefinitely.

It was not until 1823 that the Newton venture emerged from its state of suspended animation. By that time conditions in the industry had been materially improved by tariff protection, machinery improvements, and some general business recovery from five years of depression. New textile factories, some of them very large, were being planned or set up at East Chelmsford and Southbridge, in Massachusetts; at Bath, Maine; at Somersworth, New Hampshire; at Philadelphia; and at several places in Connecticut.[22] The profitable example of the Boston Manufacturing Company was before all. Perkins went ahead with his plans, and the Elliot Manufacturing Company became a reality. Its inception followed a familiar pattern. Capital was provided by Boston merchants of the Perkins, Cabot, Lawrence, and Lee families.[23] Frederick Cabot, a commission drygoods importer and a cousin of Francis Lowell, was made treasurer. One of the old snuff mills was torn down, and on the site, some time in 1823, the foundations for a cotton factory were laid. As at Waltham, the time had now arrived when the merchant owners needed a "practical man." Perkins, like Lowell, drew on the abundant resources of native mechanical ability and profited by the tempering to which such ability had been subjected in the earlier textile mills.

Otis Pettee, a village mechanic with a smattering of experience in cotton manufacture, was given the position of superintendent of the reborn company. He embarked at once on that traditional first step in the manufacture of cotton cloth — the erection and outfitting of a shop to build the machines required to make the cloth.

By the time this enterprise at Newton was fairly under way, other events of great significance in Saco-Lowell's history were occurring in a distant village in Maine.

3. 1825: The Falls at Saco

Maine did not share in the cotton-factory fever which brought prosperity and then ruin to so many mills in Massachusetts, Rhode Island, and elsewhere, and in the heat of which the Boston Manufacturing Company and the Elliot Manufacturing Company were conceived. When Francis Cabot Lowell was experimenting with his loom and General Elliot was drawing up the deed of sale for his snuff mills, the site of Saco-Lowell's third parent company was the scene of extensive lumbering operations. Maine at that time belonged to an earlier economic age. The exploitation there of magnificent timber resources continued well into the nineteenth century to command the attention of venture capital. While cotton factories were operating and being built on less remote mill sites to the south and west, the splendid rivers of Maine were still highways for logs, down which floated the virgin white-pine forests of the back country. As late as 1823 there were said to be but three cotton factories in the entire State.[24]

Here and there a prophetic voice was raised.[25] It was obvious to most who viewed them that the falls at Saco surpassed in adaptability to manufacturing purposes most of those water courses which had long since been channeled through the penstocks of Massachusetts and Rhode Island cotton factories. The Saco River poured out of New Hampshire's White Mountains and wound south and east a hundred and sixty miles to enter the ocean some ninety miles above Boston. Its course and nature presented numerous opportunities for industrial exploitation. At Saco Falls, four miles above the sea, the river split itself on several rocky islands into two precipitous channels and roared over drops totaling forty-two feet.

This was the historic domain of the aristocratic merchant Sir William Pepperell, whose purchase of a sawmill site and 4,500 acres of land in 1716 commenced the systematic and large-scale plunder of the pine stands along the river. The settlement on the east bank of the falls accordingly took the name of Pepperellboro, which was later changed back to the old Indian designation, Saco. Lumbering operations progressed steadily up-river, and two substantial communities grew up around the falls. Even before 1800, the population of Pepperellboro came to exceed 1,500 persons. Three sawmills were in operation there, drawing water from the channel between the east bank and the islands. On the west bank, dominated by towering bluffs, lay the village of Biddeford, with four sawmills, and, by 1790, a population of 1,000. Seven other sawmills were located on the three principal islands known as Indian, Gooch's, and Spring Islands, which lay in the river between the two villages. Grist and fulling mills were also located in the area; somewhat later, shops which manufactured clapboards, shingles, and laths were established there and shipbuilding was successfully undertaken. Lumber formed the basis for an extensive trade with the seaboard ports and with the West Indies.

The forest-nourished industries at Saco Falls had more than local importance. Reserves of capital were accumulating, and a population apt with machinery was growing up. As natural resources gradually became depleted, these communities found within themselves the prerequisites for conversion to a manufacturing economy.

By the second decade of the nineteenth century the incredible had occurred — the timber was gone, or at least gone beyond the reach of the small operator. From about that time onward, lumbering became an increasingly costly operation involving long tote roads into the interior and treacherous log drives down the narrow tributary streams. The cream had been skimmed, and enterprising men with small capital saw, for the first time, greater profits in iron than in wood.

On Indian Island the whole course of local history had been transacted in miniature. Here, from prehistoric times, the Pequawket sachems brought their annual fishing cantonments to feast on the swarming salmon and revel in the passing plenty. Then came the sawmills, and the stores and warehouses of the merchant, to profit from a different sort of plenty which proved even more transitory than the salmon. Here, in 1811, was built an iron works — the first symbol of the third phase.

The Iron Works at Saco Falls could appropriately be called a step-parent to Saco-Lowell's machine shop in Maine. This early venture contributed management, machinery, plant, water power, and possibly some capital to the company which was later to build the first textile-machine shop at Saco Falls. The Iron Works, however, was conceived in response to the crying need of countryside and towns alike for nails, a necessity of life in America without which the millions of board feet of native lumber were almost useless. The enterprise was an equal partnership between two merchants, Thomas Cutts from Saco and Josiah Calef from Boston.

Thomas Cutts had served his apprenticeship in the countinghouse of Sir William Pepperell and later bought land on Indian Island on which to erect a store. His operations expanded into shipbuilding, shipowning, trade with the West Indies, and operation of a saw- and gristmill.[26] Cutts belonged to that class of merchants who, like Thomas H. Perkins, were unwilling to give up their established trade and equally unwilling to deny themselves the increasing profits from the manufacturing ventures which they saw growing up around them on all sides. Like Perkins, Cutts invested capital in manufacturing, but abstained from active management. On December 5, 1811, Cutts conveyed to Josiah Calef, a Boston merchant, one undivided half of certain land and water privileges on Indian Island, for the purpose of erecting a rolling and slitting mill and a nail factory. Calef paid $550 for this interest and assumed active direction of the enterprise. Cutts, with customary Yankee caution, safeguarded the rights to water for his saw- and gristmill, and included the provision that at the end of fifteen years he should be allowed to purchase back the half-interest, if he so desired.[27] Cutts, however, died in 1821. A year later Calef secured to himself the Cutts half-interest. In eleven years the price of one undivided half of the company had increased from $550, Calef's original investment, to $6,220, the price paid by Calef to the heirs of Thomas Cutts.[28]

This beginning of relatively large-scale industrial enterprise was of immediate practical value to Saco and Biddeford. The historical significance of the Iron Works, however, lies in the introductory nature of the venture. On February 3, 1825, Josiah Calef obtained a charter for a new company, the Saco Iron Works Company, to manufacture iron, steel, and cotton goods. A reliable contemporary source says that the capital behind the venture came principally from Boston.[29] Calef probably invested some of his own money too, but the extent of his financial participation is not known. In May of the same year Calef sold the old Iron Works and privileges to the new company for $105,626.[30] A year later the name of the company was changed to Saco Manufacturing Company, and the authorized capitalization extended from $350,000 to $1,000,000.

This was the beginning of cotton manufacture and textile-machine building at Saco Falls. It was also the beginning of the drift of large cotton factories of the Waltham type to Maine — a drift which was soon to become a mad scramble for water rights and which was destined to plunge Maine into an orgy of land speculation such as the country up to that time had rarely seen. It was Josiah Calef and his nail factory which either directly brought, or indirectly attracted, the new type of enterprise to Saco. Calef may well have been the moving force behind the new company and a substantial financial backer as well. Whether he was or was not does not affect the importance of his work at Saco Falls from 1811 to 1825. A large metal-working establishment had been created and the water power harnessed to operate it. Trained mechanics were available, men who knew wood and water and iron. The Saco Manufacturing Company took over a going concern and secured for itself a substantial revenue to help tide over the period while cotton machinery was being set up. Without such a combination of attractions Saco might well have waited longer for its Industrial Revolution, and for the setting-up of the two industries which were to dominate the industrial life of the community from this time on — the manufacture of cotton cloth and of textile machinery.

4. The Founding Pattern

Saco-Lowell origins are not to be found in the expected places — among the early independent machine shops. After 1790 the evolution of textile-machinery manufacture followed a dual pattern of development. Here and there specialized machine-makers appeared whose shops were devoted to the manufacture, not of cloth, but of machines to make that cloth. This was a development which held more promise for the future than importance at the time. Most of the early cotton mills had machine shops in their basements. It was no mere coincidence that this plan of construction was universally followed. Such machine shops, of necessity, were set up in advance of the mills which they were to serve. The basements, being finished first, were quickly fitted out to produce and assemble equipment for the unfinished floors above. This practice, at first required by the scarcity of specialized machine-makers from whom equipment could be purchased, may, in turn, have somewhat retarded the development of such specialization. The cotton manufacturer's custom of constructing his own machines was certainly well rooted, and was to continue until the 1820's, at least, as a dominant characteristic of the industry. These circumstances explain why Saco-Lowell's three parent companies were primarily cotton factories and only incidentally machine shops. Since the first interest of these companies was in the manufacture of cloth, rather than of machinery, many phases of their subsequent operation bear slight reference to Saco-Lowell's early history. The founding facts in each case are interesting and pertinent. Once the manufacture of cloth has commenced, however, we are directly concerned less with the operations of the companies themselves than with the subordinate machine shops of those companies.

This chapter has traced the remarkably uniform founding pattern of the three parent companies — a pattern in which the figure of the merchant promoter is dominant. The following chapters treat of the emergence from factory basements of a tremendously energetic industry. The emphasis changes. Promotion yields to operation, and administration yields to invention. Regional isolation breaks down and the machine shops begin to compete for business. Boston offices are set up, and the widening gap between ownership and management inaugurates a century of intermittent internal corporate strife. The mechanic, having already provided vital services in setting up the enterprises, goes on to become the crucial figure in the mills. In the years following the foundings of the three companies, the marvelous skill at the workbench overshadows all other aspects of their history. These companies go on to play a prominent part in giving America not only more and better cloth than had been known before, but in providing men, machines, ideas, and inspiration for phenomenal growth in all the mechanic arts.

CHAPTER II

OPERATING AS A COTTON-MILL DEPARTMENT
WALTHAM, 1814–1825

1. Equipping the Waltham Shop and Mill

While the creative talents of Francis Lowell and Paul Moody were being concentrated upon the problems of the power loom, the administrative capacities of Patrick Tracy Jackson were directed at the equally vital problem of organizing the Boston Manufacturing Company. The basic requirements of Jackson's task were crystal-clear. In the first ledger book of the company five accounts sufficed to record Jackson's activities during the first twelve months. The general founding necessities were conceived by the company to be land and water power, buildings, machinery, labor, and administrative supervision. How successfully these factors could be combined by unpractised men to turn out an unfamiliar product on equipment not yet invented was far from clear.

In September of 1813 Jackson purchased in his own name but for eventual transfer to the Boston Manufacturing Company the land, buildings, and water rights of the paper mill of John Boies on the Charles River at Waltham.[1] With the purchase of 6,000 feet of planking from stockholder Uriah Cutting on November 26, 1813, construction of Mill Number One commenced. On the same day the first charges were made to the machinery account — the first machine shop in Saco-Lowell's history received as its initial equipment a humble order of files, vises, assorted blacksmiths' tools, and an anvil.[2]

Plans for the new mill called for a brick structure of four stories above the basement, which was to be 90 feet long and 45 feet wide. This was an ambitious undertaking in comparison with the much smaller New England mills of the day, though of a size by no means uncommon in New York and Pennsylvania, and frequently surpassed in England. In this mill was contemplated, however, a scope of operation which may have been unique in the world. Up to this time American cotton mills had been accustomed to perform preparatory and spinning processes only, putting the yarn out to be woven in homes and finished in independent shops. Slater had brought some weavers into his mills, but had never achieved complete integration of processes within his earlier establishments. In England subdivision of labor was carried much further than in America, and the division of manufacturing processes among independent mills was even more pronounced. The manufacturing plan at Waltham, credited to Francis Lowell, called for integration within the one company of all processes in the manufacture of cloth. History has emphasized this feature of the Boston Manufacturing Company, and justly so, for it established a pattern that had a profound effect upon the industrial organization of the country. The plan also had far-reaching implications for the machine shop in the basement of the mill. In the long run this plan stimulated creative mechanical effort in many directions, forcing Moody and his assistants to study, master, and then improve not just the power loom but most of the machines then known to cotton-textile manufacturers.

No such far-reaching effect, however, is discernible during the first years of the Boston Manufacturing Company's existence. The basement of the new mill could more properly be called a workshop than a machine shop. The handful of men employed there in 1813 and 1814 were not machinists but carpenters, blacksmiths, and masons. Experiments on the loom presumably were continued here, but there is no evidence that any other machinery was constructed on the premises. Efforts throughout the first year were confined to raising the structure of the mill building and installing the power transmission system. Company policy in respect to machinery other than the power loom began to crystallize in December of 1813 when an order for spinning and carding machines was placed with Luther Metcalf & Company, of Medway, Massachusetts. At this point it becomes clear that the Boston Manufacturing Company initially contemplated mechanical innovation in the weaving process only. For the rest it was content to utilize machinery already being manufactured by established companies.

While no significant amount of machinery was manufactured at Waltham in the first year of operations, the ledgers record the slow building-up of the tools and equipment which eventually were to make such manufacture possible. Early constructive efforts appear to have been exclusively the product of hand labor, and the common file was the most prominent feature of early tool orders. Large numbers of files, together with many carpenter tools and quantities of blacksmith-shop fixtures, nails, cast steel and Russian iron, oak planking, timbers of red cedar and mahogany, castings, mill gears and shafting were carted in over the turnpike road from Boston. Then certain other tools began to arrive at Waltham which offered formidable challenge to the supremacy of the file. In June of 1814 the company settled a bill with the foundry of General Shepard Leach at Easton, Massachusetts, for a roller lathe, a fluting lathe, and a cutting engine. Unfortunately, the growing mechanization of the Waltham machine shop cannot be continuously traced by means of such purchase records, for after this date the company appears to have built most of its own machine tools. Neither can these machines be described. The Leach purchase is a significant event in itself, however, for it shows that at the time when the Waltham venture was launched, American mechanics had already begun to emerge from the handicraft stage of manufacture.

For the year ending November 30, 1814, expenditures for tools of all kinds totaled $1,081; for sundry machinery, $251; for a blacksmith shop, $449; for expense incurred in constructing a power loom, $1,428.[3] Throughout this year, work on the new mill was pushed forward with energy. Considerable improvement was made in the existing water privilege, and many purchases of gearing and shafting were made from the small forges of neighboring towns. Paul Moody made several trips to neighboring manufacturing centers and traveled to Amesbury to consult with his old employer, Jacob Perkins. Perkins rendered the company important assistance, and installed a patent water wheel at Waltham which was designed to eliminate the back water occasioned by freshets and high tides and to produce a more stable flow of water to the wheel.[4] By the end of November, 1814, Jackson had expended, in addition to the amounts for tools and equipment previously noted, approximately $13,600 for buildings, $4,200 for water wheels and mill work, $2,100 for two houses, $4,900 for water privileges, and $9,200 for dam, flume, and raceway. He had advanced $3,600 to contractors and had about $5,000 in cash on hand.[5] Except for the installation of machinery the mill was completed, and in December of 1814 the first order for cotton was placed. It was a good start, and one which gave promise of enlarged activity in the machine shop. The completion of mill construction relieved the shop of heterogeneous functions. The perfection of the power loom some time late in the fall and the arrival of the Metcalf machinery in December gave direction and stimulus to activity in the basement of the mill. From this time and for some months to come, the machine shop was devoted to the building of looms and the installation and repair of purchased machinery.

2. A Decade of Success: 1814–1824

The Metcalf machinery, augmented by other orders for drawing frames, a stretcher, and additional spinning machinery, had been installed and was operating early in 1815. At that time only one loom was operative,[6] and the quantity of cloth which first reached the market in September of 1815 was small.[7] Operations expanded rapidly thereafter, however, and the success of the Boston Manufacturing Company as a cotton-cloth factory is intimately linked with the development of the basement machine shop.

That success came at a time when the distress of other American cotton mills bordered on catastrophe. The flood of cheaper foreign textiles which followed the ending of hostilities in 1815 was only a part of the grim economic picture. The tariff of 1816 levied a 25 per cent duty on all imported foreign cloth, but business distress spread with the depreciation of Western currency and attendant financial disorders. When Francis Lowell and Nathan Appleton visited Pawtucket to discuss the terms of the new tariff with Rhode Island manufacturers, they found that the machine shop of David Wilkinson, which had been taxed to its utmost capacity during the war years, was completely idle. Wilkinson told them that scarcely a spindle was running in Pawtucket.[8] In Massachusetts only six new manufacturing companies received charters in the years from 1817 through 1820. Many mills failed outright; others closed down for varying periods. Cloth prices declined sharply, and even the price of Waltham sheeting was forced downward from thirty cents a yard in 1816 to twenty-one cents in 1819. The fall in price of other types of cloth more susceptible to market conditions was far greater, and reflected far less than did the Waltham product any increase in operating efficiency.[9]

In 1815, the first year in which cloth was marketed by the Boston Manufacturing Company, sales totaled $2,987. For the year ending August 30, 1817, the figure had jumped to $34,432. By 1822, annual sales had reached a peak of $345,000.[10] Profits were large. Francis Lowell is said to have remarked that the only circumstance which made him distrust his cost calculations was that they always came to a result too favorable to be credible! [11] The physical assets of the plant expanded rapidly. In 1816 a second mill, of greater size than the first, was commenced and in the next few years many other substantial plant additions were built or acquired. Total assets grew from $39,000 in 1814 to $771,000 in 1823.[12]

There were many obvious and some subtle reasons for this remarkable performance in a period of chronic bad business and in a stricken industry. The technical advantage accruing from the power loom was a dominant factor in creating profits. The cloth for which that loom was best adapted was a staple article well suited to the public demand, and it competed so successfully with the imported India cottons that the tariff of 1816 probably was not necessary for the success of the enterprise, though it made that success more pronounced. Marketing techniques employed by the company, though more the result of chance and necessity than of foresight, were highly successful. There were other important factors in the success of the Boston Manufacturing Company, and such of these as directly concern the machine shop must be studied. At this point, however, it will suffice to note that the shop expanded partly because it was a vital department in an expanding organization.

3. American Cotton Machinery in 1814

In 1790 America was completely dependent upon England for knowledge of the new water-driven textile machinery, and by 1814 the dependence had scarcely lessened. The slow spread of Arkwright's system of power spinning over the New England countryside and its implantation in New York, New Jersey, and Pennsylvania was effected by American mechanics employing English knowledge — or by English mechanics using American capital. By 1812, native mechanics, adept, energetic, and adaptive though they were, had scarcely progressed beyond the most elementary stage of the slow learning process — imitation of the teacher. The war years that followed produced dual misfortunes: the surreptitious flow of trained men and of technical knowledge from England to America was interrupted, and the American textile mills were freed from foreign competition. Native inventiveness, in consequence, became starved for inspiration and anesthetized by a booming market. The record of new textile inventions for the 1812–14 period indicates that creative mechanical effort had deteriorated to the status of tinkering, and that the wide gap between British and American manufacturing skill had not been appreciably narrowed, but may have widened still further.[13] For the whole period from 1790 to 1814, Americans contributed only two original inventions of recognized importance in the field of cotton machinery.[14] The fruition of native mechanical skills, however promising, was yet to be achieved, and the machine-building skills of 1814 were closer to those of 1790 than to those of 1820.

The Boston Manufacturing Company is credited with developing a whole new series of machines which differed so widely in principle and detail from what had hitherto existed and from what contemporary machine-makers were turning out that they came to be labeled the "Waltham System." It is important to note, however, that this system (which in its broadest definition embraced manufacturing techniques and labor policies as well as machines) took several years to develop, and that the first mill of the company was equipped, in 1814, with the Slater-type machinery in use in contemporary mills. This machinery, with which Slater had introduced the first successful water-power spinning in America in 1790, was directly patterned after that with which Sir Richard Arkwright had accomplished a similar result in England two decades before. Slater and the American machinery builders who immediately followed him, moreover, were not the last to be indebted to the eighteenth-century English mechanics. The great historical importance of the first English power-driven cotton machinery lies in the fact that the cumulative work of generations of machinists was to produce great improvements in the machinery itself but only minor changes in the functions which that machinery was designed to perform.

Opening and Picking Machinery

Earliest records of the Boston Manufacturing Company make no mention of opening or picking machinery, and it is possible that the company had none. The cleaning of cotton preparatory to carding and spinning was a less complex task in 1814 than it was later to become, because cotton as it arrived at the mill was less firmly compressed and could be serviceably prepared by relatively simple processes. In 1814 hand picking was still common in England. In America this practice was customary at that time, and was destined to persist for many years. The usual technique employed was to spread the cotton on a frame which was covered with small cords fixed at both ends and parallel with the two sides of the frame. The cotton was then beaten with switches. The cotton fibers were thus opened and the dirt fell down between the cords. Impurities and dead cotton that did not fall through the frame were then picked out by hand.[15] In some instances the chore was not even performed in the factory. Many American companies put cotton out to be hand-picked in the homes of the countryside.[16] Machines to loosen the matted cotton and shake loose the impregnated leaf, seed, and dirt had been invented, however. These machines took many forms, but all depended on revolving paddles, arms, or teeth which acted upon the cotton somewhat as had the hand-wielded switch. Basic concepts of pickers, willows, openers, and whippers of various kinds came from England to America, and minor American modifications appeared in increasing number after 1807. Machines for opening the tightly packed bales of cotton came to be differentiated from those for picking and cleaning, though the one process closely supplemented the other and in many mills both opening and picking were accomplished on one machine. Just as the Boston Manufacturing Company finished building its first mill, Creighton's combined opener and lapper appeared in England. This machine delivered the cotton in the form of a continuous and more or less even lap, or web, which was wound by the machine on a wooden roller ready for the carding process to follow. Formerly the cotton had been taken from the opener and spread by hand on the feed apron of the carding machines. The important economies effected by Creighton's machine did much to stimulate mechanization of the preparatory processes in England, and widespread adoption of machine techniques in America was only a matter of time and acquaintance.[17]

Carding

In contrast to opening and picking processes, the carding process which followed initial preparation of the cotton was mechanized in all mills in 1814. The carding machines utilized an ancient principle — that of combing out the matted cotton so that the fibers lay roughly parallel and in a form suitable for drawing and twisting into yarn. As early as 1748 this carding action was accomplished in England by passing the cotton around a cylinder covered with a multitude of projecting fine wire teeth. The main cylinder revolved against similar cylinders of smaller size or against stationary strips of wire-studded wood to perform the carding action. By 1790 double carding was being practised. Slater had a breaker card for rough initial work and a finisher card for final working-up of the fleece into a sliver, or loose rope of cotton. Both types of cards consisted of a main cylinder eighteen inches in diameter, with a fixed arch of wire-studded "top flats" against which the main cylinder brushed, and a doffing cylinder which removed the fleece from the main cylinder and delivered it in a continuous sliver. They were small in size, simple in construction, and inexpensive to make, but had to be stopped every fifteen to thirty minutes to allow the top flats and main cylinder to be stripped by hand of their accumulated dirt. The quantity of sliver produced per card was small and the waste was considerable, but on the whole the carding was well done. After 1790, additional "urchins," or small auxiliary rollers, and more top flats were added, and a number of doffing improvements made, but the carding machines set up by Slater were closely imitated by other mills and used without important modification for more than fifty years.[18] It was this type of card which the Boston

Manufacturing Company set up in 1814, and later built for sale to others.

Drawing and Roving

In 1814, drawing and roving machinery in use in America was substantially the same as that patented by Sir Richard Arkwright in 1775 and brought to America by Slater in 1789. In the drawing process lengths of the sliver produced by the carding machines were combined and fed to the drawing frame, where the action of three or more pairs of rollers turning at different speeds drew the sliver out. This drawing process, often repeated a number of times by doubling the sliver produced by the drawing frame, carried to greater perfection the parallelization of fibers already commenced by the action of the cards. After drawing, the sliver was subjected to the roving process, during which further doubling and drawing took place, and a twist was imparted to the sliver to give it the cohesive strength necessary to withstand the action of subsequent processes. Several different roving frames were in use, but they varied only in details. The lantern, can, slubbing, and skeleton frames of the period all imparted some twist to the sliver by means of revolving cans, into which the sliver was fed from the rollers of the machines. After twisting, the sliver (called "roving" once it had gone through the roving frame) was made ready for spinning by being wound, either by hand or by crude winding machines, on bobbins which fitted the creel of the spinning frame. The roving process in particular, though so long unchanged, was recognized at a comparatively early date as unsuited in many respects to high-speed, low-cost production. The revolving can method of imparting twist did not produce roving of uniform strength, and the necessary additional task of winding the roving on bobbins was costly. Arkwright himself tried to eliminate the winding process by designing a roving frame which wound the roving directly upon the bobbins by means of a rotating flyer arm similar in principle to that employed on his spinning frame. The solution lay in this direction, but Arkwright's theory was too far in advance of his times to be made practicable. He failed to solve the basic mechanical problem of regulating the speed of the bobbin so that winding-on of the roving took place at a rate neither faster nor slower than that at which the roving was fed through the rollers of the frame — a problem immeasurably complicated by the constantly increasing circumference of the bobbin as it filled with roving. The difficulty in providing for variable bobbin speed defied solution until 1813. In that year a patent was issued in England to Joseph Raynor, of Sheffield, which marks the birth of the so-called fly frame. Raynor's frame, however imperfect, appears to have been the first successful attempt to provide for variable bobbin speed, and it was followed in the next twenty years by a host of inventions directed at winding the final product of the roving process directly on bobbins.[19]

Spinning

Spinning techniques of 1814 were in a position analogous to that of roving. The American machines of 1814 were not much changed from those of 1790, which, in turn, still bore strong resemblance to the earliest English machines. Slater spun both his warp yarn and his filling on the so-called water-frame — named from its source of power. Some time between 1790 and 1814 the gearing of this frame was altered to produce a simpler machine requiring less power to drive. The improved machine was called the throstle (allegedly because the noise of the spindles resembled the song of the bird of that name), and was destined, in that form, to be a dominant feature of American mills until after the Civil War.[20] A contemporary development concerned a different type of spinning, also destined to become important in America. The mule spinning frame, which was better adapted than the throstle for spinning the soft weft-yarn, or filling, and the finer counts of all yarn, was introduced into America in the 1790's, and by 1814 it had become common practice, particularly in Rhode Island factories, to spin the warp on throstles and the filling on mules.[21] The Waltham system, however, was to be guided in a different direction by the inventions of Paul Moody.

Weaving

In England the power loom was slowly overcoming the passive opposition of cynical mill masters and the virulent hatred of the hand-loom weavers. In 1813 there were said to be 2,400 power looms in use there, and recognition of the economies of the new device was growing.[22] These economies resulted from a reduction in the number of loom attendants required, the employment of relatively unskilled attendants, and an increase in output as compared with the hand loom.[23] Furthermore, the quality of such cloth as the early power looms could produce was higher than comparable cloth from the hand loom, due to the mechanical regularity of the "beating-up" process. In America spinning, carding, drawing, and roving processes all were geared to the water wheel by 1814, but the yarn produced in such abundance still was being "put out" to be woven by hand. The weaving of cloth was still a home industry, and the hand loom, equipped with a fly shuttle, produced virtually all of the domestic cloth. The last stage in the mechanization of textile manufacture in America waited upon the efforts of Paul Moody and Francis Lowell at Waltham.

4. A Decade of Technical Progress in Waltham 1814–1824

The power loom of the Boston Manufacturing Company affected the American cotton textile industry as no other innovation since 1790 had done. It signalized the awakening of American mechanics from war-induced torpor and, though the loom came from England, its introduction to America was an indication that mechanics here could rise above slavish dependence upon the mother country. This loom will remain only a vague symbol of progress, however, for almost nothing is known about it. Francis Lowell and Paul Moody could have patterned their loom after any one of several English loom-types of the period. It is possible that they utilized a combination of English and American ideas, and probable that Moody incorporated original concepts of his own. Nathan Appleton, who had ample opportunity to observe and judge, states that the first Waltham loom was different from any existing English looms but he does not say that it was better.[24] Available evidence indicates that it was inferior to the Horrocks, or Scotch, loom of 1814, which was the best and most widely used of the British machines.[25] In 1813, when Horrocks patented his final improvement, Lowell's English trip of investigation had ended.

Whatever the merits of the Waltham loom in comparison with its British contemporaries, it introduced to America the economies of power weaving. It secured to the Boston Manufacturing Company the immediate technical competitive advantage without which existence itself might have been denied the company. It was, therefore, a recognizable factor in the establishment of the Waltham machine shop. After 1814, however, this machine played a progressively less significant part in the development of the Waltham shop. In its first functionings the Waltham loom was a reflection of Moody's mechanical genius. Once the loom was operative, Moody's attention shifted to other machines and no important loom improvement subsequently originated in Waltham. Temple improvements were made on the Waltham loom, but they were purchased from other mechanics.[26] Credit must be assigned elsewhere for the steady improvement which took place in the American loom, and the Scotch loom introduced to the Rhode Island factories in 1817 was so superior in mechanical action that the Waltham model was eventually superseded. Waltham effort was forced in other directions.

The patent for the loom was issued in the name of Francis Lowell and Patrick Tracy Jackson. The earliest patent which bears Paul Moody's name was granted May 19, 1816, and was for a winding frame. A more important machine, however, for which Moody received a patent on January 17, 1818, was one which dressed the warp yarn preparatory to weaving in the power loom.[27] England was slow to accept the power loom as a proven advance over existing weaving techniques. A part of this reluctance arose from the fact that the power-weaving process before 1800 was not much, if any, cheaper than the older methods. The great obstacle to the success of the power loom was that it had to be stopped frequently in order to dress the warp as it unrolled from the warp beam. This required that an attendant be employed for each loom. The dressing process — impregnating the warp yarn with sizing — had not been necessary when weaving was done with the slow-moving hand loom. With the introduction of the power loom some preparation of the warp to give it greater rigidity and strength became necessary. This need was met in England in 1803 and 1804 by the invention, by Horrocks and others, of machines for dressing the warp

Patrick Tracy Jackson
First Agent of the Boston Manufacturing Company

Saco-Lowell's Most Historic Machine Tool
A lathe built in 1820

before it was set up in the loom. Francis Lowell brought back with him from England a drawing of Horrocks' dressing machine, and Moody was given the task of making it operative. Since efficient power weaving was dependent upon the dressing process, Moody's work on the dressing frame was almost as vital to the company as his work on the loom itself.

That work could not be successfully accomplished without great mechanical skill, considerable experience in the handling of cotton fiber, and a general knowledge of the progress of other mechanics, both in England and in America. An additional factor, which on more than one occasion meant the difference between success or failure, was luck. A lucky conversation solved for Moody one of those exasperating problems which frequently halted progress in the improvement of early machines. The incident illustrates a vastly significant situation inherent in the mechanic arts of the day — a situation where the thinking of brilliant men often far outran the manual skills of their environment, and where improvements in mechanical principles often were forced to wait upon improvements in the physical means of realization.

In his efforts to solve the mechanical complexities of the dressing machine, Moody was plagued by a simple trifle. The problem centered in the wooden rollers which conveyed the yarn into the sizing solution. Being constantly wet, these rollers swelled and became so warped that they would operate only imperfectly — or not at all. Moody tried various remedies and at length attempted to cast a shell of pewter around the rolls. His conception, however, was beyond the manual skill of his foundrymen, who encountered difficulty in constructing molds in which to cast the shells. Moody turned to this new problem of molds and consulted with his brother David, who suggested the use of a soapstone mold for the casting. This advice sparked a new idea. Moody made the rolls themselves of soapstone and thus solved his difficulties inaugurating the feature which was to be characteristic of the Waltham dresser for many years.[28] That dresser was a far greater mechanical success than the loom, and surpassed in efficiency the English model from which it was adapted. Unlike the Waltham loom, it continued in use without substantial change at least until the late 1850's.[29]

Work in the machine shop of the Boston Manufacturing Company progressed through several distinct stages, and it reflects the carefully planned efforts of the company to achieve maximum production in the shortest possible time. The necessary initial concentration of effort on weaving and dressing techniques was made possible by the purchase of roving, drawing, carding, and spinning equipment, however imperfect, from others. After 1817 Paul Moody was able to turn his attention to improving these latter processes, and it was with them that he achieved his greatest successes.

In America the first departure from the revolving-can type of roving frame was made by Paul Moody and Francis Lowell with the Waltham double speeder, for which the first patent was issued to Moody on April 3, 1819, and subsequent patents on December 30, 1820, and February 21, 1821.[30] This roving frame was hailed as an invention, but, like most of the Waltham machinery, it represented original thinking applied to machinery conceived in England. Here, again, the original contributions by the Waltham men appear to have been considerable, but they cannot be definitely identified. The Waltham double speeder effected changes in the speed of the bobbin as it increased in diameter by means of a compound or epicycloidal train of gearing. This gearing system may have been original. Certainly Francis Lowell performed remarkable mathematical calculations to guide Moody in constructing the model. America's most eminent contemporary mathematician, Nathaniel Bowditch, stated that the calculations involved in this machine were such as he supposed hardly a person in New England (and hence, by inference, in America!) could make.[31] From 1819 to 1823 the double speeder manufactured by the Boston Manufacturing Company appears to have been unchallenged in the American market. The sale of this machine to other companies probably did much to stimulate the large number of improvements in roving frames which began to be patented in America after 1823.[32]

The double speeder completed, Moody appears next to have commenced improving the spinning process in the Waltham mill. The greatest of his improvements had long been an obvious need, but the final stimulus to act came as a result of Paul Moody's attempt to bluff a shrewd competitor. The Boston Manufacturing Company was following the usual practice of mills spinning the coarser counts of yarn — spinning both warp and filling on the old-style throstle frames. After the filling yarn had been spun onto bobbins in the throstle frame, the full bobbins were placed in a winding machine which wound the filling yarn onto a different type of bobbin for the loom shuttles. One of the pioneer Massachusetts cotton manufacturers, Silas Shepard of Taunton, had patented and was using a winding machine which Francis Lowell considered far preferable to the one in use at Waltham. Lowell, accordingly, took Moody with him to Taunton to see if arrangements could be concluded for lease of the invention at a reasonable price.

Shepard, the son of a Yankee farmer, was not one to let an honest dollar escape him.

"You know, Mr. Lowell, you must come to my terms," he said, refusing the first offer of the Waltham men.

Moody must have known that cotton manufacturers respected his inventive talents. "I was just thinking, Mr. Shepard," he replied, "that I could spin the cops direct upon the bobbin."

This threat of Moody's to do away entirely with the winding process carried weight. "You be hanged!" shouted Shepard. "Very well, I accept your offer."

"No!" replied Lowell, suddenly breaking into the conversation. "No, it is too late."

Moody and Lowell departed. Once inside their carriage, Lowell informed Moody that since he had suggested the plan of spinning the filling directly upon the shuttle bobbin, he must now make the idea practical. Moody then confided to his companion that his remark to Shepard was purely for bargaining purposes. Nevertheless, he felt, the idea was a good one and he would see what he could do. The result was the filling frame, patented May 6, 1819, and February 19, 1821 — an invention of unquestioned originality which contributed much to the steadily decreasing cost of cotton manufacture in America.[33]

Moody's second important contribution to spinning techniques was the invention or the introduction of the so-called "dead-spindle" system of spinning.[34] The origins of the dead spindle are obscure, but its future in America was to be important. Rhode Island mills clung to the live spindle of the old-style throstle frames because of the superior quality of yarn produced. Northern New England mills adopting the Waltham system, however, preferred the higher speeds of the dead spindle. Not until the final triumph of ring spinning long after the Civil War did the dead-spindle throstle frame first introduced at Waltham pass from the American scene.

Of Moody's minor inventions, no complete record has survived. It seems safe to assume that the half-dozen or so patents which constitute Moody's claim to fame represent at best only the small climactic part of his total work. Even on the basis of incomplete information, however, Moody stands out as the foremost innovator and inventor of the 1814–24 period, and these ten years, together with the decade which followed, possibly constitute the most dynamic period in the entire history of the American cotton machinery industry. From 1814 to 1824 Moody's inventions and adaptations of English inventions were the dominant development in the American textile industry. Almost single-handed he produced sweeping changes in manufacturing techniques — changes which primarily benefited the Boston Manufacturing Company, but which came to be shared by all cotton mills.

There was no creative effort of comparable scope either in the Blackstone Valley or in cotton-manufacturing centers to the south. Quiescence in these areas suggests a preoccupation with English techniques and machines then existent. Certain individual contributions of significance, however, were made by others, both in the Waltham-dominated area and elsewhere. Amos Whittemore of Cambridge, Massachusetts, had been turning out card clothing on automatic machines since 1797. Ira Draper of Weston, Massachusetts, had patented his self-acting loom temples in 1816. A year later William Gilmour had placed the Scotch loom in successful operation in Rhode Island. Pickers and openers, either invented locally or copied from English inventions, had been placed in operation in a number of mills and were being improved almost as fast as they were introduced. In 1823 Asa Arnold of Providence, Rhode Island, patented a greatly improved compound gear for roving frames and indicated by his example that Blackstone Valley mechanics had begun to stir. The sum total of these efforts amounted to a technological revolution in the areas affected. Of all the processes involved in American cotton manufacture, only carding and drawing failed to be radically improved in this decade.

Mechanical leadership at Waltham, coupled with sound business management, could have but one result. These ten years saw the Boston Manufacturing Company temporarily established as the greatest cotton mill in America, and the machine shop of the company as the most potent single force in the trade which was making great mills possible.

5. Operations in the Machine Shop, 1814–1824

The machine shop of the Boston Manufacturing Company was conceived as a necessity, but with the passage of time the urgency of that need declined. Serving initially as an unspecialized workshop, it built the first company mill and installed the power generating and transmission system. During the 1814–15 period the shop commenced the manufacture of looms for the company's own use and gradually assumed responsibility for the construction and installation of other types of machinery. Company policy in respect to the machine shop in these first years is clear. Certain types of equipment could not be purchased at all. Other types which could be purchased were not satisfactory, except to meet emergency needs. Only by building its own machinery could the company achieve its ambitious manufacturing goals. In 1816, however, with the first mill in operation and the second mill far advanced in construction there was a change in policy, and company action reflects a broadening view of the potentialities of the shop. Early in 1817, orders were first taken from other manufacturers for the construction of machinery.

Machinery Sales to Other Factories

The new practice of selling machinery to others offered the twofold advantage of utilizing machine-shop facilities and personnel no longer engaged in company work and also of providing an additional source of revenue. Available records fail to indicate which of these considerations was dominant, but the advantages of maintaining an active machine shop are clear, and the profits realized were in themselves a substantial justification for the new policy.

Another motive which in at least one instance prompted the company to sell machinery to others was a desire to dispose of obsolete equipment. The first substantial sale of machinery, however, was actuated by a desire to acquire some knowledge of the machinery of another manufacturer. On June 9, 1816, Francis Lowell wrote to David Greenough, part-owner of two small Massachusetts cotton mills, "The original proposal which I made to you and to which you acceded, was that we might see your machinery and copy from it as far as we pleased provided we would permit you to have the use of our patent Looms and warping machine and permit you to copy our Dressing machine."[35] Lowell went on to state, "It is perfectly indifferent to us whether you relinquish this bargain or not if you think our prices too high build for yourself or if you think the price of your frame too low keep it." This professed indifference seems to indicate that the company at that time had not committed itself to the policy of building machinery for others, but this attitude was soon to change.

There is a further possibility that the policy of selling machinery to others was motivated in part by a philanthropic urge on the part of Francis Lowell to share the fruits of his enterprise with the industry, though not, of course, at a pecuniary sacrifice. The merchants who turned from commerce to manufactures were sound men of business with uncompromising attitudes toward a bargain. But many of them were also highly patriotic citizens keenly interested in the progress of the new nation. This was particularly true of Francis Lowell, whose spirit of public service and vision of making America economically independent of England is well authenticated. That this motive was shared by his associates is indicated by Nathan Appleton's statement that, although in the beginning he did not share Lowell's optimism regarding the financial potentialities of the enterprise, nevertheless he was quite willing to lose the full amount of his subscription in order that so important an experiment might be tried.[36] These considerations are overshadowed by the evident self-interest of the men involved, but they must not be neglected as a contributing force in the determination of their business policies.

The first outright sale of textile machinery in Saco-Lowell's history was made on February 21, 1817, to Poignand Plant & Company, of Lancaster, Massachusetts, and was made at a profit of 20 per cent. This transaction and others which soon followed are of great historical interest, for they yield what are probably the earliest detailed records yet published of profits in the American textile machine industry. Boston Manufacturing Company ledgers record the Poignand Plant transaction in itemized form:[87]

Machines Sold	Amount Received from Poignand Plant & Co.	Cost
4 looms @ $90	$ 360	$ 360
4 looms with iron rockers @ $95	380	380
1 dressing machine	813.50	500
1 warping machine	250	200
1 bobbin machine, 50 spindles	175	150
20 yarn beams @ $5	100	80
Total	$2,078.50	$1,670

In the seven months ending August 31, 1817, the company sold, in addition to the first Poignand Plant order, 18 looms, 2 warping machines, 2 dressing machines, a drawing frame, and a bobbin machine.[88] Dollar volume of sales for the period amounted to $7,498, and a profit of $2,030 was recorded. These sales followed a pattern which reflected the almost primitive state of the cotton textile and machine industry of the day.

The Boston Manufacturing Company experimented with prices, and found that the market was willing to pay more than the figures first set. After the first sale of machinery, prices on looms, warpers, and dressing machines were extended by inclusion of a patent fee. Once these initial adjustments had been made, prices and costs became well stabilized. The relationship of one to the other can be measured, but not explained. Prices after 1817 were set to allow an extremely generous profit margin, but a margin which varied considerably from one machine to another. Profits on individual machines, expressed as a percentage of selling price and usually reflecting the inclusion of a patent fee, ranged from 20 per cent on yarn beams to 50 per cent and more on warpers, dressers, drawing frames, throstle spinning frames, and double speeders. Looms were usually priced to yield 28 per cent profit.

Existing records do not clearly reveal the components of the cost figures against which sales were measured to arrive at profit margins. Inability to criticize the company's accounting in the light of present-day concepts, however, is not a serious handicap. However they were made up, these profit figures are valuable because they represent what the company believed to be their profit. In spite of the small volume of machine business done, and in spite of the existence in the record books of standard machine cost quotations, the company recognized and recorded the most minute variations in the day-to-day costs of building machinery. The concept of inflexible, standardized costs adhered to by generations of petty capitalist artisans was transcended.

These costs and selling prices have only a relative significance in history, and they are of value only to the extent that they can be compared with later costs and prices in the same company or with the contemporary costs and prices of other companies. There is no cost information on which to base comparisons between the Waltham machine shop and other shops in America and England, and very little comparative price information of a specific nature. In 1820, prices of cotton machinery in America were said to be double those in England,[39] and one competent observer states that in the American market the Waltham patents were being held at a high price.[40] The Gilmour loom is known to have undersold the Waltham loom by as much as $55, but this is probably the only direct comparison possible between the machines of contemporary manufacturers. A comparison of Waltham prices with those of earlier machine-makers in an attempt to establish the trend of machine prices is subject to the same difficulties arising from lack of specific information. Rare price lists of cotton machinery in Philadelphia and New Jersey in the years from 1808 to 1815 are available.[41] These data indicate that the Waltham prices on certain machines from 1817 to 1823 substantially exceeded those of the earlier period.

Almost as soon as it commenced the manufacturing of machinery for sale, the Boston Manufacturing Company found profit possibilities in licensing agreements, and in June, 1817, inaugurated the policy of charging other mills for the privilege of building and using the Waltham patent machinery. The first mill to enter into such an agreement was the Peterborough Factory Company, of

Peterborough, New Hampshire, which purchased "the patent right to use 16 looms at their Factory" at a rate of $10 per loom. Subsequent agreements were made, however, at a rate of $15 per loom. In most cases licenses were granted to build and use relatively small numbers of Waltham machines at a standard price set by the company. Such transactions usually involved only one or two types of machines, and were in the nature of an outright sale. In certain instances, however, broader agreements were entered into with other mills, and these were formalized in legal documents. Such an agreement between the Boston Manufacturing Company and the Dover Factory Company, of Dover, New Hampshire, dated October 12, 1821, furnishes an illustration of the terms involved.

By the terms of this agreement the Dover factory was granted the right to use all machinery patented by the Boston Manufacturing Company and all machinery not patented but in use at Waltham. The agent of the Dover Factory Company was given free access "to examine the buildings, works, tools, implements, machinery, modes of operation, processes, improvements and modifications as well relating to the making and using machinery, as to the general manufacture of cotton goods." The Dover company was also granted the use of "such patterns for castings as the Boston Manufacturing Company may from time to time possess." The rights specified were limited to the construction of a 6,000-spindle mill by the Dover Factory Company for their own use and were restricted to a term of five years. For these privileges the Dover company agreed to pay $6,000; and the agreement contains the further provision that they "will not communicate to others, or for the interest of others, such information as they may receive under this agreement, but will adopt such measures as the said Boston Manufacturing Company shall communicate for the purpose of preventing publicity to such things as the said parties shall require not to be made public." [42]

In February of 1822 a much broader agreement was made with the newly formed Merrimack Manufacturing Company, under the terms of which the Boston Manufacturing Company granted all the privileges included in the Dover agreement, but placed no limitations of time or quantity and agreed to let Moody work for Merrimack at such times as he could be spared from his Waltham duties. The price paid by the Merrimack Manufacturing Company was $15,000. On October 1, 1823, a third contract of this nature was made by the Boston Manufacturing Company. This contract was with the Elliot Manufacturing Company, of Newton Upper Falls, and was similar to the Dover agreement.[43]

The Waltham licensing agreements constitute an early example of a business technique which did much to hasten the industrial development of the country. The practice of selling manufacturing rights enabled small machine shops to get their machines produced in greater volume and over a wider area than would have been possible had they utilized only their own manufacturing facilities. To the independent inventor with no production facilities at his disposal, licensing offered a solution to his fundamental problem of making money from invention. The sharing of patents came to be widely practised, and went far toward breaking American manufacturing enterprise loose from the suffocating restrictions of small size and provincial isolation.

There is no evidence to show that the licensing of inventions to other manufacturers in the cotton textile industry was practised on any significant scale before the time of the Boston Manufacturing Company. Widespread knowledge and use of Samuel Slater's machinery in the 1790's came about as a result of actual theft of machine plans by workmen. The fact that two decades later Waltham machinery was made available to the industry largely through legitimate channels of sale and patent leasing indicates, not that Americans were becoming more scrupulous, but that patent rights and laws had now come to carry weight. The licensing agreements testify to the small scale of operations at Waltham; also, they constituted an effort on the part of the company in its formative years to utilize for its own profit the productive capacities of other manufacturers.

The nature of the company's machinery customers and the terms under which business was conducted with those customers present further evidence of small-scale operations in a localized industry, and indicate that no clear-cut policy had evolved in the matter of discounts and credit. From February to August, 1817, sales of machinery were made to five cotton mills. By 1823 the list had grown to twenty-three customers. One sale was made to a company in Matteawan, New York, and another to a Maryland manufacturer. These two cases were not typical. The bulk of the machinery business from 1817 to 1824 was done with customers located within a radius of fifty miles of Waltham — in Dedham, Milford, Winthrop, Taunton, Dover, and other Massachusetts and New Hampshire communities where survivors of the old "cotton-factory fever" days struggled on.[44]

For such a small amount of textile machine business as existed in the lean years from 1815 to 1822 the Boston Manufacturing Company had scant competition. There were a number of mechanics north of Providence who could and did produce one type of machine, but these independent craftsmen generally failed to develop into important machinery manufacturers. One exception was Ira Draper, but the Draper shop developed later and existed then only as a specialized establishment. The Scholfields, who commenced in a promising fashion soon after 1800 with the manufacture of machine cards, confined themselves to woolen machinery and were not a factor in the cotton-machine market. Elsewhere in Massachusetts cotton-textile machines were built only in the insignificant machine shops of small cotton mills, and little of this work appears to have entered the general market.

Rhode Island had an active textile machinery industry with at least two independent machine shops in the Providence area after 1810, and considerable machine-building activity in the many mills of the Blackstone Valley. The Rhode Island and the Waltham markets were virtually non-competing, however. The fact that two different manufacturing systems and divergent technical viewpoints evolved in the two neighboring areas is an indication of localized trade and essential independence. Transportation difficulties may explain this phenomenon of isolation. Trade in heavy equipment actually grew up more rapidly between seaports hundreds of miles apart than between inland towns separated by a few dozen miles of abominable country roads. A further and very simple explanation for the lack of competition between shops of the two areas, however, is that the Rhode Island machine shops and the shop in Waltham were not as yet large enough to feel pinched by their environment. There was business to be had at home.

There were many machine-builders in New York, New Jersey,

and Pennsylvania, and extensive machine shops existed at Paterson, but these, too, served a local market. Until after 1823 there appears to have been virtually no regular movement of textile machinery between these various centers of cotton-manufacturing activity, and very little movement within each. The cotton mills themselves were building a substantial part of their own machinery.

In the matter of terms of machinery sale the policy of the Boston Manufacturing Company reflected the mercantile background of the company management. Francis Lowell and Patrick Tracy Jackson in their old capacity of merchant dealt, of necessity, in both short-term and long-term credits. Often they waited many months for returns from their investments. As manufacturers they brought the long-range viewpoint into the merchandising of both cloth and machines. In the former case they set up standing accounts with their selling agent; in the latter they extended liberal credit direct to their customers. In the years from 1817 to 1822 it is doubtful whether machinery could have been sold to the credit-stricken industry on any other basis.

An examination of the machinery sales accounts for these years reveals little consistency of credit policy and no discernible trend. Roughly 16 per cent of sales were for cash, and in a few cases cash discounts ranging from 1½ per cent to 3 per cent were granted. Credit of from one to three months was extended on 26 per cent of all sales; 15 per cent more were made on four to eleven months' credit; 37 per cent on credit of twelve to twenty-four months; and 5 per cent on credit of longer than twenty-four months. There appear to have been few losses from bad debts, although credits were frequently extended beyond the contractual limits.

In Table 1 is presented the statistical picture of marketing operations from 1817, the time when the company first began selling machinery, to 1823, when such operations were curtailed. One fact revealed here tends to be overshadowed by the seeming insignificance of the figures involved. However small the volume of business done, the company learned in these years that the manufacture of textile machines could be independently profitable. The table also points to wide fluctuations in sales from year to year. These fluctuations undoubtedly reflect the changing fortunes of the

TABLE 1

SALES, PRICES, AND PROFITS: TEXTILE MACHINERY OF THE BOSTON MANUFACTURING COMPANY

Product	Cost	Price[a]	Sales (By number of machines; year ending August 31) 1817	1818	1819	1820	1821	1822	1823
Looms	$ 90	$ 125	26	0	33	0	0	1	18
Bobbin Machines	150	175	2	...	...	...	...	...	...
Cards	150	175	...	...	...	...	8	5	...
Warper	200	600	3	2	8	1	...	1	1
Double Speeder	950	2,000	...	2	4	...	2	3	...
Dresser	500	1,000	3	3	7	1	...	1	1
Throstle Frames									
Warp (per spindle)	5	8	(No. of spindles)		...	...	256	1,920	...
Filling (per spindle)	7	10–12[b]			256	...	640	1,024	...
Drawing Frames	200	300	1	1	2	...	1	...	...
Picker	400	...	...	...	...	...	...	...	...
Rights to build and use:[c]									
Loom	...	15	16	23	24	12	...	32	130
Double Speeder	...	300	...	...	...	...	3	2	...
Warper	...	300	...	...	...	...	3	...	...
Dresser	...	300	...	...	...	...	3	1	...
Throstle frame (per spindle)	...	2	(No. of spindles)		...	...	...	384	...
Sales of Machinery & Parts[d]			$7,338	$8,698	$28,806	$1,807	$11,547	$33,513	$3,455
Less Cost			5,467	3,980	14,774	900	11,229[e]	23,184	2,440
Profit on goods manufactured			$1,871	$4,718	$14,032	$ 907	$ 318	$10,329	$1,015
Profit as per cent of sales			25	54	49	50	3	31	29
Add other income:									
From patent fees			160	345	360	180	2,400	3,369	1,540
From sale of general manufacturing rights			...	...	...	...	...	21,000	5,000
Total profit in dollars			$2,031	$5,063	$14,392	$1,087	$ 2,718	$34,698	$7,555
Total profit as per cent of sales			28	58	50	60	23	103[f]	219[f]

[a] Prices most frequently charged.

[b] Price from August, 1819, to June, 1821, was $12; thereafter, $10.

[c] Exclusive of general rights granted Dover Factory Co., Merrimack Manufacturing Co., and Elliot Manufacturing Co.

[d] Figures for sales, cost, and profits are computed or taken direct from the Boston Manufacturing Co. Sales Machinery account. This account was credited with machinery sales and income from patent fees and manufacturing rights. Charged against the account were standard costs of machines sold and a small number of miscellaneous items such as legal expenses in patent suits, drayage, etc. The balance of the account — which appears, with minor adjustments, as "Total Profit" above — was credited to the personal account of P. T. Jackson on the books of the company.

[e] Includes cost of $2,000 incurred in sending representative to England.

[f] These profit figures reflect special transactions more in the nature of capital gain than of normal operating profit.

Source: Computed from Boston Manufacturing Company Ledgers, Journals, and Accounts Current.

textile industry, but they also indicate periodic concentration by the machine shop on orders for the parent company. Product trends are hinted at — the minor importance of loom, card, and drawing-frame sales; the growing volume of patent-right sales; the steady emphasis on dressing, warping, and roving machinery; the increasing popularity of the Waltham throstle frame. The great significance of this product information, however, lies less in the changes in emphasis than in the fact that the Waltham shop was producing a general line of cotton machinery and could come close to outfitting a mill complete. This policy, first becoming effective in 1821, was consciously followed by the two successors of the Waltham shop for nearly a century; it constitutes the axis around which much of the Saco-Lowell history revolves. In 1821 the policy of diversification was not new to the textile machine business — it had been forecast as early as 1793 in New York, 1808 in New Jersey, 1810 in Rhode Island and Pennsylvania, and 1813 in North Carolina.[45] Nevertheless, it constituted an important local departure from the specialization of mechanics upon one or two machines which generally characterized the trade of the times in northern New England. It was an important and consistent feature of the Waltham psychology of manufacture.

Tools and Price of Materials

The record books of the Boston Manufacturing Company emphasize the fact that the primary function of the machine shop was to construct machinery for the company. There is no evidence to indicate that the management contemplated extensive cultivation of the textile-machinery market, and there is considerable evidence to support the conclusion that, initially, a minor rôle was contemplated for the shop, once the company building program was completed.

During the 1814–16 period, when no machinery sales were being made to other companies, all expense incurred in the construction and acquisition of machines was charged to an expense account labeled "Machinery." The machine shop was charged with no capital assets, and, insofar as the formal records of the company are concerned, did not even exist. Some capital assets, consisting of a small number of machine tools, were acquired or built, but these were charged to the expense account. Even when the machine shop was moved to a new building (in 1818) and began to make machinery for others, no separate account was used to record its activities. All expenditures — current and capital, direct and indirect — were still charged to and the cost of machines sold was credited to the machinery account. This account, then, is the key to machine-shop operations. From it may be had glimpses, but glimpses only, of manufacturing activity from 1816 to 1824.

The acquisition of many hand tools is recorded, but in most cases the sources of supply cannot be identified. A surprisingly small number of machine tools were purchased. These came from the Leach foundry in Easton and appear to have been used as models from which the company built its own tools. An inventory of the machine shop taken in February, 1817, lists the equipment with which the 2,000 spindles of Mill Number One had been placed in operation, and which at that time was being turned to the construction of machinery for the 3,500-spindle Mill Number Two.

TABLE 2

TOOLS AND EQUIPMENT OF THE MACHINE SHOP, FEBRUARY, 1817

Description	Valuation[a]
3 anvils with blocks	$ 100.00
2 forge bellows	55.50
New files	194.50
2 cutting engines	390.00
1 fluting engine	80.00
4 roller engines	730.00
1 polishing machine	50.00
8 lathes for turning	800.00
19 vises with benches	380.00
Carpenter's chest of tools	105.35
9 small and 2 large grindstones	19.00
6 grindstones & frames	30.00
Patterns for castings	300.00
1 pair large shears for cutting iron	30.00
Sundry small tools & benches	1,500.00
Miscellaneous	102.87
Total	$4,867.22

[a] Valuations placed by the company reveal the lack of any fixed depreciation policy, but indicate that management was aware of this cost. All equipment was written down in value at various times, and the loss charged to expense of the period. The term "depreciation" does not appear in the record books of this period.

Source: Boston Manufacturing Co., Accounts Current.

Prices for materials purchased by the company declined more or less steadily from 1817 to 1824.[46] The few cases where earlier comparisons are possible indicate declining prices after 1815. Brass wire which cost $1.00 per pound in 1817 cost 80¢ per pound in 1824. Over the same time-span coal declined from 28¢ to 21¢ per basket; blistered steel from 18¢ to 12¢ per pound; shuttles from $1.23 to 40¢ each; and iron wire from 18¢ to 4¢ per pound. Cast steel, for which the company paid $1.35 per pound in 1814, had declined to 33¢ in 1816, to 26¢ in 1817, and to 21¢ in 1824. Emery, which sold for 32¢ per pound in 1814, cost 25¢ in 1817 and 15¢ in 1824. Block tin declined from 50¢ per pound in 1815 to 25¢ in 1824. The descriptions of iron bars and shapes vary so widely over the period studied that comparisons are difficult. From the records it is evident, however, that the company was using large quantities of English, Swedish, and Russian iron, the prices of which also appear to have declined considerably between 1817 and 1824.

Entries in the machinery account recording the purchase of castings are highly significant. Most important, they reveal the fact that the Boston Manufacturing Company had no foundry. For the entire 1814–24 period the company purchased its castings. The two principal suppliers were Charles L. Leonard, of Canton, Massachusetts, and Shepard Leach, of Easton, Massachusetts. Leach completed by far the larger amount of work. Orders placed with the Easton foundry grew from $5,000 in 1817 to $26,000 in 1824, and the Boston Manufacturing Company numbered among its assets "Patterns at Leach's Furnace." The price per pound for castings declined from 8¢ in 1814 to 6¢ in 1824. This decline undoubtedly reflected declining metal prices, but increasing foundry skill and possible economies from larger orders may also have played a part.

Accounting

The question inevitably arises as to what the Boston Manufacturing Company considered as costs of building machinery. Unit costs which reflected allocation, on one basis or another, of all overhead costs were not computed for either cloth or machinery. Certain costs were not charged to the machinery or cloth accounts at all, but were posted, along with the machinery and cloth-account balances, to a central clearing account, which alone served to show what the over-all costs of doing business and the total profits from the enterprise were.[47] The cost-per-machine figures given in Table I are therefore artificial to the extent that they fail to include some overhead costs. The margin of error is not large, however, for the company allocated portions of a large percentage of its total costs to the production accounts. There was a painstaking tabulation of all direct costs, together with a careful allocation of such costs to the department of the business in which they were incurred. Labor costs, for example, were not only broken down between cloth, machinery, and other accounts, but were even further prorated to the various types of machines under construction or repair. A definite attempt was made to charge many overhead costs to the production accounts. An outstanding example of this attempt to assign such costs to the department in which they were incurred is provided by the company's treatment of executive salaries. The salaries of Paul Moody and Patrick Tracy Jackson were spread over several different accounts, and the allocations were varied from period to period as the supervisory attention of these men shifted. Presumably the basis employed in making these charges was the number of hours (probably estimated rather than tabulated) devoted by the agent and the treasurer to the various phases of the business.

There are few contemporary examples against which to measure the accounting methods of the Boston Manufacturing Company. A tentative appraisal, which could be confirmed or denied only by an extensive study of American accounting practice, indicates that in bringing to manufacturing industry the conscientious record-keeping of the merchant countinghouse the company made a vastly important contribution to American business techniques. This contribution should be assigned a value equal to that of the Waltham precedents in production organization, mechanical effort, and labor policy.

Labor and Wages

Much has been written about the Waltham labor policies — the employment of young women of the countryside, the payment of cash wages, and the construction of company-owned boarding houses, store, school, and church. This story is more pertinent to the history of the cloth-manufacturing activities at Waltham than to a history of the machine shop. In general it may be said that employment in the machine shop exhibited far less of the new and revolutionary than did employment in the mill. The record books, however, preserve only statistical fragments of the human side of the machine-building business.

A question of primary interest is where the mechanics employed by Moody came from, and where they received their training. One reputable authority states that all workmen in the early machine shops were native Americans taken from the common trades and farms, who came into the shops unskilled.[48] From the rates paid at Waltham, however, it may be inferred that many of the mechanics there were skilled and experienced when they reached Waltham. These men may have come from the Blackstone Valley mills, which in 1814 were still the primary training ground for textile mechanics. Additional evidence that skilled native labor was available is provided by entries in the record books of expenses incurred in advertising for foundrymen. In only one case does the company appear to have imported skilled labor from abroad. In March, 1816, the expenses of a passage from England for a Thomas Faulkner were paid by the company. This man was subsequently paid a substantial salary of $1,000 a year, which was charged to the machinery and spinning accounts.[49]

In May, 1817, when detailed labor statistics first are given in the company records, employment in the machine shop was expanding. In this month the total number of Boston Manufacturing Company employees was one hundred and twenty-five, of whom twenty-five were machinists and the remainder either maintenance men or mill operatives. (Table 3 presents a detailed analysis of the company working force.) Under the impetus of the company building program the number of machinists increased to a peak of sixty-five in July of 1818. The very marked downward trend of employment after that date indicates that the building of machinery for other factories had failed to sustain a high level of activity in the machine shop. The downward trend also coincides with the sharp recession in general business activity in America which occurred in 1819. From the July, 1818, high point the number of machinists declined to a low of twenty-nine in September, 1819, and then rallied in the following months to a level of about thirty to thirty-five men. In 1823 employment in the shop expanded under the impetus of machinery orders from the Merrimack Manufacturing Company, and by February, 1824, a total of forty machinists were employed. In March of that year machine-building activities were all but halted, and about half of the machinists moved on to a new scene of operations.

Wages in the machine shop were computed weekly and distributed in cash semi-monthly. In 1817 all wages (except in the case of Moody and Faulkner, who were paid annual salaries) appear to have been based on a straight day rate. These rates were quoted in shillings, but the total computations were given in dollars and cents. Throughout the entire 1817–24 period most of the machinists whose names appear in the records were credited with full-time employment of six days per week. It would appear that when there was not enough work to provide reasonably full-time employment, machinists were laid off rather than kept on in a part-time status. Day rates continued to be the main basis for wage computations; after 1817, however, piece rates assumed increasing importance. Often a combination of the two kinds of rates was used. A machinist's weekly earnings, for example, might consist of two days' work on spindle repair at a rate of nine shillings per day, plus a sum representing completion of two dozen double speeder shafts at 20¢ per shaft.

Table 3 represents the various wage scales in effect in all departments of the Boston Manufacturing Company; it is subject to the usual bias attendant upon the use of average figures which include both the highest- and the lowest-paid employees. There is, however, a close correlation between daily rates and actual earnings because of the fact, before noted, that most of the employees were on or near a full-time work schedule.

In the wage rates paid to individual workmen there was surprisingly little variation over the 1817–24 period. A few rates were raised, but cuts were rarely made. The attempt to trace the rates paid to individual workmen over a period of time reveals a high turnover of employees. Of the thirty-one machinists employed in May, 1817, only five were still on the payroll in September, 1823.

A possible explanation of this turnover is that Waltham-trained men were now in as great demand in the industry as Slater-trained men had been earlier. In the few cases where piece rates can be traced over several years, little change is observable and no clearly defined trend appears. Year-to-year comparisons are difficult, however, because of rapid changes in job classifications.

TABLE 3

CLASSIFICATION OF WORKERS AND WAGE RATES, MAY, 1817
BOSTON MANUFACTURING COMPANY

Classification of Employee	Number	Average Daily Wage
Machinists	26	$1.43
Carpenters	2	1.42
Laborers	4	1.02
Millwright	1	1.41
Picker	1	1.25
Carders	17	.44
Roper[a]	1	2.31
Double Speeder Operative[a]	1	1.12
Spinners	12	.51
Warpers[a]	3	.54
Mule Spinners[a]	2	3.14
Dressers[a]	4	.94
Drawing-in Operative[a]	1	.84
Winders[a]	6	.58
Weavers[a]	36	.62
Cloth Picker	5	.43
Watchmen	2	1.05
Teamster	1	1.00

[a] Average daily earnings on piece-rate basis.
Source: Boston Manufacturing Co., vol. 80, Payroll.

The average daily wage of machinists had a slight downward trend after 1817, and in February, 1824, the shop average had declined to $1.20 per day.[50] This decline did not come about as a result of individual pay cuts, but because of a general shift toward employment of new help at lower rates. In May, 1817, 16 per cent of the machinists were paid at a rate of $1.75 or more per day; 74 per cent were paid from $1.00 to $1.75; and 10 per cent were paid less than $1.00. In February, 1824, the percentages for the three pay brackets had shifted to 10 per cent for the highest, 73 per cent for the middle, and 17 per cent for the lowest.[51] This shifting downward of wage rates seems to indicate that machine-building techniques were being systematized to permit the replacement of highly skilled machinists by lower-paid, more specialized, and less skilled men. Such a conclusion is strongly supported by an examination of piece-rate records for the period. These records reveal a marked increase in the subdivision of jobs in the machine shop. A growing concept of machine-building as a series of related but specialized operations becomes evident. From the time in 1814 when the completed machine was the basic unit of cost, the Waltham manufacturing system had progressed to a point where costs were first expressed in terms of parts and the minutely specialized procedures involved in the manufacture of those parts. A fundamental element in this system and an evidence of the increasing scope and subdivision of manufacture was the practice of numbering patterns for castings. This practice first became a necessity early in 1817. By 1823, mass-production techniques clearly were being applied by the Boston Manufacturing Company to the manufacture of machinery as well as cloth.

6. The Concluding Phase of Machine-Shop Operations 1822–1824

The final phase of machine-building operations at Waltham involves the formation of the Merrimack Manufacturing Company and the transfer of the Waltham machine shop to Chelmsford, Massachusetts.

Chapter III deals with the background of the Merrimack Manufacturing Company, and it is sufficient to note here only that this company, a promotion of the Boston Manufacturing Company stockholders, was in the process of being organized during 1821, and on February 6, 1822, was duly chartered by the Commonwealth of Massachusetts. Mention has already been made of the February, 1822, agreement, under the terms of which the Boston Manufacturing Company granted the Merrimack Manufacturing Company broad rights to build the Waltham machinery. Late in June of 1823 Patrick Tracy Jackson received the following letter:[52]

Chelmsford June 20, 1823

Sir/

The Merrimack Mang. Co. being anxious to establish a shop at Chelmsford for the construction of machinery on the principles now in use at Waltham, are desirous to purchase of the Boston Mang. Co. all their patent rights, patterns &c, together with all their spare tools, & the services of such of their mechanics as the BMCo. can dispense with.

In the event of the BMCo. consenting to treat for the same, a committee has been appointed to adjust the terms, consisting of Mr. Dutton & myself.

I am sir
Yr Obt Sert
Kirk Boott Agent M. M. Co.

The plans and needs of the Merrimack Manufacturing Company appear, by 1823, to have grown beyond the point where they could be satisfied by the 1822 agreement. This agreement was the most extensive entered into by the Boston Manufacturing Company up to that time, but it provided for no mass transfer of workmen or tools or patterns, and the Merrimack Manufacturing Company would have had to build a machine shop in order to exploit the patent rights acquired. The offer advanced by Kirk Boott in his letter contemplated, in fact, the physical transfer of a substantial part of the machine-shop assets and the full-time employment at Chelmsford of Paul Moody and others. On August 9, 1823, an agreement between the two companies was drawn up to achieve these objectives.

By the terms of the 1823 agreement the Merrimack Manufacturing Company acquired the title to all Waltham patent rights and the privilege of building, using, and selling all Waltham machinery, patented or unpatented. The Boston Manufacturing Company retained the right, however, also to build, use, and sell that machinery. Patterns for castings were sold outright to Merrimack, with the provision that the Boston Manufacturing Company might use them at any time. Such tools as Merrimack might require were to be transferred by the Waltham company. Paul Moody's contract with the Boston Manufacturing Company was to be canceled, leaving him free to make a new contract with Merrimack. The Boston Manufacturing Company, nevertheless, was to have the privilege of consulting Moody, and also was to have the benefit of all inventions and improvements that Moody might make at Chelmsford. For these rights and privileges the Merrimack Manufacturing Company agreed to pay the Boston Manufacturing Company $75,000, payable on or before October 1, 1824.[53]

The decision of the Boston Manufacturing Company to dispose of the machine shop and to terminate extensive machine-building activities at Waltham is colored by the virtually complete identity of ownership of the two companies.[54] The most important factor in the action taken was the desire to start spindles turning in a new location that offered unlimited possibilities for exploitation. The old concept that the machine shop was an indispensable appendage to new construction still prevailed. Clearly, the building of textile machinery had not yet been divorced from the cotton-mill basement, and had yet to evolve from a subsidiary function to an independent industry.

Construction of the machinery for the Merrimack Manufacturing Company's first two mills had been commenced in Waltham more than a year preceding the agreement to transfer the machine shop to Chelmsford. After August, 1823, charges to the Merrimack account recording the progress of machinery construction became increasingly heavy. By February, 1824, Merrimack's first mill was completed, and charges to that company totaled more than $100,000. At that time the physical transfer of the machine shop appears to have taken place. In that month Moody ceased to be referred to as "Agent" on the books of the Boston Manufacturing Company. A portion of his salary, however, continued to be charged to the Waltham company. Thomas Borden, superintendent of the machine shop, moved to Chelmsford at that time, and the dropping of fifteen other machinists from the Waltham payrolls possibly signifies a mass transfer of personnel. Machinery built after February, 1824, continued to be charged to the Merrimack account on the books of the Boston Manufacturing Company, but there is a strong possibility that it was actually constructed in a new shop commenced by the Merrimack Manufacturing Company in Chelmsford in the spring of 1823.

By February, 1825, the agreements between the Boston Manufacturing Company and the Merrimack Manufacturing Company both as to transfer of machine-shop assets and as to construction of machinery had been completely fulfilled. The ledgers of the Boston Manufacturing Company reveal the results of the concluding phase of machine-shop operations in Waltham.[55] During the period from August, 1822, through February, 1825, the Boston Manufacturing Company built machinery for the two Merrimack mills consisting of a total of 7,168 spindles. The price charged Merrimack was $28 per spindle, with an additional charge of $5,000 for extras. On the total order of $205,704 for machinery, plus a transfer of approximately $25,000 of tools, equipment, and other assets, the Boston Manufacturing Company realized a profit of some $52,000 in addition to the $75,000 fee paid by Merrimack under the terms of the 1823 agreement.[56] Despite Patrick Tracy Jackson's professed fear that the profits of the company would be reduced by the transaction, the Boston Manufacturing Company in January, 1825, declared a 15 per cent dividend, marking it "Extra from profits on sale of machinery."[57]

With the transfer to Chelmsford of Moody, Borden, and other machinists, as well as a number of machine tools and all patterns, and with the completion of the Merrimack order for machinery, machine-building at Waltham was virtually suspended. A shop was maintained and a score of machinists employed, but only local repair and maintenance work was undertaken. After 1824 the Boston Manufacturing Company ceased to be a factor in the development of American textile machinery, and the initiative was deliberately passed to other hands.

7. The Essence of Management

The operating results achieved by the Boston Manufacturing Company and by the machine shop reflect a virile, purposeful, and imaginative business management. Of the three dominant personalities responsible for success Francis Lowell indicated the goals, Paul Moody provided the means, and Patrick Tracy Jackson applied Moody's means toward the fulfillment of Lowell's goals.

Francis Lowell was not a key figure in the management of routine company affairs. His legal connection with the company was limited to his position of stockholder and director. He held no active office and he accepted no pay. The force of his personality cannot be appraised, and his premature death in 1817 leaves unanswered vital questions of his influence on managerial policy. He appears to belong to that class of business men who sincerely identify their own with the public interest. He operated in full view of society and concerned himself primarily with the basic economic, social, and political aspects of the business. He was, in short, a new type of manufacturer in America.

In contrast to the shadowy figure of Lowell, Patrick Tracy Jackson's personality sparkles in company affairs. There was commanding dignity in his rangy figure and there was Irish humor in his face — he was a man instantly liked and trusted by other men. His actions and letters show foresight, a grasp of both principles and details, a strong sense of self and company interest, and a profound (and sometimes uncritical) enthusiasm for promotion. A planner himself, he appears to have been the perfect agent for the execution of the plans of other men. His concern with Moody's mechanical efforts was immediate, and he was never far removed from scenes of operation. In 1814 and 1815 Jackson was engaged not only in welding the organization together, but in supervising construction, keeping accounts, and making purchases. His salary was never charged wholly to administrative expense, but was allocated to machinery, gearing, buildings, mill, and other operating accounts. After 1815 he appears to have withdrawn somewhat from machine-shop affairs, relinquishing to Moody the supervision of routine matters there. To Patrick Tracy Jackson the Boston Manufacturing Company, and hence the machine shop, owed much for its successful course after 1814. His influence on the American textile industry was exceeded only by that of Lowell.

Moody lacked the vision of Lowell and the sparkle of Jackson. He was the work-horse of the enterprise — a nimble-fingered Yankee with a single-mindedness of purpose. So great was his value to the company that he could have bargained for a top position in management, yet he remained a mechanic to the day of his death. His supervisory talents were adequate to enable him to manage the machine shop, but since that shop was not an independent operating unit the need was for mechanical rather than business judgment. His indispensable value to the enterprise can be entirely measured in terms of the machines which he produced. The application of production-line techniques to the manufacture of textile machinery was a great step forward, but one which savors as strongly of Jackson's talents as of Moody's.

The success of the Boston Manufacturing Company was the success of the machine shop, and many of the factors contributing to that success were new to American manufacturing enterprise. The promoters of the Boston Manufacturing Company were merchants, and they carried over to the manufacturing field the strengths and weaknesses of the system of mercantile capitalism under which they had established their fortunes. Those strengths were potent indeed.

One great asset possessed by the company was a large and fluid capital. This was associated with a concept of large-scale enterprise hitherto almost unknown to American manufacturers.[58] The concept of great size, large capital, and wide markets was a direct legacy from the merchant world. Applied to the manufacturing world it dwarfed contemporary undertakings and laid open a new and timely vista to American capitalists, to whom big business had previously been associated with sailing vessels, countinghouses, lumber, rum and molasses, trade and barter.

If the chief physical asset of the Boston Manufacturing Company and of the machine shop was capital, the chief skill was managerial — a facility in putting that capital to productive use. This, too, was a legacy of the system of mercantile capitalism which, above all else, demanded of its merchant disciples a fine touch in the control of goods and agents, plus an unlimited capacity for making rapid adjustments to changing conditions.

The accounting controls of mercantile trade were here adapted with outstanding success to the requirements of an industrial system. Mercantile accounting could scarcely be applied to a manufacturing business without substantial alterations. These alterations were made, but the concept of close control through the keeping of adequate records was carried over intact. The accounting system of the Boston Manufacturing Company was a classic influence in the New England textile industry and may, upon further study, prove to have possessed even wider significance.

A corollary to the scope of operations contemplated at Waltham was the necessity that management weigh most carefully the effects of national policy upon its business. Since earliest colonial days manufacturers had turned to government for special assistance. The artisans of the countryside first looked to community or State government, however, and it was the merchant with his national and international interests who made the first successful attempts to influence national as well as local government policy in his behalf. Francis Lowell probably did as much as any other one man to bring to manufacturing enterprise the broad political viewpoint of the merchant. His successful lobbying for tariff protection in 1816 was an accomplishment which few contemporary mill owners had the influence to accomplish. This was certainly a meaningful precedent.

The wealth of the Boston Manufacturing Company and the powerful social contacts of its promoters and managers made possible a managerial practice which the tiny mills of southern Massachusetts and Rhode Island could scarcely have afforded, and which manufacturers in general had hitherto neglected. This new technique was the employment of professional consulting experts. It is a remarkable fact that within a short space of time the Boston Manufacturing Company employed Daniel Webster, Nathaniel Bowditch, Jacob Perkins, and Loammi Baldwin — men of preëminent reputation in the fields of law, mathematics, mechanical engineering, and construction engineering, respectively. Company policy went beyond the mere employment of expert talent. Webster, Bowditch, and Baldwin were all given an opportunity to subscribe to the closely held stock of the company, thus reinforcing their professional interest with a personal one.

The practice of employing experts was, in part at least, a defensive mechanism designed to compensate for a fundamental weakness of the merchant managers. However strong the merchant might be in finance and management, his technical deficiencies could not be denied. Though both Lowell and Jackson had unusual mechanical aptitude, neither was essentially a technical man. The employment of expert mechanics could successfully remedy the deficiency only so long as the advice of those mechanics was judiciously heeded. In the years following 1824, unfortunately, collaboration between top management and technicians was not always close, and when a break occurred there was abundant opportunity for disaster.

Few of the policies put into effect by the Boston Manufacturing Company were individually new, but taken as a whole they represented a type of business administration new to American industry. Far more significant than the "Waltham System" of manufacture was the Waltham system of management which guided the company's manufacturing experiments. Machine techniques changed rapidly — Moody's great innovations became obsolete and were superseded. The managerial principles adopted at Waltham, however, not only established basic precedents for the guidance of the machine-building trades, but also set the pattern for the development of big business in America.

CHAPTER III

THE SHOP THAT BUILT A CITY

Proprietors of the Locks and Canals on Merrimack River — Lowell, Massachusetts, 1823–1845

1. The Larger Plan

The founding and early history of the city of Lowell, Massachusetts, has become inseparably associated with noble social objectives on the part of the founders. It was an essentially simple business situation, however, which transformed the tiny village of East Chelmsford into this once thriving "City of Spindles."

The Boston Manufacturing Company had been making more money than the stockholders had dreamed possible. In 1820 and early 1821 the decision to expand operations and thereby secure still larger profits was not a difficult one to make. A new company could be formed to make the old product, but this would involve competition with the existing organization. Instead, it was suggested by market-wise Nathan Appleton that printed calicoes be attempted. Another vital decision involved the choice of a site more adaptable than Waltham to the water-power requirements of a large factory. If these decisions, necessitated by the drive for greater profits, required that the face of civilization be changed — then let it be changed. If social benefits as well as dollar profits accrued — so much the better. Francis Cabot Lowell would have said that such a result was not only good, but good business. Thus it was that the self-interest of an eminently practical group of men founded a city, stimulated an industry to new heights, and energized profound social movements. As in 1814, the machine shop was the keystone of the contemplated structure.

There is a continuity in this important branch of the Saco-Lowell history which defies both corporate and geographic change. The machine shop of the Boston Manufacturing Company was moved to Lowell, to perform there the same task of mill-building that had been undertaken at Waltham, though on a vaster scale. As first set up in Lowell in 1824, the machine shop existed as a department of the Merrimack Manufacturing Company. This cotton-mill alliance clearly was derived from the earlier Waltham pattern. In 1825, machine-building operations were transferred to a development company known as the Proprietors of the Locks and Canals on Merrimack River. The traditional link between machine shop and cotton mill was not severed by this move, for by this time the Locks and Canals Company (as it has always been called) was closely controlled by the Merrimack Company. After 1837, however, the machine shop became increasingly independent of domination by any one cotton-manufacturing company. With the formation of the Lowell Machine Shop, in 1845, actual as well as legal independence was achieved.

Because, for the period covered in the present chapter, the machine shop was not an independent operating unit it scarcely can be studied apart from its parent companies, nor, indeed, from the general industrial development at Lowell which it both created and throve upon. In Chapter II the machinery contract between the Boston Manufacturing Company and the Merrimack Manufacturing Company was outlined, and the transfer of the machine shop from the old company to the new was noted. It is now necessary to consider the sequence of events occurring outside Waltham which lay behind that transfer and that contract.

Having made the decision to expand operations, Jackson, Appleton, Moody, and other stockholders of the Boston Manufacturing Company commenced a search for water power for a new factory. That search ended one day in the autumn of 1821 when Paul Moody descended from his chaise to view the magnificent Pawtucket Falls of the Merrimack River at East Chelmsford, a scanty twenty-five miles north of Boston.[1] The site was nearly ideal. It offered a powerful flow of water with more than a thirty-foot fall. It offered a canal connection with Boston — unlimited room for construction — and a canal around the falls which would be invaluable for mill purposes. The lack of a supply of labor in the area was no obstacle. Francis Lowell had already shown, at Waltham, that country labor would flock to the factories and occupy company-built housing.

Moody reported his "discovery" to Jackson and made a chalk diagram of the area for him to study. Jackson's active imagination responded with a scheme far more ambitious than the original desire to build a new factory. He conceived the plan of developing a huge manufacturing center which would encompass many factories—a plan on a scale untried and scarcely comprehensible in the light of experience to that time. Immediate action was initiated to put this larger plan into effect.

The Merrimack Manufacturing Company was formed to secure and develop the Pawtucket Falls area, establish a machine shop to supply both its own needs and those of such factories as should later be built, and engage in the manufacture of cloth. Many of the details involved in the formation of this company are not pertinent to a history of the machine shop, and it is sufficient to note only the presence of new capital from the Boston mercantile firm of Boott & Sons and the consequent appointment of Kirk Boott as agent and treasurer of the Merrimack Company.[2] Boott was to play an exceedingly important part in the affairs of the machine shop and in the general development of Lowell. His background will be considered in detail in that part of the history where his personality came to dominate company policy.

Moody's preliminary investigations of the East Chelmsford site revealed encouraging possibilities for acquiring the water rights and property at a reasonable figure. A substantial part of those rights was vested in the Proprietors of the Locks and Canals on Merrimack River, a company which had been formed in 1792 to operate a canal around the Pawtucket Falls to facilitate the passage of lumber and produce down-river. This project had been of some value to the shipbuilding interests of Newburyport at the mouth of the river, but the returns to the stockholders had not been large. Consequently, by 1821 the Locks and Canals stock was not selling at a high price, and there appears to have been little enthusiasm or optimism among the stockholders. The remainder of the land in the area was owned by a small number of farmers. There were some small mills at the falls, but these were renting water power from the Locks and Canals Company and their existence presented no serious additional problems.

So unconscious was America of the value of its water power that

Jackson with very little difficulty succeeded in acquiring a majority of the stock of the Locks and Canals Company and title to the key farmlands.[3] The prices he paid for land and stock were fair for the times—few indeed could foresee the cosmic change in standards of value implicit in the success of the Waltham venture. Those who did thus anticipate profited as few in New England had profited before. The acquisition in 1821 of the East Chelmsford lands at existing market rates and the increment in value of those lands thereafter exerted a dominant influence on the financial history of the machine shop and of all the Lowell mills.

2. The Lowell Development

Early Progress and the Division of Functions, 1821–1825

Having acquired title to the East Chelmsford lands and water rights, the Merrimack Manufacturing Company at once commenced to render the area suitable for large-scale manufacturing. A dam was built across the Merrimack River, the old Pawtucket Canal was widened and deepened, new locks were installed, and two additional canals were started. This activity was on a grand scale. Five hundred Irish laborers were sent in to dig and blast the main canal. Shanty villages sprang up in the pastures, and the peaceful hamlet was transformed into a boisterous construction camp. Kirk Boott exchanged letters with Myron Holley, engineer of the Erie Canal, and received valuable advice on the construction of dams and locks.[4] The enlarging of the Pawtucket Canal alone cost $120,000—more than the entire capital of most American cotton mills up to that time. On September 1, 1823, the task was completed, and water was let into the canal.[5]

In Waltham the machine shop of the Boston Manufacturing Company was busily engaged in building machinery for Merrimack's first two mills. By the fall of 1823, plans to move the machine shop to East Chelmsford were far advanced. A site for the shop had been picked at the Swamp Locks, and the construction of a building to house the machine shop had been started there. By early autumn of that year the first machinery in the Merrimack mills was ready to operate.

Paul Moody had planned a breast wheel of noble dimensions, and Kirk Boott recorded in his diary the beginning of operations:[6]

Thurs. Sept 4, 1823 After breakfast, went to factory, and found the wheel moving around his course, majestically and with comparative silence. Moody declared that was "the best wheel in the world." N. Appleton became quite enthusiastic. . . . Both Moody and Borden [Moody's assistant] said "they never saw machinery start better."

This was the beginning of Patrick Tracy Jackson's larger plan, and events which were to profoundly influence the machine shop transpired in rapid sequence after 1823.

A third factory for the Merrimack Company was commenced, the machinery being built not at Waltham but in the still unfinished machine shop at East Chelmsford. In May of 1824 the Merrimack directors were authorized to build two more factories at the Swamp Locks, on the opposite side of the Pawtucket Canal from the machine shop.

There is evidence that the initial plan for the development of the area was to have the Merrimack Company not only develop and regulate all water power but also operate all the factories which it might build and the machine shop as well. By 1824, however, it had become evident that such a program was beyond the capacity of one corporate body to administer. Plans for the Swamp Locks factories were abandoned, and two basic changes in policy were made. Some time in 1824 the Merrimack directors decided that new companies should be allowed to participate in the East Chelmsford development. Even more pertinent to the Saco-Lowell history, the directors further decided that the functions of cotton manufacturing and machinery building were better separated, but that machinery building and the regulation of water power and real estate could well be combined.[7] Future activities were predicated upon these assumptions.

The over-all industrial plan was carefully worked out on the basis of available water power, and a standard unit for the sale of that power was set up. Taking the second mill at Waltham as a model, the Merrimack Company divided its water rights into fifty mill powers. Each mill power carried with it the right to use water sufficient to drive a mill of 3,584 spindles and the right to purchase approximately four acres of land for a mill site.[8] Not only were the mill sites thus standardized and charted, but the outlines of an embryonic city were indicated in the form of plans for streets, bridges, operatives' housing, and certain civic buildings. This concept of a planned industrial community was far in advance of contemporary thinking, and it exerted a tremendous influence on the subsequent industrial growth of New England communities such as Lawrence, Chicopee Falls, Springfield, Biddeford, Nashua, Manchester, and many others.

In 1823 and 1824, negotiations were conducted relative to the formation of the first of the new companies to which mill power was to be sold. On January 26, 1825, the Hamilton Manufacturing Company was incorporated.[9] The Merrimack Manufacturing Company, having as yet divested itself neither of the machine shop nor of title to the water privileges, contracted to supply the Hamilton Company with machinery and buildings for two mills (7,168 spindles) at a cost of $26 per spindle. Water privileges and land were charged at the rate of $4.00 per spindle additional, and an annual water rental of $300 per mill power was agreed upon.[10] Before work on this contract had fairly begun, the Merrimack Company took the final step directed at divorcing itself of all but cotton-manufacturing functions.

The Proprietors of the Locks and Canals on Merrimack River had become inactive after the purchase of its stock by Merrimack in 1821. The charter, however, was still in force. The Merrimack directors therefore decided to revive this company and to transfer to it the machine shop and all lands and water rights, reserving only such property as was necessary for the Merrimack Company in the conduct of its cloth-manufacturing business.

New capital was required to enable the Locks and Canals Company to purchase the machine shop, real estate, and water rights and to carry out the general plan of development at East Chelmsford. This capital was promptly supplied by the Merrimack stockholders. Optimism was rampant. Stockholders in Jackson's enterprises refused premiums of 25 per cent for Boston Manufacturing Company

Kirk Boott
First Agent of the Merrimack Mills and Machine Shop

First Machine-shop Building, Lowell, Massachusetts

and Merrimack shares.[11] Stock in the Hamilton Company had been snapped up so quickly that few new stockholders had been able to secure shares. Times were good, and there seemed no limit to the possibilities for profit.[12]

In this spirit the revitalized Locks and Canals Company was launched. Kirk Boott was made agent and treasurer of the company, retaining both these offices in the Merrimack Company. Paul Moody was named superintendent. Thus the management of the machine shop remained the same as it had been while operating as a department of the Merrimack Company. The following transfer of assets between the two corporations was recorded:[13]

Transferred from Merrimack Manufacturing Company to Proprietors of the Locks and Canals on Merrimack River:

Locks and Canals stock	$ 60,000	
Water power and factory sites	358,400	
Other land (400 acres)	75,000	
Machine shop, tools, and buildings	215,016.91	
		$708,416.91
Less: Property retained by Merrimack Manufacturing Company		
6 mill powers at $3.00 per spindle	$ 64,512	
3 mills with machinery	279,552	
		344,064.00
Balance paid in cash by the Proprietors of the Locks and Canals to Merrimack Manufacturing Company:		$364,352.91

With the consummation of this transfer early in 1825 the pattern for the next twenty years was established. The corporate separation of cloth manufacture from machinery building was final — and the alliance of the latter with water-power ownership established a precedent that was closely followed in other manufacturing centers in New England. In this year, too, the machine shop was completed — five stories of new brick and gleaming white trim crowned with a slate roof and a graceful bell cupola.[14] There was great activity in shop, mill, and town. Two hundred and sixty laborers and mechanics under Moody's supervision hastened to set up machinery in Merrimack's third mill. Orders for the two mills of the Hamilton Manufacturing Company gave assurance of at least two years of peak activity, and there were rumors of more mills yet unplanned.

The community of East Chelmsford stood on the industrial frontier of America, and in 1825 it exhibited many of the characteristics of a true frontier settlement. The land bore the scars of construction with scant grace, and the shanty dwellings of canal-building days were now crowded with the families and even the livestock of the laborers. Where two hundred persons had lived in 1820 there were now twenty-five hundred, and lodgings were at a premium as each stage from Boston brought new arrivals. Contemporary observers viewed the scene with enthusiasm — a typically American enthusiasm for financial achievement and material triumph over natural obstacles.[15]

Building the Mills, 1826–1835

In 1824 the village of East Chelmsford secured a town charter. The question of a name was raised, and Nathan Appleton suggested Lowell. This was appropriate and fitting, for the plan envisaged by Jackson and executed by his associates and lieutenants differed only in scope from the pattern established at Waltham by Francis Cabot Lowell. Large capital; large mills, integrating many processes; wide markets; houses and civic services for the operatives — it was in this direction that Lowell evolved. This was a pattern of feudalism in which the mill was the castle and the agent was the bailiff. Some would have said that, on the one day in the week when he visited the mill, the treasurer was the Lord High Executioner. Operatives were not tied to the land as vassals, to be sure, but wages provided a more popular bond than law. The machine shop was the castle forge, which hammered out the tools and weapons that made a degree of self-sufficiency possible. Like early feudalism, the system was a remarkably efficient solution to problems of the day, and before deterioration set in, it provided notable advantages to all who sought its shelter.

The years which followed 1826 brought a succession of new mills created in the image of the Boston Manufacturing Company, each growing out of the success of antecedent ventures. Most of the machinery for these mills was built by the Locks and Canals Company. In most cases the machine shop was responsible for constructing the mill buildings and the housing for the operatives as well, together with many of the civic necessities for a booming community. No enterprise could locate advantageously in Lowell except on Locks and Canals land, and no wheels could turn except by means of Locks and Canals water. More advantageous circumstances for this company's operations could scarcely be imagined.

Throughout 1826 and the first six months of 1827 the Locks and Canals Company was engaged in constructing machinery for the two Hamilton mills. These were both in operation by the summer of 1827, and Hamilton at once purchased two additional mill powers and sought to contract for machinery for a third mill. At the same time, the Merrimack Manufacturing Company made plans for an additional mill. An agreement was made between the Locks and Canals Company, Merrimack, and Hamilton that machinery would be furnished for a Merrimack mill followed by machinery for a Hamilton mill and then for another Merrimack mill. In 1828, however, one of the original Merrimack mills burned, and Merrimack paid Hamilton $50,000 so that the order of contracts could be altered to permit the Locks and Canals Company to build machinery for the two Merrimack mills first.[16]

While Hamilton and Merrimack were clamoring for machinery, two new companies were forming. On February 4, 1828, the Appleton Company was incorporated; four days later the Lowell Manufacturing Company was organized. The latter proposed to manufacture carpeting, and the specialized machinery for this type of manufacture was not built by the Locks and Canals Company. The Appleton Company, however, was a customer for machinery. There seemed to be no end to the market opportunities in sight, and it was profitable business for the machine shop. The contract for one of the Merrimack mills specified 3,584 spindles at a price of $18.40 per spindle. An abatement from this sum was to be made by the Locks and Canals Company if the profit on the contract exceeded 25 per cent.[17] Kirk Boott was authorized by the directors of the Locks and Canals Company to settle the Appleton contract "on such a principle as will leave to the Proprietors a clear profit of twenty-five per cent on the cost of the machinery." [18]

By 1830 the Hamilton and Merrimack orders had been completed, and there was a lull in mill-building activity.[19] This lull was temporary; possibly it grew out of a sharp depression in 1829, which, while failing to shake the heavily capitalized Lowell companies, nevertheless hit the textile industry hard. By the end of 1831 the machine shop was plunged into an era of renewed activity. New capital was flowing from Boston to Lowell, and three new companies were incorporated — Proprietors of the Tremont Mills, the Suffolk Manufacturing Company, and the Lawrence Manufacturing Company.

The Tremont and Suffolk companies secured somewhat more advantageous contracts than had the earlier companies. The easing of terms may have reflected unsettled business conditions which prevailed in 1831 and 1832, but there is a possibility that mill-power prices were lower for the less advantageous sites. Kirk Boott offered Tremont two mill powers at a price of $3.00 per spindle, $1.00 less than the previous standard. He later offered two additional mill powers at a price of $2.50. He also offered to build machinery for two mills at such a price as would yield 20 per cent rather than 25 per cent profit. Although the Lawrence Company secured similar terms on its machinery, it appears to have paid the usual price of $4.00 per spindle for its mill powers.[20]

These contracts, plus additional work for Merrimack, kept the machine shop humming after 1831. By March of 1832, 10,240 spindles were in operation in the Suffolk mills. By July of 1833, 11,136 spindles were in operation in the Tremont mills, and two mills for Lawrence appear to have been completed. Lawrence hesitated briefly in 1833, then ordered machinery for two more mills.[21]

Some conception of the size and nature of these contracts may be gained from the Lawrence Manufacturing Company records. Far more than machinery was involved. By February, 1835, at which time four mills had been completed, the Locks and Canals Company's account with Lawrence consisted of the following items:[22]

Machinery and furniture	$342,119.36
Mills and gearing	213,515.91
Houses	102,663.86
Bleachery	57,008.72
Real estate, land & privileges	34,512.00
Storehouses	19,322.84
Interest	4,100.57
Total	$773,243.26

The year 1835 was one of high prosperity and excellent prospects. The machine shop had completed its large mill contracts, but another large contract was being negotiated with the newly formed Boott Mills. Abbott Lawrence, one of the promoters of this enterprise, cheerfully confided to Kirk Boott that the stock was all gone and "more than gone." The stock subscription situation, in fact, was "quite out of control." Subscribers to large blocks of shares had been asked to split their blocks to allow friends and relatives to participate — and had refused.[23]

The machine shop now employed nearly 300 men, and it was no idle boast that the complete machinery for a mill of 5,000 spindles could be turned out in four months.[24] In the decade following 1825 the population of Lowell had swelled from 2,500 to 15,000. Where 11,000 spindles had turned in 1825 there were now 120,000.[25] The best mill sites had been sold, but there were many other sites left, and little was now heard of the original plan of converting the machine shop to a cotton mill when all the potentialities of the area had been exploited.

Not the least of the causes for optimism was the revolution in transportation. Progress in communication had been steady since the earliest days, when passengers to Lowell took the Boston to Amherst stage and changed at Billerica to make the Lowell connection. In the middle 1820's a direct connection had been made with Boston and a daily stage inaugurated. Service for passengers had been improved by a six-horse stage, but still the trip consumed five hours in bad weather. By 1835 there were forty to forty-five stages leaving and arriving at Lowell daily. Lodgings were scarce, and the thirteen hostelries were always crowded. Some freight traveled to Boston by way of the Middlesex Canal — a twenty-seven-mile trip which took seven or eight hours if time consumed in teaming to and from terminals was included. High tolls and inadequate canal boats, however, prevented maximum utilization of this method of shipment. When the canal was frozen, freight traveled by ox teams — at great cost and over bad roads. Teams leaving Lowell in the morning did not reach Boston until late the following night, though the average pace was said to be fifty miles in twenty-four hours.[26]

It was small wonder, then, that the opening, in 1835, of the Boston and Lowell Railroad was considered an event of major importance in Lowell's history. There were skeptics, of course — and opponents. A spokesman for the Proprietors of the Middlesex Canal stated, on the floor of the General Court in Boston, "Railways, Mr. Speaker, may do well enough in the old countries, but will never be the thing for so young a country as this." [27] Patrick Tracy Jackson was, as usual, the leader of the promotion, and in outlining the geographical disadvantage of Lowell, he recorded the most telling argument for a railroad: "I have always estimated water power within ten miles of Boston as worth Double the price of the same quantity of water at Lowell." [28] With the railroad in operation, Lowell was brought closer to the metropolis, and it appeared that the last major obstacle to unlimited expansion had been removed.

The Boott and Massachusetts Contracts, 1836–1841

The last two contracts between the Proprietors of the Locks and Canals and major Lowell mills are of particular interest. Fortunately they have been preserved in sufficient detail to furnish information about costs, profits, and the contractual relationships between the Locks and Canals machine shop and the Lowell mills. Of even greater value is the picture given by the Boott contracts of the machinery components of the large mills of the day.

Work commenced on the Boott mills in 1835. The first mill was in operation in July of 1836, the second in May of 1837, and the third by December of 1837.[29] The Locks and Canals Company realized a profit of 27 per cent on machinery for the first mill and 31 per cent each on the second and third mills. The details of machinery components, prices, and costs of these three mills are presented in

Appendix 1, Table A. This information at once invites comparison with components and prices for earlier and later mills.

Machinery for the first Boott mill was priced at $12.59 per spindle; for the second and third, $11.00 per spindle. In 1839, two years after the completion of the third Boott mill, the Locks and Canals Company was quoting machinery for a mill outside Lowell at the rate of $12.20 per spindle. Machinery for a typical American mill of about this time is represented by a competent authority to have cost $11.58 per spindle. In Table B of Appendix 1, a comparison is drawn between the 1839 Locks and Canals' mill and the "typical" American mill of the day. The summary figures above and the figures in Appendix 1, Tables A and B, indicate that Locks and Canals machinery was being sold at a price very near current market prices. This fact is of interest in view of the charge made that Lowell mills were built at a high cost in comparison with mills in other manufacturing centers. This charge appears to have been true, but must be qualified by the important amendment that such high costs did not have their origin in machinery prices.

A comparison has been attempted in Table C of Appendix 1 between one of the Boott mills and a mill set up in 1814. This table shows a price per spindle (pre-weaving machinery only) in 1836 of $9.45, as against a price for comparable machinery of $11.11 per spindle in 1814. Stated in a slightly different way, machinery for a spinning mill in 1814 cost almost as much per spindle as pre-weaving and weaving machinery combined in the mills of the 1836–39 period. This table fails to reflect the increasing complexity of the individual machines, but it does show an amazing similarity in the manufacturing processes — a similarity which was destined to persist for a century to come. A comparison of output per spindle in 1814 and in 1836 would give an insight into the increasing efficiency of machinery which went hand-in-hand with the decreasing cost. Unfortunately, lack of information renders such an analysis impossible.

In January of 1839 the Massachusetts Cotton Mills was incorporated, and a contract was made with the Locks and Canals Company for four mills, to be commenced immediately. The major points of the contract were typical of the Lowell development.

The Locks and Canals Company agreed with the Massachusetts Cotton Mills as follows:[30]

1. To supply four mill sites comprising 11½ acres of land together with water equal to nine mill powers, 24 hours per day, at an annual perpetual rental of $2,400 — $84,023.
2. To procure materials for and erect four mill buildings, including gearing and such other buildings as may be wanted, but not to be responsible for delivery at any specified date — at cost.
3. To furnish machinery and tools for the same price as charged the Boott Mills. Any improvements over the Boott machinery to be installed with the consent of the Boott Mills management — $72,500 per mill (of approximately 6,000 spindles).
4. Machinery for Mill Number One to be completed in 14 months; machinery for Mill Number Two to be completed in 20 months; machinery for Mill Number Three to be completed in 26 months; machinery for Mill Number Four to be completed in 32 months.
5. Payment for machinery to commence three months from date of contract and be at the rate of $35,000 every three months.

This appears to have been the last big building contract between the Proprietors of the Locks and Canals and new mills at Lowell. Both the Lowell Bleachery and the Prescott Manufacturing Company mills were built after this time, but neither of these undertakings was on a scale comparable to preceding contracts and neither employed the facilities of the Locks and Canals machine shop to any significant extent. Though additions and alterations continued to be made, by 1840 the task of building the Lowell mills had largely been completed, and the attention of the machine shop had been diverted in other directions.

3. Details of Operation, 1825–1845

New Machines and the Revolution in Power

Between 1825 and 1845, American textile machinery was immeasurably improved. Many inventions or adaptations of great value and universal application were made. The strange fact about these inventions is, however, that few of them originated in Lowell, in this period the greatest textile-manufacturing center in the country.

There is no certain explanation of why the leading position of the Boston Manufacturing Company in developing new textile machines was relinquished by the Proprietors of the Locks and Canals. Paul Moody died in 1831, and his successors may have been less imaginative mechanics. Other possible explanations lie in the unparalleled prosperity of the Locks and Canals Company, its domination of the booming Lowell development, and the preoccupation of the shop with physical problems of mill and canal construction. The fact remains that in this period many new machines equal or superior to those developed earlier at Waltham were being built by machine shops outside Lowell — and even outside New England.

In the years from 1814 to 1824 the power loom, the Waltham dresser, double speeder, and filling frame, the self-acting loom temple, and various types of pickers and openers effected a major revolution in the American textile industry. Most of these machines, as we have seen, grew out of earlier improvements in England. From 1825 to 1845 a whole series of new machines carried the advance almost as far again. In this later period, as in the earlier, English inventions gave rise to American adaptations. There was evidence, however, of increasing American originality.

Two American inventions of primary importance were directed at eliminating the clumsy flyer arms of the throstle spindle. In 1828 Charles Danforth of Paterson, New Jersey, brought forth a so-called cap-spinner which, for certain counts of yarn, surpassed the common throstle both in economy and in quality. The invention stirred the American trade and even invaded the English market.[31] Two years later John Thorpe of Providence, Rhode Island, introduced a method of winding yarn on the bobbin by means of a ring around which a metal guide or "traveler" revolved carrying the yarn. Imperfections in Thorpe's early ring-spinning devices delayed market acceptance, but the invention was destined to become one of the most important in the history of the textile machinery industry.

Thorpe's machine was overshadowed by the development, first in England, then in America, of the self-acting mule — an invention which did for mule spinning what the power loom had done for weaving. In the early 1830's the first successful automatic mule had been turned out by the English firm of Sharpe & Roberts. By 1837 William Mason, who was to found a famous machine shop at Taunton, Massachusetts, had succeeded in producing a self-acting mule, patterned after the Sharpe & Roberts model, which could successfully compete with the English mule in the American market.

These refinements of the spinning process were coupled with several other inventions to materially speed and cheapen the manufacture of cloth. Several improved speeders or roving frames appeared after 1824. Samuel Batchelder, agent of the Hamilton Manufacturing Company, invented a stop motion for drawing frames which automatically halted the machine when the sliver broke. John Whitin of Northbridge, Massachusetts, was attracting the attention of mill managers with his picker-spreader, patented in 1832. In 1833 W. B. Leonard, of the Matteawan Machine Shop in New York, patented the so-called "railway drawing head," an important step forward in the integration of yarn-manufacturing processes.[32]

The Locks and Canals Company participated in this progress, not as inventors but as agents. Demands from customers induced the company to build under lease from the inventors the most popular of the new machines being perfected outside Lowell. Transactions are recorded which illustrate the leasehold relationship between the Locks and Canals Company and other machine shops. Of primary interest is the fact that these transactions show the beginning of a breakdown in local and regional isolation and the beginning of an inter-regional movement of mechanical ideas. As we shall see later, an inter-regional movement of machinery was the inevitable consequence.

The promoters of the Lawrence Manufacturing Company became interested in the new Danforth cap-spinning frame, and in 1832 Kirk Boott was authorized to bargain with Godwin Clarke & Company, of Paterson, New Jersey, for the patent rights. The patent holders demanded $10,000 plus fifty cents per spindle, then modified their price to $3,500 and fifty cents in order to ensure the adoption of the spindle in the famous Lowell market.[33] This is the earliest known instance in which the Locks and Canals machine shop agreed to install other than its own machinery.[34] The practice, widely followed after 1832, gave implicit recognition to the fact that no longer could a machine shop, however large, enjoy an unchallenged local demand for all its products.

Lowell in 1825

Large structure at left is first machine-shop building of the Merrimack Manufacturing Company. Merrimack Mills in center rear. Kirk Boott house right rear

Warp Throstle Spinning Frame

Built by the Locks and Canals Company about 1830 and installed in Merrimack Mills

However far behind competitors the Locks and Canals Company lagged in developing new machines, it was second to none in the continuing search for greater efficiency in the generation and transmission of water power. Since colonial days American millwrights had been learning to control water. The skill in practical hydraulics thus built up was probably the most potent single factor in the American Industrial Revolution, and continued until the early years of the twentieth century as a major influence on the growth and progress of American manufacturing enterprise. Over a period of a century and a half, the Proprietors of the Locks and Canals on Merrimack River made outstanding contributions to man's ability to apply water power to industrial use. During the span of years in which the Locks and Canals Company operated the machine shop at Lowell two great changes in power generation and transmission were introduced. The first of these was revolutionary in every sense in which the word is used when speaking of mechanical innovation.

When Paul Moody commenced the construction of the Appleton mills in 1828, he did away with the heavy English-type gearing which had creaked and groaned in every American mill from 1790 on. In its place he substituted lighter-weight shafting driven by belts rather than gears. As a result of increasing skill in metallurgy and casting, there already had appeared in England a tendency to adopt higher-speed, lighter-weight shafting. To be sure, this trend had not gathered momentum by 1828, but it probably was from England that Moody received the idea. Nor was the use of belting original with Moody. Such claims to invention must always be carefully appraised, for the origins of mechanical principles are devious, deep-rooted in the past, and usually obscure.[35] Moody may well have been the first in America to apply belting in moving large quantities of machinery. The important fact is that the use of belting in the Appleton mills touched off a new American style which soon came to constitute an important distinction between English and American mills. American mechanics, far behind the English in metal-working skill, had struggled long and without success to imitate the smoothly running gearing of the English mills. The use of belting providentially relieved them of this handicap of inferiority, and Moody's belt-drive system was rapidly adopted. Moreover, belting made higher machine speeds possible. This was a primary mechanical objective in America, though less important to the English style of manufacture.[36]

In the early 1840's there was increasing interest in America in the turbine water wheel — a wheel type long familiar in primitive forms to American millwrights. In this field of endeavor the Locks and Canals machine shop shared the credit for pioneering work with others, but the experiments conducted at Lowell, particularly after 1845, were a primary influence in the widespread adoption of the turbine in America.

In its first attempt to market a turbine wheel the Locks and Canals Company followed the familiar policy of leasing a patent. Rights to build and sell the Howd turbine, patented in 1838 by a Geneva, New York, inventor were acquired for a fee of approximately $1,200.[37] The commercial success of this venture does not seem to have been large, and it remained for an inventor in the Locks and Canals Company to design the first turbine successfully employed at Lowell.

Uriah A. Boyden, assistant to the engineer of the Locks and Canals Company, designed a turbine patterned after the Fourneyron model, first used in France in 1827. The Boyden turbine was installed in the Appleton mills in 1844, and was found to develop up to 78 per cent efficiency. The old breast wheels of the Lowell mills, developing only about 60 per cent efficiency, were destined for obsolescence; in the years to come, they were gradually supplanted by the turbine.[38]

Here was a typical example of the course of industrial progress. The great breast wheels, the individualistic work of the master millwright, slowly yielded place to the higher efficiency and lower cost of the turbine — manufactured in standard sizes for standard installations. The millwright himself — a craftsman existing by tolerance in an age which had grown away from handcraftsmanship — was to disappear with his wheels, his place in the industrial system being taken by the hydraulic engineer.

Manufacturing Diversification, Methods, and Facilities

From the scattered information available about operations in the Locks and Canals machine shop a picture of exceedingly diverse manufacturing effort emerges. The machine shop built or supervised the building of canals, locks, dwelling houses, mill buildings, streets, bridges, and a hotel. As has already been pointed out in connection with the revolution in power, the Locks and Canals Company must be closely identified with many technological developments quite apart from textile machinery. Noteworthy improvements were made in Lowell in the fields of fire protection, mill heating, lighting, and sanitation — improvements which the Proprietors of the Locks and Canals were instrumental in planning and which were widely adopted elsewhere.[39]

Contracts with the Lowell mills and others reveal what was made in the Locks and Canals machine shop, but relatively little is known about the methods, tools, and materials employed in manufacture. The first machine tool to be employed extensively in the Locks and Canals machine shop and elsewhere in America was the lathe. It will be recalled that this tool was purchased and built in Waltham and constituted the principal machine tool in use there. Some of these lathes, however, were manually operated. In the 1820's the Locks and Canals Company was using a power-driven lathe capable of handling very large shapes. With a few exceptions such as this, hand-craftsmanship in the machine shop had not been replaced to any substantial degree by the late 1830's. Small turning jobs were all done on hand tools, and the shop blacksmith made all bolts and cut the threads by hand. Leather belting for the mills was made in the shop — where hides, purchased from tanners, were cut and stretched, trimmed, cemented and stitched together or pegged together with wooden shoe pegs. Most of the tools, dies, and small parts were also made in the shop. The mechanic, who still was more a craftsman than a machinist, made his own hand tools.[40] The lack of heavy power-driven tools (other than lathes) capable of working large shapes is noticeable.

After 1840, great improvements in metal-working skills were brought about by the importation from England of new machine tools and by the cumulative improvement of tools already familiar in America. In 1839 the Locks and Canals Company imported a Whitworth planer from England. This machine virtually eliminated the old process of hand chipping with hammer and chisel. The machine shop also purchased from Whitworth in 1839 a "self-acting upright drilling and boring machine." This counterpart of the modern drill press is one of the earliest known to have been set up in America.

The Locks and Canals machine shop was self-sufficient to a surprising degree, and this self-sufficiency did not begin to break down until the manufacture of locomotives in the shop after 1834 introduced the necessity for sub-contracting on a large scale.

The chief dependence of the Locks and Canals machine shop on outside suppliers was for raw materials, castings, and the latest ideas in machine tools. Much of the iron used in the shop was imported from England, either by direct negotiations with English foundries, through New York agents of such foundries, or through American commission merchants in New York. It is of interest to note that by the early 1840's there were a number of agents through whom supplies could be readily secured. The growth of American industry had encouraged the growth of a host of useful business auxiliaries.[41]

Some American pig iron was purchased, principally from Philadelphia suppliers or from the Fall River Iron Works. It was generally felt, however, that the best American iron was not much cheaper than Scotch pig, and the imported article was generally to be preferred. Kirk Boott signified his intention of using a better quality of metal than was customarily used in machinery — in fact, a quality inferior only to the best tool steel. There is little consecutive information at this time, however, on prices paid for iron or on grades and quantities purchased.[42]

All purchases for the machine shop appear to have been handled through the Boston office of Patrick Tracy Jackson. Until 1840, when a foundry was built at Lowell, all castings were still being secured from the old Leach furnace at Easton and from a newer one at North Chelmsford or from Lasell Perkins & Company at Bridgewater. The price ranged close to four cents per pound. Miscellaneous supplies such as files and grinding stones, unobtainable locally in the grades desired, were ordered from England. Lumber came by boat from Waterville, Maine, to Boston, where it was transshipped to Lowell by railroad. A few textile-machine sub-assemblies, such as card clothing and spindles, also appear to have been purchased from others, rather than manufactured at Lowell.

Manufacturing facilities were expanded somewhat during the 1825–45 period, but the need for great physical expansion of plant was somewhat obviated by the large size of the main shop building erected in 1824. The principal addition to plant in this period was the erection in 1840, at a cost of $30,000, of a large foundry. Water power was supplied by two of the old-style breast water wheels, thirteen feet in diameter.[43] In 1845 the machine-building facilities of the Proprietors of the Locks and Canals, consisting of four shops, a smithy, and a foundry, were said to comprise the largest textile-machine shop in the country.

Management, Industrial Relations, and Labor

The personality of Kirk Boott dominated the management of both the Merrimack Manufacturing Company and the Proprietors of the Locks and Canals, and indelibly impressed itself on the early history of Lowell. An American by birth, Boott had served in the British army under Wellington and brought to his positions of mill agent of Merrimack and agent and treasurer of the Locks and Canals Company the strong English traditions of class consciousness and stern discipline. Boott, in addition, was a trained engineer and draftsman, though inexperienced in manufacturing enterprise. He was remembered as a man of more than medium height, very erect, with open and intelligent features, and a high forehead crowned with a shaggy mane of hair. There was a decided military air about him and a stiffness in his gait which was later so increased by rheumatism as to require the use of a cane (which on occasion is said to have been used on more yielding objects than pavements!). He spoke in an undertone, but every word was charged with energy. His orders were given briefly and with decision, and he expected answers of a like nature. His taste was impeccable, his language abusive on occasion, and his manner imperial. He sought to dominate not only the business affairs in his charge but the religious, political, and social affairs of the community. Because this combination of characteristics enabled him to drive over all obstacles and because his devotion to duty was absolute, his managerial achievements were great. It has been customary to say that a less powerful man could not have succeeded in his place, and this may be true. The precedent he set, unfortunately, was followed by less able men, and much of Lowell's subsequent labor unrest may be traced to the permanent prejudice against mill agents which took root in the minds of the operatives during the reign of Kirk Boott.[44]

Boott served as agent and treasurer of the Locks and Canals Company until his death in 1837 and was succeeded briefly by Joseph Tilden. No less a man than Patrick Tracy Jackson, however, was required to fill the void left by Boott's death. In 1838 Jackson was made agent and treasurer of the Locks and Canals Company. He remained as treasurer until 1845, but relinquished the office of agent in 1838 to William, younger brother of Kirk Boott.

Kirk Boott had handled many of the details of the business, and his letters reveal his close contact with purchasing, selling, and finance. Dominant and forceful though he was, the Locks and Canals Company was not a one-man organization. In the second rank of command, Paul Moody served under Boott in apparent harmony, and had complete charge of the technical details of the machine shop until his death in 1831. Under Moody the management of the technical branch of the business had been divided into two vaguely defined divisions, conforming to the two main functions of the company. Thomas Borden, a skilled mechanic who came with Moody from Waltham, supervised machinery building and installation. The construction and maintenance of locks and canals was closely supervised by Moody himself. In this function Moody appears to have been assisted by Joel Lewis, of whom little is known except that he was referred to both as an "engineer" and as a "surveyor." In Moody's time a high degree of specialization of managerial function had not yet become a necessity. Moody was able, because of his personal ability and the relative simplicity of operations, to possess the knowledge and perform the duties of the hydraulic and the mechanical engineer. This situation changed after Moody's death.

The inception of locomotive building in 1834 required a new division of the Locks and Canals management, and this phase of activity was placed in charge of George W. Whistler, an engineer possessing the specialized skills required. The primary emphasis of management, however, was not shifted. Moody's place was taken by George Brownell, a textile-machine mechanic who had been trained in the tradition of Waltham. The position first occupied by Joel Lewis was filled in 1834, after the death of Lewis, by James B. Francis — a young Englishman of promising talents. Francis had a background of experience in railroad engineering which proved useful, but it was in the field of hydraulics that he was to become famous. Under Francis a clearly defined department of hydraulic engineering developed. By 1840 the organization of the Locks and Canals Company had crystallized into three distinct though not mutually independent departments — locomotive building, hydraulics, and machine-building.

During Kirk Boott's life the form of management adopted by the Locks and Canals Company was not typical of the Lowell mills, which customarily operated under a resident agent and a treasurer in Boston, the latter being the actual though not the titular head of the company. After Jackson became treasurer in 1838, this conventional pattern of management was adopted by the Locks and Canals Company.

Operating policies were formulated in some detail, both in the Lowell mills and in the Locks and Canals Company, by the boards of directors. At this point in New England's industrial history the position of director often carried with it an obligation to participate actively in company affairs. Agents and treasurers, although not deprived of opportunity for exercising initiative, were closely supervised by the directors, acting either as a Board or individually. This managerial system was highly effective as long as the interests of key directors were not spread too widely. With the multiplication of cotton mill companies both in Lowell and elsewhere, however, this very diffusion of interests came to pass. A basic criticism of the system was that the directors no longer possessed the knowledge to match their responsibilities and that Boston treasurers no longer comprehended the operating requirements of their Lowell companies. A further weakness developed in the form of conflicts between treasurers and agents. Virtually all the large New England cotton mills experienced varying degrees of difficulty attributable to such causes. The Locks and Canals Company to 1845 seems to have avoided trouble — largely through the energies of Patrick Tracy Jackson. He dominated the company from 1821 to 1845, first as a director, then as treasurer. Despite his multiple interests he served the company well and kept himself and the other directors closely informed about operating conditions at Lowell.

Those conditions often were of a complex and delicate nature. The position of the Locks and Canals Company was one of legal independence of the Lowell mills. This legal position was fiction in point of operating policy. Control of the Boston Manufacturing Company, the Merrimack Manufacturing Company, the Proprietors of the Locks and Canals, the Hamilton Manufacturing Company, and the Appleton Company was vested in one small group of Boston capitalists. There was a slow diffusion of stock ownership and the members of this group did not always work harmoniously together, but in general the policies of each company were guided in coöperating paths. For the Locks and Canals machine shop this fact spelled a guarantee of large orders and the strongest possible financial backing.

After 1830 a new group of Boston financiers, headed by the brothers Amos and Abbott Lawrence, entered the Lowell picture. A new spirit of competition and occasional conflicts of interest arose, but the monopoly position of the Locks and Canals Company in respect to mill sites and water power was sufficiently strong to prevent "outside" interests from entering the development except on terms advantageous to the Proprietors. In the light of these financial alliances and the business consequences of a highly effective monopoly, the Locks and Canals Company can scarcely be said to have succeeded in the textile machine business on its merits alone. The question should be raised as to whether those merits were sufficient to have made success possible in a less sympathetic environment. There can be no certain answer. The company unquestionably fell behind competitors in developing new textile machinery. On the other hand, the financial, marketing, and administrative aspects of the business appear to have been exceptionally well handled, and, as will be pointed out later in this chapter, a very real efficiency was achieved in the manufacture of steam-railway locomotives.

There is no doubt that the early Lowell mills benefited immensely from the presence in their midst of a large and active machine shop. Mechanical talent was employed in the mills, but not to an extent sufficient to permit independence of the Locks and Canals Company. The mill agents in charge of the Lowell establishments were generally non-technical men. Paul Moody and his successor, George Brownell, served as technical advisers to all the companies, and would allow no company to trifle with the machines which they set up. The Locks and Canals Company further reserved to itself the care and regulation of water power and allied facilities.

In matters concerned with the price and regulation of mill powers, relations with the Lowell mills were not always harmonious. Water-power obligations of the Locks and Canals Company were carefully defined by contract with the individual mills, but the rise of unforeseen circumstances precipitated occasional disputes. The Locks and Canals Company was suspected of favoring the older mills with which it was so intimately linked by ties of ownership. Kirk Boott, moreover, was peculiarly vulnerable to charges of partiality by virtue of his dual position as agent of both the Merrimack Manufacturing Company and the Locks and Canals Company. The old alliance between cotton mill and machine shop had been formally severed in 1825, when the Merrimack stockholders revived the Locks and Canals Company, but the lingering on of this tie in the form of a common agent embarrassed the latter company on more than one occasion in its dealings with other Lowell mills.[45] After Boott's death no such obvious connections were reëstablished. With the growth of the machine shop's business both in and outside Lowell came a necessary correlative trend toward actual as well as nominal independence. Even with the employment of neutral judges to arbitrate water-power disputes and with the evident attempts to quote equally fair machinery prices to all, the difficulties of serving more than one master became increasingly evident.

In contrast to the industrial relations of the Locks and Canals Company, which were frequently commented on by contemporary observers, almost nothing is known of managerial policy in respect to labor in the machine shop. This was the era in which the paternalistic labor policies of the Lowell mills were attracting wide attention in America and even in England. The machine shop, with its relatively permanent force of skilled and semi-skilled male help, appears not to have been an integral part of the Lowell system, but rather exhibited an arms-length relationship between management and worker. However, it would seem probable, though the connection cannot be positively established, that machine-shop labor shared in the general trends characteristic of all Lowell labor — the slow but steady increase in English-Irish help and those symptoms of unrest and dissatisfaction which in the early 1840's forecast the end of the golden era of the Waltham-Lowell labor system.[46]

Mechanics in the machine shop enjoyed a stronger bargaining position than operatives in the mills, if for no other reasons than the relative scarcity of mechanics and the length of time required to train competent machine-shop employees. As late as 1845, executives of the Locks and Canals Company were explaining that delay in the delivery of machinery was occasioned by a lack of skilled help. That lack could be remedied by enticing skilled men from shops in other locations, and there is evidence of considerable movement of mechanics into Lowell from other manufacturing centers. The ethical implications of the "black-list," however, militated against the practice. Lowell mills had instituted the custom of furnishing discharge papers to employees who left the mills for reasons deemed fair and adequate by the management. By reciprocal arrangements with other mills no experienced operative could be hired unless possessing such a certificate from his last employer. The system was loosely administered and not fully effective, but it may have been adopted by the Locks and Canals Company. Since there were far fewer mechanics than mill operatives and a relatively small number of machine shops compared to cotton mills, it would appear that the black list could be more effectively employed by the Locks and Canals Company than by its larger neighbors. Apparently, there have survived but two bits of evidence that indicate recourse to the system. In 1829 Ebenezer Hobbs, superintendent of the Boston Manufacturing Company, wrote a letter to Paul Moody in which he stated, "We received yours relative to the young men discharged, & will see that they are not employed here." Ten years later General Shepard Leach, owner of the Easton furnace, in a letter to the agent of the Locks and Canals Company, urged enforcement of the rule that foundries should not hire men without their presenting a regular discharge certificate.[47]

The normal and approved method of acquiring skilled help was to take in young men and train them. The apprenticeship period was three years, and the apprentices appear to have been bound not to the company but to skilled mechanics employed on job work for the company. For the apprentices there was much honor but little pay involved. In 1827, for example, Paul Moody answered the letter of a mother who anxiously inquired whether her fifteen-year-old son could be trained as a mechanic and whether he would be paid as well as trained. Moody replied that the boy was, indeed, acceptable — that he would be paid at the rate of $25 per annum during the first year, $50 during the second, and $74 during the third — and that "Proper care will be taken that the money which he earns as above be not expended by him unwisely." [48]

The position of the unskilled or semi-skilled laborer in Lowell was one of considerable economic and social subservience. There was a strong obligation to belong to the same church and lodge as the overseer and company agent — and it would have been a bold man or woman who openly favored General Andrew Jackson for President in defiance of Kirk Boott's uninhibited pronouncements on the subject. The skilled mechanics and overseers in the machine shop were far less subject to these petty tyrannies. This class constituted a workingman's aristocracy which jealously guarded its rights and on occasion took independent group action to improve its position. These men were respected by laborer and agent alike as masters of a trade. They contracted with the Locks and Canals Company for the performance of specific jobs and enjoyed considerable freedom in the fulfillment of their contracts. The job hands and overseers hired and discharged their own help, trained their own apprentices, made rules among themselves to protect the institution of apprenticeship from increasing abuses, and by their own efforts and on their own initiative did much to advance the science of their calling. In 1825 these men formed the Middlesex Mechanics Association, a trade gild devoted to the support of needy members, the control of apprentices, and the encouragement of good craftsmanship and invention. This association constituted a clear indication of group consciousness, group pride, and group independence. Unlike the various associationist movements which swept the ranks of mill operatives in the years following 1845, this organization did not seek to set the power of group action in opposition to company management. Instead, the interest of the group was felt to be identified with the interest of the company, and benefits for the members were sought and achieved by increasing the value of those members, as individuals, to the corporation. Such an association could be effective only at a time when pride in workmanship was a dominant characteristic of the members; while that situation prevailed, its effectiveness was great indeed.[49]

It is well worth while to pause and appraise this virile class of overseers and skilled mechanics, for the course of the textile machinery industry throughout most of the nineteenth century was directed by their hands. The strength of these men, in Lowell and elsewhere in America, was first derived from their ability to absorb English ideas and improve them. This ability to learn rapidly fostered a growing independence of England and inevitably resulted in original inventions of importance. These were relatively few in number, however. A great part of the evolution of textile machinery consisted of innumerable minor improvements. In this tremendous capacity of American mechanics for effecting steady technological improvement lay the great strength of American manufacturing enterprise. A serious weakness lay in the managerial deficiencies of many of these same technicians. These deficiencies, however, were remedied at first by the brilliant direction of mercantile-trained administrators such as Boott and Jackson.

4. Diversified Ambitions and Opportunities

Sales outside Lowell and New Products

In the period from 1825 to 1845 the building of textile machinery evolved from a trade to an industry. Many new and independent machine shops were formed, and of these some commenced to sell a large variety of machinery over a wide geographical area. Available evidence points to the Locks and Canals Company and the Matteawan Machine Shop in Fishkill, New York, as the two leaders in this branching-out process. The Locks and Canals Company had an undoubted advantage in being associated with the development at Lowell, and both profited from being among the very few shops in the country where a complete line of cotton-textile machinery could be purchased.[50]

The textile industry advanced in size by leaps and bounds. In 1831 there were said to be 1,200,000 spindles in operation in the country; in 1840, 2,300,000.[51] In the 1820's and before, the expanding demand for plant and equipment appears to have been supplied by local machine shops. Sales of machines by the Boston Manufacturing Company illustrate this stage of development. In the 1830's and early 1840's the demand began to outgrow the ability of local shops to supply. In some cases textile mills sprang up in areas where no machine shops existed. These circumstances, coupled with the reputation of the Locks and Canals Company, attracted orders from all sections in the country where cloth was manufactured. These orders were not large in comparison with total sales, but they did indicate that management had begun to regard the company as more than a tool for the development of the Lowell area.

In the late 1830's and early 1840's the Locks and Canals Company was filling orders for P. Whitin & Sons and the Blackstone Manufacturing Company in the Blackstone Valley; for the Nashua Manufacturing Company and the Salmon Falls Company in New Hampshire; and for mills in Vermont, Ohio, Louisiana, and the middle Atlantic States. In 1838 an order for $25,000 of textile machinery was shipped to St. Petersburg, Russia, and in the same year work was commenced upon the machinery for the first mill of the Amoskeag Manufacturing Company in Manchester, New Hampshire. In 1844 a large variety of machinery was being supplied to the Great Falls Manufacturing Company in Somersworth, New Hampshire. Loom sales featured prominently in most of these orders, and there appears to have been considerable demand for the Smith mule made by the company.

In 1838 a new market experiment of considerable interest was initiated. A southern physician by the name of Alexander Jones had invented a sixty-saw cotton gin, which the Locks and Canals Company agreed to make and sell. The company also built a cotton thrasher to be sold with the gin. The market for these machines lay exclusively in the cotton-producing areas, and the company placed several of them in the hands of Maunsel White & Company, a cotton broker in New Orleans. By December of 1839 the Locks and Canals gin was in use at Vicksburg and Natchez, Mississippi, and in Mobile, Alabama. The gin was priced at $550, and sales were slow. The agents demanded a commission of 5 per cent, which was not exorbitant, but shipping and handling costs of the heavy machine were almost prohibitive. There was also the threat of a patent suit by Jacob Perkins, who claimed infringement on his own gin patent. This combination of circumstances apparently discouraged further experiments along this line, although gins were still being sold as late as 1842.

The Locks and Canals Company began to diversify the product line. The first evidence of this diversification appears in 1833, when the machine shop was making a four-color printing machine for a Fall River customer and a calender for the Lowell Bleachery. In 1838 the company signified its willingness to build woolen machinery when demanded and, in the years following, a considerable number of small planing machines and steam boilers were made, together with such products as grinding wheels for a powder mill, mill shafting, window weights, and castings for force pumps and water wheels. The most spectacular departure from the established line of cotton machinery, however, was made in 1834, when the manufacture of steam-railway locomotives was commenced in Lowell.

Locomotive Building in the Machine Shop, 1834–1845

The beginning of locomotive manufacture by the Locks and Canals machine shop is closely associated with the organization and construction of the Boston and Lowell Railroad. This road was essentially a promotion of Patrick Tracy Jackson and was incorporated in 1830, the year in which the Baltimore & Ohio Railroad opened to travel the first length of steam railroad in America. Support for the Boston and Lowell was half-hearted, in spite of the fact that the Locks and Canals Company subscribed to $250,000 of stock in the enterprise. It was not until the company offered a bonus of $100,000 to the stockholders that other investors could be induced to extend adequate financial backing.

Like the early textile mills, the first American railroads drew heavily on English skills. In England Robert Stevenson and others by 1830 had developed the steam locomotive to the point where it was commercially practicable. Public incredulity turned to enthusiasm, and in both England and America the era of railroad promotions was ushered in with glowing prophecies. Patrick Tracy Jackson, as usual, was several years ahead of most of his contemporaries.

In 1832 Jackson imported two of Stevenson's famous "Planet" locomotives, and shortly thereafter he made plans for building locomotives in the Locks and Canals machine shop. In a letter to Stevenson he revealed the conditions which led to this decision:[52]

> I should have supplied myself further and entirely from you, but we have a large machine shop at Lowell, and finding that but few more tools would be required for building than repairs, we determined to build Engines for ourselves and for those in our neighborhood who would purchase of us. We have followed your pattern thinking it the best we have yet seen, either from England or built here.

In order to engage in this branch of manufacture, Jackson sought a man with sufficient experience and knowledge to copy the Stevenson engine. In April of 1834 the Locks and Canals directors voted to make an engagement with George Whistler to come to Lowell in the capacity of engineer to supervise the building of locomotives. He was offered a salary of $3,000 per year, with a rent-free dwelling. Whistler, with his West Point engineering training augmented by a study of the new locomotives in England and four years of experience on three American railroads, was well qualified for the hard task demanded. He was one of a very few in America competent to make the attempt.[53]

In June, 1835, the first Locks and Canals engine was completed and delivered to the Boston and Lowell Railroad. This engine was to be named after Patrick Tracy Jackson. The first suggestion was to call it the "Jackson," but this name was politically inexpedient in a Whig community. The engine was christened the "Patrick." Two months later the directors authorized the agent to erect such additional workshops as he might deem necessary for building locomotive engines and cars.

In the whole country in 1834 there were a scant half-dozen machine shops capable of meeting the demand from a large number of newly incorporated roads. Matthias Baldwin, a textile-machinery manufacturer in Philadelphia, had anticipated Jackson by two years, and William Norris, in the same place, soon turned to locomotive manufacture. In New England the Locks and Canals Company had, for a time, a virtual monopoly of the manufacture of engines.

The trade in its infancy was on a regional basis, the heavy shipping costs of locomotives tending to confine builders to supplying their immediate locality. Most of the early Locks and Canals engines went to the short new lines which were being commenced in several places in New England. There were orders from other sections of the country as well. In 1835 at least seven engines were placed in operation, five in Massachusetts and two in New York. The following year fifteen engines were turned out, and the expansion of plant appeared to have been justified. Fourteen of these engines were for New England customers.[54]

For the railroads the decade of the 1830's was as difficult as it was hopeful. Road-building costs invariably exceeded estimates. Equipment was expensive and costly to maintain in operating condition. To the burden of heavy first cost, slow construction, large maintenance expense, and small initial operating revenues were added that of specie shortage and then the acute panic of 1837.

In that year the Locks and Canals Company had built four locomotives for the Baltimore & Susquehanna Rail Road. The panic embarrassed both the Locks and Canals Company and the railroad, the latter being caught in the midst of founding efforts when the only hope for survival lay, not in curtailment of equipment purchased, but in further expansion. The Locks and Canals Company was in an awkward, though by no means desperate, position. The Pensacola Rail Road, an earlier Locks and Canals Company customer, defaulted on its notes to the extent of $10,383, and the Baltimore & Susquehanna account stood at $14,846, with little prospect of settlement in either case. It is not surprising that this experience with defaulting customers, coupled with a sharp decline in locomotive sales, brought about a decision on the part of the Locks and Canals directors to cease the manufacture of locomotives altogether. Attempts were made to collect outstanding railroad ac-

Stevenson Planet-type Locomotive
Model for the first Locks and Canals engines

THE ROGER WILLIAMS IN THE 1850's
One of the first six locomotives built by the Locks and Canals Company

counts, but the panic deepened into depression, and the company was only one of many creditors.

Reviving hopes and some new orders in 1838 led the Locks and Canals Company to begin to manufacture locomotives again. The locomotive account for the year ending July 31, 1838, the only year for which this record has been preserved, indicates that eleven engines and eight tenders were delivered, nine engines were on hand, and $10,000 of job work had been performed on locomotives. Total sales credited to the locomotive account were $83,800. The price charged for a locomotive and tender was $7,000, and the profit on each locomotive and tender was approximately $2,200, or 31 per cent.[55]

For the year 1838 information is available which serves to illustrate the position of the Locks and Canals Company in the industry. A report by the Secretary of the Treasury on the subject of steam engines indicates that the Locks and Canals Company, with thirty-two locomotives in operation in the country, trailed only Baldwin (with seventy-eight engines) and Norris (with thirty-four engines) of the domestic manufacturers.[56] Of the thirty-two locomotives listed to the credit of the Locks and Canals Company twenty-four were built for New England roads and the remainder for roads in New York, Philadelphia, and Maryland.[57]

The building of locomotives had been dealt a severe blow by the depression which followed 1837. Customers pointed to the generally prostrate position of railroads in the country, a position which was generally ascribed to the strain of completing their ambitious undertakings. Moreover, in the Southern markets at least, the wood-burning engines of the Locks and Canals Company were far less popular than Baldwin's coal-burners. From 1839 through 1845, however, the company had placed in operation forty-three new engines and had built the running gear for more than a thousand coal cars.[58] Of these engines thirty-one had been built for New England customers.

In the manufacture of these locomotives, tenders, and coal cars the Locks and Canals Company relied from the beginning on the advice of others and on specialized suppliers of parts. Matthias Baldwin himself was consulted by Jackson when plans for locomotive manufacture were being formulated. In 1835 Baldwin was furnishing wheel castings to the company, which had not yet learned the art of making cast-iron wheels with wrought-iron rims. Cranks, axles, and "tyres" were purchased from several foundries in Connecticut, New Jersey, and Maryland, and from Lasell, Perkins & Company in Bridgewater, Massachusetts. A considerable number of wheels and parts were ordered from the Bury works in Liverpool, England, and in 1839 George Brownell, the company agent, was sent to England to make purchases and seek the advice of the English masters.

The manufacture of locomotives in the machine shop was carried on as a department distinct from the manufacture of textile machines. Similarly, the techniques employed in the marketing of locomotives came in many instances to bear slight resemblance to methods employed in marketing the company's regular line of textile machinery. These specialized techniques grew out of the panic of 1837 and took the form of contractual safeguards against bad debt losses.

In drawing up a contract with the Baltimore & Susquehanna Rail Road in 1839, the Locks and Canals Company accepted the usual notes in payment. Charles Howard, president of the road, suggested that "in addition to the notes, this company would also prefer that the Engines should remain the property of the vendors until the payment of the notes, so as to give you the additional specific lien upon the property itself, besides the obligation of the company." [59]

The retention of equipment title until final payment was a new technique to the Locks and Canals Company, and certainly did not arise out of any precedent in the textile machinery business. It is perhaps significant that this mechanism was suggested by persons outside the Jackson financial circle.

Three years later, further refinements in methods for safeguarding the company's creditor position had been worked out. In a contract made in March, 1842, with the Philadelphia & Reading Railroad, the equipment was delivered in trust to two men in Philadelphia. Should the road fail to meet its obligations, these trustees were to take over the equipment and dispose of it at public sale for the benefit of the Locks and Canals Company. In addition, bonds of the road were deposited as collateral security for fulfillment of the obligation, and the road agreed: "to reserve out of the toll or freight of each and every ton of coal transported in said cars . . . the sum of twenty-two and a half cents and to apply and pay the same to the said party of the second part [Locks and Canals Company]. . . ." [60]

In another contract with the Philadelphia & Reading Railroad made six months later the number of trustees was enlarged to three, two of whom were associates of Jackson. Thus, effective control of the trust passed from the railroad to the manufacturer.

In these Locks and Canals contracts lies valuable evidence that the techniques which became standard contractual practice in post-Civil War railroad financing were conceived in some detail in the first decade of American railroad history. The Locks and Canals Company by 1842 had failed to use only one major device from among those which later became important. Still to be developed was the practice of shifting to the investing public by means of equipment-trust paper the financial burden of the transfer period. The use by Jackson of strong mortgage security, lien on income, retention of equipment title, and transfer middlemen indicates a very great advance in marketing techniques and a decided versatility in meeting changing market conditions.[61]

In appraising the locomotive building and marketing activities of the Locks and Canals Company two factors merit primary emphasis. Referring to the Philadelphia & Reading contracts in 1842, Jackson told the directors: "The object in making these contracts, is to give profitable employment for our shop and foundry at a time when we have little else to do." [62] This was almost sufficient justification in itself for the undertaking, but the second factor of importance is that this branch of manufacture was independently profitable. Beyond this, it seems safe to say that economic benefits accrued both to the firm and to New England from the Locks and Canals Company's part in stimulating the growth of the railroad network.

5. Operating Results and Sale of the Machine Shop

The prosperity of the Locks and Canals Company in the twenty years from 1825 to 1845 was great, though not uninterrupted. Assets increased steadily, liberal dividends were paid in all but two years, and the final division of profits in 1845 was handsome. This prosperity accrued from four main sources: the sale of machinery, the sale of locomotives, the liquidation of natural resources (land) at steadily increasing prices, and the improvement and rental of natural resources (water power). The very nature of these sources of wealth imparted financial stability to the business. Capital of the company in the form of land and water power increased steadily, though at varying rates and with minor reverses, through good times and bad. The locomotive and the textile machine business were compensatory, in that one occupied the personnel and facilities of the shop while the other was under a temporary cloud.

Company records do not reveal the relative contributions of each of the four sources of income. For only one year are operating profits available in detail. Though these figures cannot be considered as typical for all years and are not clear-cut from an accounting viewpoint, they do present an interesting analysis of the relative importance of the different phases of Locks and Canals business in this one year. For the year ending July 31, 1838, the company showed operating profits as follows:[63]

From mill rents account...........	$ 7,579.53	or	11% of total
From other rents account..........	5,126.04	or	8
From machinery account..........	40,009.23	or	58
From locomotive engines account...	15,722.24	or	23
Total Operating Profit........	$68,437.04		100%

The general increase in assets, the liquidation of real estate, and the increment in value of the mill powers under lease are shown in Chart I.

The course of business through 1836 was steadily upward, but in this year currency was scarce. The company was forced to pay 2 per cent a month for money in Boston, and it was felt that this situation "must materially affect the profits of the company."[64] The great financial strength of this company and of the Lowell mills, however, enabled them to survive the panic and ruin of 1837. On at least one occasion, funds were passed from one corporation to another to alleviate temporary specie shortages. Late in 1836, when the financial crisis was building up, the Locks and Canals Company became overdrawn in its accounts with the Suffolk Bank, in Boston, to the amount of $20,000. John A. Lowell, the nephew and son-in-law of Francis Cabot Lowell, was a director of the Suffolk Bank. He was also treasurer of the Boston Manufacturing Company and of the Boott Cotton Mills and was a large shareholder of the Locks and Canals Company. Lowell informed Kirk Boott of the overdraft in these reassuring words:[65] "As however I have had funds to a larger amount to the credit of the Boott Cotton Mills in the same bank, the one hand has weighed the other."

CHART I

Mill Power, Real Estate, and Net Asset Values
Locks and Canals Company, 1827–1844

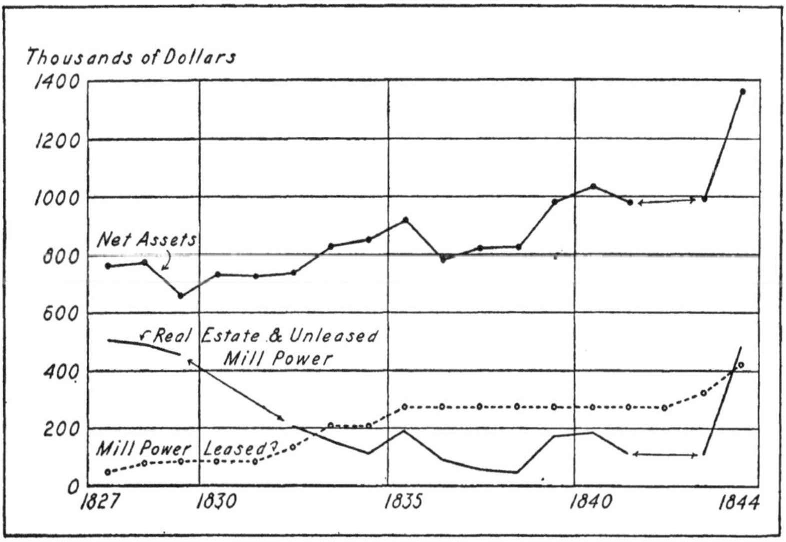

Stock of the Locks and Canals Company, with a par value of $500, which had sold in 1835 for as high as $1,820 per share, declined to a low of $900 in 1837, in which year the regular dividend was passed for the first time.[66] In the ensuing depression, which shook the confidence of American business men to its roots, the stock continued to decline, despite orders for machinery from the Massachusetts Cotton Mills and the payment of regular dividends in 1838, 1839, and 1840, and an extra dividend in 1841.

In September of 1841 Jackson reported to the directors that the profit for the year ending July 31 had been $114,923, but that the Massachusetts Cotton Mills contract had been completed and the only work on hand was an order for five locomotives. Company stock declined to a new low of $785. It was at this point that the two large contracts with the Philadelphia & Reading Railroad promised to alleviate the acute situation. These contracts, however, presented a problem. Together, they represented orders for more than $300,000 of equipment, but a two-year credit had been extended to the road and the working-capital requirements of these contracts were so extensive that there was no cash left for a dividend in 1842. Locks and Canals stock fell to $754, and Jackson rose up in the directors' meeting to chide the timid stockholders. He pointed out that profits for the past year had totaled $105,744, a third of which arose from the Philadelphia & Reading coal-car contract, which was only two-thirds completed. The relatively low price of Locks and Canals stock on the market was unjustified by facts. "We have divided 52 per cent of profits and 10 per cent on sale of water power since I was Treasurer," Jackson declared. The Proprietors, he concluded, evidently did not realize the value of their property.

The depression continued into 1843, and it began to appear that Jackson's optimism was not justified. He admitted that after the completion of the Philadelphia & Reading contract, in the summer of 1843, there were no further prospects of business. The Philadelphia & Reading, moreover, was having difficulty meeting its obligations. Three dividends were paid in 1843, but Locks and Canals stock declined to $700.

The year 1843 appeared to be the bottom of the downtrend. Business revived thereafter. Although the following year brought little locomotive business, it introduced a greatly accelerated demand for textile machinery. Locks and Canals mechanics were being enticed away by offers from smaller machine shops. Early in the year the company was "very much engaged." By November the agent was declining to guarantee delivery of textile machinery in less than six months. Soon afterward, however, a new slump in business left the company with few orders on the books.[67] At this point serious negotiations for the sale of the company were commenced.

Whatever the fate of the company after 1844, the stockholders had little to complain of. The investor who had purchased a share of Locks and Canals stock in 1825 for $500.00 could add up $1,422.50 received in regular dividends in nineteen years — an average return of close to 15 per cent per year throughout a period which included two depressions, one of which had been the most costly in American history up to that time. The value of his stock in terms of net assets of the company must also be considered. That value was soon to be determined by an actual division of those assets.

TABLE 4

PROPRIETORS OF THE LOCKS AND CANALS ON MERRIMACK RIVER
DIVIDENDS 1825–1844
(Capital Stock: 1,200 shares of $500 each.)

Dividend Number	Year	Amount per Share	% of Par	Cumulative % Realized per Share
1	1827	$ 62.50	12½	..
2	1828	62.50	12½	25
3	1829	30.00	6	31
4	1830	30.00	6	37
5	1831	62.50	12½	49½
6 & 7	1832	165.00	33	82½
8	1833	100.00	20	100½
9	1834	75.00	15	115½
10	1835	100.00	20	135½
11 & 12	1836	200.00	40	175½
[a]	1837	[a]	..	....
13	1838	50.00	10	185½
14	1839	60.00	12	197½
15	1840	75.00	15	212½
16 & 17	1841	125.00	25	237½
[a]	1842	[a]		
18, 19 & 20	1843	150.00	30	267½
21	1844	75.00	15	282½

[a] Dividend passed.

Source: Locks and Canals records, Directors' minutes.

Proposals to sell or convert the machine shop first began to be heard in the depressed period between the completion of the Massachusetts Cotton Mills and the signing of the Philadelphia & Reading contracts. On September 21, 1841, Jackson told the directors that in view of the lack of orders it would be well to sell the machine shop. However, Jackson doubted if such a course could then be followed "to advantage." He proposed an alternate plan of converting the shop to a twist mill. Reviving business caused this proposal to be tabled until October of 1842, when "owing to cessation of demand for new machinery and reduction of work of repairs, now generally done in company shops," it was again considered, and again tabled.

In November, 1843, a committee consisting of Abbott Lawrence, part-owner and director in several mills, William Appleton, brother of Nathan, and Thomas B. Wales, active in the affairs of the Western Railroad, requested Jackson to state the terms on which the Locks and Canals Company would dispose of the machine shop. On September 25, 1844, Jackson offered to sell the machine shop and foundry, with land and two mill powers, for $200,000. Lawrence countered with an offer of $175,000, and this was accepted. The Locks and Canals Company went about terminating its affairs.

There is no way of telling why the decision to sell the machine shop was made. Business since 1837 had been full of uncertainty. The most lucrative property had been sold, and the Lowell mills had been built. It would appear that the directors were content to skim the cream of the business, take their profits, and withdraw. A further possibility is that a need was felt for separating the water-power and machine-building functions of the company in order that both might be developed to maximum advantage.

By the terms of the 1845 reorganization the machine shop was sold to a new corporation, to be known as the Lowell Machine Shop. The Locks and Canals Company sold $600,000 of real estate to the various Lowell corporations, called in its stock, and divided its assets among its stockholders. A new company called, like the old, the Proprietors of the Locks and Canals on Merrimack River, was formed to regulate the water power at Lowell. Stock for this company was subscribed by the Lowell corporations on a basis proportionate to the number of mill powers owned by each.

With the division of assets in 1845 the complete picture of operating results stands revealed. Liquidation dividends amounting to $1,582 per share were distributed to the stockholders in 1845 and 1846.[68] The division of assets added to dividends previously received totaled $3,004 per $500 share — an average increment from 1825 to 1845, inclusive, of 24 per cent per year. This record of success covered a period when the trend of commodity prices in American markets had more or less steadily declined, and when the difficulties of conducting business had been aggravated by that downtrend and by frequent and severe depressions.

Even measured in non-monetary returns, the accomplishments of the Locks and Canals Company had gone beyond the most optimistic of the early plans. Almost literally, the machine shop had built the city of Lowell, where (in 1845) 30,000 people lived and 200,000 spindles turned. Developmental costs had been high, but the heavy first cost of water power had been paid for largely by the sale of city lands. Managerial techniques had been developed which were copied by other textile centers, as was the whole concept of a planned manufacturing development centering in a water-power privilege.

Locomotives from the Locks and Canals machine shop sped the growth of industrial New England. In 1830 Patrick Tracy Jackson had confessed that he valued water power within ten miles of Boston at double the price of the same quantity of water at Lowell. By the mid-1840's mill men were stating: "The advantages of a factory at Lowell in consequence of its nearness to the metropolis are generally admitted to be sufficiently great to be an offset to the increased cost of the land and water power." [69] Most important of all, perhaps, was the fact that between 1825 and 1845 the textile machinery industry flexed its muscles and snapped the bands of regional confinement. The advantages of early entry into the textile-machinery market had been realized and the great developmental profits had been pocketed. After 1845 the prosperity of the machine shop at Lowell was to depend upon the ability of that shop to compete on equal terms in an open market with a growing number of textile-machine shops all over America.

CHAPTER IV

BIRTH OF TWO INDUSTRIES AT SACO AND BIDDEFORD, 1825–1850

1. Cotton Manufacture and Machine-Building in Saco 1826–1839

The upward course of American business can be spelled out in terms of successive waves of optimism. In the textile industry the unfathomed mass psychology of the business man had produced a spurt of mill construction in the early 1800's; another in the years from 1812 to 1815. In the middle 1820's the depression psychosis which had prevailed in varying intensity since 1816 was finally shaken off. The subtle transition to recovery took place, and, almost imperceptibly, enthusiasm for the promotion of cotton manufactures revived once again.

The Locks and Canals machine shop at Lowell grew out of this latest revival of hopes and prospects, and over the course of two decades following 1825 it evolved from a cotton-mill department to an independent position of importance in the national market. Over approximately the same span of years Saco-Lowell's corporate forebears in Maine were experiencing a comparable, if more feverish, evolution. In the background of this development lies a period of metal-working operations in Saco extending back to 1811. As at Lowell, however, it was the optimism of the early and middle years of the 1820's that brought the twin manufactures of cotton cloth and textile machinery to the falls of the Saco River.

The Lowell pattern was closely followed in Saco and Biddeford. A machine shop was called into existence to create a cotton mill. A manufacturing community was planned, and a water-power company was organized to create and promote it. Machine-building functions were transferred from cotton mill to water-power company. As at Lowell, the formative period of machine-shop operation ended when initial contracts for the local mills had been completed and the machine shop was forced to look beyond the immediate environment for continuing success. That the form of the Lowell plan was empty without the energizing substance of managerial skill was proven at Saco, however, where great resources, both natural and human, initially produced not profit but bankruptcy and ruin.

The Saco Manufacturing Company, 1826–1830

The Saco Manufacturing Company was organized in 1826 for the purpose of building a cotton factory on Saco Falls. As related in Chapter I, the first step taken by the newly organized company was to secure the property, equipment, and water privileges of the old Iron Works, established on Factory Island in 1811 by Thomas Cutts and Josiah Calef.

Information contained in long-forgotten records suggests that approximately one-half of the capital for this first cotton factory and machine shop at Saco came from the firm of Waterston, Pray & Company, commission merchants and importers in Boston.[1] Isaac Pray, a banker and a partner in this firm, was named treasurer of the Saco Manufacturing Company. The remainder of the capital was locally subscribed in Saco and Biddeford, some of it by Josiah Calef, who, if he was not actually the moving force behind the whole promotion, was at least an influential and active participant. The source of capital for the Saco venture is of interest as further evidence of the important part played by the accumulated mercantile wealth of Boston in financing the early New England textile industry. Of equal interest is the fact that local business men in the smaller communities outside the primary cotton-manufacturing districts were by now willing and anxious to invest their small accumulations in the new field.

Plans for the company's factory were drawn on a scale which indicated that the planners had carefully observed the advantages of large-scale operation as practised at Waltham and Lowell and had hoped, by building an even larger mill, to multiply those advantages still further. A mill of truly heroic dimensions was commenced — a seven-story wooden structure measuring 210 feet by 47 feet, to house 12,000 spindles and 300 looms.[2] This mill building, completed in 1826, was more than twice the size of those currently under construction in Lowell and was by far the largest in the country.

A machine shop was set up in the mill and "a large number of experienced and skillful workmen were employed in the construction of the necessary machinery, much of which was executed with skill and ingenuity seldom equalled."[3] These mechanics must of necessity have been imported from the older textile centers, but their identity and training are unknown. In the fact that large orders for castings were placed with the foundry of Shepard Leach lies a hint that the machinery was patterned after Waltham and Lowell models. The machine shop appears from the records to have been surprisingly large — its size an indication of the scope of the company's ambitions. In 1827 the shop was carried on the books at a valuation of $170,802, an amount $68,000 larger than the valuation of the Locks and Canals shop of comparable date.

Although the mill building was completed in 1826, the first sale of cloth was not recorded until June, 1829. The delay was occasioned by failure to turn out machinery on schedule, coupled with delays in canal construction. Some of the water wheels and gearing, in fact, were not completed until February, 1830. The evidence of poor planning and unexpected technical difficulty is clear. During these three years of delay, however, the old nail works and a sawmill were operated by the company and produced some welcome revenue, though scarcely enough to meet the heavy costs of construction.

The timing of the Saco enterprise could scarcely have been worse. Had the mill been placed in operation on schedule, it is possible that cash reserves could have been accumulated to carry the company through the depression of 1829. Neither did the company possess capital resources comparable to those of the Boston Manufacturing Company and the Merrimack Manufacturing Company. Despite charter rights permitting a capitalization of up to $1,000,000, the Saco Manufacturing Company was forced to borrow heavily from Boston banks to finance construction. Just at the time when the company began to turn out cloth, the cloth market became depressed — flooded by the wares of Waltham, Lowell, and other established mill centers. In the six months ending in December, 1829, the Saco Manufacturing Company was able to market only $35,000 of cloth. Debts of the company exceeded $300,000, almost the entire amount of which was in the form of notes held by the American, City, Atlantic, and Globe banks of Boston and the Saco Bank in Saco. On December 30, 1829, the creditors took over the company and drew up an agreement by which the company management was to operate the property in trust for the benefit of the banks concerned. The situation was desperate, but liquidation was not immediately contemplated. Instead, the banks directed the management to complete the construction of machinery with all possible haste. The indenture agreement between the banks and the company indicates that only half of the machinery was in operation in 1829.[4]

Were it not for this financial crisis, much information of value might never have been preserved. The creditors, however, caused a complete inventory of company assets to be recorded. Monetary values are missing from the inventory, but the picture of what a 10,000-spindle cotton factory consisted of in 1829 is reasonably clear. Machinery components are accurately indicated, and while the list of machine-shop tools reveals a general lack of power-driven equipment capable of working large shapes, the abundance of specialized small tools, both manual and power-driven, is noteworthy. A comparison of this tool inventory with that of the Boston Manufacturing Company inventory of 1817 suggests some advance in metal-working techniques throughout the period — a multiplication of both numbers and kinds of small machine tools.

On a bleak Sunday evening in February, 1830, the minds of the company creditors were relieved of the burden of pondering the future of the prostrate enterprise. At 3:00 P.M. the factory bell commenced to peal a dreaded tune. Villagers running from their houses saw smoke pouring from the basement windows of the machine shop. Watchmen and volunteers rushed to the forcing pumps to turn the valves which would deluge the mill interior with water from tanks in the attic. They were met with a solid wall of flame at the door of the pump room. The mammoth wooden mill became an inferno, and soon the tenements and outbuildings were blazing. No

TABLE 5

FIXED ASSETS OF THE SACO MANUFACTURING COMPANY
DECEMBER, 1829

BUILDINGS

Cotton factory 210 x 46 feet
3 picker buildings and cloth house
Wood machine shop
Grist mill containing 4 pairs stones
Trip-hammer shop
Rolling mill
Nail factory
3 coal houses
4 wood sheds
Lumber house
Warehouse
Joiners' shop
Lime shed
3 barns
Mansion House (a hostelry)
Undisclosed number of dwelling houses
9 wooden tenements — mainly one-story
1 four-family brick tenement
1 ten-family brick tenement

MACHINE-SHOP TOOLS

1 fluting engine
2 polishing engines
1 bevel gear engine
1 cylinder gear engine
5 spindle engines
3 single roller engines
1 main-shaft hand lathe
1 filing engine
1 sloping engine
1 spiral gear engine
1 drilling engine
8 double roller engines
1 main-shaft double engine
12 large hand lathes
12 polishing lathes
44 bench vises and other small tools

MACHINERY

Completed	*Unfinished*	*Total Planned*
1 picker	...	1
1 lapwinder	...	1
2 lapwinders & pickers	2	4
2 mixers	1	3
72 cards	48	120
12 drawing frames	8	20
12 double speeders	8	20
4 grinders	2	6
96 spinning frames (6,144 spindles)	72 (4,608 spindles)	10,752
180 looms	120	300
11 warpers	7	18
11 dressers	7	18

Source: Saco Manufacturing Company, Journal, Dec., 1829.

hand could stay the disaster, and in a short time what had been called "one of the noblest monuments of New England enterprise" was a ruin of charred timber and twisted metal. The damage was estimated at $300,000, of which a third or less was covered by insurance.[5]

This was the end of the Saco Manufacturing Company, an enterprise boldly conceived but poorly planned and poorly supported — a venture which showed only too clearly the fatal hazards of bad timing in the unstable manufacturing economy of the day. The history of textile-machine building at Saco Falls, however, had scarcely commenced to unfold.

Early Years of the York Manufacturing Company, 1830–1836

In August, 1830, the creditors of the Saco Manufacturing Company sold the entire Saco property, water rights, and ruins at public auction. The buyer was Charles Bradbury, a Boston publisher and lawyer who paid a total of $60,600 — a price which, as the creditors ruefully pointed out, barely covered the value of the buildings still standing and which, in effect, constituted a gift to the purchaser of all the land and water power. On March 16, 1831, Bradbury and several associates incorporated themselves as the York Manufacturing Company and announced plans for an 8,000-spindle cotton mill, to be built at an estimated cost of $200,000, on the foundations of the old mill. Bradbury then sold the recently acquired Saco property to the new company (at an apparent profit to himself of $15,000).

Capital stock to the amount of $300,000 was subscribed, and by July, 1832, it was fully paid in. The three hundred shares of stock were distributed among eighteen stockholders, all of whom were Boston men. It is worthy of note that the name of no Appleton, Lowell, Jackson, Lawrence, Perkins, or Boott appears in the list of original stockholders. The venture was exclusively a promotion of middle-class business men — bankers primarily, but also stationers, shopkeepers, provisioners, and small-scale commission agents and importers — petty capitalists whose local operations had provided a surplus for investment.[6] The eager participation of this class of business man is further evidence of the all-pervading optimism with which the manufacture of cotton cloth was regarded at the time. It remained to be seen whether such men, with adequate capital but lacking the practical experience now possessed by their more famous contemporaries at Lowell, could successfully compete with the large mills already in existence. However great the confidence of the participants, the venture was clearly of a most speculative nature.

Charles Bradbury appears to have been the moving force behind the formation of the York Manufacturing Company. Bradbury subscribed to forty-two shares of stock, the largest single block, and was elected president of the board of directors at the first meeting of the Board in April, 1831. The directors took immediate action to secure a skilled and experienced agent to build and operate the factory at Saco. On August 16, 1831, a contract was concluded which brought Samuel Batchelder from Lowell to Saco.

Batchelder, like Paul Moody, came from solid country stock and from boyhood had earned a living with his hands. Like Moody, Batchelder proved to be a talented mechanic and he had turned his attention to the field of cotton manufacture at an early age. Batchelder was endowed with a rare combination of abilities. He proved to be not only an expert technician but a capable administrator as well. These qualities enabled him to operate a small New Hampshire mill so successfully that in 1825 he was engaged by the Jackson interests to superintend the Hamilton Manufacturing Company at Lowell. After several years there, one of those frequent conflicts between resident agents and Boston treasurers embittered Batchelder and rendered him susceptible to the extremely liberal terms offered by Bradbury on behalf of the York Manufacturing Company. Batchelder agreed to go to Saco and act as the "principal Agent" of the company, to erect one or more manufactories, to contract for machinery, to superintend all establishments built, and to collect rents and real-estate income as due.[7]

By the summer of 1832 the first York mill was in operation on the site of the Saco Manufacturing Company factory. Business prospects appeared good, despite strong political hostility toward monopoly and protectionism. Moderate prosperity prevailed, and Americans showed a lively disposition to indulge in any enterprise that gave even a remote promise of riches — be it wild lands, silkworms, or a new machine. The textile industry was rapidly expanding. Far from being unaware of the potential value of water power, American promoters by 1834 had come to place preposterous valuations on every creek and stream which could conceivably turn a water wheel. Whole townships were purchased in Maine, sight unseen, and Boston land speculators filled the hotels of Portland to overflowing. It was a joke in Bangor that boarding houses were so full of Boston men that late comers were forced to pay high prices for the privilege of leaning overnight against a fence-post.[8] The York Manufacturing Company, its fine properties and water privileges acquired for a song, was in an extraordinarily advantageous position to profit not only from good management but from a highly favorable set of external influences.

Little is known of the early operations of this company. The only evidence that a machine shop was in existence in 1832 or that machinery for the first mill was built locally lies in the fact that in 1832 the company was employing 108 machinists, at an average wage of $1.20 per day.[9] Notwithstanding fears of the cautious that competition from the great number of cotton mills under construction in Maine would operate to reduce the profits of all, the York directors voted, in September of 1833, to build a second factory.[10] In January, 1834, a 20 per cent stock dividend was declared and $180,000 of new capital (all but $11,000 of which came from the original stockholders) [11] was subscribed to finance the second mill. In 1835, cash dividends totaling 12 per cent were paid, and an additional $60,000 of capital was paid in, this last to help finance extensive purchases of land and water privileges in Saco and Biddeford. In 1836, 10 per cent in dividends was paid, the foundations laid for a machine shop "equal in size to that at Lowell," and a new cotton factory started. Additional capital to the amount of $150,000 was paid in.

So far the operating plan at Saco had closely followed that put into effect at Lowell. An excellent water-power privilege had been acquired at low price, and surrounding property bought up as rapidly as possible. Relatively large amounts of capital had been poured into the venture and used in an ambitious building program. Expert management had been hired by the non-technical promoters,[12] and a machine shop had been commenced to serve company needs. Operating results at Saco, as at Lowell, had proven highly satisfactory. Boston bankers and tradesmen, it would seem, were proving themselves as successful in the field of manufactures as the Boston merchants who preceded them at Waltham and Lowell. Credit for the splendid operating results achieved, however, must be ascribed to the genius of Samuel Batchelder — whose loss Lowell was to have increasing reason to regret.

2. Formation of the Saco Water Power Company, 1836–1839

In 1836 the York directors took a step which unmistakably was inspired by what had been accomplished earlier at Lowell. On November 1, 1836, they voted "that it is deemed expedient to make a division of the Company's Property at Saco and Biddeford, forming a Water Power Company for a part thereof." Batchelder was appointed to a committee of stockholders to submit a plan for the division. On March 22, 1837, an act to incorporate the Saco Water Power Company in the State of Maine was approved. This charter was brief and general. It allowed the company to purchase and hold real and personal estate to the amount of $500,000 and fixed no limit to the liability of the stockholders. By its terms the company was granted permission to engage in virtually any type of manufacturing and real-estate transactions in the towns of Saco and Biddeford, provided that navigation on the Saco River was not impeded.[13]

Those conditions of financial stringency which in 1837 had caused the Locks and Canals Company in Lowell to pass its dividends operated with equal force at Saco; there they had the effect of delaying the organization of the Saco Water Power Company. Symptoms of distress became evident as early as November, 1836, at which time the York directors found it necessary to send the treasurer as far as New York to secure the best terms he could for a $25,000 loan. At the same time, Batchelder was requested to suspend building contracts in Saco and discontinue as many expenditures as possible. These difficulties were considered to be transitory. Late in the year $250,000 more capital was subscribed, and early in 1837 a 6 per cent dividend was paid out. Thereafter business matters took a turn for the worse.

The difficulties at first were monetary. There was no money to be had except on exorbitant terms. Failure by the weakest individuals and companies to honor their paper as it came due had the effect of relaying the stringency from man to man and house to house, until even the strongest wondered whether they could muster capital to meet their obligations. Caught in this vicious circle, the York Manufacturing Company found itself with $37,000 of suspended notes on hand. Operations at Saco were curtailed. A committee of directors visited Saco to examine into means of reducing expenditures. A recommendation was made that construction of Mill Number Three be slowed down. In April, 1837, half of the spindles in Mill Number Two were stopped, and construction work on a dye house and bleachery was suspended. In May all spindles in Mill Number Two were stopped. In December the stockholders were called upon to stand ready to endorse the treasurer's notes up to $200 for each share of stock held, should such action be necessary in the company interest. When it was learned that Lowell and other large cotton centers had reduced the wages of all operatives by one-fifth, a similar course of action was followed at Saco. Orders for cotton were rescinded. In this fashion and by reason of these widely practised defensive tactics the monetary panic gave way to a severe general depression.

By June, 1838, a degree of recovery had set in. Two of the York mills were in full operation again and half of the third was busy, employing a total of 736 men and women. By February, 1839, all three mills were in operation, with 1,000 men and women at work. Three months later the question of forming the Water Power Company was again raised. A committee was appointed by the York directors to effect the organization, the directors stipulating that the Water Power stock be offered first to York stockholders, on a share-for-share basis. On June 25, 1839, this committee reported that 936 shares out of the 1,000 authorized for the Water Power Company (with par value of $500) had been subscribed by York stockholders.

Since 1830 some interesting changes had occurred in the ownership of York shares which were reflected in the initial Water Power Company subscription. Diffusion of ownership had steadily taken place, as the eighteen original stockholders sold off shares or willed them to members of their families, and as new stock issues failed to be entirely taken up by the old stockholders. By 1833 the number of shareholders had doubled. In 1839 the offer of Water Power stock to York shareholders resulted in the splitting of the 1,000-share issue into 142 blocks, of which the largest block controlled by one family was only 56 shares. The average holding was seven shares. This diffusion of ownership, which was occurring simultaneously in the Boston Manufacturing Company and in the various corporations at Lowell, was the natural consequence of company growth and the splitting of large blocks by inheritance. It called forth a new managerial technique — the proxy vote — and it ushered in a new era in which management of many companies came to depend not on ownership but on control.

Significant new names had also appeared on the York stock lists after 1830. Benjamin and Elijah Loring, Boston stationers and merchants, had bought into York, and in 1839 they came to own the largest block of the new Water Power Company shares. Nathan Appleton also had purchased a few York shares, and in 1838 Batchelder had reported, "I am very glad to find that Messrs. Lawrence & Co are getting an interest in our stock, and have no doubt it will have an effect in bringing forward purchasers for any shares that may be for sale." Symbolic of the trend of the times was the fact that Henry Lee, one of the most bitter merchant antagonists to protection for infant industries, had come to hold stock in York and in the Water Power Company.

The alliance of these powerful families indicated the esteem with which Batchelder's operations in Saco were held and imparted further strength to the enterprise. Of the original subscribers to large blocks of York stock, only Bradbury, with forty shares, and Cartwright, with twenty-five shares, appeared as holders of sizable blocks of the Water Power Company stock. Batchelder and his family owned forty-five shares of the new stock. Since the York stockholders were almost exclusively Boston men, it followed that ownership of the Water Power Company was similarly vested. Less than forty shares were owned by stockholders claiming Maine as their residence.

The Saco Water Power Company, like its parent, the York, was

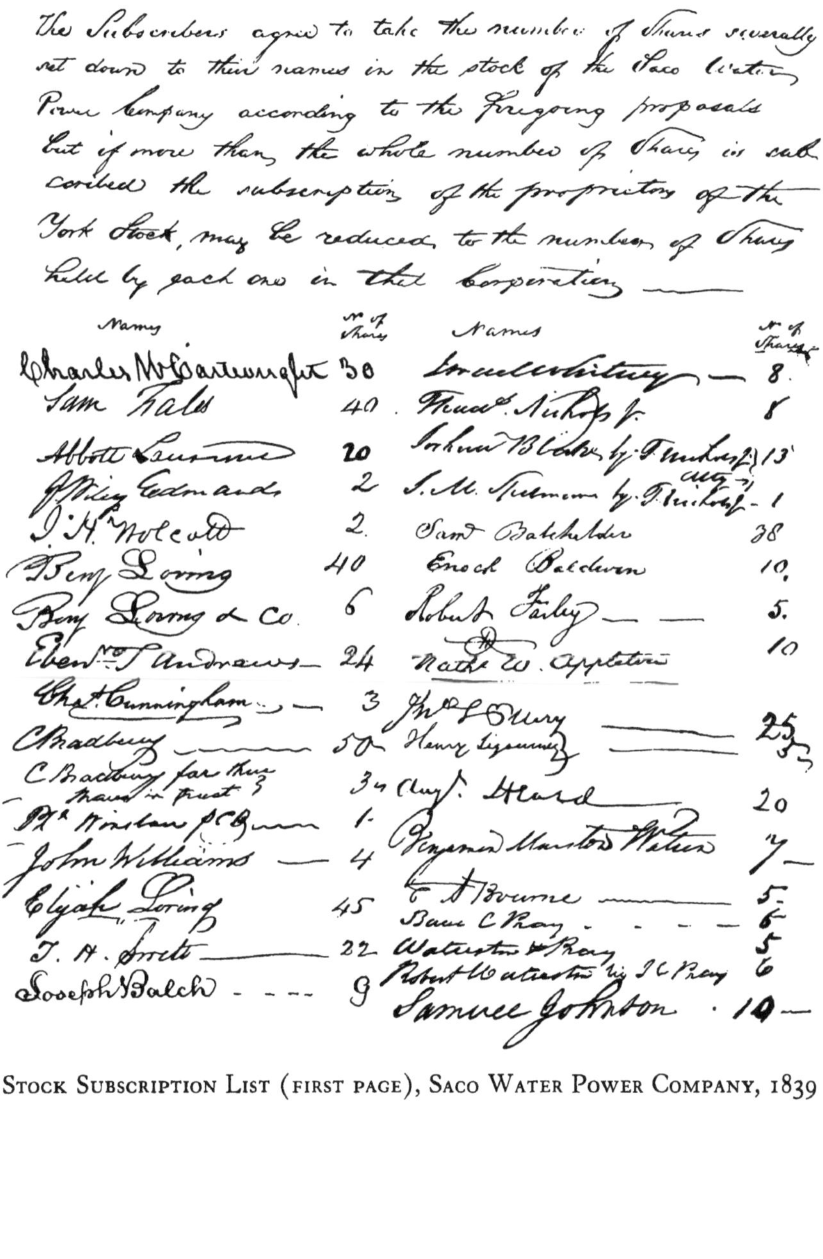

The Subscribers agree to take the number of Shares severally set down to their names in the stock of the Saco Water Power Company according to the foregoing proposals but if more than the whole number of Shares is subscribed the subscription of the proprietors of the York Stock, may be reduced to the number of Shares held by each one in that Corporation —

Names	No of Shares	Names	No of Shares
Charles W. Cartwright	30	Israel Whitney	8
Sam Hale	40	Thos. Nichols Jr	8
Abbott Lawrence	20	Jotham Blake by T. Nichols Jr atty	13
J. Wiley Edmands	2	J. M. Stedman by T. Nichols atty	1
J. H. Wolcott	2	Saml Batchelder	38
Benj Loring	40	Enoch Baldwin	10
Benj Loring & Co.	6	Robert Farley	5
Ebenr. T. Andrews	24	Nathl W. Appleton	10
Chas. Cunningham	3	Jno L. Emery	25
C Bradbury	50	Henry Sigourney	5
C Bradbury for shares in trust	34	Augs. Heard	20
Wm. Winslow	1	Benjamin Marston Watson	7
John Williams	4	E. A. Bourne	5
Elijah Loring	45	Bain & Pray	6
J. A. Smith	22	Waterston & Pray	5
Joseph Balch	9	Robert Waterston by J C Pray	6
		Samuel Johnston	10

Stock Subscription List (first page), Saco Water Power Company, 1839

intimately linked with Boston financial institutions. At the first meeting of the stockholders, held on July 18, 1839, in the old Cutts mansion on Factory Island, Joseph Balch, president of the Merchants Insurance Company and a director of the Suffolk Bank, was elected president of the Water Power Company. Enoch Baldwin, president of the Shoe and Leather Dealers Bank, was elected treasurer. Nine directors were chosen, six of whom were Boston bankers, importers, or merchants. The other three were Balch, Baldwin, and Samuel Batchelder. At 4:00 P.M. on July 29, 1839, the first meeting of the Saco Water Power Company directors was held at 87 State Street in Boston, and important steps were taken to activate the company.[14]

The first move of the directors was to appoint a committee to treat with York for the purchase of land, buildings, and water power. The treasurer was authorized to employ an engineer "to make surveys, plans & estimates of the land & water power contemplated to be purchased." An assessment of $100 per share on the Water Power stock was voted. The treasurer was also authorized to borrow $50,000 from the York Company. (This loan was approved by the York directors at a slightly later date.) The directors then voted: "That Samuel Batchelder, Enoch Baldwin & Josiah Calef be a committee to examine the premises contemplated to be purchased of the York Manufacturing Company & to select there upon a proper location for a Machine Shop & Foundry and that the same committee be authorized to proceed forthwith to the building of the same & to furnishing the same with all the requisite Machinery & Apparatus. . . ."

3. INITIAL OPERATIONS, 1839–1843

Purchase of Land and Privileges

A perplexing question arises as to how two companies, owned by virtually the same group of men, could come to have serious disagreements or seek to advance the interests of the one at the expense of the interests of the other. This anomalous and puzzling situation had occurred earlier at Lowell (being evidenced, for example, by sharp bargaining between the Boston Manufacturing Company and Merrimack — both controlled by substantially the same group of stockholders). It became noticeable in Saco immediately after the organization of the Water Power Company, whose relationship with York became increasingly strained with the passage of time. As we shall see later, conflicts between the Water Power Company and intimately related interests in another company were to precipitate a crisis in company affairs.

The first sign that complete coöperation did not inevitably follow from common ownership occurred when the Water Power Company attempted to settle upon terms for the purchase of property from York. A price was readily agreed upon, but the York directors interjected conditions which the Water Power Company committee held to be in violation of preliminary agreements. To those shareholders with an equal interest in both companies there must have been an element of humor in the situation, as they mused upon whether their left pocket would be enriched at the expense of their right, or vice versa.

The initial disagreement between the two companies, though not serious of itself, had serious implications. This curious disharmony in a closely related group illustrates the fact that even when men owned stock in both companies they tended to ally themselves firmly with either one or the other, and willingly robbed Peter to pay Paul. Personalities undoubtedly were involved in these alliances, but of even greater importance was the factor of professional reputation. Enoch Baldwin, for example, held stock in York, and in May, 1839, was a member of the York committee to bargain with the Water Power Company over the terms of the property sale. In July he appeared as a member of the Water Power Company negotiating committee! What had happened in the three months to make Baldwin switch allegiance is obvious — he had been elected treasurer of the Water Power Company, and on the success of that company depended his reputation and future.[15] There were, moreover, a few stockholders who held shares in only one of the companies. Their number increased as time went on, and they vociferously resisted bargains in which their particular company came off second best. A more significant group was that which, while owning stock in both companies, held larger blocks of shares in one than in the other. Men in this situation, of course, tended in cases of controversy to advance their greater interest at the expense of their lesser. This information suggests why differences could and did occur between York and the Water Power Company despite the fact that over 90 per cent of the stock of the latter initially was owned by York stockholders. Percentage-ownership figures, moreover, became progressively less significant as the number of shareholders increased — as the time approached when ownership and control ceased to be necessarily synonymous. At all times the significance of joint-ownership figures must be carefully appraised in order to avoid over-emphasis on the degree of coöperation which actually existed in the large textile centers.

Samuel Batchelder himself, like Kirk Boott at Lowell, attempted to serve two masters, and found himself in an awkward position when disputes arose between the two. He was, of course, a large shareholder in both enterprises and active in the management of both. Wisely he refrained from participating in the property dickering in 1839 and 1840, and for some time thereafter he appears to have remained aloof when disputes were brewing between the two companies.

An agreement for the transfer of York property and privileges to the Water Power Company was finally reached in July, 1840, and was incorporated in a contract dated October 17, 1840. The purchase price agreed upon was $200,000, and the property involved was described as follows:[16]

> All the land and buildings and water power of the York Mfg. Co. lying in Saco & Biddeford except that part of Cutts [Factory] Island lying northwesterly of the middle of the road leading from the Saco Bridge to the lower Biddeford Bridge with sufficient water powers for the existing works of the York Mfg company and for one other factory of about 6,000 spindles and machine shop for repairs, to be built. . . .

The contract attempted to define the complicated matter of water rights in such a way as to minimize the possibility of subsequent disputes. According to measurements made in 1838 by an engineer employed for the purpose, the Falls at low water could furnish sixty mill powers. A third was deducted from this figure "in order to make a safe estimate at the very lowest state of the water. . . ." From the forty mill powers thus calculated to be available, York reserved the privilege of drawing eleven mill powers during eighteen hours of the day. The remainder of the mill powers, calculated to be sufficient for fifteen cotton mills of the same dimensions as the Lowell factories, were to become the property of the Water Power Company. The influence of the Lowell development is clearly manifest throughout this contract. Not only was the Lowell unit of power measurement adopted, but past experience at Lowell inspired a clause in the Saco contract setting up a board of arbitration to preside over water-power disputes.[17]

The real-estate and water-privilege transfer was extraordinarily complex. The Saco Manufacturing Company and then the York Company had aggressively expanded the original property and privilege of the old Iron Works. These purchases subsequent to 1825 sought not only more land, but also a clear title to the water privileges already claimed. This latter was difficult to acquire, in consequence of an unusual local custom. Ownership of the sawmills, which originally controlled the water rights, was divided not into shares or partnerships, but into "days" or "hours." Proprietors of the sawmills appear to have sold others the right to use the mill for so many hours in each day or so many days in a month or year. This was not a lease, but an outright sale — an equity in the mill which could be sold or passed on to heirs as though it consisted of shares of stock. These rights were widely sold, and further split by inheritance into fractions sometimes as small as minutes! To gain undisputed title to a mill privilege, therefore, each day, hour, and minute which had ever been disposed of by the original owners must be bought in. York County records are filled with deeds chronicling the distribution of these rights and subsequent efforts to reacquire them. Clear titles to some properties were not obtained for generations — a problem not faced by the Lowell promoters.

Table 6 below reveals the slow accumulation of property and rights which had taken place since 1825, and which came, with minor variations, to be vested in the Saco Water Power Company in 1840.[18]

New Machine Shop and York Contract

On July 23, 1839, the York directors had decided that it was expedient to construct a fourth mill and voted "that Mr. Batchelder

TABLE 6

VALUATION OF REAL ESTATE & WATER POWER TO BE CONVEYED TO SACO WATER POWER Company[a]

JUNE, 1839

Mill privileges:	
Purchased by Saco Mfg. Co., May 1825–November 1827.	
33 days in Cole Mill & $44\frac{5}{24}$ days in Eddy Mill	$13,908.05
Purchased by York Mfg. Co., 1830–1840	
$14\frac{8}{24}$ days in Cole Mill	3,191.67
14 days in Gooch Mill	1,463.00
36 days in Bog Mills	3,777.00
$46\frac{3}{4}$ days in Pepperell Mills	27,700.00
Spring Mill	5,400.00
Total Privileges	$55,439.72
Land:	
Purchased by Saco Mfg. Co., 1825–1830	
32 acres in Biddeford	....
31 acres in Saco	6,575.56
Purchased by York Mfg. Co., 1830–1840	
$312\frac{1}{2}$ acres & 27 houses (almost all in Biddeford)	56,549.21
Total Land	$63,124.77
Other:	
Expenditures in finishing & repairing houses	11,027.44
Land contracted for, at expense of York	20,000.00
York expenditures on brick block of 5 stores and houses	20,240.15
Remainder of Island (except York property): wharf & wharf lots, mill sites for 6 mills, with expenditures on canals, dams, bridges, & streets	30,167.92
Total Valuation to Be Conveyed	$200,000.00

[a] It should be understood that these purchases were in addition to the main purchase by the Saco Mfg. Co. in 1825 of the Iron Works for $106,000, most of which was retained by York. The Pepperell Mills referred to above were sawmills and should not be confused with the cotton mill of later date.

Source: York Mfg. Co., Directors' records.

be requested and directed to contract with the Saco Water Power Company for such of the machinery required for the new mill as he may be able to obtain from said company on such terms as he may deem reasonable." At this time the Water Power Company had not concluded its property transfer contract with York, and, of course, was far from commencing to build its own machine shop.

Correspondence and committee reports of the Water Power Company record the sequence of events in 1839, but the situation which existed at this time in respect to machine-building at Saco is not entirely clear. York Company records indicate that the foundations for a new company machine shop had been laid late in 1836. There followed a year of delay, probably occasioned by the depressed state of business. Negotiations at length were opened by York with Rufus Nichols, a local machinist, "for the purchase of his machinery & tools, & for the employment of himself to superintend the building of machinery, machine shop &c. . . ." [19] Nichols offered to sell his tools and fixtures for $4,500 and to accept an annual salary of $1,500 for a term of five years. This agreement between Nichols and the York Company became effective in February, 1839; by that time, of course, York had conceived the idea of a machine shop operated by the Water Power Company. York's contract with Nichols was therefore transferred to the Water Power Company and was changed to date from October 1, 1839.

Although the plans for the York machine shop which had been drawn in 1836 and furthered in 1839 by the agreement with Nichols were not carried through, there is clear evidence that in 1839 (and probably in earlier years as well) Nichols had been operating a fully equipped and independently housed machine shop in Saco. It was in this shop that the Water Power Company commenced its machine-building activities. A letterbook of the Water Power Company gives evidence of limited machine-shop operations from August, 1839, and apparently conducted in the name of the new company. The letters consist of reports from Nichols in Saco to Baldwin, the treasurer, in Boston. In August Nichols was ordering steel, but no machine-building was going on. A wharf was being constructed for use by the Water Power Company. Nichols commented on the unfavorable monetary situation and told Baldwin that nothing further could be ascertained about the order for York's fourth mill. The York directors, in fact, had just instructed Batchelder to stop half the spindles in Mill Number Three. In November Nichols reported that not a solitary individual was at work in the machine shop, and that it was perhaps a good time to lay in some new tools. The limited scope of operations is indicated by the fact that from August through

December, 1839, Nichols had received only $2,400 in cash from Baldwin and had expended $2,165.63.

On December 30, 1839, Nichols sat down and penned the following paragraph to Baldwin:[20]

Sir:
I have the painful necessity of informing you of a fire which broke out in our machine shop this evening about ¼ past 6 o'clock, and in less than two hours the whole machine shop, grist mill, and two boarding houses on the hill nearby, with two other buildings used as storehouses were enwrapped in flames and nothing of any consequence saved from any of them.

This event inevitably delayed the plans for the new York mill, and if the Water Power Company had hoped to commence machine-building operations immediately those hopes were seared in the flames of the only machine shop at the Falls. Three weeks later Batchelder offered Nichols the lower floor of York's planing-machine building and gave the Water Power Company a small order for turning engines. In April, 1840, Nichols complained to Baldwin that the eight machinists working would soon be unemployed. He urged Baldwin to let him begin building lathes and other tools for their own machine shop. This letter is of considerable interest, for it indicates that almost all the machine tools in use were still being built by the shops themselves, rather than purchased from specialized suppliers. The same situation prevailed at Lowell as well, with the exception of certain importations from England.

This was certainly a precarious time for the Water Power Company. Business was depressed, the York Company undecided about expansion and unwilling to conclude the sale of property upon which the Water Power Company's very existence depended. At least two orders for machinery from outside Saco had to be refused for lack of tools or facilities to manufacture. For the three months ending March 31, 1840, receipts from rentals totaled approximately $1,500. Baldwin had advanced $3,500. Expenditures for machinery, building materials, and labor were slightly over $5,000. The Water Power Company stock was selling at a low figure in Boston, and Nichols remarked, rather unnecessarily, that "we need something to enhance the value of our holdings."

By December, 1840, however, affairs looked more hopeful for the company. The property transfer from York had been effected, and a site for a machine shop had been selected on the Biddeford side of the Falls. Batchelder had agreed to install old machinery in the new York mill, thereby allowing the Water Power Company time to erect a machine shop and commence upon the York order. Nichols optimistically reported (in March, 1841) that he would build a machine shop as large as that at Lowell—to be ready in the autumn. Expenditures, to be sure, had greatly exceeded receipts, but this was to be expected in the early stages of development. The fact that any income was being received was an encouraging sign. The statement below shows operating results from the opening of formal company records in November, 1839, through December, 1840:

Receipts:		
Rentals	$6,286.36	
Sale of machinery	688.08	
		$ 6,974.44
Expenditures:		
Repairs & Improvements	$1,648.53	
Wharf	4,960.52	
Machine tools	1,018.32	
Paid to York Mfg. Co.	4,302.61	
Machinists' payroll	1,007.29	
Miscellaneous materials	3,996.67	
		16,933.94
Excess of expenditures over receipts		$ 9,959.50
Add cash on hand in Saco		5,686.45
Total applied to operations from stock assessments		$15,645.95

The state of manufactures generally, however, remained depressed, and it was a time of great uneasiness. Politicians from other sections of the country were urging tariff reduction. Idealists of many hues were denouncing "the corporations," and labor was restive. Factory regulations had begun to chafe, and wage cuts had come with alarming frequency. In many large mill centers there were outbursts of varying degrees of violence. On March 23, 1841, Samuel Batchelder had posted a notice on the doors of the York mills that all operatives should henceforth live in company tenements or be discharged. On March 20 the operatives staged a "turn out"—peaceful but determined. A banner with the inscription "We scorn to be slaves" was paraded by several hundred of the female operatives. Batchelder, supported by his overseers, acted with "firmness and moderation," and the outbreak resolved into submission to company rules. A contemporary observer reported with sly if unconscious humor, "No grievance could justify proceedings so incompatible with the retiring delicacy of the female character."[21]

Despite the distractions of the day, Nichols reported, in November of 1841, that the machine shop was nearly finished. In this month Batchelder and Nichols put their names on the contract for machinery for the York Company's fourth mill. This contract called for the following:[22]

Machines	Prices	
24 cards @ $160.00 each	$3,840	(Cost $109.02 each to make.)
8 drawing frames @ $225 each	1,800	(" $139.00 " " " .)
8 fly frames, 48 spindles @ $1,200 per frame	9,600	(Cost $701 per frame to make.)
32 warp, 24 filling } frames, 96 spindles @ $360 per frame	20,160	(" $242.88 " " " " .)
6 warpers @ $150 each	900	
10 dressing frames @ $375 each	3,750	
168 looms @ $50 each	8,400	
Total Price	$48,450	
Price per spindle	$9.00	

The differences between these prices and those of the Locks and Canals Company of similar date seem to indicate conclusively that machines of basically different construction were being built in Biddeford and in Lowell. The Water Power Company's card and loom, in particular, were much less costly than those built by the Locks and Canals Company, while the Biddeford fly frame appears to have been considerably more expensive than the Lowell speeder. In view of the strong resemblance in many respects between the two textile centers, this suggestion of deviation in machine design is worth noting. The full implications of this deviation were to become apparent by 1850.

The Water Power Company appears to have outdone its contemporary at Lowell in mark-ups charged on machines. The average Water Power mark-up on cards, drawing frames, fly frames, and spinning frames built for York was approximately 54 per cent over cost. The comparable figure for the Boott contracts of the Locks and Canals Company was 33 per cent. In one respect, however, the York contract was very similar to those drawn at Lowell. A definite time schedule was written into the agreement, and a penalty clause inserted for failure to supply machinery on schedule. The per-spindle price of the Water Power Company's machinery was considerably below average, but this deviation appears to arise from the inexplicable absence of opening and picking machines from the York order.

Since the York contract called for the first machinery to be delivered in July, 1842, construction work on the new machine shop was pushed with all possible haste. On December 18, 1841, water was let into the machine-shop canal. Up to this time $15,000 had been spent on the shop and another $4,000 on the foundry. The buildings and fixtures had been insured for $30,000. Total expenditures for the year exceeded $40,000, and Baldwin had forwarded over $30,000 throughout the year to Nichols to finance construction. This money came from assessments on Water Power Company stock and was in the form of drafts on the Manufacturers Bank in Saco. Baldwin also paid many company bills from his Boston office. No machinery had as yet been produced, but Nichols reported an income of about $5,000 for the year from the rental of local properties.[23] A committee of directors audited the books and summarized the company's business from the beginning through November, 1841, as follows:

Treasurer's Account		
Collected from assessments on stock............		$242,500.00
Paid Out by Treasurer		
To York Mfg. Co. for real estate............	$200,000.00	
To Amos Chase for real estate...............	900.00	
For incidental expenses.....................	1,971.94	
For interest................................	598.35	
To the Superintendent.......................	24,233.97	
On Hand—Treasurer's Account		
U. S. Stock.................................	10,004.50	
Balance in Shoe & Leather Dealers Bank.....	4,791.24	$242,500.00

Superintendent's Account

Received by Superintendent from Treasurer	$ 24,233.97	
Income from rents	9,865.22	
Interest income	15.18	
Income from machinery sales	771.73	
Draft on Treasurer not recorded	2,075.00	$ 36,961.10
Cash Paid by Superintendent		
Wharf	$ 3,170.53	
Purchase of Bog Mill	850.00	
Machine tools and manufacturing	7,036.35	
Canals	2,372.70	
Streets	103.50	
Repairs & improvements—real estate	6,840.83	
Materials for building	10,676.89	
General expenses	2,092.11	
On hand—Superintendent's Account	3,818.19	$ 36,961.10

In January, 1842, the directors instructed Nichols not to expend any more money than was absolutely necessary and to confine himself exclusively to the York order. In April the machine shop was completed, and Nichols moved his men and machines into the new brick building—a solid structure 145 feet long, 46 feet wide, and five stories high, the same size as the Locks and Canals machine shop—equipped with the latest type of oil lamps and the supreme luxury of a steam-heating plant.

As early as May it was obvious to Nichols that he would not be able to finish the York contract on schedule. A request was made for a six months' extension of time. This request was granted by York without invoking the penalty clause in the contract, but there was little optimism in either Biddeford or Boston. For a time in 1842 it had appeared that the long depression was about to end. In June Nichols was authorized by the directors to finish two streets on Corporation land which had been started earlier and abandoned, to put in guard gates and river walls for the lower canal, and to build a counting room and storehouse. In January of 1843, however, the necessity was being urged upon Nichols for "curtailing the expenses of the company in every possible manner." Few men had the courage to believe once more that this was to be the last in the series of business crises. There was much gloom in manufacturing circles, and there were no prospects for machinery orders. In March, 1843, at about the same time that the directors of the Locks and Canals Company were considering the sale of their machine shop at Lowell, Rufus Nichols reported to Baldwin that the York order would soon be completed and that he was ready to close the doors of the Water Power Company shop. Nichols must have looked long and unhappily at his splendid new plant as he regretfully admitted that such a course was necessary in order to conform with the times.

Administrative Checks and Balances

Methods of business administration in this period of initial operations were relatively simple, but in more than one respect those methods were not completely effective. The basic system of checks and balances is set forth in the bylaws of the company. These bylaws conform closely to those of the York Company and the Lowell corporations.

The bylaws provided for nine directors, a president, treasurer, superintendent, and clerk. As was customary at the time, the position of president carried few responsibilities. His only formal duties were to preside over meetings of the stockholders and directors and to affix his signature to stock certificates and other official company papers. Joseph Balch, the president, however, was active in the affairs of the company by virtue of his position as a director.

Control of company affairs was vested in the board of directors, whose administrative powers were broadly defined in the bylaws. In actual practice the board of directors could assume great responsibilities or could relegate itself to a minor administrative rôle as it wished. That the Water Power Company directors followed the former course is indicated by the fact that directors' meetings were held monthly or oftener and that committees of directors were appointed to look into every major course of company action. These men were most capable in the field of finance, but at all times the Water Power Company appears to have had at least one technical man (like Samuel Batchelder) on the directorate. Often the non-technical men, such as importer Tasker H. Swett and banker Joseph Balch, developed a grasp of the operating details of the business which was as useful as it was surprising.

The treasurer occupied a key position in the company. His duties nominally consisted of managing the financial and legal affairs of the company.[24] These consisted of collecting stock assessments, settling bills, discounting notes received in settlements, keeping and managing company funds, reviewing the detailed operating figures furnished by the superintendent, and furnishing the directors with summary figures and operating information. The treasurer stood in an intermediate position between the policy-making board of directors and the superintendent at the Biddeford shop. Initially, the treasurer received a very small salary ($300 per year in 1839; raised to $500 in 1840), and this fact suggests that he devoted only a part of his time to company affairs. Once operations became full-scale, however, both his salary and his attention to the management of the Water Power Company were increased. It became his function to exercise general direction over the company's day-to-day activities, and this involved far more than financial responsibilities.

The traditional location of the treasurer's office in Boston arose from the necessity, in this era of slow communications, for close physical proximity to the financial district. This location was also dictated by the fact that most of the stockholders and all the directors were Boston men. There was an additional advantage in having the central offices located closer than Biddeford to the sources of material supply, and in the field of procurement the treasurer assumed important responsibilities. The records of the company indicate that all purchases, except of lumber and some small supplies, were made by his office, upon the request of the superintendent in Biddeford.

The superintendent was a paid employee of the company, working under a relatively long-term contract. He did not attend directors' meetings, but he usually owned a small block of stock in the company. It was his function to carry out the policies of the board of directors and the instructions of the treasurer. His primary qualification for the position was technical skill. If he was a good administrator as well, so much the better, but his knowledge of men was conceived to be of far less importance than his knowledge of machines. This criterion often, though not inevitably, gave rise to local irritations.

In the Locks and Canals Company at Lowell the separation of machine shop and company office appeared to have caused little administrative difficulty, principally because of the extraordinary ability and exertions of Patrick Tracy Jackson and Kirk Boott. In the affairs of the Saco Water Power Company, however, the separation was a constant source of minor troubles. Instructions from the directors and the treasurer frequently were slow in arriving at Biddeford and often were ambiguous or inadequate to meet local conditions. In such cases delays occurred. On the other hand, the treasurer complained on at least one occasion that the superintendent's accounts had not been received in Boston in time for the directors' meeting. Frequently materials ordered through the treasurer's office were not satisfactory to the superintendent, and exchanges and returns consumed time. Altogether, there is considerable evidence in the correspondence of this period of a lack of close coördination between activities in Boston and Biddeford. Nichols continually urged the treasurer and directors to come to Maine and view the various problems at first hand. This the Boston gentlemen were understandably loath to do, particularly in mid-winter when the coal grates and fireplaces on Beacon Street were particularly enticing. Two days at least were ordinarily required to take a stage both ways and allow a few hours for business in Biddeford. Early in 1843, however, a railroad connection was established with Boston. This was a fact of great significance not only because of better freighting but from an administrative point of view. Nichols triumphantly wrote to Baldwin, "I suppose you have learnt that you can start from Boston and make us a visit and return the same day and be with us five hours in the best part of the day."

The railroad brought Biddeford and Boston closer together, but there remained a psychological cleavage between the two places. The same situation prevailed at Lowell, and in both places improved transportation facilities never fully succeeded in producing the feeling of complete identity of interest between treasurer's office and shop or mill. Nichols' letters to the treasurer are obviously addressed to a man of higher social position. Often these letters criticize and chide the "Boston folks," but always they are couched in a highly respectful tone. Distance tended to lend awe, if not enchantment, to the Boston office and the well-groomed men associated with it. On visits to Biddeford the treasurer and the directors were treated with supreme deference, and there are many evidences of the feeling that these men were of another world. This feeling did more for the ego of the directors than it did for the wise administration of the company's business. A common thought was that the Boston capitalists were concerned only with their dividends and that the Biddeford management could see no further than technical problems and steady employment. It was to be many, many years before the two attitudes were reconciled to any extent. In the early years of operations both at Biddeford and at Lowell any new policy decided upon by the directors was likely to be viewed at the shop or mill as a manifestation of greed or, at best, as evidence of technical ignorance. By the same token, recommendations of resident agents and superintendents were frequently thought by the directors in Boston to involve unwarranted extravagance with the stockholders' money. Since both attitudes occasionally were justified by facts, the mutual suspicion though usually well concealed became deep-rooted.

Business records necessarily were divided between the machine shop at Biddeford and the treasurer's office in Boston. At the former place the superintendent kept day books, journals, and ledgers recording daily receipts and expenditures. Once the business was established, Nichols was far too busy to engage in bookkeeping. In March, 1841, Thomas Quimby was hired to serve as company surveyor, engineer, and bookkeeper. This rather startling fact is less a tribute to Quimby's diversified talents than it is a commentary on the relatively simple requirements of the business at this time.

At the Boston office were kept the stock-transfer records, the minutes of directors' and stockholders' meetings, and a Treasurer's Balance which recorded summary receipts and disbursements. Nichols furnished the treasurer with monthly receipts and expenditure accounts — these, he confided, were a nuisance and should only be required quarterly. Every six months the books at Biddeford were balanced and a trial balance forwarded to the treasurer, who incorporated the summary into a semiannual Treasurer's Balance which was presented, together with the superintendent's trial balance, for examination and approval by the directors. Quarterly the treasurer furnished the superintendent with a statement of bills paid and drafts honored. This was reconciled with the superintendent's records of the same transactions.

The accounting system of the company grew out of contemporary small-business practice and was formalized in a set of detailed instructions drawn up by a committee of two directors in November, 1841. Both these men were bankers, and this fact may account for the relatively unspecialized nature of the accounts. Records of the company are not complete, but the fragments indicate a lack of detailed costing procedures, which contrasts strongly with the accounting methods employed by the Boston Manufacturing Company twenty years before.[25] Direct and overhead costs were allocated to the various types of machines and to the various activities of the company, but not, as at Waltham, to the component parts and processes. This came later, and may not have been considered necessary when only one contract was on the books and activities were on a limited scale.

The stockholders' and directors' only check upon the honesty of the treasurer and the superintendent was in the form of a semiannual audit of the accounts by a committee of directors. These audits were necessarily of a perfunctory nature and were ineffective as a method of control. One of the first reports of the Saco Water Power Company auditing committee reads as follows:

> Boston, February 22, 1841. The subscribers a Committee of the Directors of the Saco Water Power Compy. to whom was referred the examination of the Treasurers a/cs. beg leave to report that they have performed that duty as far as they had the means by access to a few statements & find them correctly stated — with a balance due to the York Manfg. Co of Ten or twelve thousand Dollars which they recommend to be paid forthwith.
>
> Jos. Hall Jr.
> T. H. Swett

The next report, dated November, 1841, voices the fundamental weakness of this audit system and suggests the remedy which eventually was adopted voluntarily and then made compulsory by law:

The undersigned, having been appointed a Committee to Examine the accounts of the Saco Water Power Company and to arrange a System or plan for keeping the accounts of said Company Report
That they have Examined the accounts of the Treasurer and the accounts and Vouchers of the Superintendent in part - so far as they could attend to the same - and so far as they did Examine the accounts appeared to be Correct and Satisfactory - they are of opinion however that some alterations may be made hereafter in the arrangement of them, when the Buildings and Works now in progress shall have been completed and Suggest the following for consideration - as regards the accounts kept at Saco

First. That all sums laid out and Expended on Buildings and Estates belonging to the Corporation for repairs of ordinary use and Natural decay be charged to an account to be denominated Repairs on Real Estate, and that the Entries in the journal be so made as to designate the Building or Estate to which the Expenditure was applied - and to describe the nature and object of the repair or Expenditure.

Second. That all sums laid out and Expended for purchase of Land and Buildings - for Erection of new Buildings and for additions and improvements to Buildings already Existing of a permanent character - partaking of the nature of New investments be charged to an account to be denominated Real Estate with like Specifications in the Entry in the Journal.

Third - That all sums Expended for the construction of Canals, Bridges Wharves, Streets and Highways be charged to accounts to be kept with Each respectively

Fourth - That all sums Expended for Fixtures Machinery Utensils Tools and Furniture designed for use in the New Machine Shop or appurtenant to that Establishment be charged to an account to be denominated Machine Shop

Fifth - That all sums Expended for Fixtures Machinery Utensils Tools and Furniture designed for use in the Blacksmiths Shop or appurtenant thereto to be charged to an account to be so denominated.

Sixth - That all sums Expended for Fixtures, Machinery Utensils Tools and Furniture for the Grist Mill and appertaining thereto be charged to that Establishment - and in like manner for every other separate concern -

~~Seventh~~ Eighth. That all Expenditures of a general character or not applicable specifically to any one of the separate Interests into which the Concern may have been divided be charged to an account to be denominated Expense account

~~Eighth~~ Ninth - That all sums paid or received for use of funds or Credit be carried to Interest Account and all sums received for Rents be carried to an Account to be denominated Rent account -

~~Ninth~~ Tenth - That there be a Profit & Loss account to which all losses and gains are to be Carried once in Six months when the accounts are balanced say in January & July - all Entries being previously made.

~~Tenth~~ Eleventh - That all Entries in the Journal contain such specifications and references as may be necessary for the purpose of Enabling a Committee Examining the accounts to ascertain therefrom the cost of Each Building or Separate Establishment, and the cost of the Contents of Each Building - and of every Bridge Canal Road or other object of Expenditure.

Directors' Committee Report on Accounting Procedures, Saco Water Power Company, November, 1841

To have gone into a full and thorough examination of the Vouchers for all the expenditures in detail would have required more time than your committee could bestow on the subject, they however did examine the vouchers for many of the accounts and finding them correct they feel great confidence that the others are so, and they think the general aspect of the accounts & the methodical manner in which they are arranged is such as to confirm their opinion & is very satisfactory. Should it be thought proper, however, as it may be, to have a more thorough examination they recommend that some competent accountant be employed for this service. . . .

There were, of course, no legal requirements to be observed at this time in respect to record-keeping or reporting, except the laws which required publication of notices of corporate meetings and a law passed in Maine in 1837 requiring every corporation to report annually to the assessor in every Maine community in which company stockholders lived the number of shares owned by such stockholders and the amount of capital paid in per share. A yearly report of this nature was also required to be filed with the Secretary of State.

A conservative appraisal of these various administrative checks and balances employed by the Water Power Company leads to the conclusion that the company had much to learn from contemporaries about the effective control of operations. Many of the weaknesses actually were remedied, as the trial-and-error period of management yielded to experience and seasoning. Others, such as the difficulty of coördinating activities in Boston and Biddeford, persisted for generations, and not in this company alone. In general the techniques of management were adequate to meet the requirements of a relatively simple and leisurely business situation. The real test of management was to lie in its ability to adjust to increased size and a rising tempo of activity which came about after 1843.

4. Emergency Plans and the Laconia Contract, 1843–1847

In May, 1843, the directors voted two measures designed to produce additional revenue and to utilize the now idle machine shop. On May 23 the directors instructed Nichols to build a new dam and to build and furnish a gristmill to be located on the Saco side of the Falls. This was a counsel of desperation. On May 30 the directors voted unanimously "that the Superintendent be instructed to proceed forthwith to make about five thousand spindles with the Machinery for Carding & preparation in proportion, with a view to filling the two upper stories of the Company's Machine Shop with Machinery for the Manufacture of Yarn or Twist. . . ."

Conversion to cotton manufacture was the traditional remedy for an idle machine shop, often proposed but never executed at Lowell. At Biddeford, however, there was every indication that the partial conversion voted in May would be made. Nichols drew up specifications, and in July a committee of directors returned an appraisal of the financial position of the company and of the capital requirements of the new plan.

Perhaps the most striking fact revealed by the correspondence between the superintendent and treasurer was the rapidity with which managerial attitudes toward business prospects fluctuated in the 1839–43 period. In this respect the Water Power Company management reflected the general feeling of insecurity — the rapidly alternating hopes and despair — which pervaded American business. At Saco and Biddeford pessimism invariably persisted as new policies were initiated. Then optimism revived as those polices became translated into solid brick and stone, or tidy new machines. The consummation of policies and contracts usually brought deepest pessimism. These fluctuations in attitude and the condition of the company itself closely conformed to the cyclical pattern of general business in this period.

Events in the summer of 1843 indicated that in Biddeford and in Boston optimism had supplanted the despair of early spring. The financial report presented to the directors undoubtedly had much to do with the reversal of attitudes. This report revealed that for the $275 paid in on each share of stock the stockholders had an equity in tangible assets to the amount of $301.47 per share.[26] The report went on to point out that on the basis of prevailing rent incomes and the sale of a nominal amount of machinery ($10,000 per year) the stock should return 5 per cent to its holders. Moreover, the committee reported, "it is to be borne in mind that a large portion of the value included in the first purchase is unproductive property — from which no immediate income was expected . . . and much of the subsequent expenditures partake of the same character, being made with a reference to future operations, rather than to those already existing — such as the expense of canals — dams — streets &c made for the use of Mills and other buildings contemplated to be built at some future time."

At this time a conflict over future policy came to a head. The original plan to convert the upper floors of the machine shop to a spinning mill had been endorsed by only 474 out of the 1,000 votes of the stockholders.[27] In the July 20 report of the financial committee a significant qualification was appended that 6,000 spindles would be placed in the machine shop *unless* "a purchaser should appear who is willing to pay a satisfactory price for it." By August 2 the transition to a new scheme was completed when the directors voted to "proceed forthwith to the extension of the Canal & the laying of a foundation for a Factory. . . ." This plan to build a new factory rather than to set up spinning machinery in the existing shop was the logical outgrowth of reviving optimism, but it precipitated a further conflict in the ranks of directors and stockholders.

The question at once arose as to whether the new factory should be owned and operated by the Water Power Company or by a separate company. Both sides of the dispute had strong arguments. On the one hand, the Lowell precedent of separation of functions could be pointed to. On the other hand, there was the overwhelming temptation to secure profits from the manufacture of both machines and cloth. Samuel Batchelder appears to have been the leader of the separate-ownership group, and Baldwin may have been the leader of the opposition. Batchelder and Nichols, acting in their own names but at the instigation of the Water Power Company, had secured a charter in 1841 from the State of Maine for a new company to be known as the Laconia Company. Possibly a long-standing desire to activate this company lay behind the opposition to Water Power Company ownership of the proposed factory. Whatever the motives involved, the Batchelder group succeeded in forcing the adoption of their plan.

On November 15, 1843, the directors voted to approve the plans and estimates prepared by Batchelder and Nichols and signified their willingness to sell the water power and land necessary to effect the contemplated arrangement with the new Laconia Company. Baldwin was not present at this meeting; although he resigned two weeks later for stated reasons of ill health, he retained his place on the board of directors. The office of treasurer was filled by Jonathan Chapman, active in Boston banking and one who had proven his financial abilities during a term as mayor of Boston. On December 29, 1843, the directors voted to get up a new company under the Laconia charter, "the stock therein to be first offered to the Stockholders of the Water Power Company. . . ."

An alluring picture was painted for the Water Power Company stockholders in a circular dated January 1, 1844, and signed by Chapman, the new treasurer of the Water Power Company:

The Stockholders have authorized the Directors to call in the remainder of the Capital Stock, viz: $200,000,—which they have determined to do, and proceed forthwith to build a Cotton Mill, to be carried on by the Water Power Company, unless a new Company, exclusively for manufacturing purposes, should take up a portion of the power, and employ the Water Power Company to erect its buildings and machinery.

This latter course is far the most desirable, as keeping the appropriate business of the Water Power Company distinct from manufacturing. To this end, the Directors have secured a valuable Charter, granted by the Legislature of Maine, incorporating the *"Laconia Company,"* for the purpose of carrying on manufacturing at Biddeford (directly opposite Saco). The position of this place, *upon navigable waters and accessible also by Railroad from Boston,*—its abundant and never failing water power,—and its excellent mill sites,—render it one of the most desirable locations; and it is confidently believed that a cheaper and more profitable manufacturing establishment can be erected there, than now exists. And in this new Manufacturing Company, will not only secure its advantages, but reap also the collateral benefits accruing to their present Water Power property, and be relieved from further assessments thereon.

The circular went on to silence possible objections from stockholders who might not wish to subscribe their share in the proposed $200,000 Laconia stock issue. If the new issue was not subscribed, Chapman stated, the authorized $200,000 assessment on Water Power Company stock would be levied at once. There was little choice. Neither was there any longer the powerful obstacle of general hard times, for business had visibly improved in New England. In two weeks the Laconia stock subscription was completed. Chapman was elected treasurer of the newly organized company, retaining at the same time his position as treasurer of the Water Power Company.

The initial agreement with Laconia signed in January, 1844, called for the immediate sale of sufficient land for a cotton mill, together with the right to five mill powers for the first mill and an option on locations and power for subsequent mills which might be built. The contract for the first Laconia mill specified machinery for a 10,176-spindle mill.[28] Like the contracts of the Locks and Canals Company at Lowell, and unlike the York contract of 1841, this agreement with Laconia called not only for machinery but for the erection of the mill building, a counting house, a picker house, a cotton house, a packing house, and three blocks of tenements. The Water Power Company agreed to construct machinery and buildings at the lowest possible cost, taking a 5 per cent profit on the machinery only, and promising that the machinery should be built "at as low prices as can be done elsewhere." The whole was estimated to cost the Laconia Company $200,000.[29] A similar agreement concluded a month later for Laconia's second mill specified a 5 per cent commission on both machinery and buildings. These contracts, with a far lower profit margin than was customarily taken in Lowell, were exceptionally advantageous to the Laconia Company — a fact undoubtedly explained by the close relationship between the two companies.[30] The significance of the Laconia contracts lay in their size, for only a machine shop of a size comparable to the one at Lowell could fulfill the terms involved. The decision of the Water Power Company to remain a machine shop and to incorporate separate companies to utilize the power privileges of the area for cotton manufacturing closely followed the example of the Locks and Canals Company. The results of these contracts were to be five years of activity and profit for the machine shop at Biddeford.

5. The Pepperell Affair

By the end of 1845 the first Laconia mill was in operation and early in 1846 the second mill was completed. In the fall of 1846 the Laconia Company contracted for a third mill, which was in operation a year later. From 1844 to 1847 these Laconia contracts, together with certain civic improvements which will be detailed later, occupied the entire attention of the Water Power Company. Once again the star of the business man was in the ascendancy. Not only were times good, but enthusiasm for textile-mill promotion was so great as to once again be labeled "mill fever." In western and southern Massachusetts — on the Merrimack below Lowell — in Maine — in New Hampshire — great new developments or enlargements of existing manufacturing facilities were being executed. Locally the York Company was distributing magnificent dividends, and Laconia, though scarcely come of age, had already declared a dividend. The Water Power Company itself was more prosperous than it had ever been before — its stockholders had money and an apparent desire to employ it to create greater wealth. Conditions were propitious for a new venture.

At the annual meeting of Water Power Company stockholders, held July 15, 1847, the treasurer of the company clearly defined the course which was to be followed after completion of the Laconia contract. The leading interest of the company, he stated, was "to extend the use of its water power by procuring, in some way, the erection of more mills." The Saco Water Power Company, then, was considered primarily as a developmental company, whose machine-building activities were subsidiary to the main task of creating, enlarging, and profiting from real-estate and water-power values. This philosophy of management, which if followed through to its natural consummation could only mean the abandonment of large-scale machine-building, had been discarded at Lowell in 1845 and perhaps much earlier. Either conditions at Biddeford were different or the Saco Falls development was still at an immature stage.[31]

Much of the company's real estate, the treasurer went on to report, was still unutilized. With space for 100,000 spindles, only 12,000 were actually in operation. Faith alone would not build up the local population — business establishments must come first. The mills already in existence and employing local people had not attracted new residents. Even the railroad, concluded the treasurer, "which looks so sharp after every source of business, has hitherto passed us by as not worth stopping even to look at." The course

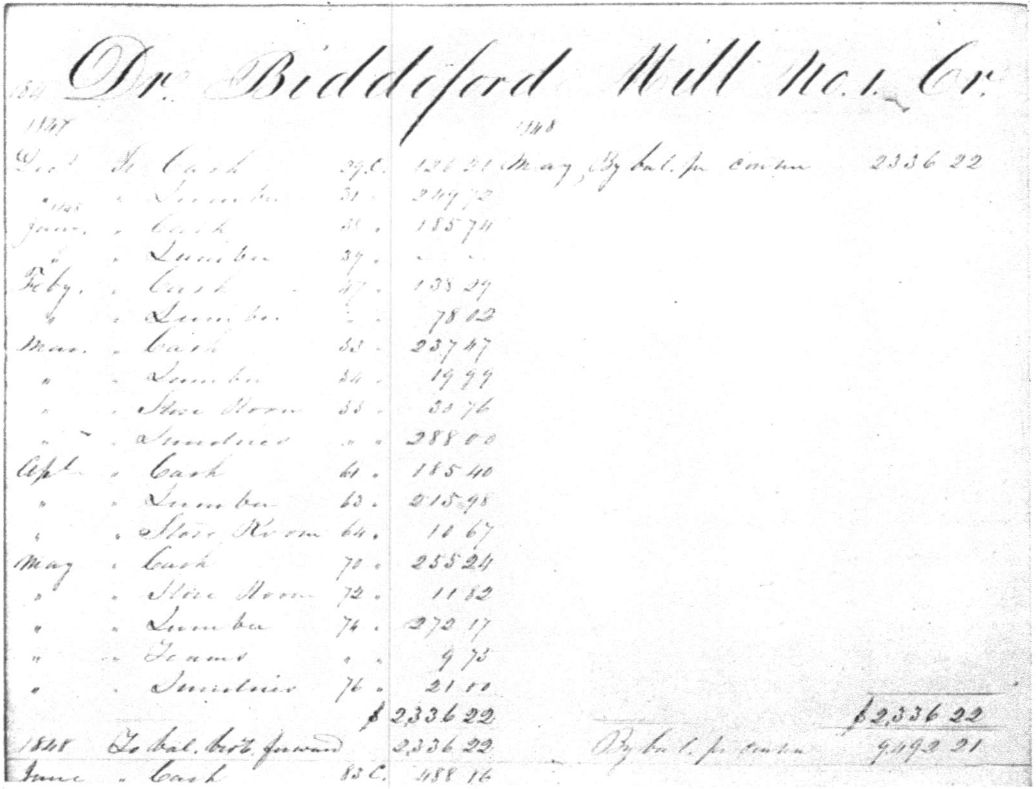

Dr. Biddeford Mill No. 1. Cr.

1847				1848		
Dec.	To Cash	27C.	1262 21	May,	By bal. per contra	2336 22
"	" Lumber	31 .	249 72			
Jan.	" Cash	31 .	185 74			
"	" Lumber	37 .	[illegible]			
Feby.	" Cash	37 .	138 29			
"	" Lumber	.	78 02			
Mar.	" Cash	53 .	237 47			
"	" Lumber	54 .	19 99			
"	" Store Room	55 .	30 76			
"	" Sundries	" .	288 00			
Apl.	" Cash	61 .	185 40			
"	" Lumber	63 .	215 98			
"	" Store Room	64 .	11 67			
May	" Cash	70 .	255 24			
"	" Store Room	72 .	11 82			
"	" Lumber	74 .	272 17			
"	" Teams	" .	9 75			
"	" Sundries	76 .	21 00			
			$2,336 22			$2,336 22
1848	To bal. brot. forward		2,336 22		By bal. per contra	9492 21
June	" Cash	83C.	488 76			

Entries on Saco Water Power Company Ledger Recording Commencement of Pepperell Mill Number One, December, 1847

was clear: the Water Power Company must build more mills, thereby enhancing the prosperity of the community and the value of existing company property and making subsequent disposals of that property easier and more profitable. The company itself could operate the mills, or dispose of them should a purchaser be found.

The specific plans advanced in the summer of 1847 called for two mills to be constructed simultaneously on company property. Capital to commence this ambitious undertaking was secured in part from the Water Power Company stockholders and in part from new investors. The remainder of the existing capital stock in the amount of $100,000 was now assessed. At the same time, the legislature of the State of Maine was petitioned for an increase in the authorized capitalization of the company from $500,000 to $2,000,000. When this petition was granted, 1,000 new shares of stock with a par value of $500,000 were issued.

At this point serious dissension appeared in the company. The main issue appeared to be the wisdom of an expansionist policy. A hint of lack of unanimous support for the proposed plan is contained in the fact that existing stockholders took only 28 per cent of the new stock issue. The remainder was subscribed by a large number of Boston merchants, bankers, and manufacturers and a few local men. Treasurer Jonathan Chapman was a strong proponent of expansion. An angry committee of minority stockholders was later to comment on the fact that at the 1847 annual meeting at which the enlargement of capital stock was approved, Chapman, owning but five shares of company stock, cast 238 votes. In September of 1847 four of the nine directors resigned, including the staid and conservative Bostonian Henry Lee and Enoch Baldwin. These resignations were not exclusively a protest against expansion. Baldwin, in fact, was a member of the directors' committee which originally had recommended the plan. The old controversy of company ownership versus sale to a new company, however, had already commenced to split the directorate. Baldwin, in 1847 as in 1843, wished to retain and operate the mills to be built.

In addition to these disputes it appeared that affairs were not going smoothly in Biddeford. In the fall of 1847 Superintendent Rufus Nichols exchanged places with Otis Holmes, the agent of the

Laconia Company. Whether this change resulted from opposition on Nichols' part to the new plan in whole or in part is not clear, but the timing of this unusual shifting of key men is, if not significant, at least highly coincidental. Holmes, who had come to Laconia from the Springfield Arsenal in 1844, appeared to be a capable machinist fully able to fill the important position.

On September 25, 1847, the board of directors voted "That the Superintendent be instructed to proceed at once to lay out the whole proposed Mill site in reference to the four Mills that can be placed upon it, and to cause the Canal raceway, and all the underground work to be made in reference to the whole number of Mills, and to cause two of the Mills and other necessary buildings to be erected, as soon as the same can be done." Thus was determined the site of what was to become the Pepperell Manufacturing Company.

By November of 1847 the excavation for foundations had commenced. Plans called for the erection of two mills of 15,000 spindles each, a picker house, a countinghouse, a cotton house, and a tenement block 400 feet long and 2 stories high.[32] By the end of 1848 most of this work had been commenced, and Mill Number One, together with attendant millwork, was well on its way to completion. Construction work on Mill Number Two had been started in November, 1848. Two months earlier a contract had been made with the Lowell Machine Shop, successor to the machine shop of the old Locks and Canals Company, for all the machinery for Mill Number One. This contract undoubtedly was inspired by the inability of the Water Power Company, even with expanded facilities, to perform unassisted all the work for both mills.[33] Machinery for Mill Number Two, however, was built by the Water Power Company itself, commencing in April, 1849.

The year 1848 was one of peak activity, with all facilities of the machine shop employed to their utmost capacity. The year also produced an important change in the office of company treasurer. In May Jonathan Chapman died. Samuel Batchelder was elected treasurer pro tempore of the Water Power Company and Laconia. In July William Dwight was elected treasurer of the two companies. Dwight's background and experience were promising. The son of an influential family in Springfield, Massachusetts, Dwight had been graduated from Harvard in 1825 and then had studied law. He entered the family mercantile business in the Connecticut valley and had served as a representative in the State legislature.[34] It is not clear how Dwight came to be selected, but once he was installed as treasurer he appears to have devoted great energy to completing the projects undertaken by his predecessor.

By May, 1849, almost $400,000 had been expended on the new mills, and over $500,000 more was required to complete them. The existing financial resources of the Water Power Company were strained. From its expenditures on the mills the company could expect no return for many months. Construction of both mills and machinery had fallen behind schedule. Liquid assets were insignificant in amount, and the possibility of bank loans to continue construction was probably limited by the existing indebtedness of the company, which amounted to more than a quarter of a million dollars. This indebtedness had gradually been built up over the past two years by heavy drafts on the Biddeford Bank, on the Massachusetts Bank, the New England Bank, the Shoe & Leather Dealers Bank, and the Globe Bank in Boston. All drafts on these banks had been paid as they fell due, but the steadily mounting volume of outstanding paper indicated that new capital must be subscribed.

At the annual stockholders' meeting in July, 1849, far-reaching measures were adopted, and thereafter events moved swiftly to a climax which was to split the company asunder. The stockholders voted to increase the capital stock of the Water Power Company $500,000 by creating 1,000 new shares. This step had been foreseen two years before when an amendment of the company charter had raised the authorized capital to $2,000,000. The new capital provided would enable the mills to be completed. Also in conformance with the original plans the stockholders voted that, should the old shareholders fail to subscribe the new issue and provide the needed funds, the mills would be sold at such price and on such terms as the directors should determine. In the event that this latter course became necessary it was agreed that a separate company, the Pepperell Manufacturing Company, would be activated to take over the new mills.[35]

Subscriptions were opened for the 1,000 shares of new Water

Power Company stock, and September 15, 1849, was set as the final date for subscribing. This issue met with a far different reception from that of the 1847 issue, however: by September 15 only 229 shares had been signed for. Lack of confidence in the company may have been a factor in the failure of this subscription, but a more plausible explanation is that a severe monetary reaction to the boom of the preceding three years was militating against the disposal of securities. The directors decided to extend the time of the subscription.

On December 31, 1849, William Dwight reported that debts now totaled $350,000 and that they would be over $500,000 before the mills were completed. Legislative action was successfully invoked to enable the company to expand its working-capital loans. By the terms of an act passed by the Maine legislature in 1844, stockholders of corporations incurring debts exceeding one-half the amount of their paid-in capital became individually liable for the excess debts. William P. Haines, the company's lawyer (who had great influence in the legislature because of a law partnership with the governor) lobbied for a liberalization of this restriction and succeeded in having the act amended to allow debts equal to one-half the paid-in capital plus "their other property and assets." Dwight, however, expressed doubts that the new mills could be operated by the Water Power Company while under such a burden of debt, unless the money market improved sufficiently to permit a long-term loan to be negotiated; he asked the directors to decide whether this was not the time to sell the properties — even if it was necessary to sell them for less than cost. The directors, however, hoped that in the spring the Water Power Company's new stock issue could be floated. By March it had become evident to all that there was little hope. In April the directors, having referred the matter to the stockholders at a special meeting, offered the mills to the Pepperell Company for $600,000 — property which the directors stated had and would cost $790,000. Having failed to raise money to operate the mills, the Water Power Company was now forced to offer them for sale at a discount sufficiently large to attract capital to the Pepperell Company.

The Pepperell Manufacturing Company was duly organized in

April, 1850, and William Dwight was elected treasurer. Samuel Batchelder, who had been elected president of the Water Power Company in 1849, was elected a director of Pepperell. The other Pepperell directors were either past or present Water Power Company directors or stockholders. A stock issue of 2,000 shares was authorized and a subscription paper opened. According to agreement this stock was offered first to Water Power Company shareholders on a share-for-share basis. It is not surprising that the Water Power Company stockholders, having refused to put more money into their own company likewise refused to put money into another company formed for an identical purpose. By June 15, 1850, Dwight had obtained subscriptions for only 427 shares of Pepperell stock. The directors of the Water Power Company, acting under their general powers but not under specific instructions from the stockholders, then lowered the terms of sale to $500,000 in order to increase the attractiveness of the Pepperell Company to reluctant venture capital. A new subscription paper was opened. On July 10, 1850, the last day of the subscription period, only 1,236 shares had been taken. Dwight, apparently acting in desperation, personally signed for the remaining 764 shares and the formation of the Pepperell Manufacturing Company was accomplished.[36]

For William Dwight, personally liable for assessments on a third of the entire capital stock of Pepperell, this was a period of "extreme anxiety." Dwight and the Water Power Company directors, moreover, were vulnerable to serious charges. Those Water Power Company stockholders who had not purchased Pepperell stock would suffer the loss accruing to the Water Power Company from the transaction without reaping the compensating advantage which they would have enjoyed had they purchased Pepperell stock. The final cost of the property conveyed to Pepperell for $500,000 was $826,004. But this, stated a committee of stockholders at a later date, was only the cash value put into the construction of the properties and included nothing for the real estate conveyed, nothing for depreciation on Water Power Company tools and machinery, and nothing for rent of the property. The committee claimed that, figuring these in at a conservative rate, the value of the property conveyed actually was $1,104,254.[37]

Unfortunately these charges are difficult to confirm or deny, and the entire controversy is befogged by the inter-relationship of the two companies. Substantially more than half the Water Power Company stockholders had been unable or unwilling to subscribe to Pepperell stock. Had Dwight and the directors betrayed their fiduciary position by negotiating a sale which sacrificed the interests of a majority of stockholders in favor of benefits for the minority? Or had the repeated refusal or inability of the stockholders to subscribe to either Water Power or Pepperell stock and their approval of the sale to Pepperell relieved those officers of further responsibilities? One fact is clear: in pleading with his stockholders on occasion after occasion to support their company William Dwight presents ample evidence of honest intent. His was the unfortunate and not unfamiliar situation which could so easily arise from being the responsible official in two companies whose interests suddenly clashed. In 1850 he was in the embarrassing predicament of owning a large block of shares in a company which by his own action had received a handsome endowment, at the expense of a company in which he held very few shares. Dwight subsequently made desperate efforts to persuade others to purchase his Pepperell stock, and this effort constitutes a further denial of selfish interest. At no time in this trying period following the property sale was Pepperell stock inaccessible to any of the Water Power Company stockholders. It was not until some five years later, in fact, that an organized protest against the transaction was made. This protest might be classed with that made two decades earlier by landowners at Chelmsford when the farms which they had sold to the Merrimack Company increased a hundredfold in value.

The Caesarean operation by which the birth of Pepperell was effected left the mother company in a delicate condition. This condition, however, was quite compatible with the concept which had prevailed to this time, that the primary function of the Water Power Company was the development of the local textile industry. The events of 1850 altered that concept. With its choice mill sites sold or committed, the Water Power Company henceforth was dependent upon machine-building activities to augment its rental income. There were machinery orders yet to be filled in Biddeford, but the

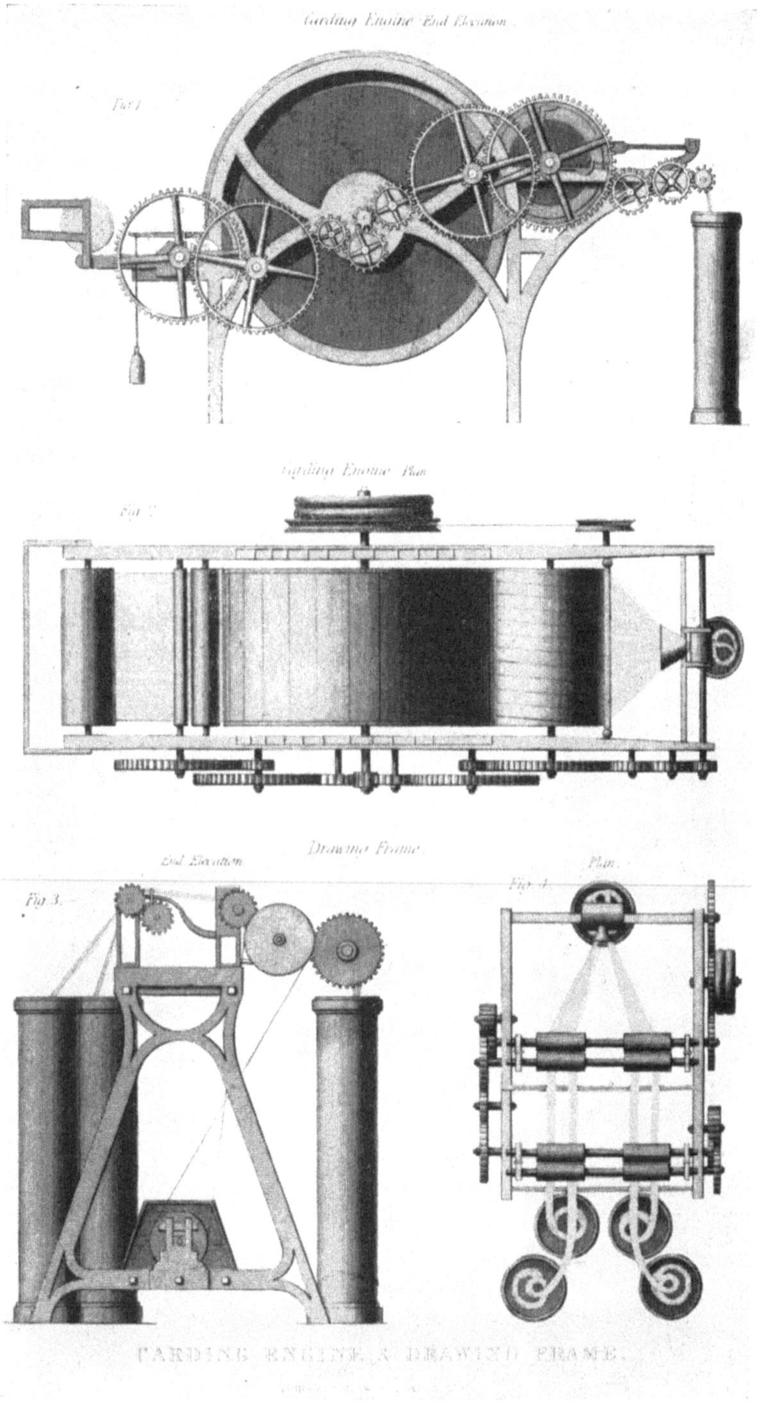

Carding Engine and Drawing Frame
Type built by Saco Water Power Company about 1840

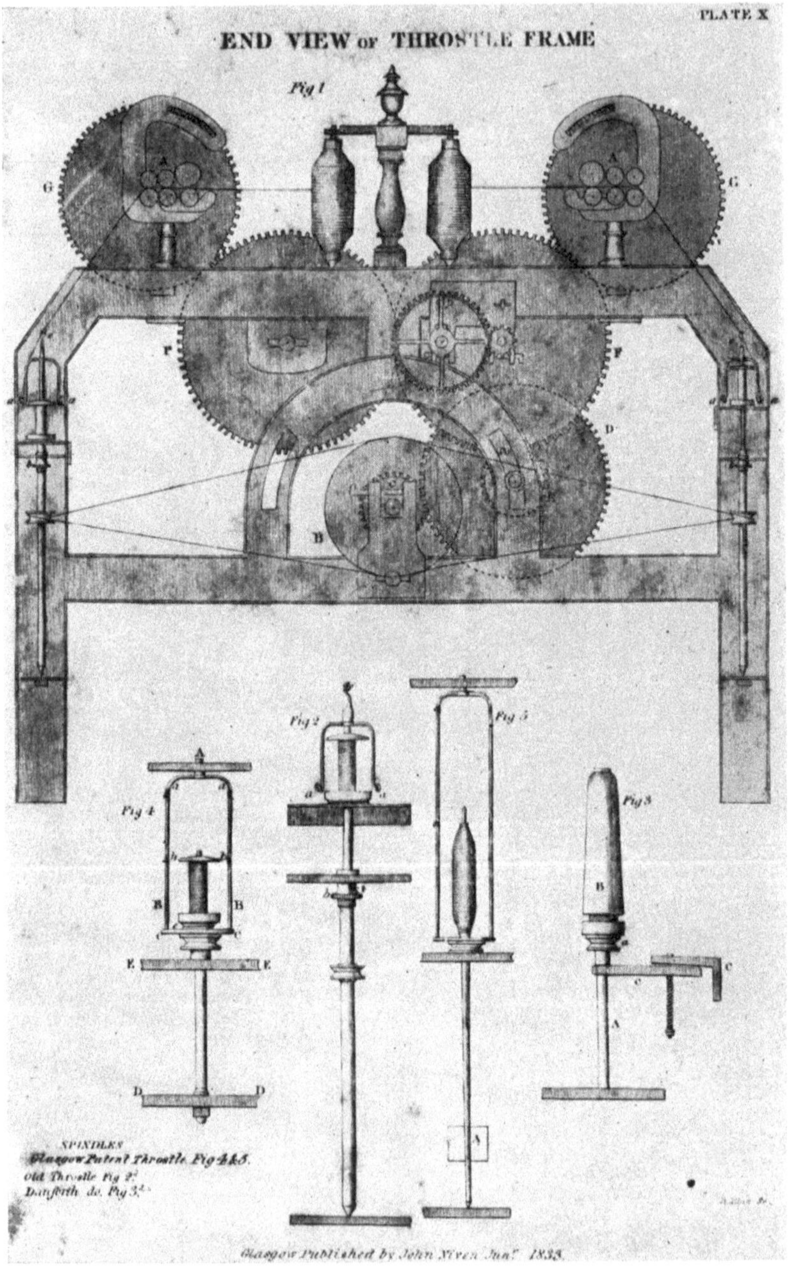

Throstle Spinning Frame and Spindles
Types built by Saco Water Power Company about 1840

fact was clear that future business with Laconia and Pepperell could not support the Water Power Company in the manner to which it had become accustomed. To 1850 not a spindle had been built for mills outside Saco and Biddeford. After this time the Water Power Company turned of necessity to the open market and became an eager and respected competitor for textile-machinery contracts wherever they could be found. The formative years were over. At Biddeford, as at Lowell, the end product of experimental corporate and functional relationships was a company whose primary objective was the manufacture of textile machinery for the American market.

6. PROGRESS OF THE COMPANY, 1844–1850

Growth and Profits

Under the stimulus of the Laconia contracts the Water Power Company steadily increased its machine-shop facilities and real-

TABLE 7

ASSETS OF THE SACO WATER POWER COMPANY, 1840–1850

	Dec. 31, 1840	May 30, 1846	Jan. 1, 1850
Machine shop, building & site[a]....	$	$ 33,738	$ 80,272
Machine tools..................	1,018	21,520	43,151
Carpenter's shop................	......	......	11,503
Blacksmith shop & fixtures........	......	6,177	10,481
Counting & storehouses...........	......	2,888	6,955
Dams, canals, & real estate........	200,000	281,313	521,687
Total assets.....................	224,628[b]	661,395	1,484,422

[a] Machine-shop site, building, feeder, millwork, and fixtures.
[b] Estimated.
Source: Saco Water Power Co. records: Superintendent's ledger balances and treasurer's financial statements.

estate holdings. In 1847 the machine shop was enlarged to almost double its original capacity, and in this same year extensive purchases of land and privileges were made to secure for the company unrestricted use of the power at Saco Falls and flowage and reservoir rights above the Falls. This expansion was financed by stock assessments and payments from the Laconia Company. To administer adequately the increased real-estate holdings a separate land department was organized in the company and placed in charge of William P. Haines. Henceforth the superintendent was responsible only for construction operations and the maintenance of the canals and dams.[38] By 1850 the machine-shop establishment consisted of a building 271 feet long, 46 feet wide, and five stories high; and a blacksmith shop, a carpenter shop, a lumber house, a storehouse, a countinghouse, and a sawmill. Table 7 records the cost valuation of selected company assets in 1840, 1846, and 1850.

Operating statistics for the Water Power Company are available only after 1846. These show the importance of rentals from company property in the period after completion of the Laconia mill contracts. Profits from the land department and from the machine shop from 1848 to 1850 were as follows:[39]

6 Months Ending	Land Department	Machine Shop
Nov. 30, 1848.........	$ 7,689	$16,103
May 31, 1849.........	13,391	15,181
Nov. 30, 1849.........	8,986	2,394
May 31, 1850.........	11,674	523
Nov. 30, 1850.........	12,234	1,282

The first Water Power Company dividend was paid in June of 1844. This dividend was in the amount of 6 per cent of the paid-in capital, and the 6 per cent rate was paid in every year thereafter through 1849. The loss from the Pepperell sale resulted in passing both semiannual dividends in 1850. This dividend record is not impressive in view of the prosperity of the textile industry of the period and in comparison with the record of the Locks and Canals Company in Lowell. The Saco Water Power Company had expanded its shop and holdings to valuations comparable with those of the Locks and Canals Company, despite the fact that mill powers initially available for sale at Saco were less than half as numerous as those at Lowell. The possibilities of multiplying the Biddeford-Saco mill sites were substantially less than at Lowell, and the canal footage actually constructed at Saco Falls was, in fact, very small in comparison with canal construction at Pawtucket Falls. In ten years the Locks and Canals Company had placed 120,000 spindles in operation at Lowell, while over a comparable length of time since its formation the Saco Water Power Company had been able to promote approximately half that number. Although the investment in machine-shop building, tools, and fixtures appears to have been justified by the fact that these assets were fully employed from 1842 to 1850, the heavy investment in real estate (much of it unproductive) would seem to reflect undue optimism on the part of the management as to the immediate returns which could be realized from such property. Moreover, while Kirk Boott had stated that initial land purchases at Lowell had cost about $100 per acre, the Saco Water Power Company had paid $168 for its land.

The price of Water Power stock indicates a general lack of enthusiasm on the part of investors, even in periods of great business optimism and when prospects of the company were brightest.

TABLE 8

MARKET PRICE OF SHARES, SACO WATER POWER COMPANY, 1845–1850

Year	High	Low	Par (paid-in) Value
1845	$400	$300	$400
1846	425	325	400
1847	450	375	500
1848	480	400	500
1849	410	335	500
1850	350	250	500

Source: Martin, *Boston Stock Market, 1835–1861*, p. 42.

The Machine Shop in 1850

For the period from 1839 to 1850 little reliable information has survived about the organization of the machine shop or about the men who built the machines. Scattered references to the shop and its people tell that, in the peak years of activity on the Laconia contracts, 600 men labored in the shop and on the buildings and canals. Reminiscences of an old machinist relate how work in the shop was done by contract, with experienced machinists taking certain parts of a machine to do by the job, employing cheap help, many of them boys, to perform over and over again one small task. "In this way, even boys would become so adept in a single process as to be quite profitable to the contractors employing them, yet would obtain but little real knowledge of the machinists trade. . . ." [40] Another reference of interest, contained in a letter from the superintendent to the treasurer, notes the scarcity of labor in 1847 and mentions the fact that handbills asking for men had been placed in thirty towns and that the superintendent himself would make a trip into what he rather picturesquely called "the interior" to obtain help. In another letter in this same year the superintendent indicates that the influx of Irish laborers, already noted at Lowell, had reached Biddeford, and, as at Lowell, had provoked the antagonism of the "natives." The superintendent noted that they had had a good deal of disturbance and one "pretty decided riot."

These bits of information are augmented by a detailed account, written by the superintendent and dated January 31, 1850, of the machine shop as it then existed.[41] At that time, the superintendent stated, the machine shop was stocked with tools, engines, and machines of all kinds requisite for carrying on the manufacture of cotton machinery and the building of mills. An overseer was employed by the company who had entire control, under the superintendent, of all persons employed in the shop and whose duty it was to examine and approve or condemn all work done.

The superintendent's description confirms other reports concerning the contract system of employment. He said that he contracted for the different kinds of work in the shop with men "who employ their own hands, make contracts with them and pay them." These contractors and their employees worked in the shop and were furnished by the company with all the tools and materials necessary for carrying on their work. When the work contracted for had been completed to the satisfaction of the superintendent, the contractors received payment in accordance with the terms of their written contracts. Apart from these contractors, the company employed some hands directly, the number varying according to the quantity of work to be done.

A man was employed by the company to keep the time of all who were employed in the shop, together with an account of the kind of work upon which each hand was engaged. The timekeeper made his rounds four times a day; he was responsible also for delivering tools and materials to the employees and contractors. All articles such as files, wire, screws, vitriol, pig lead and tin, glue, borax, emery, et cetera, needed in the shop were kept in a storeroom attached to the countinghouse. Each article delivered to the shop was recorded and charged to the particular kind of work upon which it was used; or, if for the use of one of the contractors, it was charged to his account.

The contractors, reported the superintendent, were paid monthly according to the time they and their hands had worked, receiving eight shillings ($1.00) per day for themselves plus whatever they paid their hands. It is worth noting that this rate was lower than the average daily wage of all machinists in the Boston Manufacturing Company in 1817 and was considerably lower than the rates received by skilled machinists elsewhere in New England at the time.

A forging and blacksmith shop was operated by the company in conjunction with the machine shop. At the head was an overseer appointed by the company, who had exclusive charge of this department under the superintendent. The overseer of the blacksmith shop marked out all work to be done and supervised its execution. He weighed out all iron and steel used in work for the machine shop and charged each piece of work with the quantity of materials used. Four times a day the overseer also took the time of all men employed, noting the kind of work each was engaged upon. Work in the forging and blacksmith shop, the superintendent stated, was all performed on a day basis, there being no contractors employed in this department.

At the end of each month a distribution sheet was made out in the counting room, which showed the exact time occupied by every man and boy in both the machine and blacksmith shops upon the various kinds of work being done. Also attached to the machine-shop staff were two watchmen, one of whom was on duty at all times, night or day. The superintendent noted that at the time of his report there were sixteen contractors at work in the shop, employing one hundred and thirty men and boys. How many other hands were employed directly by the company was not stated.

In the schedule of machine tools presented in the superintendent's report of 1850 the old-style hand lathes and fluting engines are still noted, but they had been augmented by machine tools capable of heavy work — vertical drills, squaring machines, planers (the largest was 26 feet long, capable of planing 3½ feet wide), card cylinder turning engines, shaft straighteners, heavy slabbing machines, and engine lathes with a two-foot swing. This inventory (presented in Appendix 3, Table B), as compared with that of the Saco Manufacturing Company in 1829, reveals that in the two decades ending in 1850 tremendous progress had occurred in American metal-working techniques, the advance being particularly noteworthy in the facilities for accurate, power-driven machining of large shapes.

An Appraisal of the Water Power Company in 1850

One major policy error emerges in an examination of the Saco Water Power Company in 1850. This error, unconsciously and pardonably committed in the years from 1844 to 1850, was destined to plague not the Saco Water Power Company of 1850, but the Saco-Lowell Shops of modern times. In this six-year period the Water Power Company, obviously conceiving for itself a limited future as a textile-machine shop, sold off its mill sites wholesale. The Laconia and Pepperell contracts condemned the Saco-Lowell Shops to a cramped existence on a narrow half-moon of land on the banks of the Saco River. In 1850, however, such a consideration, had it been foreseen, would have attracted scant attention amid the more pressing troubles of the day.

The financial condition of the Water Power Company following the Pepperell sale was poorer than the directors had anticipated. In May, 1851, the first date on which the records fully reflect the transaction, debts of the company amounted to $276,000, having been reduced by payments by Pepperell from a high point of close to half a million dollars in 1850. Total assets had decreased to $1,284,000 from a high of $1,641,000, and the stockholders' equity in the business was to be further reduced to liquidate a deficit of $328,000.

These factors were directly attributable to the Pepperell sale, but the several careful examinations made of the company's assets at this time revealed other disturbing facts. On April 25, 1850, the board of directors reported to the stockholders that the machine

MAINE REGISTER.

BIDDEFORD MACHINE SHOP.

he Water Power Company,

BIDDEFORD, ME.,

MAKE ALL KINDS OF

TON MACHINERY, SHAFTING, MACHINE TOOLS,

MILL GEARING AND IRON CASTINGS.

ALSO, KEEP CONSTANTLY ON HAND,

WD, BRADBURY AND SPIRAL VENT WATER WHEELS,

AND ALL KINDS OF

MILL WORK, FENDER POSTS, SAW GANGS, &C.

rticular attention paid to Self Acting Mules, Fly Frames, Drawing Frames, and Shaping Engines.

DWIGHT, Treasurer,
Boston, 20 State Street,

WM. H. THOMPSON, Supt.

Early Advertisement of the Saco Water Power Company
Maine Register, 1856

shop had depreciated as a result of "the too great multiplication of machine shops and machinery within the last few years." A later report of the directors candidly admitted that in 1850 the machine shop was obsolete, because of the technological changes in the industry. These changes appear to have been the great increase in popularity of the automatic mule, the widespread adoption of the railway drawing system, and the use of intermediate roving frames. Each of these developments in American textile machinery characterizing the years from 1839 to 1850 had been ignored in Biddeford, where not even opening and picking machinery had been built until 1849. Unlike the Locks and Canals Company, the Water Power Company did not avail itself of the opportunity of building the most modern types of machines under lease from the inventors. The basic technological error in Water Power Company policy was complete preoccupation with the machinery for only two textile companies. In a period in which the textile industry was turning from the traditional coarse goods to finer types of cloth the Water Power Company's attention had been confined to the old types of machines and processes. When the necessity arose for competing in the open market, the Water Power Company was faced with the choice of raising new capital for modernization or closing up the machine shop. At Biddeford as at Lowell, and to a far greater degree in the former place, the servicing of a narrow market had produced technical stagnation of dangerous proportions. In 1850 the great necessity for the future was to secure technological skill comparable to that in other machine shops and to present evidence of that skill to the textile industry outside Biddeford.

CHAPTER V

OTIS PETTEE AND THE END OF THE FORMATIVE PERIOD

1. The Struggle for Survival at Newton, 1823–1853

In their formative years Saco-Lowell's parent machine shops at Lowell and at Biddeford faced common problems and followed generally parallel paths. That part of Saco-Lowell's early history which centered in the shop of Otis Pettee at Newton Upper Falls, however, differed in some important particulars from the pattern of development which has been outlined in the preceding chapters. Otis Pettee's story is somewhat more personal, possibly more dramatic, certainly more typical of the age and the industry in which he made his mark.

Each of Saco-Lowell's three parent companies was a promotion of Boston mercantile capital managed by former Boston merchants or bankers. Each machine shop had been created to build one or more local mills. At Lowell, at Biddeford, and at Newton there were, initially, no plans for the manufacture of textile machines for the national or even the regional market. The Perkins-Lee-Cabot interests, which in 1814 had contemplated and in 1823 had commenced the construction of a cotton mill at Newton, however, had envisaged the creation of a single company only. The very nature of the area precluded any grandiose scheme for the development of land and water privileges into a great manufacturing center. Thus the dominant motive in the Lowell and Biddeford promotions is not to be found at Newton.[1]

Independent American textile-machine shops evolved in one of two ways. In western and northern Massachusetts, in Maine, and in New Hampshire the most important shops grew out of land-and-power development companies. Shops of this type, of which the Locks and Canals Company at Lowell was the largest and best known and the Saco Water Power Company was also an example, fed upon their environment and grew rapidly in size, almost irrespective of their intrinsic machine-building abilities. In southern Massachusetts, Rhode Island, Connecticut, New Jersey, New York, and Pennsylvania many smaller machine shops came into existence as a result of the initiative and skill of a single mechanic. Some of these shops were unaffiliated from the beginning with any cotton mill or industrial development. Others had been born in the basement of a cotton mill and had severed the connection in infancy. These shops sold machines to anyone who would buy. Many perished, and for each of them the handicap of limited capital was severe. Such of these as survived and succeeded did so because of the inherent worth of their machines. For shops of this second type expansion was often slow and painful. From such beginnings, however, grew the Whitin Machine Works, the Draper Corporation, Fales & Jenks, and other important machine shops which were to become the spirited competitors of the Lowell and Biddeford companies. The shop of Otis Pettee grew along these lines, partaking, after an initial period of dependence on a cotton mill, of the vicissitudes, the handicaps, and the strengths of the small unaffiliated shops.

Pettee's Early Experience, 1823–1831

In all of Saco-Lowell's early history there is no individual comparable to Otis Pettee, the mechanic in whose charge was placed the construction of the Elliot mill. At Waltham and Lowell, Paul Moody and his successors never rose above the position of superintendent. The same was true of Rufus Nichols and Otis Holmes at Biddeford. All these men were probably equal and in some cases undoubtedly superior to Pettee in technical skill. Yet, either through lack of initiative or of administrative ability, or possibly through lack of opportunity in the large organizations of which they were a part, these men never became business leaders. Samuel Batchelder, to be sure, had risen from the ranks of the mechanics to become a dominant figure in top management. His interest, however, swung to the management of cotton mills. A question of immediate interest, therefore, is how and why Pettee, a back-country mechanic, succeeded by his own efforts in founding a machine shop and in laying the groundwork for the growth of a great machine shop.

Otis Pettee's only surviving portrait (facing this page) reveals a grim-visaged, close-mouthed Yankee. Such details of his life and character as are known are completely in keeping with the impression rendered by this uncompromising picture study. His story is the typical American success story, the delight of local moralists and historians — a career which effectively exemplified New England's favorite truism: Waste Not, Want Not.

Otis Pettee was born in the town of Foxborough, Massachusetts, twenty miles southwest of Boston, in the year 1795. His father, Simon, was a blacksmith and gunsmith by trade, an inventor by disposition, a man of good judgment, and a leader in civic affairs in his native town. By the time Otis was old enough to be constructively interested in the mechanic arts — that is to say, at the age of ten or twelve — interest in textile invention had permeated even this small community. Simon Pettee himself had secured a patent for a loom in 1813, and by that time Otis had already availed himself of the opportunity of probing into "the works" of a carding machine in operation in a neighbouring gristmill and digesting its marvelous intricacies.

In his youth Otis was employed at his father's forge or on the farm. A few weeks in each winter were devoted to the rudiments of common school education, the objective of which was to instill an elementary ability to read, to write, and to distinguish between Puritanical concepts of good and evil. Otis Pettee's real education, like that of his contemporaries, came from an insatiable curiosity about the workings of his world, eager but desultory perusal of books on the mechanical and natural sciences, and the eminently practical teachings of a hard-working father. This casual educational system produced thousands of plodding, narrow-minded farmers. At the same time, it produced hundreds of mechanics of great and varied dexterity. For the few like Otis Pettee, who possessed great initiative and better than average native imagination, this seemingly limited environment could scarcely have been more favorable.

Early in his life Otis determined to confine his efforts to the field of textile machinery. Before he was twenty he had set a thread mill

Otis Pettee
Founder of the Pettee Machine Works

in operation in Foxborough and had established a local reputation for ability and honesty. In 1819 or 1820 he accepted a call from a Rufus Ellis to take charge of a cotton factory at Newton Upper Falls for the term of one year. Little is known of this venture, except that at the end of the year Pettee returned to Foxborough. It was this employment, presumably, which brought Pettee to the attention of the proprietors of the Elliot Manufacturing Company. In 1823, when that company was at last incorporated, Pettee was called once again to Newton Upper Falls and entrusted with the building of the first Elliot mill and machinery.

By 1824 the Elliot factory was in operation, turning out thirty-six-inch-wide cotton sheetings, to which the company thought it necessary to affix the label, "The whole process of manufacturing these goods is performed by water power machinery, which makes them more even and uniform than can be done by hand." Unlike the Lowell companies, the Elliot Company performed only the weaving process, purchasing its yarn from other manufacturers.

This was a strenuous and trying period of operation. During the summer, that is, from March 20 to September 20, machine shop and mill alike were opened at four o'clock each morning. A half-hour was allowed for breakfast and three-quarters of an hour for dinner. At seven o'clock operations were suspended for the day. From September 20 to March 20 breakfast was taken before the machines were started at daybreak, and they were run until seven-thirty in the evening, except on Saturdays, when the working day ended at dark. These hours were customary in machine shops and mills of the day, but were nonetheless fatiguing because of that fact.

Otis Pettee's rugged country physique was equal to the strain of great physical exertion; in fact, he found time from his daily labors to experiment with machine improvements. It is said that even before Pettee went to Newton for the first time he had become interested in improving the existing roving frames. He, like Moody at Waltham, began work upon the baffling problem of providing for variable bobbin speed that must be solved in order to permit roving to be spun on bobbins rather than into the old-style revolving cans. Like Moody, though six years later, Pettee patented an invention to accomplish this end. Pettee's double speeder, patented in 1825, was more remarkable than Moody's, however, to the extent that Pettee worked out his solution unassisted by any such gifted mathematician as Francis Cabot Lowell. Little is known of this invention except that it substituted metallic gearing for the treacherous leather belts on conical drums which characterized the English-type fly frame. Pettee's double speeder received considerable acclaim from both scientists and manufacturers, and it appears to have been widely used in the industry for at least twenty-five years following its invention. Pettee followed up this invention with another — an improvement in the flyers of the double speeder, patented March 28, 1834. These were his only patented inventions, but each was valuable and successful. A most important consequence of the patents was that Otis Pettee became known throughout the country as a gifted machinist.

Pettee's labors, responsibilities, and difficulties multiplied after 1824. As soon as the first Elliot mill had been completed, the directors voted to equip a second mill for the production of sheetings. Even before the installation of the looms, however, plans were changed. The directors decided (possibly for financial reasons) to install spinning machinery only, for the production of thread. Since Pettee had engaged in this type of manufacture at Foxborough, he was placed in charge of the second mill — he was already head of the mechanical department of the company. By 1825 this mill was in operation, but after some initial success the thread market became satiated with the offerings of the many small thread mills of Rhode Island and southern Massachusetts and the directors decided to revert to the original plan of producing sheeting. To this course of action Pettee objected, but to no avail. By the time the looms were in place, a year later, Pettee's fears had been realized — the market for sheeting had become stagnant while that for thread had revived, and Elliot, like many other mills, went out of production. This was only one of the differences which had occurred between Pettee and the top management of the company.

The basis for Pettee's trouble with the directors and the treasurer was a common one. While nominally investing Pettee with great responsibilities, the owners of the business exercised dictatorial powers which at times embarrassed their agent. A failure on the part of the directors to understand the working details of the business made Pettee's life still more unpleasant; and, worse yet, the directors could not even agree among themselves. These difficulties were aggravated by the question of building machinery for other mills.

Pettee had filled several small orders for machinery from neighboring mills. In 1829 he undertook his first extensive order for machinery for an outside mill. This order was to supply machinery for the Lowell Manufacturing Company at Lowell. The contract was an imposing one for a small and virtually untried shop to undertake, but special circumstances were involved in the placing of it. The Locks and Canals machine shop was completely occupied at the time with the construction of the Appleton mills. Moreover, Samuel Cabot, who held a large block of stock in the Elliot Manufacturing Company, had been put in charge of the Lowell Company. This personal contact brought the machinery order to Newton, where it was completed to the apparent satisfaction of all concerned.

In 1830 the Elliot Company contracted to supply the Jackson Company of Nashua, New Hampshire, with machinery for their new mills. Many obstacles stood in the way of completing this contract, not the least of which was that, despite success with the Lowell order, the Elliot directors were unenthusiastic and were persuaded only with great difficulty by Pettee to accept the order. The troubles anticipated by the directors proved to be very real. Materials had to be carted in from Boston and Providence, since there was no access by navigable water to Newton. No foundry had as yet been built there, and castings had to be ordered from foundries at Walpole, Foxborough, and Easton. Materials were slow in arriving, and delays in securing castings upset the manufacturing schedule. Pettee had difficulty in securing skilled and unskilled labor alike. Faced with these obstacles and seemingly with a lack of progress (much of the early work being performed outside Newton), the directors became apprehensive that the order would not be completed on time. Pettee explained that even though little headway was evident to the unpractised eye, he had every confidence that the machinery could be finished. The directors, however, ignored this advice, and informed the Jackson Company that, owing to limited transportation facilities and the scarcity of materials and labor, they must cancel the contract and transfer it to some other shop. Pettee thereupon offered to assume complete responsibility for completion of the machinery. The fact that this offer was accepted by the Jackson Company indicates something of Pettee's reputation for skill and integrity.

This was the significant turning point in Otis Pettee's career, but the details of it are not well known. Presumably Pettee continued to use the facilities of the Elliot machine shop. Money to finance machine-building operations may have been advanced by the Jackson Company — an arrangement not unusual between machine-builders and customers at this time as well as later. Whatever arrangements Pettee made to bring about the continuation of construction, it is clear that he had little to lose and everything to gain. His success in completing the contract on schedule elicited a glowing tribute from the Jackson Company. The sweet taste of independence and the flavor of personal profit made Pettee determined to sever all connections with the Elliot Manufacturing Company and to set up in business for himself.

The Shop of Otis Pettee, 1831–1853

When it became publicly known that Pettee had decided to leave the employ of the Elliot Manufacturing Company, he received a number of invitations to locate his machine shop or accept employment elsewhere. The Nashua Manufacturing Company was anxious to have him come there; manufacturers in western Massachusetts and eastern New York held out inducements for him to locate among them. The citizens of Foxborough urged him to return and set up his business in his native town. To these importunings Pettee had a simple response: "My home is here [in Newton], my land is in a good state of cultivation, fruit trees are beginning to bear, flower gardens and greenhouses are in a flourishing condition, and my family are comfortably situated. I see no reason why I cannot do as well here as anywhere else." It is not often in business history that the personal, non-economic motives so frequently underlying important policy decisions stand so clearly and frankly revealed.

After looking about for a suitable location on which to build a shop, Pettee finally decided to purchase land bordering on both sides of South Meadow Brook, a small stream which coursed its way down to the Charles River about half a mile above the Elliot mills. A mile up the brook from the river was an old dam and flume, built in colonial times by some long-forgotten millwright. Pettee saw the possibility of repairing this dam and of flooding a hundred or more acres of swamp land above it for a storage basin. A short distance from the river the brook fell twenty-five feet, and there was a natural opening between two hills for a dam. It was here that Pettee planned to locate the new machine works.

The first purchase of land, a trifle over twelve acres, was made on March 2, 1832, from Asa Williams and his wife. The price paid appears to have been $1,200, of which $200 was in cash and the balance in the form of a mortgage.[2] Laborers were immediately employed to build a dam across the brook and valley to the headlands on either side, from which gravel for the dam embankment could be hauled by wheelbarrow. Millwrights were employed in setting sheet piling and building flumes, together with penstocks and other waterways. Stone masons were put to work building retaining walls for wheel pits and setting foundations for shop buildings, while carpenters labored on the frame buildings of the shop itself. A temporary work building was erected in which to build water wheels and perform other mill work, and a single-story forge shop, fifty feet long and twenty-seven and one-half feet wide, was built on the east side of the brook. A small water wheel for temporary use was placed in the raceway just outside the main shop.

When Pettee left the Elliot Company the directors had decided to have no more to do with machine-building, and at length they offered their entire stock of tools and patterns for sale. This was most fortunate for Otis Pettee, and the eventuality may not have been unforeseen by him. Pettee was the principal buyer and removed the greater part of the equipment to his new forge shop, where it was set up ready for business. Four months after Pettee had left the Elliot Company's employ, wheels were set in motion in his own shop and workmen were engaged in building machinery.

The first section of the main machine shop, sixty-four feet long, twenty-seven and one-half feet wide, and three stories high, was constructed of wood on the west side of the raceway in line with the forge shop. A permanent water wheel soon replaced the temporary one. The space between the forge and the main shop was enclosed by a two-story building thirty-two feet long. This completed construction for the first season. The next year an addition of forty feet was made to the machine shop, and steam was introduced to augment water as a source of power. In 1835 eighty feet more were added to the shop. In 1836 a ninety-foot addition reached to the hill on the west side of the works; it was so constructed in relation to the high ground as to provide a ground entrance to each story for loading machinery. A track was laid and a flat car provided for carrying lumber to the circular saws and planing mills in the attic.

Castings were still ordered by Pettee from the furnaces at Walpole, Foxborough, and Easton, and occasionally work was done for Pettee at the new Leach furnace at Chelmsford. The attendant scattering of patterns and delay and expense in delivery of finished castings proved to be as annoying as when Pettee had been working on the Jackson Company order. Pettee came to the same conclusion which was to be reached at Lowell at a slightly later date — that a foundry was an indispensable part of any well-ordered machine shop. He therefore built a foundry, and the first castings were poured in August, 1837.

During these early years of operation Pettee found it necessary to compromise with his neighbors in disputes arising from the flowage of land. These disputes resulted in the purchase of some additional acreage above and around the storage reservoir. The machine shop was a particular source of annoyance to Amasa Winchester, a wealthy retired merchant who had fled the bustle of Boston to seek quiet and repose in the Newton meadows. When the clamor of the new machine shop there disturbed his meditations and the back water from the machine shop dam flooded his pasture, Winchester appears to have felt that industry in its relentless advance had singled him out as a special victim. He settled the flowage question with Pettee by an exchange of lands, but when the railroad pushed through his boundaries a few years later Winchester gave up his country retreat and returned to Boston.

The most poignant question which this outline of shop expansion raises is how Otis Pettee, with obviously limited resources, was able to finance the undertaking, at least until such time as profits began to accrue from machinery sales. Pettee must have had some capital of his own — possibly the profits from the Jackson Company contract. Of this there is no record. It is known, however, that substantial sums (substantial, that is, in relation to the initial small-scale nature of the venture) were raised by mortgages on real estate and equipment. In the first three years Pettee recorded four mortgages totaling $4,200. One of these covered the first purchase of real estate. Two others were held by Boston merchants affiliated with T. H. Perkins. Frederick Cabot, treasurer of the Elliot Company, was a co-holder of one mortgage which appears to have covered a part of the purchase of the Elliot machine tools. In 1834 Pettee raised $6,000 on a mortgage of the machine-shop tools and certain real estate. This loan was made by William Gardiner, son-in-law of T. H. Perkins.[3] Apparently Pettee's past differences with the owners of the Elliot Company had not created permanent ill will, for it was these men who supplied the bulk of such capital as Pettee found necessary to borrow.

The Gardiner mortgage deed is of particular historical value because it not only illustrates how machine-shop operations were financed, but also reveals much about the machine shop itself. The schedule of property attached to this deed (see Appendix 3, Table A) presents a further opportunity for ascertaining what a well-equipped machine shop consisted of in this early period and for comparing the tools in use at Newton in 1834 with those at Waltham in 1817 (Chapter II, page 49), at Saco in 1829 (Chapter IV, page 108), and at Biddeford in 1850 (Appendix 3, Table B).

In addition to his ability to raise capital and obtain tools ready-built from former business associates, Pettee found that the years with the Elliot Manufacturing Company were to return additional and even more substantial benefits. He had left the company at a time when all American mills were struggling with the problem of rapid obsolescence. Never at any subsequent time were so many major alterations in so wide a variety of machines required as in the two decades ending in 1830. Far from being hailed as a blessing, rapid technological advance was decried by many mill owners and labeled as a major obstacle to profits.[4] The Elliot Company, in taking stock of its equipment in 1831, found that the plant which had cost $96,151 was then worth $77,000, despite continuing improvements.[5] In 1832 modernization was necessary, and the first contract of Otis Pettee's new shop was with his old employer.

Pettee's outlook for new business, however, was severely restricted by the still localized nature of the machine-building trade. The unusual circumstances which enabled the Lowell Company order to be secured in 1829 could scarcely occur again. Not only had the Locks and Canals Company a virtual monopoly in Lowell, the principal market for textile machinery in America, but that company was itself by now reaching out for business. To the immediate south and west the shop of John Whitin and several smaller shops in Pawtucket and Providence were firmly in possession of the Blackstone Valley trade. The Fall River market had yet to experience its great growth, and local shops there were firmly entrenched, too — their position reinforced by the factor of high transportation costs from Newton. The question of what lay beyond the immediate horizon was soon to receive an unanticipated answer.

The intensely nationalistic interest of the United States in fostering home manufactures had begun by the middle 1830's to be echoed by her neighbor to the south. The Mexican government was embarking on a policy of encouraging infant industry by means of discriminatory tariff legislation. Foreign machines but not foreign manufactured goods were welcomed.

For twelve years Ithamar Whiting, a native of Dover, Massachusetts, had been prospecting for gold and silver in Mexico. When a company was organized in Tepic to promote one of Mexico's first cotton mills, Whiting was engaged as a contact man and sent to the United States to secure machinery. The proximity of Whiting's native town to Newton may explain why Otis Pettee secured the Tepic contract. Among the stipulations of this contract, which was signed in 1837, were the following:

We want machinery that will produce 750 yards of sheeting from no. 16 yarn in a day: including all supplies of whatever kind to put it in operation, including water wheels, shafting, plans for factory buildings, window frames, sashes and glass, door frames and locks. The machinery when finished, must be taken apart and packed securely in strong boxes to be shipped via Cape Horn and the Pacific Coast to San Blas; and as far as possible the gross weight of each package must not exceed 175 pounds for convenience of transportation on mules' backs from the port of entry to Tepic, a distance of about sixty miles.

This mill in Tepic, the Mexican counterpart of the Boston Manufacturing Company, was highly profitable and inspired many imitators. Pettee's second large order came from Durango in 1839; his third from Guadalajara in 1840. He supplied not only the machinery and factory accessories, but also machinists and cotton spinners, without which the American machinery would have been useless. Orders from Mexico, augmented by occasional contracts with new factories in Tennessee, Georgia, the Carolinas, and Maryland, appear to have been the principal source of business for the Pettee shop from 1837 to 1853, when Otis Pettee died. The Mexican orders constitute the earliest known exportation of any considerable amounts of American textile machinery and anticipate by more than half a century the next great exodus of such equipment. The contracts with mills in the cotton-growing area of the United States are also of considerable interest, for they reflect that significant though abortive first attempt to implant the textile industry in an area of cheap labor and accessible raw material. This experiment, too, was destined to be attempted again a half-century later, under different conditions and with far different results.

From what is known of Otis Pettee's trade, therefore, it would appear that he followed a course diametrically opposed to that pursued by the Locks and Canals Company and the Saco Water Power Company. The local market, which provided the bulk of business for the Lowell and Saco shops, was largely neglected by Pettee, through either chance or necessity. After 1832 Pettee's contacts with New England mills appear to have been confined to the sale of rights to manufacture his patent double speeder and his speeder flyers. Like his Lowell and Saco contemporaries, however, Pettee emerges even at the very beginning of his career as the builder of a complete line of cotton-textile machinery.

The financial results of operations at Newton from 1831 to

1853 are difficult to appraise. The expansion of the machine shop and the growth of Otis Pettee's personal fortune reflect a large measure of prosperity. Throughout the whole period, however, expansion on borrowed capital and entry into the cloth manufacturing business in 1840 tends to obscure the results of machine-building activities.

In 1839, Pettee, who at the time seems to have been on the verge of great success as a result of his Mexican contracts, received a severe blow. At 7:00 P.M. on a summer evening in 1839 a spark from the boiler-house chimney ignited the shingles of the machine shop. So rapidly did the flames spread through the wooden structure that some of the workmen were forced to leap from windows to safety. Only the foundry escaped destruction in this fire. The loss was placed at $100,000, with only $20,000 of covering insurance.

The events of 1839 and 1840 reveal Pettee's amazing vitality, energy, and optimism, so typical of many manufacturers of the day who waged a continual battle against hard times, physical disaster, and the handicap of scanty capital. Like many of his contemporaries, Otis Pettee's greatest assets were supreme confidence in his own ability, an almost blind faith in the future of his industry and his country, and an unquenchable energy in the pursuit of personal gain. Some months before the fire Pettee had discharged the $6,000 Gardiner mortgage with money raised on a new mortgage loan of similar amount from the Boston mercantile firm of Thomas Howe & Company. The fire loss resulted in no further mortgage loans, and the expense of rebuilding may have been met out of accumulated capital. In 1840 Pettee, far from being crushed to earth by his misfortune, was laying plans to purchase the Elliot Manufacturing Company!

Fluctuations in the price of cotton in 1840 had caused a diversity of opinion among the Elliot stockholders which finally resulted in the closing of the mills. In September, 1840, Pettee purchased the entire Elliot properties for the sum of $46,000.[6] Of this sum $38,000 was in the form of a mortgage held by the old owners, while the balance appears to have been paid in cash. Pettee proceeded to put in 250 new looms and to remodel the two mills, substituting the production of print goods for that of sheetings. When these alterations had been completed, the company, which Pettee named the Elliot Mills, was weaving 60,000 yards of calico cloth weekly and was reputed to be the largest weaving establishment in New England.

Coming in the midst of generally hard times this expansion would appear to have been more optimistic than wise. In 1843, the low point in the depression for most of New England's textile companies, Pettee was forced to make an assignment to his creditors of all mill and machine-shop properties.[7] The burden of debt by which and under which Pettee had operated appears, at this point, to have become intolerably heavy. Moreover, the practice of paying old mortgages with new borrowings was scarcely practicable in a period of financial stringency. Pettee's creditors, however, had sufficient confidence in him to keep open the machine shop and the Elliot Mills, and agreed with Pettee that three years should be allowed in which to pay off the debts.

Some concrete reasons for the confidence in Pettee appear in the inventory attached to the creditors' agreement of 1843. This inventory reveals a pattern of growth in the machine shop and the existence, in 1843, of an extremely well-equipped and modern plant. Since 1834 the capacity of the machine shop had been increased perhaps 25 per cent. Important tools appear in the 1843 inventory which had not been in use in Newton in 1834. These included a trip hammer, three cutting engines, two screw machines, a filing machine, a punching machine, and five planing machines. The trip hammer, ancient forebear of the modern power press, had been in use in America for a century, but its presence in a textile-machine shop indicated progress in the direction of rapid, automatic production of standardized parts. The appearance of planing machines at Newton followed closely upon the importation of the English Whitworth planer into Lowell. The screw machines were also a highly significant new addition to the American machine shop and, unlike the planer, they represented the results of native invention. The 1843 inventory also reveals that the number of lathes had increased greatly and that another steam engine had been added to the two in use in 1834. The use of steam power was thus well established at Newton long before it had become usual in the textile machine industry, though this fact was not occasioned so much by advanced manufacturing techniques as by the inadequacy of the local water supply. The inventory of machinery in the Elliot Mills showed 250 looms and about 5,000 spindles in place, indicating that Pettee had commenced to produce at least a part of his own yarn.

No information has survived about the course of business at the Newton shop in the decade following 1843. Pettee must have shared to some extent in the prosperity of the textile industry, for the assignment on his property was finally discharged in 1850. Otis Pettee himself had become a man of substance and standing in the community — a selectman, owner of thirty dwellings in the Upper Falls village, and proprietor of a fair-sized mansion on the hill overlooking his machine shops. Not a man of great charities or social grace, he commanded, nevertheless, the genuine respect of his contemporaries. "What a hum there would be in the world if everybody was as active as Otis Pettee," exclaimed one observer. "A man of energy and no mistake. The grass will never grow under his feet. If he is in Boston today he may be a thousand miles distant next week, if business requires it. No snails are allowed to crawl on his premises. He operates by example more than by precept. Always says 'Come,' not 'Go!' "[8]

This description of Otis Pettee, inadequate to the extent that it ignores the intimate motivations that made his life what it was, is nevertheless of value in explaining the tremendous vitality of the Newton enterprise. Pettee came close to being the model or typical successful business man of the period. The mold of the environment had produced, in his case, a near-perfect image. Even the details were clearly defined, for Pettee was both a temperance man and an abolitionist. In his community activities he drove to effect practical civic improvements which would benefit his business. These activities were pursued with a hard-headed realism that bordered on obstinacy. In 1844 Pettee was instrumental in preventing the Boston & Worcester Railroad from extending a branch from West Newton to the Upper Falls. Pettee pointed out that this connection would involve a fifteen-mile haul to Boston, instead of the ten-mile connection which was theoretically possible by a straight-line route. The Falls people, therefore, continued to use the daily stage to Boston for eight more years — until the Charles River Railroad was constructed on the only route which Pettee felt to be practicable.

In 1853 Otis Pettee died, at the age of fifty-seven years. The last three years of his life had been both prosperous and troubling. By 1850 the capacity of the Elliot Mills had been enlarged to 9,000 spindles by the addition of self-acting mules. The machine shop was active, employing 300 machinists. The Upper Falls community numbered 1,300 inhabitants, most of whom were still of native stock, dependent for their livelihood on Pettee's enterprises and living in Pettee's houses. From these people at various times had come demands for reduction in the length of the working day, first to twelve, then to eleven, then to ten hours. Pettee, in his relations with his employees, appears to have been no better and no worse than his contemporaries in Lowell and elsewhere. Employee demands were ignored until social pressure had been built up by precedents in the federal employment service and the influence of the English Factory Acts to a point where further opposition would have been dangerous; then employers yielded with many misgivings. These periodic contests, however, do not appear to have disrupted the community and left no discernible scars. There is no evidence that the reform and associationist movements of the middle 1840's were championed by the Newton workmen. There is, however, a hint of continuing business difficulty after 1850. In 1851 Otis Pettee raised $11,000 by a mortgage on his home. This loan was extended by Henry Billings, who appears rather abruptly on the Newton scene at this time, emerging out of obscurity as a young man of considerable means and the successful pretender to the hand of Louisa, Pettee's daughter.

Otis Pettee's will provides the final bit of information on operating policy and results. The inventory of assets accompanying this will, according to the Chief Judge of Probate of Middlesex County, was the largest, irrespective of business liabilities, that had ever been filed in the county to that time. Those business liabilities, however, were heavy and indicate that the debts by which expansion had been financed ever since 1831 had not been liquidated. The total estate, real and personal, amounted to $232,175.[9] Debts totaled $84,003. Listed among Pettee's real estate were "The valuable machine shops — about 12 acres of land with several large and some lesser machine shops, an iron foundry or blacksmith shop, and sundry other shops for various mechanical purposes, 2 dwelling houses, water privileges, steam engine, etc. etc." Also listed were the Elliot

Mills, including all machinery and 13 dwelling houses "mostly adapted to several families each," and "a valuable paper mill, 7 acres of land, and a rolling and slitting mill, nail factory, saw mill and grist mill" in Needham, Massachusetts.

All of this mill property was offered for sale in order to liquidate the debts outstanding at Otis Pettee's death. The Elliot Mills were sold to a group of Boston promoters and were never thereafter associated with the machine shop. The miscellaneous mill property at Needham was also disposed of in the settlement. The sale of the machine shop to a partnership comprised of George and Otis Pettee, sons of the founder, and Henry Billings, the son-in-law, completed the liquidation of the estate. As nearly as can be ascertained from the available legal records, the sale of mill properties accumulated by Pettee during his life yielded $90,501, or about $6,000 more than enough to pay off the debts incurred in acquiring and operating those properties.[10] Pettee's personal estate, amounting to $105,339, was not touched in the debt-liquidation process, and represented unencumbered and unexpended profit which had accrued to Pettee over the years.

The death of Otis Pettee and the settlement of his estate ended the formative operating period of the Newton shop. The shop had been established; markets and manufacturing methods had been probed; and the financial burdens of founding and expansion had been carried and finally resolved. The new partnership, Otis Pettee & Company, formed in the year of Otis Pettee's death by his sons and son-in-law to carry on the business, took over an experienced, unencumbered organization. At Newton, as at Waltham, Lowell, and Biddeford, this first period was one in which technical and financial problems were dominant. Competition had not been a primary concern of management. At Lowell and at Biddeford local monopoly situations had provided the bulk of orders. At Newton exploitation of a unique foreign market was the basis of a thriving business. Each of Saco-Lowell's three parent companies faced an identical situation at the end of the developmental phase of operations. The Lowell Machine Shop in 1845, the Saco Water Power Company in 1850, and Otis Pettee & Company in 1853, all were faced with the necessity of seeking business in the open American market.

Skill in making and selling machines under conditions of rapidly increasing competition was henceforth to be the requirement for profitable existence.

2. The Formative Period in Saco-Lowell Origins: Analysis and Retrospect

The death of Otis Pettee in 1853 marked the end of the formative period in Saco-Lowell origins. What may be said of this period in retrospect? Shielded from clear view by the haze of years, this era unquestionably stirs the imagination. So perishable are great segments of business history that often there is difficulty in imparting the breath of life to the body of fact — in rounding out in all its segments the story which history has to tell. In Saco-Lowell's early history there are many hints of drama and questions of great interest which can never be answered by the historian. How vital a part in the building of the nation was played by the leather-aproned men who, in the interest of personal gain, labored with infinite patience on their flimsy machines? Might it not be true that, in presenting the pageant of early nineteenth-century America, historians have paid too much attention to the roar of cannon on the high seas and the echo of the long rifle in the hills — too little to the rattle and crash of the trip hammer in the forge? What was the substance which lay behind a dozen shadowy personalities at Waltham, Newton, Lowell, and Biddeford? Was one of America's great business statesmen buried in the grave of Francis Cabot Lowell? How should history appraise the relentless, heavy-handed efficiency of Kirk Boott? What was Otis Pettee's life, that behind such taciturn features so bright an enthusiasm burned? To the novelist this period presents a thousand exciting possibilities — to the historian, as many limitations. To leave questions such as these unanswered is regrettable; to refrain from pointing out the deficiency, however, would be misleading.

Many vital questions about this period fortunately can be answered, and the pith of the history preserved thereby. To the historian the preceding studies of the three parent companies suggest significant conclusions and the need for exploration in greater detail of certain fields which must be passed by in a history which follows three companies for more than a century. It is of particular and immediate importance for a proper understanding of events in Saco-Lowell's history, however, that the machine shops at Lowell, at Biddeford, and at Newton be made to appear in their proper place and perspective in the American business scene and in their true relationship to each other and to the textile machinery industry.

The Evolution of the Textile Machinery Industry

Over the years encompassed by the incorporation of the Boston Manufacturing Company and the death of Otis Pettee — that is to say, from 1813 to 1853 — there was a stirring among all American machine shops. In these years this stirring was little felt by the men at Lowell, at Biddeford, and at Newton, yet it was destined to become vastly important to them in succeeding decades. In these years the manufacture of textile machinery evolved from a local trade sporadically practised by many small shops to an industry characterized by a few large shops and an increasing number of smaller, more specialized shops, all of which were beginning to compete vigorously for business on a national scale.

In 1813, textile machines were being produced under diverse auspices. There could scarcely be said to be an industry recognizable as such. Many blacksmiths were turning out textile machines as a side line. A great many cotton mills were making their own machinery. At the same time, many highly specialized machine shops were plying their trade, concentrating their attention on one or two machine types. The machine shop which could build a mill complete, however, was in a strong competitive position in the open market compared with the specialist, and this fact accounts for a definite movement toward diversification in the industry. This movement was well under way in the 1840's. Some specialists commenced adding to their lines as rapidly as available capital would allow. The trend toward diversification went beyond the goal of a complete line of textile machinery, and some shops, such as the Locks and Canals Company, began building machine tools, locomotives, stationary engines, and a wide variety of other metal products. This tendency in the direction of diversification had not matured by 1853. Neither was it all-inclusive or even the dominant trend in the industry.

Many machine shops began or continued to specialize successfully, basing their success on unusual manufacturing skill or on the possession of a prized patent.

The trend toward diversification by certain segments of the industry became noticeable at about the same time that the textile industry began to depart from its original highly localized basis, and it seems entirely plausible that one cause for diversification was the increasing competition which characterized the decade of the 1840's. The position of the Locks and Canals Company was challenged. Through the 1820's and 1830's this company, by virtue of its association with the great Lowell development, was the best known and largest of the non-specialized American textile-machinery manufacturers. In 1845 the Locks and Canals Company was still the largest in the industry, but many other machine shops which had become powerful locally had begun to make their competitive strength felt.

The Matteawan Machine Shop had become famous in the New York area and was active in the importation and improvement of the latest English inventions. From the scanty evidence available it appears that this shop took the lead over all others in the industry (including the Locks and Canals Company) in selling a full line of textile machinery over a wide geographic range. The Bridesburg Machine Works, founded in Pennsylvania in 1810 by a disciple of Samuel Slater, was equipping mills in the Central Atlantic States and to the south and was reputed to be one of the most important textile-machinery manufacturers in the country.[11] The firm of Gay & Silver at North Chelmsford, Massachusetts, and the shop of Otis Pettee at Newton Upper Falls were typical of the smaller companies building a wide variety of textile machinery and becoming successful in specific marketing areas. In 1840 the construction of the huge Amoskeag Machine Shop was commenced at Manchester, New Hampshire. Slightly later a large machine shop was established at Lawrence, Massachusetts. By the end of the decade these shops, following the example of the Locks and Canals Company, were turning a speculative eye on the general market. In addition to these actual or potential competitors for complete mill orders, two important specialists were beginning to diversify their line. By 1849

John Whitin, who had become well known for his pickers, had added facilities for the manufacture of a nearly complete line of textile machinery to his shop at Northbridge, Massachusetts.[12] At Taunton, Massachusetts, William Mason, whose attention was first concentrated upon the self-acting mule and the ring spinning frame, had also begun to seek diversity.

Many other textile-machinery manufacturers, both specialized and non-specialized, were plying their trade in the 1840's. Some of these, like the Saco Water Power Company and the machine shops at Springfield and Chicopee, Massachusetts, and at Paterson, New Jersey, though producing nearly complete lines of machines, had exerted little apparent influence on the competitive market. Others — for example, the Providence Machine Company and Fales & Jenks in Pawtucket; E. C. Kilburn & Company and Hawes, Marvel & Davol in Fall River; the Crompton Loom Works in Worcester; Davis & Furber in Andover; and George Draper & Sons in Hopedale — were either specialists or were soon to become specialists. Their position in the industry in the period under consideration is difficult to appraise, but their influence was to be felt in the near future. The emergence of these shops made one fact clear: by 1853 the construction of a machine shop by a cotton-mill company had ceased to be the prerequisite for the construction of the cotton mill.

Even a casual examination of the important machine-makers with whom the Saco-Lowell parent companies came face to face at the end of the formative period at once reveals the fact that diversification of product line had not been an essential characteristic for survival. Neither, apparently, had been location. The concentration of the textile industry in New England had produced a similar concentration in the textile machinery industry, but other cloth-producing areas to the south also supported successful machinery manufacturers.[13] Gone, however, were the tiny shops of 1813 with their smithy tools and hand-turning engines. The successful manufacture of textile machinery had become more and more a product of large shops housing heavy, expensive machine tools and employing machinists of increasingly specialized skills. This had been a natural evolution which the most successful machinery manufacturers had accomplished as a matter of course. Those who could not afford to keep pace with technological advance were quickly left behind. In perhaps no other period in the history of either the textile industry or the textile machine industry was the necessity for rapid adjustment to change so acute.[14] This necessity was universal. There were a variety of other attributes, however, which were combined in various ways to yield profits, or at least to permit survival.

The textile-machine shops which emerged from the obscurity of the first three decades of the nineteenth century to become important competitors in later years survived and prospered either because of monopoly situations, skill in invention, skill in manufacturing, forwardness in adopting the inventions of others, or by a combination of these characteristics coupled with sound business management. Thus, though the Locks and Canals Company produced no important new textile machines, it enjoyed great success as a result of its semi-monopoly position at Lowell, and because of its alertness in the introduction of improvements effected by others, great manufacturing skill, and sound management. The Saco Water Power Company owed its existence almost exclusively to its monopoly position in Saco and Biddeford. In 1850, as we have seen, that company was in no position, either technically or financially, to compete on equal terms with other machine shops. The shop of Otis Pettee profited by the special opportunity provided by the unusual Mexican market, but this shop, like the one at Lowell, appears to have been efficiently equipped and ably operated. It is of considerable interest to note that of Saco-Lowell's three parent companies only the shop of Otis Pettee depended to any appreciable degree on market aggressiveness for success in this period.[15]

There were factors even more fundamental than these to the success of the various machine shops. Behind the evolution in form and growth in size of the textile machinery industry lay the sensational growth of the textile industry itself. The fact that spindles in the United States increased from under 100,000 in 1811 to approximately 3,600,000 in 1850 is basic to any study of textile-machinery history in this period.[16] This increase was one phase of the general increase of the material wealth of the country — an increase manufactured out of rich resources by a tough-fibered, hard-working, ingenious population, using the tools provided by the English and American Industrial Revolutions. The struggle for existence of each individual firm was conditioned by this broad, powerful, favorable trend.

There were counter-currents. From 1815 to 1843 there was a rapid, though irregular, decline in the general price level.[17] Severe depressions shook the country, and the years of recession and depression outnumbered the years of recovery and prosperity. Vigorous new industries, to be sure, resisted the trend. A number of textile companies suffered comparatively little in the 1819–21, 1829–30, and 1837–43 depressions. The Locks and Canals Company and the other Lowell corporations are noteworthy examples of strength in times of general weakness. Nevertheless, the fall in textile prices over the 1815–43 period was pronounced and the challenge of hard times was felt in varying degrees by all.[18] This environment was particularly favorable for the development of textile-machine shops. Falling prices and increasing competition were, in part at least, the product of technical improvements. The existence of these conditions, however, was an impelling stimulus to effect further improvements and to put such improvements to immediate use. The competitive necessity on the part of textile mills for ever lower production costs appears to have been a factor of some importance in explaining the growth of the textile machinery industry and the survival of individual machine shops in this period.

Another aspect of an environment which was conducive to technological improvement and friendly to the machine shops was the high cost of labor in America. The farm and the frontier competed with the manufacturer in his quest for cheap labor, the supply of which was particularly restricted before the great waves of immigration commencing in the late 1840's. The extent of the demand for labor-saving machinery — for rapid, automatic production — was therefore a unique characteristic of the American economy. This demand was the more easily met because of America's cheap and abundant power, the existence of which directed American economic development along a somewhat different path from that followed in England. In 1840 James Montgomery stated:[19]

Driving machinery at high speed, however, does not always meet with the most favorable regard of practical men in Great Britain; because in that country where power costs so much, whatever tends to exhaust that power, is a matter of some consideration: but in this country, where water power is so extensively employed, it is of much less consequence.

A less widely recognized but important stimulant to the introduction of automatic textile machinery was the recalcitrant attitude of certain groups of foreign skilled laborers who were employed in American mills. William Mason himself reported the complaints of mill owners about the disorderly habits of English jack spinners. The owners told Mason, "We need a self-operating machine, which can be run by a boy, and will make [us] independent of the unreliable class of workmen we are compelled to employ." The response to this appeal, said Mason, was the construction by four different American inventors of as many self-operating adjustments which could be added to the jack frames.[20]

The consequence of these various forces was the most prolific period of innovation in the history of the textile machinery industry. Before 1830 the incidence of revolutionary inventions was particularly high. After this time progress was less spectacular and, with important exceptions such as the self-acting mule and the ring spinning frame, manifested itself in the form of innumerable improvements of existing machine types. The cumulative effect of these improvements over the next two decades, however, was probably as profound as that produced by the sweeping changes of Paul Moody's day.

These innovations and improvements were the work not of scientists but of practical mechanics, working by trial-and-error methods. In America science had scarcely descended to the level of the workbench, and contemporary writers held that want of sufficient and accurate acquaintance with the sciences on the part of the nation's ingenious and originating minds was hampering progress.[21] The great service performed by organizations such as the Middlesex Mechanics Association, at Lowell, was in attempting to remedy this very real deficiency.

Improvement in textile-machinery design went hand in hand with great progress in American machine-building techniques. This progress was neither confined to nor exclusively the product of the textile-machine shops. A great and quite independent contribution to the American Industrial Revolution was being made in the first half of the nineteenth century by the firearms and clock factories in Connecticut and by the federal arsenals at Springfield and Harper's Ferry. In these places was being evolved the "American System"—the technique of interchangeable parts manufacture. This system and the closely related technique of working to extremely fine tolerances had but a limited usefulness in the manufacture of textile machinery and was not an integral part of the increasing efficiency of the textile-machine shops. That efficiency and the growing skill exhibited in all American manufacturing enterprise was, to a large extent, the result of yet another contemporaneous development—the widespread adoption of new machine tools in the 1830's and thereafter. The planer, the heavy lathe, the drill press, and the milling machine all came into general use in this period. The emergence of specialized machine-tool manufacturers in the 1840's was to result in an even greater rate of progress after 1853. In 1775, appliances for cutting metal were little better than those of the Middle Ages. By 1850 most of the basic machine tools in use today had been invented.[22]

In this 1813–53 period the American textile machinery industry had been vitally dependent on England for models of new machine tools and textile machinery. Despite the repeal of the British Restrictive Acts in 1845 the English textile machinery industry still remained, in 1853, a source of inspiration rather than of competition. Throughout the entire period under consideration and particularly in the 1840's and 1850's American machine-shop owners were sending their ranking mechanics to England to purchase, to observe, and to learn. The testimony preceding the repeal of the Restrictive Acts presented ample evidence, however, that America was beginning to repay her debt—that the Acts, while conceived to prevent the spread of the Industrial Revolution abroad, had actually fostered a vigorous and increasingly original development of skills across the Atlantic.[23] One historian has stated that America had become the land of originality, England the land of experience, and that unconsciously and undesignedly the two countries coöperated with and supplemented each other in advancing the world's technical progress.[24] This judgment appears to have increasing validity for the years following 1830. Nevertheless, originality should not be confused with superiority. In 1853 English metal-working skills still surpassed those to be found in America. Scotch pig iron was still the basic ingredient in American machines, although the time was near when the American iron industry was to provide domestic consumers with domestic metal. English machine tools far surpassed their American counterparts in design and workmanship. English textile machines exhibited a similar superiority in workmanship and in addition were produced at lower cost, the result of minute specialization in the English industry and differences in the cost and use of labor. A comparison of the output of English and American textile-machinery manufacturers must take into consideration the differing characteristics of textile production in the two countries. England surpassed in the manufacture of fine goods, while America had already become famous for mass-production techniques and by 1853 was making rapid progress in overcoming the lead of the English in other fields.[25]

Like the machines themselves, ownership and managerial practices in the American textile machinery industry exhibited an evolutionary pattern. A very great majority of the early textile-machine shops were proprietorships or partnerships, managed by the owners. The Saco-Lowell parent companies, all three of which were incorporated at the beginning and in which ownership and management were separated in varying degrees, appear to have been typical neither of the textile machinery industry nor of contemporary American business in general. The Elliot Manufacturing Company, to be sure, soon abandoned this pattern, and the company set up by Otis Pettee was of the type most common in the industry. Growth in the industry and familiarity with the corporate form of business did not materially increase the number of incorporated machine shops nor greatly alter the ownership-management relationships which had prevailed. Proprietorships and partnerships continued to dominate, the principal exceptions being provided by a few large promotions modeled after Lowell, such as those at Manchester, New Hampshire, and at Lawrence and at Holyoke, Massachusetts.

With the growth in size of individual machine shops the professional agent or superintendent came to be a fixture in the industry. In some cases, as at Biddeford and at Lowell, he had sole responsibility for shop operations and reported to owners who had little grasp of the technical side of the business. In other cases he acted as an assistant to owners active in management. By definition he was a technician, and his duties included only minor aspects of financial administration. In contrast to many industries where top managerial positions were a stepping-stone to setting up in business, these professional machine-shop agents or superintendents seldom appear to have established their own shops, though many of them held shares in the companies whose shops they managed. Otis Pettee's career was by no means typical and was not often imitated after 1830.[26] Instead, the progress of these men was from a small shop to a larger one, and the best of them climaxed their career as resident agents enjoying a large measure of responsibility for administering the technical affairs of the business.

The employment of professional technical management was the first break in the traditional system of owner-managed enterprise — the resident agent was the ancestor of the professional manager and the harbinger, in many companies, of a divorce between ownership and management. In the Lowell corporations in the first half of the nineteenth century only the position of treasurer, which was habitually filled by an important stockholder, stood in the way of complete divorce. Toward the end of this period even the office of treasurer had come close, in some instances, to achieving a professional standing. It was no mere coincidence that administration by means of agents first appeared in those companies promoted by mercantile interests. The mercantile capitalist had developed great skill in the use of this system of administration and quite naturally applied it to his ventures in the manufacturing field.

One factor which helps to explain the increasing importance of the resident agent in the incorporated machine shop was the slow but steady diffusion of ownership which had occurred. This tendency is admirably exemplified by the Boston Manufacturing Company, the Merrimack Manufacturing Company, the York Manufacturing Company, and the Saco Water Power Company, much of the stock of which had become in the 1840's the property of persons outside the realm of business.[27] Control of such companies as these tended to pass into the hands of coalition groups of minority stockholders whose key to power was the proxy vote, while management became more firmly professional in nature. The widening gap between ownership and management and the discrepancy between ownership and control unquestionably left room for conflict and inefficiency to develop. This appears to have occurred in the Saco Water Power Company to some extent, but in most companies new administrative techniques were generally successful in meeting the changing characteristics of the corporate enterprise.

Of the relations which existed in the textile machinery industry between management and labor in the years before 1853 almost nothing is known. With the exception of the more famous mechanics who patented machines, very little is known of the men who worked in the machine shops. One fact stands out with considerable force and clarity. From the 1820's on, the skilled mechanics in American textile-machine shops were native-trained.[28] The flow of skilled English artisans which had first stimulated the manufacture of textile machinery in America and which, in 1853, was still nourishing the textile industry had long since ceased to be a dominant factor in the evolution of the textile machinery industry. After Samuel Slater, the Scholfield brothers, and their contemporaries, invention and improvement were, to a very large extent, products of the hands, if not the minds, of American mechanics. The earliest of these, recruited from the ranks of a highly ingenious artisan class, were trained by the English masters. Thereafter, the process of transmitting skills became largely an indigenous one, and foreign-trained mechanics participated only when a new process or machine, imported from abroad, required a foreign expert. This situation is not easy to explain, particularly in view of the fact that a great many of the overseers in American textile mills were foreign-trained. It would appear that, though the supply of skilled mill operatives and skilled mechanics alike was small, the latter could better be trained than imported. Perhaps the task of making a workman who had never seen a mule into a proficient mule spinner was greater than that of making a textile-machinery mechanic out of a millwright, a shipwright, or a blacksmith. Then, too, there is a suggestion that English-trained mechanics with their highly specialized skills did not fit readily into the pattern of the average American machine shop, where functional specialization, though increasing, was never to equal that of the English shops. There was, moreover, a definite prejudice against foreign-trained mechanics. This feeling went beyond the ordinary dislike based upon competition for jobs and differences in living standards which existed between the native and the foreign laborer. The English mechanic was accused of being unimaginative and suspicious of change. One contemporary commentator expressed a widely prevailing attitude when he stated:[29]

From the habits of early life and the diffusion of knowledge by means of free schools there exists generally among the mechanics of New England a vivacity in inquiring into the first principles of the Science to which they are practically devoted. They thus frequently acquire a theoretical knowledge of the processes of the useful arts, which the English laborers may commonly be found to possess after a long apprenticeship and life of patient toil. For this reason the American mechanic appears generally more prone to invent new plans and machines than to operate upon old ones in the most perfect manner. The English mechanic, on the contrary, confining his attention simply to the immediate performance of the process of art to which he is habituated from early youth, acquires wonderful dexterity and skill.

This estimate may well have been colored by the intense nationalism of the day, but the rational validity of such sentiments mattered little. The prejudice took root and flourished.

This same nationalism underlies all aspects of the development of the textile machinery industry. Americans were boastfully proud of their accomplishments. Their attitude toward England was a mixture of deference and defiance. In the field of business, as in politics, a sense of Manifest Destiny became strong. Political and economic events in England and Europe in 1848 nourished this feeling in America and provoked sentiments which were glowing but prophetic. Well-informed men were saying:[30]

. . . the present disastrous state of things in England betoken that the sway of the old world is broken, and that the United States will inevitably become the leading nation of modern times.

This was the larger frame of reference within which the Saco-Lowell parent companies and the textile machinery industry had evolved. What was the true relationship of these companies and that industry to the growth of American business enterprise? The manufacture of cloth was America's greatest industry. For a considerable part of the 1813–53 period the manufacture of textile machinery appears to have been America's greatest heavy goods industry, occupying the primary position in point of size and value of product among all industries which fabricated metal. Size, however, is not the most critical measure of importance. From the textile mills and the textile-machine shops came the men who supplied most of the tools for the American Industrial Revolution. From these mills and shops sprang directly the machine tool and the locomotive industries, together with a host of less basic metal-fabricating trades. The part played by the textile machinery industry in fostering American metal-working skills in the early nineteenth century was a crucial one. It is for this reason that considerable attention has been devoted to the early years of Saco-Lowell's history. In an industry of considerable importance in the economic evolution of America, the story of the three Saco-Lowell parent companies assumes particular significance. The machine shops at Biddeford and at Newton serve to illustrate the characteristics and vicissitudes of a large segment of the industry. The part played by the Boston Manufacturing Company and the Proprietors of the Locks and Canals on Merrimack River in developing machines, techniques, and organization and in training machinists was perhaps without rival in their time.

Part Two

THE ADVENTUROUS MIDDLE YEARS

Saco-Lowell's Parent Shops from 1845 to 1912

To the machine shops at Biddeford, Lowell, and Newton maturity imparted little of the stability associated, in men and institutions alike, with middle age. The difficulties surmounted in the formative period of Saco-Lowell's history, great though they were, did not surpass those of the succeeding years. After 1845 the old challenges of depression, war, and inflation were encountered again, each of these essentially normal business situations being greeted with incredulity by management. The ability of textile-machine shops to survive and prosper, however, was contingent upon skill not only in meeting normal business challenges, but also in adjusting themselves to a sweeping change in the textile machinery industry — the increasing competition for business.

This competition was already being felt in 1845. It accelerated steadily and reached a climax in a bitter and, for a time, unrestrained fight for new machinery markets after 1874. This struggle molded the form of the textile machinery industry and set the organizational pattern of the modern Saco-Lowell Shops.

In the six chapters which follow, the history of the Lowell Machine Shop, the Pettee Machine Works, and the Saco Water Power Company is traced through the era of so-called free competition.

The financial and technological problems which dominated the developmental phase of these companies in the first half of the nineteenth century are encountered again, but the core of the history is to be found in the field of marketing and finance. In this eventful half-century of Saco-Lowell's history the up-surge of the Newton and the Biddeford shops and the first drawing together of hitherto independent business units in the industry occupy a primary position. The middle years are climaxed in 1905 by a surprising reversal of the position and relationship of the three parent companies.

* * * *

CHAPTER VI

SPECIALIZATION IN AN EXPANDING MARKET

The Lowell Machine Shop, 1845–1879

1. The Ante-Bellum Shop, 1845–1860

Formation of the Company

The formation of the Lowell Machine Shop early in 1845 told much about the prospects of textile-machinery manufacture in America. The Lowell mills had been built, and the great profits from sale of land and water power had been pocketed by the stockholders of the old Locks and Canals Company. The decision of a group of astute and wealthy investors to set up a company which should be devoted exclusively to the manufacture and sale of machinery indicated faith in an expanding textile industry — confidence in their own ability to find business outside the immediate environment.

While the directors of the Locks and Canals Company were declaring their handsome liquidation dividends and laying plans for the formation of a new Locks and Canals Company which would continue to regulate the water power for the Lowell mills, a small group of men were busily engaged in the formalities of corporate organization. On January 29, 1845, Governor Briggs of Massachusetts signed an act incorporating the Lowell Machine Shop. Before that date there had been the usual mystery as to the identity of the "interests" with whom Patrick Tracy Jackson had been bargaining for the sale of the Locks and Canals machine shop. The Lowell Machine Shop charter partially resolved the mystery. It carried three names well known in Lowell: Nathan Appleton, John A. Lowell, and Abbott Lawrence.[1] At the first stockholders' meeting of the new company the remaining investors were identified. This meeting was held at 11½ Tremont Row in Boston on March 12, 1845, and was taken up with the acceptance of the charter, the adoption of bylaws, and the election of officers. John A. Lowell was elected president of the Corporation, and J. Thomas Stevenson was elected treasurer. The directors consisted of the president, the treasurer, Abbott Lawrence, Nathan Appleton, Ebenezer Chadwick, John Clark, and Homer Bartlett.[2]

In this directorate the Boston mercantile interests which had built much of New England's textile industry predominated. Boston's most potent financial institutions were represented. John A. Lowell was both nephew and son-in-law of Francis Cabot Lowell. After a mercantile apprenticeship in the firm of K. Boott & Son, he had succeeded Patrick Tracy Jackson as agent and treasurer of the Boston Manufacturing Company and had gone on to become treasurer of the Boott Mills and Massachusetts Cotton Mills in Lowell; the last two positions he held in 1845. J. Thomas Stevenson, a retired East India merchant, had been treasurer of the Lowell Manufacturing Company prior to assuming the similar position with the Lowell Machine Shop. Abbott Lawrence was wise in the ways of finance and textile manufacturing long before he invested in the Lowell Machine Shop. Lawrence, too, came of mercantile background and had established his fortune in the famous mercantile house of A. & A. Lawrence. In 1845 he was an active partner in the firm of J. W. Paige & Company, a Boston cloth-selling house which acted as agent for many large New England mills. His investments in the mills at Lowell had been heavy, his participation in national politics successful, and his dominance of such Boston financial institutions as catered to the textile industry remarkably complete.[3] Nathan Appleton, who had so reluctantly invested in the Boston Manufacturing Company in 1814, had ridden the crest of the Lowell tide. Like Abbott Lawrence, Appleton turned from foreign trade to the marketing of domestic cloth; he was actively engaged in selling cotton goods in the commission house of J. W. Paige & Co. at the time he helped to organize the Lowell Machine Shop. Also like Lawrence, Appleton was active in politics, both State and national, and his banking connections were impressive. John Clark and Homer Bartlett were serving as mill agents at Lowell, and Ebenezer Chadwick was active in mill promotions in Maine and in the affairs of the Boston & Lowell Railroad.

The list of stockholders who on December 7, 1845, affixed their signatures to the subscription list for Lowell Machine Shop stock is impressive. Of the 600 shares of $500 par stock issued, the Lawrence family owned or controlled 150 shares. Nathan Appleton and his cousin William owned or controlled 76 shares. John A. Lowell owned 50 shares, and William Sturgis, of the Boston brokerage house of Bryant & Sturgis, owned 30 shares. The remainder was split into smaller blocks among 36 other stockholders also drawn from the cream of Boston's mercantile aristocracy.

The Lowell Machine Shop could scarcely have enjoyed a more regal sponsorship. The wealth of the directors alone was sufficient to guarantee adequate capital for the venture. The political, financial, industrial, family, and social connections of the stockholders linked the Shop to every important Boston financial institution and every large cotton mill in northern New England.[4]

The character of ownership and top management of the Lowell Machine Shop in 1845 was such as to leave unanswered but one question relating to the probable success of the venture. That question was: Could the Lowell Machine Shop build machinery? Neither wealth nor influence would, for long, ensure the sale of an inferior product in an increasingly competitive market. A part of the answer to this question was implicit in the nature of the property acquired from the Locks and Canals Company.

The change in ownership from the Locks and Canals Company to the Lowell Machine Shop produced few immediate changes at the operating level. The tools, the buildings, the power, and, with two exceptions, the men who had built the Lowell mills passed to the new company. Even while the Governor was signing the act to incorporate the Lowell Machine Shop, machinery was being loaded into cars on the Boston & Lowell siding in the shop yard at Lowell. The storage yards on both sides of the Merrimack Canal stood ready stocked with lumber and iron. There were unfilled orders on the superintendent's books in the tiny counting room which sat astride the entrance of the shop yard. The Lowell Machine Shop was, from the moment of its inception in January of 1845, a going concern.

For this property and for intangible values arising out of the machine shop's established reputation the organizers of the Lowell

Machine Shop agreed to pay to the Locks and Canals Company the sum of $175,000. Land and tenements owned by the company were $50,000 additional. The transfer of title from the old company to the new took place on April 1, 1845, and at this time a new superintendent was brought to Lowell.

James B. Francis, the gifted engineer who had presided over the affairs of the Locks and Canals Company, did not remain to serve the Lowell Machine Shop. As an hydraulic engineer his future lay with the regulation of water power, and he was made agent of the new Locks and Canals Company. George Brownell, who had served the Locks and Canals Company as superintendent of machine-building since 1831, retired. Brownell's career went back to the very beginning of machine-building at Waltham, but in 1845 he was only fifty-three years old. His retirement or dismissal hinted at dissatisfaction with the manufacturing methods of the Shop as then practised; it also implied the desire of the new owners to make a break with the past. William A. Burke, master mechanic of the Amoskeag Manufacturing Company, was appointed superintendent of the Lowell Machine Shop and was charged with the responsibility for managing all company affairs at Lowell.[5]

The Course of Business

The Lowell Machine Shop was launched in a period of considerable business optimism which reflected the recovery from the great depression of 1837–43. The dividend rates of several of the large New England textile mills had jumped in 1844 and again in 1845.[6] Railroad securities were enjoying a mild boom. There was movement in the business world and progress in the scientific. William Mason was building a textile-machine shop in Taunton. The ambitious cotton-mill promotion at Lawrence, Massachusetts, had been launched with the fervid hope that here, twelve miles below Lowell on the Merrimack River, another Lowell might be created. The first telegraph line connecting Baltimore and Washington had been pronounced a success. Charles Goodyear was experimenting with rubber, and Elias Howe with a sewing machine. Cyrus McCormick was looking for a wider market for his reaper.

The promise implicit in the times was not generally fulfilled in

William A. Burke
First Agent of the Lowell Machine Shop

Main Shop of the Lowell Machine Shop
Probably in the 1860's or early 1870's

the months which followed the incorporation of the Lowell Machine Shop. The recovery movement of 1844 was attributed by Whig manufacturers in New England to the protective tariff of 1842. In 1844 Democratic James J. Polk had been elected to the Presidency, and in 1845, soon after his inauguration, there was disquieting talk of modifying the tariff to a revenue basis. No other single topic of the day occupied so fully the contemporary business mind, and the uncertainty which began to be evidenced in New England late in 1845 undoubtedly reflected anxiety over tariff schedules then under discussion.[7] Though optimism was not lacking, business trends were mixed, and a "wait-and-see" attitude prevailed. The first year of its business, which had commenced with such auspicious omens, proved to be one of merely nominal activity for the Lowell Machine Shop. Sales for the twelve months ending March 31, 1846, totaled only $177,787, but a part of this low volume may have been attributable to extensive factory alterations which interfered with production. The directors felt sufficiently confident of the future of the company to declare a 12 per cent dividend in April of 1846.

The ensuing year brought continued business uncertainty, but the reasons for the optimism of the directors became apparent. Late in 1846 some large orders had been booked, and the flow of orders continued at a comfortable level well into 1849. Chart II reveals the leap in sales which succeeded the hesitant first year of operations and shows the general trend of Machine Shop sales thereafter to 1860. As a measure of comparison, this chart also shows Warren and Pearson's index of wholesale commodity prices in the United States, one of the few available statistical series reflecting general business activity of the period.[8]

The dividend records of the Lowell Machine Shop, which are preserved in both the minutes of directors' meetings and company receipt books, confirm the trend of business revealed in Chart II.

The record of the Lowell Machine Shop in the 1845–60 period was occasionally at variance with the trend of contemporary business. Depressed conditions prevailed generally in 1846. In the following three years, which saw a thriving activity in the Shop, New England textile mills reported hard times. To President Polk's assertion that capital, under the new tariff of 1846, was yielding adequate

CHART II

Lowell Machine Shop Machinery Sales, 1846–1860

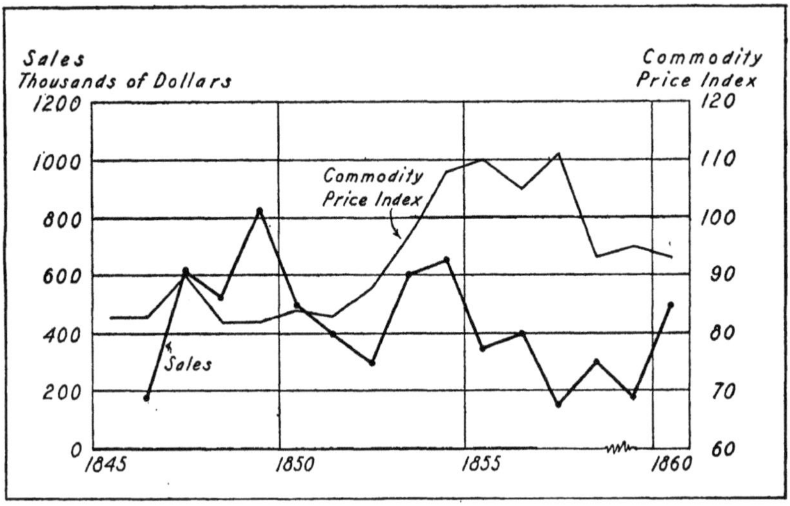

TABLE 9

DIVIDENDS, LOWELL MACHINE SHOP, 1846–1860

Year Ending March 31	Dividend[a] In Dollars	Dividend[a] As % of Capital Stock	Year Ending March 31	Dividend In Dollars	Dividend As % of Capital Stock
1846	36,000	12	1854	48,000	8
1847	125,000	25	1855	none	none
1848	100,000	20	1856	48,000	8
1849	60,000	10	1857	18,000	3
1850	36,000	6	1858	none	none
1851	24,000	4	1859	none	none
1852	18,000	3	1860	30,000	5
1853	36,000	6	....	......	....

[a] Average dividend, 1846–60: 7.3%.

Source: Lowell Machine Shop records, Directors' records.

and fair profits, the Lowell Whigs tartly retorted, "Our manufacturing interests have seldom or never been more prostrate." [9] The Mexican War expenditures were not popular in New England, and Lowell men were advised by the Whig *Journal* not to enlist. While Machine Shop stock was selling at a premium of from $125 to $150 over par in 1848, there were reports of low dividends and inactivity in the textile industry.[10] The Lowell companies which were purchasing heavily from the Shop in 1847 and 1848 were probably taking advantage of bad times and low prices to improve their mills.

After 1849 Machine Shop sales and dividends reflected little of the prosperity which prevailed throughout the country for the next four years. Lowell Machine Shop stock prices in the Boston market declined to a low of $200 in 1851 and did not go above par at any time until 1864. The entire decade following 1850 was one of confused trends. Business men looked for encouragement to the discovery of gold in California in 1848, the deluge of new inventions which poured into the United States Patent Office, the completion of 50,000 miles of telegraph lines, the extension of the railroad network, the modest but steady rise in commodity prices to 1857, and the increase in spindles in the United States from slightly more than three and a half million in 1850 to more than five million in 1860. Opposed to such favorable influences were the great political struggles of the day, in which many of the Lowell Machine Shop officers and stockholders participated actively. Lowell and Boston manufacturers were elated by the Whig triumph in 1848, but their elation was short-lived. In 1852 the Democrats were returned to office, and renewed attacks on the tariff ensued. If the general trend of business prosperity from 1850 to 1860 was upward, the Lowell Machine Shop generally failed to conform with the rise, while at the same time suffering greatly in the sharp reversal which took place in 1857 and 1858.

One indication of the prospects of the Machine Shop as appraised by investors at the time is provided by the trend of prices for the company's stock (Chart III). As in Chart II, the index of wholesale commodity prices is included for purposes of comparison.

Even a cursory examination of the Lowell Machine Shop in its environment reveals the necessity for looking beyond the broad trends of the day for an explanation of the company's performance. At the same time, the effect upon the Shop of those trends must be acknowledged, though it cannot be measured in terms of sales and profits. There is little doubt, for instance, that the generally unfavorable political climate of the day was a depressing influence on New England cotton mills, and hence on Lowell Machine Shop

CHART III

Trend of Lowell Machine Shop Stock Prices, 1845–1860

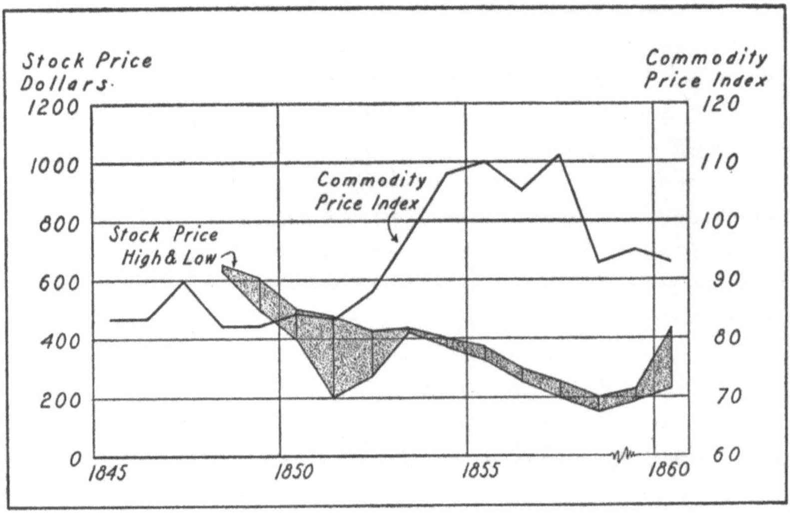

sales. The discovery of gold in 1848 had inflationary implications, yet the gold rush which followed stripped the city of Lowell of hundreds of its young men, and hampered operations in both the mills and the Machine Shop. The increase in the size of the textile industry held forth a promise of larger machinery orders, yet that very expansion led to bitter mill competition in the depression of 1857–58 which curtailed machinery sales. Beyond these indeterminable factors, however, lay other and more immediate reasons for the often puzzling variations in Machine Shop business.

Serving the Narrow Market

The Locks and Canals Company had made a start in tapping markets outside Lowell, but until 1845 by far the larger part of its business was confined to New England. This was also the case in 1846 and 1847, the first years for which information on Lowell Machine Shop customers is available. For the year ending March 31, 1847, sales were $617,000. Of this total $541,292, or 88 per cent, was accounted for by the Lowell mills alone.[11] Almost all of the remainder represented orders from the Boston Manufacturing Company at Waltham, the Essex Company at Lawrence, and the Great Falls Manufacturing Company and the Nashua Manufacturing Company in New Hampshire. Sales in Massachusetts comprised 95 per cent of total sales. No customer outside New England ordered so much as $1,000 of machinery. The tendency to seek orders outside Lowell, first noted in the Locks and Canals Company in the 1830's, had not progressed far. Like its predecessor, the Lowell Machine Shop was doing business on a restricted regional basis.

By 1860 the market for Lowell Machine Shop products had broadened, but only slightly. From 1854 to 1860, years for which sales information is available, Massachusetts customers accounted for approximately half of the machinery sold. Company order books showed customers in twenty-one States, Canada, and Mexico, but in these years 95 per cent of the Lowell Machine Shop machinery went to New England customers. This shift in emphasis from the Lowell market to the New England market was an entirely natural process arising out of the great expansion of the textile industry in other New England localities. That the shift was not more pronounced may be ascribed, in part, to the fact that although no large new mills were promoted in Lowell after 1846, expansion of existing mills there almost doubled the number of spindles in Lowell in the decade ending in 1855.[12]

From 1850 to 1860 the textile industry expanded at a greater rate than did the sales of the Lowell Machine Shop. Over this period total spindles in the United States increased by a third, while Shop sales were unstable and exhibited a tendency to decline. The restricted area serviced by the Shop may be an explanation, though statistics for both the Shop and the industry are too few and untrustworthy to prove the point. Such expansion as took place outside New England in this period resulted in few orders at Lowell. Even in New England, however, the Lowell Machine Shop was selling to a restricted market. The Providence and Fall River areas were in the orbit of competing shops such as Fales & Jenks, the Providence Machine Company, Whitin, and the Fall River Iron Works. Neither was the Shop strong in western Massachusetts, where large building programs were being launched. The concentration by the Lowell Machine Shop on a handful of very large mills in Massachusetts, Maine, and New Hampshire may have been poor policy at a time when other areas and other mills showed unmistakable signs of progress.

Products and Technology

Between 1845 and 1860 the Lowell Machine Shop added one new series of products to its line, dropped another, and gave added attention to a third. This period and the war years which followed saw the greatest diversification of product in the history of machine-building at Lowell. In this period it was said of the Shop that everything from a jew's harp to a locomotive was made there. The statement was almost literally true. In these years, however, technological progress, both at Lowell and in the industry, was exceptionally slow in comparison with preceding years.

A steady flow of inventions was recorded in the textile industry after 1845, but few of these were individually important and none had the effect of revolutionizing the industry. None of the more important inventions appears to have originated in the Lowell Machine Shop, which continued the Locks and Canals policy of purchasing manufacturing rights from inventors outside the company. The textile industry, however, was far from being technologically static.

Perhaps the most significant movement under way in these years was the shift from throstle to ring spinning frames. In 1855 the Lowell Machine Shop sold 112 spinning frames comprising 14,336 spindles. All were throstle frames. Before five years had elapsed, orders for ring spinning had become larger than for the old-style frames. The advantage of the ring over the throstle frame was not so great, however, as to make the substitution a sudden necessity for the industry.[13]

The most important single invention of the period was that of the so-called "self-stripper" for cleaning card flats, patented by George

Wellman in 1854 and built under licensing arrangement by several machine shops soon thereafter.[14] While this invention was a relatively inexpensive attachment and did not materially assist in raising the volume of orders, it did represent a definite technological advance and perhaps opened the way for the development at a later date of the revolving flat card. Unlike the Wellman stripper, however, the various improvements in looms which were being made at this time did result in large machinery sales. No one of these loom improvements produced widespread changes in the textile industry, but the cumulative effect appears to have been a more rapid rate of obsolescence in looms than in any other type of machine.[15] What part the Lowell Machine Shop played in this progress cannot be ascertained. In 1855, loom sales constituted the largest part of the Shop's business, and in the ten succeeding years they increased steadily in relation to the rest of the line.

An important evolution in the roving process was forecast in these pre-Civil War years and reflected in Lowell Machine Shop sales, but did not gain momentum until later. The essence of this evolution was the introduction into America from England of greatly improved roving frames, which were destined to replace the American fly frame or speeders. The English machines were of three types, but all were designated as "English bobbin-and-fly frames" or, simply, "English fly frames." The change was directed primarily at producing the finer yarns required by the market and at remedying the inflexibility of the old-style speeder, which could be changed from one size of roving to another only by an intricate adjustment of bobbin and spindle.[16] A few of the new type of machines were built and sold by the Lowell Machine Shop as early as 1857. The speeder, however, continued to be manufactured and sold for some years after the Civil War.

In the field of picking and opening machinery a new firm began to make its products known. The shop of Richard Kitson in Lowell was producing an improved cotton opener, and Kitson's picker was pushing Whitin's out of the field. This development was of no particular significance to the Lowell Machine Shop, however, for Lowell had rarely built pickers or openers and owned no patents that could be made obsolete by Kitson's improvements.

Any appraisal of the rate of technical progress in these years is difficult, and conclusions derived from such an appraisal must be tentative. It would seem, however, that from 1845 to 1860 technical evolution was slow and confined to improvements which a mill could conceivably postpone for several years without endangering its competitive position. If this was actually the case, the weakness of the replacement market (in contrast to the market provided by new mills or the expansion of old mills) may present an additional explanation for the indifferent sales record of the Lowell Machine Shop between 1850 and 1860.

There appears to have been a conscious effort on the part of the shop to build up sales volume in these uncertain years by the addition of new product lines. Since the very beginning the Shop had built many of its own machine tools. The extension of this practice to the building of tools for others was therefore a natural step, and one which appears to have been undertaken immediately upon the formation of the Lowell Machine Shop in 1845. William B. Bement was brought by Superintendent Burke from Amoskeag and began immediately to design a line of basic machine tools for sale by the Shop. Bement's work in Lowell from 1845 to 1851, when he left to form his own machine-tool company in Philadelphia, was outstanding, and the machine tools of the Lowell Machine Shop enjoyed a reputation comparable to those of the specialized toolmakers in the Providence area.[17]

In 1857 the Shop commenced the manufacture of a complete line of paper machinery. This, too, was a natural step to take. This machinery was well within the capacity of the Shop to build, and the market for the machinery lay close to the textile-mill areas where most of the Shop's cotton machinery was being sold. This instance of product diversification, coming as it did in the midst of a severe depression, suggests even more than does the manufacture of machine tools a conscious reaching out for new markets to supplement the sale of cotton machinery. Unfortunately there is no adequate record of the success of the new line. Paper-machinery sales appear, however, to have constituted but a very small portion of total sales.

Diversification brought its problems in an age in which the intricacies of manufacturing techniques were increasing and specialized effort was being advanced as a competitive necessity. Locomotives were the first of the Lowell Machine Shop's products to feel the effects of specialized competition. The experience with locomotives probably would have marked the turning point in company product policy had not the Civil War intervened to postpone the inevitable simplification of the line.

Between 1845 and 1854 the Lowell Machine Shop produced sixty-one locomotives.[18] Orders were particularly heavy in the early 1850's, reflecting the flow of capital and the extension of rail lines into the Upper Mississippi Valley. Activity in the nation's railroads, however, had encouraged a great expansion of locomotive building. In 1855 there were forty-four locomotive works in the country.[19] As in the past, some textile-machinery builders had entered the field. In 1855 the Amoskeag, Lawrence, and Mason shops were all turning out locomotives. By this time, also, the specialized builders in New Jersey and Pennsylvania were beginning to forge ahead. The decline of New England's promising locomotive industry was foreshadowed by the rise of large locomotive shops close to coal and iron supplies and strategically located in respect to the expanding railroad market in the Middle West. The triumph of specialization over part-time effort was clear-cut in the rapidly changing technology of locomotive manufacture. After 1855 the Lowell Machine Shop appears to have devoted little attention to locomotives, and after 1861 it withdrew from the field entirely.

2. The Shop at War, 1861–1865

On April 19, 1861, the Sixth Massachusetts Regiment was attacked by mobs as it marched through Baltimore on its way to the defense of Washington. For Lowell, represented in the "Bloody Sixth" by a company which included many Machine Shop men, this was the beginning of the Rebellion. A week later, the directors in Boston were appraising a greatly altered business situation.

There was much confusion, and the venerable Merrimack Manufacturing Company took the lead in what was to be immortalized in Lowell history as a "stupendous blunder." Sharing the common Northern belief of "peace in sixty days," Merrimack closed its mills, dismissed its operatives, and began to liquidate its cotton at the rapidly rising prices which prevailed. Cowley, the Lowell historian, says, "The blunders of the older company were not only copied, but exaggerated and intensified to a fatal degree." [20] As the War went on, many efforts were made to start up the mills, but from 1861 to 1865 two-thirds of the spindles at Lowell remained idle and large sums were lost by experiments with cassimeres and hosiery. Not all the largest Lowell Machine Shop customers followed the precedent set by the mills at Lowell, but Shop records show a sharp decline in orders for textile machinery in 1861. Nevertheless, after a period of readjustment lasting through 1861, the War was, in historian Cowley's words, "improved by this company to the utmost advantage." [21] Table 10 shows orders during the War years for the three most important types of textile machines made by the Shop.[22]

TABLE 10

SALE OF LOWELL MACHINE SHOP LOOMS, CARDS, AND SPINNING FRAMES
1860–1865

	1860	1861	1862	1863	1864	1865
Looms............	1,049	141	1,111	314	978	1,838
Cards..............	274	252	219	204	none	192
Spinning Frames....	358	48	59	83	17	185

In 1860, the best year since 1855, the Shop had 500 employees. In 1863, when the Lowell mills were generally inactive and the 10,000 mill operatives released by the closings were seeking reëmployment in Lowell or elsewhere, the Shop had 800 men on the payroll and was doing an active business.[23] Sales increased from about $500,000 in 1860 to over $1,000,000 in 1865, the first year in the company's history in which the output of the Shop had reached the million mark. Dividends for these five years were 5 per cent in 1860, 8 per cent in 1861, 6 per cent in 1862, 9 per cent in 1863, and 8 per cent in 1864 and 1865. Company stock rose in price from an 1861 high of $375 to $550 in 1864, from whence it declined in 1865 to par ($500). Compared to the record of many Northern manufacturing concerns in the war years this prosperity was far from spectacular. The performance of the Shop warrants explanation, however, in view of the disruption of normal textile-machinery markets.

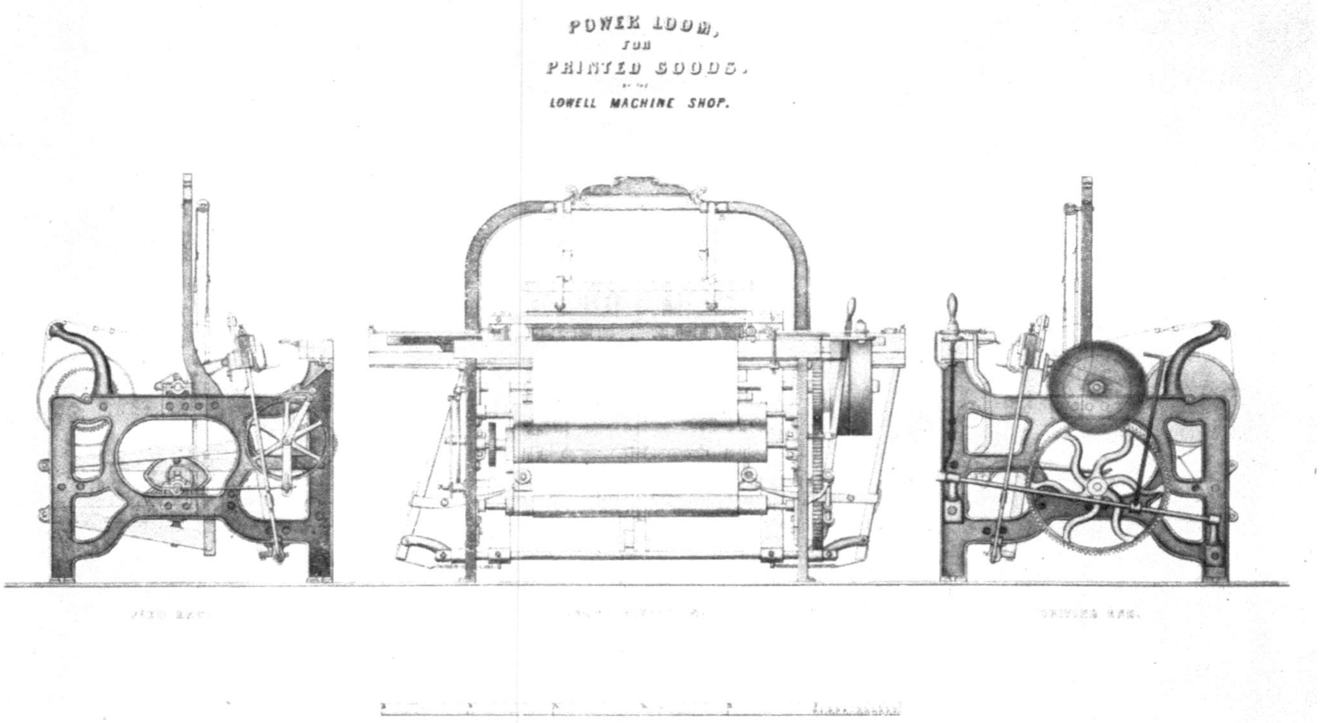

POWER LOOM FOR PRINTED GOODS
As built by Lowell Machine Shop in the 1840's and 1850's

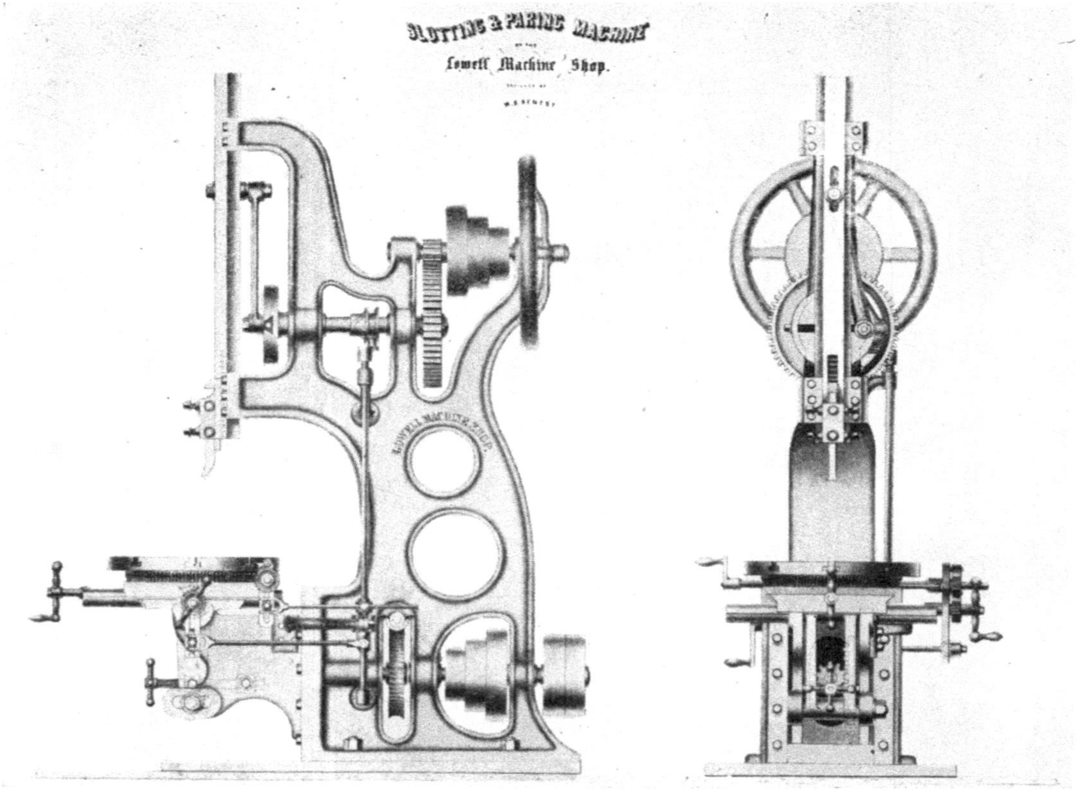

Slotting and Paring Machine

Designed by William B. Bement and built by Lowell Machine Shop in 1850's and 1860's

The Shop took few direct war contracts from the United States Government. This policy was in contrast to that of the Mason Machine Works and the Amoskeag Manufacturing Company machine shop, both of which turned out many thousands of rifled muskets and carbines under government contract. The Holyoke Machine Shop of John C. Whitin, however, pursued a policy similar to that of Lowell, accepting relatively few government contracts, and confined these chiefly to machine tools for the Springfield Arsenal. The Lowell Machine Shop filled one order from the Springfield Arsenal for 25,000 steel ramrods, and company tradition has it that the great turrets for the famous ironclad *Monitor* were turned in Lowell. Unfortunately, company records do not confirm this claim. In September, 1864, the Lowell Machine Shop contracted with one James Tetlow of East Boston to "Finish work for 2 turrets for the Quinsigamond according to plans and specifications to be furnished by him."[24] If this 3,200-ton ironclad was ever completed, it appears not to have been commissioned as a United States warship, for there is no record of its subsequent career. It was probably this contract which gave rise to the *Monitor* story, a forgivable perversion of historical fact inspired by pride in a notable engineering feat.[25]

Certain other contracts were placed with this same Tetlow for specially designed machine tools. These contracts were written, but later changes were verbally authorized by a Naval officer who subsequently embarked upon a four-year cruise and was unable to substantiate the Shop's claim on the government for reimbursement under the amended contracts. A controversy wore on through an interminable exchange of correspondence and finally was settled in 1871 to the mutual dissatisfaction of all parties concerned and an actual loss of $2,200 to the Lowell Machine Shop. War business, even in those years, was not without its tribulations.

Under the impetus of war demand, sales of machine tools and miscellaneous other products expanded greatly. These sales were made to various foundries and railroads, rather than to the government or its various agencies. Orders for drills, lathes, shapers, planers, and slotting machines increased noticeably, and many new products were turned out. In 1863, in addition to the almost complete line of cotton machinery and the complete line of paper machinery which were being built, the Shop turned out Jonval and Swain turbine water wheels, hydraulic presses, boilers, locomotive tanks, railway switches, hydrants, pill-dispensing machines, indigo grinders, sugar mills, sewing-machine needles, set screws, factory elevators, fire escapes, iron bridges, force pumps, locomotive and steamship cranks, double gang saws, pony steam engines, fire engines, ventilator fans, rotary pumps, wool cards, and a wide variety of mill gearing, shafting, and miscellaneous iron construction shapes. In this year also the Shop supplied the Commonwealth of Massachusetts with derricks, stone and striking hammers, shafting, pulleys, couplings, and cranks for the construction of the Hoosac tunnel.

No one of these products was sold in large quantities, but the cumulative volume of business which they represented helps to explain the activity of the Shop in the war years. Sales of textile machines, moreover, continued in fair volume, despite the disruption of the prewar market. Many mills continued to operate as best they could with the restricted cotton supplies. Other mills reopened and operated a limited number of spindles. Many of the Shop's old customers took advantage of large profits, realized from liquidation of inventories, to replace obsolete machinery or even expand their facilities. Some orders for machinery resulted from attempts by various mills to turn out new products or to utilize low-grade Indian cotton. Much repair work was also done, and the sale of replacement parts for machines was unusually heavy. A considerable part of the repair business consisted of replacing the wooden frames of various machines with iron frames, adding the Wellman attachment to cards, and otherwise modernizing old machinery. In the summer of 1862 the Boott Mills commenced to modernize two of its five mills, and in the next two years purchased $212,000 of machinery alone, in addition to large amounts of gearing and mill work. This order is clearly reflected in the figures for 1862 in Table 10. The Lawrence Manufacturing Company in Lowell and the Pacific Mills in Lawrence also added much new equipment, and there was a steady trickle of orders from other companies in Lowell, Lawrence, and Nashua. By 1864 the cotton supply had ceased to be critical, and by April, 1865, the demand for textile machinery was greater than at any time before in the Shop's history.

3. HIGH PROFITS AND A GREAT DEPRESSION: THE SHOP FROM 1865 TO 1879

Reaping the Harvest

The twenty years which followed the end of the Civil War were the most prosperous in the history of the Lowell Machine Shop. Not since the days when the Locks and Canals Company was exploiting the Merrimack Falls had such profits been made. Unlike the earlier experience these profits accrued from machine-building activity alone. As had been the case a generation before, however, a remarkable record was achieved in the face of general business uncertainty.

Lowell Machine Shop sales broke sharply from the record high of over a million dollars for the year ending March 31, 1865, declining a third in the following twelve months. This falling-off of business was general. There was monetary instability and a declining price level. In 1866 the prices of textile products broke, and in that year and the next business suffered a postwar recession.[26] The Lowell Machine Shop had emerged from the War period in a healthy financial condition, and the modest reserves built up by the prosperity then ending carried the Shop through the period of adjustment which followed 1865.

Conditions following the postwar depression of 1866–67 favored the machine-builders. Against a background of high tariff protection American business in general and the textile industry in particular entered a period of feverish activity. The number of spindles in the United States increased 45 per cent between 1860 and 1874, and the industry became more firmly entrenched than ever before in the large mills of New England — that very segment of the industry where the Lowell Machine Shop had always been strong.[27] From 1870 to 1874, when spindles in the United States increased 25 per cent, these conditions combined to produce the greatest activity the Shop had yet experienced.[28] The fact that John C. Whitin at this same time was advising customers of the Whitin Machine Works to order English machinery suggests that the activity was general throughout American shops.[29] In 1873 Lowell Machine Shop sales

CHART IV

Trend of Lowell Machine Shop Stock Prices, 1861–1879

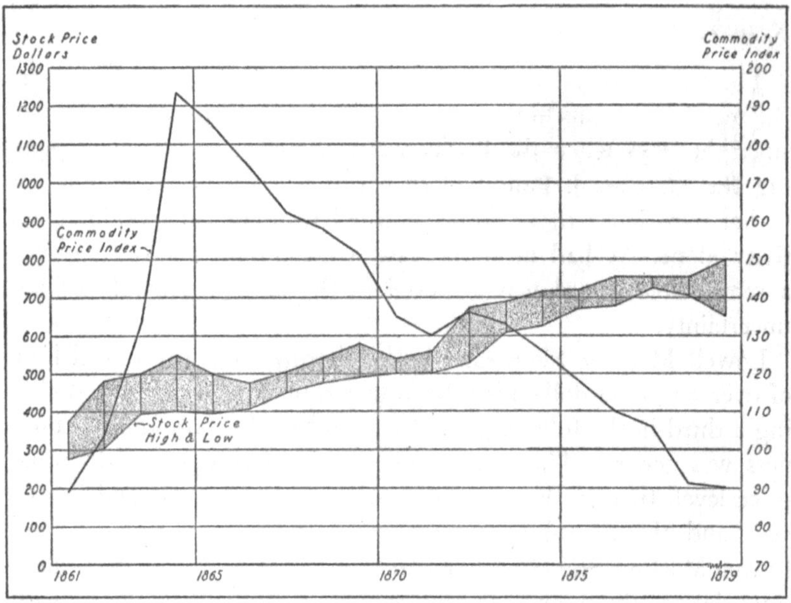

exceeded one and a half million dollars. A 20 per cent dividend was distributed and sales remained high, but the peak had been passed. The profits and activity of 1874 reflected contracts placed in 1873, before panic had struck a crushing blow at business confidence.

The six-year depression which followed the monetary collapse in the fall of 1873 cut at the very heart of American business. Failures and near-failures were numerous among the customers of the Lowell Machine Shop. In November, 1876, the treasurer advised the superintendent, "From present appearances there is no great hope or expectation of many or lucrative orders, and we must go along and make as small a loss as possible." By 1877 the orders for machinery were only a third of the 1873 peak, and the treasurer was confessing, "We are pretty hard up at the Shop for jobs." In 1879 an even lower total was recorded. Nevertheless, profits as a percentage of sales were higher in the depression than in the five years preceding it, and dividends from 1874 to 1879 averaged slightly more than 22 per cent of capital. In 1879 the accumulated surplus on the books was larger than it had been in 1873. The crash of security prices in 1873 left Lowell Machine Shop stock unaffected. From a new high of $690 per share in 1873 the stock rose steadily through the depression to $800 in 1879, while the margin between bidding and asking prices narrowed appreciably. Chart IV shows the trend of stock prices as compared with the Warren & Pearson commodity-price index.

What lay behind this out-of-season prosperity? One obvious answer is the sound, conservative financial policy of the Shop. This policy will be considered in detail in later paragraphs. Another explanation is suggested by a letter to George Richardson, Shop superintendent, from General Stevenson, the treasurer. This letter, dated November 14, 1873, gives a good feeling for the times and provides an insight into Shop product and employment policy as well:

> I have yours of the 13th inst., with schedule of such machy as you would like to go on and build in the absence of orders. While I see many objections to departing from our rule, which is to build no machinery excepting such as may have been ordered & contracted for by purchasers, I should be ready to make an exception on account of the probabilities involved in the present gloomy prospects of our principal customers, the cotton manufacturers, with a view to furnishing employment to a portion of our hands.
>
> But, being satisfied that one of the necessary and certain results of the existing state of things must be a very serious reduction in the wages of labor, I should not feel justified in building machinery in anticipation of future orders (for the sole purpose of furnishing occupation to the hands) unless it could be done (the work) at a reduction of at least ten per cent from the prices heretofore, recently, paid. With this concession (10%) I should justify you in going on & building the machinery specified in your schedule after having filled all existing orders for such machines, although I cannot doubt that the permanent reduction of wages will be much larger than 10%.

Appreciation of the need to cut costs sharply and quickly is reflected in this letter. Success in doing so is indicated by the subsequent maintenance of a high profit level in the face of declining sales. The specific economies in manufacturing operations which brought this about will be considered later.

A comparison of the performance of the Lowell Machine Shop with that of the Shop's customers in this depression indicates that the short-term prosperity of the Shop was not completely dependent upon the existence of prosperity in the textile industry.[30] The more solidly entrenched mills often seized upon periods of inactivity to modernize their manufacturing facilities, for in such periods machinery prices were usually low and plant alterations could be made without serious work stoppage. Moreover, the very fact of severe depression in the textile industry may have provided a cushion against a correspondingly severe collapse in the textile-machinery market. At this time (1874–79) technological improvements were being promoted by the machine shops which could neither be ignored nor postponed for long by any mill which wished to maintain its position in a bitterly competitive market. Competition in the textile industry had always been a strong ally of the machine shops. In this particular depression period, adoption of improved machines became almost mandatory in cost-conscious mills and may well have compensated for lack of new mill construction.

Contemporary observations support this explanation for the relative prosperity of the machine shops. A protest was raised by mill owners against the foisting of further improvements on the textile industry by the textile machinery industry. This was not a new cry — nor did it die out in the nineteenth century. The protest was unfair in that it failed to admit how many of these improvements had actually originated in textile mills rather than in the machine shops. If this complaint against the necessity for discarding so much machinery so long before it had worn out was short-sighted, it was, at least, understandable.[31] In the depression year 1866 the protest was extended into a forthright charge that machinery orders were being obtained under duress:[32]

In mills of large capital, influence of many kinds exerted by various parties, constrain the managers to great expenditures for frequent costly changes of machines and modes of operation, to the throwing out of much still serviceable and valuable machinery. . . . Whether we are unduly influenced, in this regard, by the pertinacity of inventors, patentees, dealers in patented articles, or parties interested to keep machine shops running, or the pride of our help and overseers in making a good show and using nice appliances, it is scarcely proper to spend time now in enquiring. Suffice to say, that complicated machines, and complicated processes for doing simple things, are fair objects of opposition.

Of all the textile-machine shops in America at this time the Lowell Machine Shop was the most vulnerable to such a charge. Of no other shop could it be said, in 1866, that its directorate and ownership was so constituted that pressure could be brought to bear on most of northern and western New England's largest mills. The fact that the charge was made by Franklin Forbes, agent of the Lancaster Mills, is particularly interesting. Lancaster was a Lowell Machine Shop customer in which Lowell Machine Shop directors and stockholders were financially interested.[33] Unfortunately, although the extent of inter-relationships in the New England textile industry have been studied, the true operating results of the inbreeding and cross-breeding will probably never be known and this interesting charge cannot be easily confirmed or refuted.[34]

Table 11 presents a summary of operating results of the 1865–79 period. The paragraphs following describe the important operational details underlying those results.

Markets and How They Were Reached

The narrow geographic limits of the Lowell Machine Shop market had begun to break down to a noticeable extent by 1879. The chief excursion outside the New England area was into the expanding Southern market. This story will be reserved for the following chapter, for it was not until after 1880 that the growth of this market became a matter of dominant importance in Shop affairs, as in the textile machinery industry. At this point it is sufficient to note that for the five years from 1866 to 1870, inclusive, 74 per cent of sales were made in New England and the Middle Atlantic States (in contrast to 99 per cent in New England alone in 1847), 15½ per cent in States south of the Mason-Dixon line, and 10½ per cent in the Middle West or in foreign countries.

In 1879 the Lowell Machine Shop sold machinery to three hundred and eighty customers in twenty-six States, Mexico, and Canada, in comparison with two hundred and twenty-five customers

TABLE 11

SALES, PROFITS, AND DIVIDENDS, LOWELL MACHINE SHOP, 1865–1879

Year Ending March 31	Sales[a]	Net Profit[b]	Net Profit as % of Sales	Dividends	Dividends as % of Capital
1865	$1,220,000	([c])	....	$ 48,000	8
1866	766,700	([c])	....	72,000	12
1867	1,082,800	([c])	....	72,000	12
1868	943,900	([c])	....	72,000	12
1869	869,500	$ 85,300	9.8	72,000	12
1870	1,042,900	108,000	10.4	72,000	12
1871	981,800	129,700	13.2	72,000	12
1872	1,262,000	145,800	11.6	72,000	12
1873	1,598,600	152,100	9.5	120,000	20
1874	1,573,400	280,200	17.2	174,000	29
1875	760,800	127,700	16.8	72,000	12
1876	824,200	119,400	14.5	72,000	12
1877	583,200	100,400	17.2	240,000	40
1878	815,600	95,000	10.4	60,000	10
1879	571,100	62,100	10.9[d]	240,000	30

Total sales, 1869–79	$10,883,100
Average annual sales, 1869–79	989,373
Total net profit, 1869–79	1,405,700 (12.92% of total sales)
Total dividends, 1869–79	1,266,000
Average annual dividend as per cent of capital, 1869–79	18.27%

[a] Sales for 1865 estimated; other years actual. These figures represent gross sales of all machinery and parts. Returns and allowances appear to have been negligible. Sales of paper machinery and miscellaneous products are included, but were so small a percentage of the total that the figures above may be considered to indicate without appreciable bias the trend of cotton textile machinery orders.

[b] Balance of Profit & Loss account.

[c] No data.

[d] After $34,000 loss on defaulted order.

Source: Lowell Machine Shop records, Ledgers and journals.

in twenty-one States and Canada in 1860. Immediately following the Civil War the large orders came from Lowell and New England mills. In the late 1870's these mills still accounted for most of the large orders, but an occasional sale of comparable dimension was made in the South. (See Appendix 10.) As in the past, few sales were made to the Rhode Island market, where competitors were strongly entrenched. Neither does the Shop seem to have participated in the tremendous building program in Fall River, where (between 1870 and 1872) fifteen new mills were organized and the number of spindles in operation doubled.[35]

There is no way of ascertaining to what extent the gradual expansion of markets was a result of direct action by the Shop or how much a natural consequence of an expanding textile industry. The latter seems to have been the stronger influence, for selling methods in the 1865–79 period were far from aggressive. No marketing organization existed and no salesmen or agents were employed. Customers came to Lowell to buy their machinery, and although the treasurer carefully answered all inquiries for machinery, there are comparatively few letters in the correspondence files which were written unsolicited to potential customers. Personal contacts by the treasurer, the superintendent, and the directors served in lieu of sales promotion.

When the Shop began to outgrow its adjacent market areas some advertising was done. This took two forms — paid advertising in trade journals and participation in the various regional and national fairs and exhibitions which became so numerous in this period. Few trade-paper advertisements have been found prior to 1880. After 1872 the Shop was advertising in *Dockham's Directory,* a yearly catalogue of textile mills and mill suppliers. The Boston *Journal of Commerce* also carried Lowell Machine Shop advertisements in the 1870's, and the correspondence of the treasurer indicates that by 1877 the Shop was advertising in Southern papers. Though some machine shops at this time were illustrating their advertisements with cuts of machinery or plant, the Lowell Machine Shop confined itself to the more usual unadorned listing of the products manufactured.

Fairs and exhibitions occupy a prominent place in the evolution of American marketing, serving as they did to place the products of American manufacturers before the public in the best and most direct way possible in the pre-catalogue era.[36] Several regional and national organizations devoted to the promotion of domestic manufactures sponsored yearly fairs. One of these, the American Institute Fair of 1850, in New York, is the earliest at which the Lowell Machine Shop is known to have exhibited. The notice of this exhibit, published in the *Scientific American,* was probably as good advertising as the Shop could have aspired to at the time.[37] In 1876 the Philadelphia Centennial Exhibition stirred the entire country, for both the extent and the quality of American products shown. The Lowell Machine Shop is said to have exhibited machinery there, although the extent of the exhibit is not known.[38]

Such scanty information as can be found about promotional techniques shows that the Lowell Machine Shop was more conservative than some competitors but, in general, tended to approximate industry practice. Whether the same could be said of the terms granted customers is problematical, since little is known about this phase of marketing in the textile machinery industry. A comparison with the Whitin Machine Works is possible, however, after 1870.

In the prosperous early 1870's the Lowell Machine Shop was pursuing a one-price-for-all policy. No deviation is discernible in prices, length of credits, or interest charges between large purchasers and small, old customers and new. The treasurer constantly reiterated the desire of the Shop to sell for cash only, but many sales, including most of the larger ones, were settled by the payment of one-third to one-half of the order in cash and the remainder by notes of from six to twelve months, bearing interest at 7 per cent. Cash sales appear to have commanded no discount, but the definition of cash was a loose one and left the customer at least thirty days of grace. Payment was due upon notice that the machinery had been completed and was usually made by a draft payable at a Boston bank. Drafts payable in other cities than Boston or New York were not acceptable. This was partly a matter of convenience and partly a reflection of the long-standing Boston distrust of country banks.

If the customer was one in which the Shop had complete confidence, notes given in partial settlement of accounts were required to be endorsed only by the treasurer of the purchasing mill. On new accounts, and particularly on accounts with Southern mills, the endorsement of all the directors was demanded. No capital stock, bonds, or cotton were accepted in part payment of machinery, and for a time conditional sales contracts were demanded of new Southern customers. These protected the Lowell Machine Shop by retention of title to machinery until final settlement. Occasionally mortgage liens on plant were demanded as security for machinery sold on credit.

These terms were similar in nature to those granted by the Whitin Machine Works and, as with Whitin, were liberalized during the depression of 1873–79.[39] The easing of terms after 1874, however, was not marked. In 1877 Treasurer Stevenson was writing:

> Of course each case must stand upon its own merits but where parties can give us satisfactory reference and have mills and machinery in profitable operation, not encumbered by mortgage we are willing to sell on the payment of ⅓ or ¼ cash before delivery of machinery, the balance in two or three equal payments in notes of 6, 9 or 12 months secured by mortgages of the machinery, with 7% interest — note payable in Boston.

Preferential treatment in the matter of prices and terms also became a necessity, but the Shop reduced the cash down-payment only for the best of its customers. In 1876, for example, the Atlantic Mills in Lawrence purchased $200,000 of machinery for 10 per cent in cash, the balance payable 5 per cent monthly. In at least one case where a customer obtained cash for machinery payments by borrowing from a Boston bank, the Lowell Machine Shop "went on" the customer's note, guaranteeing thereby that the bank would be paid and the customer protected in case the bank called for payment before maturity.[40] Even in the depths of the depression, however, the Shop was conservative in quoting terms. A few credits of from twelve to twenty-four months were given, but most sales were still made on shorter-term notes.

Other terms quoted customers were similar to those being extended by Whitin. All customers were charged 5 per cent to cover boxing, freight from Lowell to wharf, and placing on board. Insurance charges were paid by the customer, as were the traveling expenses and board of the erectors who were sent from the Shop to get the machinery running in the customer's mill.[41]

The liberalizing of credit terms after 1874 was one indication of increasing competition in the textile machinery industry. Before this time competition for markets had not been an important factor in the affairs of the Lowell Machine Shop. The severe depression in the 1870's, however, marked the end of the virtually continuous sellers' market in machinery which had existed for almost a half-century. Regional influence was to continue; regionalism itself, which saw the flourishing of local monopolies in the machinery-building trade, was ended. The end had long been forecast by the steady improvement of transportation facilities and by growth in the machinery industry itself.

In 1879 that industry had assumed a definite pattern, in which the Lowell Machine Shop occupied a unique and powerful position. The strength of the Shop lay not in its size but in the fact that it made and sold a complete line of cotton-textile machinery and furnished mill plans and engineering service. Few other shops in the country could match the Lowell line, and the few that did aspire to match it appear not to have been strong competitors or comparable in size and general reputation.[42] The completeness of the line was a challenge as well as a boon. The convenience and economy of ordering a complete cotton mill from one shop was great, but not great enough to permit that shop to offer machines of a quality substantially inferior to that of machines built by the more specialized shops. When such inferiority developed, as was the case with the various pickers and openers which the Lowell Shop was making in the early 1870's, the basis of the Shop's chief advantage was threatened. If more than two types of Lowell machines were so poor that buyers were forced to get them elsewhere, the claim of being a supplier of complete mills was meaningless. The Lowell Machine Shop, however, maintained its somewhat precarious position. Although for almost every type of machine some supplier could be found who excelled the Shop in quality of product, this fact did not spell trouble as long as the superiority was not too great, and as long as the various specialists did not merge. When this latter circumstance actually came to pass at the turn of the century, the Lowell Machine Shop found itself in a hopeless competitive position.[43]

The chief competitors of the Lowell Machine Shop in 1879 were those machine shops which manufactured most, but not all, of the important machine types. The Mason Machine Works in Taunton was one of these; the Whitin Machine Works was another. Both these shops lacked only roving machinery, and both were rapidly achieving a size comparable to that of the Lowell Shop.[44] Some specialized manufacturers such as the Providence Machine Company (roving and spinning machinery) provided sharp but limited competition. Another group of shops concentrated their efforts upon one machine. The Fales & Jenks Machine Company (spinning) and the Crompton Loom Works were competitors of this type. By 1879, too, a new competitive element was present in the form of the specialized mill engineer, such as A. D. Lockwood, of Providence, who stepped into the industry to offer not machines but plans and technical advice. Thus the Lowell Machine Shop found itself ringed with competitors, no one of which produced so many types of machines and no one of which sold, in total, so much machinery, but each of which was encroaching on some segment of the Shop's business.[45]

The trend of the textile machinery industry had been toward a steadily increasing number of specialized shops and a great expansion in total output. Census statisticians reported that the number of establishments manufacturing cotton and woolen machinery in 1870 was 176 per cent greater than in 1860, and that the product of those establishments was 272 per cent larger. Between 1870 and 1882, despite the depression intervening, output nearly doubled again, but few new companies were entering the field and many had been forced to retire.[46] Competition was becoming keen, and was centering in the larger shops.

The English had also entered the American market. Just when foreign competition became troublesome is not clear. The legal bans imposed by England on machinery exports were lifted in 1845. By 1870 the machine-makers had become intensely interested in tariff rates, not only as they affected customers but as they affected themselves. In that year the treasurer of the Lowell Machine Shop wrote:

> . . . the severest competition with which we have to contend is with the English Machine Builders, who are enabled to underbid us on the lower rates of interest, the lower price of materials (chiefly iron) and the lower wages of labor in England as compared with this country.

At a later date William A. Burke, then treasurer of the Shop, stated that although virtually no English machinery had been installed in Lowell mills, yet from 1868 to 1875 two-fifths of the machinery installed in American mills was English, and from 1875 to 1878 one-fourth was English.[47]

These estimates by the machine-builders themselves of the extent of English competition were possibly exaggerated for political purposes. There is no doubt, however, that English competition in post-Civil-War years was keen in specific types of machines such as the mule, the fly frame, and the slasher. Moreover, at least one English firm, that of Howard & Bullough, was offering a complete line of cotton machinery to American mills. The presence of English machinery in the American market aggravated a competitive situation which, in the late 1870's, had already begun to call forth far greater marketing efforts than had ever been required before. The climax of the English threat came after 1879, however, and is considered in Chapter VII.

Machinery Improvements

In the years from 1865 to 1879 four major developments occurred in textile machinery. The first of these was the introduction of the English slasher in 1870; the second was the invention of the Foss & Pevey card, patented in 1875. The third was the further adoption of the English fly frames — a movement which had its origin in earlier years and its conclusion later. The fourth and most important was in the field of spinning. The change from throstle to ring spinning had been made in many mills by 1860, but the spinning frames installed then were made obsolete by the revolution in spindles in the late 1870's and the continuing improvements thereafter. The number of important inventions patented in this period was small in all fields except spinning. Nevertheless, the treasurer of the Lowell Machine Shop reported, in 1880, that nearly all the machinery in use in Lowell mills in 1860 had been replaced and that 25 and perhaps 30 per cent of the cotton machinery built by the Shop was to take the place of obsolete machines.[48]

The Lowell Machine Shop did much to hasten the adoption of both the English slasher and the Foss & Pevey card. Both came at a providential time and were welcomed as a source of revenue in time of depression. So large and complex was the former machine that there was no rush on the part of American shops to build it. The Lowell Shop was the first to undertake its manufacture, soon after 1870, and never relinquished the lead thus obtained. So efficient was this machine in performing the function of sizing the warp yarn that in less than ten years the old-style dresser had been driven from the market.[49]

The American Foss & Pevey card was an answer to the comment that the cards then in use in American mills were, with the exception of Wellman's automatic stripping device, the same as those used in Samuel Slater's day.[50] This statement, of course, was not literally true, for many improvements such as the lickerin (to separate the cotton fibers being fed into the card) and more and larger flats to increase the carding area had been added. The basic principles of Slater's card, however, had not been changed — nor were they in the Foss & Pevey card, which, by the addition of flats on the under as well as the top side of the main cylinder, increased the carding area still further. The Lowell Machine Shop may have assisted in the development of this card; it was said to have been the first to build it.[51] In 1879 the Shop sold three hundred and twelve of the new type of card, in comparison with two hundred of the old.

In the 1865–79 period the Shop continued to expand its sales of coarse, intermediate, and fine speeders — the answer to the new specialized English fly frames. The English type of frames were occasionally built by the Shop, but the claim continued to be made that the speeder, as modified, was superior to the imported fly frame. The Shop also participated, in these years, in the still spreading popularity of the mule for spinning filling. In 1870 a peak in mule sales of 24,648 spindles was reached, as compared with 52,808 ring frame spindles. In 1879, sales were 13,317 mule spindles as compared with 56,672 ring frame spindles. The declining proportion of mules to ring frames in the latter year indicated that the trend had run its course.[52]

These fields of technical advancement were all of minor importance in comparison with the evolution of the spindle — unquestionably the most important and spectacular development in the industry since the prolific 1820's. The spindle evolution changed the course of two industries and culminated in the near domination of one by the firm of George Draper & Son, of Hopedale, Massachusetts.

The background of the spindle story is technically complex, but the essence lies in the substitution of a light-weight, high-speed spindle for the heavy spindle hitherto used, with tremendous attendant gains in productivity and savings in power.[53] Textile mills were immediately faced with the necessity of making the change or being driven out of business. Textile-machine shops scrambled to copy the new idea, fought the Draper domination of the spindle field with every means at their disposal, and lost.

The spindle battle of the 1870's grew out of the not unusual situation where several inventors, working independently, produced similar devices at nearly the same time. The controversy directly involved three inventors, Pearl, Sawyer, and Rabbeth, and three machine shops, Fales, Jenks & Sons, Whitin, and Draper. From 1860 to 1870 both Whitin and Fales, Jenks had made many experiments with light-weight spindles, and in 1869 the Lowell Machine Shop was building the so-called Whitin ring frame.[54] The Lowell Machine Shop had, up to this time, done no important work on the ring frame, having concentrated apparently on improving the speeder.

In 1866 the first Rabbeth spindle was made and subsequently developed by Fales, Jenks, who controlled the patent in 1872. In 1870 Oliver Pearl, overseer in the Atlantic Mills at Lawrence, perfected his spindle and personally retained his patent. On April 19, 1871, Jacob Sawyer, agent of the Appleton Mills at Lowell, presented his spindle before a gathering of the New England Cotton Manufacturers Association in Boston. George Draper & Sons, which before 1870 had operated on the fringe of the textile machinery industry as a manufacturer of twisters, spoolers, warpers, and various parts and attachments for looms and other machines, acquired control of the Sawyer patent and in 1872 formed the Sawyer Spindle Company to promote it.

Hot controversies raged in the industry over the merits of the various spindles, and Draper aggressively went about acquiring rights, by sale or suit, to the various improvements which were being effected. In 1874 Fales, Jenks capitulated to Draper on a charge of patent infringement, and in 1879 a new and vastly superior Fales & Jenks Rabbeth spindle also passed to Draper by amicable agreement. Watching Draper's progress anxiously, George Richardson, superintendent of the Lowell Machine Shop, took action to attain for the Shop an independent position in the ring spinning field.[55]

When Oliver Pearl was developing his spindle he came to Richardson for help. Richardson agreed to take an interest in the patent and for a time served as Pearl's technical adviser. The two differed, however, and Pearl felt that Richardson was too conservative. A quarrel ensued, after which Richardson consulted with A. G. Cumnock, agent of the mill in which Pearl was overseer, and in 1871 designed the so-called Richardson-Cumnock spindle. Richardson's own testimony indicates that this spindle was based on Pearl's idea, with Richardson's improvements. In all this experimenting Richardson's basic desire was, as he expressed it, to "beat Draper."

Pearl, undaunted by the palpable theft of his spindle, obtained a judgment against the Lowell Machine Shop in 1872 which declared the Richardson-Cumnock spindle to be an infringement of the original Pearl patent. The Lowell Machine Shop was then faced with a choice of paying royalties of 20 cents per spindle to Pearl for the Pearl spindle, or of 38 cents per spindle to Draper for the more popular Sawyer spindle. Actually both royalties were paid, for customers were demanding both types of spindles in Lowell Machine Shop frames. Meanwhile, Richardson tried again. In the summer of 1875 the Lowell Shop brought forth the "Jackson" or "Experimental" spindle, and Oliver Pearl not only brought suit for infringement again but revoked the Shop's license to make the Pearl spindle. Thereafter, when customers wished Pearl spindles in Lowell frames, it was necessary for them to apply directly to Pearl for a license.

In 1877, with the Pearl suit pending, the Lowell Machine Shop was caught in a vicious cross fire. Pearl charged not only that the Jackson spindle was an infringement on the Pearl spindle *but that the Sawyer spindles which Lowell was building under license from Draper infringed the Pearl patent.*[56]

This latter point was simultaneously being raised in a suit brought by Pearl against the Appleton Company, namely, that the Sawyer spindle infringed the Pearl patent. This was the basic question of the day, and it was of vital interest to all machine shops which had been building Sawyer frames under license from Draper. If Pearl won this suit, not only Draper but all who had built the Sawyer spindles would be liable for damages. The contention of Pearl that the Jackson spindle of the Lowell Machine Shop also infringed the Pearl patent now became a minor issue, in comparison with the Pearl-Appleton suit, for the Shop had built relatively few of the Jackson spindles, whereas in the first six months of 1878 alone it had contracted for or built frames containing 100,000 Sawyer spindles.[57]

On July 17, 1880, Judge John Lowell rendered a far-reaching "No infringement" verdict, and Draper had won a great triumph.[58] The Lowell Machine Shop and all other shops were free to build Sawyer frames under Draper's licenses. Lowell's fight with Pearl over the Jackson spindle seems not to have come to trial — nor, indeed, was there any necessity for a further fight. The Sawyer spindle had, by 1879, won the market on the basis of technical superiority.[59] The *Pearl* v. *Appleton* decision was a Pyrrhic victory for Lowell and the other builders of ring frames. Saved from paying damages to Pearl by the ruling, the Lowell Machine Shop, having failed to develop a spindle of its own, had no choice but to pay royalties to Draper for the Sawyer spindle until such time as the now all-powerful company at Hopedale could be challenged with some new spindle improvement.

The spindle revolution of the 1870's points to an interesting conclusion — and one which might be considered to have validity for a period extending at least as far back as 1845. The important inventions in textile machinery were not being made in the large machine shops. No better proof exists of this conclusion than the record of the Lowell Machine Shop and its predecessor, the Locks & Canals Company, from 1824 to 1879. This shop and others effected innumerable refinements in machinery, to be sure, but the original ideas — the new principles — were being worked out elsewhere.

There were three main fountainheads of mechanical innovation. The first was England, as exemplified by the slasher and the fly frame. The second was the textile-mill overseer or mechanic, such as Oliver Pearl and Jacob Sawyer. The third was the independent inventor, who set up a highly specialized shop to exploit his improvement or licensed others to build it. This source is best illustrated by the various loom-builders. The second and third sources, of course, could be, and often were, synonymous. Why were the large shops, with such ample facilities in the way of capital and skill, so slow to initiate major improvements?

One answer might be that a sellers' market for machinery which existed prior to 1874, while having little effect on the small inventor who had everything to gain by effecting an improvement or introducing a new idea, was not conducive to the initiation of change by established shops. George Draper himself indicted the industry in these words in 1878:[60]

> I find in all cases, almost without exception, that all of the principal machine shops are opposed to the introduction of improvements for the reason that it is costly for them to make the necessary changes, and it takes the personal attention of the leading men to the details that are required, and every point has to be considered, while in order to duplicate machines they have only to give the order; the patterns and the drawings and everything being ready for it and their hands being accustomed to do it.

Draper, with his aggressive improvement and merchandising of spindles, was to prod the textile industry as it had scarcely been prodded since Paul Moody's day, and in 1878 he could well afford to chide his fellow-machine-makers. The part played by the large shops, however, in advancing new ideas conceived elsewhere was both creditable to them and indispensable to the inventors.

The sum total of invention and improvement in the textile industry to 1879 was impressive in terms of lowered costs and improved quality of cloth; and of these benefits, in the presence of high competition in the textile industry, a substantial part was passed on to the consumer. Appendix 9 conveys some idea of the trend in prices, costs, and productivity. The hours of labor in textile mills had decreased, a result which was attributable directly to social pressure but which was perhaps facilitated by the increased productivity of machinery. In 1879 the textile-machine shops could stand on their record and admit that George Draper's accusation was substantially true without being damning.

By 1879, too, the Lowell Machine Shop had committed itself to the policy of specialization in the field of cotton-textile machinery. Despite advertisements which called attention to the turbine wheels, mill gearing and shafting, paper machinery, hydraulic presses and pumps and mill elevators, the Shop's chief interest was cotton machinery. In 1879 the line of machine tools followed the locomotive, and the treasurer was stating:[61]

> The fact is . . . steam engineering has become a specialty, as also other things we used to make, and we have filled all our shops with special tools adapted to making cotton machinery, and while we are able to employ 800 to 1,000 men on cotton machinery it gives us as much business as I certainly want or have the capacity to manage.

A change in superintendents in this year made the treasurer's statement of policy effective. For the next two decades the Lowell Machine Shop was to yield to the prevailing necessity for intensive effort in a single field — a policy which seemed to go hand in hand with prosperous times.

4. Shop, Shop Management, and Men, 1845–1879

One large segment of Lowell Machine Shop history can scarcely be touched upon. The record of laborers, foremen, and manufacturing methods, hard to reconstruct from even the most complete shop accounts, must, in the absence of any pertinent records whatsoever, be passed by. The forced omission is unfortunate, for this was a period of significant trends: rising wages, omnipotent foremen, increasing specialization of function at the workbench, shorter hours, adumbrations of organized bargaining, and new racial groups of workmen.

Employment in the Machine Shop expanded more or less steadily from a force of 300 in 1845 to 1,250 in 1880. If this working group partook of the changing characteristics of all labor in Lowell, as seems probable, a preponderance of native-born workmen in 1845 gave way in the 1850's to the large increase in Irish help in the unskilled and semiskilled positions, particularly in the foundry. French-American and French-Canadian unskilled help definitely came into the Shop in numbers after the Civil War, and competed with the Irish for the unskilled jobs. In 1879, however, the foremen and job-takers, or contractors, were almost exclusively native-born men. No payroll records of the Shop have survived. In 1864, however, John C. Whitin made the interesting remark that he was paying 25 cents per spindle more for labor than did Lowell.[62] A wage differential in favor of the Lowell Shop over Whitin might be inferred from the relative abundance of labor in the city of Lowell as compared with the town of Whitinsville.

In 1850 the twelve-hour working day was universal. In Lowell there was much agitation for a shorter day, which culminated in a bitter local election campaign in 1852 and the triumph of Democratic Benjamin Butler, self-styled champion of the ten-hour-day movement. The Massachusetts legislature to which Butler was sent was adamant, however, and unrest among workmen and operatives in Lowell increased. In 1853 one-third of the employees of the Lowell Machine Shop struck for a shorter workday, but were said to have been unsuccessful.[63] However, in this same year the Lowell corporations adopted the eleven-hour day. This action was carefully labeled "voluntary"; it was actually a necessity brought about by force of public opinion and the manifest political strength of the ten-hour movement. Despite these occasional and short-lived disturbances, Lowell was remarkably free of labor strife, although by 1879 several unions were active there.[64] No hint of trouble in the Shop other than the 1853 demonstration is to be found for the entire 1845–79 period.

Work in the Shop continued to be performed, as in the past, by the contract system. Job-takers worked in the Shop under contract and under supervision, but exercised, nevertheless, much independence. They were paid a daily rate and supplied with materials and they employed, supervised, and paid their own assistants as needed. On large orders formal contracts were signed with the job-takers; on small orders, or what the superintendent referred to as the "peanut trade," verbal orders were deemed sufficient and binding.

In tracing the changes in top-level management in the Lowell Machine Shop the functions of the superintendent are most appropriately studied as an adjunct of affairs at Lowell and should carefully be distinguished from the managerial prerogatives exercised in the treasurer's office in Boston. The superintendent was a machinist, up from the ranks. As such, and lacking any over-all grasp of the financial necessities of the business, he tended to side with the labor force against decisions from Boston. It is significant that in the depression following 1873 the suggestions of manufacturing for stock in order to maintain employment came not from Boston but from Lowell.

Four men filled the position of superintendent from 1845 to 1879. William A. Burke, whose career has already been noted, left the Shop in 1862 and was succeeded by W. C. Bryant, who died shortly thereafter. Andrew Moody, a grandnephew of the famous mechanic of other days, succeeded Bryant. Nothing is known of Moody's capacities or achievements. He was succeeded in 1870 by George Richardson, of whom the treasurer found it necessary to say to an irate customer, "Mr. Richardson sometimes, under the pressure of business perplexities, incident to the business he has in charge, may use stronger expressions than he really intends." He was, the treasurer added, rather unconvincingly, the "last person to entertain aught but amicable relations with all our friends and customers." Despite a shortness of temper and the forthright Yankee penchant for saying what was in his mind, Richardson was more than competent. In nine years he effected a major overhaul of manufacturing facilities which was to serve the Shop well in the following decade of active business. Richardson's career from its beginning as a yard sweep to its climax on the witness stand in the Pearl versus Appleton case was colorful. Appendix 7 presents excerpts from his testimony — a rare, graphic, and valuable story of the life and training of an old-fashioned mechanic. His death in 1879 marked the end of that era in Shop affairs in which one man could master the technical intricacies of almost anything made from iron.

The career of each of the several Shop superintendents had one thing in common: each undertook to improve upon the manufacturing facilities inherited from his predecessor. Superimposed on this periodic overhauling was a more or less steady program of plant expansion, specifically authorized by the board of directors.

In terms of dollar valuation Lowell Machine Shop plant assets, including real estate, tools, shops, tenements, and water power, increased from $224,296 in 1846 to $400,000 in 1880. The rate of expansion varied; see Table 13, page 229. Most of this growth took place between 1845 and 1855. From 1845 to 1850, plant assets increased 92 per cent in valuation. In the five years following

1850 the increase was 22 per cent. Thereafter, a more or less steady decrease occurred as obsolete plant write-downs exceeded the valuation of new improvements and alterations.

The great increase before 1850 was a result of new capital and new management at work in the Shop. The need and the objective were voiced by William A. Burke, shortly after he had assumed the position of superintendent in 1845:[65]

As it appears to be decided that we shall occupy our present buildings for some time to come, certain repairs and additions seem to be very necessary to enable us to compete successfully with other Machine Shops and also to give us what I suppose is the expectation of the owners, the *first* establishment in the country.

One avowed purpose of the alterations was to increase available storage space for metal and casting in order, as Burke stated, "to supply ourselves beforehand with castings so that we can go on without such a daily dependence on the movements at the Foundry as we now experience," and so that the Shop would "be better able to secure the purchase of the articles wanted at proper season and advantageous prices."

When Burke presented plans to the directors for three substantial new buildings in 1847, he made an interesting commentary on machine-shop practice of the day:

These rooms in Nos 2 & 3 for setting up machinery it is supposed will be sufficient to accommodate a complete set of machinery for 5 to 6 thousand spindles. Since iron frames have taken the place of wood more fitting is necessary in setting them up and adjusting the several parts; when this is done in the mills it is very annoying to the managers, converts the rooms of the mills into machine shops, and also takes many of our hands from the control of the rules of the shop and tends to break up the order which we ought to observe. When the time comes that we shall build machinery to go abroad we shall find these rooms of essential importance.

The dollar valuations in which plant expansion is traced are, at best, useful only in tracing general trends. In terms of production the Shop expanded from an annual capacity of $230,000 in 1845 to a capacity of close to $2,000,000 in 1880. Unfortunately, no reliable index of machinery price changes exists against which this change in dollar volume of production can be measured, but foundry output increased over the period from 100 tons to 650 tons of castings per month.[66] On the following pages these figures are translated into reality by a visual record of plant changes as seen through the eyes of contemporary artists. These buildings no longer exist. It seems well worth while, therefore, to preserve in all possible detail the plant record of the Lowell Machine Shop — in its middle years shown herewith as one of the most famous machinery-manufacturing establishments in America.

5. Conservative Finance and Financiers, 1845–1879

The Treasurer's Office

The gap which existed between Lowell and Boston has been pointed out on several previous occasions. The division of managerial functions between treasurer and superintendent worked as well for the Lowell Machine Shop as it had for the Locks and Canals Company. That this was so is attributable, in the later company as in the earlier, more to the abilities of the men involved than to such inherent worth as the system possessed. The administrative difficulties involved were greatly lessened by improvements in transportation (more trains and faster trains) and communication (the telegraph). In 1879, however, the treasurer was still transacting routine business with the superintendent by means of letter and the traditional Thursday visit to Lowell.

J. Thomas Stevenson, the first treasurer of the Lowell Machine Shop, must go down in history as a type rather than as a personality. In the pre-Civil-War New England textile industry the treasurer's office usually implied a Harvard College degree and a background in foreign trade, or a clerkship in one of two or three Boston cloth-selling houses. The demand was not for a conservative man but for one who would not be left behind by a tremendously dynamic industry. Of necessity, the successful Boston treasurer of the period was a progressive. His success depended largely upon his ability to expand wisely. His contribution to New England manufacturing

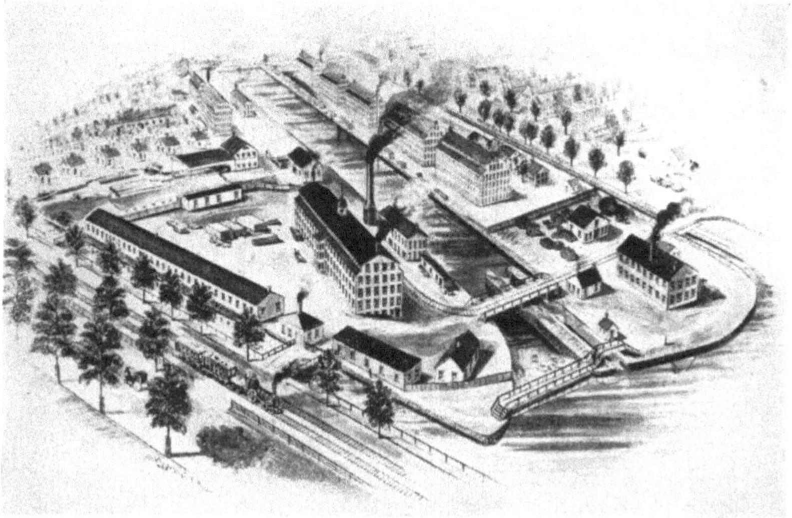

The Lowell Machine Shop in 1870

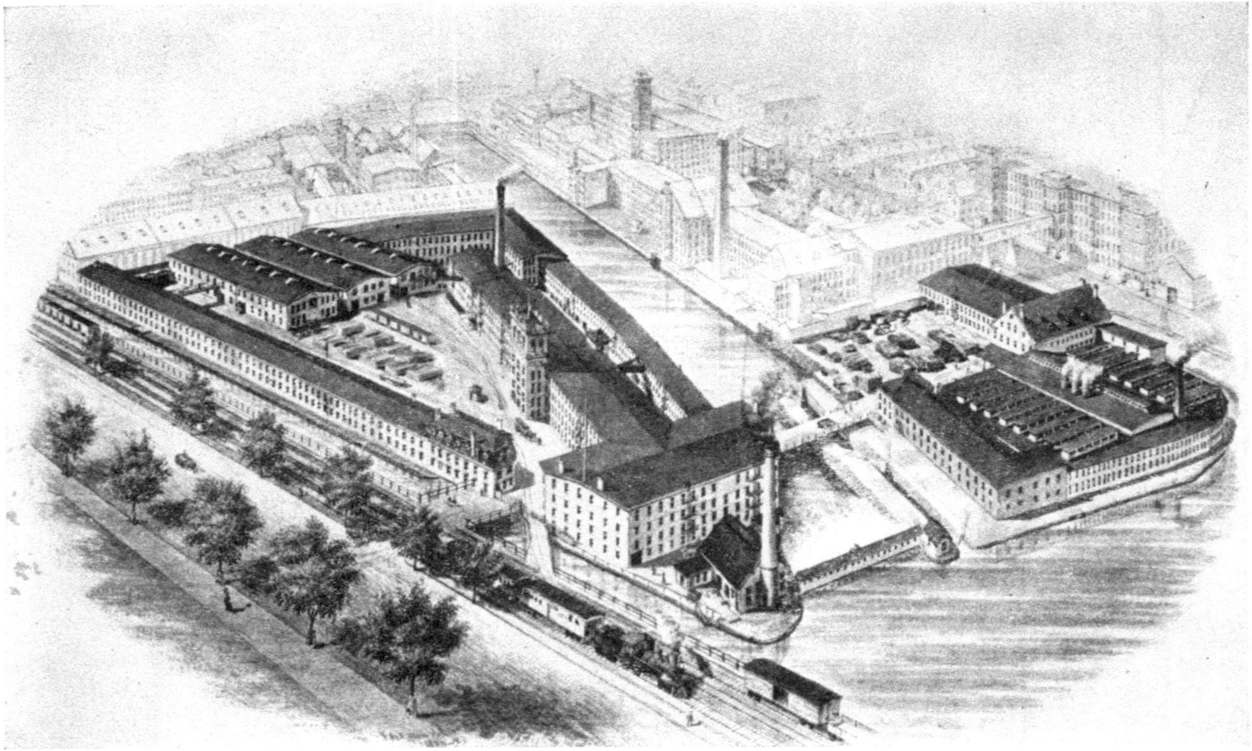

THE LOWELL MACHINE SHOP IN 1893

enterprise was the managerial adroitness which he brought from the countinghouse. His greatest assets were his relatives, friends, and business associates. Stevenson conformed to this pattern. He was, moreover, a man of great and persuasive eloquence, a conservative Whig, and, in common with many of the Shop directors, a member of the Massachusetts legislature (1839, 1851–53). Stevenson served the Shop for thirty-one years, and his career there inspired the directors not only to pay the usual tributes to a man of skill and good judgment, but also to comment on a quality of general sympathy which endeared him to his associates.[67]

Stevenson was succeeded briefly by his son, R. H. Stevenson, and on September 20, 1876, William A. Burke was made treasurer. Since leaving his position as Shop superintendent in 1862, Burke had made the difficult transition from technician to administrator. After six years as agent of the Boott Cotton Mills, he became treasurer of the Suffolk Manufacturing Company and the Tremont Mills. Two years later he resigned these posts to become assistant treasurer of the highly successful Great Falls Manufacturing Company and the Dwight Manufacturing Company. He returned to the Lowell Machine Shop, therefore, with a rare background of experience in building and operating machines. If Burke was less endowed than his predecessor with influential contacts in Boston, he repaired the deficiency by a knowledge of operations at Lowell which Stevenson could never have had.

With the growth in size and wealth of the Shop the duties of the treasurer increased in complexity, but not until after 1876 was the salary paid commensurate with the responsibilities of the position. In 1845 the post commanded the nominal annual salary of $3,000. This was not changed during all the years that Stevenson held office. Burke was paid $5,000 when he became treasurer, and in 1879 his salary was raised to $7,500. The duties performed by the treasurer were virtually the same as those associated with the office in the Saco Water Power Company and outlined in detail in Chapter IV. The treasurer made purchases, collections, and payments; arranged loans; determined credit policies; and was responsible for the preparation of summary financial statements. Much of the detail work was performed by a clerk, but the treasurer signed (and presumably read or scanned) every letter which went out of the office. Correspondence with customers demanded more time of the Boston office than all other functions combined, for the treasurer was, in effect, the sales manager of the Shop. While there is no means of ascertaining the treasurer's day-to-day activities, his correspondence may be indicative of the nature of the demands upon his time. In a representative month in 1872 Treasurer Stevenson sent forty-three letters. Of these, thirteen were to the superintendent at Lowell, four were to banks, twenty-seven were to customers, and six were to suppliers. Over half the letters sent dealt with credit terms or collections. Detailed attention to many phases of business activity was the dominant characteristic and principal demand of the office.

The Board of Directors

Appendix 11 is a record of officers and directors of the Shop. From 1845 to 1879, important new names were added to the directorate as the older members resigned or died.[68] A pattern is discernible in the type of man chosen, though it is doubtful if any set formula was resorted to in picking a new director. Throughout this period (and after 1879 as well) a majority, at least, of the directors were men who were prominent in Boston financial institutions and whose investment interest reached out to most of the northern New England textile mills. In addition to these, at least one textile mill agent and one partner in a Boston textile commission house were included. The Board also included a partner in one of the commission agencies through which the Shop obtained its iron, and for most of the period some director was a member of the Massachusetts legislature or was high in the councils of the Whig party. The potency of a Board so constituted could have been great, provided that it was active. There is ample reason to believe that the Lowell Machine Shop directorate was both powerful and active — an effective implement for binding the Shop to its suppliers and its customers and a decisive factor in the success of the Shop.

The efficacy of this directorate is not reflected in the minutes of its meetings — which were usually concerned with routine affairs. The most important official function of the Board was the selection of capable treasurers and superintendents. The Board also approved (but did not initiate) plans for plant expenditures. In exceptional cases (such as manufacturing for stock and expanding the line in time of depression) operating policy was discussed and approved. Official financial responsibilities included authorization of changes in capital, approval of large loans (either to or by the Shop), audit of the treasurer's accounts, and approval of changes in property valuation. Acting as individuals rather than as a Board, the directors advised the treasurer as the occasion demanded. There are many examples in the treasurer's correspondence to show that official action was taken after unofficial consultation with directors, particularly in respect to credit policy of the Shop in particular cases.

Trends in Ownership

The records of capital-stock ownership indicate that the Lowell Machine Shop was predominantly a promotion of partners of the cloth commission houses, A. & A. Lawrence and J. W. Paige & Company. Though the initial dominance of the Shop by these firms became weakened somewhat in terms of stock ownership, their influence was still firmly entrenched in 1879. Tracing this influence is a difficult task, which can be accomplished only by examining the holdings of the Appleton and Lawrence families and of such other stockholders as are known to have been commission-house partners. This method, however, may well result in an understatement of the extent of the influence, through failure to take account of shares which, though not owned directly, were readily controlled by these partners.

In 1846 the Lawrences, Appletons, and J. H. Wolcott, partner in the firm of A. & A. Lawrence, owned 35 per cent of Lowell Machine Shop stock. In 1876 the same group owned 18 per cent of the stock. Either holding was probably sufficient to control the Shop, even without reinforcement from shares which may have been held by other members of the commission houses.

Control by a small group became progressively easier as the number of shareholders increased and the average size of the holdings diminished. This dilution of ownership is clearly shown in Table 12, in respect both to family groups and to the entire stock ownership.

Because of the longevity of the original stockholders the process of dilution was not fairly started until after the Civil War, and even then it was not rapid. "It is very seldom the stock is offered in the market," stated the treasurer, "most of the transfers being on a/c of settlement of estates, and but few of these." [69]

TABLE 12

CHANGES IN OWNERSHIP OF LOWELL MACHINE SHOP STOCK, 1846–1876

Year	Size of Average Holding (No. of shares)	Total Number of Stockholders	Percentage of Total Capital Owned by Appletons	Lowells	Lawrences
1846...........	9.5	63	14.6	9.6	16.6
1856...........	9.4	128	13.3	10.4	12.2
1866...........	8.8	137	7.4	6.1	13.4
1876...........	8.0	151	([a])	([a])	([a])

[a] These percentages are progressively less meaningful, since family blocks were split by inheritance among many heirs who were actually members of these family groups but who bore different names. I have ended the family group percentages in 1866, the very latest date at which the original family names have any statistical validity.

Source: Lowell Machine Shop records, Stock lists.

An interesting question is raised by the character of the Shop ownership. The Boston commission houses controlled by the Lawrence and Appleton families had reached out in a process of vertical integration to control the mills which were their suppliers — even to set up mills to produce goods for sale. Was the Lowell Machine Shop promotion a calculated further step in the integration process — a reaching back to protect the cloth supply by guaranteeing good machinery at nominal cost? If this had been the case, the normal expectation would have been that profits in machine-building would have been kept at a minimum in order to benefit the mills from which the selling houses derived their prosperity. As we have seen, however, this was not the case. Contemporary observations lend credence to the surmise that the ends were being played against the middle — that profits in cloth merchandising and machine-building fed off the fat of the textile mills. Until more companies in the Lawrence-Appleton-Lowell group can be studied in detail, these challenging observations must be advanced as possibilities only. The discovery of a strong movement toward vertical integration in the textile industry at a relatively early date would scarcely be surprising. It is not illogical to surmise that the textile industry, which led all others in the American Industrial Revolution and which set the pattern for large-scale corporate enterprise, now was establishing organizational precedents which the Rockefellers, the Carnegies, and the Morgans were soon to make famous.

J. C. Ayer, a wealthy patent-medicine manufacturer in Lowell and a large Machine Shop stockholder, found something sinister in the system:[70]

> From a clique of twelve or fifteen men in Boston, Directors enough are taken to make a majority of each board in most of the great manufacturing corporations of the State. . . .

Ayer charged mismanagement, nepotism, and disregard for the wishes of the minority stockholder in the affairs of the Hamilton, Boott, Middlesex, Bay State, Merrimack, and Massachusetts mills in Lowell and Lawrence, and in the Lawrence Machine Shop. He indicted, by implication, a majority of the Lowell Machine Shop directors, but significantly enough omitted any inference of mismanagement or irregularity in the affairs of the Shop.

That Ayer pointed out genuine abuses and present perils, few could deny. His protest was that of the small man — the outsider — the resident of Lowell — who saw the omnipotence of the Boston group and his own helplessness. It came at a time (1863) when the Lowell corporations were particularly vulnerable to attack by reason of their classic blunder in the war market. His charges were biased and unfair in that they failed to admit that stockholders like himself, though occasionally subject to loss, had generally profited from the system he attacked. In terms of cloth prices the public, too, had benefited — benefited perhaps from the zealous promotional activities of the very commission houses whose activities Ayer found so distasteful. His protest was significant — an early example of the one-sided attack upon American business which, because neither heeded nor effectively refuted, was to build up such a tremendous pressure by the turn of the century as to alter the pattern of business in general and to influence the course of Lowell Machine Shop history.

Financial Policy and Practice

Conservatism was the keynote of Lowell Machine Shop financial policy. From 1845 to 1879, assets tripled while invested capital doubled, and the stockholders' equity in the business rose from $564 per share in 1846 to $891 in 1879. The expansion of assets for the period amounted to $709,000, of which $300,000 represented additional capital paid in ($200,000 in 1846 and $100,000 in 1848) and the remainder reinvested earnings. Over the thirty-five-year period dividends totaling $2,294,000 had been paid out.

The great need of the Lowell Machine Shop in active times was for working capital. Orders taken by the Shop were individually large, tying up substantial sums for periods ranging from three to nine months. This capital was obtained in part from customers, suppliers, and Boston banks. No records exist to indicate the extent of advances by customers on contracts under construction. Credit from suppliers was frequently obtained until the middle 1850's, but this was a costly source of capital since such credit involved not only interest charges but loss of cash discounts. The Shop, in consequence, came to rely more and more on short-term bank loans. These loans were obtained, naturally enough, from the banks and institutions in which Shop directors were actively interested. These included the Railroad Bank at Lowell (the principal source of working capital from 1865 to 1880), the Boston Bank, the Provident Institute of Savings, and the Massachusetts Hospital Life Insurance Company, all three in Boston.

From 1855 to 1879, inclusive, a total of $6,246,000 was borrowed from these sources and from metal supply houses. These notes ran from three to nine months and were usually paid upon maturity, though occasionally extended. The largest loan was negotiated in 1855 with the Massachusetts Hospital Life Insurance Company — a two-year note for $100,000, a quarter of which was extended to 1858. In the depression following 1874 very little money was borrowed. In three years (1876, 1877, and 1879) no money whatsoever was borrowed. This condition probably was a consequence of the Shop's ability to finance the small orders which then stood on the books.

Great caution was exercised in extending credit to customers. Company policy in this respect was made easier by the fact that by far the largest part of the orders taken were from well-known mills in the New England area. The credit of new customers was carefully checked by reference to local bankers, and, as previously stated, credit sales of machinery were well secured. The best indication of this caution is provided by the record of bad debts written off in the 1874–79 depression. During these six years bad debts charged off totaled some $5,000, as compared with total sales of slightly more than $5,000,000.

A hint that the same caution was practised in valuing Shop assets is contained in the fact that in 1876 and again in 1877 all stock accounts were arbitrarily reduced 60 per cent in value — an amount far in excess of any possible inventory loss arising out of declining metal prices. There is no means of ascertaining definitely whether plant values were understated or not in this period, though the high property tax rate in Lowell certainly provided an incentive for such a step.[71] Periodic plant write-downs were authorized by the directors, but these probably reflected an antiquated method of recording depreciation which is of some interest and importance.

In the 1870's few manufacturing concerns recognized depreciation as an annual cost of doing business. The English practice was far ahead of American in this respect. In 1876 it was said that, though some companies set up reserve funds to replace obsolete machinery, others employed large numbers of mechanics to keep machinery up to its original value and took original cost as the equivalent of present value.[72] The Lowell Machine Shop conformed to general practice in charging no depreciation for several years and then charging off the total estimated deterioration of manufacturing facilities at some such time as the Shop could best afford to do so. It was not until 1878 that a reserve account appears to have been set up for replacement of machinery, and this was not maintained for long. Plant accounts were carried at original cost and stood unchanged on the books for as long as seven years. In 1860 the directors ordered a reduction in plant valuation of $39,000. Write-downs of $30,000 in 1866, $17,000 in 1868, and $100,000 in 1876 followed. In between these dates no changes were made in the plant accounts, despite the fact that additions and alterations are known to have been made.

This was rule-of-thumb accounting, and clearly unsatisfactory by present-day standards. A major deviation from modern practice was the loose treatment of capital expenditures. The system of charging many capital expenditures to current operations and making depreciation a periodic capital expenditure militated against an accurate statement of worth and profits in any one year. Over a period of time, however, these rule-of-thumb methods were not ineffective. Neither operating practice of the day nor existing tax laws required any greater accuracy. In this period, when top management was close to the details of the business, personal knowledge took the place of complicated accounting procedures. The treasurer depended less on the figures on his balance sheets than on the word of his superintendent. That, to all practical intents and purposes, was all that was needed to run the business, provided that the superintendent was trustworthy and the business did not expand beyond the point where one man could be completely cognizant of the various facilities which comprised the manufacturing establishment.

Financial records were maintained primarily for the benefit of the directors. Since the Massachusetts State tax on corporations was based on the market value of capital stock and the Lowell city tax was based on assessed valuations of plant assets, record-keeping was designed for internal use only.[73] A nominal check was maintained on the integrity of the treasurer by an annual audit of the books by a committee of two stockholders appointed by the directors. This audit, which was purely perfunctory, was performed without the benefit of outside experts.

In Table 13 is presented a series of balance sheets as they appeared in the treasurer's annual report to the directors. Though the accuracy of the figures as a measure of company worth at any given date may well be questioned, the trends revealed justify the presentation.

Like most financial statements these figures give but an imperfect picture of company condition and provide no information as to the important factors in company progress, or lack of it. Clearly, the

TABLE 13

BALANCE SHEETS OF THE LOWELL MACHINE SHOP[a]

	1847	1860	1879
	ASSETS		
Real Estate	$190,624.50	$133,584.24	$ 118,000.00
Water Power	33,139.85	35,581.60	35,000.00
Tools	15,000.00	105,922.83	60,000.00
Machine Shop	....	76,324.10	48,000.00
Locomotive & Turbine Shop	....	49,350.00	32,000.00
Tenements	....	61,600.00	50,000.00
Foundry	....	43,540.00	40,000.00
Storehouses	....	29,250.00	17,000.00
City of Boston Bonds	....	....	50,000.00
Cash	6,866.62	11,832.75	21,489.70
Nashua Mfg. Co.	....	17,181.00	....
Notes Receivable	....	57,840.72	178,714.63
Bills Rendered	....	18,308.73	186,259.47
Superintendent's Account	323,232.96	177,791.36	164,337.28
Machinery Suspense	....	....	70,000.00
Miscellaneous Assets	76.00	827.96	....
Total Assets	$568,939.93	$818,935.29	$1,070,801.08
	LIABILITIES AND NET WORTH		
Notes Payable	$179,095.60	$150,218.93	$ ....
A. Lawrence	20,000.00	....	....
J. T. Stevenson	30,500.00	....	....
Miscellaneous Liabilities	901.44	1,000.00	2,050.00
Capital Stock	300,000.00	600,000.00	600,000.00
Profit & Loss	38,442.89	67,716.36	248,751.08
Reserve for Dividends	....	....	220,000.00
Total Liabilities and Net Worth	$568,939.93	$818,935.29	$1,070,801.08

[a] Figures are for March 31 of each year.

Source: Lowell Machine Shop records, Directors' minutes.

Lowell Machine Shop in 1879 was in a strong financial position. In retrospect this state of affairs appears to have grown out of thirty-five years of conservative business administration. In these years the Shop made few spectacular efforts in any field. Invention lagged and market aggressiveness was noteworthy for its absence. The Lowell Machine Shop, however, made no serious mistakes. It profited from growth in the textile industry and it retained the inherited strength implicit in a full line of cotton machinery. Manufacturing skill, both inherited and fostered under competent superintendents, enabled the Shop to turn out machines of good quality. Specialization in the field of textile machinery enabled that skill to be concentrated. Alertness in securing manufacturing rights to the most promising new inventions compensated for lack of inventive originality within the Shop. In 1879 the Lowell Machine Shop stood on the verge of the greatest era of expansion and change the industry had yet experienced. It remained to be seen whether financial strength and a conservative philosophy of business administration could survive a drastic realignment of competitive forces growing out of an equally drastic shift in the market for cotton-textile machinery.

CHAPTER VII

THE GREAT YEARS OF THE "BIG SHOP"

The Lowell Machine Shop, 1880–1897

THE two decades following 1880 found American business at its best and worst. The expansion of existing industrial units and the creation of new units went on apace. Production of industrial equipment increased as never before, giving America more, faster, and better machines than any other nation. Manufacturing enterprise grew and competitive struggles shook the business world. The business man fought domestic competition with aggressive marketing and aggressive cost-cutting; in the political arena he fought foreign competition. Marketing organization and the modern art of advertising were born. When voluntary agreements failed to curb annihilating competition, the industrialist turned to merger and trust. The investment banker moved in to save business from its own excesses. Labor was aggrieved in the grinding down of costs, and was not soon to forget the rebuffs which met its protests. The public rebelled against the consuming struggle, even while pocketing the proceeds in the form of better goods at lower prices. In this blustery environment the Lowell Machine Shop — "The Big Shop" to generations of Lowell workmen — throve brilliantly, while hastening to the end which inflexible management in changing times made inevitable.

1. OWNERSHIP AND TOP MANAGEMENT

In the years from 1880 to 1897 the essence of Lowell Machine Shop ownership was stability. Management, too, shared that characteristic and was marked by outstanding conservatism. Changes, however, inevitably occurred in both ownership and management.

The ownership of the Lowell Machine Shop became still more widely dispersed, but the process of diffusion was not rapid. Lowell stock seldom appeared on the market, and, as in the past, the increase in shareholders came mainly from the splitting of blocks through legacies. The number of stockholders increased from 151 in 1876 to 286 in 1896, and the average size of holdings declined in this period from 8.0 to 6.2 shares. The splitting-up of stock among holders in the same family but with different names effectively prevents a continuation of the statistical data on family group ownership presented in Table 12, Chapter VI. In 1897, however, the Lawrence and Lowell families still were strong in the company. The Appleton family had become less prominent in company affairs.

The most startling aspect of Shop ownership was the growth of non-business stockholders. In 1874, women, minors, and trustees of estates had controlled 38 per cent of Lowell Machine Shop stock; in 1904 this group controlled 76 per cent of the stock. The family group no longer was the important unit in company ownership, and control became effectively dissociated from ownership. The continued influence of the Lowells and the Lawrences, as well as the rising importance of the Stevensons, Wolcotts, Coolidges, and Lymans, was predicated upon ownership of very small percentages of the total stock outstanding.

Top management of the Lowell Machine Shop from 1879 to 1897 was exercised by supremely competent financiers. The Boston iron-merchant firm of Stevenson & Peirson provided the Shop with treasurers, following the retirement of William A. Burke in 1884. General R. H. Stevenson, son of the first treasurer of the Lowell Machine Shop (1845–76), held office from 1884 to 1888. Succeeded by Charles L. Peirson, he resumed the office in 1891. Stevenson's chief abilities appear to have been financial. A precise, impeccable, and dignified man himself, he administered the affairs of the Lowell Machine Shop precisely, impeccably, and with dignity. Serving under these treasurers was Superintendent Charles L. Hildreth, who resided at Lowell and was entrusted with the management of shop operations. Hildreth's career was distinguished by more than its length (1879 to 1905). An old-time bench-trained machinist, Hildreth soon came to share the conservative sentiments of the men under whom he served, and although primarily a technician he developed a sympathy for the stockholders' interests which was far from usual in a man of his position and background.

The board of directors had a strong financial cast, its members continuing to link the Shop with the most important Boston financial houses and the most important New England textile mills. T. Jefferson Coolidge, mill treasurer and financier, an active Republican, and at one time U. S. Minister to France, provided the traditional contact with political affairs at the national level. Roger Wolcott, governor of Massachusetts, supplied a strong link with political affairs in the Commonwealth. Wolcott, in addition, provided the legal background for the directorate. Charles L. Peirson held a civil engineering degree and appears to have been the only director who was close to manufacturing problems. The active and investment interests of Arthur T. Lyman, J. H. Wolcott, Richard D. Rogers, Charles W. Amory, Augustus Lowell, Samuel Snelling, Edward Hooper, and George P. Upham covered an amazing range, but the heavy emphasis was concentrated in the New England textile industry.[1]

The distinguished directorate of the Lowell Machine Shop was a homogeneous group. Most of these men were mill treasurers, bankers, or cloth-selling-house partners and were associated with each other on the directorates of dozens of Boston-sponsored companies. All were Boston men, many were related by blood ties, most were Republicans, and almost all were graduates of Harvard. This last-named bond was sealed in 1901, when A. Lawrence Lowell, president of Harvard and an interested participant in industrial enterprises, was made a director. The question as to how the responsibility of these men for the administration of the affairs of the Lowell Machine Shop was actually exercised takes on considerable importance in view of events in the years following 1897. The pre-Civil War directorates had been active in the interests of the Shop, and there is no evidence to show that later directorates were substantially less so. In 1886 Percival Lowell, who was close to Shop affairs, made a remarkably clear statement of the duties of directors as then conceived:[2]

A director does not care to examine every book. It is the more important duty of directors to attend to the general progress and success of the business; it is not the custom for them to scrutinize all the details of management. You have to trust something to a man's honor. If the directors attend faithfully to the general policy they do their duty.

By this definition the directors of the Lowell Machine Shop did their duty and more than their duty. Minutes of the invariably well-attended meetings indicate that the Board considered not only the usual matters of dividends and annual reports, but also questions of labor and product policy, plant expansion, credit terms, and important contracts to which the Shop was a party. In 1886, responding to startling defalcations which were occurring in supposedly reliable business offices, the Board instituted a significant change in auditing procedures. The committee of stockholders, which hitherto had performed a purely perfunctory annual examination of the treasurer's accounts, was empowered and directed to employ an expert from outside the company. This measure preceded by some ten years the earliest State regulations which eventually made the practice universally compulsory.[3] This incident was only one of many which illustrate the financially astute and eminently cautious character of top management of the Lowell Machine Shop in this period. Under the stable direction of these men the Shop survived depressions of major magnitude, and in periods of prosperity garnered large profits.

2. Prosperity and Solid Worth

From 1880 to 1884 the Lowell Machine Shop experienced unprecedented activity and profits. Annual sales came close to the two-million-dollar mark; profits ran as high as 26 per cent of sales; and dividends for the five years equaled 185 per cent of invested capital. This prosperity was general throughout the business world, and producers of industrial goods of all kinds strove to fill orders which had been postponed through the depression years preceding 1880. Activity in the textile-machine shops was stimulated further by the rapid obsolescence of the common spindle and the rise of the Southern textile industry. After this great boom of the early 1880's the business of the Lowell Machine Shop took on a new pattern. A more accurate statement would be, perhaps, that after 1884 the Shop began, for the first time, to yield to the pressure of the prevailing business pattern.

CHARLES L. HILDRETH
Superintendent of the Lowell Machine Shop, 1879–1905

Prosperity was characteristic of the Shop from 1880 to 1897, excepting only the depression years of 1885 and 1886. The dividend record was maintained unbroken throughout the period, and Lowell Machine Shop stock did not fall below par, even in time of general economic crisis. The reputation of the company was spread throughout the land, and Lowell machines were well regarded wherever cotton spindles turned. In the 1880's the prestige of the Shop was probably higher than at any other time in its history, and was surpassed by none. These were truly the greatest years the Lowell Machine Shop was ever to know.

Conservative financial policy preserved the earnings of good times for use in bad, maintained the plant in excellent operating condition, and kept the company clear of encumbering debt. These were no mean achievements under the fluctuating conditions of the day.

Earned surplus on the company books on March 31, 1881, amounted to $605,600, declining from that level to $156,200 in 1885. Thereafter, surplus rose more or less steadily to a high of $400,600 in 1897.[4] The balance sheets in Table 15 show the position of the Shop at the peak of a boom (1881), in the depths of a depression (1886), and at the end of the period under consideration (1897).

Throughout this period the Lowell Machine Shop had infrequent recourse to the capital market for either long-term or working-capital loans. In 1881, $300,000 more of capital stock was issued, the proceeds of which were used for plant expansion. The boom in business of the early 1880's, however, was financed without bank borrowing, nor were any loans negotiated until 1887. Between 1887 and 1899 the Shop borrowed a total of $1,470,000, or a yearly average of slightly more than $120,000. By way of contrast: from 1855 to 1877, when the volume of business was smaller, yearly working-capital loans averaged $250,000. Increasing wealth appears to have resulted in greater financial independence. After 1880 no substantial credits were sought from raw-material suppliers, and all banking was done in Boston. The Merchants National Bank supplied most of the working capital that was borrowed, although loans were also placed with the Massachusetts Hospital Life Insurance Company, the Old Boston National Bank, the National Union Bank, the New England Trust Company, and the City Trust Company. Shop direc-

TABLE 14

SALES, PROFITS, AND DIVIDENDS, LOWELL MACHINE SHOP, 1880–1897

Year Ending March 31	Gross Sales	Net Profit[a]	Net Profit as % of Sales	Dividends	Dividends as % of Capital
1880	$1,198,900	$166,800[b]	13.9	$240,000	30
1881	1,606,200	421,200	26.2	480,000	80
1882	1,943,900	358,900[c]	18.5	360,000	30
1883	1,845,000	259,200[d]	14.0	360,000	30
1884	819,400	120,000	14.7	135,000	15
1885	558,700	17,300	3.1	54,000	6
1886	521,800	8,800	1.7	54,000	6
1887	850,000	31,200	3.7	54,000	6
1888	970,600	93,500	9.6	90,000	10
1889	1,436,500	168,300	11.7	90,000	10
1890	1,461,100	89,600	6.1	90,000	10
1891	985,600	50,500	5.1	90,000	8
1892	932,800	33,100	3.6	63,000	7
1893	1,171,100	78,200	6.6	63,000	7
1894	1,210,900	70,100	5.8	63,000	7
1895	1,036,700	79,600	7.7	72,000	8
1896	1,730,600	156,200	9.0	90,000	10
1897	1,047,900	102,400	9.8	81,000	9

Total Sales	$21,327,700
Average Annual Sales	1,184,872
Total Net Profit	2,304,900, or 10.81% of total sales
Total Dividends	2,529,000
Average Annual Dividend as % of Capital	16.05%

[a] From Profit & Loss account, company journals.
[b] After $95,000 charge for plant improvements.
[c] After $86,900 charge for plant improvements.
[d] After $175,200 charge for plant improvements.
Source: Lowell Machine Shop records, Ledgers, journals, order books, and directors' minutes.

tors, officers, and stockholders were prominently identified with all these institutions.

Despite large dividends and the accumulation of substantial reserves, much money was reinvested in the business in the form of plant alterations and repairs. This policy was well recognized by the nineteenth-century industrial capitalist as an elementary require-

TABLE 15

BALANCE SHEETS OF THE LOWELL MACHINE SHOP

	1881	1886	1897
ASSETS			
Real Estate	$ 118,000.00	$ 118,000.00	$ 120,780.00
Tools	60,000.00	60,000.00	60,000.00
Water Power	35,000.00	35,000.00	35,000.00
Machine Shops	80,000.00	80,000.00	80,000.00
Foundry	40,000.00	40,000.00	40,000.00
Tenements	50,000.00	50,000.00	50,000.00
Storehouses	17,000.00	17,000.00	17,000.00
Bills Rendered	408,130.55	169,157.19	238,042.79
Notes Receivable	135,415.62	228,248.06	505,057.93
Superintendent's Accounts	274,975.39	207,440.12	176,104.43
Cash	87,178.70	138,998.88	86,811.97
Patents & Insurance	....	2,268.00	10,000.00
	$1,305,700.26	$1,146,112.25	$1,418,797.12
LIABILITIES AND NET WORTH			
Capital Stock	$ 600,000.00	$ 900,000.00	$ 900,000.00
Profit & Loss	605,625.26	165,067.25	400,644.21
Reserve for Dividends	100,000.00	81,000.00	....
Miscellaneous	75.00	45.00	75.00
Bills & Notes Payable	....	....	118,077.91
Total	$1,305,700.26	$1,146,112.25	$1,418,797.12

Source: Treasurer's reports to directors.

ment for successful operation in a competitive market. Like much of contemporary manufacturing enterprise, the Lowell Machine Shop diverted earnings into expanding plant to meet the boom market of 1880–84. Thereafter, much of this capacity could not be utilized and was an unwelcome burden until the turn of the century, when business volume once again called it into profitable use. The practice of carrying larger manufacturing facilities than demanded by the average volume of business may have been uneconomic; failure to expand to meet boom peaks, however, would have threatened the competitive position of the Shop. As it was, many customers, who of necessity were refused in periods of great activity, formed permanent affiliations with other machine shops. Moreover, the profits which could be realized from this excess capacity far outweighed the cost of carrying it in slack times.

Shop balance sheets give little or no indication of the true value of the fixed investment at Lowell. Between 1880 and 1897 only one plant account (real estate) out of seven was altered by so much as a penny. Tools, machine shops, tenements, water power, foundry, and storehouses were carried at an unchanged valuation for the entire eighteen years. The question is immediately raised whether the Lowell Machine Shop was not actually in even more prosperous condition than is shown by the figures in Table 15. If repairs and improvements did not greatly exceed plant depreciation and obsolescence, then the condition of the Shop in 1897 was probably more accurately reported than the artificial appearance of plant accounts would lead a casual observer to suspect. In fact, there is substantial evidence that assets were greatly understated.

The motive for such understatement was twofold. First, there was the somewhat ill-defined desire to "be conservative." Conservatism for conservatism's sake was a motivation of no little importance in the New England (and particularly in the Boston) business world. A second and much more real reason for undervaluation was local property taxation. For some years before 1880, Lowell corporations had complained of an unjust tax burden and had taken such measures as were available to combat it. The tax advantage in understating assets was psychological, since taxes were laid on assessed and not book valuations. The Shop (and other companies), however, employed the book figures as a lever in bargaining, and assessors could scarcely avoid being influenced by these figures.[5]

The specific evidence of undervaluation of plant accounts lies in the journals of the Lowell Machine Shop. These journals show substantial yearly charges for plant repairs — charges which varied with the prosperity of the Shop, but which in aggregate appear to have been sufficient to preserve the general level of manufacturing efficiency. No depreciation charges as such were recorded, the Shop subscribing to the contemporary belief that depreciation occurred only when a machine failed to function. In addition to large repair charges, the Shop made heavy capital expenditures for plant improvements. As in the past, and in accordance with the informal (and not altogether illogical) general practice of the nineteenth century, these expenditures were made in prosperous times and charged to operating expense. From 1880 to 1883, inclusive, $422,-416 was spent on "improvements." These included a new counting-house, a new Harris-Corliss steam engine, two new tenement blocks, a new machine shop (Number One Shop rebuilt at a cost of $156,559), a new smithy, and various extensions and enlargements of existing plant. Not one of the asset accounts which purported to represent the various plant divisions was altered in the slightest degree.

Undervaluation was not confined to fixed assets. In each year from 1882 through 1897 the year-end inventory of raw material and goods in process was arbitrarily marked down in value by the treasurer by amounts ranging from 18 per cent to 40 per cent of the cost value. Since the year-end value of stock on hand seldom was less than a quarter of a million dollars, the deductions were considerable. There was no tax advantage to be derived from this practice, and one object of inventory devaluation may have been to insulate the company against falling metal prices. In general, however, these discounts were so manipulated as to understate profits in good times and overstate them in bad, and this was the primary objective of the practice.

For generations the business man has looked at property undervaluation as a useful tool of conservative fiscal policy. The most serious objection to the practice comes from those outside the business who have of necessity relied upon conventional business statements, and, all too often, have accepted them without question. Consistently applied, the undervaluation of assets imposes no serious barrier to the understanding of trends in the history of a company. Almost by definition, however, undervaluation has not been consistently undertaken, and the student of business must exercise particular care to qualify his analysis. The Lowell Machine Shop was not only solidly prosperous throughout much of the 1880–97 period, but was even more secure financially than its summary financial statements showed.

There were, nevertheless, discordant notes — an uneasy counterpoint to the main theme of prosperity. Viewed through the eyes of contemporary Shop management the difficulties of the period could scarcely have been regarded as ominous or prophetic. More than likely, they were noted as natural manifestations of a trying business environment shared by all alike. Only when viewed in retrospect could certain trends in Shop operations possibly be identified as symptoms of serious internal difficulty.

CHART V

Trend of Lowell Machine Shop Stock Prices, 1880–1905

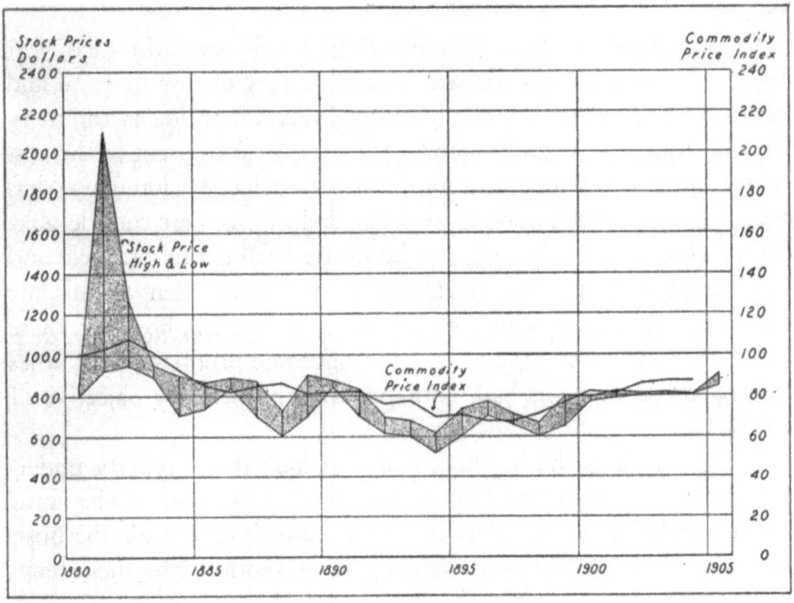

The fact was that prosperity, though great, was not so great as it had been, relatively speaking, before 1880. The business of the Lowell Machine Shop was larger after 1880 than before in terms of average annual sales: higher peaks were reached and more men were employed. Yet net profits were lower (10.81 per cent of sales for the 1880–97 period, as compared with 12.92 per cent from 1869 to 1879), and were at a markedly lower level after 1884 than before. A comparison of Tables 11 and 14 reveals the significant difference in the degree of prosperity (as reflected in the relations of profits to sales) which existed between the earlier period and the later.

If business after 1880 was more active than ever before, the fluctuations from peak to valley were more violent. The dividend record was maintained unbroken, but the average annual dividend from 1880 to 1897 was 2 per cent less than that from 1869 to 1879. In many years dividends exceeded earnings. This had seldom been the case before 1880 — only twice had this happened from 1869 to 1879, as against eleven times from 1880 to 1897. In 1886 an actual loss ($8,600) was recorded on machinery sales — the first in at least seventeen years and probably even longer.[6] The fact that this loss was offset by rent and interest income, so that operations for the year resulted in an over-all profit, does not detract from the significance of the event.

Lowell stock prices provided a lucid clue to the altered circumstances of the Shop, and suggested that the Lowell Machine Shop was no longer so successful as it had been in defying the broad movement of American business. The reader will recall (Charts III and IV) that after 1859 the trend of Lowell Machine Shop stock prices had been steadily upward, defying two major depressions, several sharp monetary crises, and a more or less steadily declining level of business prosperity. This contradictory performance was climaxed in 1881, when Lowell stock sold for $2,100, or 420 per cent above par ($500). Though the stock never sank below par thereafter, the trend in prices, shown in Chart V, was steadily downward.

There is manifest contradiction between these symptoms of difficulty and the solid financial position of the Lowell Machine Shop. The financial statements, however, echoed but faintly those tremendously significant events which were molding the shape of company history. The fate of the Shop lay not in the size of the earned surplus account but in the markets where textile machinery was bought and sold.

3. THE REVOLUTION IN MARKETS AND MARKETING

Rise of the Southern Market

The Southern States had shown a decided interest in cotton manufacturing long before the Civil War. Considerable enthusiasm was generated in the 1840's by factories built in Georgia and South

Carolina. The Southern promoter was told of the ease with which a complete factory and a man to run it could be obtained from machine shops in the North.[7] The advantages to be derived — principally cheap and plentiful labor — were clearly recognized. The movement, however, gained momentum but slowly. Lack of skilled operatives and lack of interested capital (in both North and South) were restraining factors. There was a strong local antipathy to the movement which was shared by all but the visionary.

The Lowell Machine Shop, offering not only a complete machinery line but mill plans and engineering advice as well, was in an unrivaled position to serve this market, provided that the opiate of large local orders did not deaden the awareness of opportunity. A lack of records between 1846 and 1856, however, forestalls the interesting question as to whether any complete mills were set up by the Shop in the South in this period. A few small orders from mills in Maryland, Georgia, and Louisiana are known to have been filled from 1856 to 1860. The Civil War put a temporary end to further development.

The great spurt in Southern mill construction came after 1880, when the confusion of Reconstruction had abated. The Lowell Machine Shop, however, had made such large sales in the South prior to 1875 as to suggest that it played an extremely important rôle in the early development of this market. Table 16 and Chart VI show the volume of sales in the various Southern States and the importance of this market relative to the Northern market. These figures have been carried forward to 1905, the last year for which detailed information is available.

Until 1870, small orders constituted the bulk of the business. The largest order had been for a complete mill of 2,880 spindles, for the Great Falls Manufacturing Company in Rockingham, North Carolina. In 1870 the first large Southern order was placed by the Langley Manufacturing Company, of Langley, South Carolina. Between 1870 and 1873 some $113,000 of machinery for a mill of 9,600 spindles was sold to this company. Thereafter, large orders for complete mills followed in accelerating succession. These orders are shown in Appendix 10.

The Atlanta Cotton Exposition of 1880 awoke the South. North-

F. A. LEIGH & CO.

57 Sears Building, - - Boston, Mass.,

IMPORTERS OF

HOWARD & BULLOUGH'S SLASHER,

With Important Patent Improvements,

PATENT SELF-STOPPING WARPER,

Green's Patent Fuel Economizer,

PATENT BLEACHING AND WASHING APPARATUS,

ENGLISH CARD CLOTHING.

LOWELL MACHINE SHOP,

LOWELL, MASS.,

MANUFACTURERS OF

COTTON MACHINERY,

Turbines, Mill Gearing,

CASTINGS, MACHINISTS' TOOLS, PAPER MACHINERY, &c.

J. THOS. STEVENSON, Treasurer. GEO. RICHARDSON, Sup't,

OFFICE, 82 MILK ST., BOSTON, MASS. LOWELL, MASS.

PLATT BROTHERS & COMPANY,

(LIMITED)

Hartford Works, Oldham, Lancashire, England,

ENGINEERS, MACHINISTS, MILLWRIGHTS,

ROLLER AND SPINDLE MAKERS, &c.

MACHINERY FOR OPENING and GINNING SEED COTTON. MACHINERY for preparing and Spinning Cotton, Wool and Worsted. MACHINERY for Carding and Spinning Silk Waste. POWER LOOMS for all descriptions of Plain and Fancy Cloths in Cotton or Wool. SIZING, DRESSING, WARPING, BEAMING, WINDING and REELING MACHINERY. CLOTH FOLDING and MEASURING MACHINES. HYDRAULIC and CAM BUNDLING PRESSES for Cloth. COMBING MACHINES for Cotton, Hellman's or Whipple's patent. CRIGHTON'S PATENT OPENING MACHINES for Cotton. HARD WASTE BREAKING-UP MACHINERY. PATENT BURRING MACHINES for WOOL. PATENT BRICK-MAKING MACHINERY. FORGING MACHINES, HORIZONTAL and VERTICAL DRILLING MACHINES, PLANING and SHAPING MACHINE, CHOPPING MACHINES, SAWS, and other Tools for Mechanics' and Smiths' Shops. BAR, HOOP, and ANGLE IRON, SHAFTS, FORGINGS and USES, &c., &c.

SAMUEL WOOD, Agent, No. 14 Devonshire Street, BOSTON.

EDWIN ASHTON, 113 Chestnut Street, PHILADELPHIA.

TEXTILE-MACHINERY ADVERTISING IN THE 1870'S

ern commentators, while not actually belittling the progress in manufacturing that had been made, professed to see no threat to the Northern industry. The Exposition itself, however, was too strong a stimulant to be nullified by the Northern speeches made there. A remarkable exhibit of Southern manufactures and Northern machines (including a sampling of the Lowell Machine Shop line) indicated more clearly than words what lay ahead.

CHART VI

Geographic Pattern of Sales, Lowell Machine Shop, 1847–1905

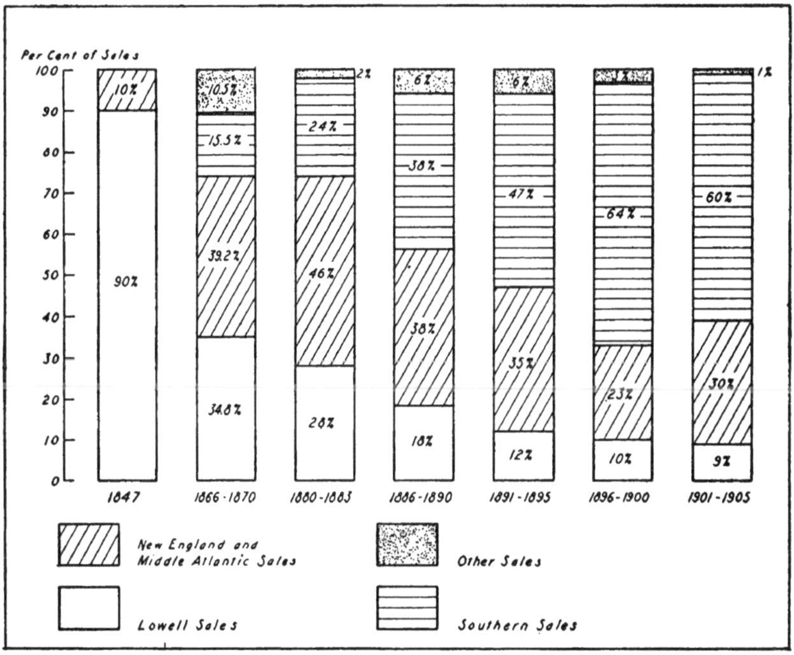

From 1870 to 1880, Southern spindles increased 65 per cent. From 1880 to 1890 the increase was 178 per cent. The building of mills in the South became a patriotic mania unmatched in America since the "cotton-factory fever" days in early nineteenth-century New England. The progress was jubilantly hailed in the South and viewed with ill-concealed alarm in the North. Competition from

Southern mills in coarse goods became noticeable — then acute. The rudimentary air-conditioning systems which began to be manufactured in the 1880's opened the possibilities, later to be realized, of entry into the fine-goods field. Northern machine-makers flocked to the harvest.

TABLE 16

SOUTHERN SALES OF THE LOWELL MACHINE SHOP AS A PERCENTAGE OF TOTAL COMPANY SALES IN SOUTHERN STATES, 1866–1905

Years	Ga.	N. C.	S. C.	Md.	Va.	Tenn.	Ala.	La.	Miss.	Ky.	Texas	Ark.
1866–70.......	45	10	..	33	..	2	..	..	10	..	..	..
1880–83.......	39	16	17	3	4	10	2	2	7	..	..	..
1886–90.......	28	19	24	2	11	3	8	1	2	2	..	..
1891–95.......	25	27	22	2	13	1	5	4	1	[a]	[a]	[a]
1896–1900.....	38	11	21	1	1	5	14	..	6	3	..	..
1901–05.......	45	11	8	1	1	2	16	..	3	3	6	1

[a] Under 1%.
Source: Lowell Machine Shop, Order books.

The question as to which machine shops were most active in the South cannot be answered positively, nor can the extent of English competition there be appraised.[8] Only the records of the Lowell Machine Shop and the Whitin Machine Works are available for study. These records suggest that these two companies played an extremely important part in the Southern growth — possibly more important than that of all other shops combined, measured in terms of machinery sold. This domination probably reached a climax in 1895, in which year the Lowell Machine Shop installed 25 per cent of the new spindles erected in the South, while the Whitin Machine Works installed 31 per cent.[9]

In 1880 the Lowell Machine Shop was strongly entrenched in the Southern market. The greatest competitive advantage that a machine shop could possess at this time was a number of relatively large mills in operation in the South, all equipped with that Shop's machinery. These show places for prospective customers the Lowell Machine Shop had — the Augusta Factory, the Sibley Manufacturing Company, and the Enterprise Manufacturing Company, in Augusta, Georgia; the Langley Manufacturing Company, in Langley, South Carolina; and many other complete, though smaller, mills in Georgia, South Carolina, and Maryland. The Lowell Machine Shop may have possessed an early advantage over Whitin by virtue of prestige accruing from the number of large installations already made, and because a Southern promoter could purchase all his machinery and plans in Lowell. If this was the case, that advantage soon weakened and then disappeared. After 1883 first one shop and then the other took the lead. By 1885 Whitin was offering mill plans to its customers, thereby overcoming one advantage previously enjoyed by the Lowell Shop. George Marston Whitin confessed, however, as late as 1895 that the lack of completely equipped Whitin mills in the South which could be shown to mill promoters was a disadvantage to him.[10] Total Southern sales by the two shops for the 1880–97 period were virtually identical in volume. For much of this business, however, the two shops did not compete with each other directly. Whitin concentrated upon the North Carolina market; the Lowell Machine Shop was strongest in Georgia.

The rapid rise in the 1880's of the Whitin Machine Works to a position equivalent in importance to that of the Lowell Machine Shop was extremely significant. Whitin's sales, both in the South and elsewhere, began to equal those of the Lowell Shop at a time when the reputation of the latter was at its zenith. The great promise implicit in the advantages of size and reputation of the Lowell Machine Shop in 1880 had not been fulfilled by 1897. The Shop had not yet thrown away its lead — but now that lead was being shared, and shared at a time when it might well have been increased to unchallenged supremacy in the American textile-machinery market. Conservative financial policy had shut the door in the face of an opportunity which was never to present itself again.

On February 7, 1882, the treasurer of the Lowell Machine Shop wrote J. D. Burke, of Magnolia, Mississippi, the following letter:

My Dear Sir:

Your esteemed favor of the 3d inst. is received — I cannot entertain your proposition to take stock in your projected Cotton Mill, and besides our Shop is now so over-crowded with orders for Cotton Machinery from our regular customers that we should probably decline for the present contracts for new parties.

Yours very truly
Wm. A. Burke Treas.

The greatest obstacle to the development of mills in the South appears to have been lack of capital. Mill promoters had little initial success in attracting Northern capital — time and again in the 1880's the treasurer of the Lowell Machine Shop told these men that Boston was no place to seek to market their stock and bonds. Faced with a scarcity of capital, Southern entrepreneurs sought the longest possible credits on their machinery. They asked and obtained advances from cloth commission selling houses for working capital. They asked the Northern machine shops to accept stock and bonds in partial settlement for machinery purchased.

The refusal of the Lowell Machine Shop to accept stock in Southern mills was absolute and was consistently followed through the years. This policy reflected deep-rooted conservatism and an unfortunate earlier experience with railroad bonds which had been accepted in settlement of locomotive contracts. The short-term implications of the policy were not serious. In the prosperous early 1880's the Lowell Machine Shop could well afford to deny requests for stock settlements. Denial was easy: the treasurer of the Shop pointed out that most types of Massachusetts corporations were prohibited by law from holding stock in other corporations.[11] The problem was present as soon as the growth of the Southern textile industry became accentuated after 1880. It was not to become acute until competition itself became acute in the depression of 1897. Nevertheless, the groundwork for failure in the Southern market had been laid by the Lowell Machine Shop.

There is no question but that the Shop made a strong bid for supremacy in the South. Short of accepting stock or undertaking any foreseeable financial risk, every inducement was extended to Southern customers. Credit policies were liberalized and more active marketing policies instituted. In 1882 the Shop's first illustrated catalogues were issued. These were of some use in serving distant markets, though probably no machinery was ever sold from a catalogue alone. Advertisements were placed in leading Southern periodicals, and both the treasurer and the superintendent made occasional trips to visit customers and prospective customers. An extensive correspondence was carried on by both the Lowell and Boston offices with Southern promoters. Buyers were liberally entertained and taken to view Lowell machinery in operation. Many scores of mill plans were drafted at the request of prospective mill owners. These plans were not standardized, but they were made to fit the individual desires of promoters and were charged at the nominal rate of $250 per mill — deductible from the bill for machinery if the order was placed. Most of these mill-plan requests came to nothing, the treasurer confessed with some irritation. Nevertheless, the practice was an essential part of Lowell's merchandising.

The lack of a specialized marketing division in the Lowell Machine Shop was one which seems to have been characteristic of the industry before 1890. Nor did either Lowell or Whitin seek to sell machinery through agencies in this period. The treasurer of the Lowell Machine Shop pointedly refused an agency offer in 1883, stating that customers preferred to do business directly with the machine shops. The "trip North" became a deep-rooted custom of the Southern mill managers, just as the "trip South" became a seasonal function of the machine-shop treasurers and superintendents. Always, the most potent selling aid was the demonstration of machinery successfully at work in a successful mill, together with the testimonials of satisfied mill managers and overseers.

This being the case, the Northern machine shops found it necessary to furnish one other type of service. If scanty capital was a serious problem in the South, so, too, was the lack of trained mill managers. Frequently these men were recommended by the shops which built the machines. Some were machine-shop overseers, others were overseers in Northern mills with whom the shop managers were acquainted. From 1880 on, the treasurer and the superintendent of the Lowell Machine Shop made many such recommendations. The demand which came oftenest was for young men possessing from $10,000 to $15,000 of capital. Superintendent Hildreth replied to such requests that to find young men was difficult, but that to find young men with capital and knowledge was next to impossible.

The great debt of South to North was not for capital but for skill. That skill was provided of necessity, for without it the Northern machines could scarcely operate to advantage. Once the initial machinery order had been placed, the greatest concern of the machine-shop superintendent was that competent overseers be obtained by the ordering mill. Superintendent Hildreth went so far as to suggest the removal of men who he felt were abusing the Lowell machines and failing to get the most out of them. A poorly run machine was little better than a poorly built machine.

The treasurer and directors of the Lowell Machine Shop grudgingly began to give way to customers in the matter of terms. Both Northern and Southern buyers began to receive longer credits. Whether the pressure from the South was an opening wedge here is not clear, but the liberalizing of terms to all customers definitely coincided with the growth of the Southern textile industry after 1880. In the 1870's the usual terms had been one-third to one-half payment in cash, the balance by six-, nine-, or twelve-month notes bearing interest at 7 per cent. After 1880 the Shop still insisted on a comparable cash payment, but notes for the balance were allowed up to thirty months, and interest became fixed at 6 per cent. Exceptions became more frequent. Old and proven customers in both South and North often gave a smaller cash deposit or no cash at all, and interest charges were trimmed. Less and less standardization of terms became apparent, and bargaining increased. Once a Southern customer had proven his reliability, he might expect terms comparable to those offered in the North, provided that his orders were as large as those of the Northern mill. Great care, however, was exercised by the Shop in dealing with new customers.

The difference between the attitude of the Lowell Machine Shop and that of its competitors toward the Southern market appears to have been one of degree. Lowell did everything that competitors did except to take Southern stock, but did not go quite so far as other shops. The difference was a subtle one, and vastly important. It centered in the extent to which each of the machine shops was willing to assist the Southern mills to become established on a firm basis. George Marston Whitin cautiously began to accept selected Southern stock in payment for machines, taking this stock in his own name until such time as Massachusetts corporations felt legally secure in holding the stock of other companies.[12] Both the Whitin Machine Works and the Lowell Machine Shop professed a strong desire to encourage new Southern mills. The Lowell Shop, however, seems not to have been able to venture boldly. An abiding fear of loss on credit sales cost Lowell its early lead in the Southern market. This fear was indigenous — a fundamental characteristic of the "Boston Treasurer." An experience which culminated just as the great new market was unfolding reinforced this fear and seemed to justify a policy of extreme caution.

The ACF Affair

So frequently did the name Atlanta Cotton Factory begin to appear in the records of the Lowell Machine Shop that soon the clerks in Boston and Lowell were able to refer to it, with no danger of confusion, as the "ACF." These initials came to symbolize all the worry, the danger, the trouble, the loss that was inherent in a venture into untried fields. They spelled out unsecured risk — loss through lack of caution. The ACF affair provides an unusually detailed insight into the difficulties attending the growth of textile manufacturing in the South at a time when the maladjustments of Reconstruction were still acute and the new enterprises which were the hope of the South were starving for lack of capital.

On September 24, 1875, J. T. Stevenson, treasurer of the Lowell Machine Shop, dictated the terms of the Atlanta Cotton Factory contract. This was an important order — the largest yet taken in the South by the Lowell Machine Shop and possibly one of the largest, if not the largest, placed in the South by any machine shop up to that time. This 11,000-spindle mill was to be a model for Georgia to follow — the showroom for Lowell machinery in the South. Every energy at the Shop was strained toward technical perfection, and the carloads of machinery which moved out of the yard in the summer of 1876 were the culmination of generations of machine-building experience — in Superintendent Richardson's words, "as fine a lot of machinery as this Shop has ever turned out."[13]

The ACF contract was drawn for machinery "amounting to about $100,000." Terms of payment were unusually lenient. Ten per cent of the amount of the order was to be paid in cash on January 15, 1877 (six months after delivery). The balance was to be paid at the rate of 5 per cent monthly thereafter, with interest on the unpaid balance at 7 per cent per annum. Title to the machinery was to remain with the Lowell Machine Shop. On this latter point Georgia law was vague. In 1857 the title of a vendor in a conditional sales contract had been sustained by the Supreme Court of the State. Beyond this there was no precedent, and the Lowell Machine Shop was advised by counsel to have the contract recorded as a personal mortgage. The contract was reworded, however, and the legal conclusion was that:

> The agreement as now drawn will in legal effect constitute a mortgage, if not valid as a conditional sale and therefore no alteration in it will be necessary to be recorded as a personal mortgage.

Two erectors departed from Lowell to set up the machinery. H. I. Kimball, president of the Atlanta Cotton Factory, wrote Treasurer Stevenson that he had placed $5,000 of fire insurance on the machinery. Stevenson telegraphed back an emphatic demand that the full value of the machinery be covered. In September of 1876 William A. Burke, the new treasurer of the Shop, pressed Kimball for more insurance coverage. Kimball complied, and confided that the Atlanta Cotton Factory would be turning out cloth by Christmas. In November Kimball asked the total amount of the Factory's bill. "One hundred eighteen thousand five hundred," telegraphed Burke in reply. In December Kimball wrote a startling message:

> The unsettled condition of business throughout the country will render it impossible for the *ACF Co.* to carry out their part of said contract. They desire however to so coöperate with the said Lowell Machine Shop that both parties may be protected and for that purpose make the following proposition to the end that the Lowell Machine Shop may be more fully secured and protected and that the ACF Co. may be enabled to start up and run said machinery successfully.

Kimball's proposition comprehended five- to ten-year loans totaling $140,000. These were to be placed with the aid of the Lowell Machine Shop, if not actually made by the Shop. From the proceeds of these the Shop was to receive $45,000 in part payment of the contract. The remainder was to be used to liquidate other debts and provide working capital. Treasurer Burke did not even answer Kimball's letter. A representative of the Shop, James W. Burke of Alexandria, Virginia, was dispatched post-haste to Atlanta, armed with power of attorney and instructions to hire reputable local counsel and gather information. His report was not encouraging.

The Atlanta law firm of McCay & Trippe — "lawyers and gentlemen of high standing both having been on the Supreme bench of the State of Georgia but resigned the judgeship to practice law" — had examined the ACF contract and confirmed Lowell's title to the machinery. James Burke had gone through the factory incognito and found all well there. In addition to its obligation to the Lowell Machine Shop, however, the Factory owed at least $60,000. Political suspense and consequent financial depression had prevented the collection of stock assessments as well as the sale of additional stock. There was a strong feeling in Atlanta against Kimball personally, which was keeping some local capital out of the business. The directors, reported Burke, were men of integrity and high standing in the community. "But unfortunately," he wrote, "they have not provided as they should have, the funds for putting their mill in operation." His recommendation was that "the Mill be not started till Capital enough is paid in to make at least 50% sure to the Shop of what is owing it."

Here was exemplified the basic difficulty of the early Southern mills. Hazardous ventures at best, they could hope in their formative stages to attract little Northern capital. The savings of local bankers, merchants, doctors, and lawyers were often inadequate to both build and operate a cotton mill. Hope was continually frustrated by inexperience. Total capital requirements were all too frequently underestimated. Too often the goal of local fund-raising campaigns was the erection of the mill and the purchase of the machinery, with no adequate provision made for working capital.

January, 1877, brought the expected default on the first payment specified in the contract. The Lowell Machine Shop was faced with an awkward choice. Strict legal protocol indicated that formal possession be taken of the machinery. Yet, stated Treasurer Burke, it was the Shop's policy to encourage the ACF to "go forward." There was still hope that capital would be raised, and any aggressive action by the Lowell Machine Shop at this time would seriously affect the standing of the ACF. The new year brought proposals and counter-proposals, while the machinery stood idle. Treasurer Burke traveled personally to Atlanta. A proposal was made by the Atlanta Cotton Factory to commence operations and run for a year with no payments to the Shop — the profits, if any, to be turned over at the end of that time. This was rejected by Treasurer Burke on the grounds that the machinery would be worth only half price after twelve months of use. Burke's minimum demand was that the ACF secure adequate capital to pay off all except the machinery debt and provide adequate working capital, guaranteeing at the same time a cash payment of $30,000 on the machinery in six months. Under any other terms than these the Shop refused to allow the machinery to be started. In April of 1877, the ACF having insufficient funds to meet the bill of $275, the Lowell Machine Shop found it necessary to pay the insurance premiums then due. In July the Factory offered a preferred stock issue to the Shop in partial settlement of the Shop's bill for machinery. Treasurer Burke declined to settle on these terms. An unsuccessful attempt was then made by the Atlanta Cotton Factory to sell the stock in the market, but all efforts to raise working capital during the year failed, notwithstanding Kimball's resignation as president.

Throughout 1877, relations between the Lowell Machine Shop and the ACF were amicable. Attempts to reach an agreement were wholehearted, and the mutual desire to coöperate sincere. Representatives of the Shop who went to Atlanta to check on local conditions were carefully instructed to do nothing to annoy the ACF directors, and were courteously treated by those men. The ACF simply was unable to raise money, and the Lowell Machine Shop was unwilling to permit the venture to be launched without sufficient capital to ensure its success. The Shop studiously avoided participation in the local quarrels which were impairing what little hope there was left of a successful termination of the affair.

On January 16, 1878, a new contract was signed, under the terms of which the ACF was to pay the Lowell Machine Shop $18,000 by

January 25. Payments on the balance were to commence in July, 1878, and to be made at the rate of approximately $18,000 per year until final settlement in 1884. Security for the contract was a first mortgage on the entire mill. Even as this contract was being signed, however, it was evident to all that cash to start the mill was not to be had. The selling house of Coffin, Altemus & Company, of Philadelphia, refused to extend credit for the purchase of cotton. Stockholders had no cash to pay assessments and gave notes instead. The ACF offered these notes to the Lowell Machine Shop in settlement of the initial payment due on January 25, but the Lowell directors decided they must stand on the original agreement.

The affair now reached a climax, and the patience hitherto noted on both sides wore thin. Lowell's representative in Atlanta telegraphed on January 26 that the ACF was likely to go ahead and start the machinery without the Shop's assent. Three days later the machinery actually was started. The Lowell Machine Shop immediately caused a restraining order to be issued and an injunction to be served. This legal action stopped the operation of the machinery, and the mill property passed into the custody of the local court. Treasurer Burke was indignant, and labeled the action of the ACF as "a great wrong," saying that it would be "to the injury of Southern Manufacturing interests generally so far as their credit with machine builders at the North is concerned."

The Shop now moved to secure legal possession of the machinery. The local judge was not disposed to favor the Shop, but in February, 1878, a decision was given by the Georgia Supreme Court which prompted Burke to state, "It appears now that there is in the Georgia Courts some security for property held under the condition of our contract." At the same time he confided to a customer that the directors of the Lowell Machine Shop were almost ready to cut off all credit to Southern customers. Local feeling in Atlanta against the Lowell Machine Shop was bitter, but some parties stated privately, "We feel you are wronged and ought to have justice but our interests are all here and we must sustain public opinion."

Negotiations with the Atlanta Cotton Factory were continued, in the belief that the best remedy still lay in securing capital to start the mill. In June Treasurer Burke stated that the Shop would consider no proposition involving the taking of stock for a part of the claim. The efforts of the Atlanta men to sell more stock again met with failure. Ex-Governor Brown of Georgia had become active in ACF affairs and was unfriendly in word and action. His charge that Lowell's prices were high was answered by Burke with the statement that machinery prices in general had declined greatly since 1876. Burke offered to settle all claims for $90,000. By November, Ex-Governor Bullock had joined the list of notables interested in getting the Factory started, and relations once again became characterized by amicability and a spirit of coöperation. The Shop declined, however, to undertake the sale of bonds issued by the Atlanta Factory or to accept them in settlement of claims. "It has always been the policy of the Shop," stated Burke, "not to be interested in any way in the management or ownership of property outside their own."

The ACF bond issue precipitated a final crisis. Burke discovered that all the ACF property, including Lowell's machinery, had been pledged as security for the bonds. Burke threatened legal action to stop the sale of the bonds. McCay & Trippe, the Atlanta counsel, advised against the course; "a declaration of war would make them furious, even if they intended to be honest & still more furious if wrong was intended." Burke had planned to place a public advertisement warning prospective bond purchasers that machinery pledged was not the property of the ACF, but at the urging of his legal advisers he agreed to abstain from this measure. Personal notices to this effect, however, were served on the bond trustees.

With the machinery removed from the schedule of property pledged, the bond issue was virtually worthless. By April of 1879 the situation had become hopeless. The Lowell Machine Shop began to sell off as much of the machinery as possible to other mills in the South and made preparations for shipping the remainder back to Lowell. By July two-thirds of the equipment had been sold (principally to the Bibb Manufacturing Company in Macon) and the rest returned to the Shop. An entry was made on the Lowell Machine Shop books charging off a $34,000 loss on the machinery returned to the Shop. The machinery sold resulted in an additional loss of about $12,000 on the basis of original list prices.

There was much ill feeling in Atlanta, and Governor Bullock was indignant at what he termed interference with the sale of the Atlanta Cotton Factory bonds. Burke and the Lowell Machine Shop directors were severely criticized. These reactions were the natural culmination of three years of frustration, and the Shop was made the scapegoat for failure to launch the undertaking. An impartial study of the entire affair, however, can lead to only one conclusion: the actions of the Lowell Machine Shop were legally and ethically unimpeachable. This was sound, fair, and conservative business policy — but was it good business policy? The repercussions of the ACF affair were heard longer in Lowell than in Atlanta. Southern mills continued to seek Lowell machinery, but the Lowell directors never forgot the Atlanta experience.

The English Threat and Its Consequences

The statement has already been made that after 1845 American machine-builders had become vitally interested in the tariff not only as it affected their customers, but also as it affected themselves. The English threat became increasingly real after the Civil War.

A basic reason for fear of English competition lay in the undoubted superiority of certain English machines over their American counterparts. Only in spinning frames and looms were the American shops unchallenged. The trend toward production of fine goods in America tended to force competition into fields in which the English were at their best. Moreover, there is evidence to indicate that as late as 1886 the historical American preference for anything of foreign (and particularly English) manufacture was operating to the disadvantage of American cotton-machinery builders.[14]

Statistical evidence of English competition in the textile machinery industry is both scanty and unreliable. Annual reports of the United States Bureau of Statistics show that total importations of machinery from England up to 1879 were consistently averaging less per year than the annual sales of the Lowell Machine Shop alone.[15] Despite the apparently low level of importations, however, the treasurer of the Lowell Machine Shop had complained (Chapter VI, page 211) as early as 1870 about foreign competition. Two lines of resistance were available to the American shops.

The English incursions were combated by American technological progress. This progress is more fully discussed in Section 4 of this chapter. It was not until after 1890, however, that the preference for American over English machines became firmly established on a widespread basis, and much of that preference may have arisen out of the ability of American shops to service the industry more efficiently than could the English. A second and more immediately effective course of action lay in the political arena. The necessity for concerted political action had important repercussions in the textile machinery industry.

In 1870 the Lowell Machine Shop was presenting high-tariff arguments in Washington through the same James W. Burke who participated in the Atlanta Cotton Factory negotiations. There is little doubt that Burke was serving as a resident lobbyist, representing (as far as can be determined) only the Lowell Machine Shop. By March, 1872, a Committee of Machinery Builders had been formed to represent the industry in tariff discussions then under way. This committee constitutes the earliest known instance of collective action in the industry. The formation of the committee occurred on the eve of the discovery by American business that free competition did not preclude coöperative effort in solving common problems.

No information has been found about the Committee of Machinery Builders other than that both the Lowell Machine Shop and the Whitin Machine Works were members, and that a lobbyist was being employed. In 1877 a more formal combination had been effected in the form of the American Cotton Machinery Builders Association. Like the earlier committee, the association was formed to present the tariff viewpoint of the industry in Washington. Josiah Lasell, treasurer of the Whitin Machine Works, was treasurer of the association, and William A. Burke, treasurer of the Lowell Machine Shop, was chairman.[16]

The committee and the association were formed in 1872 and 1877, respectively, to meet specific threats of tariff reduction. (On neither occasion were the proposed rates on machinery lowered from the existing levels: ad valorem rates of 35 per cent on parts of the machines made from iron, and 45 per cent on parts made from steel.) Between these two dates the organization remained inactive. In 1880, however, a bill was introduced to Congress by Southern textile interests to reduce the duty on cotton machinery. Lasell wrote Burke to inquire about the matter, but the threat was apparently not real enough to necessitate a meeting of the Executive Committee of the Machinery Builders Association. A lobbyist (J. S. Hayes) was dispatched to Washington to look after the interests of the machine shops.[17]

By 1882 action was required. Imports of English machinery had approximately tripled since 1879. Other manufacturing industries as well were clamoring for higher duties, and in 1882 a new Tariff Commission was hearing arguments. The Cotton Machinery Builders Association was called by its secretary, William H. Bent (treasurer of the Mason Machine Works) to a meeting to be held at the Boston office of the Lowell Machine Shop on February 15, 1882. The services of lobbyist Hayes were retained, and an assessment was paid by member shops of $250 each. The Lowell Machine Shop's William Burke himself went to Washington and personally presented the arguments of the machine-builders.[18] These arguments followed the classic line which has echoed in Congressional committee rooms down through the years:[19]

> If you relieve the foreign maker of machinery of the duty he would put his price up at once, and I do not believe the American manufacturer would be relieved at all by the taking off of such a duty, while, on the other hand, I think it is to his interest to have it continued. As a manufacturer, I think the American machinery is superior and that it is better to protect the American maker and stimulate him to improve the machinery than to depend upon the manufacturers abroad for it. It is not a very profitable business in one sense. Hardly any new establishments have been erected in some years, and many who were in business have been obliged to retire. The protection has not been sufficient to make it profitable to build new machine shops.

Stockton Bates, of the Bridesburg Manufacturing Company in Pennsylvania, added that labor constituted 50 per cent of the value of textile machinery and that English mechanical labor was 40 to 50 per cent cheaper than American:

Large quantities of English machinery have been imported, almost, if not quite, defying competition under the above conditions. Cotton manufacturers have bought the English machinery on account of the low prices at which it could be obtained, while generally conceding the superiority of the American.

By the terms of the Tariff Act of 1883 the duty on manufactures made from iron was raised from 35 per cent to 45 per cent, ad valorem. On April 28, 1883, Burke addressed a letter to the Honorable William A. Russell, of Lawrence, Massachusetts, representing the Seventh Massachusetts district in Congress, which read, in part, as follows:

The result of legislation on the Tariff Bill in the last session of Congress as it affects the interests of Builders of Textile Machinery in this country, is very gratifying and highly satisfactory—all that could be expected, I had almost said or desired. . . .

For the next ten years the Machinery Builders Association appears to have been almost dormant, although there was some exchange of correspondence in 1888 relative to a proposed tariff on jute machinery. On January 20, 1890, Treasurer Peirson of the Lowell Machine Shop addressed a letter to the members of the association:

At the suggestion of Gen'l Draper, I write to ask you to meet informally some of the principal builders of machinery at my office, on Friday next at eleven o'clock, to see if any concerted action is necessary on our part for protecting our interests at Washington.

This meeting resulted in the appointment of General Draper and William Bent to represent the machine-builders at Washington, and the members agreed to share expenses equally. No marked effort was made as a result of this meeting, and no change was made in the tariff on textile machinery. Peirson's letter is of interest, however, in that it contained a list of the machine shops which presumably were represented by the association. These shops were: the Crompton Loom Works, the Davis & Furber Machine Company, George Draper & Sons, the Fall River Machine Company, the Fales & Jenks

Machine Company, the Franklin Machine Company, the Lewiston Machine Company, the Mason Machine Works, the Pettee Machine Works, the Providence Machine Company, the Saco Water Power Machine Shop, and the Whitin Machine Works.

The introduction of the Wilson Bill shortly after Cleveland's inauguration in 1893 presented a new threat to the machinery builders, and the group organization was quickly activated. English competition had increased despite the high tariff. Imports in 1893 were approximately double those of ten years earlier. The high-tariff interests had a staunch supporter in the House of Representatives in General William F. Draper. Treasurer Stevenson urged Senators George F. Hoar and Henry Cabot Lodge to oppose attempts in the Senate to reduce machinery rates. An assessment was laid on member shops equivalent to 1 per cent of their capital stock. Treasurer Stevenson, of the Lowell Shop, addressed frequent letters to General Draper. A memorial was drawn up and presented to the Tariff Commission by the Machinery Builders Association. William Bent, still secretary of the association, testified personally before the Commission, as did a relatively new figure in the industry, R. P. Snelling, treasurer of the Pettee Machine Works. Bent reiterated long-familiar arguments and sounded a significant new theme:

> Cotton machinery manufactories have been for fifty years, and are now, the nurseries and training schools from which many of the best mechanics in the country have graduated. . . . we are not in any sense monopolists, nor do we enrich ourselves at the expense of the common people . . . there is not now and never has been any trust or combination of cotton machinery builders. . . .

Snelling pointed out that machines which the English had formerly exported to America were now being built by American shops, to the great advantage of the textile industry, and that the attendant investment in new tools made by those shops should be protected. English prices, said Snelling, were as low as American, and the American shops were vitally dependent upon the tariff.

Countering these arguments were statements that a strong preference existed in America for English machinery. The best efforts of the Machinery Builders Association were insufficient to prevent a 10 per cent cut in the tariff, and English competition appears to have been severe until technical progress, aided by a restoration of the tariff cut in 1897, gradually reduced the foreign threat.

Competition from abroad was not serious to American shops in periods of prosperity, when demands of the textile industry generally exceeded the ability of American machine-builders to supply. It was in the depressions following 1873, 1883, 1893, and 1897 that competition had the effect of aggravating the serious, though temporary, over-capacity which existed at those times. High protective tariffs unquestionably were useful in excluding competition from English shops in those depression years, but proximity and local influence, the great advantages of domestic machinery producers, guaranteed a major share of the American market for American shops irrespective of national tariff policy.[20] The most important results of the English threat were to stimulate technical improvement and to give birth to an industry consciousness in America. The possibilities of group action, first discovered in the fight against foreign competition, were soon to be applied to the resolution of excessive competition between domestic machine-builders.

4. Improving the Manufacturing Processes

Technical development from 1879 to 1897 was more a matter of improving existing machines than of inventing new ones. Two outstanding new machines of the period were the revolving flat card, introduced in numbers into America from England in the early and middle 1880's, and the Northrop loom, developed by George Draper & Sons and placed on the market in 1895. Both these machines entirely displaced existing machines, though the process of displacement varied in rapidity. By 1900, for example, the Lowell Machine Shop had completely abandoned the old-style cards,[21] but even as late as 1905 competition from Draper in the loom field had not reduced loom sales appreciably.

The new card and loom exemplified the means by which the American textile processes were being improved, and indicated clearly how the American shops were meeting the English challenge. No new formula was involved. Even in these mature days of the machinery industry, progress was the combined result of original conceptions and copying from the English. Perhaps by the end of the nineteenth century the balance had swung to predominance of native American improvements, but the debt to England was still heavy.

Change was the essence of the 1879–97 period, yet, since that change involved few new machines, these years have not been accorded their proper significance in the unfolding panorama of cotton-textile machinery improvement. Deep-rooted trends matured. The English system of roving entirely displaced the American speeder. The Lowell Machine Shop had produced its first English-type fly frame in 1879, but few of them had subsequently been made. In 1885 the claim was still being advanced that the Lowell speeder made roving equal to that of any fly frame, and that it was extensively used all over the country.[22] By 1893, however, the speeder had been virtually abandoned in favor of a new line of fly frames.[23]

The late nineteenth century also saw the virtual end of the mule in spinning coarse and medium yarns for filling.[24] Improvements in the ring spinning frame which rendered it adaptable to the production of the soft weft yarn as well as warp yarn doomed the mule. Here was one case, among many in nineteenth-century America, where the traditional conflict between quality and speed was resolved in favor of speed. Once a certain minimum standard of quality had been achieved, the greater productivity of the ring frame as compared with that of the mule was a telling argument, and the mule was retained for only the finest work. Speed was not the only factor in the decline of the mule, however. The difficulty in obtaining skilled mule operators was very real. So, too, were the troubles which the predominantly English group of mule operators generated. Having brought with them from England a strong propensity for organization, the mule spinners were not only in themselves perpetually troublesome to management, but the early precedent of the Mule Spinners Association was felt to be dangerous, and undoubtedly was influential in stimulating other labor organizations. In 1893 the Lowell Machine Shop was making few mules; by 1899 it had entirely discontinued their manufacture. The decline of the mule in America may have been the primary cause of an important alteration in competitive forces in the industry. The Mason Machine

Works, a strong contender for business in the three decades following the Civil War, had done more to develop the mule and was more intimately linked to the fate of this machine than any other shop in America. The decline of this great shop to a position of impotence in the field of cotton-textile machinery can scarcely be dissociated from the fate of its most notable textile-machine product.

In 1886 the Pettee Machine Works had commenced to build the English revolving flat card, and the great success which attended the efforts of this firm inspired immediate reactions from the Whitin Machine Works, the Mason Machine Works, and the Lowell Machine Shop. Lowell appears to have won the race among these three to be the second American shop to build this card, and was in production in the early 1890's.

The revolution in spindles, sponsored so effectively by the firm of George Draper & Sons, continued and culminated in the years following 1880. The old-style heavy spindle was completely superseded by the light-weight, high-speed, self-centering spindle. The famous lawsuits of the 1870's had resulted in overwhelming triumphs for Draper, but the textile machinery industry was not yet ready to capitulate. The Lowell Machine Shop, having failed once on technical grounds with the Jackson spindle, now came forward to challenge George Draper as it had once challenged Oliver Pearl.

The immediate stimulus for the challenge may have been the exceptionally advantageous arrangement which the Whitin Machine Works had made with Draper for sale of Draper-controlled spindles. This arrangement came about as a result of the Whitin Gravity Spindle, developed by Whitin in the early 1880's. This spindle resulted not in a lawsuit with Draper, but in an agreement by the terms of which Whitin contributed its gravity spindle patent to the Draper spindle patent pool and in return paid very low royalties to Draper for the spindles it produced (eighteen and one-half cents per spindle, in comparison with the forty-five cents paid by other shops).[25] This Whitin-Draper arrangement naturally gave Whitin a strong competitive advantage over other shops. The sequence of events suggests that the Lowell Machine Shop sought some other spindle the manufacturing rights to which it might secure on comparable terms.

On August 2, 1887, the Lowell Machine Shop entered into a contract with the Eureka Spindle Company, of Ayer, Massachusetts, for the exclusive right to make and sell the improvements in spindles patented by Charles H. Chapman, known to the trade as the Eureka spindle. This contract specified that a price of ninety cents per spindle be charged, of which thirty cents was to cover cost of manufacture, twenty-five cents to represent the profit of the Shop, and thirty-five cents to be paid as royalty to the Eureka Spindle Company. This price might be changed to meet the market, the profit to each varying according to changes made. The Eureka Spindle Company guaranteed to protect the Lowell Machine Shop from lawsuits which might arise (namely, the inevitable conflict with Draper), and the Shop agreed diligently to promote the sale of this spindle.[26]

Draper had brought suit for infringement against the Eureka Spindle Company even before the agreement with the Lowell Machine Shop had been signed, and the Shop threw its resources in the form of money, technical knowledge, and legal experience into the fight. This suit revolved around the interesting point that the patent which Draper claimed was being infringed was one which was not in use in any form. Nevertheless, on February 7, 1888, Treasurer Stevenson telegraphed Superintendent Hildreth, "Don't make any more Eureka spindles. Decision against Eureka Spindle Co." Draper had added one more impressive victory to a formidable record of victories and had, in effect, acquired one more spindle. Complicated negotiations followed in which the Lowell Machine Shop paid Draper $7,528.36 for 27,400 Eureka spindles sold prior to the decision, and was reimbursed for the damage by the Eureka Spindle Company. Henceforth, royalties on the Eureka spindle were raised to forty-five cents, payable in their entirety to George Draper & Sons. This was the last challenge offered to Draper by the Lowell Machine Shop, which continued, after this date, to install Draper spindles and pay the royalties.

The Whitin Machine Works offered one more challenge, which resulted in perhaps the most famous lawsuit of all.[27] Whitin brought out a second patent on its gravity spindle and claimed that, on the basis of that patent, it no longer had to pay Draper any royalties whatsoever. In 1893, after a spectacular exchange of testimony, the suit was decided in Draper's favor, and Whitin was forced to resume paying the same royalties exacted by Draper from other companies in the industry. Treasurer Stevenson, hailing the termination of the preferential royalty rates hitherto enjoyed by Whitin, wrote General Draper, "I congratulate you on your success in the Whitin case."[28]

The firm of George Draper & Sons emerged from the Whitin suit in a position of extraordinary power in the textile machinery industry by virtue of the absolute control exercised over the best spindles in the world. In the remarkable rise to dominance of this firm, antagonisms had been fired, and there was a definite feeling that the Drapers drove hard bargains.[29]

From the textile industry itself came half-serious protestations against the accelerated obsolescence of machinery resulting from the inventive and promotional genius of the firm at Hopedale. Nevertheless, there appears to have been a keen awareness in the Draper organization that its own prosperity was directly tied to that of other textile-machine shops, and the various agreements covering the sale of Draper-controlled products by other shops were predicated upon this realization. No history of any textile-machine shop is complete without an adequate recognition of the effect upon the industry of George Draper & Sons. In Eben S. and William F. Draper the industry found great leaders, whose influence in technology and politics alike was profound. The firm itself probably did more than any other textile-machine shop in the last three decades of the nineteenth century to improve the processes of American cloth manufacture.

Near the end of the 1880–97 period significant changes and experiments in product policy were initiated by the Lowell Machine Shop. These were chiefly in the direction of diversification and are taken up in the following chapter, since they carried over into the years after 1897. In the 1890's, too, some attention was paid to the improvement of manufacturing processes.

The presence of young and able men in the organization saved Superintendent Charles L. Hildreth from some of the ignominy of imposing upon the shop those rigidities often associated with aging management. In 1893 Frederick A. Flather was brought from the Pettee Machine Works to work on designs for the Lowell revolving flat card. Flather found inefficiencies and encountered difficulty in persuading Hildreth to institute needed design alterations. Under Flather's direction much progress was instituted, first in the card department and then throughout the plant. Hildreth was further aided by the more than competent efforts of Channing W. Whitaker, professor at the Massachusetts Institute of Technology, who built the shop's patent department into what was reputed to be the best in the industry.

Some of the improvements in manufacturing techniques effected in the 1890's were in response to Shop needs; others reflected general trends which were industry-wide or nation-wide. Flather bought many new machine tools. "They came into Lowell by the freight car load," reported one of the men then employed at the shop.[30] Significantly enough, these tools came, not from England, as they would have come two decades earlier, but from the Rhode Island firm of Brown and Sharpe. In 1883 three molding machines had appeared in an inventory of shop tools, and orders for more were being placed in the early 1890's. This was a trend of importance in the foundry trade, in which improvement had been stifled for generations by a rigid tradition of handcraftsmanship.[31] At the same time that machine molding was being introduced, the old practice by which each machine shop used distinctive screw sizes (in order, it was alleged, to monopolize repair and replacement demands for its machines) was beginning to give way to the evident advantages of standardization. The Lowell Machine Shop appears to have abandoned the Whitworth Standard of screw sizes in favor of the U. S. Standard in the middle 1890's. This standardization was one aspect of an increasing interest in applying the principle of interchangeable parts to the manufacture of textile machines. By the 1890's the Lowell Machine Shop was advertising that certain of its machines were made with interchangeable parts. The application of this system was limited, however, by the lack of standardization among textile machines themselves. In this field the textile machinery industry had much to learn from other metal-fabricating industries. That the lesson had not been learned earlier is a tribute to the strength of customer demands for specially designed machines.

Some lessons in the field of product policy had been well learned, and at no little expense. The need for a specialized patent expert in an age of increasing legal complications was appreciated and fulfilled. The necessity for new, young talent had been recognized as being as great as that for new, improved tools. Above all else, in these years of rich and varied experience the value of sound, enduring machines had been proven. On occasion, prices might safely be lowered; standards of quality never. The Lowell Machine Shop continued to incorporate all the accumulated skill at its command in turning out solid machines, and herein lay its greatest strength. In the 1880–97 period it was a strength which, when coupled with cautious business policy at the top levels of management, was enough to create high profits in prosperous times and avoid crippling losses in the dark years of business.

CHAPTER VIII

THE YEARS OF DECLINE
The Lowell Machine Shop, 1897–1905

By 1897 the Lowell Machine Shop had become a fat and lazy giant, surfeited with good living, its senses dulled and its muscles grown flabby from too infrequent and too easily repelled challenges. When the final challenge came this hulk once stirred was formidable in size but lethargic in action — no match for battle-hardened rivals. The years from 1897 to 1905 witnessed the decline and fall of the Lowell Machine Shop.

The decline came not as a result of financial or technological weakness, but from failure in the field of marketing. This failure must be linked with the Boston office and the complacent agreement of top management with Boston shareholders that this was a New England institution and hence, by definition, steadfast against all change. The prevalence of this attitude has been exaggerated, but it had pervaded no small part of Boston-controlled business in the late nineteenth century and was a marked change from the earlier daring which had built great companies and great fortunes together. It cost few companies their lives, for its essence was ultraconservative business policy, but it was a factor in hastening the loss by Massachusetts of her industrial leadership.

1. The 1890's: Uncertainty and Change

The hard years from 1890 to 1898 marked a turning point in the history of the textile machinery industry, and possibly of American business as well. There was much in the general business scene to worry the directors of the Lowell Machine Shop. These men had made a supreme effort in 1888 to elect a Republican president and thus end the attacks on the tariff which had characterized the preceding term of office of Grover Cleveland. The campaign was a success, but Harrison's election provided only momentary relief. T. Jefferson Coolidge, who had served as president of the Shop and as a director for many years, probably voiced the fears of his associates.[1] Securities, he said in 1890, were declining continuously, business was uncertain, Massachusetts was being heavily taxed, and gold was being hoarded. Cleveland's reëlection in 1892 brought further discomfiture, though Cleveland himself was not unacceptable to New England business leaders. He wanted good money, Coolidge conceded, but had too little experience and knowledge to be able to judge so difficult a matter. In 1893, Boston banks issued clearing-house certificates. "Business affairs continued bad and the Boston railroads, the Atchison, the Union Pacific, and the New York and New England, were in the hands of receivers. When they were taken out the management was transferred to New York, whose immense wealth is gradually absorbing the whole country." The year 1894 brought the Pullman strikes, Eugene Debs, and the specter of labor organized. Mill wages in the South were said to be 30 per cent lower than in the North. The Presidential campaign of 1896 provoked greatest anxiety. Mills were closed down and railroads lost business. Bryan delivered his "Cross of Gold" speech — "the dread of repudiation by the free coinage of silver hung like a pall over us."

The depression of 1896–98 climaxed three decades of declining prices and increasing competition. Aggressive marketing had failed to provide a universal remedy, and business turned with increasing enthusiasm to various forms of combinations within industries and between industries. Methods were sought by which available business could be shared at something better than ruinous prices. Business made new enemies and aroused old. The shadow of monopoly was cast whenever two business men talked together. Experiments in public regulation of the railroad industry pointed a way by which the advantages of free competition might be ensured to the buying and voting public. In 1890 the Sherman Anti-Trust Act had been passed, and the "trust-busting" days were not far off. Companies continued to strive both within and outside the framework of industry-imposed and government-imposed regulations to promote volume business by active marketing.

The form of the textile machinery industry was changing. From a mere handful of shops in 1820, the number of machine-builders had multiplied rapidly and steadily until about the 1865–73 period (no one year can be established as the turn of the trend). Rapidly thereafter many of the smaller shops began to disappear, and by 1896 most of the business was firmly entrenched in some fifteen large shops, of which one was in Maine, four were in Rhode Island, and ten in Massachusetts. Two of Saco-Lowell's parent shops had merged in 1897 to form the Saco and Pettee Machine Shops. The Lowell Machine Shop, the Saco and Pettee Machine Shops, and the Whitin Machine Works led the industry in point of size and completeness of line. In addition to the fifteen leading shops there were a number of specialists who made and sold one type of machine or machine parts only. Parts specialists appear to have been increasing in number. The industry picture is completed by the inclusion of the mill engineer, offering plans and advice rather than machines and competing with the mill engineering departments of the Whitin Machine Works and the Lowell Machine Shop.

Specialization among the large shops offered only minor disadvantages when the concentrated New England textile industry was being served. The rise of distant markets in the South — the great increase in orders for complete mills — further modified the form of the machinery industry. The immediate stimulus for this further evolution may have been provided by the severe depression of 1896, during which the machine shops were impelled by the scarcity of orders to adopt every conceivable measure which might improve their competitive position.

In 1896 and 1897 the specialized machine-makers began to draw together. The purpose of this move was to secure to the participating shops the advantages attendant upon offering buyers, particularly in the South, a complete line of machinery. The method of accomplishment was the employment of resident Southern agents, through whose offices were funneled the combined output of a number of shops.

The Charlotte Machine Company may have been the first of these agencies, for it was in existence at least as early as 1893.[2] In 1896 this agency was handling Atherton pickers; Pettee cards and drawing; Providence Machine Company roving; Fales & Jenks spinning; and Knowles looms — a complete line of cotton-textile machinery. In 1894 the Whitin Machine Works was represented in the South by Godfrey's Textile Machinery Agency and by D. A. Tompkins. By 1895 S. W. Cramer, Tompkins' assistant, had displaced these agents and was employed by Whitin on a salary basis. Cramer offered Whitin's machinery, reinforced by Woonsocket Machine Company's roving and Kitson pickers — another complete line.[3] After the merger of the Pettee Machine Works and the Saco Water Power Company in 1897, the roving and spinning of the latter company displaced the corresponding machinery of the Fales & Jenks Machine Company and the Providence Machine Company from the Charlotte Machine Company agency, and the two displaced companies formed an alliance with the A. H. Robbins agency, securing picking, carding, and looms wherever possible to offer a third complete line of machinery in the South.[4]

After 1897 the competitive position of the Lowell Machine Shop began to deteriorate rapidly. The great advantage hitherto enjoyed by the Shop in the Southern market was the almost exclusive possession of a complete line of machinery. The resident-agency system effectively and completely nullified that advantage by enabling the specialists (some of whose machines were probably superior to the Lowell machines) to compete effectively for complete orders. Aside from the three agencies named above, the Lowell Machine Shop found itself competing with Mason's resident agent Tompkins after 1897. In that year the English firm of Howard & Bullough built an American plant near Providence and also began to offer a full line of machinery through a resident Southern agent. Two other English lines, complete or nearly so, were being offered through resident American agencies. In addition, competition from mill engineers began to be felt by some shops. The most powerful of these engineering firms, Lockwood Greene & Company, directed very few orders to Lowell. The increasing influence of this firm swung chiefly to the Pettee-Charlotte Machine Company group.

With at least six full lines of cotton machinery being offered in the South at a time when business was generally depressed, competition for orders became deadly and relentless. This situation was faced by much of American business in the 1890's. For some, foreign markets had provided an outlet for excess productive capacity — a safety valve for the mounting competitive pressure. This source of relief was closed to the textile machinery industry by the almost complete dominance of the world market by the English shops. There is ample evidence of the omnipotence of the English machine-makers. In 1883 the *British Trade Journal* reported that the Americans were about to make a determined effort to introduce cotton machinery into Russia. Treasurer Burke, of the Lowell Machine Shop, reported to the United States consul in Moscow at about the same time, however, that American machine-makers could not hope to compete abroad with cheap English labor and materials. The Continental market was effectively supplied not only by the English, but also by the Alsatian shops of Schlumberger and Manurhin and the Swiss shops of Rieter, Sulzer, and Escherwyss. All these Continental shops enjoyed superior advantages in matters of labor and material costs, plus an additional margin provided by transoceanic freight rates.[5]

The Lowell Machine Shop and the Whitin Machine Works had exported no substantial amounts of machinery by 1905. Neither do general export figures (which, to be sure, are far from detailed) indicate any significant movement of American textile machinery abroad. This conclusion definitely does not apply to specialized American parts or to specific American machines. The American light-weight spindles, the Wellman card stripper, and the Foss & Pevey card all appear to have found an export market. American textile machinery in general, however — the complete or nearly complete lines such as those manufactured by Lowell and Whitin — found no great demand abroad.

Such sales as the Lowell Machine Shop did make in the foreign market were confined to depression years. Before 1905 there was no continuously followed policy of developing a foreign trade. Superintendent Hildreth stated the attitude of the Shop in the following words:[6]

Your favor of the 7th is received, and in reply we beg to say that at the present time we are not prepared to entertain a proposition such as you propose, viz; — the sale of our machinery in Mexico. This matter has been under consideration for some little time, and had business continued as it was two years ago, no doubt something would have been realized from it, but the unprecedented demand for machinery for mills in this country has completely filled us up with work for a long time to come, and we are in no condition now to make any sales for export. No doubt as soon as business begins to fall off again in this country we shall endeavor to make some arrangements for the sale of our machinery in Mexico.

A few large foreign orders are to be noted in the Lowell Machine Shop records prior to 1900. In 1883 an order totaling $60,000 had been supplied the Shanghai Cotton Cloth Mill Company. In 1890 a $150,000 contract had been signed with the Salvador Cotton Mills, with the assistance of the United States consul at San Blas, Mexico. In this same year $20,000 of machinery had been sold to a Brazilian mill, and about $40,000 more to the Shanghai Cotton Cloth Mill Company. Between 1890 and 1900, foreign sales were negligible. In 1900 a quickening interest in the South American market became apparent — an interest which was pervading much of American business. In this year the Lowell Machine Shop printed a catalogue in Spanish and was sending machinery to South American mills through the agency of G. Amsinck & Company, a New York commission house. Total South American sales in the five years which followed, however, were less than $50,000.

These periodic excursions into the foreign market had no immediate effect upon the competitive position of the Shop; they were significant more for the vista they unfolded than for the profit they returned. Remedies for over-competition in the textile machinery industry, if they were to be found at all, would have to be found within the protecting enclosure of American tariff walls. American shops sharpened their weapons for a close-in struggle.

2. Warfare in the Markets

It was in the decade of the 1890's that the refusal of the Lowell Machine Shop to accept the stock of Southern mills in payment for machinery became serious. This practice, reluctantly subscribed to by the machine-builders before 1897 at the urging of the Southern mills, was turned thereafter into an aggressive competitive tool by the bolder shops. The percentage of total Southern mill stock so taken by the machine-builders was certainly not large. Nevertheless, on individual orders, where the buyer's choice wavered between two competitors, the offer by one to accept partial payment in stock was almost certain to be decisive, even in the face of lower prices quoted by the other. The Lowell Machine Shop superintendent commented often, and in a rather wistful tone, on the various orders which the Shop lost through failure to make a stock offer. The policy of refusal, however, was inflexibly pursued.

The Lowell Machine Shop fought increasing competition with all the means countenanced by a conservative directorate. The first full-time salesman, E. P. Dennis, was first addressed in Shop correspondence in 1889, at which time (and thereafter) he was making periodic trips through the South, visiting old and prospective customers, quoting prices and terms, and gathering information on trade conditions and competitors. The employment of a full-time salesman, however, was in no sense a substitute for the promotional activities, such as they were, of the treasurer and the superintendent. Dennis' activities supplemented but did not replace previously existing marketing efforts.

Shop advertising was both extended and improved. By 1896, advertisements were being placed in all leading trade papers and in many Southern newspapers. These advertisements illustrated the various Lowell machines, as did the larger and more informative catalogues which were issued. The Shop continued to offer prospective customers highly competent engineering services. Under the direction of Charles C. Hedrick mill plans were drawn up on request and furnished to mill promoters at no cost, provided that machinery orders were forthcoming. In 1899 the Lowell Machine Shop opened a Southern office in Atlanta, Georgia, in the heart of the Shop's strongest sales territory.

The Atlanta office was placed in charge of a local man, John Hill, whose background and training are unknown. Hill worked on a commission basis (probably 5 per cent of sales), and the Atlanta office served as the chief point of contact with the Southern market. Hill visited customers all over the South, answered local inquiries, and investigated complaints and credit ratings. Machines were exhibited at the office, and after 1903 Hill had a technician permanently at his disposal for servicing Lowell machines in the South. Dennis, the traveling representative, worked closely with Hill, although not under his direction, and in 1900 Rogers W. Davis was attached to the Atlanta office to assist Hill further. Hill was also the agent for a line of mill supplies which augmented, rather than competed with, the Lowell line of machines. Such supplies, which included gearing, ventilating and air-moistening devices, electrical installations, and many other items, were habitually carried by the various Southern agents. This line was a convenience to Shop customers, but there was a potential danger in thus dividing the attention of the resident agent.

The question of Shop policy in the South became increasingly important after 1890. The tremendous increase in Southern spindles between 1880 and 1890 was surpassed in the decade which followed. In 1891, for the first time, the Lowell Machine Shop had sold more machinery in the South than in all other sections of the country combined. Chart VII indicates on a yearly basis the trend of the Shop's Southern sales in comparison with total sales in all other sections of the country.

On repeated occasions the Shop treasurer stated the policy of favoring old customers, both as to terms and as to delivery dates. With a few exceptions, old customers prior to 1880 meant New England customers. This constituted a self-imposed handicap, which unquestionably interfered with maximum exploitation of the Southern market. By the ties of tradition and ownership the Lowell Machine Shop was inextricably bound to a declining market. The decline of the New England mills, however, was relative rather than absolute. This fact, coupled with the generally hard times which prevailed from 1893 to 1896, may well have concealed the inherent danger in the situation. In 1880 the New England industry comprised 81 per cent of total spindles in the United States. By 1900 the ratio had fallen to 67 per cent, though the number of spindles in the North had actually increased.[7] In the period from 1896 to 1905 many of the Lowell mills experienced financial difficulties, and other Shop customers in Massachusetts, Maine, and New Hampshire began to cut dividend rates, reorganize on a smaller capitalization, or open Southern plants.[8] When the last-named remedy was adopted, the

Shop benefited greatly, of course. An example is provided by the Massachusetts Cotton Mills, an old Lowell customer, which in 1896, 1898, and 1902 built mills in the South.[9] Orders from the Massachusetts Mills in Georgia totaled $573,500 over the 1896–1902 period and included the second largest single order ever taken by the Shop to that time ($268,700 in 1895, exceeded only by the Merrimack order for $280,572 of machinery in 1848). However, Appendix 10, listing all Shop orders of $50,000 or more, clearly reveals the declining importance of the New England market.

CHART VII

Lowell Machine Shop Sales, 1880–1905

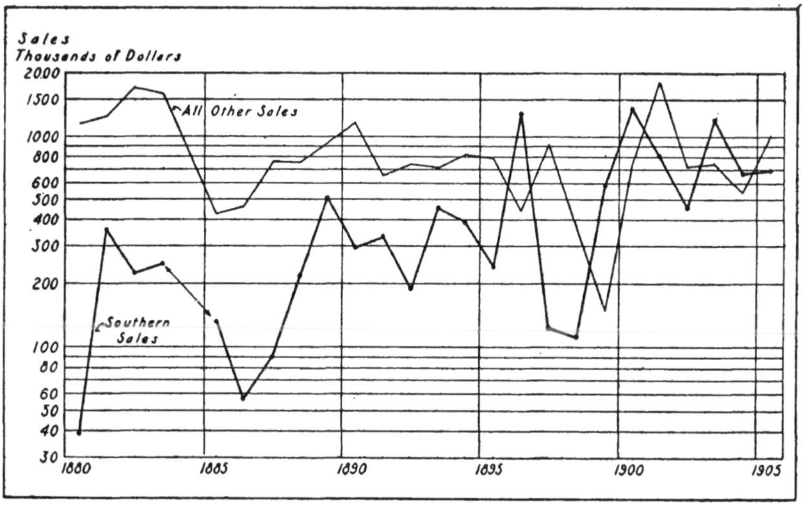

Within New England itself, ability to compete with the Southern industry varied considerably. With the lessening margin of profit, Fall River, New Bedford, and the other tidewater mills in the North gained an advantage through cheaper transportation of cotton and coal by water over the inland mills which comprised the Lowell Machine Shop's traditional market. Inability to obtain increased power from the Merrimack and other rivers to meet the larger demands caused by expansion of the industry forced the inland mills to depend more and more upon coal transported at large expense from distant coal fields, part of the way by rail.[10] Because of competitors' established strength there, the Lowell Machine Shop was never strong in Fall River, New Bedford, or Rhode Island markets and failed to realize the partially compensating benefits to be derived from the growth of these manufacturing centers.

After 1890 the competitive position of the Lowell Machine Shop was weakened by one other circumstance. Table 16 in Chapter VII shows the predominance of orders from Georgia over those from either North or South Carolina, the two other most important Southern textile-manufacturing States. Between 1890 and 1900 the number of spindles in North and South Carolina nearly quadrupled, while, throughout the same decade, the number of spindles in Georgia did not quite double. After 1900 the position of the Lowell Machine Shop in the Carolinas became progressively weaker. The Whitin Machine Works, by way of contrast, had cast its lot with the North Carolina mills at an early date and in 1902 it made a successful drive for business in South Carolina, securing a hold on these most important markets which apparently could not be dislodged. Thus, even the conservative bid which the Lowell Machine Shop did make for Southern business was rendered less effective than it might have been by an initial preoccupation with one area only — by the failure to build up an early influence in what was to become the most lucrative part of the Southern market.

In an industry in which the quality of machines produced by the various competing units varied but little from best to worst, competition was bound to revolve, sooner or later, around the matter of terms and prices. It was upon this field that the battle between the Northern machine shops was joined. The Lowell Machine Shop, a low-cost producer with tremendous financial strength, was probably better able than most to seek business on a price basis.

The inevitability of the price conflict was clinched not only by the depression of 1896, but by the emergence of new or rejuvenated competitors. Under the direction of Frank J. Hale and R. P. Snelling, the Pettee Machine Works came to life. The fate of Howard & Bullough's new American plant was placed in the aggressive hands of C. E. Riley, who had previously represented this English company in the American market. These men were all in a position where they had to fight strongly established rivals for their very existence. They competed with an enthusiasm which rocked the conservative old industry. Price warfare was certainly not originated by these relatively new competitors, but their presence and effectiveness accentuated a tendency already present.

Having experienced a degree of price competition in the depressions of 1874, 1883, and 1893, the textile machinery industry was not anxious for more. The precedent of group action in a common cause, first established in tariff fights of earlier years and carried forward by means of the American Cotton Machinery Builders Association, was now followed in meeting a still greater problem. The Machinery Builders Association apparently continued to be the vehicle by which decisions were made and industry-wide action taken.

By 1894 some agreement seems to have been reached among the principal shops setting a base price for spinning, since Treasurer Stevenson warned Superintendent Hildreth to exercise the greatest care that no departures be made from the price schedule furnished.[11] This may have been the first industry-wide price agreement in the textile machinery business,[12] although information is limited by the extreme secrecy which was exercised. That secrecy had a slightly ludicrous aspect. Customers could scarcely have avoided knowing that an agreement was in effect; indeed, they were making agreements among themselves to sustain cloth prices.[13] Much of American business was involved, in one way or another, in price-fixing, yet so guarded were the efforts that very few historical details of this important and widespread technique have survived. The secrecy engendered public suspicion and assumed a sinister connotation, which in many instances was out of all proportion to the actual evils involved in the restraint of trade. Such economic merits as the practice possessed were, of course, not made known to the public and could not be, since business men themselves usually understood only the short-term advantages to the immediate participants.

In 1895 Eben S. Draper, of the firm of George Draper & Sons, served as industry moderator in setting up minimum prices on spinning machinery, but it is doubtful if he was interested in agreements on the many types of machines which his firm did not build or supply parts for.[14]

By June, 1896, cards, railway heads, and drawing were included under pricing agreements. In this year the machine shops attempted not only to restrict credit sales to new Southern mills but also to eliminate the practice of accepting mill stocks in part payment for machinery. The 1896 agreement specified that no stock should be accepted in payment for machinery; that the most favorable terms of payment any shop should make would be one-half cash, one-quarter in six months, and one-quarter in twelve months; and that certain standard practices should be followed in dividing the machinery-erecting expense between shops and mills.[15] Northern comment on the new agreement was voiced in the following words:[16]

> We consider this an excellent move on the part of these cotton-machinery builders who have been quite free in supplying machinery and taking large blocks of stock in partial payment. . . . The principle is not a good one and is unbusinesslike, and any such arrangement should have been stopped some time ago, or, better, should never have been entered into.
>
> The probable effect of this understanding will be less cotton-mill building in the Southern States. The erection of cotton factories in the South has been overdone, and the time has arrived when conservatism should govern the ambition of the people in that section toward the erection of cotton mills. . . .
>
> We do not believe that the machinery people of New England have any desire to restrict this industry, for they know that the situation would be promptly met by the importation of English machinery, and later by the establishment of textile machinery plants in the South. We believe that this is simply a business matter brought about by the general depression, making it difficult to handle the stock of new mills.

These various agreements were scarcely in effect before they were broken. Some were broken even before they had gone into effect. The principal obstacles to successful price maintenance in the textile machinery industry, as in other industries, was the lack of means for enforcement and the severity of the competitive pressure which the price agreements strove to hold in check. The Machinery Builders Association could, at the most, only exclude a violator from membership. The expelled member would then be able to compete with members on any terms he wished. There is no record that any shop

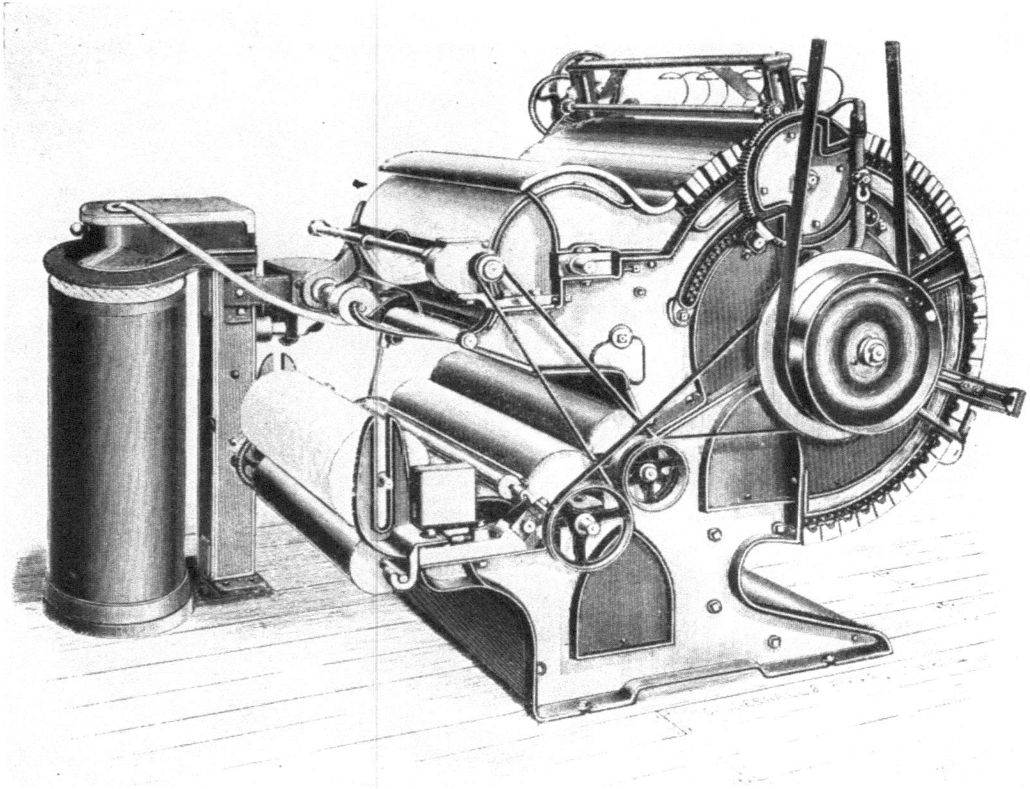

Foss & Pevey Card in 1898 — Built by the Lowell Machine Shop

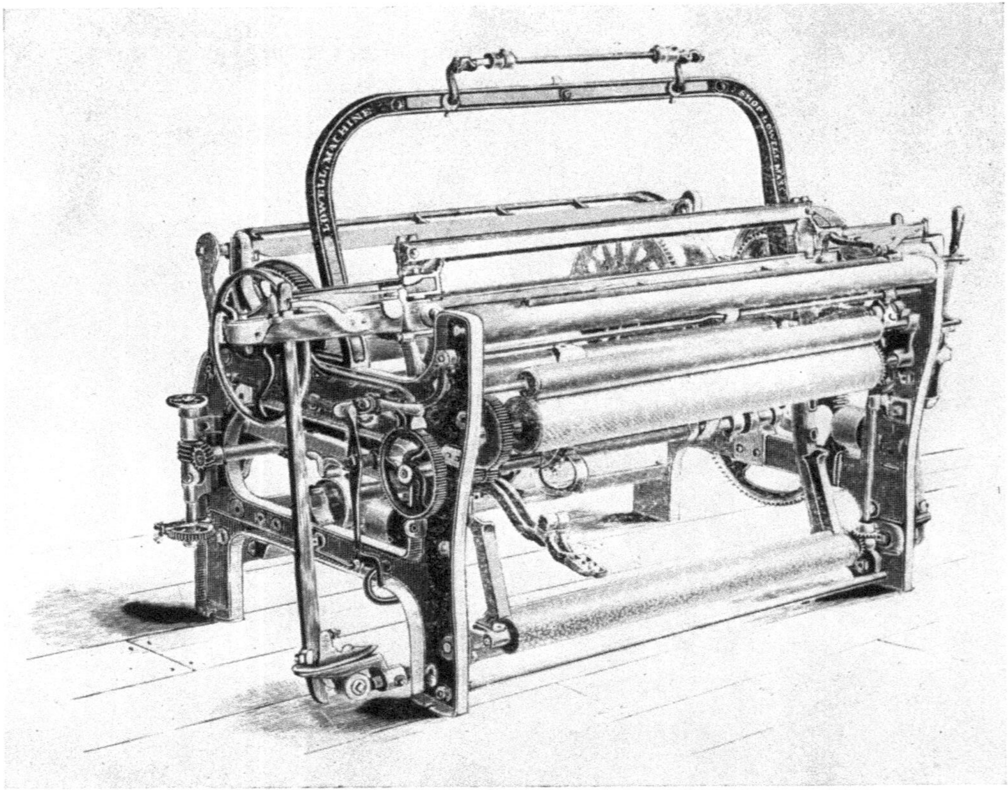

Lowell 36-Inch Sheeting Loom in 1898

ever was so penalized. The attempts to curtail credit sales and the acceptance of Southern stock by Northern machine shops were doomed from the start to be ineffective. Far from wishing to discourage mill-building in the South, the machinery manufacturers did all in their power to extend the industry there. Many, like the Pettee Machine Works, even went beyond the practice of accepting partial payment in stock and began to take an active part in the promotion of new mills.

After 1895 one price agreement after another was made, and the industry became increasingly demoralized as the means of restraining competition failed. From 1897 to 1905 George Marston Whitin, himself one of the hardest competitors, stands out as the industry moderator and leader in attempts to prevent complete chaos by maintaining prices. The Lowell Machine Shop played a passive part. Stevenson, the treasurer, participated reluctantly in the agreements, threatened to withdraw on one occasion (thereby precipitating a crisis which sent the managers of all shops hastening southward to be on hand when the agreement collapsed!), and refused to participate at all in one agreement.[17] Neither did the Lowell Machine Shop initially compete on a price basis so aggressively in the South as did some other shops.

There is no evidence prior to 1905 that the Machinery Builders Association made any attempts at a formal allocation of markets among member shops, or that such allocations were a concomitant of the price agreements. There had grown up in the industry, however, a definite, if unwritten, respect for spheres of influence. These were probably more on a customer than on a geographic basis — or, rather, the geographic basis might be transcended in specific cases. Before the 1890's a Lowell customer or a Whitin customer was not considered a prospective buyer of other machinery until he, himself, approached a competitor and asked for bids, and sometimes not even then. After 1894 the efforts of Southern agents, who were divorced from the tradition and neighborly feeling which existed between some machine-shop owners in the North, shattered the tacit respect for established customer ties.

The Pettee Machine Works and Howard & Bullough were unquestionably two of the most aggressive shops in the field. Neither hesitated to lure customers away from traditional and long-standing alliances by concessions in prices. George Marston Whitin, though obviously in favor of restraining excessive competition, was forced by the pressure of the times to give Cramer, his Southern agent, much freedom. Stuart W. Cramer was without peer among Southern agents. His stature and influence in the South were great, and he was both disliked and feared by his rivals as being a hard competitor. Hill, the agent of the Lowell Machine Shop, appears to have been less aggressive than his competitors; perhaps he was held in leash by the Boston office. The reaction of the Lowell Machine Shop to the early inroads by competitors on established markets was defensive until about 1902 — and definitely aggressive thereafter. The effect of new competitive units and new competitive verve on the part of established units was to lay the textile-machinery market open for seizure by those who were the strongest and most active.[18]

Marketing tactics became not only more aggressive, but more ingenious, particularly in respect to means of avoiding price agreements. Rebates in the form of unrecorded credit memoranda were given customers. In some cases bidders faced with a highly competitive situation would "forget" to bill certain machines on the order list.

On one occasion a salesman, endeavoring to secure an order without formally violating the price agreements, was faced with the adamant refusal of the prospective customer to listen to any arguments based on the quality of the machines involved. "I am interested in one thing only," stated the customer, *"price!"*

The salesman, requesting a few minutes to consider the matter, withdrew from the office. Quickly refiguring his quotations, he made an "error" in the calculations which resulted in a substantially lower total quotation. The order was placed. When the "error" was discovered at the home office the salesman was called in to see the agent of the Shop. "Young man," he was lectured, with mock severity, "you are a better salesman than mathematician!" That was the end of the incident, and the contract was fulfilled at the lower price.[19]

Considerable liberty was taken with freight charges, a fertile field for hidden price reductions. In some cases bids were quoted at an over-all figure with no individual prices specified. This, a favorite device for evading agreements, was used by the Lowell Machine Shop on more than one occasion after 1902. On some orders which included machines not covered by the agreements, a very low price could be quoted on such machines, offsetting, in effect, the "legal" price on the remainder of the order. The practice of giving customers options to buy at existing prices was instituted. Options were granted as soon as the machine shops felt that a new price agreement was imminent, thereby violating the agreement even before it had become effective.[20]

Once a break had occurred in the price agreements, the industry was forced to follow the downward course of bids. Thus, prices which started at an agreed-upon "list" might, by general practice, soon fall to list minus 10 per cent. Here they would pause until some shop broke through the floor to list minus 20 per cent, which price level would soon come to be the tacitly recognized minimum. When the point was reached where orders were being taken at or near the break-even point, a meeting of machine-shop treasurers and agents would be called, and new list prices established at a level which would ensure a profit. Then the downward spiral would commence again.

The history of machinery price agreements and competitive practice cannot, for lack of data, be presented in its entirety. After 1899 the story is best told in the words of Charles L. Hildreth, superintendent of the Lowell Machine Shop. The excerpts below are direct quotations from his letters to John Hill, the Shop's Southern agent. Few explanatory additions can be added, for these letters comprise virtually all that is known of the Shop's part in the agreements. Where explanations are possible, they have been inserted in brackets.

January 14, 1899: We have quoted Fulton B & C Mills of Atlanta $300 for a similar slasher cylinder including boxing. This is less than our new price list, but if we are obliged to reduce prices on these articles to obtain our fair share of the work we shall do so. If you should chance to learn the prices quoted by COHOE or PHILLIPS on slashers we shall be glad to learn them.

February 3, 1899: We enclose one of the new price lists, there have been many changes in prices outside of the combination figures [the combination of machinery builders] so please take note of same.

March 2, 1899: The Prov. Mach. Co. have notified us of their withdrawal from the combine. No further steps have yet been taken by the other builders, but we will wire you at once on any changes in price, so advise us where we shall be able to reach you by wire each day. [Upon threat of a break in the combine, each shop stood ready on a moment's notice to rush into the market with low bids.]

March 15, 1899: In reply to yours of the 13th would say that under present circumstances and conditions of trade that we do not deem it wise to make any cut in prices, as materials have advanced and are hard to obtain. We have put down the prices of the machines as taken from the regular price book. We have been covered up with orders for quick delivery on spinning and cannot promise any more frames for ten weeks, unless it is for some exceptional case accompanied with cards and Fly Frames. Our chance on the Tallassee order is good but cannot tell until order is placed.

April 14, 1899: [Telegram.] If you are satisfied others are making concessions on outside machinery, use your discretion. [Referring to practice of quoting very low prices on parts of orders not covered by price agreements.]

April 17, 1899: . . . it is very annoying to have our competitors cut prices when both they and ourselves are having all the work that we can do for several months to come. But it does not seem best to us just at this time to take any steps in regard to it, other than to protest against it, and keep ourselves informed as to the circumstances.

It certainly seems strange that when there is considerable agitation among the different shops to increase prices, they should undertake to reduce them. As we wrote to you sometime ago the cost of materials has advanced between 40 and 50 per cent., and some even are very hard to get at that price, and we think that under the circumstances our best policy is to keep our tempers, and let them take as much of the low price work as they care to undertake. [The fatal policy of the Lowell Machine Shop!]

January 18, 1900: The Laurel Miss. people have not yet closed their order, but will probably do so this week. If they gave Cramer a provisional order at lower prices, he will probably obtain it, as we are not yet making concessions of this sort.

March 29, 1900: At a meeting of the Treasurers of the Textile Builders it was agreed that the charge for erecting machinery should be hereafter $4.00 per day, per man. . . . This is not official, however, but you will probably receive official notice in the course of a few days, as soon as the committee appointed shall have reported on the matter in due form.

June 22, 1900: We enclose two copies of the new authorized edition of prices. Please take note of the various changes and additions that have been made, as there are some few items.

February 26, 1901: Replying to your favor of the 26th, beg to say, in regard to the reduction in prices, that the machinery builders had a meeting yesterday, and decided that it would not be wise to make any reduction in prices at the present time; consequently, any stories that may be reported about a reduction are not true.

Mr. Snelling [R. P. Snelling, of the Pettee Machine Works] told Mr. Stevenson that the Riverside Mills made him an offer on the Cards at a reduction in price, and that he declined to accept it.

March 29, 1901: Enclosed we give you prices and weights of the different classes of Looms called for. If necessary to do so, you may make a reduction of 10% in the prices we have given you.

April 25, 1901: If your competitors are cutting prices on cancelled machinery, you now have the opportunity of applying the same terms to the Coffee Cotton Mills' machinery in competing on mills where they are quoting prices below the combination. [Referring to practice of offering machinery ordered and then canceled by one mill to another at a reduced price.]

October 4, 1901: As regards prices, outside of terms, we think you have instructions to meet anybody's price.

May 9, 1902: . . . we are very sorry that Mr. Milstead placed his order with H. & B., but, undoubtedly, if they took stock, as you intimated they did, that it was best to have it go that way.

Most all of the shops are quite full of work taken at low prices, as you say, and there is no reason why we should not obtain a good many orders at very fair prices.

July 31, 1902: We note your remarks in regard to the discount that Whitin is giving to some of his customers, and we think by this time he would be very sorry that he has done so, as the cost of all materials has advanced almost 75%, and it is even difficult to obtain them at that figure. . . . Under these circumstances, it would be well to go slow about reducing prices, if one has any regard for the stockholders.

February 2, 1903: The order of the Gluck Mills went to Howard & Bullough, as they took stock in the mill. . . . All of the five mills that were placed here last week were stock mills, consequently we had no show.

February 3, 1903: Your favors of the 31st from Charlotte are received, and we hardly know what to say in regard to the reduction in prices at this time, until Mr. Stevenson returns, which we expect will be the first of next week. There may have been an understanding among some of the builders that they must get together and force prices up to a living basis, and for this reason there has been, as we understand it, a circulation of reports in the South which has caused the proposed mills to place their orders *at once*. As we have written you, there have been four or five large mills placed here in the East within the last two weeks; and this we are sure would not have been done so *suddenly* had not a report been spread that if orders were not placed, prices would be higher, also there has been an undercurrent feeling that there was some kind of a deal going on among the machinery builders. Of course we here in Lowell are not in a position to know any of the particulars or have any association or whatever you might call it, going on.

Prices here in the East have been run down to almost 20%, and, in some cases more, below the standard prices, and, no doubt, quite a lot of orders have been placed at these figures, besides taking stock, although we have always believed that where stock was taken, the prices were higher, but we do not know so for a fact. . . .

We are quite sure that the other shops are not getting rich out of these prices, and it seems to us that they are using the same practices as they did before the last combination went into effect.

February 13, 1903: I herewith enclose you a copy of a letter just received from the Treasurer, also a copy of the new prices, adopted by the Machinery Builders, which prices you will use in quotations on our machinery. If you have any bids out, which you think should hold, I should be glad to have you notify me of same before closing.

February 21, 1903: In regard to the matter of new prices and the quotations that you have made, would say that we should like to hear from you separately on each of these orders where you have quoted, when the parties are ready to order. We do not intend to be euchred out of any orders, and at the same time, we wish to keep fully up to the prices that have been fixed, but we wish to have each case reported on separately and dealt with separately. . . . We note the point that you make and consider it a good one, that this matter of prices was effected too quickly, and did not give us any opportunity to cover our customers or ourselves, while the other builders had ample opportunity to do so.

July 31, 1903: Regarding the making of concessions in prices, would say that if you are sure that prices are being quoted for less than the list, you are authorized to meet them, and to make such prices as will secure the work. . . . We have recently heard of some very low prices on spinning here in the North, but are rather loath to believe that our competitors would be so foolish as to make low prices when they have so much to do, as undoubtedly, many of them have guaranteed their prices against any reduction, and, of course, if we can get full prices we should much prefer to do it; but we cannot allow the shop to become slack of work by not meeting prices. I fully believe you will understand the position I wish to take in the matter and I leave it to your best judgement as to where and when to make a cut.

August 13, 1903: Referring to your favor of the 7th, we beg to say that we note it is rather difficult to obtain any positive information in regard to cuts that are being made in prices. At the same time, we feel that the time has come now where we must secure the work, even at lower prices than we have hitherto quoted. At the same time, we desire to keep our quotations as far as possible at the list price, but in case we have an opportunity to make a sale, you are authorized to make such concessions in prices as will secure the order.

September 24, 1903: I hardly know what to answer you until I know from what source you obtained the information, in regard to Mr. Twitchell's feeling disposed to give his work to the Whitins. He has been always quite favorable to us here and I do not know of any reason why he should change from the Lowell Machine Shop to the Whitin people, unless it is because of the liberality in credit which is given on the mills which they have secured the orders for.

October 19, 1903: Enclosed please find inquiry from the Lane Mills for seven slashers. We supposed that this order had been placed elsewhere some time ago. It might be well for you to see Mr. Odenheimer at once in regard to these machines and to ascertain whether there is other machinery, the orders for which have not yet been placed. Of course, if any orders have been placed for machinery, it would not be fair or good policy to attempt to take them away from other makers, and we should decline to accept orders that were given us under such circumstances.

October 23, 1903: We also have your favor in regard to the Tipton Mills and hope that you will be successful in securing the order. If possible, we think it would be better to make a lump price on this order rather than an individual price, as you are aware we are under contract with the Clifton Mfg. Co., to give them the benefit of any lower prices than when they placed their order, which was at the $6.50 basis [$6.50 per spindle base price for fly frames]. As we have sold Fly Frames at the $6.00 basis, we shall have to give them a rebate on the difference, and until they are supplied with their machinery, we think it well not to go below this price, but make the cut in some other direction, so that we can honestly say that we have sold no Fly Frames for less than the $6.00 basis.

January 11, 1904: [Hildreth authorizing a 23% discount from list prices.] I realize the fact that the prices are extremely low ones and that there would not be much profit, if any, at either of these figures, but it seems to me as if we could afford to take one or two orders at the cost of the labor and material in order to keep our men together and the organization of the Shop intact.

March 8, 1904: There is very little new work here, although there are some orders that have been taken at extremely low prices by our competitors.

March 14, 1904: We do not see how prices are to be advanced at the present time, especially on Card Room Machinery, as we have known cases of sales here in New England at even lower prices than what we gave to McClain, which, as you know, was an unusually low figure. It is probable, therefore, that our competitors will continue to make low prices until they are well filled up with work. As the matter now stands, nearly all the shops are flocking after work at some price, and we do not look for better prices until there are more orders to go around. We hope, therefore, that you will endeavor to secure the order of Capt. Kincaid, if possible. Of course, it will be absolutely necessary to protect our old customers and we shall expect you to do it.

March 21, 1904: I hope you will make every exertion to get the rest of the order from our friends at Griffin, as it is my impression that the present low prices will not last long; in fact, there are indications on the part of our competitors that they prefer to hold off on a good many of these low price orders and allow us to take certain ones of them without much competition. Up this way, Riley [Howard & Bullough] has practically backed out of the very low price orders, so far as I am able to ascertain, and the only active parties in the matter are Whitin and Pettee — especially the latter.

March 24, 1904: There is no question but what Saco-Pettee have sold at the prices you name. We do not, however, think that spinning has yet sold as low as anywhere near $2.00, although it may have sold for $2.25. . . .

We do not think that Whitin or Woonsocket look with any favor on lower prices than 20% off, and we are quite sure that they will not look at any lower prices where stock is concerned, as in the case of Chicola. There is no profit to any of us in manufacturing at much less than 20% off.

The entrance of Mason into the field with the Woodside people was quite a surprise, as it was not expected that they would take any orders for long term or stock, and Woodside had very little cash.

April 23, 1904: We also enclose copy of our quotation to Mr. Jennings of the Beaumont Mfg. Co. Our prices were altogether too high for his expectations. In fact, after making the price, the Treasurer suggested we should add five per cent more to it. The Cards and Fly frames went to Saco [The Saco and Pettee Machine Works], and the Spinning and Twisters to Whitin. Mr. Jennings' expectations were that he should get between 36 and 40% discount from list price. We do not think he got quite that, but he must have got somewhere in that neighborhood.

May 5, 1904: I telegraphed you this morning from the office here, as the Treasurer wished me to do, and I write this to say that it really seems that it is our duty at this time to come to some sort of a stand on prices, as per schedule named to you when here on the 12th of April, and that, with the exception of the $5.00 on Fly Frames, I believe that we should not accept orders, except in the case of our old customers, at such low prices as we have been taking.

May 26, 1904: We have had a telegram from Mr. Davis, regarding the machinery at the Midway and the Pee Dee Mfg. Co., and have wired him that if the prices he wished to quote were to protect our interests there, that he was to take the order. We realize the fact that this is about the only point in North Carolina where we have any very large amount of our machinery running, and we would like to keep this locality if it is a possible thing and we do not have to sacrifice too much.

June 1, 1904: We do not believe that other parties can build their Fly frames any cheaper than we can, and this seems to be shown in the fact that Woonsocket or the Providence Machine Co. are not quoting anywhere near our basis. If the Saco-Pettee desire to take Fly Frames on 5 or less basis, they are welcome to the business and the loss that it entails.

June 10, 1904: Your favor of the 7th is received, and we have wired you as follows: "Letter seventh received. Protect our trade at Athens and at Tuscaloosa Mills if not too late. Have written." The same we now confirm.

Your letter certainly does show a very discouraging state of affairs, especially in regard to prices. . . .

Of course, we do not propose to follow the lead of the other makers in regard to prices to any extent, if we have a fair amount of work to do, but at the same time it is our intention to protect our own trade as far as possible, and this we propose to continue to do, except in cases where orders are small and where we believe we should get the full price.

We should like very much, after this job is completed, if we could obtain a copy of the Saco-Pettee bid on the Athens job and on the Tuscaloosa job. We do not know whether you are sufficiently intimate with either party to have them give you this information, or whether they would consider it business-like; but if we could get hold of some bid by other builders, it might place the matter in its full light.

It is reported here that Mason and Riley have stopped taking orders at the present prices, and that Mason has gone to making printing presses, as he did some years ago.

July 2, 1904: We have not been very successful in keeping our trade in Augusta for the past few years, for some unknown reason, and it seems to us that we ought to have some of our modern machinery in that city, where we have traded for so many years with so great success and profit.

February 24, 1905: Regarding the matter of prices, would say that it is very doubtful if we should be willing to go any lower than what we have recently been quoting, as it will probably be of more advantage to us to close down than to take much further work at lower prices than what we are selling.

March 9, 1905: Do not offer any more machinery at less than the following prices:

Cards 40″	$550.00	
Cards 45″	600.00	
Pickers		10% off list
Drawing		10% off list
Roving	6.00	basis
Spinning [base price]	2.75	per spindle
Spoolers	3.00	

Withdraw any offers you may have out, or wherever you are free to do so. Prices are to be raised.

These letters of Hildreth's clearly show that the Lowell Machine Shop was prompt in meeting competitive prices. There is also the suggestion, confirmed elsewhere, that after a period of defensive action the Shop became increasingly aggressive in waging price warfare. Such a course was made possible by the financial strength and manufacturing efficiency of the Shop, and made necessary by the refusal of the Shop to accept stock. On October 27, 1904, Stuart Cramer complained to George Marston Whitin about the reckless price-cutting methods of the Lowell Machine Shop.[21] The presence of many new customers in the Shop sales records also bears testimony to market activity. This much is not hard to discern: the Lowell Machine Shop, conservative beyond the point of safety in a changing market, had been stung by the superior boldness of new and old competitors and had responded with telling blows of its chief remaining weapon — price.

Responsibility for the competitive tactics employed in the industry from 1896 to 1905 cannot definitely be placed. If the general agents, the treasurers, and the directorates of the machine shops did not initiate, they at least tolerated, but they had little choice. The environment demanded a fight for survival which at times transcended any self-imposed rules. The Sherman Anti-Trust Act, like the measures adopted by the Machinery Builders Association, sought to stem almost irresistible economic forces. It had no visible effect upon textile-machinery industry practices, which certainly violated the intent and probably violated the letter of the Act. No criticism of the actions of the textile machinery industry in this period is valid, however, that does not recognize the necessity for short-term restraint of trade in order to preserve a semblance of long-term stability and competition in the industry.

The question of the efficacy of the often-broken price agreements may well be raised. Those agreements were at least a restraining influence — at most, they may have prevented demoralization in the industry and the possible loss, through failure, of machine-making capacity, the lack of which in years to follow would almost certainly have resulted in still further restricted competition and higher machine prices. However successful these agreements were in accomplishing what was hoped of them, the experience in group action in a common cause was a valuable one to the textile machinery industry. A consciousness of industry relations was born. Perhaps this was a faltering and scarcely recognizable first step in the evolution from the complete introversion of *laissez-faire* days to modern concepts of business statesmanship and social responsibility.

3. Internal Strengths and Weaknesses, 1897–1905

In 1900 and 1901, sales volume reached the highest levels in the Lowell Machine Shop's history, exceeding the two-million-dollar mark in both these years and in 1903 as well. Abnormal business activity between 1900 and 1905 forced the company to borrow heavily ($2,225,000 over the period) but most of the credits were in the form of four-month or demand notes, and were rapidly liquidated. No fixed debts were acquired, and trade obligations were so quickly paid off that few showed on the balance sheets of even the most active years. Earned surplus increased from $400,644 in 1897 to $623,373 in 1904. Dividends, which had fallen to 6 per cent of invested capital in 1898, were increased to 10 per cent in 1900 and averaged 9 per cent over the 1898–1904 period. Operating figures are given in Table 17.

TABLE 17

Sales, Profits, Dividends, and Earned Surplus
Lowell Machine Shop, 1898–1905

Year Ending March 31	Gross Sales	Net Profit	Net Profit as % of Sales	Balance P & L a/c	Dividends	Dividend as % of Capital
1898.......	$2,468,900	$ 3,400	.137	$.....	$54,000	6
1899.......	737,800	39,700	5.4	308,800	81,000	9
1900.......	2,095,100	164,400	7.8	392,300	90,000	10
1901.......	2,636,700	301,700	11.4	604,000	90,000	10
1902.......	1,176,600	85,500	7.3	599,600	90,000	10
1903.......	2,008,100	132,900	6.6	642,500	90,000	10
1904.......	1,210,800	70,800	5.9	623,400	72,000	8
1905.......	1,698,100	136,600[a]	8.0[a]	378,700	36,000	4

[a] Loss.

Source: Company ledgers, journals, and directors' minutes.

The prosperity which these figures recorded was deceptive. The relative decline in prosperity noted in the late 1880's and early 1890's (Chapter VII, page 240) was accelerating. In the 1900–01 boom annual sales of from two to two and one-half million dollars yielded only 60 per cent as much profit as had sales of from one and a half to two million dollars in the 1881–82 peak. In five out of eight years after 1897, dividends exceeded earnings, and even in the years when sales were the highest in company history, Lowell stock prices failed to advance materially. In 1898 an operating loss of $29,000 was recorded, though it was concealed by large rental and interest revenues. In 1905 an unprecedented loss of $136,600 was incurred. This last-named loss focuses attention upon significant developments in the field of product policy.

The trend of product policy in the past forty years had been toward specialization in cotton machinery; it had been signalized by discontinuance of the manufacture of locomotives (after 1861) and of machine tools (about 1865). One further step was made by the Lowell Machine Shop toward complete specialization in cotton-textile machinery. By 1890, profits on paper machinery had fallen so low that the salary of Wyllis G. Eaton, the foreman in charge, was halved. Shortly thereafter, the line dwindled to an insignificant part of total business and was discontinued altogether. The depression of 1896–98, however, once again raised the old temptation to seek profits in other fields and initiated a trend toward diversification.

A cotton-baling press was designed and sold in considerable numbers at the turn of the century. An infinitely more ambitious venture was made in worsted machinery. Worsted drawing and spinning machinery in use in America was exclusively of foreign manufacture prior to 1898, when the Lowell Machine Shop was attracted to the field by the same deceptive similarity in manufacturing techniques which had earlier lured the company into the field of paper-making machinery and machine tools. The immediate incentive for the move was the opportunity which existed at this time for breaking the English monopoly in the American market. In 1897 and 1898, American worsted mills, unlike the cotton mills, were doing an active business and had been unable to secure prompt deliveries of machinery, for the English shops were crowded with work. Repair and replacement-parts business, moreover, was subject to the very great disadvantages inherent in the distance which separated American customers from English suppliers. This was indeed a tempting opportunity for the Lowell Machine Shop, which was currently operating half-time on cotton-machinery orders. Moreover, several of the Lowell directors were also on the Boards of important worsted mills, a factor of some importance in explaining the Shop's entry into and initial success in the worsted-machinery field.

In embarking on the worsted venture the Lowell Machine Shop employed those same methods which American shops had used for generations in their attempts to oust the English from the local market. Machines of the most approved English pattern were imported by the Lowell Machine Shop through a third party (in this case the Massachusetts Mohair Plush Company, of Lowell) and used as patterns for the new line.[22] The machines purchased were those of Prince-Smith & Stells, embodying the so-called "Bradford system" of worsted drawing and spinning. Not only were the Prince-Smith machines minutely copied, but the similarity was carefully pointed out to prospective customers — ample testimony to the dominance of this English firm in the American market. Two English mechanics, George Mintoff and Joseph Northrop, were brought to Lowell to assist in setting up the line.

The worsted venture met with considerable initial success, at least on the technical side. A worsted department was created and placed under the administrative direction of Frederick P. Shaw, former Shop paymaster. Assistant Superintendent Flather was placed in charge of the actual work of setting up the new line. One after another the Prince-Smith machines were successfully copied, and a separate catalogue of Lowell worsted machinery was printed for the trade.[23] A very low introductory price was placed on the Lowell line, and soon the worsted department was unable to fill orders on hand.

Quality and price had long been basic obstacles in all American attempts to meet English competition in the American market. Initial complaints were heard about the performance of the Lowell worsted machinery, but these were silenced, and soon customers were reporting that the Lowell machines were superior to the Prince-Smith originals. Considerations of price, however, became increasingly serious.

Lowell's introductory price, first quoted in February of 1898, had been $3.36 per spindle for spinning frames, with other machines priced correspondingly low. This price appears to have been about $1.00 below English quotations. The rush of business which ensued, coupled with rising raw-material costs, soon prompted the Shop to raise prices to the competitive level and above. By June of 1898 the price of spinning had been advanced to $4.00 per spindle, and in November, 1899, it was raised to $4.25. By September, 1905, a price of $6.00 was being asked. English prices were said to have averaged about $5.00 per spindle.

From the time of the abandonment (in 1898) of the low introductory prices, it is evident that the Lowell Machine Shop was unable to meet Prince-Smith & Stells prices, and an increasing effort was made to sell on the basis of quality and service. The Shop anxiously sought testimonials from satisfied customers and was prompt to point out the undeniably great advantage to American mills in dealing with an American machine shop. Assistant Superintendent Flather voiced this appeal in the following terms:[24]

> We regret not meeting your wishes in prices. . . . You will, of course, remember that we will set up your machinery, and perhaps do any planning or engineering that you may require, free of charge, excepting that you will pay our men's board and travelling expenses. Beyond this, it is worth something to you to have our experts call occasionally, hear the complaints, if there are any, and remedy them free of charge, which we understand no competitor does now.

These appeals must have carried weight, and the Lowell line appears to have compared very favorably with the English, for, despite higher Lowell prices, the worsted department continued to be rushed with work. By 1904, however, trouble had commenced. Flather had left the Shop to accept a position elsewhere, thus depriving the department not only of an able technician but of an enthusiastic supporter of the new line as well. Under Shaw's direction efforts were made to modify and improve the worsted line. The major technical change was the introduction of the so-called Shaw roller bearing, an invention which promised to add greatly to the efficiency of the worsted spinning machines. Shaw, enthusiastic not only about the contemplated improvements but about the volume of business done in the past five years, appeared able to persuade Hildreth, not an easily moved man, that the Shop's worsted-machinery building capacity should be doubled.

The reaction of the trade to the new worsted line was not so enthusiastic as Shaw had envisaged when he wrote one customer and said:[25]

> We have improved every part of the worsted yarn making machinery to such a point that the best English made machinery, bran new, does not even rank as a second-hand machine compared to our improved productions.

Specific claims of the Shop were that the Lowell worsted spinning frame would run 10 per cent faster than the Prince-Smith frame, using one-half the power, while the Lowell flyer redoubler would run twice as fast as its English counterpart.

Whatever the merits of these improvements (and company claims appear to have had much justification), they engendered opposition which had not been serious before. In worsted machinery, as in certain types of cotton machinery, a prejudice on the part of the large number of English mill overseers in favor of English machines was marked. So long as the Lowell line conformed exactly to that of Prince-Smith & Stells, such prejudice had little nourishment upon which to flourish. The Shaw improvements inevitably aroused the antagonism of many of these men, who were notably averse to changes of any sort and particularly to changes of American origin.

Unfortunately for the success of the Lowell Machine Shop's worsted machinery, the new line was presented to the market before it had been perfected. Throughout 1904 a large number of complaints and requests for alterations were received. These were sufficient to upset the delicate competitive balance, and more than offset the claims of the company and the occasional glowing testimonials of satisfied customers. At this same time Prince-Smith & Stells was making a vigorous drive for American business and quoting prices far below what Lowell could offer. The complaints voiced against Lowell's new line were eagerly seized upon by the English company and widely publicized.

The result of these combined circumstances was to impair seriously the prospects of the Lowell Machine Shop in the worsted field. Orders fell off (partly as a result of a general business recession), and for the first time since 1898 the Shop was forced to seek out business. The technical difficulties encountered in making the worsted improvements were gradually eliminated, but the heavy operating loss ($136,600) suffered by the company in the year ending March 31, 1905, appears to have been attributable largely to the worsted experience. In certain managerial circles Shaw and his worsted department alike were thoroughly discredited. The venture reached a climax in 1905, by which time the Shop had sold some 200,000 worsted spindles, many of which had gone to the American Woolen Company. In this year Shaw was discharged. His managerial shortcomings, coupled with technical inexperience, had come near to putting an end to the promising new department of the Shop. In 1905 few gains could be offset against the monetary losses and the dissatisfaction of customers which appear to have been the principal results of Shaw's administration.[26]

With these various product developments came changes in manufacturing techniques. The effectiveness of the plant was maintained as best it could be by continued large expenditures for repairs and the addition of new plant as needed. Assistant Superintendent Flather continued to purchase as many new tools as Superintendent Hildreth would allow. At best, however, the piecemeal growth of the Shop had not contributed to a smooth flow of production, and the orderly arrangement of processes was made difficult by the limitations of location and diversity of product line.

Shop organization had changed little since pre-Civil War days. The managerial problems involved in a large number of products were met by departmentalization and specialization. In the engineering department competent draftsmen were assigned as heads of sections set up to develop and perfect specific types of machinery. Organization at the management level was definitely on a product basis, though there were some functional specialists such as the head draftsman. Within the factory, production was split between a product and a functional basis. In the early stages of manufacture, such as casting and heavy mill work, all products passed through the same departments. The final manufacturing step, erecting, was departmentalized exclusively on a product basis. Chart VIII attempts to reconstruct the factory organization as it existed at the turn of the century.

CHART VIII

Organization of the Lowell Machine Shop in 1900

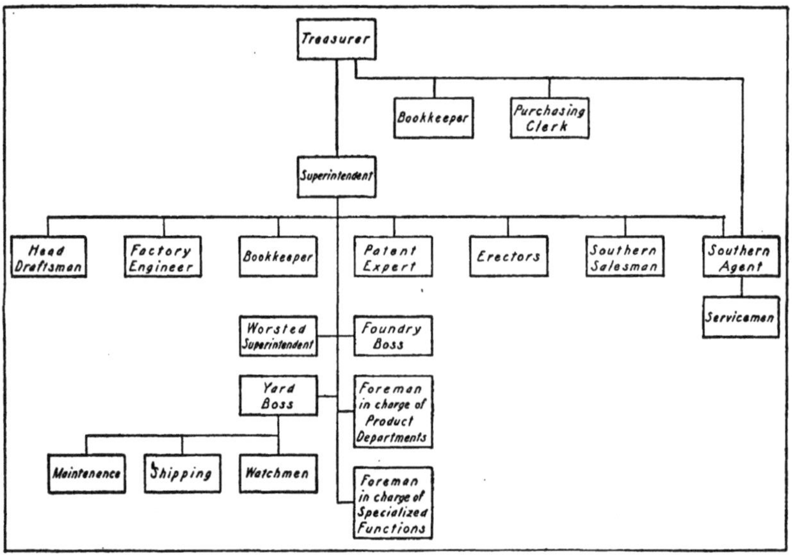

The old order was changing in the Shop. By 1890, at the very latest, the long-established system of job-takers or contractors in the plant had been abolished. Their powers of hiring, firing, and rate-setting had been turned over to the various foremen.

Trial-and-error methods of machine-making began to give way to the blueprint and the drawing-board. Men trained at the Lowell Textile School and even the Massachusetts Institute of Technology were becoming more plentiful.[27] This development weakened the technical dominance exercised by various bosses and department heads since the earliest days of the industry, but in the foreman class was still to be found that core of practical knowledge which was the first necessity of good machine-building. The Lowell Machine Shop was liberally endowed with old-fashioned, bench-trained mechanics, of whom Superintendent Hildreth counted himself one. Between 1900 and 1903, efficiency experts from outside the firm were consulted — a faint adumbration of the coming Scientific Management movement. Apparently as a result of their recommendations, the foremen were relieved of many of their job-scheduling and cost-gathering functions. Henceforth a system of job cards was instituted. These cards were passed out at the beginning of the day and returned at night to the office, with the day's progress marked on them. Customs of antique origin persisted, nevertheless. As late as 1904 an aspirant for a job in the Shop was being advised by the Superintendent that he had best go into the Shop at bell time, either in the morning or at noon, and make his inquiries of the different overseers.

Considered altogether, the scanty information about managerial techniques indicates that much was being done around the turn of the century to coördinate the rambling plant and centralize controls in the front office. The fact that Hildreth spent so much time on purely administrative tasks and devoted so much attention to customer correspondence is a further indication of a rather highly systematized manufacturing establishment. The most important adverse criticism of the Shop administration touches this very point. Regulation and systemization under Hildreth may have been carried to such an extreme that initiative in the organization was smothered.[28]

4. THE LOWELL MACHINE SHOP OF 1905

By 1904 the necessity for drastic action by the Lowell Machine Shop, in order to retain a dwindling share of the Southern business, imposed a price war of utmost severity upon the textile machinery industry. For the Lowell Shop this was the beginning of the end. Slowly but inexorably, competing shops had crowded in on territories once held to be indisputably Lowell's. Sales by the Whitin Machine Works had soared above those of the Lowell Machine Shop. Market leadership was lost, but the Lowell Shop could not even console itself with second place. The union, in 1897, of the Pettee Machine Works and the Saco Water Power Machine Shop (Chapter XI) had produced, in the Saco and Pettee Machine Shops, a new giant which outfought and outsold Lowell on almost every market front. Despite the fact that sales hovered close to all-time company peaks, the Lowell Machine Shop suffered one market defeat after another. Retaliatory efforts were made at many scattered points in the South, but these were not effective. Only a handful of the old New England customers stood firm against temptations far more seductive than the best which the Lowell Machine Shop was willing to offer.

Stuart W. Cramer, Whitin's Southern agent, reported to George Marston Whitin that the Lowell Shop had lost many an order to "the rough boys," and that lack of business judgment and tact by an "old and cranky" management was interfering with Lowell's market efforts. Haven C. Perham, treasurer of the Kitson Machine Shop, cryptically remarked that Lowell had not been able to sell "a d— thing."[29]

Thus it was that in 1905 the Lowell Machine Shop, wealthy, stable, experienced, and active, stood on the threshold of great trouble, already having relinquished a precedence in certain fields which went back to the very beginning of the textile machinery industry in America.

The heart of the dry rot which infected the company was not to be found in the shop itself, though symptoms of decay here were not lacking. The internal organization of the shop in 1905 was characterized by an unusual combination of youth and age, progress and stagnation, vitality and lassitude. Charles L. Hildreth was old in years and in experience. Undeniably he had become resistant to new ideas, and the preëminently conservative nature of shop management (reflecting the conservatism of the Boston office) was reinforced by the rigidity of old age. Younger men in the shop fought this rigidity with partial success, thus probably preventing any dangerous decline in the level of operating efficiency.

Despite the worsted-machinery venture, the Lowell Machine Shop was not, in 1905, a noteworthy originator of new ideas, and an aggressive product policy had long been lacking. Superintendent Hildreth himself stated that the Shop had always considered matters of design with a great deal of conservatism. This policy, or lack of policy, is clearly traceable to a period as far back as 1845, and possibly to the days of Paul Moody. It was characteristic not just of the Lowell Machine Shop but, in varying degrees, of every textile-machine shop in America. The age had not yet passed when the most important textile-machinery inventions were being made by the users rather than by the makers of such machinery. This fact of inventive stagnation in no way accounts for the marketing failure of the company, nor does it detract in any way from the value of the economic service for which the Shop had been so bountifully remunerated down through the years. Few great inventions emanated from the Lowell Machine Shop, but no other company had done more to spread the use of improved machines. The quality of Lowell workmanship, unimpaired and seldom surpassed from 1813 to 1905, was a constant asset to textile mills and other textile-machine shops alike. The extent of its contribution to American industry in the form of trained mechanics can only be surmised. In searching technical fields for the roots of decline we find, instead, only great success and the elements of enduring strength.

No part of the decline of the Lowell Machine Shop after 1897 can be ascribed to lack of interest on the part of either the directorate or the treasurer, yet it was at this uppermost level of management that failure occurred. What, then, was the failure, if not lack of interest or integrity or conscientious devotion to the well-being of the Shop? The answer can only be surmised. Top management had become old in the service of the company. Though far from reactionary, the directorate was outstandingly conservative. The talents which guided the company were essentially, though not exclusively, financial. The Lowell Machine Shop had many powerful and keen-minded men, but no great salesman — no figure that dominated the textile industry at the operating level. The lack of a Frank J. Hale, a George Marston Whitin, or a C. E. Riley may well have been the decisive factor. The Lowell Machine Shop was far too securely linked to the New England textile industry. The directors, to a man, were at first financially interested, not in the success but in the failure of the Southern textile industry. This interest positively did not go so far as to discourage the Shop from selling machinery to financially sound Southern mills, but it did encourage a determined refusal to concede past progress or future prospects there. This studied obliviousness was finally dissipated by the overwhelming weight of evidence, but the light came too late so far as the Lowell Machine Shop was concerned.

Nevertheless, the Lowell Machine Shop can be criticized less for what was done than for what could have been done and was not. The contribution of the Lowell Machine Shop to the vigorous new textile industry in the South was great. The reputation of the Shop's machines was excellent there, and the amount of machinery sold in the South by the Lowell Machine Shop was probably surpassed only by the Whitin Machine Works. Self-imposed handicaps, such as the refusal to accept mill stocks or to meet competitive credit terms, prevented an even more active participation; and these handicaps enabled competing shops to forge ahead. The failure of fulfillment was relative, not absolute.

Excessive caution began to be exercised at the very time when trends in the textile industry demanded daring and vision on the part of the machinery builders. By subtle degrees the spirit of perfect *safety* in all business transactions began to spread a stupefying paralysis in the Boston office. That prudence which had piled up great financial reserves ceased to be a virtue when the boldness which those reserves could have made possible was not exercised. A delicate balance of prudence and boldness had placed the Lowell Machine Shop in a dominant position in the textile machinery industry. In 1879 the Atlanta Cotton Factory affair had disturbed that balance. Thereafter, unleavened prudence was to cost the Lowell Machine Shop not only its leadership, but even its independent existence.

Conservatism at a time when competitors were being bold; the lack of a great salesman at a time when supreme marketing efforts were demanded; obliviousness in the early stages of a sensational economic trend — these were the fatal weaknesses for which the highest councils of the Lowell Machine Shop must be held accountable.

The decline and fall of the "Big Shop" encompassed a period of less than ten years. The events of this period, and particularly of the years 1904 and 1905, should by no means be allowed to obscure the earlier record or confuse the final judgment of Shop policies and performance over the course of more than half a century. For much of this period the Shop occupied a primary position in the industry in point of size and fame. Competitors and customers alike had profited from the integrity which characterized all dealings with the trade. An impartial appraisal of the history of the Lowell Machine Shop can result only in a feeling of profound respect — and a sense of the importance of such firms to the economic progress and well-being of the country.

CHAPTER IX

STATE STREET TAKES A HAND
The Lowell Machine Shop, 1905–1912

1. Fall of the "Big Shop," 1905

Some will dispute the statement that the year 1905 marked the fall of the Lowell Machine Shop, as others will challenge even the existence of decline. The fact is that decisive action was taken before the symptoms of internal decay and market failure had become readily apparent to men in the Shop. That action was surrounded with such a veil of secrecy that very few knew beyond all doubt what was happening. Nevertheless, the fall of the Lowell Machine Shop as it had been constituted since 1845, though secret, was decisive. The year 1905 marks a clean-cut division point in Saco-Lowell history which saw the dominance of one of the three companies involved supplanted by the dominance of two others, and which brought two additional machine shops into the circle of companies from which the Saco-Lowell Shops was to emerge in 1912.

In the dark months of 1904, when the inefficacy of voluntary price agreements was becoming evident to all, Stuart Cramer wrote George Marston Whitin complaining of the price-cutting tactics of the Lowell Machine Shop. He concluded his letter with these significant statements:[1]

> I merely mention all this that you may understand what the Lowell people are doing, notwithstanding what they say they are doing. I see no way of getting better prices until that shop is out of the way, and it strikes me that somebody will have to get it out of the way before you will ever get prices up again. The business is getting so terribly disorganized, at least in this part of the country, that I do not see how we can get decent prices again for a long time.

Robert F. Herrick, Sr.
President of Lowell Machine Shop, 1905–11, and Treasurer, 1905, 1911–12; President of Saco-Lowell Shops, 1923–26, and Chairman of the Board, 1927–42

Cramer's wishes did not long await fulfillment, for not only was the necessity obvious to others than Cramer, but the means and the precedent for remedial action were at hand. The combination movement had already swept through much of American business. This was the era which saw the formation of the American Tin Plate Company, International Harvester, United States Steel, and many other great combinations. Closer at hand, the American Woolen Company, in 1899, had merged nine violently competing woolen mills into one corporate entity. The United States Finishing Company combined three cloth finishing houses. The United States Worsted Company was in process of formation, as was a trust among carpet manufacturers. The American Mercerizing Company combined four mercerizing houses and one manufacturer of mercerizing equipment, and a silk trust was rumored to be forming. A knit-goods combination was being contemplated in the Mohawk Valley to remedy sharp competition there.[2]

This burst of organizational activity in the textile industry reflected those very conditions which plagued the textile machinery industry — excessive competition and the failure of voluntary associations. With the revival of prosperity in 1900, the mania for textile combinations had become less violent, but early in 1905 the textile industry began to buzz with rumors.

A combination of machine-makers, it was said, was being contemplated. The first rumors stated that the Saco and Pettee Machine Shops would take over the Lowell Machine Shop. This story was denied, and soon a new rumor was being circulated, to the effect that unidentified New York interests were trying to form a syndicate to consolidate the New England textile-machinery shops. A more explicit story was circulated that the Lowell Machine Shop, the Saco & Pettee Machine Shops, the Whitin Machine Works, George Draper & Sons, the Fales & Jenks Machine Company, and Howard & Bullough were attempting to form a combination under one management.[3] While these reports were being circulated with tremendous gusto in the trade, the directors of the Lowell Machine Shop had before them for consideration the letter which follows:[4]

Boston, March 8, 1905

Robert H. Stevenson, Esq.
Treasurer Lowell Machine Shop
28 State Street, Boston.

Dear Sir:

Having been fully authorized by my clients I now offer to all the shareholders in the Lowell Machine Shop the price of $1,180 per share with a right to a dividend of $20 per share to be declared within a short time and to be payable on May 15 next, being the regular semi-annual dividend; all upon the following conditions:

The City Trust Co. of Boston is ready at once to receive stock upon deposit under the terms of this offer and to issue proper receipts in exchange therefor. All stock dividends to be transferred ready for delivery to the satisfaction of the City Trust Co.

As soon as a majority of the stock (901 shares or more) has been so deposited the Trust Company will pay to the depositors the purchase price of $1180 a share and will also, if the depositor desires, cash the above mentioned dividend. The Trust Company will take up their receipts at the time of payment and if the depositor desires to cash the dividend an assignment of the dividend will be taken.

Unless a majority of the stock is deposited hereunder on or before April 1 next all stock will be returned without expense to the depositors.

If the stock is bought under the terms of this offer the offer will remain open a reasonable time after April 1 to such of the shareholders as for any good reason, such as absence from state, delay in obtaining signatures or authority from courts, etc. are not able to deposit their stock by April 1. I am willing that you or any person named by you shall be the final judge as to what reasonable extension of time shall be made in each case. For practical reasons, however, I am not willing that the time should in any event extend beyond Sept. 1, 1905.

Stock so bought under this offer after April 1 shall receive the same price per share and the same dividend right as that originally deposited without interest or further dividends. The above is on the understanding that until after April 1 next no dividends will be declared other than the dividend of $20 per share above mentioned and that the business be carried on in due course by the present management until a majority of the stock is purchased in accordance with the terms hereof.

Very truly yours,
[Signed] Robert F. Herrick

In a letter to John Hill, the Shop's Southern agent, Superintendent Hildreth told what he had heard, and expressed his uncertainties.

March 11, 1905

Dear Sir:

On the 9th inst. I telegraphed you to advance prices on a certain schedule of machinery; this was an order from the Treasurer's office, saying that prices of machinery were to be advanced. It appears that the advance has not been made yet, but it hangs upon a certain scheme which is now pronounced to be successful — a transaction to the sale of the stock of the Lowell Machine Shop to parties supposed to be the Saco-Pettee Machine Works. The parties make an offer of $1200.00 per share, which was made on the 8th inst., to the directors of the Lowell Machine Shop, who held a meeting that day, and unanimously voted to accept the offer, with the condition that it be promulgated that they secure their majority of stock on or before the first day of April, which is some weeks hence.

It is generally believed that this is a success, which throws the most of us into an uncertain condition of what may be the result of this transaction. . . .

The acceptance by the Lowell Machine Shop of this offer constituted surrender — the clearest possible indication that the Shop, though still able, was unwilling to prolong the market warfare further. Surrender had been rendered an easy choice for the Shop. The purchase price of $1,180 a share was generous, in view of the book value of $891 and the market value of $902 per share. The offer made capitulation profitable and therefore honorable. The decisiveness of the break with the past is indicated by the resignation on May 18, 1905, of Treasurer Stevenson and the entire directorate. A clear intent to maintain the Shop as a going concern was shown by personnel changes at the operating level. In July, 1905, a new superintendent replaced Charles L. Hildreth, "The Old Man," whose crusty devotion to the affairs of the Shop had encompassed a full generation of machinists and machinery building.

Many questions of great interest derive from the letter of March 8, not the least of which concerns Robert Frederick Herrick, who wrote it. Since the motives for purchasing the Lowell Machine Shop are reasonably clear, the questions of primary importance naturally concern the identity of Herrick's clients and the details of the 1905 maneuver. These were closely guarded secrets.

Secrecy was exercised in 1905, not because the transaction in Lowell stock was known to be a violation of anti-trust statutes; rather did it reflect widely held doubts in business circles as to what was legal and what was not. The Northern Securities decision of the United States Supreme Court in 1904 broke up a railroad empire and showed that the Sherman Anti-Trust Act could be enforced. President Theodore Roosevelt's policies promoted uncertainty and fear in business circles, just as the New Deal of Franklin Roosevelt was to do on a more ambitious scale a generation later. There was, moreover, a growing public distrust of combination which more than kept pace with the growing conviction by many business men that such combinations were essential. In an environment charged with uncertainty and distrust secrecy was inevitable, thereby adding to that uncertainty and encouraging that distrust.

By March 18, 1905, the necessary Lowell Machine Shop stock had been deposited with the City Trust Company, and the Lowell Machine Shop sale was consummated. On the books of the Saco and Pettee Machine Shops an entry was made recording the acquisition of 360 shares of Lowell Machine Shop stock, or a fifth of the total outstanding. The Whitin Machine Works also purchased a fifth interest, and George Draper & Sons probably did the same, although documentary evidence is not available to prove the Draper participation. The remaining two-fifths interest in the Lowell Machine Shop appears to have been divided among Howard & Bullough, the Fales & Jenks Machine Company, the Mason Machine Works, and the Woonsocket Machine & Press Company.[5]

The rumor that an outright merger was contemplated at one point in the negotiations was not borne out by actual events, though those events do not, of course, rule out the possibility that a merger had been attempted. The pattern is clear. The Lowell Machine Shop purchase constituted an attempt to stabilize the industry by the effective removal of a troublesome and still dangerous competitor — by the control of approximately a fifth of the preparatory machinery-building capacity of the industry in the interest of more orderly and profitable competition. A new price agreement was made in the industry, and this agreement seemed destined for greater permanence by virtue of the certainty that the Lowell Shop would no longer be a violator. It now remained to be seen whether the participating shops could exercise among themselves, and on the usual voluntary basis, that self-restraint in price-cutting which, by their joint action, they had ensured from the Lowell Machine Shop.

The purchase of the Lowell Machine Shop had a broader meaning. The textile machinery industry was both growing and concentrating. The first step in the pulling together of scattered competitive units had been the establishment of the Southern agency system. The Lowell purchase was an important second step in the process of concentration. This purchase and the price agreements which preceded and succeeded it were not phenomena, but evidences that the textile machinery industry was undergoing those changes so commonly found in American business of the time that they must be considered as normal. The events of 1905 cannot be viewed as other than immediately beneficial to the textile machinery industry. If, as has been said, too many cotton mills had been built or expanded too quickly, the higher machine prices which the 1905 purchase sought to guarantee constituted a healthful though distasteful dosage for the textile industry itself.[6] Certainly the long-range advantages to that industry of this attempt to forestall complete demoralization and possible failures in the textile machinery industry far outweighed the immediate costs, which soon proved to be small indeed.

The purchase of the Lowell Shop, however, was only a part of the negotiations which transpired in 1905, and the identity of the new owners, though of great interest, was perhaps of less significance than was the presence of Robert F. Herrick as intermediary in the transactions.

2. Robert Herrick and His Associations

By his own admission Robert F. Herrick entered Harvard College as a member of the class of 1890 possessed of means but not position.[7] The means were provided by a wholesale liquor business operated by his father, who financed a college education for the son. In 1886 Herrick secured a law degree from Boston University, practised law briefly, and decided on a return to collegiate life in a new environment.

At Harvard the activities of the stocky, affable young lawyer gave many clues to the personal traits which were to become well known on State Street. Herrick's natural gifts were a rugged physique, driving fires of energy, and a brilliantly incisive mind which he could turn with the abruptness of an electric current from one subject to another. His genius was an almost automatic affinity for the most important men around him. Prominent people sought Herrick out, however; he did not seek them, nor did he play court to prominence. The importance to Herrick's subsequent career of the Harvard background can scarcely be overstated. Herrick himself in later life placed a high premium upon these college years, while deprecating the natural talents without which that collegiate environment would have been meaningless.

In 1890 the two sports which were patronized by Harvard "gentlemen" were tennis and rowing, and Herrick soon established his mark as an oarsman. On the Charles River at Cambridge, Herrick mingled with the men who were to rise, with him, to dominating positions on State Street. For all the years of his life an active interest in the affairs of the College was instrumental in strengthening old contacts and creating new. Harvard rowing seldom had enjoyed as loyal and active a friend as Robert F. Herrick, and many remember him in his later years not as a magnate of the financial world but as a rather stoutish figure clad in a slouch hat and none too tidy business suit, crouched intently in the forward cockpit of a coaching launch on the Charles or the Thames.

Herrick could laugh, play, and relax. A member in later years of virtually every socially prominent club in Boston, and many in New York, Herrick's tremendous ability was not oppressive, nor was he pompous or unapproachable. A lawyer's caution and self-restraint marked his words, and he was "surprisingly unobtrusive in appearance and manner, not in a studied way, but quite simply."[8] His associates respected his sanity, calmness, insight, balance, and judgment, and counted on his highly developed sense of loyalty. Feared by business opponents, Herrick was honored by the deep affection of a host of friends.

Herrick's career was launched and nurtured in the field of corporate reorganization. The merger and trust movement in American business, becoming full blown in the 1890's and early 1900's, demanded new administrative skills which, for the most part, were not to be found within the framework of manufacturing enterprise. This movement, together with the reorganization of many faltering companies which had expanded not wisely but too well, placed a completely unprecedented premium upon legal and financial abilities. Investment-banking firms, which had shouldered the financial burden of many a growing company and industry, now found it necessary to step in to protect and preserve their interests. Many accused these firms of encouraging the corporate crises by which their control was extended, but it was a fact that in many instances the bankers were invited by distressed though still solvent manufacturers to do the financial and administrative job which must be done. Patent attorneys metamorphosed into corporation lawyers and became the working partners of the bankers. In the textile industry many cloth-selling houses yielded their dominant position in the affairs of the mills to the financial institutions which serviced them.[9] Behind this age of change lay the specter of over-production and excessive competition. Ahead lay public condemnation of the tremendous extension of Wall Street and State Street control and power.

Herrick's career had brought him into contact with the textile and textile machinery industries prior to 1905. Under his direction the Olympia Cotton Mills in South Carolina had been reorganized. He was friendly with William and Eben Draper and George Marston Whitin, and he had performed legal services for the Pettee Machine Works. By 1905 Herrick had established tremendously potent affiliations on State Street. A working relationship had existed between Herrick's law firm and the financial group centering in the First National Bank of Boston and the investment banking firm of Lee Higginson and Company at least by 1899, when these firms effected the United Shoe Machinery merger. In this undertaking Herrick's associate and law partner had been James J. Storrow, in 1905 a director of the First National, a partner in Lee Higginson, and already a power in the New England financial world. A strong tie was established between Herrick and Daniel Wing, who had been made president of the First National in 1903 and who was the real force within the bank. In 1907 Herrick himself became a director of the First National, in which capacity he served alongside William F. Draper, of George Draper & Sons.

Another of Herrick's early law partners was Frederick P. Fish, a director of the Old Colony Trust Company. Associated with Fish on the Old Colony board of directors were Eben F. Draper, of George Draper & Sons; T. Jefferson Coolidge, former president and director of the Lowell Machine Shop; and C. W. Amory, a director in 1905 of the Lowell Machine Shop. Herrick became a member of the Old Colony board of directors in 1907.

In addition to these significant relationships, all of which were to be of importance in the later Saco-Lowell history, Herrick served on the directorate of the Boston Five Cent Savings Bank, and was intimate with Wilmot R. Evans, who was soon to become its president. Herrick's firm also worked closely with the City Trust Company. Philip Stockton, president of the City Trust and later of the Old Colony and the First National, was Herrick's friend.

These affiliations were of more than regional scope and linked Herrick firmly to one of two wide-flung and occasionally competing financial groups. In one camp were the First National Bank of Boston, Lee Higginson and Company, the Old Colony Trust, Hornblower & Weeks, and certain other Boston financial houses. The First National group, with which Herrick's early career and much of Saco-Lowell's financial history after 1905 are linked, reached far beyond New England and was known as a member of the Morgan interests in New York. The Shawmut Bank, Kidder, Peabody and Company, and Kuhn, Loeb & Company constituted the Boston-New York axis of the parallel group.

Herrick's law firm provided legal services for many corporation mergers and reorganizations sponsored by the First National interests, but Herrick's abilities and initiative soon carried him far beyond the position of a corporation counsel. His reputation established by early legal services rendered the banks, Herrick began to participate in corporate undertakings, not as a lawyer but as an administrator. Like his partner, James J. Storrow, Herrick moved naturally and rapidly from corporate law to corporate finance. His tremendous organizing abilities led him from business law to business policy and even, on several occasions, to business management at, or close to, the operating level.

Herrick worked both with and for the banks. Wing, Stockton, and Evans called on him to assist in undertakings which they had conceived. Herrick called on these men and others to supply the financial backing for enterprises which he himself initiated. Later in his career Herrick broadened the scope of his operations still further and served with Kidder, Peabody and other erstwhile rivals of the First National group.

These facts serve as a necessary background for an understanding of the purchase, in 1905, of the Lowell Machine Shop by competing companies, and of the ensuing chain of events. Where did the initiative lie in this drastic move? To this important question there is no certain answer. Was this purchase conceived by the strife-torn industry and entrusted to Herrick to effect? Did the First National group, which included on the directorates of its several institutions representatives of the Draper and Lowell shops and in whose esteem George Marston Whitin ranked high, originate the move to ease the competitive pressure and hearten the holders of textile securities? The balance of available evidence, which, however, is far from conclusive, suggests that the Lowell purchase was instigated not from within the industry but by Robert Herrick himself. There is no suggestion that Herrick was acting on other than his own initiative. In support of such a conclusion is the fact that he was intimately informed of conditions in the industry and could readily have seen the opportunity here to promote a combination which should be at the same time profitable to himself and also of great value to the participating companies. The Lowell purchase appears to have been financed by the shops involved, with no evidence of direct financial participation by either Herrick or the First National group. Herrick received no Lowell stock, but may have looked to fee and salary remuneration for the services he offered to the industry. The Lowell Machine Shop in 1905 paid Herrick $10,000 for legal services performed, and he drew a salary from the Shop thereafter of $10,000 annually.[10] These sums were far from exorbitant, and if the participating shops paid no additional fees (there is no evidence on this point), the price paid for what was hoped would be a stabilized industry was small indeed.

One fact is very clear. Absolute control of the Lowell Machine Shop was vested in Herrick by the seven companies which purchased the Lowell stock. Following the resignation, on March 8, 1905, of all the old Lowell Machine Shop officers and directors, Herrick was elected treasurer of the Shop, and his associates were named to fill the various vacant posts. (See Appendix 11.) Moreover, soon after the Lowell purchase had been consummated, it became apparent that more had been involved than the purchase of Lowell stock.

In May, 1905, one month after the Lowell stock had changed hands, newspapers and trade periodicals announced the news that the Lowell Machine Shop had purchased the A. T. Atherton Machine Company, of Pawtucket, and the Kitson Machine Company, of Lowell, the two American producers of picking and opening machinery. Thus, through ownership of the Lowell Machine Shop, the seven manufacturers of preparatory cotton machinery sought and came near to achieving absolute control over the output of the only preparatory machines which none of these manufacturers had been able to make successfully themselves. The ownership of Kitson and Atherton by Lowell effectively guaranteed to each of the new owners of the Lowell Shop the opportunity to obtain picking and opening machinery for their customers on an equitable and impartial basis.[11]

All mention of the Atherton and the Kitson shops has been deferred to this point when (in 1905) they became crucially involved in the evolution of the Saco-Lowell parent companies. The Atherton story is little short of fantastic, but of only transitory importance, for the A. T. Atherton Machine Company plant in Pawtucket was closed down immediately after the 1905 purchase, and another Atherton plant which continued in existence until purchased by Whitin in 1913 never was a formidable competitor of Kitson. The Kitson shop, on the other hand, had played such a dominant part in the development of American picking and opening machinery before 1905, and was to figure so largely in the Saco-Lowell story after that time, that the necessity is clear for a brief backward glance into history.[12]

3. The Kitson Shop

Richard Kitson was born in Cleckheaton, near Leeds, England, in 1814, the son of a card-clothing manufacturer who held patents on needle-pointed card clothing. Kitson learned his father's business as a boy and young man, and in 1849 came to America upon the urging of a Lowell firm which was a heavy purchaser of the English card clothing.[13]

Kitson opened a shop on Broadway, Lowell, and became the first American producer of the needle-pointed clothing. Soon his attention turned to picking machinery, a field which had been dominated for many years by the Whitin picker. In 1852 Kitson brought forth a highly successful cotton opener, and a year later he began to build pickers modeled after the English machines of Lord Brothers and Walker & Hacking.[14]

The Whitin picker performed its cleaning and separating of the cotton fibers by means of a revolving blade or beater mechanism. Kitson's English-system pickers accomplished the desired effect by means of a revolving needle-pointed cylinder, which appears to have been so superior to the Whitin and other American pickers that soon Kitson was driving all other domestic machines from the market. His triumph was climaxed in the Civil War years, when Kitson machines proved able to handle Surat and other short-staple imported cotton which the mills were forced to utilize.

Until 1860 Kitson had his machines built for him. In that year he constructed on Dutton Street, across the canal from the Lowell Machine Shop, the shop which was to be the nucleus of later plant growth. Technological improvements came in steady progression from Kitson's own fertile mind, and from a succession of gifted assistants: A. S. Clarke, H. A. Davis, and A. H. Morton. The basic technical trends between 1852 and 1905 are easily defined.[15]

There was an evolution away from the use of a single machine to the employment of breaker, intermediate, and finisher machines, a trend comparable to that refinement and specialization which had taken place earlier in both the carding and the roving processes.

This evolution was stimulated by the demand for better picking which grew out of the widespread adoption in America in the 1890's of single carding on the revolving flat card.

Attempts to secure increasingly thorough cleaning and mixing of the cotton had first occupied Kitson's attention. After many improvements in this area, efforts of Kitson and his assistants were then directed at regulation of the picking process to produce the uniform and even lap of cotton so important to the carding process which followed picking. These efforts produced a number of devices for regulating the feed of cotton to the machines and for evening the lap which came out.[16] At the same time, Kitson did much to reduce the terrible danger of picker-room fires by taking the lead in developing conveyor systems which enabled the bale-breaking and mixing processes to be performed in the storehouses outside the main plant and the cotton blown through pipes to the picker room inside.

The essence of all these various changes was the reduction of manual handling of cotton, the elimination of piles of loose cotton on the floor of picking and opening rooms, and the automatic regulation of the cotton in process through the various opening and picking machines.

The Kitson shop was highly prosperous, almost from the beginning. Domestic competition was virtually annihilated by the rapid improvement of the Kitson line. Shops like the Whitin Machine Works, devoting their attention to a wide range of products, were totally unable to keep up with the technical progress of the highly specialized shop in Lowell. Both the Lowell Machine Shop and the Saco Water Power Company at one time or another had attempted to build pickers, but they were unable to compete and soon abandoned their attempts to do so. It was not until the formation of the first of the Atherton companies (about 1870) that Kitson had any domestic competition of consequence, and by this time Kitson's reputation and position was too firmly established to be shaken. English shops competed in the American market, but Richard Kitson was quick to incorporate English improvements in his machines, and so minimized the effect of such competition.

One measure of Kitson's interest in developments abroad lies in

Richard Kitson
Founder of the Kitson Machine Shop

HAVEN C. PERHAM

Treasurer of Kitson Machine Shop and Lowell Machine Shop

an unusual agreement drawn up in 1879 between Kitson and one William T. Emmott, of Manchester, England. By the terms of this contract Emmott was to direct to Richard Kitson any English inventors wishing to license picker improvements for manufacture and sale in America. Emmott charged for this unquestionably valuable service a commission of 25 per cent of the licensing fee asked by the inventor from Kitson. By reciprocal arrangement Emmott contracted to promote the licensing of Kitson inventions abroad.[17] To the charge so often voiced in the Transactions of the New England Cotton Manufacturers Association that English picking was immeasurably superior to American, Kitson could point with telling force to the fact that many of his inventions had been patented or licensed for sale abroad, and were in use in England, France, and Germany.

The shop which Kitson constructed in 1860 was a box-like brick structure, eighty feet square and four stories high, topped with an ungainly flat roof. In 1885 an addition to the shop doubled Kitson's capacity, but even with this extension the plant was unimpressive in size as in appearance. Between one hundred and two hundred men were employed, the number varying with the degree of prosperity.

Within this extremely modest establishment a high degree of manufacturing efficiency existed — efficiency made possible in part by the extremely specialized nature of the business. In 1886 H. A. Davis, then superintendent of the shop, commenced attempts to introduce a system of interchangeability of parts, replacing hand-fitting methods with machine techniques. Davis designed an 87-pattern picker with a view to building it with one of the largest planers then in existence, a Pratt & Whitney machine. This attempt was not completely successful, but Davis immediately set about redesigning the picker and by 1890 he had created a model which proved relatively simple to build with the rapidly improving machine tools of the decade.[18]

The profits which were made possible by inventive skill, manufacturing efficiency, low overhead and labor costs, and a near monopoly position in the industry can only be surmised. In 1905 this tiny shop was said to be the largest builder of picking and opening machinery in the world, producing seven-eighths of all of this class of machinery made in America. Dividends were stated to have been 20 per cent on invested capital for many years past, a large surplus had been accumulated, and a bonus incentive system had distributed a share of the earnings to employees.[19]

Kitson's corporate history had been uncomplicated. From 1849 to 1874 the company was a proprietorship, but in the latter year the extension of the business prompted Kitson to incorporate the company. Haven C. Perham, a young man who had made his start in the hardware business in Lowell, came in to assist the aging Kitson and in 1876 he assumed the key position of treasurer. In 1885, when Richard Kitson died, Perham was the active manager of the business. Much of the success of the company after this time was owing to Perham, whose greatest strength lay in the warmth of his personality. Perham's ability to make friends on all sides counted heavily in the market and promoted unity of effort in the shop. Beyond this, Haven C. Perham was reputed to be a "go-getter" and an able financier. Local legend, however, persists in assigning a share of the shop's great success after 1885 to Richard Kitson's widow. This remarkable woman kept a firm watch over what was essentially a family business. (In 1905 a majority of the stock in the Kitson Machine Company was still held by Kitson's two daughters.) Some accounts state that the Widow Kitson was not averse to taking a turn at a lathe. All concur in verifying the story that Mrs. Kitson was accustomed to sit with her knitting in the company office, maintaining a vigilant watch for tardiness and other manifestations of employee irregularity.

The terms which Herrick was forced to offer for control of this unusual company were naturally commensurate with the high earning power and prosperous current position of the enterprise, but the $300,000 paid for $150,000 par value of stock was probably one of the greatest bargains Herrick ever drove. Kitson stockholders realized, from the sale of their stock and the liquidation of certain assets not included in the purchase, about 500 per cent on their invested capital.[20] The Lowell Machine Shop acquired an almost unbelievably prolific property.

The old Kitson Machine Company passed out of existence, its place being taken by a new company incorporated under Massachusetts law on June 6, 1905, and called the Kitson Machine Shop. Herrick was named president and Haven Perham treasurer of the new company. The directorate consisted of Herrick, Perham, and Alfred B. White, a director of the Lowell Machine Shop. Haven Perham was also made treasurer of the Lowell Machine Shop. This last-named appointment was clear evidence of Herrick's esteem for Perham and provided the clearest possible testimonial to Perham's ability. Albert H. Morton, the Kitson superintendent, was made superintendent of the Lowell Machine Shop, replacing the aged Charles L. Hildreth. After this skimming of Kitson's managerial cream Herrick wisely refrained from making further changes in the Kitson organization, and the company went on as before.

4. The Lowell Machine Shop under Robert F. Herrick 1905–1912

The history of the Lowell Machine Shop from 1905 to 1912 presents a duality which makes chronological presentation difficult and raises temptations to depart from main themes. First, there is the absolute necessity of recording the progress of the Kitson Machine Shop, the importance of which was out of all proportion to its size. Secondly, as the Saco-Lowell history moves out of the shadows of the past and into the light shed by the memories of men still living, data accumulate on events in the shop. Men become men, and not names in a dusty payroll book. The shadow of personalities can be discerned behind events in the plant. In the paragraphs which follow an attempt is made to utilize this information, so regrettably missing for earlier years, without neglecting events in the Boston office, where are to be found the heart and sinews of the history for these eight important years.

The Aftermath of 1905

The effects of the purchase of the Lowell Machine Shop by its competitors and of the Kitson Machine Company by the Lowell Machine Shop must be appraised on two levels. Primary interest attaches to the question of the effects of the 1905 action upon Lowell's competitive position and upon competitive conditions in the industry. On a different plane, consideration must be accorded the internal changes which occurred at the Lowell Shop and in the Boston office. What, specifically, did Herrick's control mean in terms of company policy and management?

After March 18, 1905, when the change in ownership of the Lowell Machine Shop became effective, that Shop found itself in a strange position. To all outward appearance the Lowell Machine Shop continued to be an independent organization, functioning in the textile-machinery market as a competitor of Whitin, the Saco and Pettee Machine Shops, Mason, and the other companies which had purchased its stock. Here a distinction must be made between control of the Lowell Machine Shop as exercised in good times and in bad.

In prosperous years the Shop was active in the market. George Marston Whitin, indeed, chided Cramer, his Southern agent, for letting Lowell men beat him to orders.[21] Herrick, apparently acting with a keen awareness of the potency of anti-trust sentiments of the day, did not hold the reins more tightly than was absolutely necessary. It was in periods of depressed business, however, that the full effect of the 1905 purchase became apparent. Never again did the Lowell Machine Shop launch a price campaign comparable to that one in 1904 which precipitated the purchase of its stock.

After 1905, letters from the Shop's superintendent took on a significant new tone, and it is important to note that the Shop was now corresponding regularly with competitors who prior to 1905 had been infrequently addressed, and then curtly. The essence of the new attitude is best demonstrated by samplings of the letters themselves:

March 9, 1906.

Saco & Pettee Machine Works,
Newton Upper Falls, Mass.

Dear Sirs: —

Brenham Cotton Mills, Brenham, Texas.

Our Southern Representative is working up a trade with the above concern, to add to their mill, as it is already ours, and while the business is not very attractive anyway, we would like you to maintain present prices if asked to quote.

Very truly yours,
[signed] H. C. Perham
Treasurer.

March 9, 1906

Mr. John Hill,
Atlanta, Ga.

Dear Sir: —

Harriet Cotton Mills, Henderson, N. C.

If asked to quote on machinery to these people, do not go lower than six hundred ($600.00) dollars on Cards, and two dollar and seventy-five cent ($2.75) per spindle basis on Spinning, as a protection to Whitin, to whom this order really belongs.

Very truly yours,
[signed] H. C. Perham
Treasurer.

March 9, 1906

Whitin Machine Works,
Whitinsville, Mass.

Dear Sirs: —

Harriet Cotton Mills, Henderson, N. C.

Answering yours of March 7th. With reference to maintaining prices, if asked for a quotation on above mill, beg to say that we will not quote less than $600.00 each for Cards, and $2.75 per spindle basis on Spinning.

Brenham Cotton Mills, Brenham, Texas.

You can reciprocate for the above by quoting these people, if asked to do so, today's prices on anything they may ask for. I find that no one seems to care for Texas business, and in as much as we fitted up this plant, (and they want a little more new machinery), our Southern representative has asked us to protect him if possible. We know they are going to ask for other prices, therefore trust you will help us out.

Very truly yours,
[signed] H. C. Perham
Treasurer.

July 2, 1906.

Mason Machine Works,
Taunton, Mass.

Dear Sirs: —

Ivey Mills, Hickory, N. C.

We have not received any inquiry from the Ivey Mills, Hickory, N. C., up to this writing, and today have instructed our Southern office not to try and get this order, but to bid $2.85 and $625.00 respectively for Spinning and Cards. We feel that you, having the machinery in this mill, ought to receive the order to fill it up, hence our instructions as above.

Very truly yours,
Lowell Machine Shop.
[signed] H. C. Perham
Treasurer.

These letters, and a great many others in the company files, strongly suggest that in matters of price the Lowell Shop was strictly regulated and was allowed to compete only on the basis of quality or delivery dates. The various industry-wide price agreements which were put into effect in 1905 and 1906, however, were no more binding on Lowell's competitors than they had been before 1905. For at least a year after the Lowell purchase, these shops, and particularly the Saco and Pettee Machine Shops, continued to compete as ruthlessly as before, violating price agreements and offering every conceivable inducement to secure orders. The net effect of this highly unusual situation of a controlled company attempting to secure orders in the face of virtually unrestrained competition was that for some months following the 1905 stock purchase the Lowell Shop was almost forced out of the market. Operations were curtailed, men were laid off, and the Lowell management prayed for a resumption of prosperity which would bring enough orders to go around. The fact is, however, that this crisis soon passed. Much of the 1906–12 period was an active and prosperous era of business, with few and short-lived price wars and a marked business resilience after recession. After 1906 the Lowell Machine Shop actually reported good profits in a situation which could easily have spelled catastrophe in a period of less active business.

Because of that resilient quality of business the Shop benefited in the end from being kept out of the market in 1905 and early 1906. At this time competing machine shops had committed their manufacturing capacity for months ahead on orders placed by astute mill men at the low prevailing prices. Rapidly reviving business and increasing demand and rising prices for machinery in 1906 found only the Lowell Shop able to promise reasonable deliveries. As orders at high prices poured in to Lowell — orders which Whitin, Saco-Pettee, Howard & Bullough, and Mason had been forced to turn down because they were busy filling low-price contracts — Haven C. Perham, treasurer of the Shop, chuckled quietly and remarked, "They were hoist by their own petard!"[22]

The Kitson Shop did not share the unstable position of its owner, the Lowell Machine Shop, simply because it competed with none of the shops which owned the Lowell Shop. For Kitson this was a period of greatest activity and profit; shops like Saco-Pettee, which formerly had directed picking orders to Atherton, now found it to their interest to patronize Kitson.

Operating results for both the Kitson and the Lowell Shops reflected the generally prevailing prosperity of the times. Table 18 presents operating statistics for the Lowell Shop. These figures show clearly that the dangerous potential of Lowell's unique competitive situation was held in check by prosperity, though of course there is no way of ascertaining what Lowell's sales and profits would have been in a free market. The unusual dividends in 1911 and 1912, which do not reflect operating conditions, are explained in subsequent paragraphs.

Table 19 gives operating statistics for the Kitson Shop, and these figures speak for themselves. Both shops paid liberal dividends, but there is no evidence of substantial milking by the competitor-owners of the Lowell stock, beyond the fact that inadequate provisions may have been made for plant depreciation. Earned surplus of both the Lowell Machine Shop and the Kitson Machine Shop increased substantially over the period.

The Details of Operations

The extent to which Robert F. Herrick participated in the management of the Lowell and Kitson Shops is difficult to determine.

TABLE 18

SALES, PROFITS, DIVIDENDS, AND EARNED SURPLUS, LOWELL MACHINE SHOP 1906–1912

Year Ending March 31	Gross Sales	Net Profit[a]	Profit as % of Sales	Dividends	Dividends as % of Capital[b]	Earned Surplus
1906	$1,965,400	$ 32,200[c]	1.6[c]	$ 45,000	2.1	$ 272,400
1907	2,491,800	273,900	11.0	90,000	4.2	390,900
1908	2,682,400	458,400	17.1	135,000	6.4	759,300
1909	1,449,600	209,400	14.5	180,000	8.5	833,800
1910	2,315,500	398,100	17.2	270,000	12.7	1,051,900
1911	2,116,000	366,400	17.3	1,782,000	83.9	1,013,300
1912	1,039,900	d	...	453,600	21.4	d

[a] Before dividends.
[b] Invested capital of $2,124,000 (1,800 shares at purchase price of $1,180 per share). In 1912, $100,000 more of common stock was sold, but this was after the last common dividend of that year. In 1912, preferred stock to the amount of $1,250,000 was sold. Quarterly dividends on the preferred were paid in 1912 at the rate of 6% per annum. The new common stock issue, the preferred stock, and the preferred dividends are not included in the table above.
[c] Loss.
[d] No data.
Source: Lowell Machine Shop records, Ledger and directors' minutes.

TABLE 19

SALES, PROFITS, DIVIDENDS, AND EARNED SURPLUS, KITSON MACHINE SHOP 1906–1912

Year Ending April 30	Net Sales	Net Profit[a]	Profit as % of Sales	Dividends	Dividends as % of Capital[b]	Earned Surplus
1906	$515,000	$149,000	28.9	$ 45,000	15	$123,900
1907	679,400	230,900	34.0	90,000	30	243,500
1908	710,500	232,300	32.6	90,000	30	360,300
1909	508,700	152,400	29.9	90,000	30	484,000
1910	757,900	295,700	38.9	180,000	60	601,200
1911	569,800	174,800	30.2	532,500	177.5	144,401
1912	c	c	...	50,000	16.7	c

[a] Before dividends.
[b] Invested capital of $300,000, the price paid for the Kitson stock.
[c] No data.
Source: Kitson Machine Shop records, Auditor's reports and company ledger.

Men who knew Herrick say that he had a grasp of manufacturing problems which was unusual in a man who operated primarily in the legal and financial world. Yet, once the details of the 1905 purchase had been worked out, there were few crucial operating problems to be solved in this 1905–12 period. The Lowell Shop's relations with its owner-competitors would certainly have required Herrick's attention, and decisions such as that to accept limited amounts of mill stocks in payment for machinery were unquestionably his to make. Beyond this area of broad policy-formulation there actually was little need for Herrick's keen insight. Even financing was of a routine nature, and the details were safely left to Haven Perham. Under Perham two supremely competent superintendents handled technical shop problems.

Old employees recall that when Haven Perham took over his new responsibilities as treasurer of both the Lowell and Kitson Shops he had to be taken through the Lowell Shop to have the various types of machines pointed out to him. If the Lowell "old-timers" snorted at this necessity, they took solace in the fact that at least Perham was a textile-machine-shop man, even if that shop only built pickers. Perham quickly and effectively took charge of the Lowell Machine Shop's Boston office. His friendly sincerity and his established reputation for competence assisted in a transition which was complicated by the length of time his predecessors had held office. Perham soon came to be regarded as highly by the Lowell Machine Shop men as though he had spent his entire career with the Shop.

Albert H. Morton, the Kitson superintendent who was transferred to the position of superintendent of the Lowell shop, made no gentle transition, nor was a painless passing from old to new possible at this level. Morton was a bench-trained machinist of the old school, blunt in speech and supremely self-possessed in dealing with subordinates and superiors alike. Morton was a martinet, but he was an outstanding leader of working men. With his arrival the favoritism which had characterized the declining years of Charles Hildreth's management vanished. Morton was hard, but fair and honest. He seldom praised, but he insisted on impartiality, and though this embittered old shop favorites, it pleased the rank and file and encouraged the ambitious young men in the plant.

Morton was a highly skilled machinist and, since he was so successful in delegating managerial authority, he was able to spend much time in the shop. It is said that if, in his frequent excursions into the shop, Morton saw a job being done improperly he would seize the machine with scant good grace and show the machinist how the work should be done. One of his first acts upon coming to the Lowell Shop was to throw out the elaborate cost-card system installed at the turn of the century. "I have all the figures I need," he calmly explained. "There is just one way to control production, and that's to go out in the plant and watch it." [23] This attitude was more appropriate to the small Kitson shop than to the huge and diversified Lowell shop, but it had its merits. This was the system of visual control which had existed for generations, doomed by company growth and increasing job specialization, but existing still wherever an old-time machinist was to be found in charge of production.

Men in the shop often writhed under Morton's stern discipline, but approved of his propensity for acting decisively, if not always correctly. His approach to the problem of the nearly defunct worsted department was both decisive and correct. With a "take it or leave it" attitude, Morton raised the prices on all worsted machinery to the point where a profit was possible. He then devoted his technical skill to improving the line, and appointed a full-time field representative, Robert F. Chase, to sell and service the worsted trade.

John K. Whittier took Morton's place as Kitson's superintendent. Whittier's approach to operating problems was far different from Morton's, but different too were the problems he faced. Unlike the Lowell Shop, Kitson was a compact and smoothly operating unit. No man was better qualified than the even-tempered, well-liked, new superintendent, who had served Kitson since 1886, to preserve the high morale and high efficiency of the organization. Robert Herrick's wisdom in allowing a considerable degree of autonomy in the firm was eminently justified by Whittier's success in making profits over the eight-year period and thereafter.

There was a tightening of the reins in the Lowell Shop, and a very conscious attempt to repair the damage done to customer relations by the "old and cranky" management which had preceded Perham and Morton. Evidence that Hildreth had been lax in controlling his field men lies in a series of letters from Morton to John Hill, who continued to serve as Lowell's Southern agent after 1905.

Friction had arisen between older Lowell erectors and assistants hired in the South. "I recommend you to hire no more men in the South," wrote Morton, "as I think they [the erectors] will more readily work with men from the Shop." Morton then struck boldly at a basic source of difficulty with the erectors. "This matter of expense accounts," he confided to Hill, "is one that is giving us considerable trouble here, as I think the men are inclined to 'roast' us." [24] Morton then proceeded to challenge the erectors' expense accounts, item by item. To C. A. Whiteknact, veteran Lowell erector and repair man, Morton wrote:[25]

I cannot approve your November expense bill, and return same for correction.

Without going into too much detail at this time, question the following: Price paid for *all meals* and the *number of bus fares* charged from the time you left Mayfield, Ga., until you returned to Atlanta? Comparing with bills of others over the same territory, they are excessive, and you have evidently made a mistake.

Charges of November 1st: Stationery $1.25; and November 6th, stamps $1.00, need modifying for so short a trip. What was express charge, Nov. 2, $1.00 paid out for?

If Morton's indignation over these charges seemed petty, the fundamental motivations were far from unimportant. A man of greatest integrity himself, Morton insisted on complete straightforwardness on the part of his men. Morton's attention to minutiae, a factor which had long been lacking in Lowell management, was of greatest value in electrifying the listless organization, though individual examples of this obsession often seemed trifling or ridiculous to the parties involved.

Perham's success was outstanding in restoring customers' confidence in the Lowell Machine Shop. His contacts in the trade were excellent, for he had sold Kitson pickers to a far wider range of mills than used Lowell Machine Shop machines. These contacts and his own obliging disposition brought business to the Shop even in the face of restrictions imposed on marketing effort by the new owners of the company. Though he derived his power from Herrick, Perham was in no sense a representative of the stockholders. His sympathies lay with the Lowell Machine Shop, and he did all he could to advance the Shop's interests.

Morton, too, in his own way, helped to cement wavering customer loyalties. His was the frank approach, and mill men soon discovered that Morton was trustworthy, even to the point of admitting such deficiencies as occurred from time to time in Lowell machines. Often his frankness was disarming. For example, when a representative of the Lafayette Worsted Company stormed into the Shop to complain about the performance of some Lowell worsted machines and began to criticize the Shop's manufacturing methods, Morton emerged from his office and listened briefly. "Mr. Parnall, I would be a fool if I walked into your mill and told you how to spin worsted," Morton said. The customer at once grasped the implied parallel, but Morton was not even remotely subtle. "You, sir," he blasted, "are a damned fool!" Seizing the initiative by this spectacular deviation from traditional methods of placating irate customers, Morton then proceeded to explain and adjust, admitting where the Shop was at fault and staunchly defending it where he thought the customer was wrong. The two men emerged from the encounter fast friends.

These same tactics were employed in the field of labor relations, and with apparent success. Labor policy was heavy-handed, but less so than in many companies of that time, and from 1905 to 1912 there was virtually no labor trouble at either the Lowell or the Kitson plant. Morton discharged men on instant provocation, but granted liberal pay increases to those whose skill he thought deserved reward. Here, too, Morton's sense of justice appears to have operated to good effect. On March 30, 1905, George Theopolos, a steady, hard-working molder, was hospitalized by burns on the foot sustained in the Shop foundry. In such cases, and where the Shop was at fault, men were reimbursed for hospital expenses and lost wages by insurance policies carried by the company. Morton wrote the American Mutual Liability Insurance Company a letter setting forth the facts of the Theopolos case, and concluded:[26]

We do not need to suggest to you that the case is worthy of careful handling. Until now, the Greeks who have been in our employ have been industrious, capable, docile, trustful of us, and, apparently, confident that we would deal fairly with them in case of accident. It is worth something to us to have them retain this confidence, and, if this is a case where there is a doubt whether something should be paid to the man, we shall be glad, both because of his personal good behavior and because of the general good behavior of his countrymen, if you will give him the reasonable benefit of the doubt.

Shop policy toward unionism in its gathering strength was stated simply and rigorously enforced; in Morton's words, "We always have and always intend to maintain an open shop."[27] The freedom which the Lowell and Kitson Shops enjoyed from strikes in this 1905–12 period, however, was probably more a result of external influence than internal policy or management. Saco-Lowell's parent shops at Newton and at Biddeford fought strikes in these years (Chapter XII), but in both these communities no adequate supply of trained machinists was available outside the companies to operate the plants in case of a strike. At Lowell the machinists enjoyed no such monopolistic position, and here, moreover, a strong tradition of labor peace had grown up through the years.

At the Kitson Shop the incentive bonus system which had been instituted in the 1890's was continued after 1905. Piecework rates, of course, were almost as old as the textile machinery industry itself, but the Kitson system of distributing a bonus based on plant output appears to have been most unusual at this time. A standard of twenty pickers per month was established, and a bonus of 2 per cent of earnings was paid to all in the shop for each additional picker turned out over the standard.[28] So rapidly were machine tools and techniques improved in the 1890's and early 1900's, however, that the standard was raised. There was dissatisfaction in the shop over this change, but changing technological conditions rather than any attempt by the management to drive the men harder was responsible for the new standard, and it was soon accepted.

The change in Kitson's bonus standard illustrates the most important technical development in both the Kitson and the Lowell Shops between 1905 and 1912. This was not a period prolific in new textile machines. A. H. Morton had perfected an automatic distributor which was highly effective in controlling the delivery of cotton to the openers and pickers. The Lowell worsted line was greatly improved. Chief Draftsman Charles C. Hedrick began to develop a line of silk-spinning machinery, in answer to demands for such machines from several American mills. The Lowell Shop commenced the manufacture of a camless winder, using patterns acquired from the A. T. Atherton Machinery Company in 1905. The Lowell revolving flat card, which developed certain weaknesses, was greatly improved by E. P. Gibbs, who traveled through the South for the company adjusting the machines. These developments were important, but far from revolutionary. A strong feeling persisted that a technical zenith had been reached by most machines, or at least that only relatively minor adjustments and adaptations were required. Only the silk-spinning machinery line was "new," and these machines were, in effect, only a modification of prevailing machine types, patterned after foreign models. With prosperity came a feeling of security, and with high profits came a period of inventive quiescence. Machine tools and machine-building techniques, on the contrary, improved rapidly, and it was in this field that the most important forward strides were made in both the Lowell and Kitson Shops.

Product policy of both Shops was unchanged in the first years of Herrick's administration. Kitson continued to specialize on opening and picking machines, which, to be sure, were increasing in variety and kind. The Lowell Shop continued to diversify, and by 1912 was building the most complete line of textile machinery of any shop in America. Records are available for the three months ending January 31, 1913, which give some indication of product breakdown of Lowell sales (Table 20), though the period covered is so short that these statistics are far from conclusive evidence of the relative importance of the various machine types. The period for which this information is available, moreover, was one of depressed trade.

In retrospect Shop operations in the 1905–12 period exhibit few startling occurrences; they were characterized chiefly by an attempt to remedy the managerial laxities which had grown up in the Lowell

TABLE 20

PRODUCT SALES, LOWELL MACHINE SHOP
THREE MONTHS ENDING JANUARY 31, 1913

Product	Net Sales			
	Dollars	% of Total	Loss[a]	Profit[a]
Pickers[b]	152,400	30	.....	64,700
Cards	54,000	11	.....	16,200
Drawing	8,100	2	.....	600
Roving	42,100	8	11,600	.....
Spinning	92,800	19	37,900	.....
Twisters	20,100	4	.....	3,900
Spoolers	7,000	1	.....	200
Warpers	6,000	1	4,600	.....
Slashers	30,100	6	.....	2,600
Camless Winders	5,300	1	3,100	.....
Looms	28,900	6	8,100	.....
Total Cotton Machinery	446,800	89	65,300	88,200
Worsted Machinery	43,626	9	6,600	.....
Silk Machinery	11,198	2	8,600	.....

[a] Net sales minus direct manufacturing costs and factory overhead; selling and administrative expense not included.
[b] Kitson Machine Shop.
Source: Saco-Lowell Shops, manuscripts, Totals notebooks.

Machine Shop. Market operations saw a gradual relinquishing of the strangle hold on the Lowell Machine Shop by its new owners as business improved and orders became plentiful enough to keep the entire industry busy. As might be expected from the fact that the Lowell Shop was owned by competitors, little capital was made available for maintaining or improving physical machine-building facilities, but neither Lowell nor Kitson was plundered in the interest of the owners. These years saw colorful men come and go in the two shops at Lowell, but the most dramatic and significant event of the period occurred quietly and almost unnoticed in the offices at 84 State Street, Boston.

The Consolidation of Ownership

By 1911 the owners of the Lowell Machine Shop had become uneasy. The control which they had purchased for themselves at no small price in 1905 seemed, at this time of active business, to be of less use to them than the capital which they had tied up. Anti-trust actions by the federal government were alarming, and the benefits accruing from ownership of the Lowell stock now seemed scarcely worth the risk of indictment for restraint of trade. In short, the textile-machine shops for which Herrick operated the Lowell Machine Shop now had the proverbial bear by the tail.

Herrick stepped into this situation to relieve the embarrassed owners and to secure for himself and a partner the absolute ownership of the Lowell and Kitson Shops. On November 2, 1911, Herrick purchased, for cash, the entire capital stock of the Lowell Machine Shop at the price originally paid in 1905 by the participating shops, $1,180 per share, a total price of $2,124,000.[29] With the consummation of this transaction, ownership of the Lowell Machine Shop passed entirely from the textile machinery industry into the hands of State Street men — predominantly bankers and lawyers — who, both as individuals and as members of the rising class of financial capitalists, had been steadily becoming more active in the management of firms which they represented or had serviced.

Robert F. Herrick appears to have purchased half of the Lowell stock for himself. Wilmot R. Evans, of the Boston Five Cent Savings Bank, came in with Herrick and took the other half. Available information indicates that both men were acting for themselves and not as agents for others. Evans was made president and director of the Lowell Machine Shop, and Herrick took over Perham's duties as treasurer following the latter's death in 1911.

There was no substantial alteration in company management, for Evans apparently came in as an investor rather than as a manager. Financial policy was formulated jointly by the two men, but Evans relied on Herrick to operate the business. Herrick was forced to become more active in the affairs of the Shop, both because of his new status as owner and because of the death of Haven Perham, his trusted lieutenant.

On the surface, the purchase of 1911 appeared to terminate that cycle so familiar in American business which saw ownership and control pass from the hands of the founding manufacturer to those of financiers who were completely divorced from the business, save for their stock interest. This was not the case. Control of the Lowell Machine Shop and its predecessors back to 1813 had never been in the hands of manufacturers. The balance of control had consistently remained in the hands of merchants — merchants in foreign trade at first, then merchants of cotton cloth — men who had primary interests in other fields than machinery building. These men lost the company in 1905, when, to all practical intents and purposes State Street, representing investment banking more than mercantile interests, and personified by Robert F. Herrick, took a hand.

Thus the historic career of the Lowell Machine Shop by-passed entirely a phase of development which dominated the histories of most American manufacturing enterprises — an often protracted period when ownership remained in the hands of the technical men who had conceived the product and had made it a commercial reality. Control of the Lowell Machine Shop and its predecessors had never even come close to the hands of the men who designed, built, and sold the machines, and yet the record of this company was outstanding for more than three-quarters of a century. Frederick Ayer's denunciations of the uses and abuses of Boston-controlled corporations could scarcely be considered pertinent to the affairs of the Lowell Machine Shop, and the administrative skills which founded the Lowell, Lawrence, and Appleton fortunes in foreign trade had proven, in this instance at least, to be equally effective in the field of large-scale manufacturing enterprise. It remained to be seen whether, in a period far less propitious than the booming nineteenth century, the lawyer and banker could duplicate the success of the merchant.

The circumstances under which Herrick and Evans purchased the Lowell stock in 1911 suggest that they might have obtained a bargain. First, there was the legal urgency of breaking up the combine. Secondly, there scarcely could have been many parties interested in acquiring these large properties on terms comparable to those offered by Herrick and Evans. The tempting cash offer enabled the participating companies to dispose of their stock quickly and without loss of capital. Since dividends received by the seven stockholders had averaged 6.7 per cent annually of the original purchase price, these shops unquestionably considered that the whole affair had worked out satisfactorily and had best be terminated before trouble or actual loss occurred. What Herrick and Evans might realize from the transaction mattered little. Indeed, the participating shops, knowing almost nothing about the true worth of the company they owned, were not disposed to quibble over terms by which they might be rid of it.

On the basis of book values recorded in the ledgers of the Lowell Machine Shop the 1911 purchase represented a bargain. In 1911 Herrick and Evans paid the same price for the Lowell stock that had been paid in 1905, yet the book value of those shares had advanced from approximately $710 to $1,079 per share. Financially, the Lowell Machine Shop was far better off in 1911 than it had been in 1905. Asset accounts had not been changed greatly in value, but notes payable had declined from $450,000 to $50,000, and earned surplus had increased from $378,700 to $1,043,800.

The book figures of the Lowell Shop, however, were obviously artificial. Some asset accounts in 1911 stood at valuations which had not changed by so much as a penny since the middle 1870's. The foundry account had not been changed since 1869, despite the fact that this section of the plant had been entirely replaced, remodeled, and enlarged, not once but several times. The basic question of whether the values received by Herrick and Evans were worth more or less than the two million dollars paid cannot be answered satisfactorily by book figures alone. On the one hand, there are many evidences that the Lowell plant had actually depreciated greatly between 1905 and 1911. Counterbalancing this shrinkage in real value was the ownership of the Kitson Shop, which stood on the Lowell books at a valuation of $150,000, but which, on the basis of capitalized earning power, was probably worth ten times that amount.

In the final analysis certain events which occurred immediately following the stock purchase showed most clearly whether Herrick and Evans had been wise or foolish. On November 2, 1911, the day upon which the Lowell stock passed to Herrick and Evans, a cash dividend of $900 per share ($1,620,000) was declared by the Lowell Machine Shop. A second dividend of $15 per share ($27,000) was declared a month later, and a third dividend of $252 per share ($453,600) was declared in January, 1912. At the same time, the Kitson Machine Shop declared two dividends totaling $582,-500. The Lowell dividends alone were nearly adequate to reimburse Herrick and Evans for their purchase price. All dividends combined totaled 126 per cent of the purchase price. Even after these dividends, Lowell Machine Shop assets were deemed sufficient to support an increase in capitalization from $900,000 to $2,250,-000. An issue of preferred stock was sold, bringing in new capital and replenishing the cash disbursed in dividends. Common stock was increased from $900,000 to $1,000,000, the additional $100,000 being subscribed by Herrick and Evans in equal parts. The liquidation of accumulated Kitson and Lowell profits reduced the earned surplus accounts of both firms, but even after these distributions of more than two and one-half million dollars in the short space of three months, total surplus of the two companies showed a credit balance, and by November of 1912 it was approximately half a million dollars. Herrick and Evans had paid $2,124,000 for their Lowell stock and subscribed for $100,000 in addition. They received $2,100,600 in Lowell dividends. (The Kitson dividends went into the Lowell coffers, rather than to Herrick and Evans directly.) Thus, ownership of the two machine shops had been secured in its entirety for a net outlay of only $123,400. Whatever the Lowell and Kitson properties were worth in 1911 over and above their book value represented additional profit on the transaction.

If Herrick had consummated a highly successful transaction, the fact is also clear that his responsibilities had thereby been vastly multiplied. His problem was one of management. It seems obvious that Herrick was eminently capable of directing the affairs of the Lowell Machine Shop, as he had done since 1905, but just as obvious was Herrick's disinclination to give up a multitude of other interests to devote his time to this one venture. Faced with responsibility for providing management for both the Lowell and the Kitson shops, Herrick looked, as he was accustomed to do, for men who could, for a consideration, assume a share of the burden.

Here a break in chronology is necessary. The threads of the Saco-Lowell story must be picked up in Newton and Biddeford and traced down through the years to the time, in November of 1912, when Robert F. Herrick's search for management was crowned with conspicuous success; when the divergent paths of Saco-Lowell's parent companies at last converged, and the corporation known as the Saco-Lowell Shops was formed.

CHAPTER X

RENAISSANCE OF THE NEWTON SHOP 1853–1897

THE evolution of the Lowell Machine Shop traced in the four preceding chapters presents interesting contrasts to the development, over the same eventful period, of Saco-Lowell's parent shops at Newton and at Biddeford. These latter exemplified the struggle of the small industrial unit against the large which was going on in many areas of nineteenth-century American business. This struggle was being resolved in favor of the large, and "big business" as we know it today was being organized. In this process small companies tended to be merged, absorbed, consolidated, dominated, and, occasionally, liquidated. Too frequently they have been forgotten. This and the two following chapters present the history of the middle years of the Newton and Biddeford shops. This history offers an opportunity for examining the pre-consolidation phase of business, the factors operating to bring about merger, the merger itself, and the immediate results of this characteristic late nineteenth-century business maneuver. These two companies, moreover, were endowed with considerable individuality and personal interest.

In mid-century the Pettee Machine Works at Newton was handicapped by limited size and an undistinguished product line. At Biddeford the Saco Water Power Company was fighting to overcome that obscurity in the national market which exclusive devotion to the local and regional market had made inevitable. Both shops stayed alive primarily because of the sellers' market for textile machinery which existed in New England until 1873. Both shops appear to have profited from the rise of the Southern textile industry after that time, and each suffered the effects of increasing competition from American and English machine-makers. In the 1890's both found themselves in the typically hopeless position of being too small — too specialized to compete successfully with the formidable shops at Lowell, Taunton, Pawtucket, and Whitinsville. In 1897 the two sought strength in combination; they achieved their purpose with such remarkable success as to affect radically the form and substance of the textile machinery industry.

Between 1850 and 1897 the Saco Water Power Company and its successor, the Saco Water Power Machine Shop, exerted an increasing but still limited influence on the textile machinery industry. The interest of this branch of Saco-Lowell's history derives from the richness of business experience to be found there. The Pettee Machine Works was an insignificant factor in the American textile-machine market for more than thirty years, but the long hiatus was ended in the mid-1880's by a vigorous new management and a new machine.

1. Otis Pettee & Company

The Years of Obscurity, 1853–1882

After Otis Pettee's death in 1853 the machine shop and some of the tenements which Pettee had built in Newton Upper Falls passed to his two sons, George and Otis, and his son-in-law, Henry Billings. A partnership was formed by the three heirs, and the business was continued under the name of Otis Pettee & Company. Insufficient records have survived to preserve the detailed story of this venture, nor can the careers of the three partners be traced. The company appears to have been without great influence or fame in the American textile-machinery market. The partnership either was doing a very limited domestic business or was depending for sustenance on some foreign market.[1]

The three partners divided managerial duties among themselves in accordance with their respective abilities. George Pettee was the bookkeeper and Otis Pettee the machinist. Henry Billings took little part in factory affairs, but he served as financial adviser and appears to have dominated the partnership.[2] Billings had influential contacts with Boston banking houses and with the iron merchant firm of Appleton & Snelling, though the source and extent of his influence cannot be ascertained.

Not even a guess may be hazarded as to the success of the venture from 1853 through the great depression following 1873. The years 1878 and 1879, however, appear to have been lean ones for the partnership. A payroll book of the company shows that the highest number of employees at work in these two years was ninety, and a crisis of some sort is evident in the affairs of the partnership. In 1880 Billings offered to sell his one-third interest in the machine shop to the Pettee brothers for $10,000, or to purchase their two-thirds interest for $20,000. The Pettee brothers decided to sell, and Henry Billings became the sole proprietor of the business.[3] The price paid by Billings for the Pettee interests suggests that the fortunes of the company were at low ebb, but under Billings' management recovery was rapid. By December, 1880, the number of employees had increased to 236. In this year and the next, large orders for cards were being filled from the Lancaster Mills and the Pepperell Manufacturing Company.[4] On September 22, 1882, the company was incorporated as the Pettee Machine Works with a capitalization of $200,000, of which $75,000 represented plant and the remainder new capital paid in.[5]

2. The Pettee Machine Works, 1882–1897

A New Company and a New Crisis, 1882–1887

Incorporation of the business in 1882 was brought about by a financial alliance between Billings and his close friend Samuel G. Snelling, prominent Bostonian iron merchant, treasurer of the Lowell Bleachery, and director of the Lowell Machine Shop. Billings subscribed to 1,000 shares of the Pettee Machine Works stock; Snelling and his immediate family took 310 shares, and Snelling assisted in placing the remaining 690 shares among his friends in Boston.[6] Snelling gave his note to Billings in payment for his stock.

The enlargement of ownership interests in the machine shop at Newton Upper Falls in 1882 has a deeper significance than the mere contribution of new capital to a staggering enterprise. The formation of the Pettee Machine Works was another manifestation of the familiar New England pattern of inter-related enterprise. Samuel Snelling himself provided a link between the Pettee Machine

Works and that group of financiers who controlled the Lowell Machine Shop, but the Pettee Machine Works was not one of the Lowell-Appleton-Lawrence-controlled companies. Snelling, though a director and, for a short time, president of the Lowell Machine Shop, was closely identified with rival (or parallel) interests, which very obviously were following the precedent established by Abbott Lawrence and his associates some forty years before. At the head of this group was David Nevins, head of Nevins & Company, a cloth-selling house, and apparently a friend and associate of both Billings and Snelling. The mills in the Nevins orbit included the Methuen Company, the Pemberton Mills, and the Stevens Linen Works. Thus, the entry of the Nevins interests into the Pettee Machine Works in 1882, effected through Nevins' purchase of 100 shares of stock and his contacts with Billings and Snelling, was a step in the process of vertical integration through which control by a coterie of Boston financiers was extended backward from cloth-selling house to cotton mills; from cotton mills to a machine shop; from a machine shop to an iron dealer.[7] A close connection with one or more Boston financial institutions completed the pattern. While in extent the Nevins interests were far more modest than those of the House of Lawrence, the analogy between the two is striking in form. Chart IX attempts to suggest the form which the two parallel groups assumed, without making any claim to completeness, particularly in respect to the cotton mills and financial institutions involved. A fertile and interesting field for further study is indicated here.

The incorporation of the Pettee Machine Works in 1882 was accompanied by one noteworthy change in management. Samuel Snelling's son, Rodman Paul, had been graduated from Harvard in 1881. A condition of Snelling's financial assistance to the firm appears to have been that a place be found in the organization for his son. In August, 1882, Paul Snelling (as he was called), though without substantial business experience, was elected treasurer of the Pettee Machine Works, and presided thereafter over the office which was then set up at 70 Kilby Street, Boston.[8]

The new organization was born in a period of prosperity, but hard times soon overtook the company, which was now actively

Henry Billings
President of the Pettee Machine Works, 1882–87

The Shops at Newton in the 1880's

managed by Henry Billings, assisted by Richard Daley, an old-time machinist whose autocratic superintendency and rule-of-thumb methods are still remembered. By 1885 some measure of recovery from the depression of the preceding year had set in. New orders were being received, inquiries were multiplying, and the outlook for the future was encouraging. The company at this time was tending to specialize in carding machines, but orders were also being filled for looms, speeders, drawing frames, and railway heads.

In 1885, in response to the general American trend toward adoption of English roving techniques, the company purchased from Wm. Higgins & Sons, of Manchester, England, all the patterns used by them in the manufacture of the English type of fly frame, which then replaced the speeder in the company line. At the same time, patterns for the English Lancaster spinning frame were also imported. In 1886 business increased still further, a result of generally improving times and the popularity of the Pettee cards and fly frames.[9] In that year the balance sheet of the company showed total assets of $275,000, roughly a quarter of the amount shown on the statements of the Lowell Machine Shop at that time.[10]

Despite evidences of increasing prosperity in 1885 and 1886, however, the Pettee Machine Works was far from being in a healthy condition. Weakness on the managerial side became more pronounced as Henry Billings became less able, by reason of increasing infirmity, to attend to the business. This weakness was greatest in the marketing phases of company activity. Despite a limited amount of advertising, sales promotion was patently neglected. There were no salesmen, and no one in the company took an active interest in marketing. Paul Snelling's activities were confined chiefly to keeping the book of stock-transfer records, and he evinced no inclination to take a firm hold of managerial responsibilities at Newton. English competition, moreover, particularly in cards and fly frames, was becoming increasingly serious. It was none of these factors, however, but a sudden and unexpected blow from a different direction which actually precipitated the crisis in the affairs of the company.

In July, 1886, Samuel Snelling made an assignment in bankruptcy, and a large amount of his paper, including his note to Billings covering the purchase of Pettee Machine Works stock, was suddenly

CHART IX

Vertical Integration in the Textile Industry

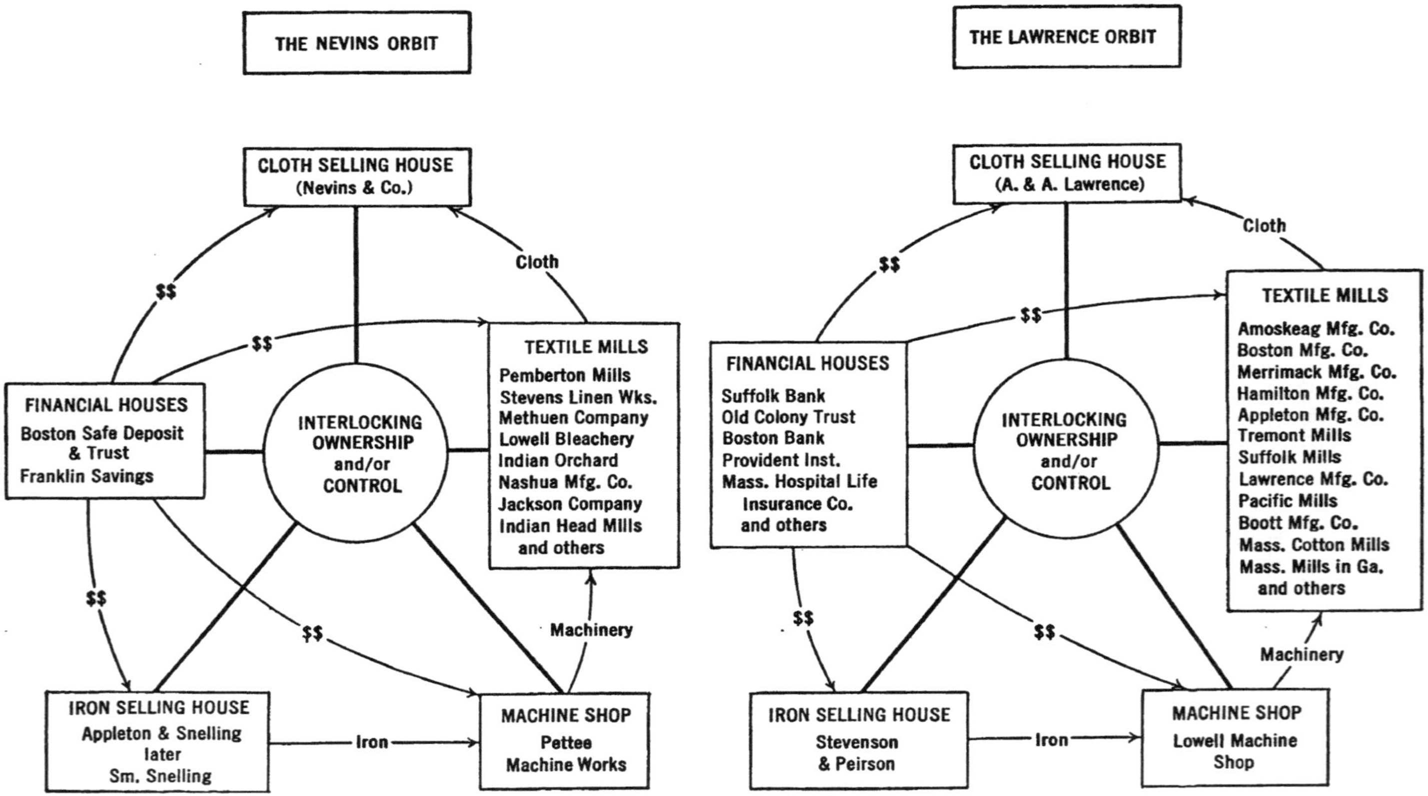

CHART IX

Explanatory Note

The contents and implications of this chart should be defined somewhat. First: the primary purpose of the chart is to place the machine shops in their proper orbit and not to probe in an exhaustive way corporate interrelationships in the textile industry. Second: the basis for including companies in either group is indefinite. Mutuality of interest cannot be assumed from the fact that companies had one or two directors in common. Common officers are perhaps a safer indication of mutuality of interest. It is this latter basis which was relied on most in compiling the above data. Whatever basis is adopted, errors are inevitable. Usually these will be on the side of assuming a lesser degree of interrelationship than actually existed. Third: the inclusion of a company in one group or another should not be taken to mean that that company dealt only with other companies in its own group. This may have been the case in respect to the relationships between cloth selling houses and mills, but definitely was not true of the machine shops. The shops unquestionably favored mills in their own orbit, but did not abstain from making sales to mills in the rival or parallel group when opportunity presented. Fourth: initiative in the process of vertical integration lay with the cloth selling houses. After about 1900 the position of dominance appears to have been assumed by one or more of the financial houses which served the group. Robert Herrick's rise to power in the Lowell Machine Shop illustrates this significant transition.

These qualifications might seem to reduce the usefulness of this chart to a minimum. This is not the case. The contribution which this chart makes to existing knowledge is in pointing out some of the specific companies which appear to have been involved; in broadening the known sphere of influence of Boston financial groups to include machine shops and iron selling houses; in emphasizing once again the significance of these groups in New England's industrial history; and in calling attention to and defining a parallel to the familiar Lawrence-Appleton-Lowell group.

found to be worthless. Billings, a loyal friend, quietly wrote off Snelling's note.[11] To cover the loss to the Pettee Machine Works involved in Snelling's assignment, Billings turned in to the company treasury, without compensation, more than five hundred shares of the company stock which he himself owned. These shares were then offered for sale. The response to this appeal for funds provides ample evidence of the influence of Billings and the Snellings and of the esteem with which they were regarded in high places in Boston. The company in this precarious plight could attract no large new investment. It was, instead, a host of friends who saved the situation by purchasing from one to fifty shares of the surrendered Billings stock. Distinguished Bostonian names were entered in the transfer books of the Pettee Machine Works — Burnham, Linzee, Amory, Wright, Weld, Lowell, Rotch, Sears, Ames, Lee, Fay, Higginson, Chase, Bryant, French, Whitney, Glidden, Weeks, and others. The number of shareholders increased from twenty-one in 1886 to fifty in 1887, and the result of this sudden broadening of ownership was to consolidate control of the company firmly in the hands of David Nevins. Nevins doubled his stock holdings in 1887 to become, with 200 shares, the owner of the largest single block of shares outside the Billings interest. At the same time Henry S. Shaw, Nevins' assistant, increased his holdings from fifty to one hundred shares. Henry Billings' death in 1887 completed the transfer of control, and David Nevins was elected president of the company to succeed Billings.

Young Men, 1880–1887

David Nevins took little part in the management of the Pettee Machine Works. The scope of his interests, like those of Abbott Lawrence and other leading financial industrialists, was too broad for this. Like Lawrence, his method was to control without managing. Then, as now, the technique depended upon the selection of able operating lieutenants.

There was need for capable new management at Newton. Already, in the last days of Billings' management, a tremendously promising idea was fomenting in the shop. This idea required fresh, specialized mechanical knowledge. The condition of the company demanded alert and vigorous administrative effort. The dual need for both technical and administrative skill was supplied by four competent and ambitious young men. Frank J. Hale, who had commenced work in the shop as office boy in 1880, had shown such capacity and likeableness that he soon became Billings' indispensable assistant, David Nevins' favorite, and Paul Snelling's friend. He advanced rapidly from office boy to paymaster and, in 1888, to sales agent. The old superintendent, Richard Daley, had been replaced in 1885 by George Tappan Francis, another young man of great promise and one whose mechanical abilities were to be a vital factor in the subsequent history of the firm. In 1887 Francis brought Frederick A. Flather and Oscar E. Nutter to Newton to assist him in technical problems then being faced.

Here was a break with tradition. Not one of these four young men had been trained at the workbench. Frank J. Hale had come to the shop from his family's farm, which was adjacent to the Machine Works property. Hale knew the shop well from earliest boyhood, for his father had taken on many an unemployed machinist as a temporary farm hand during slack times. He served no long technical apprenticeship, but was engaged almost from the beginning in the administrative end of the business.[12] This was the most difficult path to success that a farm boy without connections could select. George Tappan Francis, on the other hand, had excellent connections and good mechanical training. His father had been active in the affairs of the Indian Orchard Company, the failure of which so impaired the family fortunes that Francis was forced to forego a college education. He attended a school of mechanic arts sponsored by the Massachusetts Institute of Technology and assumed the superintendency of the shop after a short period of training under Daly, the old superintendent. This example of a school-taught mechanic assuming managerial responsibilities early in his career was far from usual at the time, but the mechanical genius of Francis, too, was far from usual. Frederick A. Flather was the son of a skilled machinist and was teaching evening drawing school at Nashua, New Hampshire, when the call came from Newton. Flather brought to the company not only some practical knowledge of machine designing, but a keen feeling for change which was not always found in the experienced and seasoned machinist. Oscar E. Nutter came to the firm immediately after graduation from the Massachusetts Institute of Technology with indispensable specialized knowledge. Nutter's scholastic specialization had been in the field of mechanical and textile engineering — his thesis subject had been carding.[13] This infusion of young blood was one of the most significant events of the entire middle period in the Newton shop history. The promise implicit in this unusual array of talent was obvious, but the problem of finding room in a small organization for the expression of the respective personalities was great.

The Revolving Flat Card

In the early 1880's a great controversy was raging in American textile circles. The basis of this controversy was the reputed superiority of English carding methods over American. There is no question that in this department of cotton manufacture the English mills were far ahead of the American, and that the English machine shops were turning out cards which were vastly superior in design and workmanship to any made in America. American carding techniques were under severe attack, both at home and abroad. Lack of care, it was said, in the mixing, opening, and picking processes meant that the carding machines were forced to clean as well as card the cotton, to the detriment of their primary function. It was also said that less improvement had taken place in the carding room of American mills than in any other branch of the manufacture. Critics pointed to the fact that the Wellman self-stripper was the only important improvement in forty years — that the main cylinder still was being stripped by hand, and that the American cards were lacking in that accuracy and exactness in workmanship which was to be found in English machines. Even the Wellman card, stated one observer, was as crude a machine as any to be found in a cotton mill of that time (1884).[14]

The immediate point at issue was the relative advantage of single over double carding. American mills had come to prefer the latter, which involved the use of two cards in sequence and which favored the American demand for high productivity in the increasingly fine sizes of yarns which were being worked. English mills were single carding with a different type of machine — the revolving flat card.

Bachrach

Frank J. Hale

General Agent of Pettee Machine Works, 1889–97; General Agent of Saco and Pettee Machine Shops, 1897–1912; General Agent of Saco-Lowell Shops, 1912–23, Vice-President, 1923–32, and Director, 1912 to present.

Bachrach

R. Paul Snelling

Treasurer of Pettee Machine Works, 1882–97; Treasurer of Saco and Pettee Machine Shops, 1897–1912; Treasurer of Saco-Lowell Shops, 1912–23, and Vice-President, 1923–32

This card was not new, but its impact on the textile industry, first in England and then in America, was revolutionary. So superior was it to the old style of card that within a decade following 1885 the stationary flat card was hopelessly obsolete. The Pettee Machine Works was the first American machine shop to build the revolving flat card, and from this machine the firm derived both fame and wealth.[15]

There is evidence that out of the confused state of company affairs in 1886 sprang the realization that the firm was not wealthy enough to build a wide line of machines, and already there had been a tendency to specialize in carding machines. Some time in 1885 the attention of Superintendent Francis was called by his friend Frederick Amory, agent of the Jackson Company of Nashua, New Hampshire, to some revolving flat cards which had been purchased by Amory from Platt Bros., of Oldham, England. At this time there were very few of these cards in operation in America.[16] Francis prevailed upon Amory to send one of the cards to Newton, where it was taken down and studied and plans made to copy it.

In 1886 Snelling and Francis sailed to England to purchase the special tools necessary to commence the manufacture of the Platt card, and to secure necessary patterns. The revolving flat card *in toto* was not patentable, but Snelling appears to have concluded some kind of an agreement in England covering rights to make and sell such parts as were covered by patents. The revolving flat card was a venture of the highest order of risk, and upon the outcome rested the existence of the Pettee Machine Works. The cost of special tools alone was $60,000, and other developmental costs brought the total to $250,000 — a sum far beyond the existing means of the company.[17] This gamble was underwritten by David Nevins, and it left the company heavily in debt to him.

On March 14, 1886, the Cunard steamship *Oregon,* carrying Paul Snelling and all the precious patterns back from England, sank off Fire Island. Snelling narrowly escaped with his life, and all the patterns were lost. After many delays the patterns were replaced, but this inauspicious beginning was followed by great manufacturing difficulties. A basic obstacle was that the perfection of the English card was based on the English system of hand-fitting the parts. In order to compete with the low English wages, American shops had long since adopted the technique of machining parts. This cheaper method of manufacture had not yet been perfected to the point where the quality of work turned out by the superbly skilled English fitters could be duplicated.[18]

The assembly of the first revolving flat card at Newton involved an incredible amount of filing, fitting, adjusting, and trial-and-error experimentation. There were delays and moments of acute depression. Always the work proceeded under tremendous pressure from those whose capital was tied up in the venture.[19]

By September, 1887, the greatest difficulties appeared to have been surmounted. In this month the first order (for seven cards) was shipped to the Jackson Company, and the Pettee revolving flat card was pronounced satisfactory. Thereafter, the story was one of eliminating, one after another, the inevitable defects which showed up in operation, and of steadily improving the basic designs.[20] The increasing number of cards sold testified to the technological success of the gamble. Between September and December, 1887, fifteen cards were shipped to New England mills. In 1888 a total of fifty-two were sold; in 1889, 208; and in 1890, 1,383. By December, 1893, a total of 6,687 revolving flat cards had been installed in American mills. As the success of the card became increasingly evident, the Pettee Machine Works gradually abandoned the manufacture of all other machines except the closely related railway heads and drawing frames.

By 1894 the Lowell Machine Shop, the Mason Machine Works, and the Whitin Machine Works had all begun to produce revolving flat cards of a quality comparable to that of the Pettee card. The competitive advantage derived by the Pettee Machine Works as a result of being first in the market, however, was one of two decisive factors in the subsequent success of the firm. The other factor, without which the new machine could scarcely have been so profitably introduced, was management — a young, alert, driving, forceful new management which bowed to no obstacles and tolerated no stifling traditions.

Reorganization, 1889–1893

The managerial pattern began to crystallize in 1889, two years after David Nevins had become president of the company. The

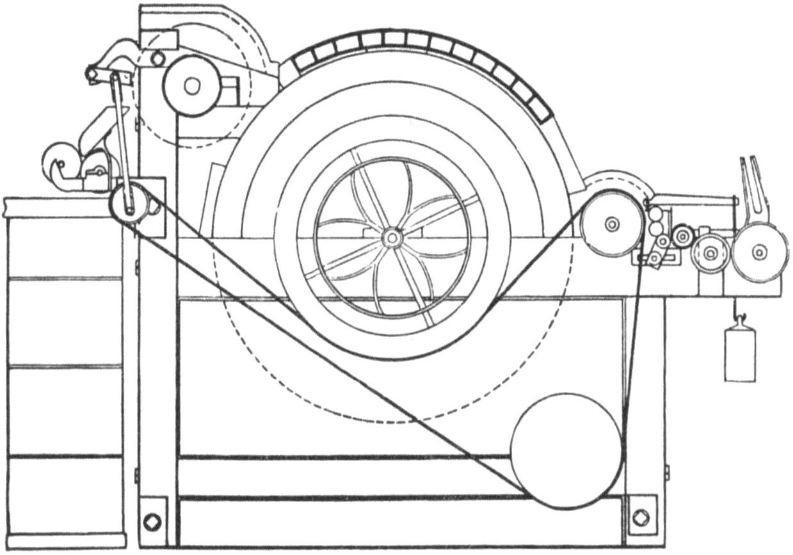

EVOLUTION OF THE CARD

Top Flat Card as Built at Lowell before 1845

Twelve top flats occupy 23 per cent of circumference of main cylinder

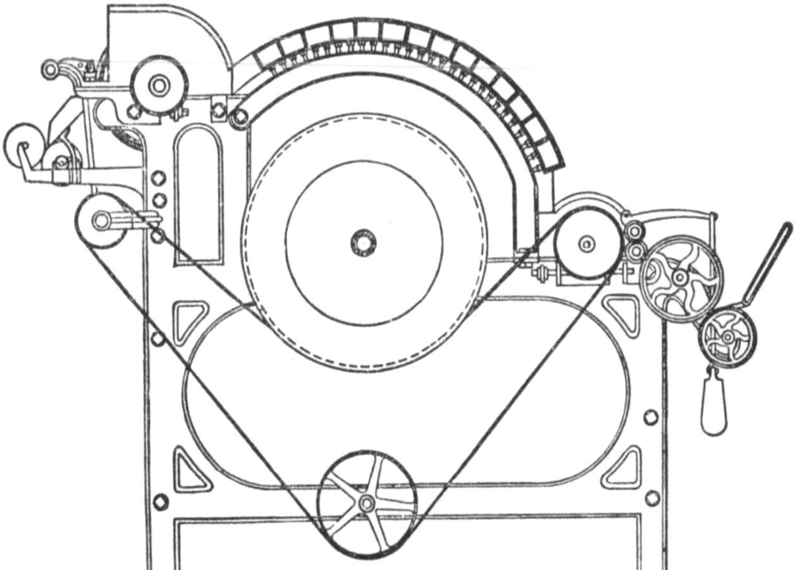

Top Flat Card as Built at Lowell Soon after 1845

Fourteen top flats occupy 27 per cent of circumference of main cylinder

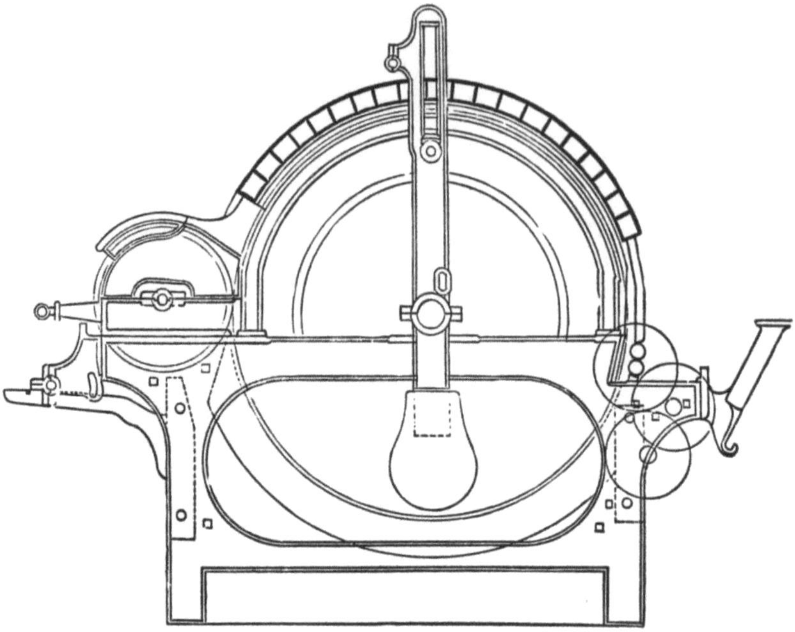

EVOLUTION OF THE CARD (*continued*):
TOP FLAT CARD AS BUILT AT LOWELL IN 1862
Twenty top flats occupy 35 per cent of circumference of main cylinder

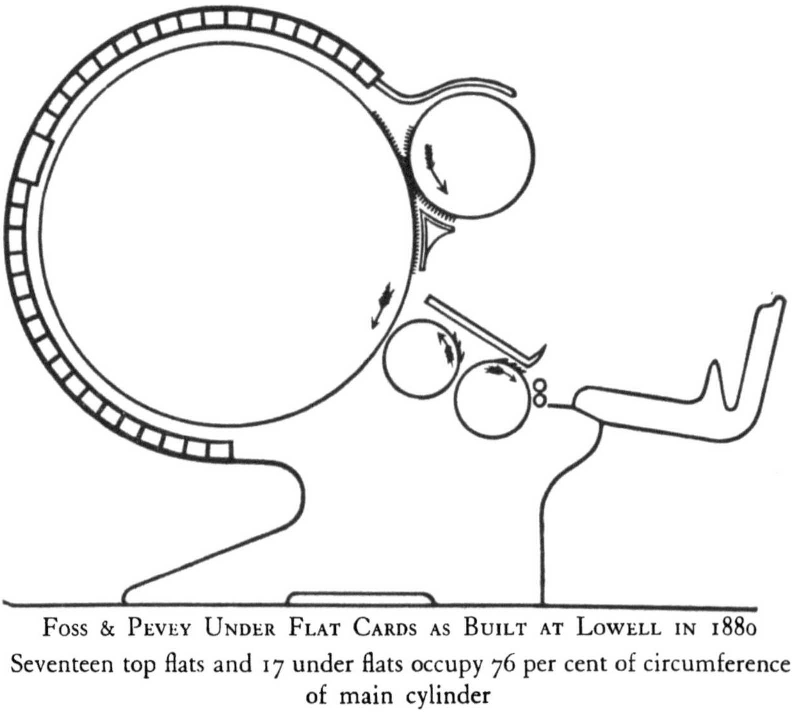

FOSS & PEVEY UNDER FLAT CARDS AS BUILT AT LOWELL IN 1880
Seventeen top flats and 17 under flats occupy 76 per cent of circumference of main cylinder

usual conflicts found in managerial reorganization were present—complicated perhaps by the entirely natural rivalry of young men striving to get ahead.

The form of the organization was altered somewhat by the creation of the position of general agent. No comparable position existed in the Lowell Machine Shop, and the precedent was derived directly from the New England textile mills. The general agent stood halfway between the treasurer and the superintendent. His duties were neither altogether financial nor technical, but administrative. In the Pettee Machine Works the duties of the position included not only the over-all management of company affairs, but the more specialized functions of sales manager as well. The choice of a man to assume the new position, of course, rested with the Nevins-Snelling interests which dominated the company. David Nevins' word was not to be contradicted when he signified his wish that Frank J. Hale be made agent. Addressing Hale in private Nevins told him, "Frank, if you make a go of this and get my name off the notes of the company I will make you a present of all of my stock!" [21]

Hale promptly addressed himself to Paul Snelling, persuading him to give up the Boston office, come out to Newton, and assume an active part in the management of the company. The close association of the two men thus commenced was to be a long, harmonious, and profitable one.

George Tappan Francis, the gifted superintendent under whose management the revolving flat card had been introduced, appears to have felt that Hale's appointment as general agent restricted his own opportunity for advancement, and in 1889 he resigned his position to accept a more advantageous one elsewhere. The loss was great, but even with this loss the net gain to the company from the reorganization was large. Frederick A. Flather was named superintendent to succeed Francis, but Flather, who had been sponsored by Francis, soon found that the company was too small to provide unbounded opportunity for his ambitions. In 1892 Flather resigned and went to the Lowell Machine Shop.[22] His place was filled by an Englishman, Charles E. Mills, who had traveled extensively erecting cards for the English firm of Howard & Bullough. Oscar E. Nutter served as assistant superintendent under both Flather and Mills. With these adjustments the reorganization of company affairs which actually commenced in 1880 with the purchase of the Pettee interests by Henry Billings was finally completed.

3. The Revitalized Company, 1887–1897

Gathering Strength in Adversity

The history of the Pettee Machine Works under the management of Frank J. Hale and R. Paul Snelling must be viewed in relation to the background conditions of increasing competition, business uncertainty, and frequent depression which existed throughout much of the 1887–97 period. Prosperous, established companies were shaken in these years. The financial record of the Pettee Machine Works does not appear auspicious, but this is misleading. The success of the firm in expanding its market, liquidating a heavy debt, inaugurating regular annual dividends, rebuilding its plant, and emerging in 1897 as one of the four dominant firms in the industry, was remarkable for the times.

The records which indicate this progress are fragmentary, though sufficient to point out the basic operating results of the new management. Table 21 presents as much of the statistical record of the 1887–97 period as can be gathered together.

These figures show the heavy burden of debt assumed by the company, first in financing the revolving flat card and then in modernizing and enlarging plant facilities. The payment of this debt in 1894, coupled with depressed conditions in the trade, appears to account for the sharp decline in assets in that year which Table 21 reveals. The financial difficulties under which the company very evidently struggled from 1887 to 1893 must be considered as manifestations of an inherently healthy internal development — one which strengthened the company in vital places, at the short-term expense of the stockholders. Frank J. Hale's philosophy of management was that, since the stockholders were accustomed to no dividends at all, he would take advantage of their defeatist attitude and put the increasing returns from the business into new plant.[23] In the last analysis, however, the stockholders gained from this policy, for the groundwork for great future strength was thereby laid.[24] With the partial liquidation which accompanied a major corporate

TABLE 21

Operating Statistics of the Pettee Machine Works, 1887–1897

Year	Sales	Men Employed	Total Assets	Dividends as % of Capital	Debts
1887	$106,000	125	$242,800	none	$ 38,300
1888	154,000	215	296,300	none	96,300
1889	238,000	250	336,700	none	136,700
1890	238,000	250	394,500	none	194,500
1891	414,000	350	425,500	none	225,500
1892	554,000	425	439,600	none	230,000
1893	697,000	510	476,500	3	249,200
1894	......	...	278,700	3	......
1895	......	...	520,700	3	......
1896	......	...	498,500	3	......
1897	297,000	...	433,500	195[a]	169,300

[a] Liquidation dividends of $70 per share in cash and $125 (par value) per share in stock of the Saco and Pettee Machine Shops.

Source: Sales and men employed from statement of R. P. Snelling before the U. S. Tariff Commission, 1890. Other figures from Pettee Machine Works records, Statements of Condition, Mass. Corporations.

change in 1897, stockholders received not only the $100 originally invested per share but additional values in cash and stock to the amount of $295 per share.

Behind this record of slowly gathering strength lay two remarkable personalities. Treasurer Paul Snelling had a dignity which commanded respect and coöperation from Boston bankers and Southern mill men alike. Snelling, it is said, could secure a loan by the way in which he walked into a bank president's office. His character was his collateral, and often he had to furnish no other. An aristocrat in bearing, soft spoken in speech, and cautious in thought and action, Snelling's greatest value to the concern was a real ability in finance coupled with personal prestige and contacts which secured both working capital and orders for the Pettee Machine Works.

General Agent Hale was a natural salesman, a tall, smiling man of contagious enthusiasms with a tremendous capacity for action and a faculty for handling men. Hale was more intimate than Snelling with plant operation, with the men in the shop, and probably with the machinery market as well. In his relations with the men under him Hale expected from all the utmost effort in behalf of the company, and his own energy and friendliness enabled him to realize his expectations while retaining the respect and coöperation of those with whom he worked. At no time was there any question as to who was in command — but this capacity for staying on top was tempered by the policy of allowing subordinates freedom for the exercise of initiative. The general agent, it is related, allowed his men all the rope they wanted, but held onto the end of it. The genuine democracy of Frank J. Hale, a quality which Snelling most certainly did not share, was a potent force in welding the organization into an effectively functioning business unit.

These two men worked smoothly together, the banker's caution and the salesman's optimism interacting here to the optimum benefit of the company. The trade came to know them as the "Heavenly Twins," an appelation which appeared to derive in equal parts from their long-continued association, the splendid figure they cut, and their willingness and ability to move Heaven and Earth to obtain orders. One old mill man was more explicit, if less delicate, in picturing the two. "When Hale took snuff," he stated, "Snelling sneezed." [25]

Marketing the Revolving Flat Card

The eventual success of the Pettee Machine Works was based primarily on success in marketing the revolving flat card. The factors involved in that marketing success are clear-cut. Foremost among these was the aggressive salesmanship of Frank J. Hale, himself. Above all else, it was said, Hale loved to sell machinery. The plain implication contained in the letters of Charles Hildreth, superintendent of the Lowell Machine Shop, was that Hale would rather sell machinery than make a profit for his stockholders. This belief, which appears to have been widely held in the trade, was based on a dangerous misconception of what was going on in the Newton plant.

Under Hale's direction an active era of promotion was instituted. Circulars, catalogues, and advertising were released to the trade. Hale was the company's most successful salesman, but under his direction a salesforce began to take form. By 1895 William V. Threlfall, W. H. Bigelow, and possibly others were acting in the capacity of salesmen, and Paul Snelling himself began to join Hale on occasional trips to the South. Snelling's activities were of greatest significance. By the middle 1890's, at the very latest, he had begun to participate actively in the formation of new Southern mills. The first of these in which there is any record of Snelling's participation was the Indian Head Cotton Mills in Alabama — a promotion undertaken in 1895 by the Nashua Manufacturing Company, with which the Pettee Machine Works had long been closely connected by personal ties. Unfortunately, there is little surviving evidence to suggest the extent of those ties or of Snelling's contacts with other cotton mills — both Northern and Southern. The most that may be said is that the active participation by Hale and Snelling in the corporate affairs of customers and prospective customers had already commenced by 1895, and may have commenced earlier. This method of influencing the placing of machinery contracts was as old as the textile industry itself, but was to be practised on an unprecedented scale by the managers of the Pettee Machine Works in the years to come. The acceptance of Southern mill stocks inevitably encouraged an interest in the fate of those mills which went far beyond the ordinary concern of a manufacturer for the welfare of his customers.

Some time between 1893 and 1895 the Pettee Machine Works formed the tremendously significant affiliation with the Charlotte Machine Company, of Charlotte, North Carolina. It will be recalled from Chapter VIII that this affiliation united the Pettee line and the products of several other more or less specialized shops in the hands of one Southern agency, thereby securing to the participants an advantage equivalent to that enjoyed in the market by the larger and more diversified shops. The necessity for such action by the Pettee Machine Works is clear. In an effort to cut Pettee out of the lucrative Southern market, the Lowell Machine Shop and the Whitin Machine Works had been quoting ruinously low prices on cards and making up the deficit on machines which Pettee did not build.[26]

The Charlotte Machine Company rapidly became a power in the South, deriving much strength from the youthful energy of its founder, H. S. Chadwick, and from an early entry into an untouched field of enterprise. Chadwick was a Vermonter, who had gained experience as an erector for the Franklin Machine Shop at Pawtucket, Rhode Island. He established his agency in 1893—at a time when few, if any, Northern machine shops were employing resident representatives in the South. Chadwick appears to have added one line after another, until, by 1896, he could furnish a cotton mill complete.[27] Like other Southern agents who became successful, Chadwick was endowed with rare personal charm and soon rose to a position of high social as well as financial prestige. Inevitably he soon took an active part in the promotion of new mills, seeking thereby to profit not only from the operation of the mills but also from the placing of machinery contracts through his own agency.

Scant regard for established customer ties was shown by the Pettee Machine Works or its agent, the Charlotte Machine Company, in the drive for business. Orders were taken wherever they could be found, and lenient inducements were extended to customers in the matter of terms and prices. Frank J. Hale was regarded in the machinery trade as a likable young fellow but one whose efforts would bring ruin upon himself, his company, and the industry. This was the usual protest of age against youth.

Driven by competitive pressure and facilitated by declining costs of manufacture, the price of cards dropped from over $800 in 1894 to slightly over $500 in 1895. In May, 1896, an agreement was reached among card-builders to sustain a minimum price of $600, but in 1897 card prices had dropped to $450.[28] Cramer, Whitin's Southern agent, reported violations of the agreement to George Marston Whitin and mentioned instances in which the Pettee Machine Works had evaded the credit regulations established in 1896.[29] Pettee, however, was but one of many offenders, and soon the 1896 agreement was being generally disregarded.

The practice of accepting mill stocks in part payment for machinery was an integral part of the Pettee market campaign. There is no positive information as to when such stocks were first accepted, but the policy once commenced was pursued with an enthusiasm which occasionally tried the patience of competitors. The claim has been made that, although George Marston Whitin had taken Southern stock as early as the middle 1870's, the Pettee Machine Works was the first to institute the practice on a large scale. This claim cannot be verified nor denied — neither can the allegation be proven or disproven that this company indulged in the practice to a greater extent than did other shops. It seems clear, however, that the Pettee Machine Works was among the most liberal in the trade in extending such accommodation to the Southern mills prior to 1897.

In a statement of ledger balances for the year 1889 no mill stocks were listed among company assets. In 1894 mill stocks were so listed, indicating that some time between these two dates the practice may have been instituted. The amount of stocks carried on the books of the company at various dates was as follows:

TABLE 22

Value of Textile-Mill Stocks Owned by the Pettee Machine Works 1894–1897

	Nov. 1, 1894	May 1, 1895	Nov. 1, 1896	May 1, 1897
Value Carried on Books..	$30,920	$30,630	$23,750	$ 58,360
Par Value..............	No data	No data	95,000	145,900

Source: Pettee Machine Works, Ledger.

All of the stock held in 1896 was of Southern mills. In 1897 approximately 75 per cent was Southern stock. The relatively small amount of these stocks carried on the books of a company known to have been among the most active in accepting stock settlements suggests that up to 1897 the financial participation of the Northern machine shops in the Southern textile industry had been limited, though not insignificant.[30]

Many questions of great interest and importance relating to the marketing efforts made by the Pettee Machine Works before 1897 cannot be answered. A gap in the records forestalls any detailed study of the terms extended to customers, the relations between the machine shop and its Southern agent, or the extent of participation by the shop in the rise of the Southern industry. The gap is most unfortunate, for the weight of verbal evidence suggests that the Pettee Machine Works was shattering industry precedents, establishing new marks in aggressive marketing, and commencing to assume a position of great importance in the South. For the period ending in 1897 these conclusions can only be stated tentatively.

Some parts of the marketing story lie outside the realm of formal records and are the more perishable, though no less valuable, for this reason. The interest and adventure attached to the early marketing efforts in the South should be reported as an illuminating chapter in the history of American business. Only a handful of men now live, however, who recall those days, and this slender link with another age has preserved only the highlights — not a consecutive narrative. These men have memories of mule-drawn wagonloads of machinery churning through the red clay of Georgia's back country. They recall the tiny last stop on many a Carolina railroad, where machinery was lifted by hand to wagons to continue a hazardous overland journey to some raw new mill town. Some remember spending wet nights on country roads beside a hopelessly mired or overturned cart. Others recall the derisive yells of "Yankee! Yankee!" with which they were greeted by the children of Alabama hamlets. All recall, in varying degrees, the personal challenge implicit in their position of machinery erectors, divorced for long periods from contact with the home office. From these ranks emerged many a mill superintendent or Southern agent. For some, however, the opportunity for dissipation and shirking was too great to be withstood. All would agree that the responsibilities involved soon determined the true caliber of a man. There can be little question that the success or failure of the Northern machine shops in the Southern market was influenced, perhaps greatly, by the abilities of these men. Their adventures illuminate a little-known episode in history — their rôle in the textile machinery industry has always been important.

Some information has survived of the mills in which Pettee machinery was being erected in the late 1880's and early 1890's. Of greatest interest is a summary recorded in one of the general agent's memorandum books in December, 1893, showing the distribution of all revolving flat cards manufactured by the company to that time. As might be expected, this summary reveals the importance of the Southern market. At the same time, it reveals heavy orders from

New England mills — orders which reflect the fact that these mills were the first to adopt the new machine on a large scale.

TABLE 23

DISTRIBUTION OF REVOLVING FLAT CARDS DELIVERED OR ON ORDER
DECEMBER 7, 1893
PETTEE MACHINE WORKS
(Covering the period 1887–1893.)

New England		Middle Atlantic		Mid-West		South	
Mass.	1,717	Pa.	118	Ind.	58	Miss.	20
N. H.	563	N. Y.	325	Neb.	42	Tenn.	83
R. I.	465	N. J.	64			Ky.	24
Maine	240					Md.	117
Vermont	16					La.	1
Conn.	272					Texas	16
						Va.	59
						N. C.	330
						S. C.	1,404
						Ala.	369
						Ga.	484
Totals	3,273		507		100		2,907

Total to Northern mills,	3,880
Total to Southern mills,	2,907

The extent of the business done by the Pettee Machine Works from 1893 to 1897 cannot be determined. Some clipping books kept by the company indicate a very heavy volume of sales between 1893 and 1896, and a serious decline in sales commencing in 1896 and extending into 1897 — a decline which reflected general conditions in the trade. A preponderance of Southern orders in 1895 and 1896 suggests that these mills did not lag far behind their Northern rivals in adopting the new card. Of the ten largest mills in the South in 1896 seven were equipped with Pettee cards, and the list of Pettee's other Southern customers is impressive in length.[31]

Much business was done in North and South Carolina. In this geographical area competition with the Whitin Machine Works was strong. Despite the rivalry which existed between the two shops, however, Frank J. Hale looked to George Marston Whitin as the elder statesman in the industry, and a friendship grew between these two hard competitors which contrasted sharply with the aloof relationships between the Whitin Machine Works and the Lowell Machine Shop. This cordiality may have been a factor in facilitating the 1905 combination. Certainly Hale's ability to fight hard for business and still retain the friendship of his rivals was a factor of some significance in the history of the Pettee Machine Works.

In marked contrast to the Lowell Shop, the Pettee Machine Works found considerable business in the Fall River and Rhode Island areas. Possibly aggressive salesmanship overcame the tendency of many of these mills to patronize English card manufacturers. Competition from England, however, was conceded to be formidable, despite high tariffs. The propensity of English-trained mill overseers and superintendents to use English machinery was an obstacle which only time, trial, and selling effort could overcome. Ironically enough, it was not the price protection held to be so vital by high-tariff protagonists which finally began to overcome the English threat but, rather, the superior performance of American machines and the better service provided by American machine-builders. The gradually increasing preference for American-built revolving flat cards which the Pettee Machine Works had done so much to bring about typified this historic abandonment of a buying habit which had its origin in the very beginnings of the textile machinery industry.

Efficiency in the Shop

Behind the active marketing efforts of Hale and Snelling lay a splendid manufacturing organization. Here, in the shop itself, lay the reason for that willingness to accept low-priced orders which Charles Hildreth and others in the industry found so difficult to comprehend. Manufacturing efficiency was a major factor in the success of the company.

Much credit for the attainment of that efficiency in this period must be credited to Hale and Snelling themselves. For these men, the one a salesman and the other a banker, to grasp the essential need for attention to shop affairs was one of the most effective possible tributes to the versatility of their management. Hale's insistence upon plowing back earnings into the plant was the foundation for subsequent manufacturing achievements. The progress thus instituted by the general agent was carried forward by extremely capable assistants with such success that after an initial preoccupation with shop affairs Hale and Snelling were able to devote their full attention to marketing and finance.

After 1886 the Pettee Machine Works enjoyed one great manufacturing advantage over the larger shops — specialization on a narrow line of machines. To this initial benefit was shortly added that of a modern plant equipped with the latest machine tools. Modernization of the old shingled buildings commenced in 1886, when a brick building was constructed to house the tools imported to manufacture the revolving flat card. The acquisition at this time of a complete line of specialized English tools of the latest design gave the company an initial advantage over competitors. This advantage was increased by the success of George Tappan Francis and Frederick A. Flather in adapting American mass-production techniques to an English hand-fitted machine. Under these men two ideas were fostered: first, to turn out a revolving flat card which would give a satisfactory performance in the cotton mill; secondly, to design the card so that maximum manufacturing simplicity could be achieved.

In 1895, extensive plant improvements were undertaken. The old wooden buildings were largely replaced by brick structures. Electric lights were introduced. A new foundry was added which increased the casting capacity from seven and one-half to twenty-two tons or more per day. Over-all plant capacity was increased one-third.[32]

The work commenced by Francis and Flather was taken up and carried forward by Charles Mills and Oscar E. Nutter. With the solution of initial manufacturing problems attendant upon the introduction of the new card, even greater attention was devoted to reducing costs and simplifying operations. Great progress was made under Mills in producing interchangeable parts — progress which was immeasurably assisted by the work of Nutter and Loren W. Penny, a draftsman and designer who was brought to Newton in 1889 from the Lowell Machine Shop and who probably did more than any other person to improve the output of the shop. Alexander Rankeillor, who had come to the Newton shop in 1890, applied the canny instinct of the Scot to designing a card grinder which relieved the company of the temporary embarrassment of paying royalties to the Lowell Machine Shop on a Lowell-controlled English patent.[33] A high degree of mechanization was achieved which enabled unskilled labor to be utilized, and the concentration of effort upon three machine types only made possible great savings in supervisory costs. In 1895 machine molding was introduced in the foundry.

The card-erecting process exemplified those methods by which low costs were made possible. Here a line of twenty machines was positioned on each side of a long room. Erectors progressed down one line, each applying one part or set of parts. When one line of cards had been completed, they were disassembled, boxed on the spot, and trucked from the room. While the completed line was being disassembled and boxed, the erectors were working on the other line, so that by the time the first line of machines had been removed the second line had been completed and the erectors were ready to commence upon a new line set up where the first had been. These mass-production techniques, made possible by the specialization of the company, were introduced at Newton into an industry which had little experience with or feeling for such methods.[34] These various technical and organizational improvements were manifestations of a highly effective managerial system in the shop. General Agent Hale gave Superintendent Mills, Assistant Superintendent Nutter, and Chief Draftsman Penny the greatest possible freedom of action, and set up no fixed classification of responsibilities. "I intend," Hale told Nutter on one occasion, "to let you three find your own levels in this company." Had any one of these men been mediocre, uncoöperative, or possessed of a discordant personality, such informality would scarcely have been possible. Mills, Nutter, and Penny worked closely together for more than thirty years without, it is said, the exchange of a single unkind word. Such prolonged managerial harmony was highly unusual and must stand as the most important single factor underlying the efficiency of the Newton shop.

The details of plant operations in this period are scanty, and almost nothing is known about labor or wages. By 1887 the traditional system of job contracting had been abolished in the plant. Labor was native-born, English, Scotch, and Irish. The names on a payroll list covering the early 1880's suggest that possibly a quarter of the men in the shop were of Irish extraction, and an even higher percentage of Irish were employed in the foundry. In 1887 about 40 per cent of the foremen were Irish, 40 per cent English, and 20 per cent native-born Americans. By 1897 the average daily rate of pay in the shop, which in 1882 had been $1.57, had risen to $1.69.[85]

The cumulative effect of decreasing labor and material costs and increasing manufacturing efficiency between 1893 and 1896 is well illustrated by the figures in Table 24. In 1897, a year of poor business and declining metal prices, cost of manufacture showed a tendency to increase. This reversal of the previous trend indicated the extent to which the shop was dependent for its cost efficiency upon quantity production. A sample breakdown of card-manufacturing costs is included in Table 24 as a matter of interest.

The Pattern of Ownership and Management

In the familiar American tradition the successful efforts of Frank J. Hale and Paul Snelling to revitalize the company resulted in great personal rewards. These rewards took two forms—only one of which is measurable. The opportunities presented for participating on favorable terms in the development of the Southern textile industry appear not to have been scorned by either man. Opportunities also were presented to each for increasing, likewise on favorable terms, their stock ownership in the Pettee Machine Works.

These latter opportunities grew out of the uncertain future of the company in the 1880's and 1890's which, when coupled with frequent general business depressions, contrived to keep down the market price of Pettee stock. Both Hale and Snelling, however, were imbued with optimism over the prospects of the company under their management and availed themselves of an offer by David Nevins to loan them money at any time that an opportunity for purchasing stock might arise.[86] From 1889 to 1897 the most significant aspect of company stock ownership was the marked trend toward

TABLE 24

REPRESENTATIVE MANUFACTURING COSTS, 1893–1897
PETTEE MACHINE WORKS

	Labor Cost			Total Cost of Manufacture		
Year	Cards	Drawing per Delivery	Railway Heads	Cards	Drawing	Railway Heads
1893	$150.00	$18.00	$60.25	$641.07 to $710.11 (Selling price $749 to $820)	No data	$112.01 to $153.64
1894	123.00	13.55	50.00	No data	$67.07 (Selling price $66.99)	No data
1895	106.85	9.90	41.00	$517.00 (Selling price $637.30)	$47.60 (Selling price $63.57)	No data
1896	100.00	9.40	33.16	$463.30 to $500.00 (Selling price $560.66)	$34.00 (Selling price $66.98)	$88.50 (Selling price $204.80)
1897		No data		$454.86 to $494.71	$46.55	$116.76

COST OF CASTINGS PER POUND

Year	Total Cost	Labor Cost
1893	$.0188	$.0082
1894	.0171	.0070
1895	.0158	.0072
1896	.0160	.0070
1897	.0163	.0072

SAMPLE BREAKDOWN OF MANUFACTURING COSTS

Cards, 1893	
Labor	$201.93
Stock	278.87
Burden (33⅓%)	160.27
Total	$641.07

Source: Memorandum books of Frank J. Hale and Oscar E. Nutter.

concentration into a few large holdings. This trend was exactly opposite the steady dispersion of ownership in the Lowell Machine Shop and had the wholesome effect of making ownership, control, and management virtually synonymous — a typical advantage of the small company over the large. Through all the difficulties of this period Hale and Snelling were backed in their managerial decisions by an overwhelming majority of stockholder votes. Neither David Nevins, the president of the company, nor the board of directors participated to any extent in management.[37] Hale and Snelling were given free rein — a fact of some importance in explaining the vitality of company policy in this period.

TABLE 25

Trends in Stock Ownership, Pettee Machine Works, 1883–1897

	Shares Held			
Principal Stockholders	1883	1889	1894	1897
Henry Billings	1,000	...	...	...
Billings Estate	...	416	...	...
David Nevins	100	194	325	400
Henry S. Shaw	50	100	215	215
Samuel, Rodman, and Eleanor Snelling	260	110	288	340
Frank J. Hale	...	90	237	290
All other subscribers	590	1,090	935	755
Total subscribers	17	50	44	34

Source: Statements of Condition, Mass. Corporations.

The financial strength of the Pettee Machine Works in 1897 is reflected in a balance sheet dated May 1 of that year.[38]

Real Estate and Machinery[a]	$539,487.89	Capital Stock	$200,000.00
Stock on Hand (75% of cost)	37,565.33	Bills Payable	169,311.54
Cash	17,432.49	Reserve for Depreciation	437,979.85
Notes Receivable	117,182.09	Profit & Loss	64,238.57
Mill Stocks (40% of par)	58,360.00		
Accounts Receivable	101,502.16		
Total Assets	$871,529.96	Total Net Worth and Liabilities	$871,529.96

[a] Included agent's house, superintendent's house, and 21 other residential dwellings.

This financial strength was a clear reflection of the character of company management. That management had succeeded in vital areas where the management of the Lowell Machine Shop had failed. Perhaps the willingness to take risks had its origin in the desperate plight of the company in the early 1880's, and in the fact that the men in control had little to lose and everything to gain; irrespective of origin, that daring contrasted sharply with Lowell policy. Aggressive marketing and a willingness to gamble heavily upon the future of the Southern textile industry, coupled with a good product and a magnificent manufacturing establishment, brought the Pettee Machine Works in the short space of fifteen years from near bankruptcy to a foremost position in the industry. By 1897, major internal problems had been solved. Financial reserves had been accumulated, a selling organization had been built, and a splendid market reputation had been achieved. The ambitions of a still youthful, still dynamic, and supremely self-confident management now turned in expansionist directions.

THE PETTEE MACHINE WORKS IN 1888

CHAPTER XI

RESURGENCE AND DECLINE OF THE BIDDEFORD SHOP, 1850–1897

1. The Saco Water Power Company, 1850–1866

While the machine shop at Newton Upper Falls was undergoing the metamorphosis from which the dynamic Pettee Machine Works was to emerge, and while the Lowell Machine Shop was waxing fat as undisputed leader of the textile machinery industry, Saco-Lowell's third parent company at Biddeford was still struggling to free itself of the encumbering fetters of the mills which it had created. Here, on the falls of the Saco River, promoters and their promotions had come in rapid sequence, some to succeed, but others destined only for obscurity. Soon after 1825 the Saco Manufacturing Company had built a machine shop and a cotton mill, but bankruptcy and fire in 1830 required a successor, the York Manufacturing Company, to make a new beginning in the manufacture of cotton-spinning and weaving machinery at the Falls. Nine years later York had created the Saco Water Power Company, which was charged with land-promotion, power-regulation, and machinery-building functions.

Resolving the Pepperell Crisis

The situation in Biddeford in 1850 was clear in principle — confused in detail. The Saco Water Power Company had accomplished the objectives for which it had been established in 1839. The Laconia Company and the Pepperell Manufacturing Company had been started, machinery had been supplied, and the best sites remaining at Saco Falls had been turned over to these two cotton-manufacturing companies. Meanwhile, the original concept of the Water Power Company as a mill promotional enterprise had clearly changed. In 1850 the intent of the Water Power Company to continue machine-building operations had been amply evidenced, but the machine shop itself was obsolete. Having built no machinery for sale outside Biddeford and Saco, the machine shop had lagged far behind contemporary technical progress. Business was depressed, machine-building operations were virtually suspended, and the financial condition of the company was unenviable. Ownership of the Water Power Company was still vested in the same group of men who controlled the cotton mills at the Falls, and these men were primarily interested in cotton manufacturing. Seven of the nine Water Power Company directors in 1850 were directors or officers of the Pepperell Manufacturing Company, and William Dwight, treasurer of the Water Power Company, was treasurer of Pepperell and Laconia as well.[1] Dwight's multiple responsibilities seemed to give little hope that the Water Power Company would receive the managerial attention that it required, and many stockholders were still angry at Dwight's apparent willingness to sacrifice the interests of the machine shop to those of the cotton mills.

In Chapter IV the sequence of events was detailed whereby William Dwight had charged the ledgers of the Water Power Company with the heavy premium necessary to make the Pepperell Manufacturing Company stock attractive to investors and attract venture capital to the Pepperell promotion. Dwight now turned his efforts to repair the damage he had necessarily wrought to the parent company. With the swift, deft touch of the experienced practitioner, he proceeded to perform the financial surgery so desperately needed by the Saco Water Power Company.

The balance sheet of the company on May 31, 1851, was considered so important that it was printed and distributed to the stockholders instead of merely being read at the annual stockholders' meeting, as had hitherto been customary. This statement reflected a loss of $326,004.37 on the Pepperell promotion. On July 31, 1851, the directors voted to charge the heavy deficit of the company against the stockholders' equity in the business. The stock outstanding was accordingly diminished in value from $500 to $300 per share. This drastic action (shown in Table 29) placed the company on a relatively stable financial basis. Future survival, however, was dependent not on financial manipulations but on the ability of the company to build and sell machinery.

Product and Marketing Policy, 1850–1866

Early in 1851 Otis Holmes, superintendent of the Water Power Company, resigned his position to seek greener pastures elsewhere. His place was temporarily filled by R. M. Chapman, engineer of the company. Chapman by his own admission knew nothing about building textile machinery. His function was to keep a nucleus of about forty skilled workmen employed until orders and a new superintendent could be obtained. Dwight hoped to find both at Biddeford.[2]

Sylvanus J. Wetherell, a local man with experience in the machine shop and cotton mills, was apparently being groomed for the superintendency as early as November of 1850, at which time he was dispatched by Dwight to England to obtain knowledge and patterns of the self-acting mules which were beginning to be adopted in America for spinning filling yarn. Wetherell wrote Dwight a frank appraisal of the difficulties which had impeded efforts to place machine-building operations on a profitable level.

Private

Manchester, Feby. 14, 1851–

With regard to your Shop—

It is a hard case, that's certain—should you make the changes herewith proposed, it would give it work enough to get through the season tolerably well. I am in great hopes you will be able to secure some work at Portsmouth as I wrote you on the 17th—and should you do both jobs it will be a relief for a time. It seems to me that as soon as manufacturing comes better—there will again be a Mill-Fever, though perhaps not rage quite as violently as in 1846 & 7. With an active, enterprising man at the head, I do not see why you should not secure work as well as the shop at Lowell or Lawrence, and there is no doubt in my mind that you can underbid either of them. The fault has been, and is, that your shop *is not known*—and persons in want of jobs do not consider you as a contracting party. Your shop has not hitherto been in the market enough as a bidder. Mr. Holmes had not much relish for this very necessary part of his business—and no one else had the authority for it. My opinion is that if you had a person of the energy and enterprise of Jarvis Williams as the head of your shop, that you would not want work when there was any in the market — Mr. Russel has not the education fit for a *Manager* but I think he has enough for an *overseer* — and as a man and a mechanic is far above his predecessor, Genl. Warren. One thing I am afraid you have never considered — that is, that after the dismissal of Mr. Nichols, every obstacle and annoyance was given to what were called the "Western men." Genl. Warren, in particular vented his spite against you, against Mr. W. P. Haines, (whom he accused of being at the bottom of the whole matter) and was especially bitter in declaiming in shops &c against your selecting "a d—d loco foco lawyer" as he expressed it to take the place of such a man as Mr. Nichols. For the first two years after the change nothing was left undone that could be done, to annoy and drive away Mr. Russel, Mr. Wheeler and myself and in fact any other "western man." Mr. Russel has often complained to me of the treatment of Mr. Quinby — and he thought a fair chance was never given him in the shop — Mr. Wheeler has been kept there only by friendship for Russel and I doubt whether you can get him away from Mr. Holmes, and he is the best man for the place he filled you can find, and I think never received credit for his *full value*. He is extremely sensitive, felt so keenly the opposition he met when he first came — that he ever after lived in a state of disgust and abhorrence of everything in Biddeford. The best man I know of for the place you mention is Mr. Stone formerly of Lawrence, now of Manchester. He is a draughtsman and thorough mechanic — but it is no use talking about him, as he knows the state of things at B. is well acquainted with Mr. Russel & Wheeler, and would not go there. Whether you keep Mr. Russel or not a good draughtsman is *very essential*, especially if the manager is not one himself, and I have thought that it might be of use to you to import one from some good shop here, I shall bear this in mind and try to find the right man against you want him. This would I think be more preferable than having an English overseer — English overseers are trained too much to one thing or machine, and do not *adapt* themselves readily to circumstances — fancy every thing wrong that they have not been accustomed to. As a more definite answer to your questions I advise you to import an English card in addition to and of different pattern to those of Mr. Clarks' — to import one "Sharp & Roberts" mule *complete* from the best shop I can find, and make what more you want in your own shop — import what Fly Frames you want at present, but be ready to contract with any future parties (especially if tariff is raised) and lastly but not least, offer J. Williams or some other competent man 5% on all orders they will get for the shop — and take any work that offers cheap, until you get your name known. It is a very general practice here to give any one 5 per cent on all work brought to the Shop. . . . I should write one or two more sheets had I time, but presume you will be glad when you get through this much. My health is much improved, the weather is mild, have had no snow and little frost.—Yours very Truly S. J. Wetherell

Wetherell's quest for information in the English shops was successful, and his well-recorded experience there throws much light not only on the universal American reliance on English skills, but also on the equally universal Yankee slyness which was employed in learning English manufacturing secrets. Wetherell confided to Dwight that entry to English shops and mills was best effected when "Master is away," and that the hard-drinking mill managers were more than sufficiently talkative after a dinner and over a glass. Wetherell brushed aside Dwight's complaint about the size of his expense account with the explanation, "I have had to operate among gentlemen more than I expected, and of course have to live and dress well . . . and when among the workmen have to fee them to get what is wanted. . . ." Wetherell stated further, "The easiest way to get along is to humor them [the English managers] in the belief that they are ahead of all creation in everything pertaining to mechanics . . . and if one is 'very green' and keeps them talking they will accidentally and carelessly drop more truth, than they will purposely give if they find you 'wide awake.' "

In the next two years the results of Wetherell's trip became evident, and the soundness of his technical advice was proven. Orders for mules for Pepperell and Laconia provided enough business to enable operations in the shop to be resumed.[3] By July, 1852, the shop had added new and improved designs for whippers, openers, drawing frames, slubbers, fly frames, self-acting mules, cloth trimming and napping machines, lathes, and drills. These were predominantly English designs, and probably had been secured by Wetherell during his English visit. By 1854 new patterns had been made for railway eveners, ring spinning frames, and narrow looms which rounded out the shop line. The condition of competitive impotence in 1850 thus proved to be a blessing in disguise. The necessity for replacing not just one or two machine patterns but the entire line had the result of making the company, by 1854, a leader in the introduction of new machines. Probably no other shop in the industry at that time could boast of so complete a selection of the most modern machine patterns. This competitive product advantage, born in 1850 of the stern necessities for complete reorganization, was tenaciously retained thereafter in the field of spinning and roving machinery. To Sylvanus J. Wetherell must be accorded the credit for effecting this most significant contribution to the well-being of the Biddeford shop.

Shortly after 1852 a policy of product specialization became evident. With the exception of a limited number of machine tools and turbine water wheels manufactured between 1850 and 1865, the common temptation to expand in periods of depression into untried fields in quest of business was, in the main, resisted. In 1857 the superintendent contemplated a venture into paper machinery, but discarded the idea when orders for cotton machinery began to come in once again. Following the collapse of the market for cotton machinery in 1863, the superintendent went so far as to go to England to procure the knowledge and designs necessary to commence the manufacture of worsted machinery. After a thorough investigation of this possibility he reported, "My opinion grows stronger and stronger that we better confine ourselves to cotton machinery mostly & now is the time to put the old shop in a suitable condition to make money hereafter."

The Water Power Company not only confined its principal efforts to cotton machinery, but soon began to specialize within that field. In 1854 the company had patterns at its disposal for a complete line of cotton machinery. By 1867, however, opening and picking machinery, looms, warpers, dressers, and finishing machines had been dropped. The company line then consisted of cards, railway heads, drawing frames, fly frames, and ring spinning frames. The increasing specialization of the Water Power Company upon the roving and spinning frames which it made best was destined to make that company a troublesome competitor of those firms like the Lowell Machine Shop which still persisted in offering a wide range of products. In this respect the Water Power Company's policy closely paralleled that of the Pettee Machine Works and other smaller shops in the industry.

Product specialization of necessity went hand-in-hand with wide markets, and the efforts of the Water Power Company to develop mill contacts outside the Biddeford-Saco area constitute one of the most important phases of the company's development. Those efforts had commenced as early as 1852, and a large part of the $200,000 of contracts on hand in 1853 was for mills outside the local area. Prior to the Civil War, business appears to have been confined almost exclusively to mills in Maine, New Hampshire, and northern Massachusetts, and orders from the Pepperell, Laconia, and York mills continued to form an important source of income.[4] After 1865 a broadening of markets is discernible, but the trend in this direction was not marked. Table 26 shows product sales for the year 1866; it presents ample evidence that, although the company was no longer dependent upon Pepperell, Laconia, and York, a narrow market was still being served.

Almost nothing is known of selling methods or terms. No salesmen were employed and little advertising was done. Like the Lowell Shop and others in the industry, the Saco Water Power Company appears to have maintained customer contacts through the personal efforts of the treasurer and the superintendent. The only known exception to this passive marketing attitude occurred in 1852, when a local paper commented that several pieces of machinery "of most elegant workmanship, made in the Machine Shop of the Water Power Company under the direction of its Superintendent Sylvanus J. Wetherell, Esq." had been on inspection at the shop and were destined for the World's Fair at New York.[5]

A glimpse of competitive practice in the machinery trade is provided by an exchange of letters between John C. Whitin and William H. Thompson, who was then superintendent of the Water Power Company shop.[6] In 1860 Whitin asked Thompson what he charged for fly frames. Thompson replied that he was perfectly willing to exchange price information, and forwarded a list.[7] On March 3, 1863, Whitin wrote Thompson as follows:

Friend Thompson:

I heard a rumor of yours a few days ago which led me to think you had a wrong impression of my work. I heard you said, Hill and Whitin have no business to come down your way to get machinery to build, as

TABLE 26

PRODUCT AND CUSTOMER ANALYSIS, SACO WATER POWER COMPANY, 1866

Customer		Location	Cards	Railway Heads	Drawing Deliveries	Mules (Spindles)	Fly Frames (Spindles)	Ring Frames (Spindles)	Grinders	Warpers	Spoolers (Spindles)
Newmarket Mfg. Co....		N. H.	...	..	..	....	....	576	..	..	100
Great Falls Mfg. Co....		N. H.	...	8	24	....	....	....	..	2	...
Exeter Mfg. Co........		N. H.	...	..	..	....	120	....	..	..	...
J. W. Little...........		N. H.	18	2	..	....	112	288	..	..	...
Belknap Mills.........		N. H.	...	..	..	....	....	....	..	2	...
York Mfg. Co.........		Maine	...	..	..	2,240	....	....	..	..	...
Bates Mfg. Co.........		Maine	30	..	12	....	....	....	..	..	...
Laconia Co...........		Maine	...	..	..	2,016	....	....	..	..	...
Hill Mfg. Co..........		Maine	46	..	..	....	620	1,152	..	..	...
Androscoggin Mills....		Maine	...	..	..	1,184	....	....	..	..	...
Woodman Dana.......		Maine	16	3	5	....	84	480	..	..	...
Pacific Mills...........		Mass.	...	..	..	....	....	5,760	..	..	...
Prescott Mills.........		Mass.	...	..	..	636	....	....	..	..	...
Shirley Yarn Mills.....		Mass.	...	..	..	1,024	....	....	..	..	...
Appleton Mfg. Co......		Mass.	...	..	..	2,368	52	....	..	..	...
Boston Mfg. Co........		Mass.	...	..	..	....	....	....	..	2	...
Everett Mills..........		Mass.	...	..	..	....	152	....	..	..	...
Robeson Mills.........		Mass.	...	..	..	....	1,780	....	..	..	...
Henry Irving & Leiper..		Pa.	...	..	..	....	....	160	..	..	...
A. Campbell & Co......		Pa.	31	8	12	....	....	....	..	..	...
Harrisburg Cotton Mill.		Pa.	...	..	18	....	....	....	..	..	...
Shaw & Knowles......		Del.	9	..	6	....	....	....	..	..	...
D. Keith..............		Ga.	22	2	14	....	340	1,920	3	..	...
Goodard Bros.........		?	32	..	..	....	....	....	..	..	...
Totals	Maine............		92	3	17	5,440	704	1,632	..	..	...
	New Hampshire...		18	10	24	....	232	864	..	4	100
	Massachusetts.....		...	..	..	4,028	1,984	5,760	..	2	...
	Total New England		110	13	41	9,468	2,920	8,256	..	6	100
	Total Other.......		94	10	50	....	340	2,080	3	..	...
	Grand Total......		204	23	91	9,468	3,260	10,336	3	6	100

Source: Saco Water Power Company records, Sales Ledger.

you did not come this way. I can assure you I have not been after work your way or anywhere else for a long time as I have had all I wish to do without, and I do not need to go after work. I do not know when I have come into competition with you, but once, for years, but I may have done [so]. . . . I write this in perfect good feeling and only wish you to understand my course exactly as it is. I think there is work enough for us all to do — all we can do comfortably at this time — Work wanted in your vicinity I shall not try to get unless it is such as you do not make. Wishing you well

Yours truly.
John C. Whitin

These letters indicate that a feeling for industry relationships existed at a surprisingly early date; they help to establish the time at which the decline of regional isolation began to accentuate competitive pressures.

Management and Ownership, 1850–1867

In the Saco-Biddeford development the process of vertical integration in which the Lowell Machine Shop and the Pettee Machine Works participated never progressed far. The Boston cloth-selling house of Francis Skinner & Company was influential in the affairs of the Pepperell and Laconia companies, and ownership and financial management of Pepperell, Laconia, and the Water Power Company remained intimately linked until 1867. The York Manufacturing Company, however, had tended to drift away from this group, but was still capable of exerting pressures on the other companies through the person of Samuel Batchelder. Table 27 suggests the intercorporate relationships which existed in the sample year 1856.

Table 27 clearly indicates the overwhelming dominance of Massachusetts investors. In 1856 approximately 86 per cent of all Water Power shares were owned in Massachusetts, 10½ per cent in Maine, and 3½ per cent elsewhere. These proportions had changed but little since 1844, the earliest date for which such figures are available. Neither had the stock been dispersed widely over this twelve-year period. In 1844 the average holding was 13.8 shares; in 1856 it was 15.5 shares.

An examination of the ownership of all Water Power Company shares shows even more clearly than does Table 27 the extent of the intercorporate relationships. In 1856, stockholders owning 992 shares of Water Power stock (49 per cent) also owned 1,073 shares

TABLE 27

STOCKHOLDER ANALYSIS, 1856
SACO WATER POWER COMPANY

Saco W. P. Co. Stockholders Owning 20 or More Shares	Location	Shares Owned: W. P. Co. 1844	W. P. Co. 1856	Pepperell 1856	Laconia 1856	York 1856
Amory & Humphreys (trustees)	Boston	..	25	..	..	40
Bowditch, J. I.	"	..	20	20	..	..
Batchelder, Samuel	"	46	22	20	..	10
Burns, Wm.	New York	10	22	..	..	7
Cartwright, C. W.	Boston	..	25	8	23	9
Dixwell, J. J.	"	..	25	5	..	..
Edmunds, J. W.	"	4	20	20	..	3
Fay, Richard S.	"	..	20	..	10	..
Goodwin, O.	"	..	20	20	13	12
Heard, A.	"	20	30	30	..	..
Hooker, Sm.	"	..	20	40	..	..
Humphrey, Benj.	"	10	20	20	12	3
Howe, George	"	..	37	..	..	..
Johnson, Sm.	"	..	48	24	..	20
Lawrence, A. (estate of)	"	10	40	30	50	20
Loring, Benj.	"	40	65	65	9	52
Lee, George	"	19	24	..	13	..
Milton & Slocumb	"	..	26	..	..	..
Pickering, Wm. D.	Salem	..	20	..	..	..
Parker, Wilder & Co.	Boston	..	25	..	..	..
Parker, Anna	"	..	20	20	..	..
Swett, Sm.	"	23	23	23	1	22
Thornton, J. B.	Scarboro	..	24	14	..	..
Wigglesworth, T.	Boston	..	24	..	15	17
Wiggin, E. R.	Saco	..	24	..	..	..

Source: Abstracts of Returns of Corporations, Secretary of State, Maine.

(50 per cent) of Pepperell stock. Most of the owners of large blocks of Water Power stock also owned large blocks of Pepperell stock, but the controlling blocks of Pepperell stock were owned by investors (principally cloth-selling houses) who had little or no financial interest in the Water Power Company. This situation appears to explain the ability and willingness of Dwight and the two boards of directors to exploit the Water Power Company for the benefit of the Pepperell Company. A very cursory examination of the Water Power

Company-Laconia relationship in 1856 indicates that the identity of ownership which had existed in 1844 had been somewhat dissipated during the ensuing twelve years. The same may be said of the Water Power Company–York relationship. In both cases, however, joint ownership in 1856 was substantial, and the principal stockholders, with a few exceptions, were the same in each of the three companies.

For the Water Power Company these relationships were a guarantee of orders, and this was the chief advantage. Correspondence between the superintendent and the treasurer reveals the many petty annoyances which arose. Quarrels over machinery contracts and water-power regulations were frequent. On more occasions than one the superintendent complained that orders had to be accepted from the three neighboring cotton mills at less than market rates. A bitter feud between Pepperell's agent and the machine-shop superintendent gave William Dwight, treasurer of both companies, many anxious moments and even necessitated the employment, on one occasion, of an outside arbitrator. There certainly are reasonable grounds for questioning whether the Water Power Company would not have fared far better on a completely independent basis.

William Dwight performed the duties of his office in as effective a manner as his divided responsibilities permitted, but his chief concern was with the financial affairs of the Water Power Company and he was heavily dependent upon his superintendent, who appears to have been entrusted with greater responsibilities than were the superintendents at the Newton and Lowell shops.

In 1854 Sylvanus Wetherell resigned the superintendency to accept a position in the York mills. His place was filled by William H. Thompson, and the $2,000 annual salary which Wetherell had received was replaced by a profit-sharing arrangement. Under this contract the machine shop was virtually divorced from operating control by the Boston office, although the treasurer continued to perform routine financial duties and Thompson was still required to furnish the treasurer and directors with semiannual operating statements and to submit all major policy decisions for their approval. By the terms of his contract Thompson received unprecedented commissions—as high as $28,000 in 1861. For the thirteen years of his service with the company Thompson received in commissions a total of $92,145.13, or an average of more than $7,000 per year.[8] A measure of Thompson's value to the company lies in the fact that, despite these high commissions, his contract was renewed again and again by the directors.

Superintendent Thompson clearly took the initiative in improving the manufacturing establishment. His demands on Dwight for new tools were frequent and insistent, and this fact is of considerable interest for, by the terms of Thompson's contract, he would personally have gained by keeping such expenditures to a minimum. Thompson consistently urged Dwight to charge adequate depreciation and to write off the books "some of our imagined property." He also complained bitterly against the practice of charging capital expenditures to current operations, though his motives here were based less on the belief that this was unsound accounting than on the fact that the practice seriously decreased his commissions. Dwight gave in on this point, and special arrangements were made to amortize capital outlays over periods ranging from three to eight years.

There is no doubt that Thompson and his relatively underpaid predecessor Wetherell were instrumental in keeping the shop alive in the difficult period which followed 1850, while Dwight's contributions to the enterprise were nominal, once his financial reorganization had been completed in 1851. More than this, Wetherell's farsighted additions to the product line between 1851 and 1854, and Thompson's refinement of the line and improvements in tools thereafter, laid the groundwork for such success as the company was to enjoy in the closing decades of the century.

Operating Results, 1850–1867

The prosperity of the Saco Water Power Company varied greatly in the difficult decade of the 1850's, which saw at least three serious depressions come and go. In 1853 Superintendent Wetherell reported that during the year past the machine shop had been put into complete and successful operation. He called Dwight's attention to the fact that in May of that year the employment mark of two hundred and sixty-two men exceeded by thirty the highest previous employment in company history (which had been reached in November,

1849, when the first two Pepperell mills were being built). Wetherell also made the highly interesting observation that contracts on hand totaled $200,000, and that of this amount only $2,400 was for machinery the patterns for which had been in existence two years previously. In this year (1853) a dividend of 3 per cent was declared, and the market price of company shares revived somewhat from the low of the previous year.

This state of affairs, however, was temporary. After 1854, wide variations occurred in activity and profits. In March of 1855 the shop was in full operation, with 330 men employed. By March of 1857 there were only 80 men at work, and the superintendent was asking permission to make machinery in advance of orders and to cut his working force in half. In July, 1857, Thompson wrote Dwight that the whole amount of work done in the year past was only $56,309.44, while in each of the two previous years the shop had done $300,000 of business. On this low volume of business, Thompson stated, he had saved $4,779.12 over and above the cash outlays made, but this had been swallowed up in overhead, which was virtually as large as when the shop was working at capacity. In January, 1858, the superintendent reported that although the shop was in better condition than ever before, work done in the last six months did not exceed $75,000. This was a time of great depression and there was talk of suspending operations, but nine months later the shop was working nights. By September of 1860 more than five hundred men were employed and orders were being refused. In September, 1860, Thompson presented a report on the operations of the year past which is valuable for the detailed information furnished. Thompson summarized the output of the shop over the twelve previous months as follows:

110 tons of shafting
179 cards and railway boxes
14 railway heads
24 heads of drawing
160 ring frames
18 mules
12 spoolers
small jobs to the amount of $33,242.

Money received from the above machinery	$319,152.02
Expended on general expenses and repairs	9,236.57
Expended on new patterns, and 1/8 the cost of steam engine and new tools	3,900.61

By the addition of $12,000 of new tools within the past two years, which in 1860 are worth twice their cost, the Shop can employ 100 more men than ever before, and facilities have been increased twenty-five per cent. Putting in a steam engine cost $11,000, but saved 50 days of production.

The Civil War years brought further uncertainties and even greater business fluctuations. Following the collapse of the market for cotton machinery late in 1862, employment at the shop declined to 200 men. For reasons not now known, no government contracts for ordnance or machinery were taken, although the superintendent considered for a time the possibilities of making shot and shell. In 1865 a sharp rise in wages and material was coupled with new tool expense and depreciation on obsolete machinery to produce the heaviest loss in seventeen years. In 1866 the treasurer recorded on his books the highest profit ever made by the company.

Table 28 shows the trend of company profits, as well as the modest record of dividends. These figures emphasize the significant duality of company functions and show the stabilizing effect of income from rentals and land sales as a counterbalance to the fluctuating level of machinery profits.[9]

The figures in Table 29 show the success of the company in working itself out of debt and accumulating a comfortable surplus, despite the vicissitudes of business.

These figures suggest a state of equilibrium in company affairs — an absence of dynamic growth. This was indeed the case, and the fact is worth noting that, even in the most prosperous years in the 1850–66 period, valuations never again rose to the level achieved in 1850. The company was not expanding, but was consolidating, reorganizing, improving its tools, and simplifying the product line. Even in the depth of the depression of 1857–58 the superintendent stated that the shop was in better condition to build machinery than ever before.

TABLE 28

Profits, Losses, and Dividends, Saco Water Power Company, 1849–1866

Year ending May 31	Land Dept. Profit	Machine Shop		Net for Company[a]		Dividends as % of Capital
		Loss	Profit	Loss	Profit	
1849	$21,081.48	....	$ 31,285.18	....	$ 28,348.00	6
1850	20,661.68	....	2,917.36	$ 24,568.36	....	[b]
1851	16,963.04	....	3,762.50	312,951.53[c]	....	[b]
1852	19,905.03	....	6,713.20	....	13,581.30	[b]
1853	22,276.62	....	13,120.85	....	27,415.46	3
1854	22,972.88	....	10,908.75	24,828.30	....	[b]
1855	25,907.90	....	53,097.44	....	56,955.65	3
1856	25,812.54	....	52,229.76	....	59,705.16	4½
1857	23,785.44	$11,826.55	....	1,261.49	....	3
1858	21,996.22	....	9,595.05	....	13,699.18	3
1859	22,660.05	....	38,992.89	....	54,841.92	3½
1860	20,348.62	....	64,807.36	....	70,429.02	6
1861	20,274.19	....	100,088.05	....	86,870.49	6
1862	19,123.10	15,037.94	....	31,699.96	....	[b]
1863	18,776.48	....	58,529.87	....	68,457.79	6
1864	16,053.76	....	37,533.54	....	28,470.87	4½
1865	16,585.82	32,350.77	....	34,019.57	....	[b]
1866	14,268.30	....	118,684.52	....	123,324.71	7½

[a] Before dividends and after deductions for superintendent's commissions and various other charges and credits not carried to the operating accounts.

[b] None.

[c] Loss on sale of Pepperell mills of $326,004.37.

Source: Saco Water Power Company records, Treasurer's reports.

In 1860, gas and steam power were introduced into the plant. In a letter to the treasurer, Superintendent Thompson clearly set forth the need for the supplementary power of a steam engine:

The past season we have been stopped 25 days in all, ranging from Aug 19th to Nov 19th & when we did run during that time it was at a very low speed; 5½ days was the longest we were stopped at any one time, & in this way our men became uneasy, some grumbled, & many went home, & others procured employment elsewhere, & all suffered more or less. This state of things broke up our organization & it was many weeks after we had plenty of water before our complement of men could be got together again & all working to as good advantage as before we were stopped.

TABLE 29

BALANCE SHEET ACCOUNTS, SACO WATER POWER COMPANY, 1849–1866

Year ending May 31	Total Assets	Capital Stock	Surplus	Notes Payable
1850	$1,641,000	$1,007,200	$ 15,300[a]	$424,700
1851	1,284,500	1,007,200	328,400[a]	276,500
1852	796,000	670,000	13,500	110,900
1853	887,000	670,000	40,900	169,000
1854	932,400	670,000	16,100	243,700
1855	983,000	670,000	73,100	236,800
1856	850,400	670,000	112,600	60,900
1857	882,500	670,000	81,100	123,800
1858	903,800	670,000	74,700	148,600
1859	875,500	670,000	109,300	89,800
1860	958,100	670,000	154,600	132,400
1861	1,133,700	670,000	201,200	254,200
1862	950,200	670,000	129,200	151,000
1863	1,038,500	670,000	197,600	166,900
1864	1,031,800	670,000	185,700	173,500
1865	987,400	670,000	121,400	195,900
1866	990,100	670,000	244,800	75,300

[a] Deficit.

Source: Saco Water Power Company records, Treasurer's reports.

Expenditures for new tools were frequent and substantial, and the visit by Superintendent Thompson to England in 1864 resulted in the acquisition of the latest English machine tools by the shop.

Despite modest dividends and evidences of internal improvements, investor confidence in the Water Power Company never was high, and Water Power Company stock prices, like Lowell stock prices, showed a rather pronounced downward tendency. Chart X compares the behavior of the two stocks. The similarity in the pattern of stock price movements between these two vastly different companies suggests that external rather than internal factors were the more important in determining the reaction of investors in the respective enterprises.

Viewed in retrospect, the operating results of the Saco Water Power Company from 1850 to 1867 bear a marked resemblance to those achieved over the same period by the Lowell Machine Shop.

Like the Lowell Shop, the Water Power Company reflects little of the expansionist trends of the times, nor do profits or activity appear to have been commensurate with the growth of the American textile industry. For both concerns the 1850–67 period was one of extreme fluctuations and indifferent financial success. If more information were available, it might well show that machinery orders gained as a result of expansion among the mills served by the two shops were effectively counterbalanced in depression years by the abnormal slackening of machinery orders resulting from generally increasing competition in the American textile industry.

The achievements and weaknesses of the Saco Water Power Company are well defined. Of the former, the break-away from the stifling confinement of a local market and the establishing of a regional, if not a national, reputation was the most important. The outstanding weakness of the company derived from the fact that the shop had not yet ceased to be subservient to a cotton mill, and that much corporate energy was still being expended in activities other than machine-building.

The realization that the machine shop had best be completely divorced from water-power regulation and land-promotion activities first appears to have come to the directors of the Saco Water Power Company in 1860. At that time a committee was appointed to negotiate a sale to the Pepperell Manufacturing Company of all properties not utilized for machine-building operations. The onset of the Civil War postponed further action until 1866, at which time the plans for splitting the functions of the company were once again considered for action. These plans were as crucial to the success of the shop as had been the financial reorganization of 1851, and were equally drastic.

2. The Saco Water Power Machine Shop, 1867–1897

Formation of the Company, 1866–1867

The disposal of the property of the old Saco Water Power Company was the final measure of exploitation of that company by the Pepperell and Laconia interests which dominated it. On September 6, 1866, the Water Power directors (most of whom were Pepperell

CHART X

Stock Prices, Saco Water Power Company
and Lowell Machine Shop, 1845–1867

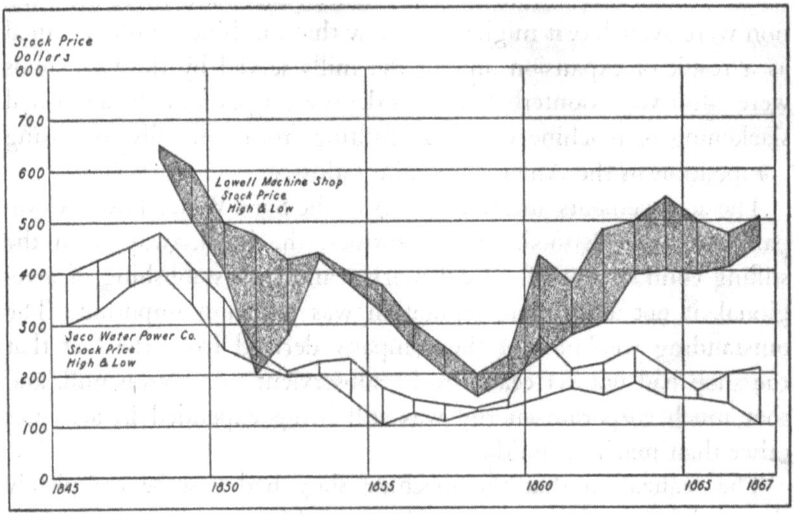

directors as well) voted to sell all property and privileges to the Pepperell and Laconia companies for the sum of $425,000, the purchasers to assume all obligations of the Water Power Company then outstanding.

There is, of course, no way of appraising the true condition of the Water Power Company at this time, or the real value of its assets. On the basis of book figures the transaction appears to have resulted in a loss to the shareholders of the Water Power Company of close to half a million dollars. For approximately half those shareholders who held stock in Pepperell this loss was offset by the gains accruing to the Pepperell Manufacturing Company from the bargain. For the remainder there were no compensating advantages.[10]

On December 18, 1866, the Pepperell and Laconia companies concluded arrangements for the sale, for $125,000, of all machine-shop properties to a new company, organized under the name of the Saco Water Power Machine Shop. This price, too, appears to have been somewhat of a bargain, in view of the book values of these properties, which were carried on May 31, 1866, as follows:

Site	$ 32,912.43
Feeder	2,308.27
Building	26,218.96
Millwork	7,310.40
Tools and fixtures	78,210.05
Total valuation	$146,960.11

As soon as the organization of the Saco Water Power Machine Shop had been completed (early in 1867), the fact became clear that this new enterprise was not independent of the old group of investors headed by William Dwight, who, though no longer treasurer of Pepperell and Laconia, was named treasurer of the new company. Some new capital and management, however, were involved.

The initiative in organizing the new company was assumed by A. D. Lockwood, who had promoted many New England cotton mills, served as technical adviser to many others (including Pepperell, since 1858), and was soon to organize the consulting service which was later to become Lockwood, Greene & Company.[11] A capital-stock issue of $300,000 was subscribed as follows:

Benjamin Bates	Boston	500 shares
William Dwight	Boston	500 "
William P. Haines	Biddeford	500 "
Josiah Bardwell	Boston	500 "
A. D. Lockwood	Lewiston	500 "
William Parsons	Boston	100 "
Edmund Dwight	Boston	50 "
James McMullan	Biddeford	250 "
S. W. Richardson	Boston	100 "

No one of these men was a stranger to operations at Biddeford. Haines, Parsons, and the Dwights were the nucleus of the old group which controlled Pepperell and Laconia. Bardwell was a partner in Pepperell's selling house, Francis Skinner & Company; Richardson had been a clerk under William Dwight and had established, with Dwight's sons, the important Boston brokerage house of Richardson, Hill & Company. Only Bates, a prominent mill promoter, and Lockwood had not been extensively involved in the industrial development at Saco Falls.

The local newspaper announced such details of the new venture as the promoters saw fit to publicize:[12]

Messrs. A. D. Lockwood of Lewiston, William Dwight, Benjamin E. Bates and Josiah Bardwell of Boston, William P. Haines and James H. McMullan of this city, have purchased all the buildings, tools and other property in and connected with the Machine Shop of the Saco Water Power Co., including the saw mills in their yard, and some dwellings on Gooch Street. . . . We are glad to learn that Mr. McMullan, who has been for several years connected in various positions with Mr. Thompson in the management of the Machine Shop, has been appointed Agent for the purchasers. He has had long experience in that business, and is not only well known to our citizens, but to manufacturers. We have no doubt but under his management the reputation of the Shop will be sustained, and we believe no better choice for the owners, or one more gratifying to our citizens, could have been made. Mr. Thompson in retiring from the position goes to Europe with his family, to be gone a year.

Management and Operating Results under James McMullan

James McMullan was one of those personalities whose force of character dominated his times, his fellow-men, and his company, to say nothing of his own real achievements. The McMullan legend is an integral part of the history of textile-machinery building at Biddeford, and the difficulty of separating legend from fact is a very real one. As with his more famous contemporaries, John D. Rockefeller, J. P. Morgan, and Andrew Carnegie, a dispassionate appraisal of McMullan as an administrator must inevitably be colored by the extreme prejudices which the man generated among his fellow-men.

James H. McMullan was born in Salem, Massachusetts, in 1832, of Scottish-Irish parentage — the son of a genial father whose first love was gambling on horses. His career started at the age of ten in local cotton mills, and a restless ambition drove the youth forward to become a proficient draftsman. A genuine Irish warmth made many friends — a biting Scotch tongue made as many enemies. McMullan himself once observed that his Irish blood was responsible for all the enjoyment he derived from life, but his Scotch blood made him successful.

James H. McMullan

Agent of Saco Water Power Machine Shop, 1867–97; President of Saco and Pettee Machine Shops, 1897–98

McMullan entered the machine shop at Biddeford in 1860 a skilled technician, a stern Episcopalian, and an uncompromising opponent of the Democratic party. Ambition, single-mindedness of purpose, and supreme self-confidence forced a realization of his presence upon all who were connected with the shop.[13] The wit and warmth and prejudice and bluntness of the man were to be amply reflected in the subsequent history of the Saco Water Power Machine Shop.

There is no information to suggest how McMullan happened to be selected by Lockwood and Dwight to head the new organization, but perhaps the force of the man is explanation enough. McMullan carried into a position of responsibility with him a fellow-draftsman, Eustis P. Morgan, who was made chief draftsman of the shop. McMullan moved at once to gather complete managerial power into his own hands and to direct the shop in a program of ruthless efficiency in the interest of maximum profits and dividends.

McMullan's administrative abilities were immediately put to the test, as were the many times proven financial skills of William Dwight. The new venture was launched entirely on credit. No cash was paid in by stockholders on the $300,000 stock subscription. Instead, subscribers gave their notes in return for the stock, and these notes appear to have been used as collateral for working-capital loans, which were secured from Benjamin Bates, William Dwight, and Richardson, Hill & Company. The indebtedness to Pepperell and Laconia of $125,000, the purchase price of the machine shop, was allowed to remain on the books and was not liquidated until 1871.

An acute depression in 1867 provided an immediate threat to the survival of this credit-based business structure. The first problem which McMullan faced was the basic one of whether to continue manufacturing operations. Dwight forwarded to McMullan his views on the question, and his letter leaves little doubt that at this time Dwight was exerting more influence upon shop operations than had been the case earlier, when he had been treasurer of three companies simultaneously.

"The truth is," Dwight observed, "when all machine shops stop you are sure of a strong demand in a reasonable time. If you keep on producing from cheap stock & labor you keep the track & make the future profits & distance competitors.

"On your mode of proceeding," Dwight continued, "you would

surely make nothing. With mine I should, when demand came, stand a chance of making something. I stand therefore by the doctrine 'the best machines from the best pattern of the best workmanship — as far as possible from special tools — produced as far as possible in uniform quantity.'"[14]

McMullan's decision was to be characteristic of all later decisions of this nature. Discarding the old argument that manufacturing for stock would preserve the organization until better times, McMullan replied to Dwight that "owing to the state of the currency and prices of labor & stock, nothing can be manufactured except on contract or with a prospect of speedy sale — however excellent in finish & workmanship the article may be, or however cheaply & perfectly it may be produced by special tools."

Company records do not reveal whether the shop remained in operation as Dwight counseled, but business soon revived and orders poured in. Manufacturing activities required heavy borrowing. Working-capital loans were negotiated with several Boston banks and increased from $129,000 in 1868 to $506,000 in 1870. Of the large 1870 borrowings $311,000 was to liquidate old obligations. Dwight and McMullan clashed over loan policies. McMullan proposed to meet a payroll by securing a personal loan from one of the stockholders. Dwight held firm to the financial reins; and, after calling McMullan's attention to the bylaws, which provided that only the treasurer should make loans, curtly stated that he saw no reason for altering the usual relationship between the treasurer and the agent.

The three years which followed the formation of the Saco Water Power Machine Shop were critical ones, despite reviving business. In 1869 an attempt was made to reinforce and perpetuate the power of the existing management by requiring all stockholders wishing to dispose of their stock to offer it first to the company. This move was defeated. In this year, too, McMullan handed his resignation to the directors and elicited from them not only a refusal of the resignation but even a strong vote of confidence. In 1870 these symptoms of managerial unrest were climaxed by a financial and administrative crisis.

On October 15, 1870, Dwight wrote McMullan the alarming opinion that, since the capital stock issued in 1867 had not been paid for by the stockholders (except by their notes), the stockholders were personally liable for all debts of the company and a suit against the company could compel them to pay up the entire capital at once. Moreover, no dividends could be paid until the capital stock had been paid for.

The measures taken to relieve the stockholders of their uncomfortable position of unlimited liability provide an insight into the much neglected legal side of business history. William Dwight summarized existing laws relating to capital stock of Maine corporations in 1870 as follows:

1. A corporation can make no dividend until it has paid in its capital stock.

2. Stockholders cannot be exempted from personal liability for the debts of a corporation until they have paid up their capital stock.

3. A corporation cannot properly issue certificates of stock until the capital stock is paid up.

4. A corporation cannot make a dividend diminishing its capital stock.

In October, 1870, capital stock stood on the company books at $300,000. Balancing this account were $300,000 of notes receivable from stockholders in payment for the stock. Since this form of payment did not make the stock legally paid up, the entire stock issue was canceled and the stockholders' notes were returned to them. A new stock issue of $300,000 was brought out, and $150,000 of it was immediately assessed. This provided cash for the payment of company debts. In April of 1871 the remaining $150,000 was assessed in order to make the stock fully paid up and thereby make possible the payment of dividends and the relief of stockholders from their unlimited liability. This second assessment, however, was no burden on the shareholders, for the company immediately declared a 50 per cent cash dividend out of existing earned surplus to reimburse them for their assessment. In the process of canceling the old stock and issuing the new, the shares of the company became much more widely dispersed. The Dwights, for example, turned in 566 shares of the old stock and failed to take the corresponding amount of new stock, apparently because they were unable to finance the 50 per cent assessment which was placed on the new stock. These shares were subsequently sold to 12 different buyers, including James McMullan, who took 60 shares.

While this legal muddle was being remedied, an attack was commenced upon William Dwight's financial management which forced his resignation from the office of treasurer. The immediate reason for this attack appears to have been a charge which Dwight made to the Profit and Loss account. This charge was an item of $35,267, and Dwight's authority for treating it as a capital expenditure rather than as current operating expense was challenged. Since there is no question that the treasurer's authority to determine accounting procedures was well established by precedent, the real issue may have been the excessive conservatism of Dwight's accounting, or there may have been even more deeply rooted reasons for the conflict within the company.

In December, 1870, Dwight resigned and was succeeded in office by his one-time clerk, Spencer W. Richardson. Dwight's once all-powerful position deteriorated rapidly. Both Dwight and Josiah Bardwell, his associate and fellow-stockholder, appear to have been in financial difficulty. On December 30, 1870, Richardson, the new treasurer, wrote Dwight:

> I am instructed by the Directors of the Saco Water Power Machine Shop to demand of you the payment of the sum of $29,693.95, the amount required to balance the cash of the Saco Water Power Machine Shop according to the Cash Book of said Company received from you on the 13th instant.

The full implications of this communication are not clear, and existing records do not indicate whether Dwight liquidated the obligation, but this was the end of Dwight's long career with the company. Any judgment of his service must acknowledge the indispensable value of his financial skill in keeping the organization alive, though there is little question that the machine shop itself and a large group of Water Power Company shareholders lost much from Dwight's preoccupation with textile-mill promotions.

Despite these disturbing events, James McMullan's report on

operations was highly encouraging. In May, 1869, McMullan reported that expenditures of $252,661 had been made in the past two years on new buildings, new tools, patterns, and repairs. In July he reported that the shop was producing machinery at the rate of $300,000 annually, and that a floating capital of at least $600,000 was needed to support this level of operations. On January 1, 1870, McMullan pointed out that operations over the past three years, after all charges, had resulted in an average annual profit in each year of $133,333, and that an earned surplus of $411,891 stood on the books.

In 1871 stock of the Saco Water Power Machine Shop was selling ten points above par and the shop was reported to be "full of work for good parties." In this year the payment of regular dividends was commenced. By 1879 the debts which apparently had been incurred in extending the business in the early 1870's and during the depressed years in the middle of the decade were liquidated. "I suppose," McMullan wrote Richardson in his usual ironic tone, "we may now be considered in good condition with no debt, and no business."

Table 30 gives the record of dividend payments. Table 31 shows account balances on two different dates.

TABLE 30

DIVIDENDS OF THE SACO WATER POWER MACHINE SHOP, 1867–1897
(Expressed as a percentage of capital)

Year	Dividend	Year	Dividend	Year	Dividend	Year	Dividend
1867	[a]	1875	20	1883	50	1891	6
1868	[a]	1876	20	1884	107[b]	1892	6
1869	[a]	1877	20	1885	6	1893	5
1870	[a]	1878	10	1886	6	1894	4
1871	50[c]	1879	20[d]	1887	6	1895	4
1872	5[e]	1880	10	1888	6	1896	6
1873	15	1881	60	1889	6	1897	60.3[f]
1874	20	1882	30	1890	9		

[a] None.
[b] Includes 100% stock dividend.
[c] To compensate stockholders for assessment of like amount of stock.
[d] Paid in stock of Lockwood Company.
[e] Paid in stock of Taft mill.
[f] Includes 2% cash dividend and 58.3% dividend (par value) in stock of the Saco and Pettee Machine Shops.
Source: Saco Water Power Machine Shop records, Dividend books.

TABLE 31

BALANCE SHEETS OF THE SACO WATER POWER MACHINE SHOP, 1870 AND 1890

	1870	1890
Assets		
Cash	$ 3,283.48	$ 26,910.89
Notes Receivable	300,000.00	54,796.00
Interest	3,682.30	1,232.48
Machine Shop and Appurtenances	374,122.98	300,000.00
Stock in Other Companies	70,000.00	29,481.72
Agent's Account	269,208.44	291,223.38
Treasurer's Account	28,984.21	....
Total	$1,049,281.41	$703,644.47
Liabilities and Net Worth		
Capital Stock	$ 300,000.00	$ 600,000.00
Returned Premiums	7,175.56	23,319.57
Notes Payable	330,213.94	652.21
Profit and Loss Account	411,891.91	79,672.69
Total	$1,049,281.41	$703,644.47

Source: Saco Water Power Machine Shop, Treasurer's correspondence.

The record of dividends suggests several important conclusions. The period which followed 1867 was obviously one of high though fluctuating prosperity, which began to decline, however, after the great activity of the early 1880's. As in the years preceding 1867, the performance of this company, measured in terms of dividends, bears a remarkable resemblance to that of the Lowell Machine Shop. From 1867 to 1897, average dividends (cash and stock) of the Saco Water Power Machine Shop were 14.8 per cent of capital annually, exclusive of the 1871 dividend, which did not reflect operating profits, and the liquidation dividend in 1897. Dividends of the Lowell Machine Shop over the same period averaged 16.6 per cent, and the pattern of peaks and valleys was virtually identical in both cases. The similarity of performance by both Shops suggests once again that external factors dominated internal ones in producing such operating results. Simply stated, these factors were the general growth of the textile industry, the expansion of the entire American economy, the rise of the Southern textile industry, and the perfection of various textile-machinery improvements which speeded obsolescence of existing machinery. So strong were these forces that the effects of the frequent and severe depressions which occurred (1866–67, 1874–78, 1884–85, 1894–95, 1896–97) were vitiated by the rising tide of activity in the Shops.

Unlike the managers of the Lowell Machine Shop, James McMullan made no effort to stabilize production, and the dividend record of the Saco Water Power Machine Shop is misleading in that it does not show the violent fluctuations which occurred in shop operations. McMullan drove the shop through periods of violent activity, and abruptly closed it down when orders ceased. There is no complete record of shutdowns, but major periods of inactivity occurred in the 1874–79 period: in 1884 (a shutdown which McMullan felt might be permanent, inasmuch as Grover Cleveland had just been elected President!), in 1885 (six months), in 1886, and in 1894. McMullan's characteristic comment upon opening the shop in 1894 was:

> We have given notice that we shall start up in June with about one half of our men and a reduction of 20 per ct. in wages. The Democratic Papers will probably hail this as a revival of business.

For many years throughout this entire thirty-one-year period the Shop literally lived from one order to another. Men were called in from farms, fishing boats, and clam flats to work at utmost capacity on orders which had been received. When the orders had been filled, and if no new orders had come in meanwhile, the men were released to get along as best they could until business revived. This practice was a common one, but appears to have been pursued by McMullan with more than usual ruthlessness.

McMullan himself appears to have suffered little from the vicissitudes of business. The story is told that in one period of great stringency McMullan was called before the directors to discuss the possibility of a reduction in his salary. Informed by the chairman that the question of salaries was now open for discussion, McMullan airily observed, "Oh, I couldn't think of accepting more money unless you raise the wages of Moses [his clerk] too!" The bewildered directors thereupon voted both McMullan and Moses wage increases.[15]

McMullan's personal financial interest in the company was never larger than 10 per cent of the stock outstanding, but he dominated the company after Dwight's resignation in 1870. The tone of the correspondence between the agent and the treasurer changes markedly after 1870. McMullan's letters to Richardson were virtual commands, covering all phases of operations, and, in certain instances, dictating the choice of company presidents and directors. One highly illuminating letter directed Richardson to withhold the financial details of a very profitable year of operations from the directors, since, in McMullan's own succinct words, "they are buyers of machinery." This letter and others indicate that the agent was taking more than a passive part in financial management — usurping, perhaps, some of the traditional prerogatives of the treasurer.

McMullan's assumption of control was undoubtedly predicated upon friendship with the Lockwood interests in the company, some of which came by inheritance to A. D. Lockwood's son-in-law, John W. Danielson. The Lockwood-Danielson interest in the company amounted to less than a majority of the stock outstanding, but since that stock became more widely dispersed this interest could well have dominated company management. The dispersion process is shown in Table 32.[16]

Product, Shop, and Labor, 1867–1897

Under James McMullan the tendency toward product specialization, already noted before 1867, was carried still further, and the astuteness of Sylvanus Wetherell in importing the patterns for English roving frames in 1850 became increasingly evident as American textile mills swung more and more toward the English system.

In 1867, cards, roving frames (slubbers, intermediates, and fine frames), ring spinning frames, mules, railway heads, and drawing frames were being built, and in that year the exclusive American rights to manufacture the English Parr, Curtis & Madeley mule were acquired.[17]

TABLE 32

Trends in Stock Ownership, Saco Water Power Machine Shop, 1867–1897

Principal Shareholders (200 or more shares)		Number of Shares 1867	1883	1890	1897
Benjamin Bates	Boston	500	...	...	...
William Dwight	Boston	500	...	...	...
William Haines	Biddeford	500	...	...	...
Josiah Bardwell	Boston	500	...	...	...
A. D. Lockwood	Lewiston	500	500	...	...
James McMullan	Portland	...	300	200	200
Biddeford Savings Bank	Biddeford	...	260	550	550
Walker & Brothie	Boston	...	220	440	...
John Berry Estate	Saco	...	...	200	...
Danielson Family	Providence	...	...	423	458
Amelia DeF. Lockwood	Providence	...	...	472	472
Eustis P. Morgan	Saco	...	...	200	200
John Parker Estate	Boston	...	...	296	...
Saco & Biddeford Savings Inst.	Saco	...	...	250	250
William Sohier	Boston	...	...	200	...
Aretas Blood	Manchester	...	...	...	270
Davis and Sargeant, trustees	Boston	...	...	...	250
E. F. Wright	Boston	...	...	...	200
Total number of shares		3,000	3,000	6,000	6,000
Total number of shareholders		9	55	73	90
Average size of holding		333	56	82	67
Per cent of stock held by institutions, women, and trustees		0	36	59	69

Source: Saco Water Power Machine Shop records, Dividend books.

Under McMullan the reputation of the Shop was greatly enhanced, and some observers stated that the Biddeford machines were not excelled by any builders of cotton machinery in America. This judgment was probably correct insofar as it related to roving frames. Here the work of Chief Draftsman Eustis P. Morgan was unsurpassed in the industry. This remarkable man suffered under the handicap of being almost stone deaf; he communicated with his fellow-men by means of a hard rubber plate, which he held in his teeth and against which his communicants talked. To Eustis Morgan must be accredited much of the technological success of the company. Evidence that a professional attitude was beginning to appear in the industry, among the designers at least, lies in the fact that Morgan was accustomed to meet regularly at the Adams House in Boston with draftsmen from the Whitin Machine Works for the purpose of comparing common technical problems and progress.[18]

Information as to the kinds, numbers, and prices of machines built by the Saco Water Power Machine Shop is fragmentary. In 1886 the product line had not changed materially from that of 1867. A large order filled for the Edwards Manufacturing Company in Augusta, Maine, consisted of the following:

209	36# cards with self-strippers . .	$110	each
179	Single Railway Troughs.	8	"
30	Double Railway Troughs.	14	"
1	Doubler and Carrying Frame. . .	600	"
7	Railway Heads.	150	"
4	Drawing Frames, 6 delivery. . . .	350	"
6	Slubbers, 60 spindle.	15	per spindle
9	Intermediates, 72 spindle.	11	" "
23	Fly Frames, 144 spindle.	5	" "
68	Ring Frames, 176 spindle.	2.75	" "
16	Ring Frames, 192 spindle.	2.35	" "
18	Mules, 832 spindle.	1.75	" "
1	Elevator and Hoisting Machine	1,050	each

Specialization was more pronounced than is indicated by the list of products which the shop could build. In June, 1887, McMullan wrote the treasurer: "Our sole business lately has been on Fly Frames and [we] shall make 300 this year — or more than ever made by us in any year."

Competition from the recently introduced revolving flat card eventually drove the Shop to discontinue altogether the manufacture of stationary flat cards. McMullan stated that, although he was envious of his competitors (presumably the Pettee Machine Works), the financial condition of the company and the available manufacturing facilities would not justify or permit his making the new card. In the 1890's the Shop, like other American shops, discontinued the manufacture of mules.

In the spinning field the Saco Water Power Machine Shop was

faced with the Draper spindle monopolies and formidable competition from Whitin and the Lowell Machine Shop. McMullan made one attempt to avoid the Draper royalties by patenting a lightweight spindle which, it was hoped, would not infringe the Draper patents. The story of this, the so-called McMullan spindle, is not at all clear, but the spindle appears to have been perfected through the joint efforts of McMullan, a nephew of his, and one Benjamin Goodale.[19] In conformance with common practice, however, McMullan had the patent (dated January 28, 1890) taken out in his own name. This spindle possessed such merit that it has been built, with modifications, ever since, but the intent to circumvent the Drapers' control of the spindle business was not realized. The famous Draper-Whitin lawsuit of 1894 convinced McMullan that his spindle would also be judged an infringement of Draper patents, and he capitulated rather than face an expensive suit which was almost certain to be decided against him. Royalties on the McMullan spindle were thereafter paid to George Draper & Sons until the expiration of the Draper patents.

The policy of product specialization, then, appears not to have been a consciously formulated and consistently pursued policy, but one which was imposed upon the company by external circumstances. An early start in producing the English roving frames, coupled with Morgan's excellent work in this field, established an unsurpassed reputation in the American textile industry for the Shop's roving machinery. Over the same period the Pettee Machine Works had dealt the Shop's card business a mortal blow, technological progress had eliminated the mule, and other shops had come to dominate the picker and loom market. Severe competition, together with failure to break Draper's monopolies, had limited the possibilities of absolute leadership in the spinning-machinery field, but the Biddeford spinning frames were highly regarded in the industry. As a result, the Saco Water Power Machine Shop concentrated its efforts upon machines offering maximum profit, and the entire plant was geared to the manufacture of a specialized line of roving and spinning machinery.

McMullan's efforts to improve manufacturing facilities and methods were sporadic, and confined chiefly to the early years of his administration. In 1868 and 1869 the size of the shop was almost doubled, and further additions were made in the early 1880's. A remarkably interesting series of letters has survived which show that in 1857 William Dwight sent Eustis Morgan to England to learn the technique of machine molding and to purchase molding machines. Considering the fact that machine molding was not universally adopted in America until the 1890's, this action of Dwight's certainly constitutes one of the earliest American attempts to introduce the process. Dwight's negotiations, which were conducted with a man named Jobson, commenced as early as 1863. The principal obstacles encountered in adopting the process, Dwight stated, were the lack of American founding skill and "the opposition of moulders, whose wages it will reduce."

After these early efforts to improve the plant and processes, little further appears to have been done by McMullan, and by 1897 the shop had become almost obsolete. The figures in Table 31 show that after 1870 the Biddeford shop did not share in the great physical expansion characteristic of so many contemporary manufacturing establishments in the industrial-goods field. Such scanty evidence as exists all points to the conclusion that earnings did not go into plant, but were reserved to meet stockholder demands for large and steady dividends. If this was the case, McMullan's policies provided a sharp contrast with those followed by Hale and Snelling at Newton over the same period.

The labor situation at the Biddeford shop could be said to be neither altogether good nor altogether bad—and in all instances it reflected the picturesque vagaries of McMullan's own personality. Hours were long and wages were low, but these conditions were universal. In the early years of McMullan's management, men worked from five o'clock in the morning to seven o'clock in the evening, with a half-hour off for dinner at noon. Apprentice training lasted three years, and apprentices were paid forty-two cents per day in their first year, fifty cents in the second, and fifty-eight cents in the third.[20] By 1897, hours of work had been reduced so that the men came to work at six-thirty in the morning and left at six o'clock in the evening. In 1886 the practice of paying wages monthly gave way to the more prevalent system of fortnightly payments.[21]

Wages in the shop in 1860 averaged $1.05 per day, with approximately 1 per cent of the men earning more than $2.00 daily. In 1870 William Dwight wrote McMullan as follows:

I should be content, if hereafter, you should see your way to bring your average rate of wages to $1.25. This would amount to a reduction of about $24,000 from the aggregate of wages before you began reduction — an amount equal to 8 per cent on your capital. The country has an idea of returning soon to specie payments, & that specie payments will bring low wages. True, but I have no faith in early specie payments, & shall be glad to see you at proper time avail of these ideas & come down to the average rate of $1.25.

By 1873 the shop average had risen to $1.70 per day, with approximately one-third of the men earning more than $2.00 daily. In 1881 the average was $1.42 per day, increasing from this level back up to the $1.70 average established in 1873. The depression of 1894, however, found the average once again at $1.40, and McMullan expressed his determination to keep it below $1.50.

Serving under McMullan was a shop superintendent, Charles Haines, who was succeeded by Gilman P. Littlefield. Both these men appear to have been competent machinists. McMullan's supervision of shop affairs continued to be vigilant, despite the presence of capable lieutenants. His omniscient attention to detail was often constructive, but rapidly killed off all initiative in the organization. No drawing left the drafting board without his personal approval, and suggestions from anyone were seldom welcomed or adopted by McMullan.

In the thirty years during which James McMullan dominated the machine shop at Biddeford he displayed some great strengths. Among these was a lack of that pomposity so frequently assumed by mill men of the day who rose to power from humble origins. McMullan was unimpressed with his own importance. Asked how he liked being agent, McMullan replied that he had been better off as a boy in the Salem mills, working for clothes and board. "Now," he stated, "I still have only enough money for clothes and board and my clothes don't fit and my board don't suit."[22] Offsetting the complete democracy of the man was his bluntness and prejudice. A lay preacher in the Episcopal Church, McMullan was once interrupted in his churchly duties. "Damn you!" he shouted at the intruder, "can't you see that I'm preparing a sermon?"[23]

After serving a term as mayor of Biddeford, McMullan was defeated in a subsequent election. Insulted by this repudiation by the citizenry, he renounced the city, moved to Portland, and harbored a lingering grudge against all who voted the Democratic ticket. So profound was this feeling that few men in the shop dared admit themselves to be Democrats, and those who were known to have Democratic leanings found little favor if already employed—little chance for employment if a Republican could be found instead. This atmosphere in the shop was a throwback to the early days at Lowell when the lives of the operatives were dominated by the religious, political, and economic views of the mill agents.

McMullan often went to amusing extremes in his efforts to advance the Republican cause, as shown by an incident in August, 1879, involving the shop payroll. At this time the cash for the monthly payroll was shipped from the treasurer's office in Boston to the Shop in Biddeford by rail express. The payroll funds were always in the form of paper currency. Each month McMullan wrote Richardson how much he would need for payroll, and specified the denominations of bills required. In 1879 the resumption of specie payments and reëstablishment of the gold standard by the federal government was a burning political issue. The Greenback movement among debtor and farmer groups was strong, and the Greenbackers hotly advocated "cheap money" in the form of paper and silver, hoping thereby to prevent the decline in prices which a return to gold-backed currency seemed to imply. On August 26, 1879, McMullan wrote Richardson, "We shall want for our Pay Roll next week $10,000 in *Gold* and $5,000.00 in bills. We must use all our influence in the coming election to defeat the Greenbackers."

Richardson appears to have registered a mild protest against the inconvenience of shipping gold instead of bills to Biddeford. McMullan replied in these words:

Dear Sir:

Yours of yesterday is at hand. We will want the Gold in tens, fives, and smaller. No doubt but the bills are more convenient but the Greenbackers tell the people they cannot get the Gold. If they are successful in the election we will pay off the next time in silver.

Very truly yours
Jas. H. McMullan, Agt.

As might be expected, these positive traits in McMullan produced a positive reaction among the men in the shop, and divided them into staunch supporters and secret enemies of the agent. The complete absence of paternalism was not an unhealthy situation, and the men in the shop appear to have taken a kind of perverse pride in the eccentricities and prejudices of their agent. There is no evidence that those eccentricities and prejudices interfered seriously with production, and there was no serious labor trouble in the shop. On the contrary, a rather surprising *esprit de corps* existed. Many came to realize that McMullan's gruffness concealed much kindness, and many took pride in his friendship. Always, however, McMullan's labor policies (in contrast with his personal friendships) were guided in the interest of maximum dividends for the stockholders. Indeed, there could scarcely be said to have been a labor policy, for labor was considered along with tools and metal as a factor of production, to be purchased for as low a price as possible in as small amounts as possible when required to fill orders on the books.

Markets and the Industry, 1867–1897

Such information as has survived concerning McMullan's marketing efforts indicates that a decided drive for business was instituted soon after he had become agent. This drive was contemporary with his attempts to enlarge and improve the plant, and it provides additional evidence of the abundant energies of the new management. As in the plant, however, those energies were soon dissipated. As the reputation of the company's machines improved, marketing became an increasingly passive matter.

The Saco Water Power Machine Shop took an early part in the development of the Southern textile industry, and by 1885 it had machinery in operation in the important Pacolet, Clifton, Piedmont, King, Langley, Matthews, and Newberry mills. This entry into the Southern market was not effected by aggressive salesmanship or advertising, for the company had no salesmen and did little advertising. The excellent reputation of the firm's machines must have been a factor of some importance in gaining customers, but the decisive factors in this market were liberality in credit and willingness to accept mill stocks in part payment for machines.

The practice of accepting payment in stock commenced in 1869, some years before John C. Whitin had taken his first stock. In this year William Dwight subscribed for 1,000 shares ($100,000) of stock in the Orray Taft mill in Connecticut, the subscription being conditional upon the placing of an order for machinery with the Saco Water Power Machine Shop.

As was later to be done at Whitin's, this stock was eventually divided among the company stockholders in lieu of a cash dividend. The extent of this participation was unusual, and no such amounts of stock in any single Southern mill were subsequently taken. In 1888 the company carried $55,000 of mill stocks on its books, of which the largest block was $20,000 of Pacolet Manufacturing Company stock. By 1897, however, the company held $152,626 of mill stocks and bonds, an indication of the increasing prevalence of the practice.

The extent of McMullan's willingness to extend credit in the South is indicated by his acceptance in 1880 of an order from the Atlanta Cotton Factory for machinery to replace that which the Lowell Machine Shop was removing from the mill because of the Atlanta Factory's failure to meet its payments.[24] The extent of that credit was formidable, if mill notes as well as stocks are taken into consideration. In 1890, for example, only $44,100 of the company's capital was tied up in mill stocks and bonds, but mill notes which ran from thirty days to five months stood on the books to the amount of $132,214, and many of these were not collected at maturity.

Requests from Southern mills for extension of credit were frequent, and usually were complied with. These requests were necessitated by shortages of working capital and inability to hire capital on favorable terms in the South. R. L. McCaughrin, president and treasurer of the Newberry Cotton Mills, in South Carolina, voiced a classic plea which summed up the difficulties of the Southern promoters:[25]

I know you do not like to hear complaints, but with the 3 years' past depression in business generally and the past year being a year of serious disasters in this state, first the cold weather of last Jan'y and Feb'y that froze out our small grain, followed by the floods of the spring & summer which destroyed all corn & crops in the river and creek bottoms & the cotton crop on sandy lands, followed by the drouth culminating in the earthquakes & low prices of cotton have left our people with but little surplus & much depressed, still we are not going to surrender but will meet the emergency as we have so many in the past 20 years, and I believe will surmount all difficulties.

McMullan, in common with many of the Northern creditors, appeared to grasp the need for maximum tolerance, and to appreciate the potential gains to be realized from forbearance. "It is not pleasant," wrote McMullan in 1885, "to be obliged to constantly renew these Southern notes but there is no escape."[26]

Table 33, showing the disposition of notes taken by the Saco Water Power Machine Shop in the sample year 1884, forcibly illustrates the difficulties attendant upon the settlement of machinery accounts.

TABLE 33

DISPOSITION OF NOTES ACCEPTED IN 1884
SACO WATER POWER MACHINE SHOP

Company	Amount	Terms	Disposition
Matthews Cotton Mills....	$ 9,000	4 mos., 6%	Renewed for 12 months
Evansville Cotton Mfg. Co.	10,000[a]	12 mos., 6%	Renewed. Paid in 1886
Pacolet Mfg. Co...........	20,000[a]	6 mos., 6%	Renewed for 6 months
Darlington Mfg. Co........	7,500	12 mos., 6%	Renewed
Aurora Cotton Mills.......	40,000	12 mos., 6%	Renewed 12 months
Pacolet Mfg. Co...........	6,000[a]	6 mos., 5%	Renewed 6 months
Lockwood Co.............	60,000	4–6 mos., 4%	$30,000 paid, balance discounted at $3\frac{3}{4}$%
Matthews Cotton Mills....	5,000[a]	12 mos., 6%	Renewed 12 months
Montreal Cotton Co........	816[a]	4 mos., 5%	Discounted at 4%

[a] Renewals of earlier notes.

Source: Saco Water Power Machine Shop records, Notes receivable book.

The effect of these extensive credits and of the relatively long periods consumed in filling machinery orders was to force the company to borrow heavily from Boston and local banks. The treasurer's office was the clearinghouse where maturing obligations were balanced against credits outstanding. The need for ready cash was met with difficulty, even though, because of the practice of offsetting needs against collections in a central clearing institution, the only significant use for such cash was to meet the fortnightly payroll.

These were essentially normal business problems, and were accepted with little comment by McMullan and his contemporaries. A far more crucial matter to them was the state of the tariff. McMullan's protectionist viewpoint and violent sentiments toward free traders are amply recorded; they coincided with those of other machine-builders. The threat of English competition was felt to be severe throughout the years of McMullan's administration, and he complained bitterly about it. In answer to one of his complaints, William Dwight wrote an exceptionally informative appraisal of the effect of the existing tariff:

March 12, 1870

Dear Sir:

I have been this morning to the custom house, in order to find how the Englishman can drive us from our own markets, on cotton machinery.

Of cotton machinery made in the United States 30 per cent of the cost is wages; 70 per ct materials. Or, certainly, wages do not, in any shops, exceed 33 per cent of the cost of machinery, leaving materials 66 per ct.

In cotton machinery in U. S. pig iron, bar iron, & steel are all imported — that is all of the materials of the machinery, except the woodwork. Pig iron, Scotch, cost, today, abroad $17.50 gold & we pay a duty of $9.00 in gold, on it. The cost of bar iron abroad today I do not know; but we pay a duty on what we import of at least 35 per ct & more on some sizes. On steel we pay a duty of 45 per ct.

All cotton machinery imported pays a duty of 35 per cent. That is, the Englishman sends his cotton machinery here at 35 per cent, or pays a duty on the pig iron bar iron & steel of which it is made of 35 per ct; while we American manufacturers pay a duty of 50 per cent on the pig iron of 35 per ct on the bar iron & 45 per ct on the steel of which our cotton machinery is made. When pig iron rules as low as $14 per ton, in England, as it does, at times, our rate of duty on pig rises to 60 per cent & above, being 9 per ton.

Our wages are 33 per cent higher than before the war & I think 70 per ct higher than English wages.

At the custom house they inform me this morning, that they are crowded with cotton machinery imported, while you complain that the Englishman offers to send cotton machinery here & put in the mill 17 per ct lower than you can place it in the mill, at cost. He can under bid you, working at cost, 17 per ct.

I think the statement I give above explains your situation, & the competition from England, which will close your shop. Your condition is worse than it would be with absolutely free trade without any duties at the ports, as you could then import your raw materials as cheaply as the Englishman could send them or as cheaply as the purchasers of English machinery can import pig iron bar iron & steel made up.

Truly yours,
Wm. Dwight

As has been mentioned in the chapters dealing with the Lowell Machine Shop, one of the most important effects of the great tariff controversies of the 1870's and 1880's was to draw the textile machinery industry together and to foster a feeling of group interest among the shops. There is little evidence to suggest that McMullan ever took a decisive part in any coöperative action in the industry, whether on the subject of tariff, customer terms, or machinery prices. McMullan's extreme individualism unquestionably held the Saco Water Power Machine Shop aloof from many of these joint undertakings, though the company was a member of the American Cotton Machinery Builders Association.

McMullan's position in the various price agreements which were made after 1894 is not clear. He apparently did not sign the agreement of 1896 which forbade the acceptance of mill stocks, but he did go so far as to make the comment that he had so much stock on hand that he would take no more.[27] An extensive correspondence has survived between Eben Draper and McMullan which indicates that the Saco Water Power Machine Shop participated to some extent in spinning price agreements. Such participation was virtually compulsory for any shop which wished to handle the Draper spindles. The story is told, however, that when Draper asked McMullan to sign one of the agreements McMullan replied, "Eben, I won't sign any agreement. I am a scoundrel, sir, and if I signed I'd never stick to it." [28]

The weight of evidence emphasizes McMullan's independent position in the industry and the fact that he did not compete vigorously on a price basis for orders. In his later years McMullan appeared to care little whether the shop ran or not, and this attitude effectively removed the company from the competitive scramble for business. Neither McMullan nor Eustis Morgan showed the slightest disposition to adjust the Biddeford spinning and roving frames to customers' specifications, but McMullan's independence was respected and his integrity was unquestioned. In the machinery industry McMullan was well liked and the products of his shop were highly regarded — sentiments which undoubtedly were encouraged by the comfortable feeling that here was no deadly rival. When business was good, McMullan took what orders came his way. When business was bad and other companies were desperately fighting for orders, McMullan closed down his shop and waited for better days.

No business could long survive this managerial attitude. McMullan's scorn of the new marketing techniques was profound. He joined no marketing group in the South and he employed no Southern agent. Informed that a mill owner in western Massachusetts was interested in his roving frames, McMullan replied, "If he wants my frames, let him come to Biddeford and get them."

By 1897 the Saco Water Power Machine Shop was a competitive nonentity. Its assets had shrunk and deteriorated, and the steady pouring-out of dividends had drained a once handsome surplus. But if James McMullan had, as many claimed, run the enterprise into the ground, he, together with Eustis P. Morgan, had also preserved its most invaluable and perishable virtue — the reputation of Biddeford machines. This was James McMullan's greatest accomplishment. Perhaps it should be allowed to overshadow all else in his administration, for it was the unsurpassed excellence of Saco Water

Power roving and spinning frames which encouraged the management of the Pettee Machine Works to promote the merger which kept the machine shop at Biddeford alive.

Rarely does business history provide so clear-cut an example of failure in the field of business administration as that of the Saco Water Power Machine Shop. Here lies exposed the fatal thesis which was the undoing of so many companies in the closing years of the nineteenth century — the thesis that manufacturing skill alone could ensure success. This was the classic blunder of the nineteenth-century industrial capitalist, still so intrigued by the machines which brought him initial success that he saw neither changing market conditions nor increasing financial complexities. James McMullan's errors were the magnified images of those of his time, but his legacy to the future — uncompromising insistence upon painstaking workmanship — was to be indispensable to a new type of management which tended to emphasize other aspects of business administration.

CHAPTER XII

COMBINED OPERATIONS: THE SACO AND PETTEE MACHINE SHOPS, 1897–1912

In the years preceding 1897 the most significant events in the evolution of Saco-Lowell's parent companies had been concerned with shops and markets; with workbench affairs and changes in marketing; with management at the operating level. Such corporate changes as had occurred were essentially simple in nature, often involving little more than a change of name. At or soon after the turn of the century, however, a broad shift in emphasis had taken place, not alone in Saco-Lowell's history, but in American business in general. The entry of Robert F. Herrick into the affairs of the Lowell Machine Shop and the textile machinery industry focused attention upon financial affairs, upon basic organizational changes, and upon management at the highest administrative levels.

The paragraphs which follow are marked by the same shift of emphasis that characterized the description of the Lowell Machine Shop in the years from 1897 to 1912. Such changes as occurred in production and marketing at Newton and at Biddeford between 1897 and 1912 were, with a few exceptions, quantitative rather than qualitative. Administrative techniques, however, were being revolutionized, and events of great interest were occurring in the field of financial management. While the years of Saco-Lowell's history from 1813 to 1873 might more or less accurately be described as the Age of the Manufacturer, those from 1873 to 1900 could well be labeled as the Age of the Salesman, and the period from 1900 to 1912 as the Age of the Financier.

1. The Merger of 1897

The causes which underlay the merger of the Pettee Machine Works and the Saco Water Power Machine Shop were simple and powerful. Neither company alone could do so well in the American textile-machinery market as could the two acting as one. This was a further instance among almost innumerable instances of the day when advantages in a highly competitive market were sought through corporate combination. In the textile machinery industry voluntary associations had been tried and found wanting. Outright merger was the next step.

Size had become almost a goal in itself in American business — a mania, a fad, a panacea for many ills. Behind the sudden growth in corporate size in the last decade of the nineteenth century, however, lay immensely practical considerations. Prominent among the causes of the movement was the need to reduce excessive competition by absorption of rival companies, or to meet such competition by achieving the economies (some real, some fancied) of large-scale operations under central management. Neither of these common causes, however, played a large part in the formation of the Saco and Pettee Machine Shops. The component companies were not direct competitors. Central direction of the two widely separated plants offered even greater administrative problems than had existed before, and the act of merger, per se, could scarcely bring greater manufacturing efficiency.

The motive for the merger was the same as that which had generated the growth of the Southern agency system: the desire, based upon competitive pressures, of being able to offer customers a nearly complete line of cotton-mill machinery. The convenience of customers, however, was not the sole consideration. Absolute control of a large variety of machine types promised far greater flexibility in meeting the competitive marketing tactics of the non-specialized shops. Demand for machinery, moreover, was seldom spread evenly over all types of machines, and a well-rounded line offered more business than a stabilized line.

Once again a sense of the movement of powerful unseen forces pervades Saco-Lowell history. As late as the middle 1880's the dictates of low-cost production were whipping the Saco Water Power Machine Shop, the Pettee Machine Works, and much of the textile machinery industry along the road toward product specialization. Within a decade the trend, so often reversed before, was reversed again. The movement then inaugurated toward large-scale business units and diversification within the field of cotton-textile machinery was destined to leave its mark on the industry of the twentieth century.

It was the desire of Frank J. Hale and R. Paul Snelling to diversify their product line by the addition of the Biddeford roving and spinning machinery which initiated the 1897 merger. The condition of the Saco Water Power Machine Shop presented an opportunity too obvious to spurn. McMullan had grown old and indifferent, and there was no heir-apparent to his throne. For seven years Biddeford dividends had been low, and the stock was selling below par. There were few orders on the books, and a shutdown of the plant was imminent. Since visible assets had deteriorated, while the greatest asset of all — the skills accumulated in half a century of machinery building — remained unimpaired, a bargain could be anticipated, for most mergers were based upon measurable values only.

Hale sought the advice of Eben Draper, and Draper urged the acquisition of the excellent Biddeford machinery line. Preliminary conversations with McMullan were encouraging, and the Boston law firm of Gaston, Snow and Saltonstall was entrusted with the details of merger. By the autumn of 1897 an agreement had been reached, and on October 30, 1897, the Saco and Pettee Machine Shops was formally incorporated under Massachusetts laws.

The new corporation was capitalized at $800,000, of which $350,000 represented Biddeford assets and $450,000 Newton assets.[1] A partial liquidation of each of the merging companies was involved. For each share of old stock held, Pettee stockholders received two and one-quarter shares of the new corporation's stock and $70 in cash. Biddeford stockholders received for each share of their old stock one half share of the new stock and about $100 in cash from liquidation of receivables and mill stocks not involved in the consolidation. There is little basis for judging the relative fairness with which the two stockholder groups were treated. The essence of this transaction may be summarized by the statement that the Biddeford group received nominally better terms than were justified by the condition of their company, but at the expense of control of the merged companies.[2]

The officers and directors of the new company came from both the component organizations, with the balance of power resting with the Pettee group. To the Biddeford group went the offices of president (James McMullan) and assistant treasurer (Spencer W. Richardson). To the Pettee group went the positions of treasurer (R. Paul Snelling), general agent (Frank J. Hale), and vice-president (David Nevins). The directorate consisted of three representatives of the Biddeford shop (McMullan, Richardson, and John W. Danielson) and four from the Pettee Machine Works (Hale, Snelling, Nevins, and Henry S. Shaw). Although control by the Pettee stockholders was absolute and obvious, the implications of that fact were very evidently misunderstood by James McMullan.

Despite McMullan's advancing age, he considered himself capable of playing an active part in the affairs of the new company for a time at least. Soon after the merger had been consummated, Frank J. Hale arrived at the Biddeford office and with characteristic energy began to issue orders. McMullan appeared, and took in the situation at a glance.

"Am I to understand that you will give the orders up here, Frank?" he demanded.

"Why yes, sir, that is the understanding," replied the younger man. McMullan then walked to his desk, gathered his papers together, and left the factory without a further word.[3] From this point on, the control of the Saco and Pettee Machine Shops by the Newton man was never seriously challenged, and activities at Biddeford were closely supervised by the main offices at Newton.

2. The Great Prosperity

In all of Saco-Lowell's history only the Kitson Machine Shop showed higher returns to the stockholders over an extended period than did the Saco and Pettee Machine Shops in the fifteen years of its existence. There is considerable basis for surmising that the Saco and Pettee stockholders received benefits substantially in excess of dividends recorded on the books of the company, and that the Saco and Pettee Machine Shops was the richest of all the Saco-Lowell parent companies. The foundation for the great prosperity was laid by the decisive action of Hale and Snelling in the wake of the 1897 merger.

The Necessities of '97

One pressing problem was that of the Biddeford plant, deteriorated to such an extent that it was entered on the books of the new company at a valuation $100,000 lower than the much smaller Newton plant. The problem of fostering efficiency in shop and office and of introducing systemization to a manufacturing establishment in which irregularity had been traditional was acute. The new management attacked the difficulties with enthusiasm and soon broke down much of the barrier of local suspicion and distrust which inevitably was raised in Biddeford against the Newton authority. The fact of merger, however, was never entirely digested by the Biddeford men, and the individuality of neither the Newton nor the Biddeford shop was submerged in the corporate body of which each was now a part.

William V. Threlfall, former sales agent of the Pettee Machine Works, was made agent at Biddeford. Alexander Rankeillor, another Newton man, was brought to Biddeford and entrusted with the vital task of teaching to the Biddeford foremen the manufacturing skills learned at Newton. James Tarr, a sea captain turned machinist in the best Maine tradition who had worked in the shop as a foreman prior to 1897, was promoted to the position of assistant superintendent. Gilman P. Littlefield, superintendent under McMullan, was retained in that position. Both Littlefield and Tarr had indispensable knowledge of local conditions. Threlfall commenced reorganizing with relentless and heavy-handed efficiency, Rankeillor with tact and understanding of the delicate nature of both the task and the personalities involved, Littlefield and Tarr with a knowledge that change must not subjugate the good while eliminating the bad.

The most important single act of the new administration in winning the coöperation of the Biddeford shop was performed by Hale, who strode into the office soon after the merger agreement had been signed and tossed a sheaf of orders on the bookkeeper's desk — more orders, it was said, than had been seen in Biddeford in a decade. Where McMullan had been weakest the new administration was strongest, and soon a flood of orders opened closed doors, lubricated dusty machines, and brought steady work and wages to a rapidly increasing number of Biddeford mechanics.

Local estimates of the new era in the Biddeford shop were heard in 1901, when it appeared that James McMullan was making an attempt to gain control of the company. This attempt was apparently not a sufficient threat to have been remembered by those active in the shop at the time, and is only recorded in the local newspaper.[4] McMullan's efforts are less significant than the editorial comment they called forth.

McMullan and Richardson, it was said, had been buying up the stock of the Saco and Pettee Machine Shops, with the result that McMullan would probably become head of the company at the next annual meeting of stockholders. The newspaper account speculated in these interesting words on the results of such an eventuality:

> It will be a matter of much local interest and importance, and while there are doubtless many of the old timers would like to see the shop back under the old management there will be more who will regret any such change.
>
> The Saco Pettee has been worth more as an industry in the last two years to Biddeford than it ever was under any half dozen years of the McMullan management. The pay roll is at present probably double what it ever was under the old management and strict as the rules are which now govern the shop there is without any doubt more of justice and equality in the present management than there was in the former.
>
> As a political institution the shop is not as valuable as it used to be but as an industry there has been such an improvement that the majority who are interested in Biddeford's prosperity will regret any change, such as is rumored likely.

Editorial comment was even more scathing:

> The reported possibility of the Saco-Pettee shop going back under the old management is not an agreeable one. Under the old management the shop was shut down much of the time when it might have been running and at its best was never as valuable an industry as it is at present. However, it is purely a money transaction and the public's wishes will have no influence. Nor will everybody take the same view of it. There are those who have very good reasons for regarding the old manage-

ment as preferable, particularly the politicians and those who used to enjoy soft snaps in the shop because of their political influence rather than because of their value as workmen.

McMullan's challenge, however, never materialized, and the plant activity in which the new management found its chief source of local favor was unfettered by any vital changes at the managerial level.

That activity stemmed from the splendid marketing organization which had been built in Newton before 1897 and which was expanded thereafter to encompass the distribution of Biddeford roving and spinning frames. The Saco and Pettee Machine Shops, however, benefited not just from innate effort but from a great and prolonged period of American business prosperity and a continued expansion of the American textile industry.

Marketing and Mill Promotion

Markets for textile machinery were expanding more rapidly than ever before. Between 1900 and 1910, total spindles in the United States increased by a third, and the industry in the South tripled in size. The excellent contacts already established by Hale and Snelling in the great Southern market now assumed tremendous importance, and were strengthened still further by the addition of the highly regarded Biddeford machines to the line. Expansion of the textile industry in southern New England was also large, and in Fall River and New Bedford the Saco and Pettee Machine Shops found much business.

When the 1897 merger was being planned, a prospectus was drawn up which included estimates of the business that might be realized by the combined companies. James McMullan glanced at these figures and contemptuously labeled them as grossly over-optimistic. Lacking the sanguine disposition of the Newton men, McMullan could scarcely have anticipated or prepared for a booming market and profited by it only fortuitously. The buoyant optimism of Hale and Snelling could have been dangerous in a prolonged downward cycle, but 1897 was the low point of a trend and prosperity lay ahead. Hale's estimates have more than passing interest, for they may be checked against actual realizations and, in addition, they reveal the product breakdown of sales of the combined companies.

	1897 Estimate of Annual Production Saco and Pettee Machine Shops	Production for Year Ending April, 1900
Cards	1,200	1,447
Drawing Frames	1,800	2,244
Railway Heads	120	144
Spinning Spindles	300,000	250,952
Roving Frames	400	734

After 1900, the first year in which the 1897 estimates were exceeded, sales volume expanded rapidly to a plateau never before

TABLE 34

Sales of the Saco and Pettee Machine Shops, the Lowell Machine Shop, and the Whitin Machine Works, 1898–1912

Year	Saco and Pettee Machine Shops			Whitin Machine Works	Lowell Machine Shop[a]
	Newton Shop	Biddeford Shop	Total		
1898	$ 495,300	$ 309,200	$ 804,500	$ 993,400	$ 2,468,900
1899	655,000	496,200	1,151,200	1,915,900	737,800
1900	1,117,100	738,700	1,855,800	3,137,100	2,095,100
1901	1,309,400	1,671,900	2,981,300	2,789,800	2,636,700
1902	758,700	1,269,800	2,028,500	2,480,200	1,176,600
1903	1,215,800	1,819,600	3,035,400	2,804,500	2,008,100
1904	1,021,600	1,765,100	2,786,700	2,397,400	1,210,800
1905	989,600	1,362,400	2,352,000	2,304,800	1,698,100
1906	1,102,500	1,138,600	2,241,100	3,022,600	1,965,400
1907	1,326,900	1,690,100	3,017,000	3,595,600	2,491,800
1908	1,366,100	1,669,900	3,036,000	2,977,600	2,682,400
1909	1,063,300	1,253,200	2,316,500	3,917,800	1,449,600
1910	1,504,400	2,367,000	3,871,400	4,645,300	2,315,500
1911	1,590,200	2,205,100	3,795,300	3,096,900	2,116,000
1912	933,700	1,685,100	2,618,800	3,281,700	1,039,900
Total	16,449,600	21,441,900	37,891,500	43,360,600	28,092,700

[a] Lowell sales 1906–11, estimated from Bills Rendered account.

Source: Saco and Pettee Machine Shop and Lowell Machine Shop, Ledgers and journals; Navin, *Whitin Machine Works*, Appendix 29.

reached by any of Saco-Lowell's constituent companies. Table 34 shows the course of sales from 1898 to 1912 and at once suggests the most noticeable result of the 1897 merger.[5] The union of these two companies, neither of which had hitherto challenged the Whitin Machine Works or the Lowell Machine Shop in point of sales volume, had produced in the Saco and Pettee Machine Shops an organization of sufficient size and power to offer serious rivalry in all markets and in all spheres of business activity to the traditional leaders of the industry.

The relationship in point of sales volume between the Saco and Pettee Machine Shops and its chief competitors is even more forcibly illustrated for the years from 1906 through 1912 by figures quoted in a Department of Commerce report on the six principal shops producing cotton preparatory machinery.[6] Sales of the Saco and Pettee Machine Shops as shown in company records, and combined net sales in each year of the Saco and Pettee Machine Shops, the Lowell Machine Shop, the Kitson Machine Shop, Howard & Bullough, and the Whitin Machine Works, as given in the Commerce Department report, stood as follows:

Year	Total Sales of Six Shops (Comprising 80 to 90% of industry output of preparatory machinery)	Biddeford and Newton Shops Combined	
		Total	Percentage of Six-shop Total
1906	$10,845,818	$2,241,112	20.7
1907	11,513,044	3,017,083	26.2
1908	8,622,966	3,036,057	35.2
1909	12,837,892	2,316,589	18.0
1910	12,803,814	3,971,458	31.0
1911	8,848,787	3,795,398	42.9
1912	8,784,222	2,618,850	29.8
Average			29.1

The absence of detailed company sales records precludes all but a general discussion of markets in the 1897–1912 period. The large sales volume which was built up was a product of the expansion of the domestic textile industry. As in periods of prosperity in the past, American machine-builders paid lip service to the possibilities of the export market, but sent little machinery abroad. Foreign sales by the Saco and Pettee Machine Shops, like those of the rest of the industry, were inconsequential.[7] Far from being able to meet the English on neutral ground, American shops were still complaining, though with less basis than in the 1880's and 1890's, of English competition in American markets.

The Southern market continued to expand at a faster rate than did the Northern. The Pettee Machine Works had taken orders wherever they could be found, but by 1905 the Saco and Pettee Machine Shops appeared to be strongest in the South Carolina market. In the first decade of the twentieth century geographical spheres of influence of the various machine shops became well defined in the Southern manufacturing districts, though the boundary lines were often ignored by ambitious salesmen. There is no evidence to suggest that these spheres of influence were set by mutual agreement. Rather, they seem to have grown up by a process of natural concentration. Whitin deliberately courted the smaller, more soundly financed North Carolina mills, and on only one occasion (1902) made any serious effort to secure the business of the large South Carolina mills which provided so many orders for the Saco and Pettee Machine Shops. In Alemance County, North Carolina, the firm of Howard & Bullough was strongest, while the Fales & Jenks Machine Company competed with the Saco and Pettee Machine Shops in the Greenville–Spartanburg area in South Carolina. The Lowell Machine Shop concentrated its effort in the Atlanta–South Georgia area, but had customers scattered all over the South.[8]

The great expansion of the textile industry in southern New England after 1900 temporarily challenged the increasing predominance of machinery orders from the South. The first large contract on record placed with the Saco and Pettee Machine Shops in southern New England was for the Soule Mills in New Bedford, in 1901. Orders for the Taber, Kilburn, and Quissett Mills in New Bedford and for the Lincoln and Luther Mills in Fall River followed soon thereafter.

The greatly increased sales volume arising both out of the merging of the Newton and Biddeford lines and as a result of increasing prosperity and growth in the textile industry demanded alterations in the marketing organization. Available evidence suggests that some time prior to 1897 the Pettee Machine Works had come to exercise strong control over the Charlotte Machine Company, their Southern selling agency. The extent of that control is indicated by events in 1897.

Among the machinery lines handled by the Charlotte Machine Company under the direction of H. S. Chadwick were those of the Providence Machine Company (roving) and the Fales & Jenks Machine Company (spinning). Immediately following the merger of 1897, these two lines were dropped and the Biddeford roving and spinning were added. If the Newton men did not actually own the agency, it is clear that they could exert sufficient influence upon Chadwick to dictate as to the lines to be carried.

Chadwick himself left the Charlotte Machine Company in 1898 to enter the army, and his place was taken by A. H. Washburn, a one-time machinery erector who had come to the South in 1881 to set up machinery in Georgia and who had stayed on to become Chadwick's assistant in 1895. In 1899 Chadwick died, and the Charlotte Machine Company as such passed out of existence. After this time the agency was carried on under Washburn's name and under the control of the Saco and Pettee Machine Shops. Repair facilities which had existed before 1897 were improved and extended, and the offices served as the base for all Southern marketing. Washburn was paid a salary ($4,800 annually, in 1912), but continued to carry the supplementary product lines of other manufacturers (as had Chadwick before him) and received a commission from those companies which augmented his income from the Saco and Pettee Machine Shops. A permanent office force of fourteen included clerks, five machinists in the repair shop, and four salesmen, A. H. Washburn, U. S. Washburn, A. K. Landau, and Ralph Webber. In addition to these, the office was the headquarters for from twenty to fifty machinery erectors.[9]

Here in Charlotte lay the core of the marketing organization — here were found those energies and enthusiasms which made that organization, though smaller than some competing offices, one of the most effective in the industry. A. H. Washburn certainly lacked the stature of Cramer, Whitin's agent, and in his later years is said to have allowed other interests than the Saco-Pettee agency to occupy his time. Nevertheless, the force under Washburn drove hard for business. The high spirit of that force and the firm conviction entertained at the Charlotte headquarters that the Saco-Pettee line was unequaled in the world may have been imparted directly by General Agent Hale, whose visits to the Southern office stimulated both the efficiency and the loyalty of the employees there.

An enlargement of the sales and service force followed in the wake of the merger, but advertising expenditures were almost insignificant in amount. The largest annual sum spent in the entire 1897–1912 period was $4,278, or about .2 per cent of sales in that year (1900). Additional sums were expended on catalogues, but even these were modest. These marketing tools, so effectively utilized in some industries, had limited value in promoting the sale of textile machinery. Instead, a major factor in the market strength of the Saco and Pettee Machine Shops (like the Pettee Machine Works before it) was the aggressive pursuit of orders and important contacts by Hale and Snelling themselves.

In 1898 a significant addition was made to the company directorate in the person of Seth M. Milliken, head of the firm of Deering, Milliken & Company, cloth commission agents. This firm had been founded in 1865, but Deering had soon withdrawn and gone to Chicago to enter the harvester business. Under Milliken's direction the business grew to a position of prominence in the textile industry, and by 1885 the company was said to have $300,000 invested in cotton and woolen mills in Maine and in the Southern States.[10] By 1897 the firm had offices in Boston, Chicago, and New York, and was the selling agent for many important textile mills. The contact with Milliken appears to have been made before 1897 by John Danielson, a director of the Saco Water Power Machine Shop; it came about as a result of Milliken's handling of the output of Danielson's mills in Maine and Connecticut. After the merger of 1897, however, a strong friendship grew up between Milliken and the Newton men.

Like most of the commission agents who had money to lend, Milliken's influence in the South was great; and he served on the directorate of many mills. He was also instrumental in placing Hale and Snelling on the Boards of some of his mills. The story is told that, once a year, Milliken would engage a private railway car and tour the manufacturing districts of the South, inspecting his mills, renewing old acquaintances, and making new friends. On these occasions Hale and Snelling frequently accompanied him, and the grand tours presented an unexcelled opportunity for meeting, under the most favorable conditions, the men who were the heaviest purchasers of textile machinery in the country.

The generally favorable condition of business from 1906 to 1912, coupled with control of the price-cutting tactics of the Lowell Machine Shop by the companies which owned it, had the effect of mitigating price warfare in the industry. That competition continued to exist and at times was very keen, however, is clearly indicated by the fact that certain promotional efforts of the Saco and Pettee Machine Shops were pursued with greater energy than ever before.

In 1904 George Marston Whitin had held $825,000 of mill securities, taken in prior years in settlement of machinery contracts. In 1905 he stopped accepting mill stocks entirely.[11] In contrast to this policy of Whitin's and a similar one pursued by the Lowell Machine Shop, the Saco and Pettee Machine Shops launched a campaign of accepting mill stock which went far beyond anything seen in the industry before or since.

Why should Hale and Snelling have accepted large amounts of mill securities at a time when Whitin was refusing to do so, and in a period of generally prosperous business? There is no positive answer to this question. Whitin, of course, may have felt that he already held too many securities; Hale and Snelling, having always followed the policy of not allowing mill stocks to accumulate on their books, were free to continue and expand the practice which had been so valuable in the past in attracting orders. With their responsibilities tremendously enlarged as a result of the 1897 merger, the Newton men may well have felt the need, even in a period of good business, for promotional assistance such as that afforded by the acceptance of mill stocks. To these possible explanations should be added one more — that the mill stocks which were being taken were proving extremely profitable in themselves.

Thus the practice which had once been deplored by machinery manufacturers as a necessary evil — it even had been forbidden by mutual agreement among themselves — now was actively encouraged by the Saco and Pettee Machine Shops. The traditional nineteenth-century aloofness of machinery builders from the financial and operating affairs of their textile-mill customers had never been observed to any appreciable extent by the Newton men, and at this time they ignored it completely. Much more interesting than this, however, were the revelations contained in company record books that much of the financial assistance so bountifully extended was at this time being channeled to Northern mills, and that the Saco and Pettee Machine Shops played an important promotional rôle in the great mill boom in southern New England.

There is no adequate record of stocks and bonds accepted in payment for machinery by the company between 1897 and 1905. For the period after 1905 considerable information is available. Between April, 1905, and September, 1912, more than two and one-half million dollars (par value) of mill stocks and bonds were taken from forty-eight different mills. This was equal to approximately 12½ per cent of machinery sales for the period. George Marston Whitin's most active period of stock-taking had been between 1895 and 1905, when he accepted mill stocks equivalent in value to 5 per cent of sales.[12]

Appendix 12 presents some of the details of stock participations by the Saco and Pettee Machine Shops. Twenty of the forty-eight mills from which securities were taken were located in South Carolina, but 70 per cent by value of the securities accepted between 1905 and 1912 were of Northern mills. The impressive total for the period came about as a result of several very large participations in both Southern and Northern mills. These were recorded on the company's books as follows:

Drayton Mills, Spartanburg, S. C.	1906–07	$149,000
Taber Mills, New Bedford, Mass.	1907–08	85,000
New Bedford Cotton Mills Corporation, New Bedford, Mass.	1909–10	158,600
Lincoln Mfg. Company, Fall River, Mass.	1908–10	121,700
Quissett Mills, New Bedford, Mass.	1910–11	227,000
Harmony Mills, Cohoes, N. Y.	1911–12	690,000
Dunean Mills, Greenville, S. C.	1912	271,500

The immediate results of these various participations were orders for machinery and, in the larger transactions, a voice in the management of the mills involved. This latter was usually in the form of a directorship for one or more of the officers and directors of the Saco and Pettee Machine Shops, which not only safeguarded the immediate creditor position of the shop but facilitated the placing of future machinery orders. By 1912 the number of contacts in the form of common officers or directors between shop and customers was formidable. Not all of these, to be sure, were the result of stock participations, but all were important as sources of business for the Newton and Biddeford shops.

Henry S. Shaw, president of the Saco and Pettee Machine Shops, was treasurer and director of two mills and president and director of two others. Director Charles E. Rogerson, primarily interested in the banking field, was a director of four mills. Directors Harcourt Amory and John W. Danielson were between them directors of a minimum of five mills (and probably many more), treasurer of two mills, and president of one. Seth Milliken was president of seven mills, treasurer of one mill, and director of fifteen others. Frank W. Hale was a director in seven mills and in two companies which controlled five other mills. R. Paul Snelling was director in nine mills and in one company which controlled five other mills.[13]

In this list of mill offices held, there is, of course, some overlapping. Both Hale and Snelling, for example, were directors of the Indian Head Mills of Alabama, of which Amory was treasurer and G. M. Draper president. Other mills in which both Hale and Snelling were directors included the Harmony Mills (Cohoes, New York) and the Lincoln Manufacturing Company (Fall River, Massachusetts). That the interest of the Newton men in textile mills had gone beyond the mere acceptance of stock in payment for machinery is evidenced by the fact that in 1909 they participated, with Myron C. Taylor and C. M. Warner of New York, in the formation of the Bay State Cotton Corporation, a holding company for the securities of four mills. In 1910 this same group organized the International Cotton Mills Corporation, which combined three earlier consolidations.[14] These latter activities relate to the history of the Saco and Pettee Machine Shops, however, only insofar as they illustrate the important position which the Newton men had come to occupy in the textile as well as the textile machinery industry. The results of their contacts in terms of machinery sold may be inferred but obviously cannot be measured.

The record of stock participation by the Saco and Pettee Machine Shops might be criticized on the grounds that it violated the dictates of conservative business practice and was an unnecessary risk. The question as to whether the company would have done as well in this period without accepting large amounts of stock is theoretical in the extreme. Whitin sold larger amounts of machinery without taking any stock, but the Whitin Machine Works was far better established in the market than the relatively new Saco and Pettee Machine Shops. There is little question that the rapid rise of the Pettee Machine Works from 1886 to 1897 owed much to liberality in dealings with customers, and much justification exists for the viewpoint that the success of the Saco and Pettee Machine Shops after 1897 was due in substantial part to the continuation and extension of that same liberality. That the practice was full of risk few would question, but condemnation must be based not on what could have happened but what did happen. The financial results of stock participations after 1905 are traced in a later section of this chapter. At this point no more need be said than that, as a result of careful selection of the mills assisted and a generally rising security market, the stockholders of the company paid few premiums for the machinery orders secured in this way. Even had the practice resulted in heavy short-term loss, the addition of new customers who would purchase machinery for many years to come would have justified the means and the expense. Questions as to whether the encouragement of further rapid expansion of the textile industry was economically sound might well be raised, but the immediate benefits to the mills thus assisted were obviously great. The part played by the Saco and Pettee Machine Shops in furthering with capital as well as with manufacturing skill the growth of the textile industry should be acknowledged.

Corporate Control and New Administrative Tools

The history of the Saco and Pettee Machine Shops was strongly influenced by two situations of basic importance. The first of these was the absolute control exerted over the affairs of the company by

Frank J. Hale and R. Paul Snelling, who between them owned less than 10 per cent of the company stock outstanding. Behind Hale and Snelling, however, powerful forces were arraigned.

One result of the merger of 1897 was to increase the total number of shareholders and facilitate control of the new company by a coalition between the Nevins interests which had controlled the Pettee Machine Works from 1886 to 1897 and the Lockwood-Danielson-Milliken group which had dominated the Saco Water Power Machine Shop for much of the thirty-year period prior to 1897. In 1910 the most important stockholdings in the Saco and Pettee Machine Shops were the following:[15]

Boston Safe Deposit & Trust Co., trustees under will of David Nevins	400	shares
Henry S. Shaw	658	"
Henry S. Shaw, trustee	153	"
Amelia DeF. Lockwood	275	"
Sarah Danielson	238	"
John W. Danielson	23	"
Seth W. Milliken	247	"
Charles E. Rogerson	181	"
Harcourt Amory	112	"
Frank J. Hale	350	"
R. P. Snelling	290	"

The total holdings of these stockholders amounted to 2,927 shares of the 8,000 shares of common stock outstanding. Of these owners Shaw, Milliken, Snelling, and Hale all were directors. Shaw, the president of the company, had succeeded Nevins at the latter's death in 1898 as central figure in the Nevins group of companies (Chart IX, Chapter X). Director John W. Danielson represented the Lockwood interests, and Director Charles E. Rogerson was president of the Boston Safe Deposit and Trust Company. Harcourt Amory, the seventh director, had a relatively small stock interest in the company, but was an officer by virtue of his connections with the Lancaster Mills, the State Street Trust Company, and other interests which had been or were becoming closely identified with the Saco and Pettee Machine Shops.

The power of this directorate was unchallenged by the large group of minority stockholders not directly represented on the

Board. That this power was wielded to the satisfaction of all the stockholders is evident from the internal tranquility which existed in the ranks of the owners. The reasons for that satisfaction are not hard to find — high profits and high dividends.

At routine annual stockholders' meetings formal business such as the election of officers was carried through by a small number of stockholders, who rarely troubled themselves to muster a majority of the potential stockholder votes. From 1898 to 1904 the largest number of shares represented at any annual meeting was 2,500 out of 8,000 outstanding. After 1904 the number of shares voting at routine meetings increased somewhat (to 4,941 out of 12,000 voting shares in 1907). When the occasion arose, however, the controlling interests in the company displayed an ability to muster without apparent difficulty more than two-thirds of the total stockholder votes.

Within the directorate itself there was a still further concentration of powers. Records of attendance at directors' meetings indicate that Milliken and Danielson were not often present, and that routine responsibilities of the directorate rested more heavily on the other five directors, two of whom were Hale and Snelling.[16] Between these two men and the other directors there existed the most intimate relationship and a feeling of mutual trust, with the result that the control of the company nominally vested in the directorate was delegated to Hale and Snelling in complete faith. The meetings of the Board were confined to business of a perfunctory nature. Important operating decisions were arrived at by Hale and Snelling, usually after informal consultation with the other directors. When necessary, these decisions received the almost automatic formal approval of the Board.[17]

In the annals of American business history this system of control had often been misused and as often attacked as being despotic and contrary to the intent of corporate law. Here, in the Saco and Pettee Machine Shops, was an example of the much-maligned system working to produce an immensely practicable method of administration: flexible, dynamic, alert to opportunity, and profitable to all who participated.

The second set of factors which exerted great influence upon the managerial techniques and the corporate form of not only the Saco and Pettee Machine Shops, but of all American business organizations, was a changing attitude in the State and national government and judiciary toward the business corporation. Between 1897 and 1912, tremendously significant concepts evolved. Certain of these concepts were restrictive in scope; many of them gave to American business new managerial tools hitherto denied.[18]

On a national scale the Anti-Trust Act of 1890 was becoming more clearly defined by judicial interpretation. As has been pointed out earlier, the general effect of these interpretations was to increase the potency of the Act and to force business into devious paths of evasion. In the 1890's the intent of government appeared to be punitive and flavored with a strong suspicion that size was *prima facie* evidence of attempts to monopolize and restrain trade. By the turn of the century, however, interpretation of the Anti-Trust Act, though still punitive, had become more selective, and a definite feeling had grown up that monopoly was not an inevitable attribute of large capitalization; hence capitalization should not inevitably be restricted. Thus the way was cleared for the growth of big business at the very time when big business was under attack.

With the Federal Corporation Income Tax Act of 1909 (a levy of 1 per cent on all net income over $5,000) came the first invasion of that privacy which business men prized next to the sanctity of their homes — the privacy of their business records. The implications and precedents of this law were greater than the immediate effects. It required certain standards and responsibilities in record-keeping which most well-ordered companies had long observed.

On the State level new statutory freedoms were being given to the business man. These were most important — possibly the most important influences in the evolution of early twentieth-century business techniques. What was happening in Massachusetts at the turn of the century was happening, had happened, or was to happen in other States.

In Massachusetts the old concept had given way that corporations were creatures of the State and must be guaranteed by it in all particulars of responsibility and management. The new concept set forth in the Business Corporation Law of 1903 was that, in the absence of fraud, corporations should be allowed the freedoms customarily granted individuals of the Commonwealth. Prior to

1902, stockholders had been treated as wards of the State; common stock was considered as a guaranteed fund for the payment of creditors; and corporations were regulated in the interest of creditors primarily, stockholders secondarily. The new concept, on the contrary, held that the State owed to persons who chose to deal with corporations no duty in looking after the solvency of such artificial bodies beyond that of ensuring that creditors and stockholders should at all times be informed of all facts about organization and management.

Specific privileges were extended as this drastic change in attitude became effective. The power of one corporation to hold the stock of another corporation was never expressly approved or prohibited by Massachusetts law, but had been exercised by many corporations as early as the late 1880's. Specific acts passed in other States (in Connecticut in 1895; in New Jersey in 1896; in Delaware, Maine, and Pennsylvania in 1901) appear to have strengthened the position of Massachusetts corporations, and by the turn of the century holding companies had become a legally practicable device.

In 1902, Massachusetts corporations were granted the power of issuing preferred stock; in 1903, wide freedoms were granted corporations in altering their capital structures without the hitherto cumbersome necessity of securing legislative approval. The form of Massachusetts business organizations was quick to reflect these emancipating forces. The Saco and Pettee Machine Shops, among others, almost immediately began to avail itself of the new freedoms. In 1901 a holding company was formed. In 1905 the stock of a competing shop was purchased and carried thereafter on the company books. In 1905, also, a preferred-stock issue was brought forth. In 1910 the capital stock of an important supplier was acquired and an extensive alteration was effected in the company's corporate structure. All these new techniques were designed to meet increasingly complex business situations. All were either made possible or at least greatly facilitated by the changes in corporate law in the late 1890's and early 1900's.

The Disposition of Mill Securities

In 1901 the directors of the Saco and Pettee Machine Shops incorporated the Eastern Machinery Company under Maine law. The purpose of this action was explained in the following words by Treasurer Snelling in a prospectus sent to stockholders in November, 1901:

> In the interests of the Saco and Pettee Machine Shops, a new corporation has been established under the laws of the state of Maine, with a like number of shares (8,000) but of the par value of ten dollars, called the Eastern Machinery Company.
>
> The Eastern Machinery Company has exchanged and made over to the Saco and Pettee Machine Shops all of its capital stock in return for certain shares of the capital stock of various cotton mills, which the Saco and Pettee Machine Shops has taken in times past in part payment for machinery, and which have been carried as of nominal value upon its books, as it has been impossible to find a market for them at satisfactory prices.
>
> Your Directors, at a meeting duly called and held on the 21st day of November, 1901, voted that these eight thousand shares of the Eastern Machinery Company should be distributed ratably share for share to the stockholders of the Saco and Pettee Machine Shops.

Several purposes appear to have underlain the formation of this holding company for the mill securities of the operating company. These securities at times had been hard to dispose of, as Snelling stated in his prospectus. Faced with a similar problem, George Marston Whitin had distributed his mill securities to stockholders in lieu of cash dividends, but this recourse was not practicable to a company with a large number of stockholders. The formation of a holding company and the distribution of the holding-company shares to stockholders of the parent company, however, accomplished the identical purpose and possessed other advantages as well. By this means large profits or large losses, either of which were eminently possible in transactions involving mill stocks, could be shifted to the subsidiary company, leaving the books of the parent company clear to reflect normal operating results. Moreover, by the judicious transfer of mill stocks to the subsidiary, the level of operating profit or loss of the parent could be stabilized.

The management, ownership, and profits of the Eastern Machinery Company from 1901 to 1910 are a part of the Saco-Lowell story, since the company was in effect but a department of the Saco and Pettee Machine Shops. The transfers of mill securities from the parent to the subsidiary are recorded on the books of the parent, but the surviving records of the Eastern Machinery Company are extremely fragmentary. With only half of the story thus available very few conclusions can be drawn, many highly interesting questions must be left unanswered, and there is no reliable basis for judging the financial results of the large mill-stock participations of the Saco and Pettee Machine Shops. The illustrations given in subsequent paragraphs of the relationship between parent and subsidiary are derived from the ledgers and journals of the Saco and Pettee Machine Shops, and from a penciled list of Eastern Machinery Company dividends which cannot be checked for accuracy or completeness.

A major objective of financial management in the generally prosperous times which followed 1897 was the understatement of profits. This was the case with the Saco and Pettee Machine Shops, and it appears to have been true of a wide segment of American business. Motivations for the practice have been discussed in previous chapters. The most obvious of these was the simple wish to be conservative. One phase of this was the frequent desire or necessity of concealing profits from stockholders in order that adequate reserves might be retained in the business and not disbursed in extra dividends. After 1909, moreover, there were definite tax advantages to be derived from understatement. There is no indication as to which, if either, of these motives prevailed in the Saco and Pettee Machine Shops. The evidence is reasonably clear, however, that, for whatever motives, mill stocks and other securities held were being used to channel off some of the profits of the parent company into the subsidiary.

The transactions in mill stocks were essentially simple in nature. Stocks were taken from mills, usually in part payment of machinery orders. These stocks were entered on the books of the Saco and Pettee Machine Shops at par value. After varying periods of time the stocks were written down in value by a charge to the profit and loss account, and were subsequently sold to the Eastern Machinery Company at the reduced valuation. This process recorded a loss on the books of the parent; however, the subsidiary, receiving the stocks at bargain prices, presumably realized a compensating profit, provided that the stocks could be sold at or near their par value. What these profits were cannot be determined in the absence of the Eastern Machinery Company records.

The formation of the Eastern Machinery Company itself illustrated the technique of transfer. According to agreement, stockholders of the Saco and Pettee Machine Shops received $80,000 par value of stock in the Eastern Machinery Company, in return for which the Eastern Machinery Company received from the Saco and Pettee Machine Shops securities the value of which was listed as $80,000. An examination of the securities transferred, however, indicates that they had a par value of $312,800. There is no way of ascertaining the market, or actual, value of these securities, but a conservative estimate would place that value at not far from a quarter of a million dollars.

Many examples might be given of stocks taken up on the books of the Saco and Pettee Machine Shops at par, written down in value, and sold to the Eastern Machinery Company at substantially less than par or market value. Total figures for the entire 1897–1912 period, however, are far more revealing than individual illustrations of the process.

Between October 31, 1898, and December 24, 1912, securities on the books of the Saco and Pettee Machine Shops were written down in value by the amount of $2,721,341.55. This loss to the company, however, was not net, for these securities had yielded dividends amounting to $225,109.40. Thus the net loss taken by the company on these assets totaled approximately two and one-half million dollars. Some perspective on the relative extent of these write-downs may be gained from the fact that total cash dividends paid to common stockholders in these same years totaled $2,852,560.

For the period from 1905 to 1912 more detailed information is available, and a direct comparison may be made between the value of securities received by the Saco and Pettee Machine Shops and disposed of by that company to the Eastern Machinery Company.

Securities on hand as of April 29, 1905, added to all securities taken thereafter, were valued on the books of the parent company at

$3,229,249.21.[19] Of this total book value, $1,669,865.29, or 52 per cent, was charged off as a loss. The balance, with certain exceptions, represented the valuation placed on securities sold to the Eastern Machinery Company.[20]

Might not these very large losses taken by the Saco and Pettee Machine Shops have reflected real losses incurred from a decline in the market value of securities held? The answer to this question is that some small part of these book losses unquestionably did so arise. However, these securities were held for very short periods — the turnover was far too rapid to have made such rapid depreciation possible, even on a declining security market. Actually the market for the securities held was very strong, despite the fact that few of these securities were listed on any security exchanges. Many of the stocks held by the company were selling at close to par, or even above par. The burden of evidence indicates conclusively that the losses were created in order to diminish the total profits of the parent company and to present the subsidiary company with securities at prices which might permit very large profits to be realized from subsequent sale on the open market.

Do these figures furnish any indications as to the over-all profit or loss accruing to the Saco and Pettee Machine Shops from the practice of accepting large amounts of mill securities? The books of the Eastern Machinery Company alone could furnish the documentary evidence necessary to answer this question. The terms of the answer would have to be carefully defined. The Saco and Pettee Machine Shops as a corporate entity obviously sustained a book loss of some two and one-half million dollars between 1898 and 1912. This, however, is an unrealistic concept. The stockholders of the Saco and Pettee Machine Shops need not have suffered any such loss. Assuming that all stockholders of the parent company retained their stock in the subsidiary (an assumption which cannot be proved or disproved, in the absence of Eastern Machinery Company stockholder records), these stockholders would have received profits from their Eastern Machinery Company stock which would have been offset against losses incurred as owners of the parent company's stock. Any stockholder who sold his Eastern Machinery Company stock, of course, would have suffered without compensating advantage — in much the same way that stockholders of the Saco Water Power Company had suffered who failed in 1850 to subscribe to the stock of the Pepperell Manufacturing Company.

Lacking complete records of the Eastern Machinery Company, we find no positive way of measuring the profits of that company against losses taken by the Saco and Pettee Machine Shops. An informed guess (based on a number of instances where market values of securities could be determined) would place the losses incurred in accepting mill securities in part payment of machinery at perhaps 10 per cent of the value of the securities taken. A loss of this size would have been eminently justified by the great expediency and lasting benefits of the practice.

The Lowell and Ashworth Purchases

Security transactions were not confined to textile-mill participations. The purchase of the Lowell Machine Shop in 1905 by several competing shops, including the Saco and Pettee Machine Shops, has already been detailed. Some interest attaches to the transaction as recorded on the books of the latter company.

In April, 1905, the Saco and Pettee Machine Shops purchased three hundred and sixty shares of Lowell Machine Shop stock, paying therefor the agreed-upon price of $1,180 per share, a total expenditure of $424,800. In 1906, twenty additional shares were acquired, and on November 2, 1911, the entire holding of three hundred and eighty shares was sold for cash to Robert F. Herrick.

The shops participating in the purchase of the Lowell Machine Shop could well have anticipated losses from the transaction, and probably would have borne them cheerfully, had they occurred, so long as the primary objective of controlling price warfare in the industry was achieved. Herrick's offer in 1911 to purchase all outstanding stock at the price originally paid by the subscribing shops, however, enabled all concerned to show as profit the dividends received on Lowell stock between 1905 and 1911. For the Saco and Pettee Machine Shops this totaled $180,500, or a little more than 6 per cent per year on the purchase price of the stock.

The purchase of Lowell stock in 1905, coupled with an ambitious program of plant expansion at Biddeford, appears to have been the cause for recourse to a new financial tool authorized in Massachusetts only three years before, the issuance of preferred stock. At a stockholders' meeting held on March 20, 1905, there was authorized an issue of 4,000 shares of 6 per cent cumulative preferred stock with a par value of $100 per share. This stock was entitled to voting rights and was redeemable June 1, 1910, or thereafter, at $110. The purpose of the issue having been accomplished and a reserve set aside from the bountiful profits of ensuing years, the issue was redeemed in June, 1910.

In 1910 the Saco and Pettee Machine Shops embarked on another coöperative venture similar in method to the joint purchase of the Lowell Machine Shop, but with a different objective. This second venture was the acquisition of the stock of Ashworth Brothers, Inc., card-clothing manufacturers of Fall River, Massachusetts. Both the Saco and Pettee Machine Shops and the Whitin Machine Works are known to have taken Ashworth stock, in return for which financial assistance they were assured a reliable supply of domestic card clothing, possibly at preferential prices.[21] Saco and Pettee's subscription to the Ashworth stock consisted of 800 shares valued at $90,000. These shares paid good dividends and were held by the company and its successors until 1929.

The formation of the Eastern Machinery Company, the purchase of the Lowell Machine Shop, and the acquisition of the Ashworth stock were ventures of widely varying importance, but each venture had much in common with the others. In each case expediency rather than direct financial gain was the motivating force, yet each transaction was smoothly handled and resulted in the fulfillment of the primary objective without appreciable cost, or even with some financial gain. Considered together, these transactions provide ample evidence of a significant new flexibility in administrative techniques — a new facility in solving business problems which is directly attributable to the new legalistic freedoms of the early twentieth century.

Accounting and Control Methods

Accounting practices evolved little in the years from 1897 to 1912. Indeed, a simplicity is evidenced in company bookkeeping methods which was reminiscent of the early days of the Boston Manufacturing Company and was not at all typical of the complex concepts which were beginning to form elsewhere in the field of corporate cost and financial accounting. This simplicity appears to have been characteristic of much of the textile machinery industry, which as late as 1916 was said to have neglected cost accounting to a great extent. At least one large firm at that date was still using a single-entry system for its general books. A smaller firm until 1912 had not taken an inventory of stock on hand for twenty-five or thirty years. Two other large concerns recorded expenditures in detail but had no unit-cost system. The Saco and Pettee Machine Shops had an excellent and detailed unit-cost system in the factory, but there was no distribution of the items of general expenses, taxes, insurance, and other overhead expenses by the general office; thus, while the factory unit costs were complete, a total unit cost could not be shown.[22]

In neither the Newton nor the Biddeford plant does there appear to have been installation of any of the so-called scientific management systems which were becoming so popular. A definite feeling existed that production methods and wage incentive systems already in use in the plants were not only satisfactory but preferable to what Taylor and his followers were teaching to American business. A visitor experienced in the new efficiency engineering systems was being shown through the Newton plant, and was asked whether some such systemization should be introduced there. "Why," he exclaimed, "you already have Scientific Management!"[23]

Profits, Dividends, and a Corporate Change

The records of the Saco and Pettee Machine Shops give qualified answers to the important questions of how much profit was made, how much was distributed, and how much retained in the business. Other sources of information permit, for certain years, a comparison between profits of the company and those of its principal competitors. The corporate reorganization of 1910 is included in this section because it was essentially a device for the distribution of accumulated profits.

A distinction must immediately be made between profits derived from machine-building operations and net profits reported on the books of the company. The latter figures contain so many charges and credits of a non-routine nature and were so conservatively recorded as to be almost meaningless as a measure of operating results. A fairly close approximation of real net profits, however, may be computed from the records.[24]

TABLE 35

NET PROFITS, NEWTON AND BIDDEFORD SHOPS, 1897–1912

Year ending April 30	Newton Shop		Biddeford Shop		Total	
	Dollars	% of Sales	Dollars	% of Sales	Dollars	% of Sales
1898	68,000	14	36,000	11	104,000	13
1899	150,000	25	42,000	8	192,000	17
1900	256,000	23	27,000	4	283,000	14
1901	361,000	28	317,000	15	678,000	27
1902	176,000	23	153,000	16	329,000	20
1903	291,000	24	296,000	17	587,000	21
1904	138,000	14	267,000	15	405,000	15
1905	113,000	11	58,000	5	171,000	8
1906	217,000	20	173,000	15	390,000	23
1907	346,000	26	417,000	25	763,000	26
1908	353,000	27	399,000	23	752,000	25
1909	212,000	18	156,000	10	368,000	14
1910	481,000	30	694,000	30	1,175,000	30
9 months ending December 30, 1910	334,000	33	419,000	32	753,000	33
Year ending December 30, 1911	208,000	20	390,000	24	598,000	22
10 months ending October 30, 1912	130,000	19	407,000	29	537,000	24
Average profit		22		17		20

Source: Saco and Pettee Machine Shops, Ledgers and journals.

For the 1897–1912 period the actual average net profit for the Newton shop was 22.2 per cent of sales annually. For the Biddeford shop the annual average was 16.5 per cent of sales. These summary figures tend to conceal the fact, however, that following extensive plant improvements, the performance of the Biddeford plant improved, and in the 1910–12 period Biddeford profits were relatively higher than those at Newton. Total operating profits for the period were $4,049,400 for the Biddeford shop and $3,836,100 for the Newton shop. These profits are detailed on a year-to-year basis in Table 35.

For the years 1906–14, inclusive, comparisons are available between profits of the Newton and Biddeford Shops and those of the Whitin Machine Works, the Lowell Machine Shop, the Kitson Machine Shop, and Howard & Bullough. The output of these six shops comprised from 80 to 90 per cent of all American-built preparatory machinery; hence the comparison omits no important producer of the type of machinery which constituted the entire business of the Saco and Pettee Machine Shops.[25]

In terms of manufacturing or operating profit the Kitson Machine Shop was by far the most profitable. Howard & Bullough was second, Whitin and the Newton and Biddeford plants were virtually tied for third place, and the Lowell Machine Shop was the least profitable. Average annual profits of the 1906–14 period were as follows, expressed as percentages of sales:

	Manufacturing Profit (Per cent)	Final Profit (Per cent)
Newton Shop	20.5	22.33
Biddeford Shop	20.26	21.84
Lowell Machine Shop	4.22	5.35
Kitson Machine Shop	34.11	35.16
Howard & Bullough	23.40	26.11
Whitin Machine Works	19.82	22.28

The chief value of these comparative statistics lies in the indication that the prosperity of the Saco and Pettee Machine Shops was not an isolated phenomenon, but was characteristic of the industry in general, excepting only the Lowell Machine Shop, which showed good profits in many of these years but suffered occasional heavy losses. The limitations of the statistics are those arising from the averaging process itself, which conceals the interesting fluctuations occurring from year to year and which permits an exceptionally good or bad year to distort the entire picture.

The fact that large profits were being made in Newton and Biddeford, larger even than those apparent to the casual observer, is easily established. The disposition of those profits, either through dividends or through reinvestment in plant, is less easily traced.

From 1897 to 1910, modest dividends were paid out, heavy reserves were accumulated in the business, and large plant expenditures were made. Since many of these latter were charged to current operating expense, the book value of plant increased far less than did the actual plant value and efficiency. Total assets increased from $1,505,734 in 1897 to $5,354,540 in 1910, but less than a million dollars was paid out in this period to the stockholders. This cautious retention of capital in the business paralleled a similar policy pursued by Hale and Snelling in their management of the Pettee Machine Works prior to 1897.

There came a time, however, when the retention of earnings seemed no longer to be necessary. On June 2, 1910, a corporate change was made to permit the distribution of earnings accumulated in the business. Certain assets of the Saco and Pettee Machine Shops were transferred to a new company, organized under Massachusetts statute and called the Saco-Pettee Company. Henceforth this company carried on the business, and the old company remained in existence for some two years pending the liquidation of such assets as were not turned over to the Saco-Pettee Company. The management and ownership of the new company was in every respect identical to that of the old, and the corporate change requires no further consideration than a statement of the financial objectives involved.

The necessity for the formation of a new company appears to have arisen out of legal restrictions against paying dividends out of capital, but the transfer of assets served other purposes. Out of the accumulated reserves of the Saco and Pettee Machine Shops, $1,872,000 was paid in cash to stockholders as liquidation dividends. Assets which had stood conservatively valued on the books of the old company at close to three and one-half million dollars were transferred to the new company at a stated valuation of $1,600,000, the balance having been charged off on the books of the Saco and Pettee Machine Shops preceding transfer. The devaluation enabled the Saco-Pettee Company to commence business with a greatly undervalued plant. Not only was this conservative business policy, but it may have permitted State and local tax savings. Even after liquidation dividends and devaluation of plant, stockholders of the old company were given $1,600,000 par value of stock in the new company in exchange for $800,000 par value of stock in the old—in effect, a 100 per cent stock dividend. On the basis of book value the new stock represented a dividend of substantially more than 100 per cent.

Table 36 shows the steady accumulation of wealth which occurred between 1897 and 1910, the details of the 1910 transfer, and the asset valuations as they stood two years after the formation of the Saco-Pettee Company.

TABLE 36

BALANCE SHEET ACCOUNTS, SACO AND PETTEE MACHINE SHOPS AND SACO-PETTEE COMPANY, 1897–1912

	Saco and Pettee Machine Shops			Saco-Pettee Company	
	Oct. 31, 1898	Oct. 31, 1905	Apr. 30, 1910	June 1, 1910	June 30, 1912
Assets					
Cash	$ 4,267.43	$ 134,151.39	$1,279,555.91	$ 100,000.00	$ 240,851.52
Accounts Receivable	353,393.82	568,416.24	743,323.56	....	980,263.73
Notes Receivable	33,584.98	751,843.68	798,830.38	....	598,718.16
Mill Stocks & Bonds	96,200.00	147,900.00	1,000.00	....	121,026.05
Lowell Machine Shop Stock	....	424,800.00	304,000.00	355,509.57	....
Ashworth Bros. Stock	....	....	....	90,000.00	80,000.00
Inv. on hand	211,258.08	317,149.87	286,890.43	286,890.43	254,599.93
Newton Plant	407,351.88	499,088.82	605,519.28	495,975.00	530,505.07
Newton Real Estate	....	17,685.33	70,970.19	....	88,785.13
Newton New Tools	....	87,948.74	152,650.39	....	28,466.01
Biddeford Plant	304,640.16	532,177.77	532,177.77	271,625.00	247,275.00
Biddeford New Tools & Bldgs	....	321,430.23	534,507.97	....	76,717.00
Power Plant	....	....	40,667.80	....	....
Miscellaneous	....	588.64	4,446.66	....	....
Total Assets	$1,410,696.35	$3,803,180.71	$5,354,540.34	$1,600,000.00	$3,247,207.60
Liabilities & Net Worth					
Accounts Payable	$ 80,415.34	$ 139,235.34	$ 225,512.05	....	$ 100,070.82
Notes Payable	251,000.00	1,090,000.00	....	....	795,000.00
Cap. Stock—Common	800,000.00	800,000.00	800,000.00	$1,600,000.00	1,600,000.00
Cap. Stock—Pref	....	400,000.00	400,000.00	....	....
Res. for Deprec.	200,000.00	600,000.00	1,636,493.40	....	204,148.21
Res. a/c Rec.	....	100,000.00	200,000.00	....	98,026.37
Res. Notes Rec.	....	....	200,000.00	....	59,871.82
Reserve Fund	....	558,917.53	800,000.00	....	....
Profit & Loss Account	79,281.01	115,027.84	1,092,534.89	....	390,090.38
Total Liabilities & Net Worth	$1,410,696.35	$3,803,180.71	$5,354,540.34	$1,600,000.00	$3,247.207.60

Source: Saco and Pettee Machine Shops and Saco-Pettee Company, Ledgers.

Attempts to approximate the returns to investors over the 1898–1912 period meet with many obstacles. Cash dividends paid are easily computed, but there were other returns which must be estimated if a realistic picture of profits is to be obtained. From 1898 to 1912, holders of the common stock of the Saco and Pettee Machine Shops and the Saco-Pettee Company received $2,852,560 in cash dividends. To these must be added what was in effect a stock dividend of 8,000 shares of Eastern Machinery Company stock in 1901. The true value of this stock was the value of the mill securities which the stock represented — possibly $250,000. To these figures should be added $1,017,119, the book value of the Saco-Pettee stock dividend of 1910 and the cash dividends of $180,000 paid by the Eastern Machinery Company from 1901 through 1912. Finally, on November 1, 1912, the Saco-Pettee stockholders received what were, in effect, profits in liquidation amounting to $1,391,000. These profits, which grew out of the formation of the Saco-Lowell Shops, are described fully in Chapter XIII. This brought the total measurable and estimable return to the Saco-Pettee stockholders to $5,690,679, an annual average return over the 1898–1912 period of 47.4 per cent on the original $800,000 investment.[26]

Table 37 presents the yearly dividend record of the Saco and Pettee Machine Shops, the Saco-Pettee Company, and the Eastern Machinery Company.

3. A Restive Spirit in the Shops

Restiveness and Normalcy

The affairs of the Saco and Pettee Machine Shops from 1897 to 1912 were charged with nervous energy. This was particularly true of top-level management, preoccupied not only with manufacturing operations on a vaster scale than ever known before, but also with many subsidiary transactions involving large amounts of capital. But it was true, too, at the factory level of management and in the shops themselves.

Effort to increase operating efficiency was the essence of the restive spirit, and the very evident strength of this drive in a period of great prosperity is not easily explained. The Newton and Biddeford

TABLE 37

DIVIDENDS

SACO AND PETTEE MACHINE SHOPS, SACO-PETTEE COMPANY, AND EASTERN MACHINERY COMPANY, 1898–1912

	Saco and Pettee Machine Shops			Saco-Pettee Company		Eastern Machinery Company
Year	Cash on Common Stock	Cash on Preferred Stock	Stock Dividends	Cash on Common Stock	Stock Dividend	Cash on Common Stock
1898....	$ 48,000	......	......	......	......	......
1899....	48,000	......	......	......	......	......
1900....	48,000	......	......	......	......	......
1901....	48,000	......	$ 250,000[a]	......	......	......
1902....	48,000	......	......	......	......	......
1903....	48,000	......	......	......	......	$ 4,000
1904....	48,000	......	......	......	......	4,000
1905....	48,000	$ 14,400	......	......	......	4,000
1906....	64,000	24,000	......	......	......	9,600
1907....	64,000	24,000	......	......	......	12,800
1908....	64,000	24,000	......	......	......	12,800
1909....	64,000	24,000	......	......	......	12,800
1910....	752,000[b]	52,000[c]	1,017,119[d]	......	......	92,800
1911....	640,000[b]	......	......	$128,000	......	14,400
1912....	512,000[b]	......	......	180,560	$1,124,000[e]	12,800
Total....	$2,544,000	$162,400	$1,267,119	$308,560	$1,124,000	$180,000

[a] Estimated value, Eastern Machinery Company shares.
[b] Liquidation dividends. 1910 total includes $32,000 representing regular semi-annual dividend.
[c] Includes $40,000 redemption premium.
[d] 8,000 shares Saco-Pettee stock, valued at the excess of book value of total issue of Saco-Pettee stock (16,000 shares) over the paid-in or par value of the 8,000 shares of Saco and Pettee Machine Shop stock for which it was exchanged.
[e] Textile Securities Company stock, book value.

Source: Directors' minutes, Saco and Pettee Machine Shops and Saco-Pettee Company; penciled dividend list, Eastern Machinery Company.

shops were not alone in feeling the force of this movement, for it was widespread in America and took many forms. Taylorism and scientific management, increasing recourse to professional specialists, the growth of professionalism within companies, the decline of rule-of-thumb accounting and production methods, the decline of the foreman, the rise of the industrial scientist, and the triumph of the blueprint, all were phases of the moving spirit of the early twentieth century. Electricity and hydroelectric power, better tools, better metals, and new supplies of labor provided abundant opportunities for turning out still better goods at still lower cost. The textile machinery industry produced few great inventions, but was fascinated by the possibilities inherent in simplification of machines and processes and in the application of the theory of interchangeable machine parts.

Perhaps the restive spirit was reactionary, a natural revulsion from the haphazard production methods and managerial techniques of many nineteenth-century business enterprises. In many industries, among them the textile machinery industry, the age of basic inventions had passed, and now was succeeded, temporarily at least, by the age of refinements. Apparent, too, in the drive for greater operating efficiency were the hands of the financial capitalists, the Robert F. Herricks of American business, who sought in balanced managerial emphasis the lower costs which would allow their firms to survive in an increasingly competitive economy.

In the shop the restive spirit was not constructive, as it was at managerial levels, but rather, defensive. While Newton and Biddeford superintendents and their assistants experimented, improved, adapted, rejected, altered, cut, and added, always under pressure from above, some foremen squirmed and some machinists grumbled. These protests were never loud, never serious, and almost never heeded. No person who was associated with the company in this era, manager or workman, attaches any deep significance to the apparently isolated and localized manifestations of unrest which occurred. Labor peace prevailed in the main. Workmen were generally satisfied, and with great frequency lived out their span of working years in the company, often bringing in their sons and grandsons to carry on a family tradition. Some of the plant managers were liked and some were despised, as was normal. Top management was generally respected and admired. Frank J. Hale was not only admired, but genuinely liked. The workmen criticized the company from within and defended it against criticism from without. The intensive pride of workmanship and devotion to the reputation of the company's products was still to be found, though it was naturally not so strong at first among the non-English-speaking newcomers who began to filter into the shops as among the old-time machinists. These general characteristics indicated that labor relations in the Newton and Biddeford shops were completely typical of the American business scene — no better and no worse than in hundreds of shops all over the country.

Normal, too, was the reaction of management in the Newton and Biddeford shops to both the occasional restiveness of employees and the very energetic attacks by government and muckraking journalists upon big business — attacks which tended to place all business on the defensive. Employee clubs were formed, clubhouse and recreational facilities provided, foremen's dinners were promoted, a hotel built at Newton for the accommodation of unmarried workmen, and many other similar projects sponsored, none of which had great long-range significance. Disability compensation and pensions were allocated on an arbitrary basis in accordance with management's estimate of the individual need. These measures were considered by management to be adequate or more than adequate to combat the restive spirit.

Despite these efforts and despite company ownership of some employee dwellings, particularly at Newton, that absence of paternalistic policies which had characterized the earlier years continued to be rather noticeable. Whitin and Draper pointed with pride to what were considered model factory communities at Whitinsville and Hopedale. A vast majority of the machinists and their families at Newton, Biddeford, and Lowell observed an out-of-working-hours independence of the companies which supported them. This condition, the result of the location of the shops in or adjacent to relatively large cities, effectively prohibited attempts by management to impose the "one big happy family" idea upon workmen, a concept which was being widely promoted at the time and which in many cases came to be openly ridiculed and deeply resented by labor. There is some evidence that the management of the Saco and Pettee Machine Shops envied and even tried to emulate the Whitin and Draper communities. The perpetuation of company-employee relations on a man-to-man basis, however, appears to have been an essentially healthy condition, allowing disputes to flare out in the open rather than smolder and spread, and avoiding the dislocations which occurred a generation later when government paternalism was substituted for company paternalism.

Plant, Product, and Processes

The greatest product development in the field of cotton-textile machinery of the 1897–1912 period belongs not to Saco-Lowell but to Draper history. The automatic loom was an invention comparable to those of Paul Moody in an earlier age: startling, unsettling, and such an undeniable improvement as eventually to make obsolete much of what had gone before. The Saco and Pettee Machine Shops made no looms, and they were not directly affected by the Draper innovation. Neither was the company concerned with the comber, for Whitin had secured so substantial a lead in adapting this European-conceived and English-developed machine to the American market that other shops made no attempt to compete.

Efforts in the Newton and Biddeford shops produced a large number of improvements, many of them patentable, but no basically new machines. In the Biddeford shop, Designer William H. Goldsmith succeeded Eustis Morgan, who retired. Under Goldsmith's direction a greatly improved roving frame was brought out in 1908. In the production of this frame the objective of substituting interchangeable for hand-fitted parts was first completely realized. Two years later the Newton shop brought forth a new lap winder, designed to meet the requirements of double carding on the revolving flat cards. An improved drawing frame was brought forth which met with great favor in the trade. The revolving flat card became standardized at 110 flats, in contrast to the 84-flat machine which had first been built. Improvements were made in all machines, principally in simplifying manufacturing operations and in introducing greater accuracy in the finishing of parts so as to eliminate hand-fitting.

The efficiency of the Newton plant, functioning smoothly in the experienced hands of Mills, Nutter, and Penny, at first far surpassed that of the Biddeford plant, where in 1897, it was said, the use of blueprints had not been introduced and pattern-makers worked directly from the draftsmen's drawings. One of Rankeillor's first innovations after his arrival was to convert the shop to United States standard screw sizes. Prior to 1897, special taps had been made for each job in the shop and special screws made to fit. Some of the older Biddeford men still remember the carefully marked paper packages of taps which were stored with each set of patterns.

In certain respects the reorganization of the Biddeford shop did not proceed satisfactorily. The sudden necessity for volume production in a shop which for many years had lived on a short-order basis produced many stresses and strains. Many of the older hands were unable to adjust themselves to the drive and vigor of the new management. Agent Threlfall was primarily a salesman; though he had excellent men under him, some failures occurred in attempting to convert the shop to a mass-production basis. The McMullan spindle constituted one of these failures. This spindle was tremendously efficient and ranked with the best of the Draper spindles when made right. When mass-production techniques were applied to the distinctive "loose-locked step" feature of the McMullan spindle, unsatisfactory results were achieved, and it was not until after 1915 that these production difficulties were resolved and the spindle became as popular as it deserved to be. Perhaps this was another instance where inventive skill outdistanced manufacturing skills.

Despite these various difficulties of adjustment, the discrepancy in efficiency between the Newton and Biddeford shops was gradually reduced and the average operating profit at Newton for the period did not greatly exceed that at Biddeford (Table 35). The situation of two plants under one central management provided certain opportunities for measuring comparative performances, and management was not slow to use standards set in one shop as goals for realization by the other.

At Newton machine-molding techniques were applied to more and more machine parts, and the Biddeford shop, where early attempts to introduce the process appear to have been unsuccessful, benefited from the experience. Attempts to increase the use of molding machines in Biddeford, however, met with such determined non-coöperation from the hand molders that new men were brought in to learn the process. On more than one occasion the heads of these men were targets for balls of molding sand, discreetly fired from cover by the older foundrymen. Active opposition never entirely subsided even when explanations made clear to all persons the competitive necessity for foundry improvements.

In this period, too, spiral gearing was employed in the manufacture of the Biddeford machines. The easy "wiping" motion of this action eliminated much of the wear which had been a major problem in the old-style gears. Designer Goldsmith was first prompted to try this type of gearing after observing the action of an old English lathe in the shop. None of the old bench-trained machinists proved capable of making the complicated calculations involved in cutting the gears, however, and it remained for Roderic Tarr, a young college graduate and son of the sea-captain assistant superintendent, to work out the mathematical problems involved.

There is no question that a high standard of quality was demanded by Frank J. Hale, enforced by superintendents, assistants, and foremen down the line, and observed by the men on the machines. One incident in particular well illustrates Hale's concern over the reputation of the company's products.

In the early years of manufacturing the revolving flat card a method was adopted of fastening the shafts into the main cylinders, which seemed efficient and satisfactory to all concerned. After these cards had been running satisfactorily in mills for ten or fifteen years, some of the shafts became loose in the cylinders, causing the cylinders to run out of true. Requests for repairs began to pour in. Hale was informed of the situation and was advised that customers had no grounds for grievance, inasmuch as the cards had performed satisfactorily for what was considered to be a normal life span. To this argument the general agent turned a deaf ear, insisting that the old cards be repaired at company expense. The cost of this decision was high in terms of dollars, but the company's reputation for guaranteeing the performance of its machines was established beyond all question.[27]

During the 1897–1912 period, plant capacity at both Newton and Biddeford was tremendously increased. In 1899 a large new shop and foundry were added at Newton. Five years later an addition measuring 509 feet in length, 65 feet in width, and five stories in height was built at the Biddeford plant, at a cost of approximately $200,000. Both plants were lighted by electricity at the turn of the century. Between 1910 and 1913 the Newton shops were enlarged still further, and a new steam-generating plant and a chimney 150 feet high were erected. As this chimney slowly rose over the litter of construction in the shop yard, General Agent Hale was enticed into a rash wager that he would not only climb the chimney but be the first to climb it. As soon as the last bricks had been laid, Hale started up the perilously small ladder. As he toiled upward word flew around the shop—"The Agent's up the chimney!" When he reached the top three cheers rang out from the crowd of men assembled below, and the general agent gaily tipped his hat. Perhaps it was human touches such as this which kept Hale, now wealthy, successful, and an important figure in the financial world, far closer to the men in the shop than most business men of comparable stature and position.

Shop Management, Labor, and Labor Relations

Company and government-compiled labor records suggest the interesting conclusion that average wages in the Newton and Biddeford shops in the first decade of the twentieth century were not much, if any, higher than they had been in the 1870's, 1880's, and 1890's. In some instances they were not so high. These records, however, are fragmentary and must be used with caution.

Average daily earnings at the Biddeford shop, for example, had varied, in the 1870–97 period, from $1.25 to $1.70. At Newton, average daily earnings had been $1.57 in 1882, a year of considerable activity. In no one of the three years (1906, 1908, and 1910) for which information is available were the high points of the earlier years equaled. In 1910, a year of great activity, average daily earnings were $1.65 at Newton and $1.54 at Biddeford. The Biddeford and Newton earnings, however, compared favorably with other shops in the industry. The Department of Commerce report of 1916 gives the information presented in the tabulation on page 443.

This same government report stated that the introduction of many automatic and semi-automatic machine tools and of machine molds in the foundry had permitted the use of unskilled and semi-

MACHINE HANDS IN COTTON-SPINNING MACHINERY PLANTS

	Earnings per Hour	Average Working Hours per Week	Average Earnings in Full-time Week
1906	*Cents*		
No. 1 (Newton)[a]............	16.46	58.00	9.55
No. 2 (Biddeford)...........	15.24	58.00	8.38
No. 3 (Lowell Mach. Shop)..	15.94	58.00	9.25
No. 5 (Howard & Bullough)..	14.68	58.00	8.51
No. 6 (Whitin).............	15.25	58.00	8.85
All Establishments..........	15.60	57.24	8.95
1908			
No. 1 (Newton).............	17.89	45.00	8.05
No. 2 (Biddeford)...........	16.91	55.00	9.30
No. 3 (Lowell Mach. Shop)..	18.36	45.00	8.26
No. 5 (Howard & Bullough)..	18.21	55.00	10.02
No. 6 (Whitin).............	18.03	51.40	9.32
All Establishments..........	17.94	49.36	8.90
1910			
No. 1 (Newton).............	17.52	58.00	10.16
No. 2 (Biddeford)...........	16.92	55.00	9.31
No. 3 (Lowell Mach. Shop)..	16.35	55.00	8.99
No. 5 (Howard & Bullough)..	17.00	45.00	7.65
No. 6 (Whitin).............	17.90	57.00	10.20
All Establishments..........	17.57	56.36	9.94

[a] Names of plants not supplied in original report.

skilled men, and had reduced the number of journeyman machinists and skilled hand molders to a minimum. This increased ability to utilize progressively less skilled labor, in place of the old-time apprentice-trained machinist, accounted in part for the failure of wage levels to rise over a period when American wages in general were increasing. An obvious conclusion to draw would be that, although average wages had been kept from rising by the use of more and more unskilled labor, individual wage rates had increased. This conclusion cannot be substantiated by the inadequate information

TABLE 38

AVERAGE WAGE RATES PER HOUR, NEWTON PLANT, 1892–1910

	Cents per Hour			Net Advance or Decline
	1892	1903	1910	1892–1910
				(In cents)
Carpenter	20.4	19.0	20.7	+ .3
Painter	13.7	13.0	12.5	−1.2
Drawing frame job	15.8	16.8	17.7	+1.9
Setting up, drawing	19.1	19.1	21.7	+2.6
Polishing Room	22.8	18.8	19.1	−3.7
Sheet Iron	16.2	15.5	16.5	+ .3
Flat Department	16.6	18.0	20.5	+3.9
Card Machine job	16.5	15.5	16.7	+ .2
Cylinder Room	19.2	16.7	17.7	−1.5
Setting up, Cards	19.8	18.4	19.8	...
Molders	22.4	18.8	20.7	−1.7
Coremakers	15.0	12.0	16.6	+1.6
Net advance				2.7

Source: Memorandum book of Oscar E. Nutter.

TABLE 39

AVERAGE HOURLY WAGE RATES, NEWTON SHOP AND FOUNDRY, 1900–1912

Year	Shop	Foundry
	(In cents)	
1900	17	25
1901	17	25
1902	17	25
1903	17	25
1904	17	26
1905	17	26
1906	17	26
1907	17	26
1908	17	26
1909	18	27
1910	18	27
1911	18	27
1912	18	27

Source: Saco-Lowell records, Totals notebooks.

which has survived. Figures for the Newton plant, given in Table 38, show that individual wage rates in 1910 were only a little higher than they had been in 1892. Average wage rates for the entire Newton shop and foundry, given in Table 39, show only a slight increase from 1900 to 1912.

Accompanying the increased use of semi-skilled labor were changes in the character of the labor force, alterations in the direction of plant operations, and a growing dissatisfaction with training methods, all of which movements were at work but none of which culminated in the 1897–1912 period.

In both the Newton and Biddeford shops in 1897 the working forces were composed almost entirely of Yankee, English, and Irish help. A few French-Canadian men had entered the Biddeford shop. After 1897, immigration increased rapidly, and a flood of families from Canada were drawn to the Biddeford cotton mills, and then into the machine shop. These men made excellent workers, though they shared the clannish propensities of most newly made American citizens. By 1912, few of them had risen to positions of high responsibility; even at this early date, however, it was evident that the requisite abilities were present and only limited experience on the part of the workers and considerable prejudice on the part of old-time Yankee foremen stood in the way of advancement.

At the turn of the century there were no workmen in the Newton plant who could not speak English, though many spoke it with a brogue or a burr or a twang. In 1901 and 1902 the first non-English-speaking workmen were hired. By 1912, 51 per cent of the workmen were Yankee, English, or Irish; 39 per cent were Polish; 8 per cent were Armenian; and 2 per cent were Italian. A high percentage (48 per cent) of the Polish and Armenian men were employed in the foundry.

In these years the foremen were shorn of some of their responsibilities, though this trend did not progress so far in the Biddeford and Newton plants as it had done at Lowell, where a high degree of centralized production control had been instituted by 1905. In both plants foremen retained much independence and, at Biddeford, the power of hiring and firing and wage setting. At Biddeford departmental independence impaired operating efficiency. There was competition between foremen for labor, and discontent arose out of differing wage rates for comparable jobs in the various departments. It was the rare foreman who had an adequate perspective on the relative position of his own department in the firm or who understood the operations of departments other than the one over which he presided.

In the Biddeford shop Agent William V. Threlfall was replaced in 1904 by E. E. Blake, a graduate of the Massachusetts Institute of Technology who had trained in Newton as a draftsman and had done some selling. Blake was a good mechanic — able, thorough, not quick to form an opinion, but sure of his stand once taken. He instituted the practice of daily meetings of all foremen, the object of which was to reduce departmental friction and impart to all the "Bosses" a feeling for over-all manufacturing objectives. These meetings were the nucleus of what was later to become a production department. It was not until 1917, however, that centralization of production controls had progressed to the point where the hiring, firing, and wage-fixing responsibilities of the foremen were turned over to a central authority, and an employment manager was engaged.[29] Alexander Rankeillor was made superintendent under Blake, following the retirement of Gilman P. Littlefield.

The apprentice training system of earlier years had fallen into disuse with the rise of the trade schools in the late nineteenth century, but it was revived when those schools were unable to supply the demand for graduates and were believed, moreover, to be favoring theory at the expense of practice. Results were far from satisfactory, however. Under increasing pressure to reduce costs, foremen preferred to put new workers on one job and keep them there rather than move them from place to place. Neither the textile training schools at Lowell, New Bedford, and elsewhere nor the apprentice training programs in the shops were satisfactorily developing machinists possessing the breadth of practical knowledge of the old shop-trained foremen, and foreman replacement was a major shop problem both at Biddeford and Newton throughout the 1897–1912 period. Hope for improvement appeared to lie only in taking the administration of the training program out of the hands of the foremen and vesting it in a central authority. By 1912 this apparently had been done in neither plant.

These various movements had both a cause and an effect relationship to a number of strikes which occurred at both Biddeford and Newton. The early twentieth century was not a period of obvious labor unrest in the textile machinery industry. Working conditions, wages, and benefits compared favorably with those in other industries, and the Saco and Pettee Machine Shops appears to have been no better and no worse an employer than Whitin, Draper, Lowell, and the other machine shops. Nevertheless, there were points of irritation, some of which were purely local and transitory, while others reflected movements of a national scope.

Between 1898 and 1905, union activity in the United States increased perceptibly and was more successful than at any time since the middle 1880's. The American Federation of Labor increased its membership, and in the metal-fabricating fields the International Association of Machinists and the International Molders' Union drove for recognition. Labor gains and labor defeats were recorded in the first decade of the century, but the tangible net outcome of the struggle was less important than the publicity accorded the struggle itself. The precedent for unionization and strong union activity was amply established in the skilled and semi-skilled trades — trades such as textile-machinery building.

On a local scale the drive for greater manufacturing efficiency in the Newton and Biddeford shops appears to have created more than the usual number of grievances, real or imagined. Evidence on this point is not conclusive, but the fact is worth noting that the most frequent and severe disturbances occurred at Biddeford in the five years following the installation of the new management, a period of wholesale adjustments within the plant.

The first disturbance at Biddeford occurred on May 3, 1898, less than six months after Agent Threlfall had commenced the task of reorganizing the shop. At this time a company union, which appears to have been formed a short time before, demanded a 20 per cent increase in pay. Threlfall replied that no answer could be made to these demands until the operating returns for the period ending April 30 had been tabulated. The union then called a strike, which took four hundred machinists out of the plant. Only the foundrymen, who had their own union, remained at work. The strike was quiet, orderly, and ineffective. The men remained out for a few days and finally returned to work after Threlfall's assurance that their jobs would be restored and an examination made of cases where pay raises seemed to be deserved. This was the first strike in the history of the Biddeford shop, and the fact that it was visited upon that management which was replacing the inequities of the McMullan era with efficiency, fairness, and order is both ironic and logical.

The foundry had been the first department of the Biddeford shop to organize a union. This was understandable, for in the heat and grime tempers flared and quarrels were not infrequent. The introduction of machine molding, moreover, introduced dissatisfactions not present earlier. In either 1898 or 1899 a strike of two weeks' duration occurred, apparently over the issue of recognition of the molders' union. Threlfall was adamant, the union leaders are said to have done little to press their claims on management, and the men privately approached Assistant Superintendent Rankeillor to ask him to get them back to work. Whether as a result of this strike or some later bargaining, the founders' union by 1900 had gained recognition and had signed a one-year agreement with the company. By this time, and possibly earlier, the local union had become affiliated with the International Molders' Union, a nation-wide organization.

On March 12, 1900, the second major strike at Biddeford commenced, after the following exchange of communications between Agent Threlfall and the Biddeford & Saco Federal Labor Union, an American Federation of Labor affiliate:

March 10, 1900

William V. Threlfall, Esq.

Dear Sir; — I have been requested to inform you by the members of the Biddeford & Saco Federal Labor Union that we as a body shall stop work on Monday noon March 12th at 1 o'clock if it is not made a union shop as requested to you by our standing committee.

Hoping to receive a favorable reply etc.

[unsigned]

To all concerned.

Answering the above request which we absolutely refuse to grant. All those that have fully decided to leave work because we refuse to dictate to anyone as to how they shall conduct their personal affairs, will arrange to do so at 12 o'clock noon, and *take their belongings with them,* as none will be allowed to return but for the purpose of going to work.

Those returning and continuing to work will be treated *fairly* at all times and *no discrimination* will be made on account of their *social,* political or religious connection.

W. V. Threlfall, Agt.

On March 13 the following notice was posted in the shop and published in two local newspapers:

Notice

All hands that left work Monday noon will be paid off in full Wednesday afternoon at 3 o'clock, at which time they sever all connections with this company. This notice takes effect whether application for back pay is made or not.

Those desirous of being rehired will signify their intentions as soon as possible, as only a limited amount of time can be allowed for applications to be made, which will be considered individually.

Saco & Pettee Machine Shops
W. V. Threlfall, Agt.

This strike, commenced in a mutually uncompromising spirit, took six hundred machinists out of the plant, leaving only the foundrymen. It came at a time of frantic demand for textile machinery. Threlfall's sentiments were emphatic. "We do not propose that these men shall run our business," he stated to a reporter for the Biddeford *Weekly Journal,* "unless they want to take the plant and pay us its value. If they are ready to do this they can have the plant." To this bit of palpable bluster the agent added that arrangements had been made to have orders on hand taken care of elsewhere. This threat of using the Newton plant was scarcely an effective bargaining tool, for it was obvious that the Newton plant, too, was rushed with work and in no case could undertake to build the type of machines produced at Biddeford. Threlfall stated, however, that if the Biddeford shop was closed down, the entire business might be moved to Newton.

Although the basic issue of the strike was the union's request for a closed shop, the precipitating factors had only indirectly involved company management. A very high percentage of the employees were members of the union. Less than 10 per cent of the 600 workmen involved in the strike were non-union men. These few non-union workers, the union claimed, took the job work which union men were forbidden to accept and then crowded the union men working under them by steadily increasing the standard output required. The quarrel initially was with these non-union workmen and not with management.

Local sentiment appeared to condemn the strike, which was laid by some at the door of agitators. Merchants refused to carry the accounts of the strikers, but the strike wore on for four weeks, despite efforts of the State Board of Trade's arbitration committee. On April 10 the workmen voted to return to work, the only concession given by Threlfall being a promise to take them back, as far as possible, on their old jobs.

Notwithstanding this overwhelming union defeat, the foundrymen went on strike four years later over the same issue of a closed shop. Their work stoppage lasted for more than ten weeks, and Threlfall refused to concede in any way or even to confer with the union committee. In this foundrymen's strike in 1904 the use of strike-breakers was resorted to, and violence flared as twenty-one of these men arriving on the train from Boston were met at the depot by the striking molders. Little information is available about this strike beyond the guarded allusions which appeared in the local newspaper. The strikers launched a damaging counter-attack to the injunction which the company secured against their picketing activities. Union molders from outside the local area secured employment in the foundry by representing themselves to be non-union men. Once inside the shop these men commenced a systematic and damaging sabotage campaign, which resulted in the destruction of many of the best patterns and the throwing of many hundreds of patterns into the adjacent river. This strike terminated in another union defeat, but at a heavy cost to the company.[30]

The arrival of a new agent in Biddeford in 1904 ushered in a period of labor peace, and it was not until 1910 that union activity on both a local and a national scale became intensified again. In that year a spokesman from the American Federation of Labor's International Association of Machinists campaigned for members in Biddeford and attacked company management in phrases which were already becoming timeworn. It was the Molders' International Union, however, which instituted effective action with a claim that a minimum wage of $2.75 a day in the foundry and recognition of a nine-hour day be formally written into the union contract. Since the company was paying most foundrymen more than the requested minimum and already had instituted a nine-hour day in the plant, the union requests involved no large costs, and in May, 1910, were acceded to. The fact that the company and union representatives were able to settle even minor differences without recourse to a strike indicated that the Biddeford management no longer entertained the earlier inflexible attitude toward unions and union demands.

At Newton the labor story was different, and the difference may well have been the lack of a man of Agent Threlfall's uncompromising disposition. Here the trouble, with one exception, was confined to the foundry, where, in the words of one of the Newton men, the molders wanted peace but were willing to fight to get it! From 1908 to 1914, there appear to have been not more than three strikes, none of which was of long duration, and all of which were settled on terms favorable to the company. Newton policy in strikes appeared to be that the dispute must be settled substantially on the company's terms, but once the men were back at work certain concessions might be granted.

At Newton, to be sure, was to be found that same implacable determination to fight organized labor which was almost universal throughout American industry. When it was discovered that a boathouse across the street from the shop was being used for labor meetings, the structure was purchased by the company and closed to such gatherings. Nevertheless, there is little question that labor relations at Newton were far more adeptly handled than they had been in Biddeford between 1898 and 1904. Possibly something had been learned from the earlier Biddeford experience. More probably, the willingness of Newton management to confer, explain, and reason with the strikers explains the better labor record. That this willingness was by no means universal in labor disputes of the day, events at the Biddeford shop had clearly shown. A part of the success at Newton in getting the men back to work without serious work stoppages is attributable to the personality of General Agent Hale, for there is no doubt that he was held in high regard by the men, even though, as time went on, his activities came to be centered in the Boston office and he consciously refrained from taking part in labor disputes. Superintendent Nutter did most of the negotiating, and his success lay in an ability to expound the company viewpoint quietly, simply, and forcibly, with none of the bluster which many so-called negotiators brought to the conference table. On one occasion the local parish priest joined with Nutter and a union committee in reaching an agreement which brought the men back to work.

The fact that in the period from 1897 to 1912 labor disputes occurred at Newton and Biddeford which had been noticeably absent in earlier years must be carefully qualified and placed in true perspective. Here were the unsettling manifestations of a concept of labor relations which the pioneering, individualistic American tradition of enterprise had ill prepared the American business man to recognize, much less to accept. Only untutored emotionalism can condemn the management of the Saco and Pettee Machine Shops for following out the dictates of two centuries of world-wide economic thinking. The death throes of *laissez-faire* were not pleasant to watch, even to those who stood to profit by its demise.

Nevertheless, the company which grew out of the merger of 1897 was outstandingly successful from all points of view, including that of the men in the shop. The basic benefit derived was a great net improvement in the competitive position of the two specialized shops which were thus united. The Newton shop derived sustenance from the addition of the Biddeford line. The Biddeford shop was forcibly torn out of a state of stagnation by the dynamic new management. In 1897 only 75 men had been at work at Biddeford. By 1902 employment there passed the 1,200 mark, more than double the number of men then at work at Newton. The process of introducing efficiency into the plant at Biddeford had been unusually trying, not only because of deep-rooted conditions and traditions there, but because the dictates of efficiency had initially been allowed by local management to submerge even the most elementary requirements of good labor relations. Central management at Boston may well have been at fault, not in insisting upon the installation of modern operating methods, but in allowing local management a free hand and assessing results only in terms of the figures sent to Newton each month. This fault was corrected, and after 1905 labor relations at Newton and Biddeford were comparable to those in other companies and industries where ways were constantly being sought to reduce operating costs — a quest which was absolutely vital to the health of companies and the maintenance of employment.

For the buyer of textile machinery and the stockholders of the company, the merger of 1897 had been undeniably profitable. The latter garnered the profits which accrued from the resuscitation of the Biddeford plant, the continued increase in efficiency of the Newton organization, and the over-all net gains resulting from the union of the two lines. The welding of the new organization into an immensely effective producer had given the textile industry no revolutionary machines. Nevertheless, this was not, as some have stated, a period of complete technological stagnation. The cumulative effect of minor improvements was considerable, though admittedly less than at many times in the past. More important than these, however, were the new machinery-building skills which were being learned — skills in precision hitherto unknown which were to make possible improvements hitherto unattainable.

The history of the Saco and Pettee Machine Shops, in short, was typical of American business of the day. The managerial and financial success of Hale and Snelling was typical of the American entrepreneur working in a period of expansion and prosperity. The profits of the business were typically large. The labor experience was typical of an age in which a growing restiveness was successfully fought and accorded only minor concessions. The great and increasing production skill of plant management was typical of years which were endowing the American people with more and better material goods than the citizens of any other nation.

General Agent Hale and Treasurer Snelling might well have

been content to perpetuate conditions as they existed in 1912. Both men could take pride in the company they had built. Affairs in Newton and Biddeford were organized to permit both men to engage in activities outside the company. Despite a geographical division of manufacturing facilities, the organization was now a smoothly operating unit. Technical and administrative problems alike had been reduced to a minimum. The directorate was tractable and trustworthy, and the stockholders were content. Here, clearly, was a point at which business evolution might advantageously be halted. Yet, even as this plateau of success was being reached by Hale and Snelling, new challenges were being formulated. Business evolution, like biological evolution, could be manipulated but not arrested.

Part III

THE SACO-LOWELL SHOPS 1912–1949

In 1905 Robert F. Herrick had assumed control of the Lowell Machine Shop and brought about the purchase of the Kitson Machine Company. Five years later Herrick translated his control over the Lowell shop into outright ownership, and began to look for someone who could relieve him of his increased managerial burden. He turned to Frank J. Hale and R. Paul Snelling, who had united the machine shops at Newton and at Biddeford into an immensely aggressive and profitable organization. The union of the Lowell Machine Shop and the Saco-Pettee Company, however, was by no means a foregone conclusion.

Hale and Snelling were not impressed by Herrick's consolidation proposition. They thought little of the Lowell Shop and less of its products. Union with this company would, to be sure, enable them to offer customers a complete line of cotton machinery, but the Saco-Pettee Company was already doing a larger business than was Lowell with its full line of cotton machinery, its worsted, and its silk machinery combined. The merchandising advantages of merger seemed scarcely sufficient to Hale and Snelling to counterbalance the managerial difficulties which would arise out of a consolidation, or to offset the disadvantages which might accrue to the Saco-Pettee Company as a result of combination with a weaker organization.

Herrick's persistence in urging his viewpoint upon Hale and Snelling was entirely in character. In office, club, and home he hammered away at the idea of merged interests. In his way stood the prejudice which existed among leaders in the industry against the Lowell Shop, prejudice which was well founded in the Shop's erratic performance over the immediately preceding decade. The picture which Herrick painted was that of a colossus in the textile machinery industry whose strengths would be the specialization of the Newton, Biddeford, and Kitson shops and the diversification of the Lowell Shop. However, the specific offer which Herrick made, rather than the prospects he drew, was the deciding factor, and Hale and Snelling finally (in 1912) agreed to participate on terms which were most favorable to their company.

The chapters which follow trace the Saco-Lowell story through a third major phase of development. The formative years of the parent shops saw technical and organizational problems met and solved. The middle years had brought great prosperity, a product of internal strengths and expansion of the textile-machinery market, but had culminated in stagnation for two of the three original parent shops. The years which follow 1912 are dominated by two major struggles: a long-continued effort to achieve unity in the Saco-Lowell organization and the cessation of expansion in the textile industry. From these two forces — one internal and the other external — came a business crisis and a managerial failure which all but destroyed the company. Then followed reorganization, retrenchment, and a rekindling of the inventive fires which had smoldered and smoked but had not flared for nearly a century. Two wars did not interrupt but rather hastened and accentuated existing trends in many areas of business activity. These chapters end, as they begin, on a keynote of reorganization and change, and it is a powerful sense of movement, both directed and uncontrollable, which forms the common bond between the earliest and the most recent years of Saco-Lowell history.

CHAPTER XIII

THE HERRICK ERA
1912–1926

1. Formation of the Saco-Lowell Shops

On November 1, 1912, the Saco-Lowell Shops came into existence to unite in one corporate enterprise the machine shops at Lowell, at Newton, and at Biddeford. The basic plan by which the Lowell Machine Shop and the Saco-Pettee Company were combined to effect this corporate unity was complicated in detail but simple in essence. The Lowell Machine Shop changed its name to the Saco-Lowell Shops. The Saco-Pettee Company changed its name to the Textile Securities Company. The Saco-Lowell Shops then issued stock to the Textile Securities Company in exchange for most of the assets and all the liabilities of the latter, and the Textile Securities Company continued in existence under an amended charter as a mill-security holding company, owned and controlled by the old Saco-Pettee stockholders.

The 1845 charter of the Lowell Machine Shop was retained by the Saco-Lowell Shops, after it had been amended to fit the new name and circumstances. Thus the 1912 transaction was not actually a merger but a purchase by the Lowell Machine Shop of the Saco-Pettee assets. The corporate line of descent of the Lowell Shop, which technically began with the formation of the Lowell Machine Shop in 1845 and actually began with the incorporation of the Boston Manufacturing Company in 1813, remained unbroken. Sentiment played a part in retaining the old Lowell charter, but there was sentiment on the other side of the family tree as well. Many at Newton looked with regret at the elimination of the Pettee name from the company title and were quick to characterize the 1912 purchase as a clear case of the tail wagging the dog.

The financial details of the formation of the Saco-Lowell Shops are found in Appendix 13. The essence of the transaction was the exchange of $1,600,000 of Lowell common stock for net assets carried on the books of the Saco-Pettee Company at $1,008,951, a book profit to the Saco-Pettee Company of slightly more than half a million dollars. If, as seems more realistic, the book rather than the par value of the Lowell stock is used in the computation, the profit was in excess of a million and a quarter dollars.[1] Control of the newly formed Saco-Lowell Shops appears to have remained with Herrick and Wilmot Evans, despite the fact that they owned only 7,500 shares of stock, as compared with the 16,000 shares turned over to the Saco-Pettee group. These latter shares were widely split, while Herrick and Evans retained their blocks of stock, which were by far the largest individual holdings in the company. Voting control, however, never became an issue of importance, for the Herrick, Evans, and Saco-Pettee interests worked closely together.

Management of the Saco-Lowell Shops was firmly placed in the hands of the Saco-Pettee group, for this had been Herrick's object in seeking the consolidation. The revised bylaws enlarged the directorate from five to nine members, of whom six (Hale, Snelling, Shaw, Amory, Milliken, and Rogerson) were former Saco-Pettee directors. The other directors were Herrick, Wilmot Evans, and James C. Howe, the last-named having come to the Lowell Machine Shop shortly before the consolidation to serve as vice-president and general manager and to relieve Herrick of some of his responsibilities. Herrick was named chairman of the board of directors. The principal officers of the newly formed company were Henry S. Shaw, president; R. Paul Snelling, treasurer; Frank J. Hale, general agent; and James C. Howe, vice-president. The officers and directors of the Saco-Lowell Shops are listed in Appendix 11, Table F.

In the lower levels of management important changes were made as General Agent Hale moved to eliminate what were thought to be points of weakness in the organization. John Hill, Southern agent of the Lowell Machine Shop, retired; A. H. Washburn, Southern agent of the Saco-Pettee Company, was dismissed. Rogers Davis, Hill's assistant, was named Southern agent of the Saco-Lowell Shops. Some important changes were made at the Newton,

Biddeford, and Kitson Shops. Superintendent A. H. Morton, of the Lowell shop, was replaced by William H. Thompson, Jr., who had been trained in the Lowell organization and was believed to be more coöperative than his predecessor. The replacement of the highly competent but unconventional Morton was admitted in later years to have been a mistake.[2]

Immediate steps were taken to eliminate duplication in the organization. The Atlanta office of the Lowell Machine Shop was closed and its business transferred to the Charlotte office which had served Saco-Pettee. A branch office which had been set up in Atlanta by the Saco-Pettee Company was retained. A new Boston office was engaged at 77 Franklin Street, replacing both Herrick's office at 84 State Street and the Saco-Pettee office at 78 Chauncy Street as the seat of top management. More important than these, however, were the product changes which consolidation implied. These affected chiefly the Lowell Machine Shop line. The manufacture of cards, railway heads, drawing frames, roving and spinning frames, and spoolers at Lowell was discontinued, though repair parts for these machines continued to be made when demanded. The Lowell shop occasionally built these machines in periods of very active business or when customers insisted on having Lowell machines, but more and more their manufacture was centralized in the shops at Newton and Biddeford. The chief function of the Lowell shop was to turn out worsted and silk machinery and the various types of cotton machinery (twisters, spoolers, warpers, and slashers) not built in the other shops. The Saco-Lowell manufacturing organization, therefore, consisted of one diversified and three specialized shops. Cards and drawing frames were built at Newton; roving and spinning frames at Biddeford; and picking machinery at Kitson. Lowell manufactured all other machines, and was given any new product line which henceforth was manufactured, becoming virtually a job shop.

The psychological effect of the formation of the Saco-Lowell Shops appears to have been considerable, both within the company and in the industry. The Whitin Machine Works could scarcely view the events of 1912 with equanimity, for the consolidation immediately usurped Whitin's position as the largest textile-machine shop in the country and probably raised fears as to the competitive power of the new company. Whitin, moreover, could no longer obtain access to the Kitson line and was forced (in 1913) to purchase the Atherton Picking Machinery Company and to develop its own picker line.

Within the framework of the newly formed Saco-Lowell Shops there was some uncertainty and considerable grumbling. Much of this feeling was not justified; a great deal of it consisted of the natural unrest which occurs whenever the mental and physical habits of men are even slightly altered. Some of the dissatisfaction pointed to significant dangers which must be overcome. The Lowell shop was being crushed, it was said, in the interest of the Newton and Biddeford shops, and Lowell men were not being recognized by a management dominated by Newton men. Only the most objective among the Lowell employees could see that the Lowell Shop was the weakest link in the newly forged corporate chain, and that it was here that the most drastic changes necessarily must be made.

Charges of such a kind were evidence of the intense individualism of the company's component shops, individualism which arose out of generations of machine-building experience under independent management and which was not to be snuffed out by a mere legal unification. So long as the four shops remained in existence, rivalry and jealousy were to be found. Rivalry, of course, could be healthy, but jealousy could certainly not be allowed to breed and spread. The consolidation of 1912 created a corporation, but left for the new managers the most difficult task of creating a unified company.

2. Control and Top Management

Control of the Saco-Lowell Shops was securely vested in the hands of Robert F. Herrick, Sr., throughout the entire 1912–26 period. That control, based upon ownership which at no time exceeded one-tenth of the outstanding voting stock, was never challenged, but it was nonetheless a determining factor in the direction of the affairs of the company.[8]

Herrick held fast to his determination to entrust the management of the company to Hale and Snelling, while he occupied himself with a multitude of other activities not connected with the Saco-Lowell Shops. Herrick, however, attended all directors' meetings and took an active part in formulating company policy. Herrick, Hale, and Snelling worked well together, and each held the others in highest esteem. Hale and Herrick were particularly close, an affinity which was natural between two self-made men, and one in which the more aloof Snelling could scarcely have a share. The 1912 consolidation was made the more effective for the personal harmony which existed between Hale, Snelling, and Herrick; in later years, when events occurred which could well have split these men apart, no rift occurred.[4]

For ten years, through a period of great prosperity, Herrick, Hale, and Snelling guided the company. The detailed management of Hale and Snelling was in every respect similar to that of earlier years in the Saco and Pettee Machine Shops. Able superintendents were chosen to operate the shops and were given great freedom from central control, although operating figures were closely scrutinized in the Boston office for evidence of developing weakness. Both Hale and Snelling, but particularly Hale, continued to give much attention to sales, and these men in person placed many of the largest orders.

The great activity of the postwar years from 1918 to 1921 indicated that the company was well organized to produce and sell machinery. Certainly it was immensely prosperous. As operations became more and more extensive and profitable, Hale and Snelling began to take a less active part in management. It was clear that the time was not far off when the company could be turned over to younger hands to manage, and it seemed best that this be done while the experienced men were still present to exercise guidance.

In 1919 Robert F. Herrick, Jr., then twenty-six years of age, came to work for the company, and was the obvious nomination of his father to assume the position of general agent.[5] There could be no dissenting voice successfully raised against this choice, for Herrick's power in the company was uncontestable. The fact that the nomination was accepted by Hale and Snelling without question, and that both men did all in their power to advise and assist the young man, was a tribute to the high esteem in which they held Robert F.

Herrick, Sr., for Hale had a son and Snelling had a nephew who, though younger than Herrick's son, might conceivably have been considered, in time, as candidates for the highest managerial positions in the company. There is some evidence, however, that the entry of Robert F. Herrick, Jr., into the company hastened the retirement of both Hale and Snelling.

Retirement of General Agent Hale and Treasurer Snelling occurred in 1923, but it was a qualified retirement. Hale and Snelling were named vice-presidents, and remained close to the business to advise the less experienced men who succeeded them. Robert F. Herrick, Jr., was named general agent, and Parkman D. Howe, who had been trained in the mill-management department of Lockwood, Greene & Company and had come to Saco-Lowell to succeed his brother James, was named treasurer.[6] In the next three years several additions were made to the directorate, but the new appointments had relatively little effect upon the course of company history. The many-generations-old Lowell policy was followed of picking sons of deceased directors, men whose names lent honor to the Board, and men who might be professionally useful. Interestingly enough, it was Paul Snelling who had the most to say about who should be a director. The dignity and prestige of the Saco-Lowell Board was Snelling's particular pride, and at least one outstanding nomination was vetoed by this conservative Bostonian financier.

The year 1923 marked the end of the tranquility which had existed in top managerial levels in the company since its formation in 1912. Robert Herrick, Jr., was eager, enthusiastic, energetic, and ambitious. He entered the company in a period of great activity and had never personally known anything but exceptional prosperity. Like most new managers he saw many things to be done, and with the financial means abundantly available and many immediate precedents to follow, he proceeded to get them done in the most expeditious manner possible. Herrick introduced new men to the company, some of them his college associates, as inexperienced as was Herrick himself in business. Quite irrespective of the abilities of Herrick's friends (and certain of them were men of high ability) friction was generated, particularly in the Lowell Shop, as men of longer experience were replaced or passed by. Other innovations by the younger Herrick produced upheavals at the operating level in all shops, and his attitude toward labor and toward many of the shop managers was uncompromising. Historical perspective reveals that the unrest which permeated the company following Robert F. Herrick, Jr.'s, appointment as general agent was normal, the seemingly inevitable by-product of managerial transition. Unrest had been noticeable at Lowell in 1912 and in Biddeford in 1897, to recall the most recent examples within the company. Such troubled periods usually were of short duration, as the new men and the old organization adjusted to each other. The sequence of events after 1919, however, sharply emphasizes the transitional difficulties which beset the younger Herrick's administration. Had the winds of business fortune blown from a different quarter, this would be a forgotten episode in a history replete with unimportant and temporary maladjustments.

There is abundant evidence that the son had inherited much of the ability of the father, but the guidance of older and more seasoned men was clearly needed. The younger Herrick of necessity sought the advice of Hale and Snelling when he first assumed office; but more and more, as he gained confidence, he went his own way. Neither Hale nor Snelling ever carried issues to Robert Herrick, Sr., or voiced to him whatever uneasiness they may have felt. Perhaps this was a mistake. On the other hand it seems difficult to believe that Herrick, Sr., was unaware of the course of events, and he may have hoped that everything would work out in time.

No break occurred between the old management and the new, but the feeling of responsibility which Hale and Snelling felt for the well-being of the company inevitably lessened as their counsel was ignored. Out of esteem for Robert Herrick, Sr., Hale and Snelling continued to give their advice when asked, but others in the managerial ranks who were bound by no such personal ties found continued coöperation impossible. The younger Herrick alienated powerful interests in the directorate. His action in withdrawing company funds from the Boston Safe Deposit & Trust Company and distributing them among other banks deeply offended Charles E. Rogerson, who represented an important contact with Boston financial circles. Parkman D. Howe, the new treasurer, in whom

Hale and Snelling had come to place great confidence and hope, left the company after serving for only a year. The office of general agent was then abolished and Robert Herrick, Jr., was named treasurer.

These conflicts were unfortunate and largely unnecessary. The impact of personal, non-business influences upon the course of business is clearly evident in the affairs of the Saco-Lowell Shops from 1919 to 1926. Rarely do these, among the most basic drives in business history, come to the surface where they can be recognized in all their importance. Herrick's inexperience and his personal conflicts alike might well have worked out satisfactorily, had there been time. In innumerable similar circumstances initial maladjustments of young men succeeding too soon to positions of great responsibility had been overcome so completely that in the course of years the experience was all but forgotten, or remembered with a smile. For Robert F. Herrick, Jr., and for Saco-Lowell there was no time for maturing experience or for the rectifying of initial mistakes.

In 1921 the market for textile machinery began to sag. By 1924 the decline had assumed the proportions of a collapse. Depression embraced the textile machinery industry and Saco-Lowell was precipitated into a desperate financial crisis — the product of high expenditures, depleted reserves, plunging sales, and a heavy outstanding debt. Hindsight reveals the poor timing of many managerial decisions in the 1919–24 period, though a contemporary judgment would have held that Saco-Lowell policy was that of a great many other manufacturing firms.

Robert Herrick, Jr., as treasurer of the company necessarily assumed responsibility for the rapidly unfolding disaster. Cut off by his own past actions from assistance from those who could have helped, the younger Herrick was in a hopelessly vulnerable position. All the power and prestige of the father could not have saved the son, even if the father had been disposed to attempt the hopeless rescue. Hitherto inhibited jealousies which the tremendous success and power of the father had engendered on State Street found an outlet in the plight of the son, who was uncompromisingly blamed for the condition of the company. In 1926 Robert Herrick, Jr., was forced from power by the financial institutions which had come

Robert F. Herrick, Jr.

General Agent of Saco-Lowell Shops, 1923-28; Treasurer, 1924–26; and Vice-President, 1926–28

to control the company through its tremendous load of debt. The office of treasurer changed hands twice in a year, but the new appointments were of transitory importance. The direction of the company had already passed to higher authorities.

Emergency meetings of the directorate were called. Robert Herrick, Sr., assumed active command. Frank J. Hale was hastily recalled from a vacation in Florida, and Paul Snelling stood by, faithful as always to the company.

The paragraphs which follow deal with these stirring events in greater detail and point out, insofar as is possible, the rapidly changing circumstances in shop and market which both determined and resulted from decisions which were made and events which occurred in the Boston office.

3. War Markets and Reaction

Summary

The year 1913 was one of slow business for the textile-machine shops and their mill customers alike. Since 1900 the textile industry had come very close to doubling its capacity for cloth production. The reaction which occurred in 1913 prompted utterance of the old charge (perhaps first heard in 1815) of "excess capacity." An expanding national economy had always invalidated these charges in the past. In the years which followed 1913 the fact seemed once again to be demonstrated that what was excess for one age was shortage for the next and that there was no norm, no stability, no limit to the expansion process.

Under the impact of war-stimulated demand for cloth at home and abroad, the number of active spindles in the United States increased from 32 millions in 1914 to 36 millions in 1921, and cloth output shot up at an even more rapid rate. Japan and China experienced a virtual industrial revolution and the textile industry grew phenomenally there, at a time when the English machine shops which had dominated the foreign market for generations were preoccupied with war work and were unable to supply the foreign demand.

These forces pushed Saco-Lowell sales from three million dollars, in 1913, to twenty-one millions in 1920. A successful entry was made into the foreign market, principally in Japan and China. The worsted- and silk-machinery lines enjoyed their greatest success, and the worsted line was enlarged.

When the textile collapse came, it was rapid. A precipitating factor was the general postwar collapse of prices in 1921. The ensuing depression cut demand for cloth and impaired mill finances, but there were even more deeply rooted difficulties. War and prewar statistics, examined with a critical eye, revealed the fact that the annual increase in spindles in place in the United States was markedly less after 1910 than before, and that an increasing percentage of spindles sold represented replacements rather than additions to industry capacity. New mill construction could no longer be counted on, as in the years before 1910, to supply a substantial portion of the machinery builders' business.

During the war years textile mills had commenced to operate on a two-shift and three-shift basis. In postwar years this around-the-clock use of mill facilities continued, particularly in the South, where labor laws were less stringent than in New England. This practice had the effect of increasing the capacity of the industry without, of course, immediately or substantially adding to the demand for textile machinery. The postwar American woman, with a fine disregard for economic consequences, discarded cotton stockings and ginghams in favor of silks and synthetics. The "flapper" era accentuated the trend toward less cloth per dress and more dresses per woman. Style factors confused the industry, a large part of which had been geared to the manufacture of standardized fabrics.

The machine shops entered this great textile depression with no new machines sufficiently improved to make existing machinery obsolete.[7] The penalty for a decade of technological stagnation was severe. Hard-pressed mills were able to maintain their competitive position, temporarily at least, without purchasing new machinery. Machine shops endeavoring to sell new cards at prices ranging as high as $1,500, for example, found these machines in competition with old-fashioned, secondhand cards priced as low as $60.

Total annual sales of the Saco-Lowell Shops plunged from the twenty-one-million-dollar mark in 1921 to less than six millions in

1926, while foreign sales broke sharply over approximately the same period from eight million dollars to less than one million. One "old-timer" in the Newton shop was heard to exclaim, "Huh! If they'd just hang Mr. Hale's old topcoat on the rack in the office, it'd sell more cards than everyone we've got here now!"[8] But not even a Frank J. Hale could sell machinery in the depth of this market. On the ebb of this economic tide, demand for new textile machinery almost disappeared.

The Domestic Machinery Market

Saco-Lowell's domestic sales were characterized by more than expansion and contraction. Qualitative marketing changes included an increasing number of customers producing cotton yarn and fabric for industrial purposes; an absolute and relative increase in sales of worsted and silk machinery; a great increase in the relative importance of repair-parts sales; withdrawal from the loom field; and an experiment in manufacturing jute machinery. Few changes took place in marketing practice and the marketing organization remained simple.

The textile machinery industry achieved a stability and simplicity which had not been known for many decades. English competition had become virtually non-existent, and in 1915, when the tariff on textile machinery was the lowest in many years (20 per cent), less than 9 per cent of the spinning machinery in American mills was of foreign make.[9] Even before the first World War the triumph of the large shop over the small was manifest. Saco-Lowell and Whitin stood head and shoulders above the other makers of cotton preparatory machinery. Saco-Lowell alone is said to have sold between 25 and 30 per cent of the preparatory cotton machinery purchased in the United States between 1910 and 1925;[10] this figure is probably conservative. Howard & Bullough remained active in the market, but had been left behind by the tremendous growth of the two industry leaders. The Mason Machine Works made sporadic sallies into the textile-machinery market, but this company was dying.[11] The Providence Machine Company and the Atherton Picking Machinery Company had been bought out by Whitin in 1909 and 1913, respectively. This left only the Fales & Jenks Machine Company and the Woonsocket Machine & Press Company of the old group of preparatory cotton-machinery builders which had competed so actively for business up to 1905. These two last-named companies did not surrender until 1930, when they were acquired by Whitin, but their competitive position had begun to deteriorate long before that date. Even some of the smaller repair-parts specialists were beginning to yield to the integrating pressure of the industry leaders. In 1919 Saco-Lowell acquired the Pawtucket Spinning Ring Company, and in 1923 the Metallic Drawing Roll Company, of Springfield, Massachusetts.[12] These acquisitions involved no large sums of money ($60,000 for the Metallic Drawing Roll Company stock and $90,000 for the Pawtucket stock), but they were significant confirmations of the trend within the industry.

This same trend had been noticeable in the loom-building field, which came in this period to be dominated completely by Draper and Crompton, Knowles. World War I marked the effective emergence of loom-building as an industry separate from that of the manufacture of preparatory machinery. Whitin and Saco-Lowell abandoned all efforts to compete in the loom field. Whitin leased its active loom patents to the Mason Machine Works, and these patents eventually were acquired by Draper.[13] Saco-Lowell sold Mason its heavy duck-loom patents, the only patents which had not already been rendered obsolete by Draper's Northrop loom.

In the active years which followed 1914, competitive pressure in the industry was negligible. Deliveries and not orders became the problem of the day. The depression which followed 1921, severe though it was, brought forth no such sharp competition as had characterized hard times in the last three decades of the nineteenth century and in 1904 and 1905. When the Saco-Lowell Shops was faced with financial disaster in 1926, E. Kent Swift, who had actively managed the Whitin Machine Works since 1915, did not exploit his advantage.[14] Swift's belief may have been that a monopolistic position would best be avoided by Whitin for political reasons. It is clear, however, that any attempt by Whitin to force its tottering competitor to the wall would, despite almost certain success, have precipitated a price war which would inevitably have been costly for Whitin. Among machine-builders the conviction grew that prices must be held to levels which would forestall ruin.

Price competition there certainly was, though it did not take the form of the ruthless price warfare of earlier days. Where textile-machine shops had once striven to outdo one another in slashing prices and evading mutual agreements, Whitin and Saco-Lowell now, in the middle 1920's, began to concentrate their competitive efforts in technological fields, and sought with new machines to gain a competitive edge and jolt the apathetic market. Beyond this, though list prices of machines were not cut, both firms extended substantial trade discounts wherever necessary to secure important orders and protect their own markets.

The fragmentary nature of Saco-Lowell's sales records in the 1912–26 period provides no serious obstacle to an understanding of company marketing trends, though many details are missing. Appendix 15, Table A, presents dollar sales for these years. Sales expanded sharply after 1913, and the 1920 peak of twenty million dollars was approximately six times as high as the 1914 level. Orders taken at the peak of the war boom far surpassed machinery deliveries. In 1920 the huge total of $38,575,000 of unfilled orders stood on the books. Cancellations in 1920, 1921, and 1922, however, totaled $15,175,000, so devastating was the textile collapse. By 1926, dollar sales had shrunk to about a quarter of the 1920 mark.

Saco-Lowell's sales boom carried far above the peak reached by the Whitin Machine Works. In 1920 Saco-Lowell's foreign sales alone almost equaled Whitin's total sales for that year. The comparative sales record of these two companies stood as follows:[15]

	Saco-Lowell Total Sales	Whitin Total Sales
1913–17	$ 26,383,800	$19,840,000
1918–23	90,217,400	54,161,000
Total 1913–26	136,815,500	90,174,000

The Saco-Lowell sales figures actually present a distorted picture of plant operations because of the rapid changes in prices which occurred over the period. Appendix 15, Table A, contains a tabulation of dollar sales as they would have been at 1913 prices. The effect of prices is amply demonstrated by the fact that while dollar sales increased 6.2 times between 1914 and 1920, plant activity (as measured by sales corrected for price increases) increased only 4.3 times.

Dollar sales in 1926 were 72 per cent higher than they had been in 1914, but plant activity was 15 per cent lower.

The base price of Saco-Lowell spinning advanced from $2.00 per spindle in 1913 (the lowest point in many years) to $6.75 in 1920. Over the same period cards jumped from $475 to $1,525. On the downward trend after 1920 textile-machinery prices showed markedly "sticky" characteristics, and the textile machinery industry was criticized both for exceeding the increase in prices of other commodities in the war years and for failing to adjust its prices rapidly and effectively to the decline in general price trends after 1920.[16] This last-named charge completely ignores the fact that, in depressed periods, list prices of textile machinery were not a reliable index of the true cost of machines to the mill customers. Nevertheless, Whitin and Saco-Lowell did avoid the excesses of price competition and did make an effort to hold the price line.

In 1926, despite the desperate condition of the company, Saco-Lowell's base price for spinning was $4.25 per spindle and cards were priced at $960, both figures substantially above the 1913 level. This situation, to be sure, was in considerable measure a result of inflated labor costs; but it appears also to have reflected a generally conservative and forbearing attitude on the part of Whitin. The point must be stressed that high profits were neither sought nor made by Saco-Lowell's pricing policies of the middle 'twenties. In this situation, where the outright and immediate failure of the Saco-Lowell Shops was involved, much justification can be found for the prevailing level of machinery prices. Both the theory (regulation in the interest of marginal producers) and the means of accomplishment (price maintenance) were later adopted by that same Federal Government which was so quick to chastise attempts by business to put its own house in order. The textile industry did well to pay the small premium which enabled Saco-Lowell to survive, and was more than compensated in later years by the perpetuation of brisk competition in the textile machinery industry.

The discrepancy between textile-machinery prices and prices for certain other comparable commodities is clearly evident in Chart XI, and the financial implications of these facts are considered in detail in later sections of this chapter.

In 1913 the company's marketing structure had taken the form it was to exhibit for many years to come. General Agent Frank J. Hale headed an uncomplicated organization, which included a Northern sales manager (H. D. Lord), and four salesmen, a Southern sales manager (Rogers Davis), and two salesmen, and a Worsted Department salesman (R. F. Chase). Contacts with the silk mills were made principally through C. C. Hedrick, who had played a prominent part in developing Lowell's silk-machinery line.

A study of orders received shows that these men were not the only getters of business. In 1913 James C. Howe, vice-president and general manager of the company, sold more machinery than any of the salesmen, and General Agent Hale was a close second. The largest order for cotton machinery was one of $173,692 from the Lancaster Mills, placed by Hale. Even the Whitin Machine Works and its Southern agent, Stuart Cramer, were credited with sales, presumably of Kitson pickers which Whitin customers occasionally persisted in specifying. The source of orders in this sample year was as follows:

Northern Division		
Lord	$219,096	
Wakefield	141,451	
Havey	152,582	
Green	34,427	
Broadfoot	14,032	$ 561,588
Worsted Division		
Chase		52,853
Southern Division		
Davis	32,251	
Cramer	11,027	
Bowe	38,340	
Washburn	9,712	
Southern office	365,850	457,180
Company Officers		
Hale (General Agent)	323,776	
Howe (Vice-President)	410,560	
Snelling (Treasurer)	21,500	755,836
Mills Direct to Boston Office		352,386
Other		25,472
Total Orders Placed		$2,205,315

CHART XI

Comparative Prices, 1913–1926

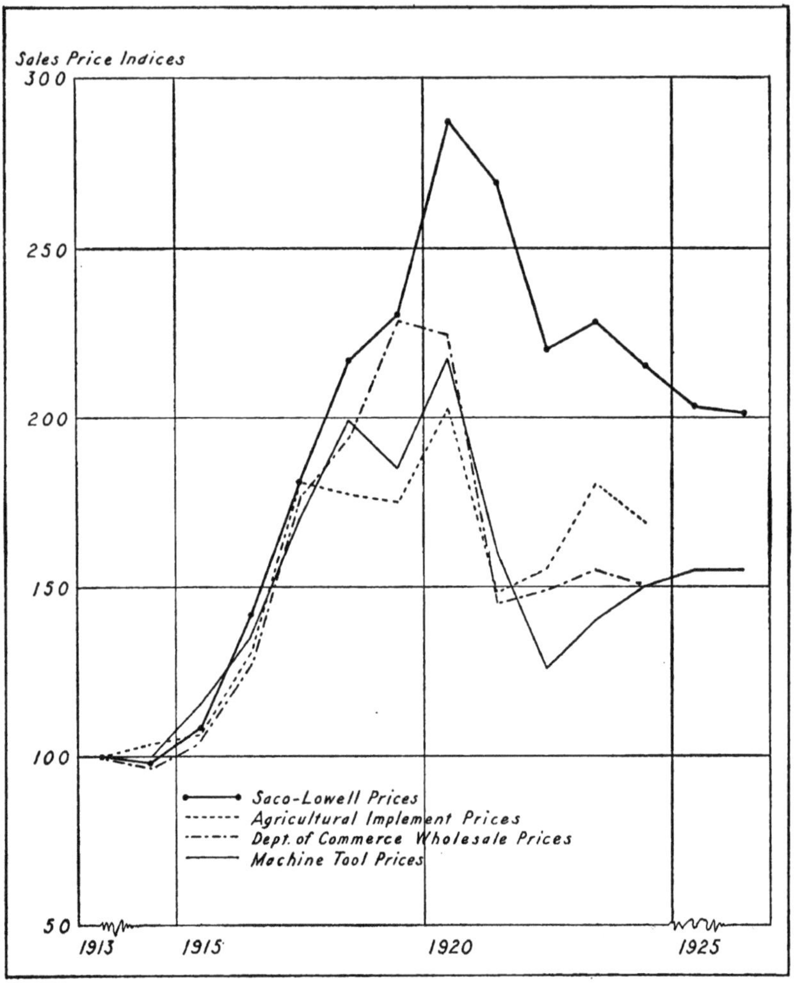

This record of sales actually understates, rather than emphasizes, the vital part played in market operations by company officers, and particularly by Frank J. Hale, who in 1914 personally was credited with $1,032,900 of the $3,062,000 of domestic orders placed in that year. It was Hale's contacts with mill men in North and South which were primarily responsible for the placing of many of the orders taken by other salesmen or sent to the shop directly from the mills. In later years Hale turned to some extent from marketing to administrative activities, but even when he was not selling, he was Saco-Lowell's greatest salesman and provided, moreover, the highest caliber of leadership to the men under him.[17]

A broad suggestion of the geographic distribution of domestic sales between Northern and Southern mills is provided by the 1913 tabulation of orders. A careful breakdown of all domestic orders into the North-South classification shows that orders from Northern mills in 1913 accounted for 71 per cent of the total, and Southern mills 29 per cent. This fact is of considerable interest, for at the turn of the century approximately 60 per cent of Lowell Machine Shop sales had been to Southern mills. This apparent reversal of a previous trend no doubt reflected the growth of the Southern New England textile industry and the increase in purchases of spinning machinery by producers of industrial textile goods, but Saco-Lowell records show that many textile mills all over New England were purchasing heavily.

In 1919, the next year for which detailed information is available, orders from Northern mills still predominated (68 per cent), but in the great postwar textile depression these mills suffered heavily in competition with the newer, better-equipped, low-cost Southern producers. Active spindles in New England commenced a more or less steady decline from a peak of eighteen million in 1922–23 to a low of less than six million in 1935–36, while active spindles in cotton-growing States increased slightly over the period. In the middle 1920's the great old mills in Lowell, Nashua, Lawrence, and elsewhere in Saco-Lowell's New England market strongholds were tottering and making plans to curtail, liquidate, or go south.[18] In 1926 Southern mills accounted for 64 per cent of Saco-Lowell's domestic sales. Appendix 15, Table B, presents in detail the geographic distribution of sales from 1919 to 1926.

The Product Line

An event of more than passing interest in the year 1913 was the agreement by the Saco-Lowell Shops to build an order of jute machinery for the Ludlow Manufacturing Associates. Little if any of such machinery had been built in America, and the small amount used had hitherto been imported from Ireland. The price quoted by Saco-Lowell to Ludlow was far less than the price of imported machinery, and the agreement between the two companies stated that all patterns were to remain the property of Ludlow and that Saco-Lowell should build no jute machinery for other parties. Ludlow orders for 1913 totaled some $383,000, and although cost information is missing, Saco-Lowell is said to have taken a heavy loss on the machinery.

The peculiarly disadvantageous conditions of the contract for Saco-Lowell, as to both price and the prohibition of sales to other mills, raise many questions. Was this another example of the familiar process of experimenting in untried fields in times of bad business? If so, why did Saco-Lowell cut itself off from all possibility of exploiting the line in America? Was the loss simply a result of cost miscalculations, or was the low price a deliberate concession to a mill from which Saco-Lowell expected substantial future orders? Whatever the answers to these questions, the transaction evidenced Saco-Lowell's willingness in this period to undertake special orders, and well illustrated the policy of making the Lowell plant serve as a job shop.

This policy was emphasized further by a decision to discontinue one of the most historic and hitherto valuable services offered by the Lowell shop, the drafting of mill plans. The American textile industry had been indebted to the drafting room at Lowell for this service since the 1840's, and possibly earlier. No other establishment in the country had performed the function of mill designing on a comparable scale over so long a span of years. This appeared to be one more instance of the triumph of specialization over diversification, and the discontinuance of this department of the Lowell shop was supported by the contention that mill-engineering firms now performed such services far more capably than could the machine shops. To this argument Lowell draftsmen replied that no one knew mill layout so well as the men who built and installed the machines. Actually, no question of the relative efficiency of the Lowell drafting room was involved in the decision to do away with it. The mill-engineering firm of Lockwood, Greene & Company, of Boston, had performed this service for the Saco-Pettee Company and the Saco and Pettee Machine Shops for some years prior to 1912. This affiliation was continued after 1912, and departments of the Lowell shop which competed with Lockwood, Greene & Company were eliminated. The change appears to have been made about two years after the formation of the Saco-Lowell Shops and came so suddenly that mill plans which were on the drafting boards at Lowell were rolled up and carried to Lockwood, Greene to be completed. When asked to assist in the transition, the Lowell draftsman who had been working on these plans stoutly refused to have anything further to do with them. The necessities of high policy were not always appreciated at the workbench level of business.

Sales of the worsted- and silk-machinery lines built in the Lowell shop over the 1913–26 period (Appendix 15, Table C) were small in relation to those of cotton machinery; and, judging from the profits of the Lowell shop in this period, neither of these lines was a money-maker. Over the 1912–26 period worsted sales averaged 7.3 per cent of the total sales; silk machinery, 2.5 per cent. Even today, however, Lowell men staunchly defend the quality of these machines and the wisdom of branching out into these fields. An impartial judgment, while admitting that the Lowell worsted and silk machinery was comparable in quality to foreign-built machines, indicates that here were two more examples of the limited financial success which, since the middle nineteenth century, had greeted all efforts to deviate from the main product line. In the active years from 1914 to 1923 the old argument was obviously invalid that such side lines, even if unprofitable, were justified as a means of utilizing excess capacity and reducing plant overhead. In the lean years between 1923 and 1926 the worsted sales, though small, were a welcome addition to sales volume. The most important economic consequence of Lowell's sally into the worsted field was destined to benefit not Saco-Lowell, but the Whitin Machine Works. As a result of the quality of Lowell work and the persistence of Lowell selling effort over a thirty-year period, some of the deeply rooted prejudice in favor of foreign-built machines had been dissipated by the time that Saco-Lowell dropped the worsted line and Whitin picked it up.[19]

A far more significant aspect of Saco-Lowell marketing in the

1912–26 period was the growth of repair-parts sales. In the era preceding 1912, when new mill construction dominated the textile-machinery market, little effort was made by the various machine-builders to push the sale of repair parts. Unlike the machine-tool industry, which charged low prices on such parts and built up a volume business, the textile machinery industry appears to have consistently charged high prices.[20] This policy seems to indicate a lack of interest in such business; it had the effect of encouraging the growth and efficiency of mill repair shops and small suppliers of specialized parts. In the years following 1915 there was a considerable relative increase in repair-parts sales (Appendix 15, Table C). This trend reflected, in some measure, the slowing rate of growth of the textile industry and indicated a fundamental change of great importance in the nature of the textile-machinery markets. There is no evidence that the Saco-Lowell Shops recognized the trend and deliberately began to court the repair-parts market. Indeed, evidence points in the opposite direction, and in 1926 the enlarged volume of repair sales was regarded as an outcome of war-delayed machinery purchases rather than as a long-range alteration in the ratio of repair sales to new machine sales.[21]

An analysis of sales by plants gives a further indication of the relative sales volume of the major classifications of machinery. Average sales of the Newton shop (carding and drawing) over the 1912–26 period were approximately 25 per cent of total sales. Kitson sales (picking and opening) were 11 per cent; Biddeford sales (roving, spinning, and spoolers) were 33 per cent; and Lowell sales (warpers, slashers, twisters, spoolers, and worsted and silk machinery) were 32 per cent of total sales. As might be expected from the set ratio of the various types of machines in the mills, these percentages varied little from year to year. Appendix 15, Table C, lists the percentages annually for the 1912–26 period, while Table D gives the total number of machines produced in the peak year (1920) and total unit production for the period.

Company records are inadequate to re-create the story of Saco-Lowell in the first World War, but no significant product changes occurred in the war period. The Lowell shop entered into a contract to supply the Russian government with 4,000,000 brass fuse casings for heavy shells, but this contract was undertaken to utilize temporarily idle machines and was canceled when textile orders began to pour in. The company undertook no other war work and concentrated on supplying the regular line, subject to government-imposed priorities in the last year of the war which directed textile-machinery orders. Whitin's experience was similar to that of Saco-Lowell, but the Mason Machine Works undertook extensive war sub-contracts for rifling and barrel-reaming drills, gasoline power generators, and other non-textile products. The difference between the policy pursued by Whitin and Saco-Lowell and that of Mason is not easily explicable, save possibly by the fact that Mason had lagged far behind the other shops in the textile-machinery market and had shown in the past a far greater disposition to enter new product fields. Saco-Lowell's World War history, in short, was merely a tremendous acceleration of existing business without perceptible change in the nature of that business.

Saco-Lowell's final experiment in product diversification — indeed the culmination for the Lowell shop of three-quarters of a century of unsuccessful straying into alien product fields — was inspired by the critical dearth of textile-machinery orders in the mid-1920's. In a desperate search for revenue, contracts were secured early in 1926 for the manufacture of refrigerators, transmission sets, oil burners, and many other non-textile products. With no experience in these lines and no basis for accurate costing, these ventures, hastily conceived in an emergency situation, were shorter-lived, far less logical, and infinitely less successful than earlier experiences in the manufacture of paper machinery, machine tools, and worsted machinery.

The regular line of cotton-textile machinery was not cheapened in any way except in price to meet depression conditions after 1921. This policy of quality maintenance, which even in the face of the most severe business crises had been consistently followed for many generations by all the machine-makers, indicates the strength of the quality motive in the textile-machinery market. Far from seeking ways to cheapen the quality of its machines, Saco-Lowell was engaged in the middle 1920's in extensive and significant product research. It was in this period that effort began to be directed at the development of long-draft spinning and one-process picking, both of which are considered in detail in the following chapter. Thus, Saco-Lowell's critical financial plight in 1926 in no way stemmed from product inferiority, nor did the technical reputation of the company suffer from that plight. Saco-Lowell machines continued to be considered in the textile industry as equal to, and in some cases (notably picking) superior to, those of any other shop. As had been the case at Biddeford in 1897, the reputation of the company's machines was probably the most valuable asset which the Saco-Lowell Shops possessed.

The Foreign Market

In 1897 it had been the temporary preoccupation of the English machine shops which had induced the Lowell Machine Shop to attempt to cut in on a share of the hitherto untouchable worsted market. In 1916 the situation was duplicated, this time on a worldwide basis. The English shops had dominated the world textile market for a century, first through technological superiority and later through great advantages in labor, material, and shipping costs. By 1916 these shops were effectively prevented from supplying their foreign customers by a combination of factors growing out of war conditions. Inquiries from mills abroad began to reach America, and found the textile-machine shops quite unprepared in the matter of experience but thoroughly willing to make an effort in the foreign market.[22]

Saco-Lowell's first large foreign orders came from China. In December, 1915, the Wah Sing Textile Company and the Yu Yuen Textile Company, both of Tientsin in North China, placed machinery orders totaling $353,600. These two orders came to Saco-Lowell through Andersen, Meyer & Company, Ltd., a New York export agency.

During the first World War Andersen, Meyer & Company, which had hitherto been engaged on a small scale in exporting, expanded enormously and specialized in the exportation of engineering equipment. With contacts and experience in China, this agency had an immensely valuable service to offer Saco-Lowell. An agency agreement was concluded in 1915 covering sales in China. By the terms of this agreement Andersen, Meyer purchased machinery outright from Saco-Lowell, reselling it in China at a price sufficient to cover shipping costs plus a commission. The value of this service was twofold. Saco-Lowell gained access to a market in which it was notoriously difficult to operate without knowledge of official and unofficial trade restrictions. At the same time, Saco-Lowell was relieved of the financial burden of dealing directly with the Chinese mills. The fact is of considerable interest that at approximately the same time that Saco-Lowell concluded this trading arrangement, the Whitin Machine Works entered into an almost identical agreement with the New York export firm of Gaston, Williams & Wigmore.

As foreign orders began to pour in, Saco-Lowell's marketing organization was shifted to meet the new circumstances. J. F. Havey, who had been selling machinery in American markets for Saco-Lowell for several years, was made foreign sales manager and departed for China. In 1917 C. C. Hedrick, who had left the post of chief engineer of the Lowell Shop to devote his efforts to the silk-machinery line, was dispatched to Japan to explore the possibilities of trade there. In 1918 these two men were joined by W. F. Lowell, who had entered the company in 1912 as an erector and had enlarged this training by subsequent employment in the Atlantic Mills, the Boston Manufacturing Company, and the Woonsocket Machine and Press Company.

Special marketing techniques and sales terms were evolved. An arrangement was made with the Yokohama Raw Silk Company for marketing machinery in Japan which seems to have paralleled that with Andersen, Meyer & Company in China. When the Yokohama Raw Silk Company failed, the Mitsubishi Company took over the agency. The presence of Saco-Lowell representatives in China and Japan was recognized by both the company and its agents to be essential for assisting customers to order, for supervising erection of machinery, and for training operatives and overseers. C. C. Hedrick's salary was paid half by Saco-Lowell and half by Mitsubishi. In 1921 Hedrick went to China, and Andersen, Meyer & Company paid half his salary while he was there.

For sales to China, Japan, and Brazil, Saco-Lowell received cash in

New York or Boston upon presentation of shipping papers to the export-agency representatives. Mills in other South American countries, in Mexico, and in Europe were reached directly, the usual terms being one-third cash in advance, one-third cash upon shipment, and the balance payable in three or six months. More liberal terms were granted to certain well-established Italian and German mills. By comparison, the strictest terms quoted in the domestic market were net cash in thirty days after average date of shipment.[23]

Certain other adaptations were made to meet this new demand from abroad. One obstacle to overcome was that such foreign mills as were already in existence were stocked with English machines, and prejudice in favor of the English systems was strong in all quarters. The Kitson picking, which was so highly regarded in the American market, met with less favor in China, and certain alterations were necessary. Japanese mills demanded two-and-one-half inch gauge spinning whereas American mills used two-and-three-quarters inch. The Japanese, moreover, wanted spinning frames of four hundred spindles — far larger than anything built for American mills. American machines were too high for the short Japanese operatives.

A part of Saco-Lowell's success in selling in the foreign market in this period lay in the insistence by General Agent Hale that the necessary mechanical adaptations be made, wherever possible, to meet the foreign demand. Many a failure of American manufacturers in foreign markets lay in a lack of such flexibility. In one important respect, however, American textile machinery failed to meet the requirements of Oriental and European mills. The emphasis of American cotton-manufacturing improvements for more than a century had been in the direction of reducing labor costs. This objective had been realized to a far greater extent than in any other country. So efficient was American textile machinery that American mills could readily afford the high initial cost of such machinery. In England, on the Continent, in China, Japan, Mexico, and South America, where labor was cheap, the labor-saving efficiency of American machines was of far less value than in America. In these countries first cost was of primary importance — hence the popularity of the English and Continental machines, which were perfectly designed to fulfill the economic needs of the situation. This fundamental weakness implied a serious limitation upon the ability of American shops to compete in foreign markets save under very special situations such as those which prevailed between 1916 and 1922.

Saco-Lowell's foreign sales boomed rapidly. Deliveries in 1919 to mills abroad nearly equaled total foreign deliveries for the entire 1912–18 period. This, apparently, was a typical experience. United States Department of Commerce figures show that in 1913 only $1,968,000 of American textile machinery was exported, and that such exports jumped from $2,705,000 in 1916 to $14,986,000 in 1919 and to $19,928,000 in 1921.[24] This latter year represented the peak of Saco-Lowell foreign sales, which totaled 39 per cent of all American textile machinery exported in 1921. Of Saco-Lowell's 1921 foreign shipments of close to $8,000,000, 65 per cent went to China, 29 per cent to Japan, and the remainder to South America, Canada, and European countries. Appendix 15, Tables A and E, presents the statistical detail of the foreign sales experience.

The export-market bubble burst in 1922. Revolution in China and earthquake in Japan accentuated the impact of the general postwar price collapse. English and Continental shops were getting back into the market, and reasserting their traditional pricing advantages. The Japanese, moreover, had commenced to copy American machinery and supply their own needs. Saco-Lowell's shipments to China fell from $2,628,000 in 1922 to $126,000 in 1923. Japanese shipments held up for a year and then declined from $1,342,000 in 1923 to $67,088 in 1924.

Both Andersen, Meyer & Company and Gaston, Williams & Wigmore, Whitin's export agency, were caught in the 1921 price collapse. Andersen, Meyer curtailed operations for a time, and Gaston, Williams & Wigmore went into receivership. Whitin assumed responsibility for fulfilling certain contracts which Gaston, Williams & Wigmore had made with foreign mills in order to prevent cancellation of these contracts by creditors of the export firm.[25] In 1923 the Saco-Lowell Shops and the General Electric Company, together with other companies which Andersen, Meyer had served, stepped in and purchased preferred stock in order to relieve the financial difficulty in which the export firm found itself.[26] This remedial action assisted Andersen, Meyer through the difficult adjustment period, but by 1926 the export market for Saco-Lowell machines had nearly evaporated.

There appears to be no statistical basis for judging the profits made on foreign sales over the 1912–26 period. At many times the realization from these sales was less than on domestic business, and in 1926 the statement was made that the chief service of this market had been to absorb overhead rather than to realize profits directly.[27] An easily recognizable and important result of the foreign-market experience was that at last substantial amounts of American textile machinery were in operation abroad. Saco-Lowell had its name before the world.

4. Production, Shop Management, and Labor

The Four Shops

In preceding chapters the evolution of manufacturing facilities of the Newton, Biddeford, Lowell, and Kitson shops has been traced in a general way. A comparison of these manufacturing establishments in 1912, when the Saco-Lowell Shops was formed, yields many interesting observations.[28]

Postponing for the moment the question of relative efficiency, an examination of plant records reveals that the Lowell shop exceeded each of the other three in size. Biddeford was a close second, Newton was only slightly larger than half the size of Lowell, and Kitson was scarcely larger than some of the departments of the Lowell and Biddeford shops.

It was the Biddeford shop, rather than the older Lowell shop, which had the dubious honor of utilizing, in 1912, the greatest floor space in ancient buildings. One-third of the manufacturing space in use in 1912 at Biddeford had been constructed before 1850. A heavy building and rebuilding program at Lowell in the middle and late nineteenth century had replaced most of the buildings which had stood on the banks of the Pawtucket Canal since 1825. On the other hand, Lowell had seen few new buildings after 1890, while almost half of the space employed at Biddeford in 1912 had been built or rebuilt since 1890. The Newton buildings were by far the most modern, most of them (89 per cent) having been built after 1890. The Kitson shop was housed almost exclusively in buildings constructed between 1850 and 1890.[29]

The age of the buildings in use at Lowell, Newton, and Biddeford tells far less about these shops than the age of the machinery employed within. In 1912 the Biddeford shop enjoyed a slight advantage over either Kitson or Newton in the possession of modern machine tools. Half the machine tools in use at Biddeford in 1912 had been added since 1900. Kitson had added 40 per cent, Newton 31 per cent, and Lowell 25 per cent over the same period. One-third of the tools at Lowell had been acquired in the decade following 1880, which was almost double the percentage of old tools in use in the other shops.[30] The origin of these tools is of particular interest, providing as it does an insight into the rise of the American machine tool industry. Of the machine tools in use at the Lowell shop in 1912, 60 per cent of those which had been put into use before 1880 had been built in the shop. The 40 per cent which had been purchased came chiefly from Jones & Lamson in Vermont. This fact is of some significance, for it suggests that the earlier dependence on England for such tools had been almost eliminated. Of the tools added from 1880 to 1912, 89 per cent were purchased and the remainder made in the shop. Thus, not only had the American machine-tool-makers apparently triumphed over the English by 1880, but these American companies had made it unprofitable for the Lowell Machine Shop to build any substantial number of machines for its own use after that date. Most of the machine tools acquired between 1880 and 1912 came from Flather & Company, Pratt & Whitney, and Potter & Johnson.

In Appendix 15, Table F, may be found a summary of plant and machinery valuations and ages which further serves to illustrate the comparative physical condition of the four shops in 1912.

After 1913 the story of manufacturing facilities is one of continuous and occasionally rapid expansion, the statistical details of which are found in Appendix 15, Table G. Between 1912 and 1926 almost $9,000,000 was expended on plant and equipment.

Floor space was increased approximately 40 per cent over that existing in 1912, and 44 per cent of the machine tools in use in 1926 had been purchased since 1912. This expansion program forms a controversial segment of Saco-Lowell's history, for much of it took place at the very peak of the market and some of it was instituted well after the disastrous course of events had begun to unfold in 1921.

Many shop people put the blame for the plight of the company in 1926 on the plant-expansion program of preceding years and further blame Robert F. Herrick, Jr., for initiating that program. Both viewpoints are to a considerable extent wrong. The financial difficulties of 1926 grew out of many circumstances, of which the building program was but one. Moreover, the heaviest plant expenditures were made in 1920, three years before Herrick, Jr., had become general agent.

In that year a new foundry was completed at Newton, a project which had stirred inter-shop jealousies. Biddeford men felt that their obsolete foundry should be replaced and that Newton, with its comparatively modern plant, had a less deserving claim to the allotment of building funds. This feeling was scarcely alleviated when expenditures on the Newton plant reached and passed the $2,000,000 mark, a figure which was said to be far in excess of estimate. There appeared to be a genuine need at this time to expand the production of cards, but the cost of the Newton improvements was claimed to be high in relation to the returns realized, and the wisdom of such perfection was later to be questioned by Saco-Lowell creditors.[31] Biddeford feelings were mollified somewhat by the completion in 1920 of two large machine-shop additions there. These new buildings along Gooch Street, added to existing shops built there in 1903, provided five stories of modern manufacturing space which extended in a straight line for a fifth of a mile.

What must be the judgment of history upon the spending of more than $4,000,000 in 1920 on plant expansion? American manufacturers have traditionally and perhaps inevitably expanded their plants at the peaks of prosperity, completing their undertakings barely in time to be blasted by the ensuing crash. The obvious conclusion is that this expansion at Newton and Biddeford was poorly timed, yet such an interpretation of events is scarcely fair or

Main Gate of the Lowell Machine Shop in the Early 1920's

The Lowell Shop in the Early 1920's
Foundry and Pawtucket Canal in foreground

accurate. There was no lack of understanding here that the high level of activity could not continue. There was, however, the hope (partially realized) that this added capacity could be brought into production in time to aid in that stock-piling of profits which the notoriously feast-and-famine textile machinery industry had found to be requisite for survival. The building program was exactly in accord with the past policy of adjusting plant capacity to meet maximum rather than average demands of the trade, a policy which in the past had been productive of near-term loss and long-range gain.

The expenditure by Robert F. Herrick, Jr., of $1,000,000 on the Lowell plant in 1923 was less justifiable than the expenditures by Hale and Snelling of considerably larger amounts at Biddeford and Newton between 1919 and 1921, if for no other reason than that by this time orders were falling off badly and company debt was increasing.[32] Caution was the proper policy, yet caution could scarcely be expected from the youthful, vigorous, and inexperienced new management which had come into power in this year. Once again the effect of inter-shop rivalries can be traced in policy decisions at Boston. The Lowell Machine Shop had been Robert Herrick, Sr.'s, company, and the son felt himself bound to this shop by personal ties. While Hale and Snelling had poured much money into the Lowell Shop, expenditures there had been less than at the Newton and Biddeford shops with which they had been so intimately associated before 1912. Herrick, Jr., determined to make up for what he appears to have felt was unjustified neglect. There is little question that the Lowell shop was in poor condition as compared with the Newton or even the Biddeford shop. There were very real grounds for doubt, however, that large expenditures at Lowell could be expected to yield returns commensurate with those realized from improvements in the other shops, and Herrick's responsibility for continuing the expansion program beyond the point of safety is clear.

Technical Progress and "Scientific Management"

Shop operations in the 1912–26 period exhibited two pronounced characteristics. Great attention was paid to production methods and controls. At the same time, a long period of inventive stagnation came to an end, and an awakening interest in machinery improvements became evident.

There is always a grave danger of underestimating the rate of technological progress in the textile machinery trade, for the reason that much of such progress has been the product of an infinite number of minor changes. Nevertheless, the rekindling of interest in the early 1920's in machinery improvements marked the end of what was probably the most unprogressive period in the history of the preparatory textile machinery industry. This era commenced soon after the introduction of the revolving flat card in the late 1880's and did not begin to draw to a close until 1920. Improvements were made, but the total efforts of the Saco-Lowell plants, Whitin, Howard & Bullough, and the other preparatory cotton-machinery builders produced infinitesimal progress when compared with the achievements of earlier and later periods or even with contemporary improvements effected in the loom field by Draper and Crompton, Knowles. This period was marked by a decided subservience to the dictum that the basic principles of yarn preparation evolved in Arkwright's day could never be substantially improved. The stagnation affected all the builders of preparatory textile machinery and is difficult to explain. In the late 1890's and early 1900's competition was keen and business was often poor, but remedies were sought in destructive marketing effort rather than in machine improvements. The fact that the period of keenest competition in the history of the textile machinery industry produced the fewest important inventions provides an interesting contrast to the commonly accepted theory that invention draws sustenance from highly competitive situations.

After 1900 much technical energy was expended (and very profitably expended) in improving manufacturing methods. It was in this period that interchangeable-parts manufacture received much emphasis. The machines into which these parts were integrated, however, were not basically changed. From 1907 to 1920, high profits and immensely active business appear to have completely stifled improvement. Textile-machinery men were eminently satisfied with the product they were selling, and so apparently were their customers.

The end of this era of complacency was abrupt. The depression which followed 1921 presented the alternatives of stimulating demand for textile machines by price warfare or by machinery improvements. The industry shrank from the first-named remedy, the disastrous results of which had been only too well demonstrated in earlier years, and adopted the other alternative. Depression, however, was not the only or even the chief stimulant of inventive progress. The textile machinery industry was being bombarded by unsettling, stimulating ideas. Experiments upon synthetic fibers were being conducted, and a whole new field was unfolding. Across the Atlantic, Fernando Casablancas and others were working out highly interesting spinning and roving techniques, and picking machinery was benefiting from creative thinking. The joint result of these forces was to cause Saco-Lowell to expend approximately $1,200,000 on basic research and design of new machinery between 1920 and 1926. The opinion of company officials in 1926 was that product improvement had, if anything, been overemphasized; that Saco-Lowell had been much more progressive than Whitin; and that the machinery of 1926 would produce from 15 to 25 per cent more than comparable machinery of ten years earlier.[33]

It was in this period that production volume so far outran nineteenth-century methods of production control and cost accounting that drastic remedial action was taken by American industry. Since the late 1890's Frederick W. Taylor had been preaching not just the revision of existing methods of wage payment but a virtual revolution in managerial attitudes. The essence of his teachings was the application of scientific exactness in determining the nature of plant operations. Out of such knowledge were to grow better incentive wage systems and more efficient work-flow plans, which would combine to effect savings in the use of labor, materials, and machines. By 1910 the name Scientific Management had been coined and applied to Taylor's techniques, and in the next five years the movement gathered great momentum.[34] Henry L. Gantt, a disciple of Taylor, effected an important modification in the Taylor system of incentive wage payments, and in 1912 he was employed by the Saco-Lowell Shops to install his system at the Lowell Shop. At this same time both Whitin and Draper called in efficiency engineers.[35]

The details of Gantt's work at the Lowell shop are not clear nor can the impact of scientific management upon the shop be appraised. There was much opposition from management to the employment of these outside consultants. A frequently voiced criticism was that Gantt's men did not understand the nature and requirements of the business. The validity of this charge may well be questioned, for it was inevitably raised whenever "outsiders" came into the Lowell shop, and even was heard on each occasion when a new superintendent was hired. That serious difficulty was encountered is suggested by the fact that R. A. Wentworth, the Gantt man who was placed in charge of the installation, finally was made superintendent at Lowell in order to give him the necessary authority to install the Gantt system. Wentworth was said to have achieved satisfactory results at Lowell, but it is significant that the Gantt system was not extended to the other shops.[36] A basic difficulty appears to have been that, owing to obsolete manufacturing conditions, installation of the Gantt system was slow. Men whose departments had not been studied became impatient to share in the earnings of fellow-workers who had already begun to work under the new system. The payment of bonuses monthly, plus inadequate reports of weekly earnings, took away much of the incentive and interest in the plan. Standards were so rapidly changed that the system soon became unintelligible to the average worker, who often found ways, through lack of adequate time-keeping equipment, to "cheat." Moreover, the Gantt system was based on time studies of existing production methods, and involved none of the improvement of those methods which was a fundamental part of the earlier Taylor and the later Bedaux systems. The entire Gantt system became discredited, and finally was abandoned at Lowell without ever having been fully established.[37]

Shortly after 1923, when Robert F. Herrick, Jr., became general agent, the Bedaux system of wage incentive payments began to be installed in all four shops by the Stevens Company, which controlled the American rights to this European-conceived system. Bedaux had gone far beyond Taylor and Gantt in designing effective and equitable methods of incentive wage payments, but the Bedaux system was complex and required careful application. This installation was one of the most significant and revealing events of the younger Herrick's administration.

Scientific management had emerged from the first World War in considerable disrepute, and the real advantages had often been submerged by inept interpretation and practice. It was in this period that labor as a whole became militantly opposed to wage incentive systems, and with good cause. In a great many cases, companies had retained only the production-increasing features of the Taylor, Gantt, Halsey, and other plans, eliminating, insofar as possible, the gains to labor which the expounders of the scientific management movement had built into their systems.

Far from attempting to offset the odium which was attached to wage incentive systems, Herrick, Jr., actually accentuated the existing feeling by his forthright action. No effective educational work had been done in the plants before the arrival of the Bedaux engineers. A crucial error was made in the failure to win over foremen and plant managers. The attitude of the four shop superintendents ranged from skepticism to active opposition. None was wholeheartedly in favor of the change. One superintendent was asked to submit his recommendations as to the need for the Bedaux system in his shop. Before these recommendations had even been formulated, the Bedaux engineers had arrived at the plant. The attempt to install the Bedaux system in the highly individualistic Kitson plant resulted in the resignation of its agent, John K. Whittier. However, such interference with the closely knit Kitson organization had been studiously avoided in 1905 by the elder Herrick, and the independent spirit had flourished since that date to such an extent that the action of Herrick, Jr., in demanding accounting conformity was probably a healthy, if immensely unsettling, influence.

Despite the abruptness with which the Bedaux installation was made, the general suspicion with which labor regarded wage incentive systems, and the opposition (both tacit and forthright) of management, no serious objection was encountered from the men in the shops. Indeed, the eagerness of the men to be placed on Bedaux where they could increase their earnings was a factor in the costly speed with which the system was applied.

At all plants the installation suffered from an attempt to avoid the delays which had so seriously interfered with the effectiveness of the earlier Gantt system. Emphasis was placed on speed of installation, at the expense of that thorough study of methods and equipment which was the most valuable feature of the Bedaux system. Thus, instead of becoming an important tool of management, the Bedaux system as installed in the Saco-Lowell Shops was based upon existing production methods and constituted merely another way of paying employees.[38]

In broad perspective the installation of the Bedaux system appears to have been a costly venture, despite the fact that this system as originally designed had great intrinsic merit. Costly errors resulted from the inexperienced and often poorly qualified company employees who were assigned to work as time-study men under the Bedaux engineers, and undue emphasis was placed upon the number rather than the quality of time studies turned in. An enigmatic situation was faced from the outset. The Bedaux system was not equally effective in all departments of the business, and yet attempts to make partial or modified applications weakened the system and multiplied the complexities. If this experience proved anything, it was that no fair way could be found of applying a standardized bonus system to all departments of the business. The temptation on the part of the company to pare down benefits to labor was not always resisted. In other cases managerial laxity resulted in setting unnecessarily loose standards. In short, it was not the system itself but the application, modification, misuse, and misunderstanding of that system which was the cause of difficulty and high cost at Saco-Lowell.[39]

Despite the manifest evidences of installation difficulties, this experience cannot be viewed in a completely unfavorable light. Here lay evidence of a sincere attempt by Robert F. Herrick, Jr., to substitute modern managerial techniques for the haphazard controls which had existed in the past. This was not the only such attempt, and neither were haphazard controls entirely eliminated. Organizational changes were effected which showed a definite trend toward centralization of production and labor control. In or about 1917, production departments were established and employment managers hired in the various shops. The purpose and essence of these innovations was to relieve foremen of responsibilities which could best be handled in the main office. The foremen, however, still continued to occupy a key position in management at each of the shops, and progress in establishing adequate accounting controls over shop operations was slow.

Financial accounting, the legacy of Boston mercantile practice, was excellently adapted to the necessity of recording the consolidated operating results of the component shops, but there is no evidence of substantial improvements in cost-accounting methods over much of the 1912–26 period. In 1926 the company's cost system was described as "rudimentary." The reasons given for this condition were the variety of products made, the complexity of the machinery itself, and the constantly changing specifications demanded by customers. At this time no dependable total cost figures could be furnished on many of the machines made, and the company was unable to state the profits made on each of the main product lines. There was, moreover, a definite failure to tabulate detailed sales statistics which would have assisted in the control of market operations.[40]

Manufacturing Costs and Comparative Shop Performance

In 1912, factory payroll (direct and indirect) totaled slightly less than half the sum realized from machinery sales. The average hourly wage in the shops was seventeen cents and in the foundries twenty-five cents. By 1924, factory payroll equaled 60 per cent of sales. For the entire period from 1912 through 1926 factory payroll averaged (for all shops combined) 46 per cent of net sales. In 1870, it will be recalled (Chapter XI), the statement was made that labor cost constituted 33 per cent of the total cost of machinery built in American shops. This figure, of course, provides only a very rough measure of comparison. Scattered evidence suggests that after 1890 direct and indirect factory labor costs had constituted from 40 to 50 per cent of the selling price of machines, and, despite rising wage levels, no major upward trend in the percentage of labor costs to total costs is apparent in the 1890–1926 period.

From 1912 to 1920, labor costs advanced far more rapidly than did machinery prices and failed immediately to follow the price

CHART XII

Cost Factors and Prices of Textile Machinery, 1900–1930

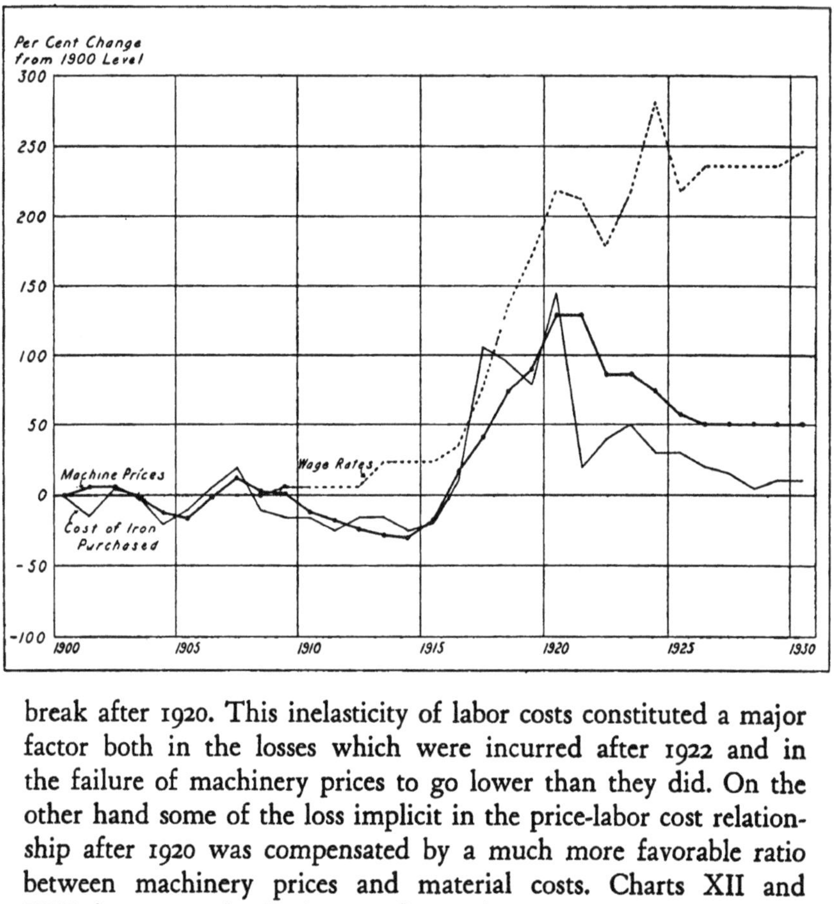

break after 1920. This inelasticity of labor costs constituted a major factor both in the losses which were incurred after 1922 and in the failure of machinery prices to go lower than they did. On the other hand some of the loss implicit in the price-labor cost relationship after 1920 was compensated by a much more favorable ratio between machinery prices and material costs. Charts XII and XIII show very clearly the significant alterations which occurred in these ratios. Figures are included for the years from 1900 to 1930 in order to better illustrate the cost trends, and Appendix 15 gives in tabular form some further information of a comparative nature for the 1912–48 period.

A comparison of the Lowell, Biddeford, Newton, and Kitson shops reveals startling variations in costs and profits. Of the four shops Kitson was by far the most profitable, Newton was sec-

CHART XIII

Cost and Profits as a Percentage of Net Sales, 1913–1926

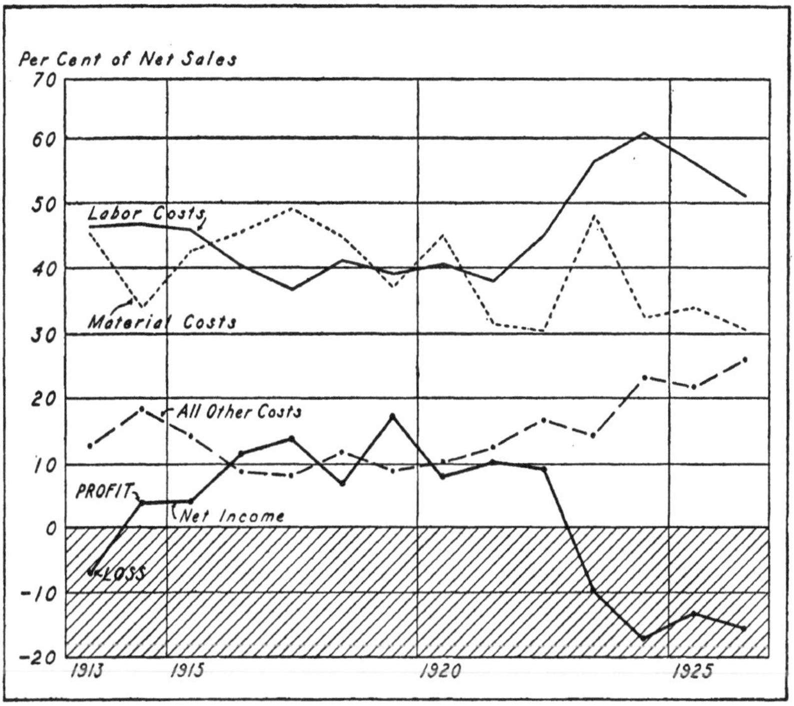

ond, Biddeford third, and Lowell a poor fourth. Over the 1912–26 period average operating and net profits of each shop expressed as a percentage of net sales of each shop were as follows:

	Operating Profit (Per cent)	Net Profit (Per cent)
Kitson	36.60	30.2
Newton	17.55	11.1
Biddeford	11.90	5.6
Lowell	4.45 (loss)	10.8 (loss)

In terms of dollars Kitson showed, for the period, a total operating profit of $5,244,000 on $16,436,000 of sales. The Newton shop showed about the same profit on twice as heavy a sales volume, and

Biddeford showed approximately the same profit on three times as heavy a sales volume. The Lowell shop recorded an operating loss of $1,902,000 for the period on net sales of $42,874,000.[41] Cost ratios varied greatly. In 1924, labor, administrative, and selling expense combined totaled 41 per cent of Kitson net sales, 45 per cent of Newton sales, 60 per cent of Biddeford sales, and 84 per cent of Lowell sales.

These random figures and the more detailed information on comparative shop performance contained in Appendix 15, Table H, reflect both variations in efficiency and variations in profit margins on the classes of machinery made in each shop. The two elements cannot be distinguished. Kitson was not nearly so efficient a producer as the profit figures suggest, for Kitson's unparalleled market position enabled high prices to be charged. The Lowell shop probably was less efficient than the others, but the job business done would not have returned high profits to even a low-cost producer. In nine of the fourteen years of the 1913–26 period the Lowell shop reported operating losses, ample evidence of the unstable nature of the type of business done there. The importance of Kitson and, to a less extent, Newton operating profits to the company after 1922 can scarcely be over-emphasized. The Kitson shop never operated at a loss. In 1923, when Biddeford and Lowell operating losses totaled $1,650,000, Kitson and Newton each returned an operating profit of close to $550,000. In 1924, Lowell and Biddeford losses totaled $950,000, Newton barely avoided a loss, and Kitson showed a profit of $462,000. In 1925 Kitson's profit of $320,000 helped to offset total losses in the other shops of $598,000.

Managerial Personnel and Attitudes in the Shop

No attempt will be made to trace in detail all the many changes in shop management which occurred between 1912 and 1926 or to give the background of the various men who managed the four shops. Efforts to discern a fixed pattern of managerial policy yield few decisive results, nor can any generalizations be drawn about the type or caliber of men selected to fill the important posts of shop agent and superintendent.[42]

While Frank J. Hale was general agent of the company (1912–23) he followed his old policy of giving the shop agents great freedom of initiative. Managerial changes in this period were not numerous. At Newton, Oscar E. Nutter succeeded the aging Charles E. Mills as agent in 1917. Mills was made consulting engineer of the company — the traditional path to retirement or dismissal. F. E. Banfield became superintendent under Nutter. John K. Whittier served as agent and Felix Langevin as superintendent of the Kitson shop. E. E. Blake and Alexander Rankeillor, both former Newton men, were agent and superintendent, respectively, at Biddeford, and Blake was given the additional task of acting as agent of the Lowell shop. Under Blake, Albert W. Thompson, former mechanical superintendent of the Amoskeag Company, filled the post of superintendent at Lowell. He was succeeded, in April, 1914, by R. A. Wentworth, who had come earlier to install the Gantt system. Wentworth was soon succeeded by William N. Goldsmith, former chief draftsman at Biddeford.

The impact of the Herrick administration in 1923 and succeeding years upon the various shop managements was profound. Robert Herrick, Jr., was likable and friendly. He could be as democratic as his father. This tremendous asset of personal charm, however, was not effectively utilized. Herrick's personality made friends; his actions made enemies. His dynamic enthusiasm and scorn of traditional methods of procedure was not calculated to enlist the support of the more conservative men in the shop, and his impatience with those who feared to follow him evoked brusque words and actions. Like the efficiency engineers in whom he placed such faith, Herrick reckoned too often in terms of factors of production, too seldom in terms of personalities. His philosophy of management was to keep a man in a position of responsibility for a time, then remove him and see whether someone else might not do better. Shop managers were shifted from one plant to another, with little regard for personal preferences or domestic convenience.

Agent E. E. Blake was the first to be replaced. A man of great administrative skill, well liked, soundly versed in mechanics, and particularly well grounded in the fields of roving and spinning machinery, E. E. Blake had rendered outstanding service for the company. Frank J. Hale advised Herrick to retain Blake in his existing status, but this counsel was not taken, and in 1923 Blake was relieved of his position as agent of the Biddeford and Lowell shops and given the position of head of patents and research. This was, in effect, a demotion — virtually an invitation to retire. In tribute to Blake it should be added that he devoted himself to the new task with conspicuous devotion and achieved important results. This story, however, belongs to a later chapter.

F. E. Banfield was made agent in Blake's place. At Biddeford Roderic Tarr, who, as assistant superintendent under Rankeillor and Blake, had worked out the production difficulties which had plagued the McMullan spindle, was made superintendent under Banfield. Goldsmith was replaced as superintendent of the Lowell shop in 1924 by E. B. Feaster, who was brought in from "outside," and whom many of the older men in the shop felt to be lacking in understanding of the Lowell line. Feaster, however, was a production man, and he successfully undertook the manufacture of flyers, thereby eliminating the company's dependence upon English manufacturers for this important part. At the Kitson shop John K. Whittier and Felix Langevin survived initial managerial adjustments, but both retired in 1926, when the Bedaux system was installed there.

There is little question that these adjustments had a stimulating effect upon the company and perhaps, if the reorganization had been allowed time to work itself out, the over-all effect would have been healthful. The fact is that valuable men were lost at a time when the highest degree of coöperation and devotion to the company interest was necessary.

Labor Policy and Wages

Saco-Lowell labor policy after 1912 was an extension of that which prevailed in the Saco-Pettee Company earlier and which has been outlined in Chapter XII. The essence of this policy was opposition to the extension of unionization in the shops and a rather militant tolerance of the established International Molders' Union, which claimed a large membership in the Newton and Biddeford foundries. There was little paternalism, and only at Newton was any serious concern manifested over housing and recreational facilities for the workmen.

The total number of men employed by the company expanded from 2,989 in January of 1914 to a peak of 6,356 in September, 1920, then declined to 2,264 in January of 1927.

Unfortunately, little adequate statistical material about wage rates and earnings has survived. Keen competition for labor in the areas surrounding the Newton and Lowell shops forced rapid increases in wages after 1913. Wages at Biddeford, where labor's bargaining position was somewhat weaker than in the active labor market in Massachusetts, appear to have lagged somewhat behind those in the other shops. The only comparative earnings figures available for the four shops are those which present total labor cost, and which have been already mentioned in connection with manufacturing cost trends. These figures fail to reflect wage differences between the shops, since the utilization of labor varied widely from shop to shop in accordance with the type of work done and the efficiency of shop management.

In January, 1914, the average weekly wage (50-hour week) for the four shops was $11.77, while the average foundry wage was $11.90. In 1921, average weekly earnings had risen to $27.93 in the shop and $34.03 in the foundries. The average working week in 1921 cannot positively be determined, but probably was close to forty-eight hours. Whitin wages appear to have approximated those of Saco-Lowell until 1917, when the traditionally lower wage rates of a factory village began to be evidenced. The number of men employed at the Whitin Machine Works, while smaller than at Saco-Lowell, was far less variable.

Average wage rates per hour are indicated in graphic form on Chart XII, and are compared there with price trends of textile machinery and iron. These rates, together with general pay increases, total employment, and certain comparisons with closely comparable Whitin figures, are shown in further detail in Table 40.

Despite the antipathy to union activity in the shops, the general attitude of management during the years when Frank J. Hale was general agent was characterized by a willingness to bargain. During the war years the company of necessity granted liberal wage increases in order to combat an increasingly critical labor shortage. With the cutback in production in 1921, however, the issue of wages once again presented a fertile field for dispute. Soon afterward Robert Herrick, Jr., assumed active direction of company affairs and commenced his program of plant reorganization. The combination of personnel changes, layoffs, modernization of plant facilities, ad-

TABLE 40

WAGES AND EMPLOYMENT, SACO-LOWELL SHOPS AND WHITIN MACHINE WORKS
1913–1926

	Average Pay Rates (Cents per hour)				Employment	
	Saco-Lowell Shops		Whitin		Saco-Lowell	Whitin
Year	Shops	Foundries	Shop	General Pay Rate Changes Saco-Lowell Shops	No. Employed on January 1	Highest No. Employed in Any Week of Year
1913	21	29	..	[a]	3,082	.....
1914	21	28	25½	[a]	2,989	.....
1915	21	30½	23	10%	2,808	.....
1916	23	34	25	21%	3,610	.....
1917	30	37	29	25%	4,086	.....
1918	40	48	37	29%	4,113	.....
1919	46	61	41	13%	4,426	2,874
1920	54	77	51	13%	5,770	3,120
1921	53	73½	58	−10%	5,970	3,252
1922	47½	61½	45	−15%	4,195[b]	3,044
1923	54	72	48	10%	4,859	2,834
1924	65	72	..	[a]	4,730	2,703
1925	54	82	..	[a]	3,123	2,300
1926	57	85	..	[a]	2,904	2,157

[a] No data.
[b] April 1, 1922.
Source: Saco-Lowell records, Totals notebooks and Directors' minutes. Navin, *op. cit.*, Appendix 24.

ditions to the product line, installation of the Bedaux wage incentive system, and fears as to the future of wage rates and jobs produced an atmosphere charged with uneasiness. Morale in the shops was not low, nor was it high. Robert F. Herrick, Jr., and his newly appointed assistants were on trial.

The Biddeford Foundry Strike

With the collapse of business in 1921 and 1922, wages in the shops were reduced over the two years by 25 per cent. In October, 1922, Local 288 of the International Molders' Union (A.F.L.) at Biddeford instituted a request for an increase in pay for the molders from $5.20 to $6.00 a day. This request clearly controverted company policy and was refused by Agent Blake. On November 2, 1922, some 150 hand and machine molders went out on strike.[43]

A week later the rumor flew about the city that strike-breakers were on their way up from Boston. The strikers grimly turned out to meet the trains, but the Biddeford *Weekly Journal* reported that Saco-Lowell management (notably Hale and Blake) had no intention of resorting to such measures. The company announced, however, that contracts for castings had been made with other foundries, and each large shipment which arrived at Biddeford was carefully reported in the *Journal*. This psychological warfare was not completely successful, for the striking molders knew as well as did management that the cost of having the foundry work done outside was nearly prohibitive.

Complications arose which interfered with the bargaining between Blake and Local 288. Announcements appeared in the local papers that Saco-Lowell had declared a 50 per cent stock dividend. This was fuel for the strikers' fire. On March 1, 1923, the foundry snaggers, who apparently were not unionized, went on strike for an eight-cent hourly increase, and they returned to work a week later after the company had granted them a four-cent increase. This settlement raised company hopes that Local 288 might accept the 10 per cent general wage increase which was made at this time and which came within eighteen cents per day of fulfilling the original union demand. In this same month Robert Herrick, Jr., became general agent of the company. Agent E. E. Blake, in whom the strikers had complete confidence (so said John R. O'Neil, national vice-president of the Molders' Union) was replaced by F. E. Banfield. Hale strongly advised Herrick to effect a compromise settlement, but this advice was rejected. A stiffening of the company's attitude toward the strike became apparent, and events soon indicated that the new management was determined to break the union.

At 4:00 P.M. on April 17, thirty strike-breakers disembarked from the Boston train and marched under the protection of armed guards from the Saco station to the foundry. Insults and angry demonstrations gave way to stones and blows. The strikers picketed the plant with renewed vigor and dispatched delegations to meet the trains. The strike-breakers (tactfully referred to by the *Journal* as "replacement molders") were quartered for a time in the plant itself. On April 20 the strikers were invited to return to work, presumably at the 10 per cent higher wage now in effect. This invitation was made directly to the men, rather than to the union representatives, and was ignored. In May more strike-breakers arrived, guarded by police and private detectives. Police protection was asked for the employed molders, and in June the police were summoned to suppress a riot at the plant between pickets and strike-breakers. Mayor Gilpatric, of Saco, stated that the strike had reached a point of open warfare.

In October, 1923, Herman Steinbeck, a "replacement molder," was shot in the back while on his way home to supper from the foundry. Ten striking molders were arrested as accessories to the shooting, and Judge George L. Emery, counsel for the company, was quoted as stating that he had sufficient evidence to justify an action for $100,000 against the Molders' Union and the city of Biddeford for conniving to interfere with the business of the company. A temporary injunction was secured by the Saco-Lowell Shops against interference by the strikers, and the International Molders' Union celebrated the completion of the first year of the strike with a banquet.

The strike-breakers formed an unruly element in the community. Many of these men were of Eastern European extraction, and racial antagonism between them and the predominantly French population enlisted community sympathy for the strikers' cause. The strike-breakers not only fought with the strikers, but also quarreled among themselves. Gun and knife play was reported on at least two occasions which had no direct connection with the strike. Local authorities maintained an official neutrality and attempted only to preserve order. The strike was reported in local newspapers in deprecating, almost embarrassed tones, as if here was a civic blight — something unclean, like a case of plague, which could well be expected to occur in some other State, but not in Maine.

The strike wore on, though many of the strikers had been replaced. On November 16, 1923, a permanent injunction was secured by the company against picketing or interference. In January, 1924, the *Journal* declared that the strike was virtually over. In

February Saco-Lowell requested the State Board of Arbitration to investigate conditions in the plant and officially declare the strike ended, so that the company might advertise for molders without stating (as required by law to do when a strike was in progress) that there was labor trouble at the plant. In March the State Board reported, to the chagrin of the company, that the strike was still in progress, a conclusion which was not difficult to arrive at, since strike-breakers were still arriving from Boston and fights were occurring almost daily at the station and elsewhere. By imperceptible degrees, however, the feeling grew that the strike was actually over. No climactic announcements marked the ending.

By March of 1924 the strikers had been completely replaced. Saco-Lowell had passed its regular common dividend, and the course of economic events had destroyed all logical basis for the union's demand for a pay increase. A very few of the strikers drifted back to work in the foundry, but most sought work elsewhere. Local 288 was broken, Saco-Lowell had incurred a disastrous direct loss of $1,250,000 from bad and expensive castings,[44] the municipal government had gained little in stature from events of the past two years, Robert Herrick's administration had been discredited in many quarters, and the seed of rancor had been planted both in the community and in the company.[45]

The question might well be raised: Was this a typical experience? Was Saco-Lowell unique in its inflexible determination to exercise the traditional domination over labor and inalienable control of wage rates? The answer to this question waits upon the compilation of more case histories of labor policy in this extremely interesting transitional period in American labor relations. One particularly close parallel might be noted in the Waltham Watch Company strike of 1924. Here was to be found the same iron-bound resolution of management; the same apparent defeat of organized labor; the same implication of the community at large.[46]

How broad was the struggle taking place in America against the increasing inflexibility of wages? Was that inflexibility an important element in the postwar depression of 1921? Was labor warfare, both then and a decade later, made inevitable by the action of stockholders and creditors of a great many harassed companies in installing new managements which took as their primary directive the immediate resuscitation of profits? Were profits and labor peace irreconcilable goals? What was the true cost of the clear-cut triumphs over labor scored by Frederic C. Dumaine, Robert F. Herrick, and other reorganizers? The answers to these questions must be most carefully qualified lest they lead to condemnation instead of understanding. Business at the crossroads could only choose the path which many decades of experience indicated to be least beset with quicksands. The challenge to classical concepts of costs, profits, returns to investors, and human relations had been articulated, but certainly had been grasped in all its ramifications by few American business men.

5. Operating Results and Financial Management

Summary Operating Results, 1912–1926

The course of financial events from 1912 to 1926 could well be the subject for a separate and lengthy historical treatise. Here lie the materials for a valuable and detailed study in American corporate financial policy and practice. The paragraphs which follow merely outline this field, touching such points as are essential to an understanding of broad trends in Saco-Lowell history and passing by, of necessity, much detailed information. In Appendix 15 may be found certain useful statistical abstracts from the records of these years. The presentation of summary operating results for the entire 1912–26 period forms a necessary introduction to the chronology of events leading to the crisis in Saco-Lowell affairs of the mid-1920's.

Summary operating results for the years 1913 to 1926, inclusive, were as follows:[47]

Total net sales	$136,815,500
Net income credited to earned surplus	5,441,000
Total cash dividends	3,772,951
Total stock dividends	4,406,250
Net income	4.0% of net sales
Average annual return to common stockholders:	
from cash dividends	5.0% of invested capital
from stock dividends	7.1% " " "
from cash & stock dividends	12.1% " " "

By way of comparison, Saco-Lowell cash dividends over the 1913–26 period amounted to 2.8 per cent and stock dividends 3.2 per cent of net sales. Dividends of the Whitin Machine Works (totaling $6,435,000, all in cash) equaled 7.8 per cent of net sales. In the peak years 1918 to 1922, inclusive, Whitin showed an annual average net profit of 23.5 per cent of sales, while Saco-Lowell's profit averaged 10.3 per cent. In the four hard years which followed, Whitin showed an annual average profit of 6.4 per cent of sales; Saco-Lowell's average loss in these years was 13.5 per cent.[48]

A comparison of even greater interest and significance may be drawn between Saco-Lowell's average annual net income in the 1913–26 period and the net profit recorded in earlier years by the various parent shops. Saco-Lowell's highest profit peaks had been 1918, 1919, and 1920, when net income had averaged 11 per cent of sales. In these years dollar sales of the Newton, Biddeford, and Lowell shops were double and treble the levels reached in any previous boom years, and machinery prices were the highest in the history of the machinery industry. The highest profit level ever reached by the Saco and Pettee Machine Works was in 1908, 1909, and 1910, when average annual net income equaled approximately 23 per cent of sales. The greatest boom years of the Lowell Machine Shop (1880, 1881, and 1882) yielded average annual net income of 20 per cent of sales.

Saco-Lowell's average net income for the 1912–26 period was 4 per cent of sales. The average for the Saco and Pettee Machine Shops from 1898 to 1912 had been 20 per cent, and the average of the Lowell Machine Shop from 1869 to 1912 had been 10 per cent. Even during the tremendously difficult years from 1898 to 1905 the Lowell Machine Shop had yielded an annual average profit of 4.6 per cent of sales. Such comparisons are suggestive but not conclusive evidence of a long-range decline in the returns realized from textile-machinery building.

These figures cannot be dismissed lightly. They indicate with great clarity the narrowed gap between Saco-Lowell's machinery costs and selling prices which was characteristic of the 1913–26 period. These figures provide a powerful justification for the level of machinery prices which Saco-Lowell demanded in this period. They free Saco-Lowell of any conceivable vulnerability to a charge of profiteering from the condition of reduced competition which existed in the textile machinery industry.

TABLE 41

COMPARATIVE BALANCE SHEETS, SACO-LOWELL SHOPS, 1912–1926
(000 omitted)

	Dec. 31, 1912 Saco-Lowell	Dec. 31, 1921 Saco-Lowell	Dec. 31, 1921 Whitin	Dec. 31, 1926[a] Saco-Lowell
Assets				
Cash................	$ 142	$ 2,082	$ 527	$ 1,518
Receivables[b].........	1,840	3,320	3,628	2,232
Inventory[c]...........	1,250	1,782	1,333	2,346
Investments[d].........	483	1,305	1,512	873
Prepaid Assets.......	58	116	.....	157
Plant Accounts[e]......	2,533	6,013	5,754	6,997
Total............	$6,306	$14,618	$12,754	$14,123
Liabilities & Net Worth				
Current Debts........	$1,889	$ 3,734	$ 1,416	$ 795
Funded Debt.........	.....	.....	.....	6,068
Capital				
Preferred Stock.......	1,250	1,250	.....	3,894
Common Stock.......	2,350	3,525	600	3,366[f]
Surplus..............	817	6,109	10,738	.....
Total............	$ 6,306	$ 14,618	$ 12,754	$ 14,123

[a] After giving effect to new financing.
[b] Net of reserves amounting, for Saco-Lowell, to $200,000 in 1912; $170,000 in 1921; and $200,000 in 1926.
[c] Net of reserves amounting, for Saco-Lowell, to $313,000 in 1912; and $200,000 in 1926.
[d] Net of reserves amounting, for Saco-Lowell, to $75,000 in 1912; and $500,000 in 1926.
[e] Net of reserves amounting, for Saco-Lowell, to $5,464,000 in 1921; and $5,392,000 in 1926.
[f] 55,875 shares of no-par stock.

Source: Saco-Lowell records, Totals notebooks. Whitin balance sheet is also taken from this source and cannot be verified for accuracy or completeness.

The fact that Whitin showed substantially higher profit margins after 1912 than did Saco-Lowell suggests that the decline in Saco-Lowell's profits was not altogether the result of broad and uncontrollable trends which equally affected all companies. Saco-Lowell appears to have been far less successful than Whitin in controlling costs, in both prosperity and depression. This generalization must be qualified, however, by the statement that operating results for the company as a whole were colored by the heavy losses incurred by the Lowell shop. The averaging process obscures the fact that the Newton shop was approximately as efficient (measured in terms of net profit) as Whitin, and that Kitson far surpassed both Newton and Whitin.

Over the 1912–26 period tremendous changes took place in Saco-Lowell asset and liability accounts. The details of these changes are befogged by arbitrary changes in valuations and by devious accounting practice, but main trends are clear. Expenditures on plant additions totaled the formidable sum of $9,291,900. A book increase in plant values of $2,282,600 resulted from a reappraisal of assets, considered in detail in later paragraphs. Capital and funded debt nearly tripled over the period, and notes payable to banks increased from $1,745,000 in 1912 to a peak of $5,640,000 in 1924. The earned surplus account, which on November 1, 1912, had stood at $1,375,300, increased to a peak of $6,109,000 in 1921. By 1925 not only had the surplus disappeared, but the common stockholders' equity in the business had been reduced by December 31, 1926, to a book value equivalent to sixty-six cents on the dollar.

These changes may be traced in the comparative balance sheets in Table 41. A Whitin balance sheet is also included for comparison and contrast.

Mounting Stringency and the Financial Crisis

The tremendous expansion and contraction of Saco-Lowell's business over the 1912–26 period almost overshadows financial events of considerable importance which were only indirectly connected with business activity levels.

The financial activities of the Textile Securities Company deserve a brief notice. This company, formed in 1912 to take over the mill security holdings of the Saco-Pettee Company, remained closely affiliated in succeeding years with the Saco-Lowell Shops, though the affiliation was not a corporate one. Officers of the two companies were identical, though the companies themselves were independent of each other. The Textile Securities Company performed the same services for Saco-Lowell as had the Eastern Machinery Company for the Saco and Pettee Machine Shops before 1912. The value of mill stocks taken by Saco-Lowell in part payment for machinery cannot positively be determined, but it appears to have been a far smaller percentage of sales than had been the case with the Saco and Pettee Machine Shops. Most of these stocks were turned over to the Textile Securities Company, on at least one occasion at a substantial discount. The Securities Company also appears to have accepted stocks directly from the mills. This company further served as a useful instrument in effecting transactions such as the purchase of the Pawtucket Spinning Ring Company and the Metallic Drawing Roll Company, together with the subsequent loan of funds to the last-named organization. The highly liquid condition of the Textile Securities Company, moreover, not only assured Saco-Lowell of a ready market for its mill securities but enabled the Securities Company to secure loans from other financial institutions, thus extending the amount of assistance which it could render the Saco-Lowell Shops. Evidence in the records, however, gives little conclusive information about the relationships existing between the two companies. In 1928 this highly prosperous offspring of the Saco-Lowell organization was sold to the Boston brokerage house of Jackson & Curtis.[49]

Another financial episode of much interest grew out of the Federal Income Tax law of 1913 and the Federal Excess Profits tax law of 1917. The Income Tax law of 1913 introduced the necessity for making regular annual depreciation charges. This law, and to a much more marked degree the Excess Profits tax law of 1917, caught Saco-Lowell and many other companies in an embarrassing predicament. Plant valuations had been so arbitrarily recorded in past years that book figures had come to bear little relation to cost or replacement values. For generations the policy of asset undervaluation had been followed by conservative New England firms. Federal tax policies after 1913 penalized this practice. Allowable depreciation rates were based on plant values, and if plants were undervalued, depreciation charges were low and taxable net income was inflated. A scramble to increase plant valuations ensued.

Saco-Lowell employed Lockwood, Greene & Company to make

a plant appraisal to determine the true cost valuation. This appraisal resulted in raising plant values in 1915 by $2,282,633, an increase of approximately 82 per cent over 1914 value. Even with this increase, plant was still said to be undervalued. The Whitin Machine Works held off until the Excess Profits tax was imminent, and on January 1, 1917, increased its plant account (after appraisal by an accounting firm) by $1,750,000.[50]

In these policy changes Saco-Lowell management reflected contemporary thinking and action. There were particular policies which reflected internal conditions and which should be mentioned as important elements in the crisis which was to come.

Capitalization had been increased by the sale of 11,750 additional shares of common stock in 1919. This issue coincided with plans for plant expansion, and was to secure new capital to facilitate those plans. In 1922, as the company tottered on the brink of the collapse of its markets, stock dividends totaling $4,406,300 were paid out. These consisted of 17,625 shares of common stock and 26,438 shares of 7 per cent cumulative preferred stock.

These dividends represented a more or less controversial solution to a delicate problem. In 1922 the company was in a highly liquid condition, as a result of the boom of preceding years. A difficult decision was involved in solving the problem of idle funds. To say that these funds should have been retained in liquid form, available to meet the unfolding depression, is both to apply hindsight and to ignore the powerful psychological effect upon the stockholders of the company's current fiscal condition. With a surplus of over $6,000,000 on the books, the pressure from stockholders for the payment of extra dividends was strong. The stock dividends of 1922 represented a compromise between these stockholder demands and the knowledge of the more conservative members of the directorate that heavy drains upon liquid capital might cause trouble.[51] The bookkeeping entry which transferred a large part of surplus into capital stock cost the company no money at the time (although it did create additional interest charges) and still conceded something to the stockholders. In view of events which followed soon thereafter, these dividends certainly constituted a serious psychological error, but the alternative of extra cash dividends would have been infinitely worse.[52] At this time it was certainly wise policy to keep as much capital as possible permanently or semi-permanently invested in the business. Justification on these grounds also exists for the heavy plant expenditures which were made, as well as for costly innovations such as the Bedaux installation. These, too, represented the "freezing" of capital in the business which might otherwise have been drained off in cash dividends.

This explanation of company policy reflects little credit on the general perspicuity of stockholders, nor is this the only incident in Saco-Lowell history when managerial decisions were palpably colored by the pressure from stockholding groups. The fact that stockholders' demands came into conflict with the dictates of conservative company policy raises questions as to the complete efficacy of Robert Herrick, Sr.'s, control of the company. This control was predicated not upon majority stock ownership but upon internal tranquility, which would preclude the rise and combination of rival minority stockholder groups. Could such tranquility, so essential to the perpetuation of existing management, be maintained only through a liberal dividend policy? Hale and Snelling had no difficulty in keeping money in the Pettee Machine Works in the 1880's and 1890's, but at that time stockholders were conveniently pessimistic and expected nothing. In 1921 — with a $6,000,000 surplus, a business which had touched the far corners of the earth, and a record of unprecedented activity in the shops — how could any stockholder be persuaded that heavy dividends should not be paid?

While Saco-Lowell's large stock dividend in 1922 was a measure of conservatism, company dividend policy in the two succeeding years, while not difficult to understand, is difficult to justify on any basis. By 1923, reserves had been depleted, expensive plant additions and reorganizations were under way, and the full force of the collapse of the textile industry was being felt. Yet, in this year and in the year following, when conditions had taken on a crucial aspect, cash dividends totaling $837,000 were disbursed. In the four years 1923 to 1926, inclusive, dividends totaling $921,000 were paid out in the face of a deficit of surplus available for dividends of more than $3,000,000. This dividend policy obviously was not in the best interests of the company, though here again it is not hard to discern the influence of pride and pressure on policy. Reluctance to admit defeat — perhaps a forlorn hope that business would be better next year — appears to have aggravated an increasingly desperate financial situation.

From the fact that the Whitin Machine Works was showing better and more stable earnings than Saco-Lowell in the 1912–26 period the inference may be drawn that the Saco-Lowell merger of 1912 had not resulted in those operating economies which mergers of small units into large were traditionally supposed to yield. There is further evidence to support this inference. Duplication existed in the organization, particularly at the supervisory level, as a result of the decentralized nature of design, purchasing, and service functions. The divisionalized plan of the plant organization not only delayed standardization of raw materials, machinery parts, and manufacturing methods, but also resulted in relatively heavy overhead, which was not materially reduced with the reduction in sales volume after 1922. Overhead costs and administrative expenses, however, were a small part of total costs (7 per cent in 1926) and cannot have been a major explanation for the company's poor showing.[53]

Failure to adjust dividend policy and selling, administrative, and overhead expenses to a dynamic business situation was coupled with an apparent failure to modify procurement policies in the face of increasing financial stringency and mounting cancellations of orders. Purchases of material in 1923 exceeded even the level of the peak year of 1921, and there was no substantial reduction in inventories even in 1924 and 1925. Saco-Lowell's borrowing policy presents still further evidence of the understandable failure to foresee the 1921–22 market collapse and the far less excusable failure to adjust company operations quickly and adequately to the new conditions as they unfolded.

Paul Snelling regularly borrowed money, even when operating capital could have been obtained without recourse to banks. This was the time-honored business practice of "establishing a line of credit," the expediency and dangers of which had amply been demonstrated in the annals of business. Recourse to working-capital loans had been heavy during the war years. Notes payable to banks stood at more than $3,500,000 in 1920, but this indebtedness had been almost all liquidated by the end of 1922. In 1923 more than

$4,000,000 was borrowed from Boston and New York banks. By December 31, 1924, notes payable to banks reached a peak of $5,640,000.

These loans grew directly out of the expansionist psychology which prevailed in the company and which was intensified rather than checked by Robert Herrick, Jr. The timing of these loans was disastrous. There was managerial failure here — failure not in appreciating the severity of prevailing economic conditions but in neglecting to provide financial safeguards against the protracted existence of those conditions. At Whitinsville, E. Kent Swift had long been pursuing the policy of keeping the Whitin Machine Works prepared for whatever might loom up through the mists of the future. Saco-Lowell gambled irrevocably on a business revival in 1924.

By January of 1925 the financial affairs of the Saco-Lowell Shops were in a critical state. The hoped-for revival in business had not materialized. Orders on the books were equivalent to about six weeks' production, and an operating loss of $1,251,000 was reported for the year 1924. Robert Herrick, Jr., had tapped every reserve, and the heavy loans negotiated in 1923 were falling due. Notes and paper outstanding on January 1, 1925, were as follows:

Irving Bank	New York	$ 250,000	Due Feb. 18, 1925
National Bank of Commerce	" "	750,000	" " " "
National City Bank	" "	250,000	" " " "
Newton Trust Company	Newton, Mass.	100,000	" Mar. 3, "
American Trust Company	Boston	150,000	Demand
First National Bank	"	500,000	"
National Shawmut Bank	"	500,000	"
Second National Bank	"	500,000	"
Old Colony Trust Company	"	500,000	"
Endorsed Paper (endorsed by Herrick, Sr., Hale, and Snelling; held by Mass. savings banks)		895,000	Various maturity dates up to Jan. 1, 1926
Other company paper		1,245,000	Before June 1, 1925
Total		$5,640,000	

Faced with an acute shortage of working capital, the directors commenced holding emergency meetings. The possibility of issuing additional common stock was considered and rejected on the grounds that common stock was not a sufficient inducement to attract new capital to the business in its existing condition. Company paper, which had always been highly regarded in Boston financial circles, began to depreciate.[54]

The crisis was staved off by loan extensions. The company literally lived on a month-to-month basis, with continued operations conditional upon thirty-day extensions of bank loans. These extensions were cajoled from creditor banks by Robert Herrick, Sr., by Snelling, and by Snelling's stepfather, Russell G. Fessenden, president of the American Trust Company and himself both a creditor and a stockholder. This was obviously only a temporary respite. A more permanent remedy was sought through the authorization of $2,643,750 of five-year, 7 per cent convertible gold notes to be issued under an indenture agreement between the Saco-Lowell Shops and the American Trust Company.[55] Proceeds from the sale of these notes were to be applied to the most pressing debts.

This gold-note issue was first offered for sale to the stockholders. Boston creditor banks agreed to underwrite $1,100,000 of such gold notes as were unsubscribed. Robert Herrick, Jr. (backed by his father), Hale, and Snelling similarly underwrote $895,000 more of the same issue, the amount needed to settle company paper which they had endorsed and for the payment of which they were responsible. By December 31, 1925, few subscriptions had been received, and the underwriters had been called to take up from 50 to 100 per cent of their guaranteed notes. The following list of gold notes outstanding on that date gives a very clear indication of the individuals and institutions that had responded to the company's plea for funds and those that had not:

	Underwritten	Subscribed & Issued
Stockholders	$	$ 122,400
Company officers	895,000	895,000
Old Colony Trust Company	300,000	150,000
First National Bank of Boston	300,000	150,000
National Shawmut Bank	250,000	125,000
American Trust Company	200,000	100,000
Curtis & Sanger	50,000	25,000
Total	$1,995,000	$1,567,400

The participation of the Boston creditor banks in this issue was commendable; though it might be argued that these banks were already heavily involved, the fact remains that they extended support at a time when the New York banks and the stockholders alike appeared to be deserting the sinking ship. Support from the stockholders was indeed disappointing, and little new capital flowed into the business to replace that which had so freely been dispensed to the stockholders in times past. The subscriptions of the Boston banks and the action of Herrick, Hale, and Snelling in making good their endorsements of company debts, however, provided sufficient capital to permit operations to continue and to provide precious time for a revival of business to rescue the company.

The revival upon which all real hope was predicated did not materialize. The operating loss for the year 1925 totaled $928,000, bringing the cumulative loss for this and the two preceding years to $3,517,000. Business in the opening months of 1926 was still slow, the indebtedness of the company was still crushing, and prospects of meeting obligations now seemed hopeless. When it became evident that the stockholders could or would do nothing to ease the crisis, the creditor banks interceded in Saco-Lowell's affairs. The resignation of Robert F. Herrick, Jr., from the position of treasurer was requested by the banks, and was accepted on March 1, 1926. Robert Herrick, Sr., Frank J. Hale, and R. Paul Snelling once more assumed the active management of the business, pending a decision by the creditor banks as to whether or not the company should be liquidated.

The Boston banks showed an inclination to allow Saco-Lowell a chance to work itself out of trouble. Possibly this attitude reflected long familiarity with the basic needs of the textile industry, and certainly Herrick's close contacts with both the First National and Shawmut groups were of greatest value on this occasion. The National City Bank of New York had a commercial rather than an investment-banking interest in Saco-Lowell and looked at the situation from a short-range, impersonal viewpoint, which contemplated the early liquidation of Saco-Lowell's indebtedness. Herrick's name, moreover, carried far less weight in New York than in Boston. The National City sent two investigators to Boston, who conducted an intensive survey of Saco-Lowell's condition and prospects.[56] This survey, completed in September, 1926, was so penetrating, impartial, and excellent that all the creditor banks agreed to use it as the basis for future action.

The most startling conclusion advanced by the National City Bank survey was that a drastic liquidation of the assets of the Saco-Lowell Shops could be expected to yield the bank creditors and gold-note holders only eighty-four cents on the dollar, wiping out the equity of the common and preferred stockholders completely.[57] Liquidation under these circumstances was not advised. The investigators concluded that the banks had best extend their notes in some form for a period of three years, provided that additional working capital could be assured for the business. The survey pointed out that the economies of a more centralized organization should be sought and that the advantages of consolidation of manufacturing facilities should be considered; the profitable Kitson organization should be legally severed from the tottering parent company in order to safeguard the sale value of the Kitson business; and careful consideration should be given the product line, with elimination of the worsted- and silk-machinery and non-textile lines as a definite possibility.

The survey had this to say about company management:

As to personnel, the present management is distinctly divided between the old and young generation. Messrs. Hale and Snelling have been connected with the Company or its antecedents for a long time and are capable and respected men in the business and in the industry which it serves. They are, however, advanced in years and cannot be expected to work actively in harness nor is it believed, because of age, that it would be possible for them to lift this Company from its troubles no matter how able they might be. Their sphere of usefulness should be largely advisory and in sales the contacts and friendships enjoyed by them with the cotton mill industry should be most productive to the Company.

The gap from them to the active administration is wide in experience and capacity. Mr. Herrick, Jr., has been the active head for some time. He is a relatively young man with neither intensive nor broad business experience prior to his coming with the Company. He is progressive in spirit and has initiated policies of a constructive and modern character but has not displayed the sense of proportion and executive capacity to guide effectively the successful consummation of these policies. He possesses an extensive and detailed knowledge of the business and reveals a thorough intellectual grasp of its requirements and conduct but has not evidenced an ability to express this grasp in sound judgment and decision.

The possibilities of new leadership from within the company were examined one by one, and this conclusion was reached:

The pressing demand in the organization is for leadership of a sound, well-poised and effective character. In other words, what is needed is the introduction of a big-visioned practical and experienced executive regardless of his particular manufacturing technical experience. And this need is regarded as a sine qua non to continued operation.

These recommendations well summarized the plight of the Saco-Lowell Shops in 1926, and forecast the changes which were to mark the beginning of a new chapter in Saco-Lowell's history.

6. The Enigma and Paradox of the Herrick Era

The opportunity for examining the influence and business methods of Robert F. Herrick, Sr., and the impact of his presence upon a particular business situation ought not to be neglected. This man was a key figure in New England finance. He represented a type of business man which had become increasingly prominent in the American economy. Not since the days of the eighteenth-century slave traders had American business methods attracted such widespread public condemnation as that of the so-called financial capitalist, the professional organizer and reorganizer of American enterprise who stepped in, with State Street or Wall Street backing, to recapitalize, regroup, consolidate, integrate, and, occasionally, to liquidate such companies as no longer seemed able to survive increasing competition or outlive the obsolete managerial techniques of existing managements. The charges against this relatively new professional business class were serious, and are repeated today with renewed vigor.

An appraisal of Robert Herrick, Sr.'s, career with Saco-Lowell takes on added interest from the fact that Herrick was publicly accused of illegal business tactics and stood, for a time, publicly condemned. The Willett-Herrick trial of 1923 and 1924 has no direct bearing upon Saco-Lowell history, but this long and famous law case focused public attention upon Herrick and his business methods. The charge against Herrick and his co-defendants, F. S. Moseley & Company and Kidder, Peabody & Company, was conspiracy to deprive the plaintiffs of their stock in the American Felt Company and the Daniel Green Felt Shoe Company and acquire control of these companies for themselves.[58] At the commencement of the trial the position of the defendants appeared to be secure against any legal challenge, although the benefits which Herrick and the investment houses had received in exchange for their financial assistance to Willett were obviously great. To the public mind the issue was not legal but moral. This clearly was considered by many as a case of State Street versus the people, and it was brilliantly presented along these lines by counsel for the plaintiff. The verdict, delivered after the longest jury trial in the court history of Massachusetts, was a people's verdict, and assessed damages in the sum of $10,534,000 against the defendants. The fact that this finding was later reversed by the Supreme Judicial Court scarcely lessened the popular prejudice against Herrick and his associates, and these men, disdaining public opinion and secure in the knowledge that they worked in the interest of business efficiency, did nothing to correct the popular judgment. Working behind the scenes, often in concert, and surrounding their activities with a barrier of legal fictions and a wall of secrecy, men of this professional class were the obvious prey of a government committed to a New Deal for the common man, whether in 1913 or 1933. Who, besides his immediate associates, could assess the business accomplishments of Robert Herrick? Must this man, standing in the shadow cast by an atrociously poor public-relations policy, be recorded in history only as the defendant in *George F. Willett, et al.* v. *Robert F. Herrick, et al.?* What light does the Saco-Lowell experience shed upon the man, his objectives, his methods, his strengths, and his weaknesses?

The enigma of Robert Herrick, Sr.'s, association with the Saco-

Lowell Shops stems from the very great difficulty of tracing the extent of his influence in company affairs. Robert Herrick, Sr.'s, control of the company was scarcely obvious, for the burden of management was carried by others and, as far as can be determined, no occasion ever arose when the extent of that control was revealed by a direct challenge. Herrick's power in the company derived less from stock ownership or the command of sources of credit and capital than from the personality of the man. Here is to be found the same intangible power of personal influence which defied the inquiring genius of Samuel Untermeyer to define and measure in the famous Pujo Money Trust Investigation in 1912 and 1913. It was the same personal influence which bound companies together without interlocking directorates, which created business ties without contracts, which established control without ownership. It would be a serious fallacy to say that ultimate responsibility for the conduct of the Saco-Lowell Shops rested with the board of directors, or with any individual or individuals other than Robert F. Herrick, Sr., whatever the source of his power or however that power was used or neglected. Herrick dominated Saco-Lowell policy just as he had dominated every situation with which he had been connected since his college years. This power, exercised in a quiet and unostentatious manner, pervaded company affairs whether Herrick was sitting in his black leather upholstered chair in the board room at Number One Federal Street or was visiting mills in China.

Herrick's object in forming the Saco-Lowell Shops in 1912 was to increase the operating efficiency, and hence the earning power, of a business unit which he already controlled by allying it with a stronger business unit. I see in this basic aim nothing that had sinister implications for society or was other than beneficial to both the textile industry and the textile machinery industry. The charge is often leveled against men who occupied positions in industry similar to that of Herrick that they sought and made profits in promotion, reorganization, and liquidation, without concern for the ultimate possibilities of profit through normal business operation. Such charges are brought to mind again and again by the testimony in the Willett-Herrick case. Not only was this not true of Herrick's latter-day participation in the affairs of the Saco-Lowell

Shops, but I even detect a lessening in the Herrick era of the old interest in profiting from price controls, together with an increasing awareness of the opportunity for profit through product development, enlarged markets, and scientific reduction of operating costs. This was particularly true of the years when Robert Herrick, Jr., actively managed the business. The elder Herrick's interest in the Saco-Lowell Shops was keen, personal, and directed at the building of a sound and permanent operating unit. Failure of achievement and criticisms of methods employed must not be allowed to obscure his objectives.

Up to 1922 there are few criticisms of the management of the company which cannot equally well be made against the Whitin Machine Works or against innumerable other manufacturing enterprises. These criticisms center in the failure to develop adequate accounting controls, to devote sufficient attention to improvement of existing machinery design, or to materially strengthen the Lowell shop by physical improvements or alterations of the product line. Such oversight in a booming war market is readily understandable. On the other hand, marketing policy had been aggressive, the Newton and Biddeford plants had been improved, labor relations were satisfactory if not conspicuously farsighted, and financial policy (including the disbursement of dividends) had been conservative. These strengths and weaknesses may be traced to Hale and to Snelling, the men to whom Herrick had entrusted the management of the business.

Robert Herrick, Sr.'s, great failure occurred after 1922, when he neglected to exercise the control which was so indisputably his, or to assume the responsibility to which his great power committed him. The failure lay specifically in not bridging the managerial gap left by the withdrawal from active management of Hale and Snelling. Perhaps the failure was more basic than this. It was the company's misfortune that Hale's advice about men and the industry and Snelling's conservative financial proclivities were uncontestably over-ruled, and that these two men and others on the directorate were placed in a position where they scarcely could feel responsible for company policy. This situation arose directly out of the lack of restraint by a proud father over an energetic but inexperienced son.

Having placed that son in a position of dominance in the company, Robert Herrick, Sr., was under the strongest obligation to guide him, or to make certain that others were guiding him.

Why was this not done by Robert Herrick, Sr., keen and able administrator that he was? A possible answer to this question lies in the vast scope of Herrick's interests outside the Saco-Lowell Shops—interests which unquestionably usurped time and energy to which Robert Herrick, Jr., and Saco-Lowell had a substantial claim. Herrick was associated with Daniel Wing, Philip Stockton, and other bankers in a large number of enterprises, which included the United Fruit Company, the United Shoe Machinery Corporation, Scott & Williams (knitting machines), Reed Prentiss Company (lathes), the Old Colony Trust Company, and the First National Corporation (investment affiliate of the First National Bank of Boston). The number of companies in which Herrick was a director was formidable, and the list of enterprises for which Herrick's law firm performed professional services constituted a virtual Who's Who of New England Business. The tremendous importance of Robert Herrick and his law firm in New England's modern industrial history is a point apart. The main issue here lies in the fact that, whatever his genius, Herrick would have had difficulty in fulfilling all the responsibilities associated with all his positions even under normal conditions, but in addition to these heavy burdens he was preoccupied with the Willett trial for thirteen of the most critical and eventful months in Saco-Lowell's history. These circumstances would seem to explain much of Herrick's neglect of an obvious and pressing duty.

There is a possibility that Herrick's failure lay in more than neglect, for it is a fact that all the mistakes of the years following 1922 were made with his knowledge and acquiescence. If Herrick's supporting votes at the Board meetings (few of which he missed) were directed by the enthusiasms of his son, then Herrick was guilty only of neglect. If he voted with full and independently acquired comprehension of operating conditions, then he must be held accountable for errors of commission as well as omission and must assume an even greater responsibility for the plight of the company. I have been unable to establish the absolute extent of that responsibility, though I suspect that the same apparent preoccupation which prevented Herrick from counseling his son also impaired his comprehension of operating conditions.

Whatever the extent of Robert Herrick's failure, the events of 1925, 1926, and subsequent years uncontrovertibly clear him of the charge of participating in the affairs of the Saco-Lowell Shops as a "business wrecker." It is true that up to 1925 Herrick had invested little — one might almost say nothing — in the company. His stock holdings in 1925 were substantially the same as they had been in 1912; the 1912 holdings, in turn, derived from his interest in the Lowell Machine Shop, which had cost him nothing. Thus, in one sense, Herrick had little to lose from bankruptcy of the Saco-Lowell Shops. Indeed, he had much to gain from liquidation proceedings, which might well have presented an opportunity for acquiring sole ownership at a low price of some or all of the properties at forced sale.

This temptation, if it did in fact exist, was rejected. Herrick, Hale, and Snelling fought to keep the Saco-Lowell Shops alive. Each man, according to his means, his responsibility, and his outside commitments, pledged new capital for the business. In 1925 these three men, as previously related, had made good their endorsements on company paper to the amount of $895,000. When new securities were issued late in 1926, Herrick pledged a quarter of a million dollars in addition to the $660,000 of gold notes he already held. These loans were not made to squeeze interest from an investment which had long since ceased to pay dividends, for they were extended at a time of gravest crisis, when word of Saco-Lowell's failure was momentarily awaited in the Boston financial district and when even optimistic Frank J. Hale despaired of saving the company.

To Frank J. Hale and R. Paul Snelling the business was an integral segment of their lives, built up painfully, adventurously, and over many trying years. Their participation in the rescue attempts of 1925 and 1926 were limited only by their available capital and, perhaps, by Snelling's declining health.

Robert Herrick, Sr.'s, position in New England financial circles had been shaken by the Willett trial and by the condition of the

Saco-Lowell Shops, for which latter he was privately blamed by many of his business associates. He rose in this time of crisis to display the highest order of professional integrity, which took the form of a determination to forestall any bankruptcy and subsequent loss to clients (in this case the bank creditors) which grew directly or indirectly out of his own actions. I am convinced that, at this point in the affairs of Saco-Lowell, Herrick and Hale would have risen to any eventuality and met any demand upon which the survival of the company might be conditioned. Having made his great mistake, Herrick now stood ready to pay any price to protect his reputation and, perhaps, to protect that of his son. Hale, bearing nominal rather than actual responsibility for the events which had occurred since 1922, stood ready to assist the company which he had done so much to build.

Paradox was the essence of Saco-Lowell's history from 1922 to 1926. Herrick, who controlled the destinies of Saco-Lowell, was farsighted and cautious, yet a poorly timed expansionist psychology flourished in the company. Herrick was a keen financier, yet near-fatal financial mistakes were committed with his knowledge and approval. Business efficiency was Herrick's profession, yet inefficiency in the form of a misdirected and faltering product policy was not checked. Herrick was liked by nearly every man, in high position or low, with whom he came in contact, yet managerial morale in the Saco-Lowell Shops steadily declined and an inexcusable and costly blunder was made in labor relations. The conclusion most favorable to Herrick to which these contradictions lend support is that the managerial prerogatives implicit in absolute control were not exercised at a time when they should have been, and that a position of utmost responsibility was filled by a man who lacked either the inclination or the time to extend guidance.

The final paradox lies in the fact that Herrick — the hardheaded realist, the buyer and seller of business empires, the bankers' lawyer — when faced with a typical opportunity to profit from corporate misfortune, appears to have turned his back on profit. Here lies final proof, if any further proof is needed, that the Saco-Lowell story is concerned not just with a corporation but with men; not just with the economic explanations of men's behavior, but also with their basic, innermost emotional motivations.

CHAPTER XIV

THE HARD CLIMB BACK
1926–1941

To INFORMED observers in Boston financial circles and to many officers in the company the plight of the Saco-Lowell Shops in 1926 seemed hopeless. A crushing debt, depleted reserves and working capital, and stagnant business had combined in ruthless force. The creditor banks had put an end to the administration of Robert F. Herrick, Jr., and now were working to avoid a costly bankruptcy. Robert Herrick, Sr., and Frank J. Hale were back in harness to save a situation which involved more than money.

The chapters which follow present the essence of what might appropriately be called the Edwards Era in Saco-Lowell's history — certainly one of the most remarkable episodes in more than a century of administrative and machinery-building experience.

1. David F. Edwards

The National City Bank survey of 1926 had stated that Saco-Lowell must secure a "big-visioned, practical and experienced executive." In response to this necessity the directors, on December 31, 1926, elected a new president of the Saco-Lowell Shops.

The agreement which brought David F. Edwards to Saco-Lowell was a liberal one, but anything short of liberality could scarcely have secured for the company a competent top executive.[1] Edwards' highly promising qualifications were already known to Herrick, and the personal impression which Edwards made upon Hale when they first met was so favorable that Hale expressed his immediate willingness to entrust the company to him.

When David F. Edwards came to Saco-Lowell he was forty-five years of age — a tall and compelling man with a disarmingly direct manner of approach. Edwards' physique was that of an athlete; his bearing and speech that of a college professor. He had been both.

His career up to 1926 had been characterized by a far from usual combination of academic and business experience, and this variety was unquestionably a source of remarkable executive strength.

Edwards was born of English-Welsh and Scottish-American parentage. After his graduation from Ohio Wesleyan University, and after two years of teaching English and history at Culver Military Academy, Edwards turned to economics as a field of study which could open avenues into either an academic or a business career. With these alternative avenues in mind Edwards studied at Harvard, where he obtained his Master's degree. In 1908, after further teaching experience, he passed his General Doctoral examination at Harvard and was appointed head of the Department of History and Economics at the Boston High School of Commerce. Then followed a year as educational director of Filene's department store in Boston, from which post Edwards resigned to become industrial secretary of the newly organized Boston Chamber of Commerce. This was the intermediate step between teaching and business, and it was here that Edwards attracted the attention of James J. Storrow, Robert Herrick's one-time partner, who had by that time turned his organizing talents and some of the resources of his firm, Lee, Higginson & Company, in the direction of the lusty young automobile industry.[2]

"Edwards, how would you like to go to Detroit and go into the automobile business?" Storrow asked.

"I never thought of it," Edwards replied. "I had thought of teaching economics at Harvard or teaching at the Business School. Do you think a man of my age can start on a new career in business?"

Storrow thought he could, and early in September of 1911 Edwards was on his way to Detroit and the beginning of his business career.

For five years Edwards worked with Storrow in the General Motors Corporation, during which time, as vice-president of the Olds Motor Works, he had much to do with restoring that company, which manufactured the Oldsmobile, to a sound and profitable operating condition. When Storrow and Nash (then president of the corporation) left General Motors in 1916, Edwards purchased an interest in and became treasurer of the Gier Pressed Steel Company, Lansing, Michigan, which he left in 1917 in order to accept a commission as major in the Army Ordnance Department. In 1919 Edwards worked at a consolidation of the Gier Company with two other companies to form the Motor Wheel Corporation. Shortly after this he became associated with John Willys and the Willys Corporation of New Jersey. This venture did not turn out to Edwards' satisfaction, and in 1921 he accepted the position of vice-president and treasurer of the Lafayette Motors Company, a promotion in which Storrow and Nash were interested and which had turned out badly. Edwards stayed with this company until it was liquidated; then, once again at Storrow's suggestion, he went to New York to become vice-president and, later, president of the Wickwire Spencer Steel Company, where he effected a badly needed operating reorganization.

Edwards' reorganizing and operating experience was thus well rounded and formed a pattern which readily accounts for his presence in the tangled affairs of Saco-Lowell. The Boston investment house of Lee, Higginson & Company knew Robert Herrick and Saco-Lowell well. The great faith which Storrow, a Lee, Higginson partner, had in Edwards, and Edwards' record in enterprises in which he had worked for Storrow and Lee, Higginson, made Edwards a natural selection to head the Saco-Lowell Shops. Here was another distressed and weakened company to be saved — or perhaps liquidated — and here was a man of experience and proven capabilities in the field of corporate reorganization who might be available for the task.

There was an intermediate step between Edwards' services for Wickwire Spencer and his acceptance of the Saco-Lowell presidency. In 1926 Wallace B. Donham, then dean of the Harvard Graduate School of Business Administration, asked Edwards to accept an associate professorship. Edwards felt that he had done all that he could do at Wickwire, and decided to see whether or not he could settle down to teaching again. Three months after his arrival at the Harvard Business School, the Saco-Lowell offer was made.

Dean Donham advised, in the strongest possible terms, that

Edwards refuse the offer. Donham, former vice-president of the Old Colony Trust Company and an informed and influential man in Boston and New York financial circles, was in a position to know whereof he spoke. When Edwards told his friend Professor Charles Jesse Bullock, distinguished member of a distinguished Economics Department at Harvard College, of his decision to forsake the Business School and take over Saco-Lowell, Bullock could only exclaim, "My *God,* Edwards!"

Behind this apparently ill-advised decision to accept what looked to be a hopeless task lay Edwards' conviction that the Saco-Lowell situation had not been correctly appraised. His confidence that there was hope for the company rested upon the realization that there was only one formidable competitor; that there always would be a demand for such machinery; that new competitors could not readily become established in this industry; and that what the company lacked chiefly was the right kind of handling.[3] Beyond these factors, Edwards' motives are best explained in his own words.

"I suppose it comes down to a question of temperament," he remarked in a reminiscent mood many years later. "I had to decide whether I was happier dealing with this kind of a situation — the excitement of it, the hurly-burly of it, the variety of it, the concreteness of it — than I would be in teaching and research, and I suppose perhaps I didn't have enough of the divine fire or irresistible urge to teach to cause me to prefer that to struggling with actual business problems. Beyond that there was this satisfaction. I have been able to take one concrete situation and so mold it and deal with it over a period of years as to convert it from something that was weak and badly demoralized into something strong, and sound, and wholly satisfactory. I think it may be something of the same kind of satisfaction that a surgeon gets from his work. If I had been born with an independent income, I think I might have been a surgeon. To take a man who is at death's door and convert him into a healthy man . . .; in some ways that is what has been done here."[4]

2. Obstacles and Aids for the New Administration

Nothing was more important to the future of the Saco-Lowell Shops in 1927 than the capabilities and personality of David F.

Edwards himself, together with the impact of that personality upon the Saco-Lowell organization. Edwards impressed Hale as being a farsighted, honest, friendly, and eminently practical executive. Herrick respected Edwards' record, but chafed with impatience as the new president worked out policies with infinite caution and meticulously avoided the quick decisions which Herrick himself liked to make. At first, Edwards' almost professorial attitude toward problems both worried and annoyed the former president. The older and more conservative members of the directorate approved of Edwards' grueling thoroughness; younger men were restless but yielding under the impact of power which derived as much from personality as from position. The organization was not long in discovering that everything which could be done to save the company would be done, and that the deep and well-modulated voice of the new president could crack with authority. Edwards commanded the respect of the organization almost from the beginning, though not all had the perception to share his grasp of the total situation.

Edwards came to the company with few limitations upon his authority. The banks insisted, however, upon maintaining close control over expenditures. Herrick himself opposed Edwards' first reorganization moves, but was over-ruled. Edwards' control was firmly established from the outset, and after this initial test of strength the directorate was, in the main, coöperative. Certain of the directors stood out as bulwarks of strength. The acquiescence of some grew out of the calmness of advanced years. The assistance of still others, who were not bound to the company by personal ties, appears to have been conditioned by their belief that the company's condition was beyond remedy.

Much support could be found for this last-named viewpoint. While the quest for new leadership for the company had been going on, an attempt was being made to secure new capital for the business. On November 1, 1926, a refinancing plan was drawn up. This plan followed the recommendations submitted in the survey made by the National City Bank four months earlier. An issue of three-year, 5 per cent unsecured notes was brought forth, and the creditor banks (holding $4,550,000 of old Saco-Lowell notes) agreed to accept these securites in settlement of their existing notes, provided that a minimum of $500,000 of new working capital could be secured. An issue of $528,750 of five-year, 7 per cent convertible notes was offered to the stockholders in order to secure this capital, upon which was conditioned the survival of the company.

As had been the case in 1925, when convertible gold notes were issued to alleviate a financial crisis, the stockholders at large once again failed to come to the aid of the company. On December 10, 1926, the American Trust Company, transfer agent for the new five-year notes, reported that only $175,000 of the issue had been subscribed by stockholders. The banks waited; maturing paper was renewed on a month-to-month basis; and, despite signs of business revival, a sense of crisis hung over the company. Once again, as in 1925, company officers came to the rescue, and on December 31, 1926, the balance of needed subscriptions was obtained. These were as follows:

Robert F. Herrick, Sr.*	$158,510
G. H. Milliken*	16,070
Robert Amory*	15,300
Philip M. Tucker*	25,000
Frank J. Hale*	60,000
Lee, Higginson & Co.	25,000
Textile Securities Co.**	15,000
Eastern Machinery Co.**	5,000
Total	$319,880

(* Saco-Lowell directors. ** Controlled by Saco-Lowell directors.)

Upon receipt of these subscriptions the refinancing plan was declared operative by the banks, and the Saco-Lowell Shops received a three-year reprieve from its most pressing difficulties.[5]

Other recommendations made in the National City Bank's survey were faithfully carried out. On November 1, 1926, the Kitson Machine Shop was legally separated from the parent company by the incorporation of a new company (also known as the Kitson Machine Shop) to which the Kitson plant and other assets were transferred. This new company remained a wholly owned subsidiary, but was placed, nevertheless, in a position where it could be separately disposed of to advantage if the parent company failed to survive.

When David F. Edwards took over the management of the company early in 1927, the refunding of the bank debts had been accomplished, but at the cost of heavy fixed charges. Working capital was still in critically short supply. The physical and financial task of consolidating plant operations seemed great, but the problem of deciding how that consolidation should be effected appeared greater yet. Balanced against these obstacles were the facts that the textile machinery business at last seemed to be reviving, Saco-Lowell's reputation in the market was unsurpassed, promising new design developments were under way, and a vast reservoir of experience in machinery building existed from which a new manufacturing organization could be built.

3. First Steps

The Edwards administration in action was not spectacular, neither were spectacular measures adopted in the first year. David F. Edwards took little for granted, and was, indeed, the antithesis of the "high-powered" executive of hallowed American business tradition. His activities ranged from daily discussions of policy with directors, bankers, lawyers, and top executives to intensive scrutiny of expense and income accounts. Edwards clamped figures in a mental vise and squeezed the essence from them. With infinite patience he built up a knowledge of the details of operations and of the peculiarities of the trade.

To help him in the task Edwards brought to the company an assistant of proven worth. R. A. Kettley was an English accountant who had come to America in 1910 and had gained a large experience in production control and controllership. Like Edwards, Kettley had progressed from one business situation to another. In 1924 Edwards had made him treasurer of the American Wire Fabrics Corporation, a subsidiary of Wickwire Spencer. Kettley's interest was industrial accounting and system work, which led naturally into broader fields of production management. In the first months at Saco-Lowell, Kettley played an indispensable part in channeling important operating knowledge into the president's office; Kettley, in turn, was greatly assisted by the detailed investigations of A. V. Stuart, his accountant-assistant who had come with him from Wickwire Spencer.

The orientation process went on through interminable hours of conferences. Dinners grew cold and lights burned late. Men called in to present information emerged from the president's office mopping their brows. Executives reported, half in admiration, half in exasperation, that David Edwards allowed no man to leave his office until he had completely assimilated that man's problems and exhaustively considered a dozen alternatives to any proposed solution. Few men immediately appreciated the tremendous potency of this growing grasp of all fields of operation when superimposed upon a proven ability to view business situations in their entirety. Even fewer realized that Edwards was teaching as well as learning, and that imperceptibly but surely the managerial staff was being molded into a new pattern of thought and action.

The strong guiding force of the new administration was soon felt. Inventories were pared down and some real estate, such as the unprofitable hotel at Newton, was liquidated. The expensive Boston offices were abandoned for a time, and the Newton plant was made the base of administrative operations. Edwards examined Stevens' Bedaux installation, and concluded not to renew the contract for further work of this nature at Newton and Lowell. His decision was influenced, in part at least, by the realization that these plants might be abandoned. A general housecleaning revealed obsolete and surplus machine tools, many of which were thereupon sold. There were, however, no immediate wholesale reductions in the working force, or in wages. Kettley and his assistants embarked upon extensive surveys of plant facilities and performance.

Organizational lines were tightened. This was not a pleasant process, but Edwards held firm to a conviction that his control over the company must be uncontested. This conviction was shared by the banks, and against such backing even important stockholders could not prevail. After initial, though minor, disagreements, the directorate evidenced its willingness to give Edwards a free hand. In March, 1927, the bylaws were amended specifically to name the president, rather than the treasurer, as the chief executive officer of the company. A new office, that of comptroller, was created, and Kettley was designated to fill this position. Provision was made for enlarging the directorate, and for setting up a three-man executive committee picked by the directorate from among its own members,

Fabian Bachrach

David F. Edwards
President of the Saco-Lowell Shops since 1926

which was to function with all the powers of the board of directors at such times as the Board was not in session. Hale, Robert Herrick, Sr., and Robert Amory were named to this committee. In 1928 Kettley was made treasurer, replacing H. B. W. Snelling, Paul Snelling's nephew, who had served in this position since 1926. These adjustments were not, however, immediately followed by personnel changes at the operating level, which waited upon Edwards' solution to the problem of plant consolidation, a problem of primary and pressing importance and one which was not long neglected.

4. Plant Consolidation — Initial Steps

On December 3, 1927, Kettley presented an infinitely detailed survey of the various means by which consolidation of manufacturing facilities might be effected. This survey hinted at the Herculean nature of the task, but it also revealed the encouraging possibility that the cost of moving (which many had felt would be prohibitive) might be substantially offset by the savings achieved in a single year of operation, plus income realized from sale of surplus machine tools and other assets.[6]

The problem as to which of the alternative methods of consolidation should be chosen was incredibly complex, and Kettley found a complete lack of adequate cost data on which to base his survey of alternatives. Consolidation of all operations in one plant offered the greatest possibilities for savings, yet this was impossible to accomplish in one move because of lack of facilities at any one place, the cost of such a move, and the attendant disruption of manufacturing operations. The next best solution was to eliminate one entire plant or more. To close only part of one plant would, it was believed, accomplish little.

The basic problem was to decide what was to be made and in what quantities. The question of production capacity involved a possible conflict between the long-term well-being of the company and the immediate interests of creditors. Kettley summarized the dilemma in these words:

> Consolidation of our manufacturing facilities can be accomplished with either of two policies in mind. One would consider only the exigencies of the moment and shrink capacity to handle only a compara-

tively small volume of sales, with no provision for a return of business in anything like the volume this company has enjoyed in the past, eliminating unprofitable lines and curtailing experimental work. Such drastic action would be the most effective in safeguarding our immediate future and protecting our creditors but would undoubtedly so restrict future output as to make unlikely the payment of further dividends. The other policy would provide sufficient capacity for future business on a large scale but would otherwise gain everything possible by consolidation.

A production capacity was planned which lay roughly halfway between the average annual output from 1912 to 1926 and the average annual output of the peak years 1917 to 1923.[7] Even under this relatively liberal schedule, however, it was estimated that Saco-Lowell's productive capacity would decline from 40 per cent to 28 per cent of the American industry's capacity.

After the decision had been made to eliminate one or more plants and after the desired capacity had been agreed upon, the difficult question was faced as to which plant should be given up. Here personal considerations and inter-plant jealousies complicated matters. There were undoubted advantages in combining Kitson with Newton, yet Kitson had a strong, almost unassailable, tradition of intense individualism. The banks, moreover, were rather inclined to preserve this organization intact and separate from the parent company to safeguard its resale value. Charges flew between Lowell and Biddeford that false figures had been given by local managements in order to influence the final decision as to which plant should be abandoned.

Abandonment of the Biddeford shop and the transfer of Biddeford operations to Lowell offered the principal advantage of concentrating manufacturing activity in a relatively small geographic area, yet such a move might interfere with the production of spinning frames, which constituted half of the company's dollar sales volume. Moreover, such a move would place a further burden on Lowell's poorly arranged plant, and make necessary the discontinuance of the worsted- and silk-machinery line. This latter consideration was a key part of the entire problem. Worsted and silk machinery appeared to have been losing money for years (there were no conclusive cost data to prove or disprove this, however). If these lines were abandoned, the company would be under strong compulsion to continue to manufacture parts for machines already in use. Yet, the manufacture of parts required almost as great a variety of tools as the manufacture of complete machines. Moreover, an inventory of raw and semi-fabricated material for worsted machinery amounting to $244,000 would have only slight value if this branch of manufacture was discontinued.

The principal alternative plan contemplated abandonment of most of the chronically unprofitable Lowell plant and the transfer of Lowell operations to Newton and to Biddeford. There was little room for expansion at Biddeford, however, and the Biddeford foundry was by far the poorest of any. If, as was suggested, the worsted business was continued in the new building at Lowell, operations would be as widely scattered as before. On the other hand, the Newton foundry, reputedly the best in New England, would be more fully utilized, with attendant savings in cost of castings (23 per cent by value of total machinery costs). Labor rates at Biddeford, too, were 4 per cent lower than at Lowell, though a counter-argument could be presented that Lowell rates were 1½ per cent lower than at Newton and that Lowell offered the most varied labor market of any of the three communities. The contention that abandonment of Lowell involved the sacrifice of $1,900,000 of plant improvements made there since 1920, principally by Robert Herrick, Jr., was partially offset by the knowledge that equivalent or larger expenditures had been made in Newton and Biddeford, and that no matter what sums had been poured into Lowell, the plant was not and apparently never would be adaptable to the economic handling of materials.

In arriving at a decision, the matter of local taxation was accorded considerable attention, though taxes formed a relatively small element of cost.[8] The Newton board of assessors exhibited a completely inflexible attitude. Perhaps they knew that the specialized nature of Newton operations had all but eliminated from consideration at this time the possibility of transferring the Newton shop. Biddeford was willing and anxious to grant tax concessions in order to preserve a vital segment of local industry. The City Council there passed a resolution granting a five-year exemption of taxes for the company, an estimated savings of $240,000 for the period. Feeling at Lowell ran high. There was strong local sentiment that the company was morally committed to remain in Lowell, as a result of certain concessions granted earlier by the city and involving the closing of Dutton Street, which separated the old Lowell plant from the Kitson shop and Herrick's new concrete building. Possibly the attitude of the Lowell City Council was tinged by skepticism that an entire machine shop could be moved — disbelief that this venerable institution which had been a landmark for one hundred and two years would seriously consider leaving. The old anti-corporation feeling was obviously at work. This prejudice derived in part from a widely held belief that the mill-controlled Locks and Canals Company had exercised its power to keep high-wage industries out of Lowell. The recent local managements of the Lowell Machine Shop, moreover, had been decidedly unpopular in some civic circles. The justification for these animosities is of less importance than the fact that they existed. The political air was far from clear. Meetings between Edwards, the Council, and Mayor Corbett, which were held at a time when there was a disposition to remain in Lowell, resulted in little satisfaction for the company. Later, a tax reduction of $25,000 for one year was extended, but this was too little and too late.

On December 15, 1927, Edwards forwarded his recommendations to the board of directors. This letter so thoroughly summarizes the complexity of the situation and so well illustrates Edwards' method of arriving at important policy decisions that it is presented in full in Appendix 16. The conclusion of Edwards and Kettley that the Lowell plant must be abandoned was approved by the banks and the board of directors, and in the spring of 1928 the move was commenced.

This move was not the relatively simple maneuver of transferring an entire plant from one location to another. Kettley's survey had revealed the fact that there were large quantities of similar tools, of different ages and in varying condition, at Lowell and at Biddeford and that both plants had a considerable surplus of tools. A primary object was to move as little equipment as possible, consistent with the policy of keeping the best and most modern tools for future use. All the complications of special jigs and fixtures had to be considered in substituting one machine for another, and the move had to be accomplished with minimum interference to production. This latter aim was materially assisted by the relatively low volume of business being done. Many difficult decisions were faced in selecting raw materials, stock in process, and finished parts for transfer and for disposal.

Abandonment of the Lowell shop meant permanent discharge for many Lowell workmen, foremen, and supervisors. This was, perhaps, the most trying part of the whole difficult operation. The hardship was greatly minimized, however, by generally prevailing prosperity and by the fact that many employees had no desire to go either to Newton or to Biddeford. Nevertheless, the choice of those to be retained and those discharged was a delicate one. It was to this aspect of the consolidation that Edwards gave his greatest personal supervision. All selections of assistant superintendents, division superintendents, accounting executives, designers, draftsmen, department heads, and foremen were finally made by the president. Selections below the foreman level were entrusted to the foremen. Efforts were made by the company to find jobs for those who were to be dismissed and who had not already found jobs for themselves. Of approximately a thousand men employed in the Lowell shop and foundry, about three hundred were transferred to Biddeford or Newton. Between twenty-five and fifty of the hundred and seventy-seven Kitson men went to Newton.

Changes and additions were commenced at Biddeford, and provision was made to augment inadequate foundry capacity during the transition period by purchasing castings outside. Before machines at Lowell were dismantled, a stock of the parts made by those machines had been shipped to Newton or Biddeford for interim storage. The consolidation literally was effected machine by machine, and customers suffered only minor inconveniences.

At Biddeford both the city and the local management rose to the occasion and made a sincere effort to assimilate the influx of machines, men, and families. Inevitably there was confusion, and there were personal conflicts as well. At Lowell a new agent, Alin

P. Greenwood, went about the task of liquidating the plant. Machines were boxed for shipment, sold, or scrapped. The decision was finally made to discontinue the worsted line, and the new concrete building was put up for sale. The decision was made that Kitson, too, should go, and six months after the Lowell move had been completed the Kitson operation was removed to Newton, as was that of the Metallic Drawing Roll Company in Springfield. The Newton organization staggered under the impact of the Lowell avalanche, and groaned when the news was received that Kitson was to come. But here, as at Biddeford, the local management rose splendidly to the emergency.

A write-down in the valuation of abandoned property of $1,000,000 was recorded on the company books in 1928. Consolidation and idle-plant expenses for the Lowell shop in 1928 and 1929 totaled approximately $375,000, as compared with the estimated consolidation cost of $384,000. The cost of the Kitson move was $101,000, as compared with the estimate of $100,000.[9] This had been an incredible task, accomplished not without waste and mistakes but, in general, with a minimum of interference with production.

The old buildings of the Lowell Machine Shop, which filled the triangle formed by the confluence of the Merrimack and Hamilton canals, were finally torn down to save taxes and upkeep. The land, once among the choicest of the original Lowell mill sites, was placed on the auction block, and the crack of the auctioneer's gavel at a bid of $100 marked the end of a distinguished episode in American machinery-building history.[10] Today this property is a vacant and overgrown mass of rubble — a scar on the face of the city and a grim monument, standing among acres of half-occupied old mill buildings, to the inexorable force of economic trends and to the consequences of municipal inflexibility in the face of those trends.

5. Old Challenges Yield to New, 1930–1933

Despite the fact that sales in 1928 were the lowest they had been since 1915 and that a net loss was registered in that year of $892,800, the three-year plan of rehabilitation was a success, if for no other reason than that in January of 1930 the company was still alive and the banks were willing to extend for another three years the unpaid balance of company notes which they held. To be sure, the equity of common stockholders had shrunk more than $1,500,000 since 1926, and unpaid preferred stock dividends had accumulated. The process of retrenchment inevitably was to be painful. Nevertheless, 25 per cent of the bank indebtedness had been liquidated, interest on the balance of the funded debt had been met, and consolidation had been effected. Operating figures had taken on a more healthy appearance. The large loss of 1928 did not reflect normal operating conditions, for it included consolidation expense. Operating losses in 1928 were actually 78 per cent less than in 1927, despite the fact that sales in 1928 had been 34 per cent less than in the preceding year. In 1929 a profit of slightly more than $1,000,000 was recorded on a sales volume only 24 per cent higher than in 1927. These figures are shown in Table 42, and the detailed statistical summary of the condition and progress of the company is presented in Appendix 15, Tables K through O.

The accomplishments of the new administration had been outstanding, and had been effected in the face of great uncertainty in the textile market. No great market boom had assisted in the saving of the company. Indeed, while many industries attained new peaks of prosperity in the late 1920's, New England mills continued, with discouraging regularity, to fail or move to the South.[11] Secondhand machinery from these mills plagued the textile machinery industry. Both active spindles and total spindles in place in New England had declined steadily and rapidly from 1921 to 1930, more than offsetting the increase in spindles in the cotton-growing States. Multi-shift operations in the mills and lack of new mill construction cut still more deeply into the potential market for new machinery. By the end of 1928, however, it was hoped that the purge had run its course, and that now, after eight years of intermittent hard times, the textile industry might begin to replace its worn-out and obsolete machinery. David F. Edwards expressed this hope in his message to the stockholders:[12]

The efficient working life of textile machinery, even when stretched to its limit under the most favorable conditions, certainly does not exceed thirty years. Assuming 30,000,000 active spindles it follows that there must be an average replacement demand alone of 1,000,000 spindles per year. This normal replacement has been deferred in large part during the last five years but cannot be deferred much longer if the equipment of the industry as a whole is to be kept up to a competitive standard of operating efficiency. When this long deferred but inevitable replacement buying starts, your Company should obtain an adequate volume of business and show greatly improved operating results.

TABLE 42

OPERATING RESULTS, SACO-LOWELL SHOPS, 1927–1941
(000 omitted.)

Year	Net Sales	Net Profit (% of sales)	Dividends (% of sales)	Outstanding Debt[a]	Balance of Net Worth Available for Common Stock[b]	Surplus
1927	$ 7,086	− 4.6	([c])	$6,608	$2,600	.....
1928	4,720	−18.9	([c])	6,068	708	.....
1929	8,777	11.4	([c])	4,908	1,757	.....
1930	4,096	−21.7	([c])	4,174	889	.....
1931	3,700	−13.1	([c])	4,191	416	.....
1932	1,982	−38.4	([c])	3,103	344[d]	.....
1933	3,717	6.1	([c])	3,749	115[d]	.....
1934	6,490	8.0	([c])	3,101	405	.....
1935	3,967	.3	([c])	2,883	416	.....
1936	6,978	10.2	([c])	2,521	1,141	.....
1937	9,026	10.4	([c])	1,050	2,083	.....[e]
1938	5,262	1.1	2.6	900	.....	$3,787
1939	6,508	5.2	2.1	700	.....	4,031
1940	9,279	9.5	4.8	350	.....	5,462
1941	11,965	0.0	3.8	350	.....	6,026

[a] Includes funded debt, accrued interest on debt, and working-capital notes outstanding.
[b] In 1938 and thereafter the old no par common stock was replaced by an issue of $5.00 par common stock.
[c] None.
[d] Deficit.
[e] Created by financial reorganization of 1937.
Source: Saco-Lowell records, Audited annual statements and annual reports to stockholders.

These hopes were partially realized in 1929, and operating results for this year bred optimism in the organization. The hard, almost hopeless, struggle to save the company appeared to have been won.

For David F. Edwards the early 1930's must have been a bitter anticlimax. Stripped of reserves and still fettered with heavy indebtedness, Saco-Lowell was scarcely equipped to meet the challenge of a great general depression.

In his annual report to the stockholders dated March 10, 1930, Edwards sounded a grim warning, prophetic of the unfolding business debacle. His reports for the three subsequent years, couched in such terms as "This brutal hammering-down of our sales volume" and "the chaotic and catastrophic conditions existing today," traced the course of the unfolding disaster. Edwards pointed to the fact that the acute and widespread depression in general business was superimposed on an already deplorable condition of excessive overproduction and price demoralization in the textile industry. He noted the heavy losses taken by mills from the plunging prices of cotton. He reminded the Saco-Lowell stockholders of the necessity for preserving intact the company's technically trained and specialized working force, even in the face of an unprecedented lack of orders.[13]

Between 1929 and 1930, Saco-Lowell sales declined 61 per cent. Not since 1914 had sales volume of the component shops been so low. Plant activity fell from 75 per cent to 33⅓ per cent of capacity, and declined again (in 1931) to 31 per cent of capacity. A drastic decline in the British pound sterling reduced British machinery prices 15 to 20 per cent in the world market and impeded Saco-Lowell's already limited ability to compete with the English shops beyond the borders of the United States. The ensuing year brought a further sickening slump. Demand for new machinery virtually ceased, and orders for parts trickled in. Plant operations were curtailed to 20 per cent of capacity, and the volume of sales in 1932 was probably lower than the combined sales of the parent companies had been at any time since the great depression of the late 1850's. "It was in 1932," Saco-Lowell's well-poised president later confessed, "that I began to lose the habit of sleep."[14]

Rigid economies were introduced as the depression deepened. Edwards personally maintained a close scrutiny upon receivables and inventory. List prices of textile machinery were not cut during the depression; but, as machinery orders became more and more difficult to obtain, these prices came to have less and less meaning. Credit terms to the trade were liberalized, and substantial discounts from list prices were granted. Competition on a price basis became more active than it had been in many years, but with the lessons of the bitter past in mind, neither Saco-Lowell, Whitin, nor the H & B American Machine Company evidenced any disposition to plunge the industry into a price war which surely would have been fatal to one or more of these three companies. In the crisis of depression Saco-Lowell's sales department rose to the need for new selling techniques and increased selling effort.

TABLE 43

PERCENTAGE CHANGES IN COSTS, PRICES, AND SALES, SACO-LOWELL SHOPS 1926–1941

Year	(Percentage change from preceding year) Total Net Sales	Factory Payroll	Material Costs	Administrative Expense	Selling Expense	Research Expense
1926	−16	−24	−34	−4	−6	[a]
1927	20	16	53	13	−14	[a]
1928	−33	−21	−28	−24	9	[a]
1929	86	42	103	5	4	[a]
1930	−53	−45	−64	21	9	[a]
1931	−10	−14	−7	−38	−21	[a]
1932	−47	−28	−24	−12	−18	−67
1933	88	30	117	−19	−5	−35
1934	75	45	27	39	91	23
1935	−39	−25	−40	−23	−12	19
1936	76	55	108	15	27	−19
1937	29	23	27	49	28	−1
1938	−42	−41	−58	−23	−12	172
1939	24	42	77	−3	20	123
1940	34	22	33	16	15	−12
1941	29	37	42	0	2	−4

[a] No data.

Source: Saco-Lowell records, Audited annual statements.

Wages, salaries, and employment were adjusted to meet the drastic decline in sales. Total employment, which had stood at 2,450 in 1926, fell below 2,000 in 1932. A part of this decline reflected consolidation operations. Reductions in wages and salaries in 1931, 1932, and 1933 totaled 35 per cent. At the same time,

Edwards noted that Saco-Lowell stood in danger of losing key executives, who had received offers of higher salaries from other firms. A stock bonus system accordingly was instituted to alleviate this threat without necessitating additional overhead expenditure.[15] Table 43 shows the impact of depression upon basic elements in the company's cost structure and reveals the inflexible nature of those elements in comparison with wildly fluctuating sales volume.

The managerial organization was streamlined to permit quicker and more comprehensive control over operations. The Executive Committee, formed in 1927 and composed of three members of the directorate, met often and conducted some business which would otherwise have awaited the regular meetings of the full Board. In 1932 the vice-presidencies, hitherto virtually honorary positions, were turned over to men active in management. W. F. Lowell was elected vice-president in charge of sales, and F. E. Banfield was elected vice-president in charge of production.

By far the most radical adjustment to depression conditions in this period, however, was the abandonment of the Newton plant, a course of action which in 1928 had been held impracticable and unnecessary. This was a bold move, superbly planned and well executed.

6. Plant Consolidation — Final Steps

In 1927 the conclusion had been reached that the Newton plant, with its splendid facilities, its specialized machines and skills, and its splendid foundry, must not be disturbed. After that time many of the factors influencing that decision changed greatly.

In October, 1931, total orders on the Saco-Lowell books stood at $724,593. Of these, $57,136, or less than 8 per cent, were for products built at Newton. The result of this disproportionate decline in activity at Newton was that while the Biddeford shop showed a nine months' profit of $144,008, the Newton shop recorded a loss of $42,275. The sale of cards, main product of the Newton shop, had fallen so low that the entire output for 1929, 1930, 1931, and 1932 combined barely exceeded the annual card-building capacity of the shop. Behind the extraordinary stagnation at Newton lurked a familiar specter — the specter of unimproved machinery.

Over a period of more than two decades the rate of obsolescence on cards in American mills had been negligible. No important improvements had been made. Moreover, thousands of sturdy Pettee cards, ten, fifteen, twenty years old and older, were turning out their sliver in hundreds of American mills almost as efficiently as the latest, shiniest creations of the early 1930's. Actual depreciation was almost as inconsequential as was obsolescence.

Other conditions, which once had made the Newton plant seem indispensable, had also changed. The modern and efficient Newton foundry was operating at 6½ per cent of capacity. For the entire month of September, 1931, the total melt was 128 net tons, only slightly more than one day's capacity. The average annual melt during the 1926–31 period was 58 per cent below that of 1921–26. Changing product policies and foundry practice, as well as prostration of the card business, explained the declining melts.

Abandonment of the worsted- and silk-machinery lines in 1927 had cut the foundry work load. New foundry techniques (savings in scrap produced) had cut tonnage output by 5 per cent. The rapid substitution of steel for cast iron had reduced output another 10 per cent. The foundry requirements for opening and picking machinery were lessened substantially by the substitution of a new steel feeder for the standard bale-breaker and cast-iron feeder. Horizontal cleaners, moreover, had been virtually eliminated because of their tendency to curl the cotton, and the one-process picker contained far less cast iron than the three machines it replaced. Thus the Newton foundry, hitherto a vital part of the company's production plan, seemed destined for permanent under-capacity utilization.

The possibility of shutting down the Newton plant until card orders began to come in was ruled out. Small orders and repair-parts orders had to be accepted; otherwise, card customers would have been driven to the Whitin Machine Works and parts customers to the small repair shops in the South. At this point, too, old arguments began to be heard about duplication in service and overhead departments arising out of geographically divided operations.

Everything pointed to the need for transferring Newton operations to Biddeford, yet such a move seemed at first glance to be completely impossible at a time when working capital was critically short and all resources were being strained to meet interest payments on a heavy debt. President Edwards was not only equal to the task of arranging the move, but he presented a plan so incredibly advantageous and timely that the directors greeted it with unconcealed skepticism. The plan looked too good to be true.

New England Industries, Inc., was a part of the Insull network of public-utility holding companies. This company had acquired control of considerable idle and vacant mill property in Maine, including the York Manufacturing Company at Saco. Efforts had been made for some time to attract new industries to these manufacturing sites, to offset the decimation of the northern New England textile industry. Edwards and Walter S. Wyman, manager of the Insull interests in Maine, struck a trade. Wyman agreed to make available 375,000 square feet of floor space in York buildings which lay just across the river from the Biddeford shop, within bridging distance, and to loan Saco-Lowell $375,000 to cover the cost of moving. Saco-Lowell was to receive a ten-year lease on the York buildings. Annual payments over the ten-year period would cover repayment of the principal of the loan and interest at the rate of 6 per cent annually. At the end of the ten years Saco-Lowell was to be given clear title to the property without further payment.

Edwards carefully explained to his directors the motives which lay behind this extraordinary offer. Wyman, he pointed out, was certain that once the company had gone to the expense of moving Newton operations to Biddeford, it would certainly allow nothing to interfere with ultimate acquisition of the leased property. Hence, the loan was basically sound; so much so that no collateral mortgages were requested of Saco-Lowell. Moreover (and this was a factor of major importance) the Cumberland Power and Light Company, the Insull subsidiary which directly controlled the York property and sold power in the Biddeford-Saco area, would benefit from greater sales of electricity to a larger Saco-Lowell plant and to a greater number of Saco-Lowell employees.[16] Implicit, though unstated, in Wyman's offer was the fact that the Cumberland Power & Light Company had been unable to find a tenant for this property and was faced with the same idle plant expenses which had prompted Saco-Lowell to tear down the old Lowell buildings. A clearer case of complete identity between industrial and public interest than this could not readily be found. This was a real Yankee dicker, in which each party divested himself of burdensome objects, and walked off gleefully fingering a pocketed prize.

As soon as these details had been worked out with Wyman, Edwards reported his recommendations to the directorate with characteristic thoroughness and decision:[17]

> Many months of hard thinking about the whole problem has convinced us that the only way to deal with it thoroughly and successfully is to consolidate the Newton plant into Biddeford and Saco. The alternative is to drift along passively with accumulating and perhaps increasing losses at Newton. This would be a do-nothing, defeatist kind of attitude which could not be taken or justified by an active management responsible for operating a business as a going concern. The timely, practical and mutually advantageous arrangement discussed with Mr. Wyman seems to offer a way out which does not involve any significant immediate expenditure of the company's cash capital. The relatively small annual payments required under the ten-year plan will be covered three or four times over by the annual savings in operating cash expenditures; the total cost of consolidation will be recovered out of savings in from two to three years and thereafter will continue as a permanent and valuable operating advantage to the company. When the cash is repaid, the company will acquire, without cost to itself, a large and valuable addition to its plant. Ultimately, it should be able to realize from the sale of its valuable real estate in Newton a sum sufficient to cover a large part, if not all, of the cost of the proposed consolidation.
>
> It is my recommendation that the Board approve the general plan for consolidation which has been presented. If the Board's action is favorable, I shall then clear the whole matter with the Creditor Banks and acquaint them fully with the proposed consolidation plans.

The consolidation was promptly approved by the directors and stockholders. The creditor banks interjected a limitation that payments on the ten-year lease be subordinated to payments on outstanding funded debt. This unbending insistence by Saco-Lowell's creditors, who in this case certainly did not share Edwards' foresight or appreciation of the advantages of the Wyman offer, might well have blocked the negotiations. The limitation, however, was offset by the action of company officers in pledging $895,000 of outstanding Class B notes (the long-standing and many times subordinated indebtedness of the company to Herrick, Hale, and Snelling) as collateral for repayment of the loan.

By June of 1932 the move had been completed. Edwards reported to the stockholders that the consolidation program had been carried through with entire success and that the expected results had been realized in full. This was the culmination of that slow-moving, but seemingly irresistible, integrating process which was set in motion by Hale, Snelling, and James McMullan when they merged their companies in 1897.

7. EMERGENCE FROM THE SHADOWS

David F. Edwards did not conceal from the stockholders the extreme gravity of Saco-Lowell's financial position, yet in each of his reports through the dismal early 1930's ran a calm theme of confidence.

In message after message he pounded into the stockholders an awareness of the increasingly acute need of the textile industry for new and better machinery and repair parts. This, to Edwards, was a fundamental and incontrovertible economic fact; the textile industry had bought comparatively little new machinery since 1922 — the pent-up demand could not be contained much longer.

In 1933 there were positive indications that the president's confidence would be vindicated. Sales and profits revived. Plant operations for the year as a whole expanded from 20 per cent to 45 per cent of capacity. Foreign sales, which had constituted a small but welcome addition to company income in the depression years, expanded sharply. The attention of Vice-President Lowell became focused on the South American market, which showed promising signs of replacing the once-flourishing but now defunct Oriental market as the primary source of foreign sales.

One factor of greatest importance in explaining the increasing confidence which characterized the textile industry was the partial control of destructive over-production and price-cutting. Early in 1931 the textile industry had made an effort, through the Cotton Textile Institute, to eliminate night work for women and minors in cotton mills throughout the country. This effort suffered from the inherent weakness of any voluntary group action. In 1933, however, governmental regulation took the place of self-regulation. The codes set up under the National Industrial Recovery Act went a step further toward eliminating the demoralization which had characterized textile production and distribution in the three preceding years. Stabilization in the textile industry inevitably reacted to the benefit of the textile machinery industry, and bore out the conviction voiced by President Edwards in 1930 that control of excessive production in the textile industry was essential for recovery of earning power.

The NRA imposed few handicaps upon Saco-Lowell, certainly none of sufficient importance to offset the great advantage of a more stabilized textile industry. The Code of Fair Competition for the textile machinery industry was approved by President Roosevelt on October 16, 1933, and was reported by Edwards to have proven fair and practicable. Company wages were well above the specified minimum rate, and the forty-hour week was no hardship to a company which was still working at half capacity. The machinery industry code had little apparent effect upon labor costs, which in 1934 were far lower than they had been in 1932.

With the revival in sales came increases in wages and salaries and expansion of employment. In July of 1933 the 10 per cent wage and salary reduction of the preceding year was restored. In November of the same year Robert F. Herrick rose in directors' meeting to point out the fact that President Edwards had not shared in this increase, and that while salaries at this time were 23½ per cent below 1929 levels, the president's salary was 34½ per cent below his 1929 rate. The directors accordingly restored Edwards' latest pay reduction.

The not uninterrupted course of business revival after 1933 may be traced in the figures presented in Appendix 15 and is tersely outlined in President Edwards' own words (Appendix 17). The urgent problem of Saco-Lowell's heavy indebtedness, however, should be noted in some detail, for in this area lay one of the greatest achievements of the Edwards administration. Saco-Lowell history in the early and middle 1930's was perhaps colored more by this load of debt than by any other single factor.

In 1930 a small part of the outstanding funded indebtedness had been retired, and the remainder refunded for an additional three years. This necessary financial procrastination enabled the company to survive, but the refunded notes fell due in January, 1933, a time of gravest crisis and depressed business. By this time, however, the original indebtedness to the banks, which in 1927 had stood at $4,550,000, had been reduced to $1,160,000. The extent to which these repayments, coupled with heavy interest charges, affected Saco-Lowell's earnings may be shown as follows:

Year	Interest Charges and Repayment of Notes	Net Loss after All Charges
1930	$ 957,500	$890,340
1931	259,888	485,951
1932	1,705,685	761,001

During this period neither any part of the Class B notes held by Herrick, Hale, and Snelling, or of the convertible gold notes which had been subscribed by company officers and stockholders in 1926 to raise working capital, was paid off. Indeed, unpaid interest on the Class B notes had accrued to a total of $106,654.

In December of 1932 a new refunding plan was approved which extended company indebtedness for another three years. This plan retired $910,000 of the Class A notes held by the banks, and provided for issuance to the banks of $800,000 of notes ("working-capital notes") in exchange for desired working-capital loans. All other indebtedness was again extended for three years. The convertible gold notes held by stockholders at large were given preference as to payment of interest over those held by officers, which were subordinated as to both principal and interest to the Class A notes and working-capital notes held by the banks. The Class B notes held by Herrick, Hale, and Snelling were subordinated as to payment of both principal and interest to all other indebtedness.

Over the next three years the Class A notes held by the banks were further reduced; the convertible notes held by officers and stockholders at large were reduced slightly; and the Class B notes remained untouched. Accumulated interest on notes held by company officers totaled $408,792 in December, 1935, but all other interest charges had been met. In this month another refunding operation extended the funded indebtedness for three more years on terms similar to those of earlier operations.

The pattern of the various financial adjustments which took place between 1926 and 1935 is clear. As was to be expected, repayment of the bank loans was given first consideration. The banks had sufficient confidence in Edwards and the company not only to renew outstanding balances but even to pledge new working-capital loans in the depths of the depression. The reduction of the bank indebtedness from $4,550,000 in 1927 to $900,000 in 1937 was facilitated by the willingness of stockholders and officers to subordinate their claims.[18] Indeed, they had but little choice.

By December of 1936 the company was nearly out of debt, insofar as the banks were concerned. The cost to officers and stockholders of liquidating the Class A indebtedness had been high. No common-stock dividends had been paid since 1925. Accrued dividends on the two classes of preferred stock stood, on December 31, 1936, at $3,037,025. On that date accrued interest on working-capital notes and Class B notes (held principally by company officers) totaled $517,382, and little reduction had been made in the principal outstanding of any but the notes held by the banks.

In 1936 it seemed, at long last, that indebtedness might soon be completely liquidated and dividends resumed. At this point, however, federal legislation caught the company in an awkward position and exacted an ironic toll. In 1935 a federal tax was levied on undistributed earnings. In 1936 Saco-Lowell earned $713,357. The fact that all of this sum and more besides was committed to debt reduction in no way limited the company's tax liability. Nor could these earnings be distributed in dividends to avoid the undistributed profits tax, for no dividends could be paid until the capital deficit of the company (consisting of the impairment of common stockholders' equity to the amount of slightly more than $4,000,000) had been eliminated. A tax of $119,657 was therefore paid, not cheerfully and not without protest.

This tax situation imparted a note of urgency to an already existing desire to simplify the unwieldly capital structure of the company and to reduce the interest charges. On May 1, 1937, an extensive financial reorganization was proposed. The basic feature of this reorganization was the issuance of three new classes of stock. A part of this stock would be exchanged for existing stock and accumulated dividends. The remainder was to be sold, and the proceeds used to retire all remaining funded indebtedness. The outlines of this plan were worked out, after many disagreements, by a committee of stockholders representing all three classes of outstanding stock and headed by Clinton P. Biddle, then Associate Dean of the Harvard Graduate School of Business Administration. The extremely complex legal details were formulated by Robert Cutler, clerk and counsel to the Saco-Lowell Shops. Approximately 96 per cent of the company stockholders agreed to deposit their stock under the terms of the new plan, and an underwriting syndicate was formed by Hornblower & Weeks for the sale of the new securities.

This plan had scarcely been declared operative when a drastic stock-market decline commenced. Hornblower & Weeks, exercising a contractual right provided in the underwriting agreement, understandably declined to guarantee the sale of Saco-Lowell securities under market conditions then prevailing, and on October 27, 1937, the original refinancing plan was abandoned.

Despite this unexpected turn of events the reorganization was pushed through under a new plan which was at once drawn up and declared operative on November 23, 1937, less than a month after the first plan had been abandoned.

This new plan differed from the old only in that the debt reduction was less than originally planned, and the underwriting agreement was eliminated. Once again, certain company officers pledged their support by guaranteeing to subscribe to enough new stock to make possible the payment of at least $900,000 of the company's funded indebtedness. The largest pledges came, as usual, from Frank J. Hale ($230,967) and Robert F. Herrick ($449,988), and were in the form of personal notes. The balance of the funded indebtedness remaining unpaid was to be liquidated by a new $1,500,000 serial bank loan at a lower rate of interest than currently being paid. This plan retained the desirable features of simplifying the debt structure and substantially reducing interest charges. A component part of both the old and new plans was the transfer of all of

Saco-Lowell's business and property to a new company of the same name, incorporated in Maine instead of Massachusetts.

Appendix 15, Table N, summarizes the multiple changes which characterized Saco-Lowell financing. The 1937 reorganization accomplished the following results:

Debt and Capital Structure Dec. 31, 1936		Debt and Capital Structure Dec. 17, 1937	
Class A Notes	$ 472,745.68		
Class C Notes & Accrued Interest	46,900.03		
Class D Notes & Accrued Interest	501,644.04	5-Year Serial Loan	$1,050,000.00
5% Promissory Notes & Accrued Interest	2,965.00		
Class B Notes & Accrued Interest	1,294,839.10		
Total Debt	$2,319,093.85	Total Debt	$1,050,000.00
Preferred 6% Stock and Accumulated Dividends	$2,112,500.00	Class A Preferred Stock	$1,543,140.00
Second Preferred Stock and Accumulated Dividends	4,818,325.50	Class B Preferred Stock	546,420.00
		Common Stock	710,010.00
Common Stock and Surplus	1,140,892.31	Paid-in Surplus	3,819,590.82
Total Stock and Surplus	$8,071,717.81	Total Stock and Surplus	$6,619,160.82

With the successful consummation of the 1937 plan, the financial rehabilitation of the Saco-Lowell Shops, necessitated by the near disaster of 1924 and 1925, may fairly be said to have been completed. What had been the final cost? All note holders had been paid in full, together with accumulated interest. Not one financial institution that stood by Saco-Lowell had any reason to regret such action. The stockholders had suffered considerable losses, though the extent of those losses is difficult to appraise. An approximate indication of the losses taken may be gained from these figures, stated in terms of single shares:

1. *Old 6% Preferred Stock Valuation*		
Redemption Value	$115.00	
Accumulated Dividends	69.00	
		$184.00
Values Received in Exchange, 1937		
3 Shares Class A Preferred Stock (at redemption valuation)	$ 75.00	
3 Shares new Common Stock (at book value Dec. 17, 1937)	31.05	106.05
Nominal Loss per Share		$ 77.95
2. *Old Second Preferred Stock Valuation*		
Redemption Value	$105.00	
Accumulated Dividends	82.25	
		$187.25
Values Received in Exchange, 1937		
1½ Shares Class A Preferred Stock (at redemption value)	$ 37.50	
1½ Shares New Common Stock (at book value Dec. 17, 1937)	15.53	53.03
Nominal Loss per Share		$134.22
3. *Old Common Stock Valuation*		
Basis (a) Original Paid-in Value		$100.00
Basis (b) Approximate Market Value, 1922		150.00
Basis (c) Approximate Market Value, 1937		11.00
Values Received in Exchange, 1937		
½ Share New Common		.....
Basis (a) Book Valuation, Dec. 17, 1937		$ 5.18
Basis (b) Market Price, Jan., 1938		5.00

These figures have validity only as a general measure of relative values. Moreover, the true worth of the new securities was actually an intangible value, deriving less from book figures than from the future prospects of Saco-Lowell as a going concern. The fact is clear, however, that bright though the future might be, those who had purchased Saco-Lowell stock at any time before 1924 had lost a substantial portion of their investment. Equally clear was the fact that the general upswing in business, coupled with deft and dynamic management, had put Saco-Lowell far along the road to recovery — an almost incredible recovery — and that those few investors who gambled on David F. Edwards stood to profit greatly. Chart XIV shows the course of market prices for Saco-Lowell common stock from 1922 to 1948.

CHART XIV

Common Stock Prices, Saco-Lowell Shops, 1922–1948

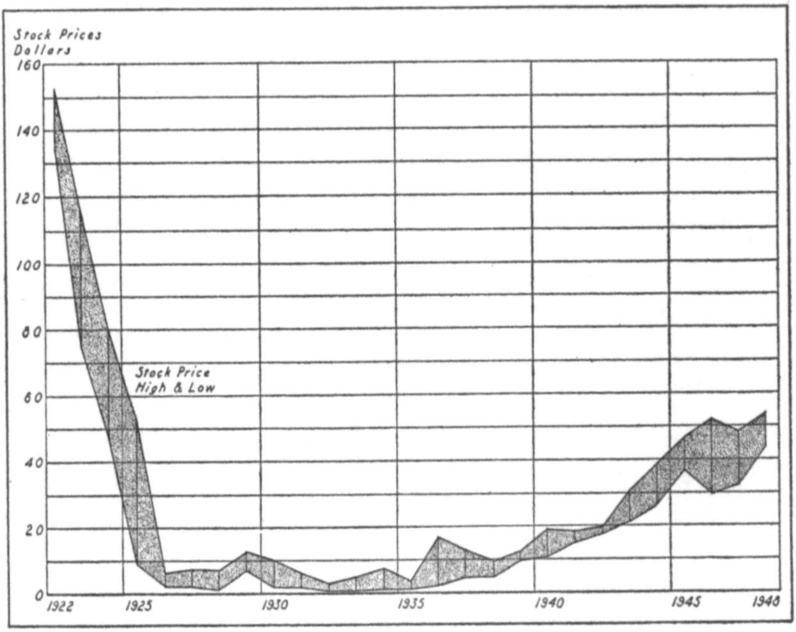

8. Aftermath of Consolidation

While these complicated financial adjustments were being made, events of considerable importance were taking place in the shop at Biddeford. Relatively few people within the organization have appreciated the tremendous burden which was placed upon top management by the combination of financial and operating problems which faced the company in the 1930's. The fact that these problems were inter-related diminished in no way the necessity for the highest order of managerial versatility. One of the great strengths of top management in this period was recognition of the need for attention to the operating as well as the financial situation. Unfortunately, however, certain limitations were imposed by the gravity of this financial situation upon efforts to effect thorough-going adjustments in the shop.

Some progress was made toward the goal of welding the recently assimilated Newton, Kitson, and Lowell shops into a smoothly working organization. In the black months of the middle 1930's, when pay was being reduced, employment was being cut, and all in the shop were exerting their best efforts to forestall layoff, morale was probably higher than it had been before or was later to become.

A surprising awareness of David F. Edwards existed in the shop — surprising because Edwards' contact with the plant was limited to occasional visits, which were largely taken up by managerial conferences. Rumors of his financial prowess seeped into the community and into the shop, and began to coagulate into a legend which Edwards' personal appearance and bearing itself helped to build. Determination and strength seemed to emanate from the powerful figure of the president, a figure so dominating as to lend ready credence to the popular belief that here was the man who had saved the company from the Boston banks. This shop estimate of David F. Edwards' particular accomplishments was woefully distorted by ignorance of the details of events in Boston and by the deep and abiding distrust with which many Maine people regarded Boston banks and bankers. Nevertheless, the great truth was known in Biddeford that Edwards had saved the company. There was a striking similarity, indeed, between the respect and esteem in which Edwards came to be held by the shop people and that accorded a former leader, Frank J. Hale.

Nevertheless, the goal of unity in the organization was not fully achieved. Component shop identities survived and even defied efforts to submerge the parts into the whole. Men were Newton men, or Biddeford men, or Lowell men — there were no Saco-Lowell men. More than all the rest, the proud Kitson group, now a small remnant of the original staff, held itself apart and bitterly resented efforts in the direction of assimilation. These difficulties were perhaps more apparent than real, but charges were often flung about the plant and whispered in the community that Lowell (or Newton, or Kitson) people were the first to be laid off in hard times; the first to be demoted; the last to be considered for positions of responsibility. This was shop talk — always loose, always bitter, and seldom fair or accurate. It is mentioned here only in support of the conclusion that moral, if not physical, disunity persisted. The importance of this factor as an influence upon the immediate over-all efficiency of shop operations is impossible to measure or estimate.

Economy characterized every phase of shop operations, and this was perhaps the most permanently damaging result of Saco-Lowell's dire financial plight. In the disruption attendant upon the 1932 consolidation an unparalleled opportunity was presented for a complete overhauling of production control and wage incentive systems — an opportunity which the company could not afford to take or to lose. The grinding poverty of the company often and of necessity resulted in adoption of the most economical rather than the best methods of plant management.

Economy was the driving need of the times. To ensure the rigid watch over costs which was essential to survival, Edwards, in July of 1935, sent his treasurer-assistant, R. A. Kettley, to Biddeford to replace Agent Banfield. Banfield was placed in charge of research, but subsequently left the company and went to the Whitin Machine Works.

Kettley was well qualified by training and temperament to perform the job at hand. His incisive, mathematical mind functioned with agility upon cost and production problems, and he characterized himself as a "monkey-wrench mechanic." Kettley's broader managerial qualifications were subtle in nature. A man of considerable reserve, Kettley was held by many to be aloof and disinterested. Associates soon found that this was not the case, though Kettley never came to be close to or understood by the men in the shop. He picked his assistants, entrusted the men of his choice with full responsibility, and backed them to the limit. Where the right men were picked, this characteristic was a source of great strength, and Kettley soon built up a staff of trusted assistants. There is no question that the combination of Kettley, entrusted with the task of promoting economy and acting as a watchdog, and Works Manager Roderic Tarr, in charge of plant operations, was an effective one in meeting the requirements of the times.

The possibility of replacing the Bedaux system completely was ruled out, for reasons of economy. Considerable efforts were made to eliminate sources of waste in the plant and to minimize the inequities arising out of faulty application of the Bedaux system. These efforts, instituted under Kettley by Plant Accountant A. V. Stuart, often encountered the bitter opposition of local management.

A system of semi-decentralized production control was adopted as providing, in a time of low business volume, the most economical method of operation. Manufacturing departments were treated almost like separate job shops and foremen were given much responsibility.

No sweeping reorganization took place at Biddeford; there was no wholesale change in managerial personnel; few outsiders were brought into the plant. This course was dictated by economy and the absolute need for avoiding excessive internal disturbance at a time when problems in other areas were acute.

Obvious success was achieved in reducing direct costs and overhead expense. This success was tempered by failure to eliminate deep-rooted abuses of the Bedaux system, or to instill into local management such organizational loyalty as would eventually minimize shop politics. The atmosphere of instability imparted by a succession of past organizational changes was scarcely cleared. Nevertheless, the important job had been done, and there was a hope and expectation that the potent managerial abilities which were to be found in the company might now, with essential tasks completed, be turned to neglected details.

9. Saco-Lowell and the Industry

David F. Edwards showed from the very beginning a keen awareness of the fact that Saco-Lowell did not exist in a vacuum. His broad viewpoint and experience, coupled with the prestige which his remarkable success with the company had built up, soon made him a recognized leader of the textile machinery industry, if, indeed, the modern industry can be said to have had a leader. Whitin's problems had never been external in the sense that institutions or investors outside the company had been called upon for help. The business, despite its size, was a family business and the interests of its managers were not often distracted from Whitinsville. The energies of E. Kent Swift, president and treasurer of the Whitin Machine Works, found an outlet in his company and in his village and

Swift had never, despite his ability and wide contacts in the trade, displayed an ambition to serve, as had George Marston Whitin, in the capacity of arbiter of industry problems.

Edwards and Swift became good but casual friends, each holding the abilities of the other in profound respect. There were also personal ties between the two competitors in the lower levels of management and, of course, some drifting back and forth of employees. Research projects and new product developments were carefully guarded secrets, but there was an exchange of information between the two firms on manufacturing controls, costs, and administrative problems. Despite a common rumor in Whitinsville that E. Kent Swift owned a controlling interest in Saco-Lowell (he actually owned, and his family still owns, one thousand shares of Saco-Lowell stock)[19] and despite personal contacts at many points in the two organizations, these two competitors remained aloof and competitive.

A strong consciousness persisted that the industry had reached a point of stability where further consolidation among major companies was not only politically inexpedient but actually offered few economic advantages. After 1930, when Whitin bought out the Fales & Jenks Machine Company and the Woonsocket Machine & Press Company, neither Whitin nor Saco-Lowell made any particular effort to absorb smaller specialists who operated on the fringes of the industry, many of whom made machines which the larger companies had dropped from their line.

Little more than rumor is known about the H & B American Machine Company, the only other American builder of a complete line of preparatory machinery. "H & B" continued to turn out machinery patterned closely after English models, and this company suffered severe financial reverses in the depression of the early 1930's. Perhaps the retirement of C. E. Riley, H & B's aggressive manager of an earlier day, affected the company adversely. Certainly this company, which since the first World War had never been a serious competitive threat, lost further ground to Whitin and Saco-Lowell in the decade of the 1930's.

In one field Whitin and Saco-Lowell did not come into competition with each other. No sooner had hard times and the necessity for plant consolidation forced Saco-Lowell out of the worsted business than Whitin plunged in — benefiting, as mentioned previously, from Saco-Lowell's thirty-year battle to build up the prestige of American-built worsted machinery. In the cotton-machinery market competition between Whitin and Saco-Lowell was both keen and clean, and each company, while willingly conceding the strengths of its rival, strove hard to outdo the other. There was no allocation of markets other than that made by the mill customers themselves, who had always shown such a pronounced disposition to patronize one shop or the other that many came in time and by their own volition to be known as "Whitin mills" or "Saco-Lowell mills."

Leadership in point of size had long been a much sought-after and much vaunted prize, and that leadership had passed and repassed between Whitin and Saco-Lowell. In the late 1930's Whitin briefly forged ahead of Saco-Lowell in volume of sales, but the margin of difference was small. A comparison of sales over the 1926–40 period yields the following results:[20]

Inclusive Years	Whitin Sales	Saco-Lowell Sales
1927–30	$19,135,000	$24,679,000
1931–35	17,944,000	19,856,000
1936–40	39,962,000	37,053,000
1927–40	77,041,000	81,588,000

One significant conclusion to which these figures point is that consolidation of plant facilities had not led to the expected decline in Saco-Lowell's share of available machinery business. This circumstance grew out of the general falling-off of machinery business in depression years and the attendant lack of pressure upon manufacturing facilities. Had business been more active, Saco-Lowell might, at this time, have been unable to fill orders and hence have lost a share of its business to Whitin.

The comparison between Whitin and Saco-Lowell cannot but lead to astonishment that in some of the most critical years of its history Saco-Lowell was able to outsell its stable and well-entrenched competitor. These figures provide a lucid commentary upon one of the great strengths of the Edwards administration — the caliber of the selling effort put forth. The strength here derived chiefly from the personal ability of Sales Manager W. F. Lowell, and from

Edwards' willingness to allow Lowell to sell. Lowell's ability took expression in the form of unsurpassed contacts in the textile industry — always the primary qualification for success in selling textile machinery. Administrative problems were of relatively minor importance where the number of customers was small, the unit sales large, and the selling staff limited in size. Saco-Lowell's need in the sales department was less for an executive than for a salesman. This need arose out of the fact that, in the absence of new mill construction, the only possible hope for selling machinery lay in persuading economy-minded mill men to replace their existing equipment. Frank Lowell proved to be an energetic and imaginative salesman, whose success was predicated, in the best Frank Hale tradition, upon the confidence and friendship reposed in him by mill men all over the world. Abandoning high-pressure methods to others, Lowell channeled his own and the company's selling efforts along creative lines, taking as a basic premise the viewpoint that Saco-Lowell must provide tangible proof to potential customers of their need for new machinery. Following this tenet, the practice of providing surveys of customers' plant layouts was inaugurated. This service was reminiscent of that provided in its heyday by the Lowell Machine Shop, when free mill plans were drawn up for prospective buyers. In the later case, as in the earlier, a marketing precedent was established which competitors were forced to follow. Lowell himself traveled on an average of about sixty thousand miles a year at this time, and was able to put Saco-Lowell machinery into many mills which had always been considered Whitin strongholds.

A comparison between operating profits of Saco-Lowell and the Whitin Machine Works over these years also yields most interesting results, and provides further evidence that the hard-hitting tactics which Edwards employed to forestall disaster had immeasurably improved the competitive position of the Saco-Lowell Shops.

	Whitin Operating Profits		Saco-Lowell Operating Profits	
Inclusive Years	Dollars	% of Sales	Dollars	% of Sales
1927–30	23,000	.1	772,000[a]	3.1
1931–35	1,674,000[a]	9.3	349,000	1.8
1936–40	3,828,000	9.6	4,786,000	12.9
1927–40	2,177,000	2.8	4,363,000	5.3

[a] Loss.

These figures, of course, do not represent final or net profits, which could not be compared because of certain inconsistencies between the statistics available for the two firms. The figures do, however, reflect operating conditions and are not biased as a measure of comparative performance by the inclusion of large, miscellaneous, non-operating revenues and expenditures. Whitin, for example, showed a very much higher net income than did Saco-Lowell over the period, but the net income figures for the two companies include considerable income from investments for Whitin and heavy interest charges for Saco-Lowell.

The comparison of profits suggests at once that despite consolidation, reorganization, and financial difficulties, Saco-Lowell was producing machinery more efficiently than Whitin. Such a conclusion could scarcely be advanced without the support of much more evidence than that provided by these figures alone, which may, for example, be colored by Whitin's developmental efforts in the worsted field. Nevertheless, they do show beyond all question the outstanding success of the Edwards administration in its efforts to put Saco-Lowell on a sound competitive operating basis, and the comparison contrasts sharply with the relative performance of the two competitors in the years preceding 1926 (Chapter XIII, p. 503).

In one other field of activity the relative efforts and accomplishments of these two shops were of great significance. Not for many years had so many promising developments occurred in textile machinery design. It was here that competition between the two industry leaders was keenest and of greatest value to the textile industry.

10. New Machines and Better Machines

Scholars pursuing the history of American invention may well be seduced into error when they come to trace the evolution of American textile machinery. The trend line seems transparently clear, and up to a certain point conforms rather nicely to the pattern in other industries. First came servile imitation of the English, an exclusively westward flow of ideas across the Atlantic. Then came the American awakening — not just American adaptations, but American inventions. English ideas continued to stimulate American machinists, but American dependence upon England became progressively less marked. Clearly, the end of the cycle was in sight. That end was demonstrable in the machine tool industry, where American subservience had yielded to mutual Anglo-American inspiration and then to near-complete American domination. Following in this pattern the textile machinery industry should have signed its Declaration of Independence in 1886, as soon as Paul Snelling had deposited the plans for the revolving flat card on Superintendent Francis' desk in the office of the Pettee Machine Works. The promise of a well-defined trend, however, was not realized in the first three decades of the twentieth century. The Atlantic Ocean continued to be a two-way street, as it had been since the 1830's. The prolific product developments of the 1920's — developments which gave both Saco-Lowell and the Whitin Machine Works new life — had their seeds in England and in Europe.

For many generations the textile and textile machinery industries had been characterized by intense preoccupations. Technological advancement had not been well rounded, and while consuming interest was manifested in one area much else was neglected, or nearly so. It seemed almost as though the textile industry was incapable of assimilating more than one major machinery improvement at a time. When the light-weight spindles began to appear in the 1870's, mill men and shop men talked, thought, and probably dreamed of spindles and little else. The revolving flat card monopolized the late 1880's, and the Northrop loom the late '90's. In the middle 1920's long-draft spinning and roving burst with pent-up force upon the textile industry, and while by this time there were wide-scale developments of interest to mill men, long draft became an absorbing subject for conversation and experimentation.

Long-draft spinning and roving was nothing more nor less than realization of an ancient ambition to reduce the number of steps through which yarn was processed to reach its final size and strength. If the drafting capacity of the spinning frame could be increased, one or more of the roving frames employed in the processing which preceded spinning might be eliminated. The difficulties which stood in the way of accomplishing such a short cut without sacrificing quality, however, were most complex.

Greatest of these difficulties was the nature of the cotton fiber

CHART XV

Elements of Long-draft Spinning

(Drawing by J. M. Scott)

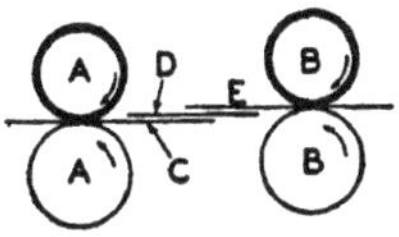

The Problem

Fiber E is being held back by the rolls BB, and fiber C, having left the grip of rolls BB, is now gripped by rolls AA and traveling at the speed of pair A. In between the nips of AA and BB is a fiber D which has already left the rear pair of rolls but has not arrived at the front pair. Usually, because of the higher speed of fiber C it exercises more control over D than does fiber E. In practice D represents a large number of fibers which will go forward before they ought to do so, the result being a thick place in the yarn followed by a thin place.

Casablancas Solution

Double revolving apron to control fibers in passage between rolls.

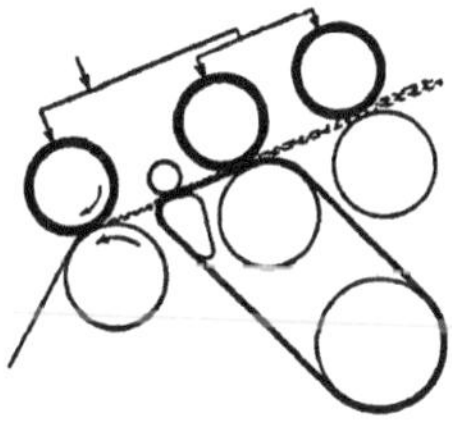

Roth Solution

Single revolving apron to control fibers in passage between rolls.

itself, which varied greatly in staple length.[21] The necessity for controlling these fibers of variable lengths in the brief interim after they had left the nip of one set of rolls and before they were grasped by the succeeding pair was immensely complicated by any attempt to increase the draft. (See Chart XV.)

Many solutions to the problem of controlling the cotton fibers during drafting had been advanced, including various methods of supporting the yarn in transit between the rolls by means of a stationary plate. A more satisfactory solution was provided by supporting the yarn by means of two revolving belts or aprons which moved at the same speed as the yarn and acted as a carrier from one set of rolls to the next. (Chart XV.) The use of belts in the drafting zone was not new, but the first man to make this device practicable was Fernando Casablancas, a Spaniard. His invention was first shown in 1913 in the School of Technology of Sabadell, near Barcelona, and stirred the European textile industry.

The first World War retarded Casablancas' work, but immediately after the war the idea spread rapidly, modifications of the Casablancas system cropped up here and there, and fantastic claims began to reach America. Saco-Lowell's chief engineer, E. E. Blake, and Vice-president F. E. Banfield went to Europe shortly after 1920 to investigate the comparative merits of the Casablancas system and a modification developed by Martin Roth at the mill of LeBlan et Cie. in Lille, France.[22]

In 1923 a syndicate was formed by American mill men for the purpose of introducing the Casablancas system into American mills.[23] For a time both Saco-Lowell and Whitin handled the Casablancas long-draft spinning installations in American mills. Few installations were actually made, however, and these introductory efforts were not successful. The sponsors did not understand the nature and limitations of long draft, and especially its application to American mill practice. The early Casablancas systems were set up for use in European mills where operations were much more closely supervised than in the high-production, highly mechanized American mills. Both Saco-Lowell and Whitin played with an alternative long-draft system — the four-roll process which was popular in England.

Chief Engineer Blake, who devoted much effort to the new development, had become convinced that the LeBlan-Roth modification was superior to the Casablancas system and all other adaptations and modifications thereof. On January 7, 1926, Sales Manager W. F. Lowell negotiated an agreement with Martin Roth which gave Saco-Lowell exclusive American rights to the LeBlan-Roth process. Blake and his engineering staff began intensive experimentation to adapt the Roth system to American conditions.[24]

Certain basic tenets were established to guide this research:

1. The future of the new development was considered to lie in the field not of longer drafting, but of better drafting.

2. The function of better drafting was to be the production of more even yarn of higher breaking strength, from a given cotton.

3. Any savings accruing from longer draft were to be considered of secondary importance, and at no time was quality to be sacrificed to attain a lower cost.

Thus the idea of *better drafting* supplanted or at least augmented that of *longer drafting*.

The original Roth long draft performed well on the soft twists used in Europe, but it required close and careful adjustments in accordance with the length and character of the cotton and the twist of the roving. Most European mill men enjoyed experimenting and tinkering with new machines, but machines for the production-minded American mill managers had to be ready to start and function perfectly as soon as the erectors had shifted the driving belt to the tight pulley. Blake was acutely aware of this and realized that, if long draft was to succeed in America, the need for all "finicky" adjustments must be eliminated. Blake's work in establishing the drafting limits for the new system constituted the basis for the success of long-draft spinning in American mills.

The first trial frames were sent out in 1926, and in March, 1928, Saco-Lowell announced its new long-draft spinning system. The immediate effect of this action was to force Casablancas into the Whitin camp, and in 1929 Whitin concluded an arrangement with the American Casablancas Corporation for the exclusive American rights to the Casablancas system. By 1930 Saco-Lowell-Roth long-draft spinning had been widely introduced. Sales of long-draft change-overs in that year totaled $501,000, or approximately 12½ per cent of Saco-Lowell's total sales. Sales thereafter, ranging from 12 to 16 per cent of total sales, went far toward relieving the pressure of depression.

Increased drafting in the spinning process effected economies in the preceding roving process. Saco-Lowell advanced modest claims for its Roth attachments, but even minimum claims indicated that on carded cottons the new system utilized drafts nearly double those possible on the old three-roll drafting element. Since more drafting could now be done on the spinning frame, it was possible to eliminate one of the three types of roving frames which hitherto had been necessary to reduce yarn for the final spinning in the average carded-yarn mill. In combed-yarn mills two, and in some cases three, roving frames could be done away with. Roving on average counts of yarn became two-process instead of three-process. Even as this change was taking place, however, engineers were working to apply the long-draft principle directly to the roving process, and do away with still another roving frame.

Whitin, through acquisition of American rights to a Casablancas-type machine developed by the German firm of Richard Hartmann Company, had gone ahead of Saco-Lowell in long-draft roving. This machine, it was hoped, would do the work of both roving and spinning frames of the conventional type. Whitin soon found that this installation was not satisfactory and began to develop a Casablancas long-draft element for roving only, which would supplement the Casablancas spinning system already being marketed, and reduce roving, as well as spinning, to a one-process system.

As soon as the Saco-Lowell-Roth spinning was made ready for marketing, company engineers turned to long-draft roving. Experiments with four-roll drafting and an apron-type frame similar to that used in long-draft spinning were not satisfactory, but in 1933 E. E. Blake learned of a promising experimental machine then in operation in the Riverside and Dan River Mills in Danville, Virginia. This was an invention of one William G. Reynolds, who had been a mill overseer and superintendent in several Southern cotton mills. Reynolds had developed his machine over a period of years, receiving financial assistance from E. A. Terrell, of the Terrell Machine Company, in Charlotte, North Carolina, in return for a half-interest in Reynolds' patent.

Vice-president Banfield, W. F. Lowell, and others traveled to Danville, viewed the machine, and talked with Reynolds. The development showed definite promise. In July of 1933 Reynolds came to Biddeford to work for Saco-Lowell and to assist the company in making his machine practicable.[25]

Blake seized upon the Reynolds idea as a providential answer to competition from Whitin's Casablancas long-draft roving frame, which since 1930 had been seriously cutting into the sales of Saco-Lowell's conventional roving frames. On December 28, 1933, an agreement was signed between Saco-Lowell and Reynolds and Terrell. By the terms of this agreement Saco-Lowell agreed to pay a royalty of 15 per cent of net sales (later reduced to 10 per cent) for all machines sold which came within the claims of Reynolds' first patent and of a second patent he was currently applying for.

It seemed clear that Reynolds had hit upon a brilliant idea, but difficulties were experienced in working it out. Experimental installations were not satisfactory, and when the machine was finally put on the market it was found that good results could be obtained only when the machine was very carefully kept clean of clogging lint and dirt.[26] Reynolds and Blake did not get on well together. The company later contended that Reynolds had been difficult to deal with and had been of little assistance in the extensive developmental work undertaken by the company to perfect his device, while Reynolds claimed that the research had been taken out of his hands. In November, 1934, Reynolds became dissatisfied and left the company. Installations of his machine (the so-called "D-2" frame) continued to be made, royalties were paid to Reynolds and Terrell, and customers continued to complain. Meanwhile, Whitin brought out an improved Casablancas frame in 1934, and gained further ground in the competitive race.

By mid-1936 Biddeford's plant manager, Kettley, became impatient with efforts to improve the Reynolds frame and instructed R. M. Jones, research engineer on cards and drawing frames, to try his hand at the roving frame. Jones was successful in his efforts, and on April 5, 1937, Saco-Lowell unveiled its new long-draft roving frame (the "J1" frame) at the Southern Textile Exposition in Greenville, South Carolina. There it was seen for the first time by Terrell and Reynolds.[27]

Reynolds' second patent application was still pending in Washington. After the "J1" frame had appeared, he filed four supplementary claims to his patent application. Saco-Lowell opposed these claims, as did Whitin, which had also developed a device which would have come under the jurisdiction of Reynolds' new claims, if allowed. Three of the four Reynolds claims were rejected by the Patent Office examiners, the fourth was allowed, and Reynolds' second patent was granted. Reynolds brought suit against Saco-Lowell, charging not only patent infringement but breach of faith as well.

Thereupon followed a suit which will long be remembered in the textile machinery industry. The action was tried in the Salisbury, North Carolina, Division of the United States District Court, and there were infinite complications.

Saco-Lowell could not claim that Reynolds' original patent was invalid (there was some evidence to indicate that his patent covered long-known principles), because of the legal doctrine that licensees under a patent might not challenge the validity of that patent. Saco-Lowell, however, pointed to the narrow construction of the patent and claimed the well-established right of using ideas disclosed but not claimed. The company presented the strongest possible arguments that Reynolds' amended second patent did not cover the "J1" frame or its later modifications, and pointed out alleged inconsistencies in Reynolds' testimony. Saco-Lowell attorneys, Hugh D. McClellan and Hector M. Holmes, carefully and thoroughly argued the company's right and need to develop a frame which could be successfully sold. This argument was impaired, however, by advertising matter which the company had issued even after the "J1" frame had been introduced extolling the "D-2," or Reynolds, frame. A strong issue was made of Reynolds' amended claims to his second patent, which Saco-Lowell counsel charged had been made *after* the "J1" frame had been seen and studied by Terrell and Reynolds at the Greenville show and which, Saco-Lowell contended, marked an eleventh-hour effort to make the pending Reynolds patent cover the "J1" frame. Saco-Lowell counsel alleged that these claims contained "misrepresentations, direct contradictions in Reynolds' own statements under oath, and misrepresentations to the Patent Office."[28] Reynolds' claim of breach of faith rested on the contention that it was he who had suggested the essential feature which distinguished the "J1" frame from the earlier "D-2" frame. This charge was vehemently denied by Saco-Lowell.

On June 9, 1943, Judge Johnson J. Hayes entered his opinion, judgment, and decree. Saco-Lowell was directed to pay $210,265 in back royalties on all "J" frames sold since 1937 and to pay royalties on all sales thenceforth.[29]

The conclusion that this judgment was based more upon moral than upon technical grounds is strongly supported by the opinion of this same court in the later case of *Reynolds* v. *Whitin Machine Works,* which likewise was decided in favor of Reynolds.[30] Some might say that Judge Hayes' decision was a triumph of justice over law. On the other hand, fine and infinitely interesting questions of justice were involved. Saco-Lowell obviously was inspired by Reynolds' original idea. Did that fact obligate the company to pay royalties to Reynolds on modifications which, it was claimed, constituted a new means of attaining the original goal? Once again the tremendous gap which existed between origination and practical realization became an issue in Saco-Lowell history. The Reynolds case, like many another such episode of the past, pointed with clarity to the essentially coöperative nature of product development. Saco-Lowell's claims were, in effect, an appeal for justice to the modifiers and improvers, without whom many an invention and inventor would have languished. Saco-Lowell's blunder was in basing its case upon fine points of patent law and infinitely complicated technicalities which no court without tremendous experience in such matters could possibly master.

The long-draft roving frame, whatever its parentage, was an outstanding success and restored the competitive balance in the industry in the roving field. The importance of this development and of the comparable introduction of long-draft spinning can scarcely be over-emphasized. Long-draft roving, which secured the necessary cohesion of fibers by the folding or condensing rather than twisting of the sliver, represented a basic change in those supposedly unalterable principles established by inventors in eighteenth-century England. The impact of long-draft roving and spinning upon the textile industry was forcible. Coming at a time when low-cost operation was essential for survival and when labor rates in the textile industry were being boosted by political action, these developments could not be ignored.[31] Positive economies were effected by elimination of costly steps in both roving and spinning processes. The end product was better yarn, while at the same time the necessity for good sliver at the roving frame forced improvements in all processes back to the opening room.

Picking and opening equipment, meanwhile, was undergoing an independent revolution. One-process picking, one of the widely heralded developments of this decade, appears to have been built by the English firm of Dobson & Barlow as early as 1913, and was in extensive use in England before it had become familiar to the American textile industry. Accounts vary as to how Saco-Lowell picked up the idea in the early 1920's. Apparently the sales department rather than the shop departments first became interested, and Sales Manager Lowell was alert to the marketing possibilities inherent in the system. There was initial skepticism in the shop, but this passed and was replaced by outstanding developmental work.

The one-process picking idea was essentially simple: it consisted of combining the primary, intermediate, and finisher machines to form a continuous-process, single machine which would save space, cotton-handling, and labor. Why, then, if one-process picking was merely a combination of existing machines, and offered such obvious advantages, had it waited so long to be adopted? The assertion that the one-process picker was actually a combination of existing machines was substantially true, but that combination could not be made practicable until effective controls had been devised to regulate the flow of cotton in the machine. The Dobson & Barlow system was said to have been unsatisfactory in this respect, and it was because Kitson engineers Robert S. Curley and William E. Shaw solved the problem of control that Saco-Lowell forged ahead of all competitors, domestic and foreign, in this field.

The first experimental installation of one-process picking was made by Saco-Lowell in 1922 in the Boston Manufacturing Company, and the first large-scale installation was made in the mills of the Langley Manufacturing Company. In July, 1928, the new system was announced to the trade at large and the Saco-Lowell picking system swept the industry.

The one-process picker, however, was only the most spectacular of many improvements effected in picking and opening equipment.

New grid bars increased the effectiveness of the vertical opener. A new lattice opener provided better cleaning than ever before. New electrical devices enabled the flow of cotton from opening to picking rooms to be controlled automatically and with great precision. These and many other improvements met the difficult challenge offered by the modern, highly compressed cotton bales and, later, by mechanically picked cotton. Progress in opening, blending, and picking techniques enabled many American mills to use cotton from one to two grades lower than those to which they had been accustomed, without loss of quality in the resulting yarn. Thus a source of savings was created which became a powerful incentive for these mills to discard their existing equipment in favor of the more efficient methods developed by Saco-Lowell.

The appearance, as well as the internal construction of picking and opening equipment changed as sheet steel began to replace cast iron. This change had been long in coming, delayed perhaps as much by prejudice as by practical considerations. A man who had been building pickers long before 1900 delivered the ultimate condemnation of the old generation against the machines being built by the new, when he exclaimed in disgust: "They looked to me like something made in Detroit!" [32]

Not long after one-process picking had been introduced, Saco-Lowell added a machine to the product line which had never before been built by the company. Whitin had stolen a march on Saco-Lowell when, in 1899, it had begun to build a comber. This English and European machine, which produced the fine yarns used in the production of high-quality cloth, was obviously destined to become a part of the American system of manufacture — a system which was becoming increasingly versatile as competition became increasingly keen. Perhaps Whitin's traditional strength in the fine-goods mill areas of southeastern New England explains that company's early interest in the comber. Saco-Lowell followed Whitin by more than thirty years, and when the decision had finally been made, stepped into the comber business in the easiest way possible. In 1933 Saco-Lowell purchased certain of the assets of the Alsatian Machine Works, of Worcester, Massachusetts, a wholly owned subsidiary of Atkinson, Haserick & Company, American agents for the English machinery-building firm of Dobson & Barlow and other European manufacturers. Harry Tunstall, an Alsatian employee, had developed a comber which was a potential competitor of the Whitin machine. Since the comber was the only cotton machine which the Alsatian Machine Works was building and because of the limited market for combers, the merchandising problem confronting the Worcester company was a difficult one. Atkinson, Haserick decided to sell its comber-manufacturing venture, and Joseph Fossel, chief designer of the Alsatian Company, came with his staff to Biddeford to form the nucleus of a comber department there. It is worth notice, as additional evidence of the skill with which David F. Edwards built up all branches of his company, that this valuable addition to the Saco-Lowell line, made at a time when opportunity knocked on empty coffers, was secured without any cash expenditure. Edwards negotiated a bargain with Atkinson, Haserick whereby Saco-Lowell paid a percentage of the difference between cost and price on combers subsequently built, until the specified purchase price of the Alsatian assets should be reached. The first Saco-Lowell combers were released to the trade in 1934. Over the next seven years three hundred and fifty-nine machines were sold, and the comber staff became established on a firm and continuing basis.

Saco-Lowell had done well, despite financial difficulties which might well have forced a less determined and farsighted management to forego the luxury of product development. Confronted by the specter of huge quantities of secondhand machinery made available for sale by the shrinkage in the number of spindles in use in American mills, Saco-Lowell took positive and most successful steps to render that machinery obsolete and non-competitive. One-process picking, long-draft spinning, and long-draft roving had been merely the most important of many new or improved products in the decade and a half which followed 1926. In this space of years Saco-Lowell had devised a new air-circulating system for opening and picking rooms, had developed a continuous card stripper, and had placed a new high-speed warper, a high-speed slasher, and a new twister on the market. Even the spindle, pride of the machinery industry, had been looked at with a critical eye and improved by needle bearings and spring-tempered blades. A start had been made on big package spinning — a development which contemplated economies through increase in bobbin capacities. Genuine contributions to scientific data-finding techniques were made in the form of a sliver-testing machine and a lap meter. With these devices the textile machinery industry moved a step nearer to understanding those perplexing variations of the cotton fiber which had impeded improvements in cloth manufacture for three centuries and longer.

In the Saco-Lowell research rooms there had been a definite awakening, inspired, like many another renaissance, by adversity. Here, possibly to a greater extent than at Whitinsville, were now to be found new fires and new faces. E. E. Blake, the superannuated agent, had done well, notwithstanding the charge (a serious one in the textile machinery industry) that he was "Hell on putting things together close." The entire research establishment crystallized into a well-defined department under Eugene Gwaltney, who came to Saco-Lowell in 1938 after extensive mill experience in the South to serve as the first director of research. The department expanded to a pre-World War II peak of thirty-five draftsmen and engineers.

In Saco-Lowell's efforts to improve its product line lay a cogent reason for the company's emergence from the shadows, and the enthusiasms and skills vested in Gwaltney's new department inspired a very real hope that the revolution had only just begun. That the origins of major technological development in the years from 1926 to 1941 lay outside the company mattered less than the obvious fact that Saco-Lowell now had the interest, the ability, and the opportunity to assist materially in leading the American textile machinery industry out of the doldrums where it had languished, technologically speaking, since the early 1900's.

11. END OF AN ERA

The first fifteen years of the Edwards administration provide no serious problems of appraisal. The obvious achievement was the rescue of Saco-Lowell from threatened bankruptcy. This accomplishment, however, is of infinitely less interest and even of less importance than the means by which it was effected. Here again, as with the Biddeford foundry strike of 1923, the parallel between Saco-Lowell and the Waltham Watch Company comes to mind.

In both these distinguished New England institutions financial capitalism was at work. In both companies Boston banks had stepped in to perform a salvage operation in the interest of creditors and investors. Both companies were placed in charge of a bankers' president: at Waltham, Gifford K. Simonds (1921); at Saco-Lowell, David F. Edwards (1927). Here the similarity ceases. At Waltham the timidity and nearsightedness of the banks, coupled with an understandable desire for self-protection, even at the expense of the company, soon precipitated another crisis.[33] A different attitude was manifest in the Saco-Lowell situation. Here, where many thought receivership was justified, the banks, including those same institutions which had been unwilling to see Waltham through, stood behind Saco-Lowell and David F. Edwards. Active financial support was forthcoming, and notes were extended, refunded, and refunded again. A conservative attitude prevailed, to be sure, when Edwards' policies involved the expenditure of money. On the other hand, when Kettley, in his 1927 survey, made what might well have been a dangerous admission that one plan of consolidation favored the creditors while the alternative plan favored the long-term good of the company, the banks made no objection to the adoption of the latter.

Why this difference in the handling of the Waltham and Saco-Lowell situations? The influence of Robert Herrick, Sr., unquestionably was a major factor. Supreme confidence in the ability of Edwards was another. The third was the apparent disposition of the National City Bank of New York to force a liquidation. This attitude sent George Armstrong to Boston to prepare a survey of the company. Armstrong's penetrating analysis of the situation was a decisive factor in the subsequent support of Saco-Lowell by its principal creditors, including the National City Bank.

At Waltham, investment-banking interests came to the rescue of the commercial banks in 1923 and a strong reorganizing management under Frederic C. Dumaine began to slash expenditures for research, advertising, and plant improvement. The result of this program was financial solvency, but the total costs have yet (in 1949) to be assessed. Saco-Lowell emerged from the financial wringer with a stronger manufacturing organization and a stronger product line than ever before. This was essentially, perhaps exclusively, the Edwards touch, but the creditor banks must be accorded credit for giving Saco-Lowell the opportunity to survive.

Balanced against these primary achievements were some errors and weaknesses. The refusal of the banks to allow Edwards to spend money in making changes in the interest of long-term operating efficiency was clearly based on the near-hopeless financial condition of the company. Investment banks, and particularly Boston investments banks, it should be remembered, are not adventurers but custodians of the funds at their disposal. The restriction which was placed upon reorganizing effort, even though seemingly essential, was unfortunate and (as subsequent events proved) shortsighted. An inequitable and inefficient wage incentive and production-control system was patched up and made to do. Efforts to smooth out the functioning of local management at Biddeford and to remedy personal conflicts there were necessarily subservient to more urgent needs. Loyalty to the Edwards legend grew markedly (even Reynolds, in his bitterest denunciations of the Saco-Lowell Shops, confessed his complete confidence in the company's president), but organizational loyalty was undermined by conflict at the local managerial level. This difficulty had devious and ancient origins — chief among them was the fact that Saco-Lowell had no tradition of stability such as Whitin and Draper possessed — but the difficulty was not, and scarcely could be, eliminated at this time. Some good men were lost and some poor ones retained, but this, of course, happens in every reorganization.

Trade and industry relations were immeasurably strengthened by the leadership which David F. Edwards exerted. This was an intangible factor, and one which cannot be fully assessed today. Few policy mistakes had been made at Boston; some operational mistakes had been made at Biddeford. One of the most costly of these was the Reynolds suit. Much can be said in defense of the action of the company, and there is no question that this suit exploded in the face of the Biddeford management. Whatever the extenuating circumstances, however, Reynolds had forced Saco-Lowell into an embarrassing breach of good public relations.

The marked improvement in the over-all condition of the Saco-Lowell Shops between 1926 and 1940 should not be ascribed in its entirety to David F. Edwards, and the tendency indiscriminately to praise and damn the general for the acts of his army must be avoided here. All down through the organization were the men who executed company policy. All these men and all their contributions cannot be named, for to name is to assess, and fair assessment of operational contributions is impossible in a work of this limited scope. Good work was done in the Saco-Lowell Shops in this period. The platitude must be uttered that, without such support, Edwards and the company alike would have failed.

Few realized at the time that the year 1940 constituted the end of an era. The company had been saved from the first challenge of insolvency. Then the unexpected second challenge in the form of America's greatest modern depression had been faced and surmounted. In 1940 an exciting vista unfolded — new machines, adventures in foreign trade, and, above all, the opportunity to examine with introspective eye the internal difficulties which still beset the organization. It was an ironic freak of fate, indeed, which now hurled a third challenge at David F. Edwards and at Saco-Lowell — the challenge of total war.

CHAPTER XV

WAR, POSTWAR, AND RETROSPECT

1. Saco-Lowell at War

The successive waves of shock, uncertainty, and optimism which engulfed the American nation between 1941 and 1945 were amply reflected in the managerial attitudes and business policies of the Saco-Lowell Shops.

In 1940, as the country moved toward war, a flurry of government textile purchases set off rumors of a runaway demand for textile machinery at sharp advances in price.[1] At year's end, however, both the textile and the textile machinery industries were sober, stable, and free from inflation in either prices or costs. This was the very end of normalcy.

War came, and with it the grave uncertainties. Was this to be another World War I, with tremendous expansion but little qualitative change in the company's output? Attitudes in Washington were all-important, and the first positive opinion that could be ascertained was that the capacity of the textile industry was so great and varied that it could stand the increased war demand without much new machinery. Then evidence of a changing concept was noted. The possibility was admitted that federal control agencies might authorize considerable amounts of new machinery. Should Saco-Lowell's specialized productive capacity be converted to the manufacture of ordnance items, only to have Washington suddenly decide that what was needed was an unprecedented amount of textile machinery?

This period of paralyzing uncertainty will not soon be forgotten by those who were responsible for the conduct of American business and on whose shoulders now descended a substantial share of the responsibility for national survival. David F. Edwards considered the alternatives, made his choice, and went before the directorate to urge the immediate acceptance of war sub-contracts for non-textile products.

For the year 1942 Saco-Lowell's contracts for ordnance items totaled 44 per cent of total dollar sales, which, in turn, were 50 per cent higher than in the preceding year. Shipments of textile machinery declined, the large backlog of orders for textile machinery evaporated, and the company became fast in the grip of material priorities. The Office of Price Administration established ceilings on textile-machinery prices, fixing them at the level prevailing on October 1, 1941. Manufacturing activities became completely dominated by the war efforts and by controls over essential materials. In 1942 the company's struggle for material became acute. A booming repair-parts business was threatened by low priorities. The first deliveries on special war products were made in the face of low priorities for steel and tools. The drift of skilled workmen into the armed services and to the highly paid jobs in the Portland and Boston shipyards precipitated a labor shortage. As these men left, their places were filled by untrained workers, many of whom were women. By the end of this year seven hundred Saco-Lowell men were in the armed forces, and total employment reached a peak of three thousand, six hundred and forty-two, a very slight gain over the highest number employed in 1941.

Managerial problems were magnified by the conversion to war. There was a mass transfer of employees and supervisors from familiar to unfamiliar jobs. A tremendous burden was placed upon all departments. New accounting controls were worked out almost overnight; unfamiliar types of contracts were processed through the offices; sales supervisors, sales engineers, and erectors were pulled in to Biddeford to face new tasks; the purchasing sections groped through the maze of official regulations; production departments wrestled with blueprints of parts and assemblies which had never before been heard of, much less manufactured. Even the genial gatekeepers now became uniformed, armed, and stern.[2]

By February of 1943 the trickle of orders for textile machinery had virtually ceased, though repair parts continued to be shipped in fair volume. Saco-Lowell was absorbed with one tremendous war contract, and negotiations were under way on another. In 1942 work had commenced upon a large order of cable assemblies for remote-control systems on 90-millimeter and 120-millimeter anti-aircraft guns. This contract was made with the Bendix Aviation Corporation, and Saco-Lowell was the first sub-contractor to enter the field. This contract illustrates two remarkable aspects of Saco-Lowell's war experience.

The first of these is the success with which the company turned to precision work. With a few exceptions, such as combers, card flats, and spindles, textile machinery had never been built to fine tolerances, yet Saco-Lowell mastered the necessary techniques in a matter of weeks. Here lay evidence of that versatility and basic metal-working skill which distinguished the American war effort.

The Bendix contract also illustrates the high degree of coöperative planning which characterized some phases of ordnance procurement. When the cable assembly program was expanded, Saco-Lowell assisted other sub-contractors (the Delco-Remy Division, General Motors Corporation; the Toledo Scale Company; and the Gilbert & Barker Manufacturing Company) to surmount initial difficulties in machining and assembling the complex and delicate instruments making up the cable system. Coöperative effort characterized subsequent relations between the cable system sub-contractors; when requirement curves began to swing sharply upward, output of the systems kept pace with demands, despite a continuing shortage of the multi-conductor cable used in the assembly.[3]

In April, 1943, Saco-Lowell went into production on the so-called "bogie-wheel assembly" for the Ford Motor Company. This subcontract called for huge quantities of wheel and track assemblies and spare parts for a mobile gun carrier. At this same time, however, when it began to appear that no more textile machinery would be built, a heavy-duty tire program vastly stimulated the demand for high-tenacity rayon cord. Saco-Lowell was directed by the War Production Board to expand its production of twisters. Because of this directive and the continuing flow of textile-machinery parts orders, Saco-Lowell never completely abandoned the textile machinery field.

Sales volume in 1943 climbed 26 per cent above the preceding year, and 72 per cent of the output consisted of non-textile items.

Labor shortages became still more acute. In March of that year 33.5 per cent of company employees were women, as compared with a peace-time average of approximately 10 per cent (13 per cent in January, 1949). Labor efficiency inevitably declined. More than a thousand Saco-Lowell men and women were now in the armed services, and President Edwards had begun to caution his stockholders about the postwar effects of fixed machinery prices and rising labor costs.

The year 1943 was doubly distinguished. On February 16, 1943, Saco-Lowell men and women were given the Army-Navy Production Award (the "E" pennant) in official recognition of their fine record in the production of war equipment. Coming at a time well in advance of the period when the "E" pennant was handed out with great freedom, this award had real meaning. The presentation was made an occasion of more than passing dignity and impressiveness, and history will not quarrel with David F. Edwards' modest statement that the company's contribution to the war effort had been made possible by the "sustained hard work of everyone in the organization in the face of difficulties which at times were very great indeed." On September 25, 1943, a second "E" pennant was awarded the company for maintenance of high standards of performance.

In 1944 the peak of the war effort was passed. Total sales increased only slightly in this year, and production of special war products declined to 63 per cent of total sales. The variety of contracts which had been undertaken by this time was imposing. In addition to the Ford and Bendix assemblies, Saco-Lowell was building or had built ground magnets, inspection covers for diesel engines, elbow telescopes, diesel-engine metering devices, machine-tool bases, outer cans for proximity fuses, telescope parts, valve assemblies, launcher grenades, cartridge containers, pump housings, spun rivets, gun mount races, and other products of an equally miscellaneous nature.

So varied and numerous did contract requests become that a selection committee on sub-contract review was set up to recommend which orders should be accepted and which refused. The following random selections from the reports of this committee preserve some of the flavor of wartime production planning:

A.O.G. Corporation
Providence, R. I.

Subject: Breech Bolt *Project No. 4040*

This project covers the above concern's requirements of a large quantity of Oerklin gun breech bolts. The selection committee studied this project very carefully and finally decided that it would not be wise to take over this project where this is only a one-piece order requiring a considerable amount of manufacturing time. Also, where we have not yet got under way with numerous other war projects demanding preferred deliveries, we are not at all certain that we could meet this concern's delivery requirements. Therefore, this project has been turned down and Mr. Kettley who came into the meeting was advised of this decision and shown the part in question.

J. S. Thorne Co.

Subject: 882,000 Cartridge Containers *Project No. 4050*

This proposition was brought before the committee again for a careful review as a slight miscalculation in our time estimate or machine capacity based on 882,000 parts could very easily cost the shops considerable money.

Mr. Carl Bohlin was called in and asked to carefully check with his department to determine exactly how many machines are available and he reports that there are 5 machines at this time which it is estimated could turn out 43,000 containers per month.

Mr. Lowell has agreed to quote a price of 18¢ each, requesting the privilege of re-negotiating if it is found after a month's run that this price is not fair to Saco-Lowell or the customer.

War Production Board, Portland Branch

M-5 Sight System
Group Drawings *Proj. No. 4237*

A large group of drawings was submitted by the Portland Branch of the War Production Board as mentioned in the review of meeting No. 26, and these have been carefully reviewed by the committee. The committee is unanimous that this proposition should be turned down.

This work would require borematics, gear cutters, and hobbers, and we have none of these machines available.

We will return the prints to the WPB.

Boston Ordnance District
Room 1501, 140 Federal Street
Boston, Mass.

PART NAME	*DRAWING NO.*	*PROJ. NO.*
Rocket P.P. 4½″ M3	None Rec'd	4367

These gentlemen told us that this project is highly confidential and is a high urgency job. Also, it can run into many more than a million pieces.

The committee discussed this project at length with Mr. Trinder and Mr. Funderburk, and it was decided that we would be interested in it.

Although we do not have the necessary equipment for making this part, nobody else has it, so the Government may as well buy it for Saco-Lowell Shops, as long as it has to be bought for whoever decides to make this part.

Mr. Trinder told us that this is one of the most urgent jobs in the country today, and for that reason the necessary machinery can be secured quickly.

They will want 4,000 or 8,000 pieces per day. He further stated that this will be a negotiated contract and that we should figure on making either 800,000 pieces or 1,600,000 pieces.

Mr. Trinder also told us that he believes the tools for making this equipment can be had by March 1, as the tools will carry a very high priority rating. The material will be allocated.

Mr. Trinder promised to give us a price range on this job, that is a maximum and a minimum price, so that we can readily tell whether we want the job.

It is my understanding that we are to advise Mr. Trinder concerning the following points:

1. Our machine capacity available.
2. Earliest month we can start delivery.
3. The month we can expect to reach maximum capacity.
4. Unit price on full capacity and unit price on one-half capacity.

Familiarity with the technique of war production did not lessen operating problems. The threat of cancellations, changes, and cutbacks in orders was always present as strategic requirements of a now fast-moving war continually shifted. Plant capacity had fallen far short of adequacy for a volume of business considerably in excess of the most active peace-time year of the preceding decade. Much work was "farmed out" to sub-contracting firms. As a result of labor shortages in the foundry the company began to purchase castings outside, often at the rate of a million pounds per month. At the peak of the war effort, sub-contracts were in force with as many as thirty-five machinery firms and fifty-seven foundries, some as far away as Pennsylvania.

But the end of the war effort was now in sight. Beginning in mid-summer of 1944, the textile-machinery builders were told with increasing frequency and growing emphasis by the War Production Board that their productive capacity would probably be taxed to the limit to meet the rapidly developing shortage of textile products. Saco-Lowell was informed that it should make no substantial new commitments for special war products until the Board had reviewed proposed contracts and eliminated those which were less urgent than the need for textile machinery. By November, 1944, all Saco-Lowell's major contracts for non-textile assemblies had been completed or canceled, although some war work continued into 1945. The grim prospect was now faced of attempting to get back into the textile machinery business at a time when manufacturing costs on most machines exceeded the government-imposed ceiling prices for such machines.

The year 1945 was one of painful reconversion. With only 12 per cent of Saco-Lowell's output accounted for by special war contracts, sales declined precipitously to half of the 1944 level. Great physical problems were faced: dislocating and costly plant rearrangement, heavy expenditures for deferred maintenance, crippling shortages of manpower and materials, increased costs of production, contract re-negotiation difficulties, and inadequate ceiling prices on Saco-Lowell textile machinery.

President Edwards moved to force the issue on prices. A forceful and urgent appeal was addressed to the Office of Price Administration, which had earlier denied an equally forceful and urgent appeal. This time, however, Edwards' letter was backed by an auditor's report which showed an operating loss of $180,000 for the month of February alone. On April 20, 1945, Saco-Lowell was granted price increases ranging from 9.07 per cent on pickers to 48.53 per cent on cards, an average increase of 21.57 per cent for the entire line.

The mental hurdle to reconversion was no less real than the problems of prices and shortages. The excitement and the glamour of the war years evaporated. The tingling mystery of guarded weapon contracts vanished. The cover of the *Saco-Lowell Bulletin* bore no more pictures of Saco-Lowell bogie-wheel assemblies grinding enemy machine-gunners into the battlefield mud. "E" pennant pins disappeared from coat lapels, and with them went the impelling stimulus to subjugate personal desires to the exigencies of the time. Absenteeism increased, attaining in the foundry the alarming rate of 12.96 per cent. Labor turnover reached a peak of 10.3 per cent of total employment. Old problems and old conflicts asserted themselves again, and a crisis in labor relations flared. With audible, visible effort Saco-Lowell returned to "business as usual."

Many operating details and certain summary statistics of the war years are contained in succeeding paragraphs. Appendix 15 presents additional statistical measures of wartime operations. Total shipments of special war products (1942–45) were as follows:

Ford Motor Company................	14,555 units Bogie-Wheel Assemblies	$17,615,101.10
Bendix Aviation Corp................	5,175 units Fire Control Systems	22,553,639.50
Miscellaneous contracts, 20 concerns....		4,421,377.14
Total sales non-textile war products		$44,590,117.74

Statistical information of this sort is essential to any account of Saco-Lowell's war experience, but the heart of the war story is not to be found in figures. He would be cynical indeed who denied the existence and importance of patriotism in the Saco-Lowell Shops between 1942 and 1945. The outstanding achievement of these years was neither the volume nor the quality of war products shipped, but rather the outstanding devotion of the shop people to the task at hand and the versatility of management in adapting itself, almost overnight, to radically changed operating conditions. By far the most significant aspect of the war years was the manifest fact that with proper psychological preparation the Saco-Lowell organization could rise to remarkable heights of performance.

2. Labor Relations and the Bargaining Table

The Edwards administration faced not only the profound problems of financial reorganization, depression, and war, but it also encountered the full impact of labor's drive for power. In less than a decade, that traditional aloofness which had characterized labor relations in the Biddeford, Newton, and Lowell shops for more than a century vanished. The remarkable feature of this transition was that the Saco-Lowell Shops, lacking a factory village and therefore having had less to do with its employees over the years than either Whitin or Draper, suddenly began to display a progressive attitude at the bargaining table which caused head-wagging in the textile machinery industry.

Unionization of the Company

Since the International Molders' Union local had been disbanded in 1923 by vigorous company action, there had been no effective organized bargaining unit among Saco-Lowell employees. Through the troubled 1930's a firm conviction was entertained in certain managerial circles at Biddeford that the company never had tolerated a union and never would tolerate one. Early in 1941 David F. Edwards received a demand from the Textile Workers Union of America (C.I.O.) for recognition as the sole bargaining agent for all production and maintenance workers in the company.[4]

The Textile Workers Union of America had successfully organized employees in local textile mills before 1941. Saco-Lowell was the only large industrial unit in the Biddeford-Saco area that had not been unionized, and the Textile Workers Union was the only powerful union organization active in that section of the State. There was no theoretical reason why this textile-mill union should not attempt to organize the workmen in a machine shop. The attempt was facilitated by the fact that sisters, daughters, and wives of Saco-Lowell workmen already belonged to the union in consequence of their employment in the adjacent textile mills.

As might well be expected, the progress of the union membership drive was watched by many with anxiety and passive hostility. The reaction of President Edwards to the union's request for recognition was characteristic, and initial negotiations between the company and the union were handled in a manner which was at once skillful and farsighted. Edwards felt that unionization was inevitable and that the union movement was destined to become a permanent feature of the American economy. He decided to cooperate with the union in every way, and he refused to block recognition. He at once established by precept and by repeated example the policy of meticulous honesty, fairness, and courtesy in all dealings with the union representatives, both national and local. The existence of this managerial attitude demands the strongest possible emphasis, for it was by no means the normal reaction of American business men, buffeted and embittered by the Roosevelt New Deal and anxious over the incredible trend of the times. As far as I have been able to ascertain, the Edwards policy was carried out with remarkable fidelity of intention, though naturally not without blunders, by those men in the organization entrusted with matters of personnel and labor relations. The policy was formulated and put into effect in the face of grave doubts, both in Boston and in Biddeford, that this was the proper way to deal with a strong, aggressive, and ambitious C.I.O. union.

After the Textile Workers Union request for recognition as sole bargaining agent had been made, it would have been normal procedure under the National Labor Relations Act for the National Labor Relations Board to determine whether the union's membership strength in the company was great enough to justify an election. Edwards offered to short-cut this official procedure by calling in the Boston public accounting firm of Haskins & Sells to ascertain the union's strength. An audit was made of union membership cards, with spot checks on membership card signatures. The cost of this audit was shared equally by the company and by the union, and the results indicated that 51 per cent of the eligible working force had joined the union. On April 18, 1941, an election was held, under the auspices of the National Labor Relations Board. Edwards insisted that each employee who interrupted his work to vote be paid his regular hourly rate by the company for a reasonable period of absence. This somewhat unusual procedure was challenged by the union and sanctioned by the Board. As a result of this move a

Saco-Lowell Spinning Frame, 1949

Saco-Lowell One-process Picking, 1949

larger vote was cast than probably would have been the case had this been time lost for pay purposes by the men. The tabulation of votes showed 1,349 in favor of and 924 opposed to naming the Textile Workers Union of America, Local 406, as sole bargaining agent for the shop employees.

After the election, negotiations immediately began between the company and the union, and on May 19, 1941, the first labor agreement was signed. In these negotiations the company was represented by Edwards, Kettley, and Assistant Works Manager Victor Beecroft. The union viewpoints were advanced by George Baldanzi, national vice-president of the union; Harold Daoust, field representative, under whose direction the membership drive had been conducted; Alphonse E. Renouf, first president of the local union organization; and other local union officers. The contract which was signed provided a 10 per cent wage increase, an open shop, vacations with pay, collection of union dues by the company from members' pay (the "check-off" clause), recognition of seniority by the company (with certain modifying clauses which diluted the strength of the provision), guarantees against strikes and lockouts during the term of the contract, and rules governing grievance procedures.

The harmonious tone of negotiations leading to this first contract and the terms of the contract itself indicated an informed understanding of labor's relatively new position in industrial affairs under the National Labor Relations Act. The check-off clause in particular bears testimony to this point. In many negotiations between companies and unions at the time, and indeed at much later dates, this feature gave rise to bitter tests of strength. That it was conceded at the outset without demur by Saco-Lowell is indicative of, and later proved to be characteristic of, Edwards' advanced grasp of labor matters.

Collective Bargaining, a New Experience

The union's response to Edwards' constructive handling of the labor situation was more marked at the national than at the local level, where it was more manifest in the personal regard of local union officers for those in the ranks of management with whom they were in frequent contact than in reciprocal concession. From the very beginning a difference in attitude between local and national union officers was apparent.

There was inexperience on both sides of the bargaining table. Alphonse Renouf, president of the local union, had been a machine molder for many years. Renouf, indeed, was one of the few striking molders who had returned to work when the International Molders' Union local was broken in 1923. There was little in his background to qualify him particularly for the responsibilities of his position, but he worked devotedly and with enthusiasm in the union cause. Beecroft, who handled initial stages of business with the union, was without previous experience in this field, and, having many other duties, was far from free to apply himself fully to these new matters. Kettley, though a man of his word, was obviously unsympathetic toward union methods and goals, as, in fact, was most of the Biddeford management.

A basic obstacle to successful labor relations lay in the nature of the Textile Workers Union itself. The unfamiliarity of this union with machine-shop operations was in evidence, though to a decreasing extent, throughout the entire 1941–48 period. The effect of this unfamiliarity was to confuse the local union organization, whose officers, although possessing an intimate knowledge of shop conditions, were directed by national officers toward the wider objectives of the national program and guided by them in tactics and procedures. Many of these objectives and tactics, though both practicable and suitable in textile mills, were less so in a machine shop. This fact the national officers found difficult to absorb and incorporate in their plans and thinking. In any case, they were versed in no other tactics and were loath to abandon or modify the objectives laid down by the national headquarters of the union. At the local level some officers realized that certain objectives, attained satisfactorily in many mills, were incapable of attainment in the Saco-Lowell Shops. Others, less thoughtful, were prepared to battle energetically for points which could not possibly be conceded. When these officers were confronted with the company's reasons for its inability to concede certain points — many of which reasons the local union leaders knew from their own experience in the shop to be sound — their confusion was manifest, and resulted in a tendency for these men to hover between suspicion of the company's guile and lack of faith in their national officers. Conversely, too, the company's operations and routine enabled it to grant certain concessions which would have been out of place in a textile mill.

New union agreements were made each year after 1941 as the old agreements expired. Each successive agreement contained adjustments of earlier clauses, and each was characterized by minor company concessions to union demands. Few basic changes in company-union relationships occurred between 1941 and 1948. In 1944 the company was forced by the War Labor Board to insert a maintenance-of-union membership clause in its union agreement. In 1945 a new local (Number 799) was formed to include shop checkers, not previously represented by Local 406. In 1946, certain clerical workers were unionized, a fact which was not without advantage to the company, since the action of Local 406 forestalled threatened organization of these workers by a much more radical union.

Late in 1947, negotiations were opened in Biddeford for a new union contract. Union demands were ambitious, but the company, now involved in a far-reaching reorganization of operating procedures, was in strong need of union coöperation in making that reorganization effective. Company-union bargaining was prolonged to the eleventh hour. A strike vote was taken by the union, and for a time the threat of a strike loomed large. The 26-months contract which was finally signed on January 5, 1948, was widely regarded as a union victory.

This new agreement called for a 10 per cent "add-on" raise in wage rates, with provision being made for eventual incorporation of the raise into the base rate for calculation of incentive earnings. A modified union shop was established; that is, union members were required, as a condition of continued employment, to remain members in good standing during the life of the agreement and all new employees were required to join the union within six weeks from the date of their employment. Employees not already union members, however, were not required to join the union. The union dues check-off clause was continued in this agreement; a sixth paid holiday was added; and existing medical insurance benefits were extended to include doctors' visits. Guarantees against strikes and lockouts were included, and the union promised coöperation in establishing principles, practices, and procedures to govern the installation and administration of a new wage incentive system. Benefits to employees under this agreement were estimated by the company to amount to $1,400,000 a year.[5]

The 1948 agreement was characterized by shrewd bargaining and illustrated well the principle of mutual concession, but the real nature of the concessions made on each side is difficult to evaluate. The modified union-shop clause, a major issue in the negotiations, had considerable propaganda value for the union, but the point gained by the union appears to have been negligible. The company had already been forced to make maintenance of union membership a condition of continued employment. Company experience showed, moreover, that 90 per cent of the new employees joined the union within 12 months of being hired, and some of the remaining 10 per cent joined later. The 1948 agreement merely formalized an existing fact. In return for the modified union-shop clause the union abandoned its demand that the pay raise be incorporated in the existing base rates. This was a dangerous request and would have imposed difficulties in any subsequent attempt to remove the inequities of the wage incentive system. The company's major point of securing a promise of union coöperation in establishing a new incentive system was felt by some in the ranks of management to constitute an exchange of words for dollars, particularly in view of the fact that the local union organization's record for coöperating with management had not been outstanding. Actually, this clause has already (September, 1949) demonstrated its efficacy, for the terms of reference under which the new wage incentive system is to be installed have been agreed upon by company and union, and work on the wage incentive system itself is proceeding in accordance with those terms.

Some obvious conclusions about labor relations in the 1941–48 period may be drawn, but no broad appraisal of the events of these years can yet be advanced. Neither does space allow presentation in the text of many interesting details of initial relations between Saco-Lowell and the Textile Workers Union of America. Some of these incidents have been collected in Appendix 18, for they have considerable value to any reader whose special interest lies in this field of Saco-Lowell's history.

These eight years clearly constitute an experimental phase in the evolution of labor policy and in the development of the local union organization — a period characterized by much groping and by repeated, though minor, tests of strength. The company's attitude was firm but scrupulously fair. National officials of the union, despite their initial unfamiliarity with machine-shop operations, were more adept at the bargaining table than local officials, and were far easier, by and large, to deal with. These officers proved to be no more lenient than the local union men, but were better informed, more understanding, and possessed of a far greater grasp of broad issues. This, of course, was to be expected, for local union leaders were struggling under the burden of unprecedented responsibilities, shouldered suddenly without prior training.

Between 1941 and 1947 there were few outstanding cases where the union helped the company in overcoming any difficulties which were not, of themselves, union-inspired or the result of union influence in plant affairs. The rift between the national and the local union organization was occasionally wide. At one time there was a strong faction in the local organization which favored severing the affiliation with the Textile Workers Union and forming a new affiliation with the United Radio, Electrical and Machine Workers Union (C.I.O.). From 1944 to the end of 1946 the company was troubled to some extent by the mutually independent actions of the local union president and the local business manager, each of whom headed a separate faction in Local 406. No serious consequence ensued from this internal factionalism, but it added nothing to the prestige of the local group and probably detracted somewhat from its bargaining power.

Over the 1941–48 period Saco-Lowell employees received tremendous benefits, tangible and intangible. Obviously, the union was in the fortuitous position of being able plausibly to claim a considerable amount of credit for Saco-Lowell's liberalized labor policy, despite the fact that over this period a prevailing sellers' market for labor and a strong pro-labor national government inevitably would have required Saco-Lowell to grant many of the basic benefits and pay increases which were incorporated in the various union agreements. In 1948, however, Saco-Lowell employees were the beneficiaries of measures which far exceeded the statutory requirements. There is absolutely no way of ascertaining to what extent the union has been responsible for these, nor what Saco-Lowell might have extended without pressure.

Between 1941 and 1947 one short-lived strike had occurred in the foundry, one official strike threat was voiced and withdrawn (1944), and wage rates had been increased by the company approximately 145 per cent. In this same span of years the Whitin Machine Works, standing fast in its factory village against the encroachment of unionization from without, fought a costly and indecisive three-months-long strike which may well have marked the end of a long, deep-rooted, and seemingly promising tradition of company paternalism.

In these years the trend of labor costs (Section 4, following) was such as to raise many questions in the mind of any farsighted labor leader. Reduction of profits and dividends through increased benefits to labor was the universal experience of American business. In an industry as unstable as the textile machinery industry and in a company such as Saco-Lowell, not fully recuperated from past reverses, the potential consequences of inflexible labor costs were inevitably alarming. The consummation of the 1948 labor agreement was marked by cordial relations between the company and the union. There were, at this time, many hopeful signs and some dangers. Factionalism in the local organization persisted, but it had been curbed to a sufficient extent to allow a united front to be presented at the bargaining table. National-local feeling, too, had been curbed somewhat, though not eliminated. The caliber of local leadership in the union had visibly improved, and the cumulative experience of local officers appeared to be imparting a degree of responsibility to the organization which had been noticeably lacking on many earlier occasions. Experience, too, had tempered Saco-Lowell's personnel departments, and there was a diminution in the feeling of frustration and exasperation which occasionally suffused the managerial organization at Biddeford. The great hope for continued labor peace and, indeed, for the future existence of the Saco-Lowell Shops lay in the ability of company and union representatives to profit by and gain in stature and responsibility from the events of the preceding eight years. The explosive potentialities of inexperience, irresponsibility, and shortsighted appraisal of company and industry trends, however, could not and cannot yet be discounted.

An impartial appraisal of Saco-Lowell's labor relations over the 1941–48 period suggests the conclusion that, considering the extremely strong bargaining position of the Textile Workers Union of America and the general atmosphere of the time, the labor policies of David F. Edwards, far from being "soft," constitute an outstanding aspect of his service with the company. Saco-Lowell wage levels in 1949 are virtually identical with those of the Whitin Machine Works. The company has weathered eight difficult years without a work stoppage, and company-union relations today are healthy. Edwards' progressive attitude has in no instance tolerated accession to unreasonable union demands, and union leaders have long since come to recognize the fact that "the Old Man" is firm and consistent in holding to his principles. Today few would question the statement that Edwards' integrity, fairness, and moderation under often trying circumstances have established a magnificent precedent for future leaders in both company and union to follow.

Organization and Techniques of Personnel Administration

Up to 1941, matters having to do with company-employee relations had been departmentalized in some detail, but there was little opportunity to coördinate these activities further than to place most of them under the general supervision of one man, the assistant works manager.[6] There could scarcely be said to have been an employee relations department as such.

The conclusion of the first union agreement in 1941 created many additional tasks, and the war imposed still more. The need for a more comprehensive and coördinated program in the field of employee relations had been in President Edwards' mind for some time, but the difficulty of detailing suitable personnel from their functions under the pressure of the company's war-work program, coupled with the scarcity of adequately trained men, inside or outside the company, postponed action in this direction.

In 1944 Assistant Works Manager Beecroft was instructed to draw up a program of coördination and rearrangement, and the Personnel Department, as it was first called, came into existence. Beecroft served as Saco-Lowell's first personnel manager.

The activities of this department were those to be found in most well-ordered personnel sections of large companies; they need not be described in detail here.[7] The fact was that Saco-Lowell, like most American firms, had Labor Relations thrust upon it. The reaction of management was occasionally hesitant and surprisingly similar to the reaction of local union officers, suddenly endowed with responsibilities and power which they were scarcely prepared by prior training to accept. Labor relations in America became a field for specialized managerial and scholastic attention in a comparatively short time, and many of the old-time employment managers, however well they knew their men, were scarcely equipped with the psychological, sociological, legal, and even medical knowledge necessary for the direction of the new and tremendously important branch of business administration. New men, specialists in a new business art, were called in by Saco-Lowell. These men knew labor relations, but in the beginning they did not know Biddeford and they did not know Saco-Lowell. Contacts between the new department and the new union officials were tinged with suspicion on the one side and a somewhat strained heartiness on the other. Between 1941 and 1947, employees were showered with benefits ranging from assistance in preparing income-tax returns to free chest X-rays. Some of these benefits were greeted with the familiar reaction which was so utterly baffling to American management of the early 1940's and which can best be described by the words often heard in the shop: "They've *got* it! Why shouldn't they?" This attitude, of course, was not universal, but skepticism certainly robbed the first-granted benefits of some of their luster. Management obviously had no choice in this labor market but to extend such benefits; employees obviously would accept them with reservations until convinced that they would not have to pay for them in some form or other. A transitional period of mutual suspicion and mutual education was inevitable, and the prevalence of such attitudes in no way reflects adversely upon either management or labor leadership. This was simply human nature at work in business, and before the 1930's few in business, aside from the foremen, realized that human nature was so vitally involved.

In Biddeford, as elsewhere in the nation, management often recorded failures in its attempts to comprehend and influence the employee mind. Full-page advertisements placed in local papers by Saco-Lowell, by the Bates Manufacturing Company, and by the Pepperell Manufacturing Company during the course of various labor negotiations illustrated varying degrees of failure in managerial attempts to reach the working man and woman. Saco-Lowell's advertisement, appearing on January 14, 1948, in the Biddeford *Journal,* was a matter-of-fact statement which avoided "writing down" to the employee level, yet Saco-Lowell employees voted 2,050 to 150 in favor of striking. Notwithstanding the fact that less than a month previously the Textile Workers Union had also run a full-page advertisement (most effectively worded), the Saco-Lowell display was widely regarded as power politics and was either ignored or resented.

These circumstances and these events marked the beginnings of labor relations — this was Saco-Lowell's new department: essential but often unpopular; groping but always hopeful; slowly, even imperceptibly, forging a new link between office and shop which has yet to be fully tested for strength and flaws.

With the appointment, in 1947, of Roger Sherman as director of industrial relations, this department virtually severed connections with the past, and work goes forward today under professional specialists. The initial shock of benefits has worn off, and subsequent improvements, such as the appointment in January, 1948, of a full-time plant physician (Dr. Frank Barden) and the substitution of a modern hospital for the old first-aid room, are accepted with little of the old skepticism.

In 1947 the first issue of the *Saco-Lowell News* reached company employees. This was the Industrial Relations Department's response to a comparatively new technique which was sweeping labor-conscious American business, the employee's magazine or news sheet. The *News* has been published monthly in the Biddeford *Daily Journal,* and thereby constitutes an interesting experiment in serving the twin fields of labor and public relations, of which the last-named had been virtually neglected by Saco-Lowell. The effectiveness of this publication in either field has been questioned by some, and it suffers badly in comparison with the expensive format and diversified content of the *Whitin Spindle,* the house organs of Pepperell and other mills, and even Saco-Lowell's own *Bulletin,* prepared for distribution to company customers. Nevertheless, a beginning has been made. In this field, where there is much to be learned, a modest start may well be wise policy. If employee publications prove their worth on a wide scale, however, Saco-Lowell may be faced with the choice of vastly augmenting this activity or abandoning it completely.

The apprentice-training program, smashed by the war, was resumed in 1946 under the direction of A. A. Alden, former director of vocational training for the State of Maine. This program combines the classroom drilling of the trade-school system with the workshop practice of old-time apprenticeship in what may well be a satisfactory answer to the formidable problem of training replacement machinists. "On-the-job" training of returned war veterans was undertaken with enthusiasm, and in early 1947 several hundred young men were receiving such instruction in the Biddeford plant.

Sore spots remain in Saco-Lowell's labor-relations program. In the present-day Industrial Relations Department, however, there is a strong and promising consciousness of things yet to be done. The policy of bringing in men from outside has imparted vigor and ambition to this vital area, and these men are coming to know the company better each day. They must come to understand not only current attitudes, but also the reasons for these attitudes, which lie deeply imbedded in Saco-Lowell's past. A dangerous failure could be recorded here if these new men overestimate the short-term efficacy of employee benefits and fail to appreciate the subtle psychological attitudes which have grown out of Saco-Lowell's unstable past. Free chest X-rays or a news sheet cannot wipe out the

Saco-Lowell Comber, 1949

Saco-Lowell Biddeford Plant Today

memory of the 1923 strike, of the financial and operating disasters of the Herrick era, or even of the ancient inequities of the McMullan régime. These events have outlived the men who participated in them.

Whether a useful tradition of employee loyalty can be generated by the perpetuation of wise and fair labor policies is another matter altogether. Modern trade unionism has consistently combated and in some cases effectively destroyed old loyalties. The only new ties that, so far, it has tolerated between workmen and management are those impersonal ones which take the form of collective action. The Edwards legend, which is grounded upon integrity and fairness even more than upon tangible accomplishments, however great, could be the instrument by which new loyalties, on the part of the individuals in the shop as well as their union leaders, might be created. This legend, however, must be broadened to include local management, and must, above all, be perpetuated and reinforced by the new managers, both in Biddeford and in Boston, who are to come.

3. Better Yarn at Lower Cost

Even during the war years, when research schedules were disrupted and research personnel was transferred to war tasks, the fact was evident that tremendously exciting product developments were under way. These developments, and in particular the work done from 1946 to 1949, have not yet become history. They must be afforded cautious historical treatment, however promising they may seem, and the observations advanced in the paragraphs following are necessarily tentative. The real importance of textile-machinery improvements is shown, neither by tests in experimental laboratories nor in trial installations, but by the experience of the textile industry as a whole over a span of years.

In 1940 experimentation in the field of long-draft roving and spinning still dominated the research effort. Saco-Lowell was selling the LeBlan-Roth drafting system on spinning frames under the well-chosen trade name of "Better Draft Spinning." The "J3" long-draft roving frame had just been placed on the market, displacing the earlier Reynolds frame and the "J1" frame. Saco-Lowell was in a strong competitive position with these models, but there were reasons for further effort. The full potentialities of long-staple synthetic fibers were becoming apparent, and Saco-Lowell's spinning and roving had been designed for cotton fiber. The textile industry, moreover, had shown an understandable disposition to purchase "change-overs" (the drafting element alone) rather than entire new frames. This market characteristic reduced the profit potential of the long-draft spinning and roving systems. Research was undertaken in the late 1930's with the twofold objective of designing spinning and roving systems which would handle synthetic fibers and which would have to be sold in a new frame. The last-named goal was not achieved; the former was attained with conspicuous and far-reaching success.

This program was placed in charge of Benjamin Shaw, who came to Saco-Lowell by the familiar route of the textile mill with an intimate knowledge of textile-engineering practice as well as theory. Work commenced in 1936 produced, over the next five years, the Shaw Controlled Draft Spinning System for fine combed-cotton yarns; the "FS2" Controlled Draft Roving Assembly for long-staple synthetic fibers; and the "Z2" Spinning System, developed by Research Engineer Benjamin Zalkind, for long-staple synthetics. The war delayed somewhat the introduction of these new developments, but the success of the new drafting systems in handling cotton fibers, synthetic fibers, and blends was obvious. This, however, was not the culmination of research effort, for no sooner were these frames ready for the market than the research organization turned to still more promising fields, which have yet to be fully probed.

A significant number of processing steps have been eliminated between the card and the spinning frame. Beyond this, the versatility of Saco-Lowell machines already on the market in handling a wide range of staple types and sizes indicates that the direction of research has changed from the traditional American emphasis on speed to an emphasis on adaptability. This factor of adaptability increases in importance with each new fiber which chemical research laboratories place at the disposal of the textile industry, and Saco-Lowell's alertness in this field may well produce further substantial competitive as well as technological changes. Whitin's strong position in the worsted-machinery business could well be challenged by Saco-Lowell machines capable of handling cotton, synthetic, and woolen fibers. Saco-Lowell may be coming into the worsted-machinery field, abandoned by the company in 1928, by the back door.

Time has yet to tell of the importance of these and other developments. The spinning of yarn in larger packages continues to hold forth promise of further reductions in textile-manufacturing costs. Saco-Lowell's baller head may eliminate the cumbersome roving cans which have cluttered cotton-mill floors for a century and a half. Anti-friction bearings with lifelong sealed-in lubricants, together with case-hardened parts which are practically indestructible, promise increased production with considerable savings in cost. Saco-Lowell has produced a new ball-bearing spindle (the New Era spindle) which is now, after many successful trials, being marketed on a wide scale.

This spindle constitutes the second major attempt to utilize the ball-bearing principle in spindle design. The first attempt consisted of an effort to incorporate bolsters and ball bearings developed by SKF Industries. These parts were purchased by Saco-Lowell and used in new twister and spinning spindles. The first Saco-Lowell ball-bearing spinning spindle, brought forth and marketed in limited quantity in 1937, was not considered satisfactory, although the twister spindle was successful. There was much skepticism among textile-machinery and mill men over such efforts to modify the traditional spindle design. The second effort, made approximately a decade later, contemplated not merely the modification of existing designs by the substitution of ball bearings, but also the building of a completely new spindle which, like the old Waltham "dead spindle," had a fixed, rather than a revolving, blade. Experimentation on this spindle was a joint effort of Saco-Lowell and the New Departure Division of General Motors, and the New Era spindle was introduced formally to the industry in the December, 1948, issue of the *Saco-Lowell Bulletin*. Claims have been advanced by company engineers that this spindle constitutes the most important alteration in spindle design since the spindle revolution of the 1870's and 1880's. The joint efforts of General Motors and the Saco-Lowell Shops on a common problem represent an interesting experiment in industrial coöperation which may well indicate the path of future improvements in some fields of product design, and which point out the increasingly specialized nature of the approach to modern technological problems.

Many other new and improved machines have come out of the Saco-Lowell research rooms — many more are on the drawing boards. No cautious and impartial historian can say at this time that a single one of these machines has yet fully established its true historical importance. No conscientious historian could fail to note, however, the fresh and vigorous research attitude in the Saco-Lowell Shops today. Neither should he overlook the promising fact that scientific means for measuring fiber characteristics and behavior have been vastly augmented over the past decade. The knowledge gained by these means, together with the willingness to utilize that knowledge, could inspire changes in the technology of textile manufacture which would dwarf those which commenced in the mid-1920's. Saco-Lowell's Research Department occupies a position of extreme importance in the company's recent history and could well dominate the course of the future.

That department has changed considerably since Eugene Gwaltney assumed direction of research activities in 1938. When Benjamin Shaw commenced work upon his spinning and roving frames in 1936, the department was set up on a product rather than on a functional basis. Shaw built his early models from the floor up, wasting valuable time in routine work which could have been done by others. Draftsmen labored in separate rooms on separate projects, with little communication between. This situation has since been modified by attempts to coördinate projects and to introduce some functional specialization within the department.

An effort has been made to bring textile-mill men into the organization — an effort which appears to derive from Gwaltney's own mill background. The personnel of the department falls roughly into two classes: fiber men (former mill men or textile-school graduates) and mechanical or process men (engineering-school graduates). Men who have spent their entire lives in textile-machinery building and designing are becoming fewer in number and exert a declining influence in the department.

The personnel problem is not a simple one, and failure to strike a proper balance between experience, inspiration, youth, and age could be disastrous. The knowledge of men who have designed and built textile machinery for two decades or more cannot be ignored, yet these men can become static. School-trained engineers and textile-mill men are prolific sources of new ideas, but they have been criticized for lack of grounding in fundamentals of textile-machinery design. These men do not know what cannot be done, and this is a healthy though necessarily expensive attitude to foster in research.

Such problems of balance are complicated by the inevitable conflicts arising out of the impact of new men upon an old organization, and of the imposition of centralized direction upon a group of individualists. This is a typical transitional experience, and is of far less importance than the question as to whether a proper organizational balance has been struck. Tangible research results suggest that it has, but this is a tentative conclusion and does not rule out the possibility that Saco-Lowell may build a still more smoothly functioning research department.

In the field of product development Saco-Lowell has forged ahead of the Whitin Machine Works and has taken the initiative in many fields. Saco-Lowell has been driven by adversity, while Whitin has indulged in financial and managerial stability. Research efforts in the Whitin Machine Works have been directed primarily at the woolen-, worsted-, and rayon-machinery markets, and those efforts have been highly successful. Woolen and worsted mills, however, account for approximately 10 per cent of the fiber consumed in cloth manufacture in America, and the market for wool and worsted machinery is correspondingly small. The rayon field is similarly limited, though expanding. Whitin has done considerable work in developing twisters for the rayon-producing firms such as Du Pont and Tennessee-Eastman; but in the field where rayon is used in staple, rather than filament, form Whitin and Saco-Lowell appear to be evenly matched. The market for cotton machinery is perhaps four times as large as for rayon and worsted machinery combined, and for this market Whitin has done comparatively little original developmental work. Saco-Lowell has not only gone far ahead in cotton, but has rapidly encroached on Whitin's earlier position of strength in rayon and worsted. The momentum of Saco-Lowell's research program is such that Whitin may not soon be able to make up the ground already lost.

A summary appraisal of Saco-Lowell's research activities from 1926 to 1948 at once reveals the importance of new products in pulling the company through years of desperately depressed business. The greatest obstacle to progress in the textile machinery industry has been the attitude that fundamental processes were not only efficient but even perfect, or at least adequate and unsurpassable. This attitude lingers on today in places, at least subconsciously, but in this period of years well-entrenched attitudes toward yarn preparation began to break down, chiefly under the impact of ideas from Europe and from textile-mill mechanics. As in the past, machine-shop engineers could claim scant credit for inspiration and a great deal of credit for making practical the ideas received from outside the company. Some men in Biddeford feel that experience has been unduly subjugated. Others hail the fresh viewpoint in research. In many quarters in Biddeford there has been inadequate comprehension of the importance of the research program, but in Boston there has been strong support for the goals sought in this program. Beyond these generalizations little can be said, and only time can reveal the true efficacy of policy and administration in the field of product development.

The enthusiasm and unorthodoxy of Eugene Gwaltney has sparked the entire research program, and to him must be awarded much of the credit for the company's great technical achievements after 1938. Gwaltney brought to his position as director of research a combination of long mill experience, a flare for new development, and great salesmanship. Willing to entertain daring theories, Gwaltney has seldom been led astray by theory, and he proved to be an eminently practical, dollar-conscious innovator. His dynamic direction of the research department caused occasional worry in the Boston office, and it is possible that other men in Biddeford could have performed the routine and perfunctory administrative chores associated with the position of department head more efficiently. Yet Gwaltney's resourcefulness and imagination proved to be priceless qualities, and were recognized as such by Edwards, who allowed this individualistic assistant the freedom requisite for creative work.

Product developments taking place in the company today under Gwaltney's direction point to broad conclusions which are best presented here, though they concern distant past as well as present circumstances.

The textile machinery industry cannot well escape condemnation for the unparalleled technological stagnation of the 1890–1920 period, but this situation was transitory. The charge that over the span of a century the large textile-machine shops have failed to keep pace with technical progress in other industries is, of course, misleading and unsupportable by any kind of specific evidence. This charge completely ignores the historic position and functions of such shops in the economy of the textile and textile machinery industries.

Out of the failure to recognize the cumulative importance of an infinite number of minor improvements has grown a severe, widespread, and substantially inaccurate condemnation of the rate of technological advance in the textile industry. Critics have naïvely assumed that since, until comparatively recent date, the basic processes of yarn preparation evolved in eighteenth-century England have not been changed, the pace of progress has been slow. The large machine shops, including Saco-Lowell and all its predecessor companies, have originated few major improvements in American textile-manufacturing processes. This fact has no derogatory implications. Too many economists have placed a premium on invention — too few have recognized the equal value of development and improvement. The cumulative importance of the many minor improvements effected by the principal machinery builders over the years, moreover, is but a part of the justification for such profits as those builders have been able to derive from their activities.

A great contribution to industrial progress has been made by the American textile-machinery shops in commercializing the creations of the independent inventor: first, by making practical and improving those creations, and secondly, by marketing them on a nation-wide or world-wide basis. I feel that this accomplishment, undramatic and consequently unrecorded by casual observers, warrants not only special notice but exceptional commendation. Today Saco-Lowell has begun to originate. As in other years, however, it still seeks inspiration from outside the company, and goes about the dual tasks of encouraging creative thinking by its own engineers and of perfecting and marketing the ideas of others.[8]

4. Operations in a Changing World, 1941–1948

Operating results of the Saco-Lowell Shops after 1940 are dominated by inflation in taxes, machine prices, material prices, and labor costs, and by capacity operations in the plant. In 1944, the peak of the war years, dollar sales were the highest in the company's history, exceeding even the 1920 peak; in 1948, dollar sales were almost double the 1944 figure. Employment expanded from approximately three thousand in January, 1940, to six thousand at the end of 1948. Behind these figures lie many disturbing factors, some of which are tempered by the caliber of the managerial effort being put forth in the company today.

Sales and Markets

Saco-Lowell enjoys today, and has enjoyed for many years, excellent relations with the trade. As in the past, this relationship has been largely on a personal basis. The friendships of men in the organization have formed a strong tie with customers. To a greater extent than ever before, however, this bond has been strengthened by effective advertising.

In 1928 Roger D. Hale, son of former General Agent Frank J. Hale, established the *Saco-Lowell Bulletin*. This concise and extremely attractive trade publication, issued monthly at first and later at irregular or quarterly intervals, appears to have been an effective medium for dispensing technical information and announcing new products. The *Bulletin* was taken over by Advertising Manager A. K. Landau, and Landau also began on an enlarged scale to issue catalogues, instruction booklets, and other direct-advertising material. Saco-Lowell appears to be ahead of other machine shops in ability and willingness to utilize this type of advertising, and the last decade has witnessed a long-delayed awakening to the possibilities of improving on traditionally conservative methods of establishing and maintaining market contacts.

Increased attention to these contacts may well be required, for the domestic market for textile machinery has ceased to feel the stimulating effect of new mill construction. Even today (1949) there are indications that the purge of New England textile mills has not completely run its course. Total spindles in place in the United States have declined by slightly more than a million since 1940 and by more than fifteen million since 1926. This industrial maturity, if it may be so called, has placed a major emphasis upon repair-parts sales, new product development, and export sales — none of which were accorded more than desultory attention by the principal machinery builders during the years when the textile industry was expanding in great bursts of new mill-building. The threat of foreign competition in domestic markets, moreover, has already been voiced in federal reciprocal-trade policies, which have resulted so far in a reduction in tariffs of from 40 to 10 per cent.

Sales Manager W. F. Lowell has evinced great interest in export markets for Saco-Lowell machinery, and under his direction the geographic pattern of foreign sales has changed in the following manner:

	Per cent of total foreign sales	
	1921	1948[a]
South and Central America	2	64
Middle and Far East	93	23
Other	5	13

[a] Seven months.

Andersen, Meyer & Company still serves Saco-Lowell in the East. Other geographic areas are reached through other agents, working on a commission basis (usually 5 per cent of sales). As in earlier periods, many direct personal contacts exist between Saco-Lowell and its foreign customers. As in the past, too, this market is volatile in nature. From 1926 through 1948, foreign sales constituted from one-fourth to one-tenth of Saco-Lowell's sales volume. Prices obtained abroad at times in the past have been less than at home, but the foreign market was served and cultivated against the day when export sales might be needed to help carry the burden of plant overhead. No estimate of Saco-Lowell's future can discount the possibility that this segment of its business may suffer a severe setback. Postwar export and exchange regulations and dollar shortages in foreign markets have already hampered sales abroad. The hope yet awaits fulfillment that the low operating cost of American machinery is sufficient inducement to overcome the lower first cost of machinery built by the English, European, and possibly Japanese shops, which have yet to get back effectively into the world market after the interruption of war years. The disheartening fact which history reveals is that although Saco-Lowell has often won out in direct competition with the English, the company's success in securing many markets abroad has been brought about mainly by removal of foreign producers from those markets by war or other temporary economic maladjustments and not primarily as a result of Saco-Lowell marketing effort, however brilliant, or the adaptability of Saco-Lowell machinery, however efficient, to the foreign demand. Large quantities of Saco-Lowell machinery are now in operation abroad, and perhaps this fact, plus a forceful policy of cultivating foreign sales, may enable the company to remain in the foreign market when normal competitive conditions have been restored.

In both the foreign and the domestic machinery markets sales performance has been strongly colored by price changes. These changes must be discounted in order to appraise Saco-Lowell's current position and compare it with past performance. If the two peak years 1920 and 1947 are placed side by side and the output of the latter year expressed as a percentage of the former, the effect of price movement becomes at once apparent:[9]

1947 Sales as Percentage of 1920 Sales	
Dollar Sales	161%
Machinery Units Sold	
(principal products)	
Vertical openers	9
Pickers	17
Cards	64
4 Roll Drawing Deliveries	54
Roving Frames	27
Spinning Frames	63
Twisters	52

The immediate effect of such a comparison is at once to negate any claim that 1947 and 1948 constitute the greatest peak of activity in the company's history. Enthusiasms engendered by dollar sales figures of these years must be tempered by the realization that fewer machinery units are being produced today than in other years. In a situation of this sort, the impact of price declines or of even small decreases in volume of machinery produced could wipe out profit margins with relative ease. The fact that Saco-Lowell is actually producing less machinery than in earlier peaks of activity suggests two principal and obvious necessities which must govern company policy in any textile-industry depression which might develop: first, for continued emphasis on product development, and secondly, for greater marketing effort than has been expended in many years. Since the characteristics of many cost elements have changed over the past decade, the necessity for maintenance of near-capacity production would seem to be much more pronounced today than it was in the 1930's. Cost rigidities exist today which did not exist before the war, and although company management has made great strides in controlling overhead costs, Saco-Lowell's ability to weather a new depression cannot be inferred too easily from the company's good record in the 1930's.

The Cost-Price-Profit Pattern

Between 1941 and 1948 the index of Saco-Lowell machinery prices increased 101 per cent. Over the same period the index of wages rose 145 per cent.[10] The trend of labor costs over a longer period is concretely illustrated by the figures on page 604, taken from a Saco-Lowell foundry report. These figures are of unusual interest because of the rough measure of efficiency provided by the index of good castings produced (column 1).

These figures, standing alone, imply a decreasing effectiveness in the utilization of labor and suggest that labor costs have become disproportionately and perhaps dangerously large. Shop performance as a whole must be considered, however, and labor costs are a relative and not an absolute factor in production. Actually, much of the tremendous increase in wage rates and wage earnings over the past decade has been absorbed either by increases in machinery prices, by improvements in manufacturing techniques, by increasing labor efficiency, or by all three. In 1927 factory payroll (direct and indirect) equaled 49 per cent of the sales dollar. In 1941 it had

Indices of Foundry Performance
(1929 = 100)

Year	Good Castings Produced	Piecework Earnings per Hour	Total Molding Labor Costs per Pound of Castings
1929.......	100 (61.72%)	100 ($.77)	100 ($.00980)
1930.......	106	99	100
1931.......	106	88	90
1932.......	103	73	87
1933.......	98	76	86
1934.......	96	87	93
1935.......	98	96	102
1936.......	103	96	81
1937.......	98	108	87
1938.......	100	112	90
1939.......	100	110	88
1940.......	102	105	83
1941.......	98	112	92
1942.......	93	126	125
1943.......	93	145	163
1944.......	85	138	162
1945.......	95	145	155
1946.......	93	151	148

fallen to 42 per cent, and in 1946 to 39 per cent. The significance of these percentages is at once apparent when they are compared with figures for the 1913–26 period (Chart XIII, Chapter XIII). In only three of the fourteen years of this earlier period did factory payroll decline to less than 40 per cent of the sales dollar, and in the years from 1923 through 1926 the factory payroll ran from 51 to 60 per cent of sales.

There is no way of ascertaining how much of the favorable ratio of labor costs to sales dollar is owing to machinery price levels and how much is the result of increasing efficiency in the utilization of labor in the shop or the increasing efficiency of labor itself. There is a strong feeling in managerial circles today that labor efficiency has declined considerably in some branches of the business, and that labor efficiency in the plant as a whole has not increased commensurately with increases in pay. Adequate measures of labor efficiency are difficult to find. One measure, admittedly limited in value, is provided by comparative ratios of numbers of machines produced per employee. Changes in the product line limit this comparison to the span of years between 1940 and 1947. In the latter year output of machines per employee was about 2½ per cent higher than in 1940, but the 1947 output, unlike that in 1940, includes some machinery built by sub-contractors outside the shop. Even if this factor is ignored, the increase in labor efficiency revealed by output per worker is barely perceptible, and lends credence to the surmise that machinery price levels, and possibly improved manufacturing techniques, rather than improved labor efficiency have borne the burden of the rapid inflation in wage rates.

These admittedly rough-and-ready comparisons do suggest that absolute increases in labor costs are far from alarming in themselves. The great uncertainty and the chief cause for concern would appear to lie not in the present level of labor costs, but rather in the flexibility of those costs over a period of declining activity. Success in holding labor costs to a safe proportion of total costs in a period of rising activity must be matched with success in maintaining the same safe ratio in a period of decline. One half of the battle only has been won, and the responsibility for the future of the company would appear to lie to an equal extent upon the shoulders of company management and of the Textile Workers Union of America. Inflexibility of labor costs may be overcome to some extent by managerial efforts to increase operating efficiency, but the limitations on such increases are obvious and the time required to make them effective is often measured in years. The Textile Workers Union must be prepared to accept essential pay reductions in any period of declining business activity. The amounts of such reductions could, of course, be influenced somewhat by the extent of the union's coöperation in extending further the productivity per worker in the plant.

If the by no means proven conclusion is entertained that labor efficiency, with some exceptions, has been at least adequate and that labor costs have been kept well within margins of safety, the question immediately arises as to why Saco-Lowell has shown such modest profits in the immensely active years from 1941 through 1948. Over this period profits after taxes have averaged 5 per cent of sales. By way of comparison, the average profit from 1933 through 1940, a period which saw low-volume operations and extremely heavy financing charges, was 6⅓ per cent of sales. Inroads made by federal taxes and by provisions for re-negotiation of war contracts explain the profit showing after 1940. The figures in the tabulation below require little comment.

Profits before and after Provision for Federal and State Taxes, Social Security Payments, and Refunds on War Contracts

	Before	After		Before	After
1941	$1,422,863	$949,478	1945	$1,107,182[a]	$1,318,162[a]
1942	2,232,431	908,054	1946	1,519,914	777,486
1943	4,539,691	704,928	1947	6,718,117	3,835,664
1944	4,478,341	830,799	1948	8,461,839	4,700,559

[a] Deficit.

Only one other major facet of Saco-Lowell's cost pattern remains to be explored. Significant changes have taken place in the past two years in the expense of administering factory operations at Biddeford.

During the depression years of the 1930's (Chapter XIV) administrative expenses were exceptionally low, owing in part to the decentralized nature of control over plant operations. The centralization and tightening of controls which followed in the wake of the 1947 plant reorganization (considered in subsequent paragraphs), coupled with an apparent decrease in the productivity of indirect labor, rapidly increased the costs of plant administration. One measure of these increased costs lies in the number of employees engaged in the various indirect (administrative) departments of the business. Between July, 1947, and October, 1948, the number of employees in direct manufacturing departments increased 12 per cent, while employment in the indirect factory departments increased 27 per cent. The tabulation on page 607 shows, on a departmental basis, the changes which occurred over a span of years.

However logical and necessary the recent trend in administrative costs may be, that trend has been watched with care by management. The low productivity of indirect labor was considered of sufficient importance by President Edwards to warrant a full page of discussion in his 1948 message to the stockholders. The feeling which exists today is that necessary increases in overhead costs are being more than offset by the economies of the new system of production controls, and that unnecessarily high overhead costs, the result of low productivity, are being brought into line. Over-all productivity (direct and indirect labor) is now felt to be as high as at any time in the past, but the real test of existing cost-control methods will not come until volume of production falls below prevailing levels. The unanswered question is whether these methods will be able to survive a major depression.[11]

The Plant

Saco-Lowell today is in a situation which bears a superficial resemblance, at least, to the condition of scattered manufacturing operations which was considered so great a disadvantage in the late 1920's. The basic difficulty has been that the plant consolidation of 1928–32 reduced manufacturing capacity to a point where a boom market simply could not be served and concentrated that capacity in an inefficient plant. This was not an operational mistake but a financial necessity.

In 1946 additional manufacturing space was acquired in Portland,

Number on Payroll; Various Direct and Indirect Factory Departments

Department	October, 1941	July, 1947	October, 1948
Experimental	[a]	44	46
Factory Accounting	80	116	112
Industrial Relations	17	42	58
Inspection	12	75	120
Methods	8	48	30
Plant Administration	2	33	45
Plant Maintenance	162	418	286
Plant Protection	...	28	38
Product Engineering	67	28	95
Production	36	63	208
Purchasing	8	16	26
Standards	78	37	47
Stores	106	160	260
Timekeepers	[a]	92	127
Percentage Increase over Previous Period			
Indirect Departments	...	85%	27%
Total Employed by Company	...	39%	22%

[a] No data.

where the so-called Thompson's Point plant was set up to assemble pickers. As the pressure on manufacturing facilities increased during and after the war years, extensive sub-contracting was done. The problem involved here was whether to let out sub-contracts for parts or for entire machines. Despite the fear by some that the latter course would eventually encourage sub-contractors to go into business for themselves, several complete machines were ordered from outside suppliers. These included combers, drawing frames, and sliver lap machines. Units in the picking system were also let out, as were filters and New Era spindles.

The sub-contracting system has possessed the great advantage of flexibility, for as capacity becomes available in the Biddeford plant the sub-contract work may be pulled back in to utilize machines and personnel that otherwise would be idle. The higher cost of sub-contract work is said to be offset by the avoidance of plant-expansion costs which would otherwise have been incurred. Some control over quality has been secured by careful selection of suppliers, and some new ideas have come from the fresh viewpoint which sub-contractors have been able to bring to the various operations. The sub-contract system can scarcely be regarded as a permanent solution to Saco-Lowell's lack of efficient plant capacity, but the adoption of this system in periods of great activity indicates a most significant departure from the traditional and hazardous practice of supporting a plant capable of meeting peak rather than average demands for machinery.

In September, 1948, Saco-Lowell purchased a plant of the Indian Motorcycle Company, located in Sanford, North Carolina, which was subsequently turned over to the manufacture of drawing frames, card strippers, and lap winders. This action raises a whole series of highly interesting questions which hitherto have scarcely been breathed aloud in Biddeford — or in Whitinsville.

Will the textile machinery industry follow the textile industry South? Speculation on this point lies outside the sphere of the present work, but factors bearing on the problem may be mentioned. Saco-Lowell today has a cramped and inefficient plant. Effective operating controls can never completely transcend the handicaps imposed by the physical arrangement of a manufacturing establishment which has grown piecemeal over the course of a century. The old multi-story buildings impose severe difficulties in the efficient handling of the heavy materials utilized in textile-machinery building. Maintenance costs are heavy, and there is no question but that lack of a modern plant is penalizing Saco-Lowell many thousands of dollars each year. This handicap, of course, is shared by Saco-Lowell's major competitors. Power is relatively cheap, but transportation costs of both machinery and raw materials are high, for both machines and materials must travel far. Approximately 80 per cent of the company's shipments to domestic customers go to the South. There is some disadvantage to Saco-Lowell, aside from transportation costs, in being so far removed from the mills where the majority of the company's machinery installations, both regular and experimental, are in operation. Customer relations and customer service unquestionably would be improved by locating in the center of concentration of cotton spindles.

From a managerial viewpoint Biddeford has seldom, since the first establishment of a textile-machine shop there, been an efficient or even tolerably satisfactory location. The record of managerial difficulties and failures in the Biddeford shop over the course of more than a century has been impressive, and it raises an interesting question as to whether some basic deficiency exists which has impaired the effectiveness of managerial effort there. In my research upon Saco-Lowell history I have encountered time and again a common criticism of Biddeford management which may well come close to a formulation of that deficiency. Men of widely varying backgrounds (some of them lifetime Biddeford residents) who agreed upon nothing else were unanimous in emphasizing the severe handicap under which the Biddeford shop has labored in its effort to secure an adequate supply of competent managerial personnel from the immediate geographic area. In late years the automobile, of course, has vastly increased the area upon which the company may draw, but there are those who feel today that Saco-Lowell has long since outgrown its environment. Saco-Lowell was charged with failure to pay sufficiently high salaries to attract the caliber of men required at Biddeford, and with relying too heavily on inadequate resident skills. For many years the company in its poverty could not have done differently, and with returning prosperity new men have been brought in and salaries raised. The managerial deficiencies incurred by the earlier necessity, however, have had to be overcome gradually.

Balanced against these disadvantages of present location are two very familiar arguments. Relations between the company and the city of Biddeford have been cordial and taxes are moderate. New England today, as for many generations past, provides an unsurpassed market for skilled machinists. These arguments are, of course, capable of modification. Southern communities could and probably would match or exceed any inducements which Biddeford has extended or might extend. The advantage of the New England labor market is tempered by an increasing utilization of unskilled and semi-skilled labor in the machine trades and a growing force of competent machine operators in the South. The intelligence of union leadership could be a decisive factor in this situation. Presumably no parties involved would repeat the mistake of the Lowell city fathers in thinking that a great machine shop could not or would not be moved.

The blunt fact is that, with the acquisition of pilot plants in North Carolina, both the Whitin Machine Works and the Saco-Lowell Shops have already taken the first step toward moving South. Whitin has heavy village commitments which might impede any effort to effect a complete shift in location, but Saco-Lowell has relatively few encumbrances. Saco-Lowell's Sanford acquisition (the so-called "Edwards" Division) encompasses a plant site of twenty-two acres. Within a radius of two hundred and fifty miles of this location are to be found approximately three-quarters of the spindles of the Southern cotton textile industry. In his 1948 message to the stockholders David Edwards reported the Sanford acquisition and rather pointedly called attention to the implications of the purchase. His statements were based upon solid and inescapable economic fact. Saco-Lowell is being driven by narrowed profit margins into serious consideration of all possible means, including a new manufacturing establishment, of reducing operating costs. The industrial engineering firm of Ford, Bacon & Davis has been retained to make a detailed examination of present manufacturing facilities and the potentialities of a new plant and new locations.

Management, Stockholders, and the Public

Financial operating results for the 1941–48 period are detailed in Appendix 15. The company's balance sheet and income statement as of December 31, 1949, are also included (Tables M and P). These summary statistics provide important evidence of the ability of the organization to convert operating assets into cash quickly and decisively in a period of declining volume—an excellent measure of managerial efficiency in the textile machinery industry. The balance sheet shows that at the close of 1949 Saco-Lowell stood in a strong financial position, with heavy reserves, conservatively valued assets, moderate liabilities, and the simplest possible capital structure. Reflected in this statement are the results of adroit financial management by Malcolm D. Shaffner, who has served as Saco-Lowell's treasurer since 1946. Beyond this, however, the 1949 statement stands as a testimonial to Edwards' career with the Saco-Lowell Shops. No more succinct or dramatic summation is possible than the one provided by a comparison between the 1949 balance sheet and that of 1926.

Saco-Lowell dividends from 1941 through 1948 were as follows:

1941	$452,781	(6.8% of sales)	1945	$ 374,363	(3.0% of sales)
1942	664,512	(3.6% " ")	1946	437,500	(2.2% " ")
1943	532,569	(2.2% " ")	1947	1,000,000	(3.3% " ")
1944	558,227	(2.3% " ")	1948	1,000,000	(2.1% " ")
				3,000,000	(stock dividend)[a]

[a] $3,000,000 represents market value; par value is $250,000.

David F. Edwards has driven hard and effectively toward a complete revision of the philosophy of profit distribution in the Saco-Lowell Shops. The old theory was that in a highly unstable industry, such as textile-machinery building, profits should be paid out liberally when earned; otherwise they would surely be swallowed up in the chaos of subsequent depression. This attitude consistently drained the coffers of the Saco-Lowell Shops, and finally (in 1925) placed the company on the brink of complete ruin. Such a philosophy has become doubly dangerous in an age when the opportunity for building up reserves has been restricted by federal taxation policies. Evidence of the new attitude is best seen in Saco-Lowell's decision to declare a stock dividend in 1948. The new concept of profit distribution is best stated in Edwards' own words, taken from a letter from Edwards to a committee of directors formed in the summer of 1948 to consider the alternative possibilities of a large cash dividend, a stock split, or a stock dividend:

This whole question must, of course, be considered against the background of the last twenty years. Unless it is so considered, no sound or informed conclusions can be reached.

Edwards pointed out the circumstances which dominated the lean years following 1926, when the company was starved for cash and maintenance was deferred:

During this period when Whitin and Draper were spending millions of dollars to replace old equipment, we were paying out even more millions in cash (in excess of $7,500,000) to cover interest charges and principal installments on funded debt. Only a few of us who actually lived with the situation day by day and fought for survival can really understand the full extent and significance of the rigid economy and bitter self-denial that we had to practice all during the 1930's in order to nurse this business back to financial health. I urge strongly and earnestly that your committee keep this background in mind at all times when considering the question of dividend policy. Unless you do so it would be very easy to arrive at a wholly wrong and even dangerous conclusion.

I know it is frequently said that in a business of fluctuating volume and earnings like ours, the time to pay big dividends is when they are being earned,—otherwise they will never be paid. I cannot share this opinion, first, because of the background already given, and second, because I think it is better to regularize and even out dividend payments over a period of years than to disgorge them in large chunks in a few prosperous years and then pay nothing in lean years.

The Edwards policy contemplates a moderate and stable dividend rate, patterned after the policy pursued by Whitin for some years. Whether it can be established as Saco-Lowell policy depends on two factors: first, whether tax laws will permit sufficient reserves to be accumulated in good years to carry dividends over poor years; secondly, whether Saco-Lowell stockholders, a few of whom in the past have occasionally failed to be farsighted or coöperative, will realize the inherent worth, the historical validity, and the absolute necessity for such a policy. The latter point depends to a large extent upon the ability of David F. Edwards and his successor to continue to set and administer the policies of the company. The changing nature of stock holdings in the Saco-Lowell Shops may facilitate continuation of that strong central control which is so essential for successful management in this company.

A marked change has occurred in the character of Saco-Lowell stockholding interests in the past decade. Ownership of the company has become rapidly and steadily dispersed, until by January of 1948 only one of the several large old ownership groups remained intact. In November, 1937, the average number of common-stock shares held per shareholder was 90, and there were 778 common stockholders. By January, 1948, after a substantial increase in the total stock outstanding, the average number of shares held had actually increased slightly (to 93), but the number of stockholders had increased to 2,679. No single holding exceeded 4 per cent of the stock outstanding. The dispersion of stock ownership took place in the face of a more or less steady rise in the market value of Saco-Lowell stock (Chart XIV, Chapter XIV) and a steady improvement in the condition of the company. This dispersion probably resulted in part from the liquidation of security blocks in the 1937 stock-market slump and in part from the natural process of dispersion of stock holdings through liquidation of estates of deceased stockholders.

This diffusion of ownership, plus the self-perpetuating nature of the directorate (a characteristic which may be traced back in company history in unbroken sequence to the earliest days of the Boston Manufacturing Company), promises to assure the Saco-Lowell directorate of freedom from effective challenge. There is, of course, no guarantee that conflicts within the directorate may not develop and interfere with effective management, though this possibility is somewhat obviated by the care with which new directors are chosen and is one which is faced by every corporation.

Despite the strong centralized control in the Saco-Lowell Shops, David F. Edwards has made a sincere effort to keep stockholders informed of events within the company and the industry. His annual messages to the stockholders constituted the nearest approach the company had made to an effort in the field of public relations before the time that this history was conceived and authorized. The annual reports have been clear, frank, and meaningful. When the picture was grim, the stockholders were warned, just as they were encouraged when optimism was warranted. Prior to 1926 there had been no annual reports worthy of the name. From 1926 to 1941 these reports were rather terse and unquestionably forbidding in form. In 1942 a highly attractive type of report was issued, and the president's message contained more details. In 1943, 1944, and 1945, appropriate illustrations were included, and the attractive format continued in standardized style. After 1946 no illustrations were included, and the reports, though lacking the colorful features adopted by some companies, continued to be attractive and readable. Financial statements have been simplified in these reports, but appear to be adequate to impart a general comprehension of vital trends. The omission of sales figures constitutes the only significant deviation from complete disclosure; this seems to infer a far better relationship between profit margins and sales than actually exists.

Under Edwards' leadership Saco-Lowell has emerged from the obscurity which for so many years has been deliberately courted by companies in this industry. The textile machinery industry has almost completely escaped public notice. At one point, when the machine-builders were actively engaged in practices which bordered on restraint of trade (1896–1912), such reticence to claim public notice was unquestionably expedient. Today only Saco-Lowell and the Whitin Machine Works have shaken off the old shyness and made faltering first steps toward establishing good public relations. Neither company in all its parts has yet completely adopted the viewpoint that aggressive frankness offers a hope of forestalling public suspicion and the unwarranted but devastating public and governmental censure which is so easily generated today by determined and skillful business enemies. The histories of the Whitin

Machine Works and of the Saco-Lowell Shops reveal a chapter in American industrial history which has been hidden by deliberate reticence; more than this, these histories evidence a new spirit and policy which is at once promising and progressive. Both these histories were authorized in the belief that a great story should be told, but the act of authorization may well prove to have been even more significant than the histories themselves.

A Final Challenge for the Edwards Administration

Possibly the most astonishing aspect of the Edwards Era in Saco-Lowell history has been the variety, number, and crushing weight of problems which have been faced. In 1946, while the company was still staggering from the shock of war, a final challenge was encountered. The word final is not used loosely, for the directorate (prompted by the president himself) has already considered candidates for the position of company president, and David F. Edwards is not far from a well-earned retirement.

In a career distinguished by courageous and energetic action, the operating reorganization of 1947–48 stands out as a conspicuous example of courage and energy. This reorganization could have been avoided by Edwards. In the traditional business-history pattern Edwards' final contribution could well have been to bring the company safely through war and reconversion. To have stopped there would have detracted nothing from an outstanding business career, and a new and younger administration could have faced the challenge of increasing operational rigidities at Biddeford.

The highly trying task of attacking those rigidities was assumed by Edwards himself. The fact that he saw them, where others were blind or fearful, tells much about the man who guided Saco-Lowell through some of the most difficult years of its history.[12]

In February, 1947, a new vice-president was sent to Biddeford to assume charge of operations there and to replace R. A. Kettley. This man was John S. Chafee. Behind the change lay a period of slowly accumulating frictions between the Biddeford and Boston offices. The Biddeford management had been hand-tailored to perform the essential task of driving the company through the stern years of depression in the 1930's. This task had been done, and the survival of the company in these years stands as a memorial to the integrity and ability of men like Kettley, Works Manager Tarr, and many others who worked devotedly for Edwards and for Saco-Lowell. The old management, like most managements which are designed to perform one major task, was fundamentally unsuited by reason of age and aptitude to function effectively in a totally different situation. Youth, energy, verve, new ideas, and optimism were now demanded, and Edwards set about to provide them.

John Chafee's business career had commenced in his family's own firm, the Brown & Sharpe Company, manufacturers of machine tools in Providence, Rhode Island. Here Chafee worked through a shop apprenticeship into the position of marketing executive. In 1943 Chafee went to Washington as Deputy Director of the Tools Division of the War Production Board, and in 1945 he became the Equipment Bureau Director of the Board. He came to Saco-Lowell at the age of fifty-one with enthusiastic recommendations from many influential men. In accepting Edwards' offer he traded a comfortable future in familiar surroundings for a new home amidst strangers and tremendous problems. With Chafee came Sven Vaule, the production engineer who was to work out the details of plant reorganization at Biddeford.

The conditions which confronted the new administration could scarcely be viewed otherwise than with alarm. A psychology of defeatism flourished. Many older, experienced men had little idea of business developments in the "outside" world, and young men worked for themselves and not for the company. Insecurity permeated the managerial organization and there was jockeying for position. Information, far from being freely exchanged, was guarded carefully by men who felt that exclusive possession of knowledge was a guarantee of job security. A scramble for power had placed some in situations where they could scarcely fulfill the multiple responsibilities they had sought and acquired. In the shop poor education, rather than nationality groupings, provided the great obstacle to the training of competent help.

Operational as well as managerial laxity prevailed. Pennies were pinched in the office, while in the shop dollars were being thrown on the scrap heap. There was occasional dishonesty—both outright stealing and the insidious so-called "government-work"—whereby employees reaped personal benefit from shop time and materials. These conditions exist, of course, in greater or less degree in every company.

The Bedaux wage incentive system had become hopelessly enmeshed in error, inconsistency, and inadequacy. Indeed, the original installation had been so thoroughly modified over the course of years that the name Bedaux could no longer be accurately applied. Multiple and varying standards existed for almost all job operations; parts lists were incomplete, terminology was inconsistent, inventory control was not centralized, and piece counts were inaccurate and highly susceptible to manipulation. The posting of job ratings, insisted upon by the union, revealed to all in the shop the inequalities of the wage incentive system. Many, if not all, of these weaknesses had been pointed out earlier to the Biddeford management, but remedial efforts had bogged down in the press of greater problems or as a result of indifference or misunderstanding or shop politics. Resistance to change was strongly entrenched and new ideas which threatened to disturb the managerial status quo were quietly sabotaged.

Edwards' instructions to Chafee were to attack these problems, but not to interrupt the rhythm of production. The difficulty of instituting major system changes in a period of peak activity was formidable, but the financial necessity for keeping the machines moving out to the trade was obvious.

Suspicion inevitably greeted the new vice-president. Even the innocuous fact that Chafee was unable to find a house in Biddeford or Saco and consequently took up his abode in Portland was cause for local comment. Possibly it was the memory of James McMullan's famous renunciation of Biddeford a half-century earlier which cast a shadow over a Portland residence.

The initial coolness with which new managers have always been received has to a very great extent disappeared, and acceptance by the organization has increased in direct proportion as the success of Chafee's methods and the soundness of his objectives have been proven. Biddeford men found the new manager experienced in solving production and administrative problems, determined, and approachable. This last-named quality has been particularly respected. Biddeford soon discovered, however, that informality was not synonymous with laxity, and that the new vice-president was willing and able to act decisively. Some felt that he had scant reverence for traditional concepts of textile-machinery building operations.

The essence of the changes which were made and are still being made was greater centralization of operational controls. This process had been under way in the Whitin Machine Works for a decade and had been completed by most large manufacturing firms in America in the first two decades of the twentieth century — in many cases earlier.

Consultant Vaule worked out new production and stock controls and a new wage incentive system. The following goals were defined:

1. Centralize control over issuing of manufacturing orders.
2. Install adequate inventory records and stores procedure.
3. Prepare process sheets for all parts, listing best prevailing shop practices.
4. Install effective timekeeping procedures to control time spent on operations and piece counts.
5. Provide sufficient space for inventory storage.
6. Repair tools and equipment.
7. Install new methods of internal transportation.
8. Make essential improvements and additions to buildings.

Chafee began to reorganize managerial alignments, defining and in many cases reducing responsibilities. Outside consultants were brought in to supply skills which were not to be found in the organization. This task of clarifying executive chains of command consumed eighteen months and only comparatively recently has it been possible to make that concerted effort necessary for building up the prestige of foremen and section hands — a far from easy task because of the fact that centralization stripped some of these men of traditional prerogatives. Chafee's expressed conviction that "there are no unimportant people in this business" appears to have been supported by his efforts in the lower levels of management. His initial attention to the foremen produced a cynical response, but cynicism has been replaced by interest and the beginning of understanding.

The new wage incentive system has yet (September, 1949) to be installed, but agreement between the company and the Textile Workers Union of America upon the conditions ("Terms of Reference") which will govern installation has been reached. The union has pledged coöperation in the important task of setting new job rates, and any failure to remove existing inequities would undermine the new system before it was even in operation. The responsibility for good faith and intelligence in the installation of the new system rests equally upon Management and Labor; and, without that good faith and intelligence on the part of both, the competitive strength of the Saco-Lowell Shops could well be seriously impaired.

Office procedures and even the offices themselves have been drastically altered. The exclusive reliance upon clerical help which, with good reason, characterized the preceding administration has been modified by the installation of International Business Machine units, which have proven satisfactory in the payroll-distribution work for which they have been utilized. The way seems clear for further mechanization of clerical procedures, should such be deemed necessary.

A great many competent men (and women) are helping to make these various changes. Some are new to the company, but most were there when Chafee entered the organization. There is no more possibility in this chapter than in the preceding one of naming them, but the cumulative importance of their contributions must not pass unmentioned.

The year 1947 marked the beginning of reorganization; 1948 was characterized by an emphasis on increasing plant output; 1949 saw a heavy emphasis on reduction of direct and overhead costs and the consolidation of gains already made. The reorganization process has not been without error. In 1948, for example, a critical situation revolved around shortages: the failure to include all needed parts in machinery shipments. The new administration has been frank in acknowledging mistakes and vigorous in its effort to correct them and prevent repetition of errors.

The impact of the new management upon the established organization has been resounding. A period of confusion and very widespread restiveness ensued. This was particularly true of the transitional months when Chafee worked with the old management. Older administrators and technical men who had grown up in the company were skeptical of what they considered an ill-advised effort to apply mass-production techniques to an industry long cursed by lack of standardized product specifications. For many years the Saco-Lowell organization had been indoctrinated with the grim necessity for economy, so well indoctrinated that the high expenditures incident to reorganization and the overthrow of old penny-pinching techniques produced in some quarters a feeling of genuine alarm. Changes became easier and were more readily accepted, however, as Chafee's knowledge of local men and conditions increased and as he built up his own staff of assistants, some of whom were brought in from outside the company. It is unfortunate, in a sense, that the new management commenced its task before the historical background of the Saco-Lowell Shops was widely known and understood. Nothing is more normal in business history than the reactions detailed above, yet many Biddeford people have regarded the events of the past three years as a unique, unprecedented, and even alarming experience. There is no cause for alarm in the fact of reorganization, or in the responses elicited by change. This is an old, old story in business. Advance knowledge of that fact might have eased the shock, which only recently has begun to wear off. Today managerial morale is higher in Biddeford than it has been for many years, and there is great hope implicit in the youth, alertness, and already evident achievements of the existing managerial staff.

Thus the chronicled history of the Saco-Lowell Shops ends, as it began in 1813, on the theme of unsettlement, internal change, and the rapid evolution of profound external forces. In a sense, this situation is unsatisfactory from the viewpoint of the historian. The story cannot neatly be summarized and ended, and intriguing questions lie for the future to answer. A sense of movement permeates the company as this historical record goes to press. By no pretext of logic or rhetoric can the year 1949 be viewed as the conclusion of anything more than the efforts of the historian himself.

5. RETROSPECT

Events of contemporary importance have a way of obscuring the past. My treatment of the Edwards Era in Saco-Lowell history has been aimed at preserving a balanced emphasis and at avoiding a very tempting tendency to regard today's problems as more profound than yesterday's. I feel very keenly, moreover, the handicaps of attempting to judge events which have just happened and of trying to place them in proper long-term perspective.

Despite these limitations, the most cautious observer would scarcely question a conclusion that the 1926–48 period should be labeled as one of the most significant in Saco-Lowell's century-and-a-third-long history. My judgment, necessarily tentative, is that the Edwards Era should rank as one of four periods of outstanding managerial accomplishment. In chronological order the other three are:

(1) The 1837–53 period of Otis Pettee's activity at Newton.

(2) The years of Lowell Machine Shop supremacy in the textile machinery industry (1845–80).

(3) The Hale-Snelling era in the Pettee Machine Works and the Saco and Pettee Machine Shops (1883–1912).

My reasons for so ranking the Edwards administration derive from the number of serious tasks faced, the energy with which they were met, the broad and long-range managerial concepts entertained and exercised, the flexibility of this administration in adapting itself quickly to new economic and social forces of great weight and import, and the freedom of David F. Edwards himself both from selfish motivations and from the ultra-conservatism which so frequently paralyzes long-established administrators.

The accomplishments (or the mistakes) of the Edwards administration are even today not completely visible. Deliberate policy decisions have forced the company out of conventional paths.

The liberal attitude of Edwards in the field of labor relations presents one area where many questions remain unanswered. However, the problem of labor relations, critical as it may seem today and critical though it has been in the years just past, might well lose its urgency in years to come. Here lies a danger which the historian, who can record only what has happened, must face. Labor relations have been reported and emphasized here because the focus of this book is primarily on past and present, rather than on the future.

Further questions are raised by trends in the product policies of the Saco-Lowell Shops — policies that call to mind the interesting fluctuations between specialization and diversification which characterized earlier years of the textile machinery industry. For some years after 1926 Saco-Lowell drove toward specialization in certain types of cotton-textile machinery. In earlier years the sporadic movements in the direction of specialization were identified with prosperous times, but in the hard period following 1926 it was not prosperity but austerity and pinched resources which lopped products off the company line.

The Whitin Machine Works, on the contrary, branched out into many fields, including some which Saco-Lowell had abandoned after long trial. In the industry generally, increasingly specialized effort has become noticeable and new firms, specializing on one machine type, have come into the market. A specific issue raised by these facts is whether the historic tendency of Saco-Lowell to seek diversification in hard times will once again assert itself. Saco-Lowell seems well prepared to conform to this tradition and, in fact, is now swinging in a new way toward diversification. In other years, diversification of markets could be achieved only by diversification in the range of machinery built. Today, the entire historic question of whether to produce cotton machinery alone seems about to lose its pertinence, as Saco-Lowell moves tantalizingly close to the goal of machinery capable of handling a very wide range, if not all types, of textile fibers.

Such considerations suggest, at many points, the crucial importance of understanding the evolution of competitive forces in the textile machinery industry. In an era characterized by considerable misinformation and misunderstanding it seems well to take advantage of the opportunity to examine a specific competitive situation in an objective way. Since 1912 price warfare in the grand old manner of the early twentieth century has been noticeable for its absence from the textile machinery industry. This situation is by no means sinister, nor does it imply either the existence of price agreements or the lack of effective competition in the industry. Care must be taken also to differentiate between price warfare and price competition, even though the actual dividing point between the two can scarcely be established. Price competition has been active in the industry in periods of depressed business — a fact which list prices of machinery, rising more or less without interruption since the early 1920's, tend to obscure. The absence of price warfare can scarcely be condemned, for this circumstance — making possible the survival of weaker firms and possibly of Saco-Lowell itself — has preserved the competitive nature of the industry. Competition, moreover, can take place in many other areas than that of price, a fact well illustrated in certain producers' goods industries, where prices move slowly and in virtual concert, and where competition centers in quality of product and service rendered. This type of competition, which has prevailed between the Saco-Lowell Shops and the Whitin Machine Works even in periods when both shops were so busy that few price concessions were offered, has been healthy, for it has showered the textile industry with new and improved machinery designed to produce cloth with less and less recourse to increasingly costly human labor. There is little doubt but that many in the textile industry would have welcomed a destructive price war in the 1930's, and would welcome it today, rather than keen competition between the machinery builders in rendering existing textile machinery obsolete. This viewpoint ignores the lesson of 1904 and 1905, when the price war launched by the Lowell Machine Shop had the initial result of removing that Shop from the competitive picture altogether and the final result of increasing substantially the prices which mills subsequently had to pay for Lowell machines. By the same token, if the health of the highly productive American textile industry is to be dependent upon a world rather than on a national market, the rapid technological progress which Whitin-Saco-Lowell competition now fosters is of supreme importance in placing American mills on a competitive plane with those of foreign countries.

These varied grounds for speculation and comparison should not be abandoned without comment on the obvious fact that the Whitin Machine Works, following a steady and conservative financial course, can boast of a consistently successful career, while before 1926 Saco-Lowell experienced vicissitudes of near-fatal dimensions, and has spent a substantial amount of time and energy since 1926 in recuperating from the earlier experiences. At this point it seems advisable to turn an introspective eye upon the broad internal aspects of Saco-Lowell's history which deal with profits, economic service, and the managerial implications of the company's unstable past.

No company alive and alert today and representing, as does Saco-Lowell, a continuous sequence of business experience over a period of a century and a third can escape judgment on the caliber of social and economic service rendered over such a protracted period. Indeed, a basic purpose of historical research is ignored if the events detailed in preceding chapters are not pointed, as best they may be, toward some such summary appraisal. A valuable opportunity is lost if these events are not used to confirm or refute the often-heard criticisms of privately owned business enterprise as it has existed in the American economy.

Even in a company such as this, which has made so many and such serious mistakes at all levels of business administration, the versatility, the strength, the energy, and the optimism of managerial effort in meeting an amazing array of obstacles have been remarkable. Only relatively unrestrained initiative of executive action could possibly have permitted survival in the dynamic and expanding society into which the textile machinery industry was born. David F. Edwards himself, whose liberal viewpoints are well known, believes that had he been faced in the years from 1927 to 1933 with the restrictions imposed on management today by government and labor, he might not have been able to save the company. This is not a stable industry, and survival in it has been conditioned upon relative freedom of executive action. Perhaps stability will come with maturity, but there is today little evidence that the necessity for prompt and aggressive adaptability is any less than it has been at any time in the past.

A bright hope for the future lies in the caliber of industrial leadership in America. Despite ever-increasing encroachments by government on spheres of executive activity in the textile machinery industry, I can detect no serious lessening of executive initiative in the Saco-Lowell Shops today. Increasing controls have modified administrative thought and action, but boldness and the desire to progress in the interest of private profit have not yet disappeared. Profits and corporate security are being sought in increasingly ingenious ways as government regulation, in this industry and in this company at least, makes both objectives the more difficult of attainment.

I cannot refrain from pointing out to those who criticize American business in general and the textile machinery industry in particular the hundred and thirty-six years which lie behind the Saco-Lowell Shops of today. This continuity could scarcely have been possible unless adequate social and economic service had been rendered. The textile industry, the men in the shops, and the investor could well have been cheated for a few months or even a few years, but not for a century and a third. Longevity in itself would seem to indicate that Saco-Lowell's selfishness has been intelligent and productive of long-term gain for many people. Anything less than fair service for the prices charged would sooner or later have brought failure. Actually, of the three interested parties named — customer, laborer, and investor — the last-named has probably fared the most poorly. The customer has received his machines, which since 1813, with inconsequential exceptions, have been unsurpassed in quality by those of any other shop. The workman has enjoyed continuity of employment and opportunity for advancement at least commensurate with what was being offered elsewhere in the American economy. For the period for which such information is available, investors in the various Saco-Lowell enterprises have realized a return on their capital which seems inadequate in view of the highly speculative nature of their investment, and possibly less than could have been secured in other industries, though information on this last-mentioned point is scant. The sum of $100 deposited in a savings bank in 1845 and left there would have shown a far greater increment than an equal sum invested at the same time in Lowell Machine Shop stock and left in the enterprise thenceforth. The long-term profits realized from textile-machinery building have been so modest, in fact, as to make any informed investor cautious of placing his funds there — save only for him who hopes, in his perspicuity, to pick one of the traditionally lush periods of activity and sell out in time to avoid the poverty which has always followed.

Over the past decade government action has effectively cut the peaks from the cycle of profits. It has yet to be conclusively proven that government control can perform the essential correlative action of eliminating the troughs of depression which Saco-Lowell in the past has found so difficult to survive without formidable reserves of accumulated profit. If this correlative mission is not fulfilled, then widows and orphans had best place their funds elsewhere.

A still further departure from general to particular implications of Saco-Lowell's history is called forth by the fact that this book is designed primarily as a study in the field of business administration. What, finally, have been the net effects of Saco-Lowell's checkered career on the administrative organization? This question seems important, for Saco-Lowell's difficulties have certainly been far from unique in the annals of business history. The answer to this question constitutes a theme which underlies the history of all the component organizations which came together in 1912 to form the present company.

A perusal of preceding chapters shows that the Saco-Lowell Shops and its forebears have consistently found their greatest strength in adversity. This is particularly true of the years of the Edwards administration. Stockholders, and labor, too, have paid an occasional heavy price for survival, but out of the staggering difficulties of the past two decades a strong-fibered company appears once again to have emerged. A tradition of survival flourishes in the company — a legacy from the past which has real meaning for the future. Today Saco-Lowell, despite its age, is young. I think no greater commendation can be given any company than this. Critical years lie ahead, in which a new administration and the company itself will be made or broken by the success with which the promise of a vigorous youth is sustained.

In glancing back over the years which separate the Saco-Lowell Shops of today from the tiny machine shops in the cotton-mill basements at Waltham, at Newton, and at Saco Falls, I have looked for unifying elements in the diverse paths and policies of the evolving companies which help to explain why the tradition of survival is so deeply ingrained in the company. The broad economic hypothesis that fair social service has been rendered is basic to any explanation for the survival of Saco-Lowell and its forebears, and beyond this there exists the more specific fact that the company's relations with its customers have consistently been characterized by devoted service and fair dealing. There is one thing more.

Cynics have stated that pride in workmanship has gone from American business. On a winter afternoon in 1948 Edwards, Chafee, and I stood on one side of a humid but spotless room in the shop to watch the operation of a new heat-treating furnace. The operator was an enthusiastic, magnificently poised man of French extraction, and he had just finished a very serious and meticulously detailed explanation of every feature of the operation. Now the instruments showed that the time for opening the furnace was at hand. The operator moved into position. As though some signal, unheard by us, had abruptly transported him into another world he suddenly became oblivious to the audience. His face became set in lines of intentness, and he drew on a heavy pair of work gloves with all the careful deliberation of a surgeon making ready for a delicate operation. He touched the controls tentatively with an intimate hand, scanned the dials before him, and waited.

Suddenly his deliberation vanished in a sequence of deft, swift moves. The furnace flew open in a blast of fumes and flame — a quick thrust on the controls lifted a hissing, glowing basket of delicately tempered steel parts to the cooling vat — another thrust plunged it in. The workman shot a critical glance along the line of instrument dials — then he relaxed, grinned, slowly doffed his gloves, and with the pride of a child in an intricate new toy turned to catch the look of respect which must have shown on the faces of the group that watched — respect which, I suppose, was not for what he had done but for what he was.

Here was no highly skilled operation, but every operation has its own standard of perfection. I cannot help feeling that down through the span of one hundred and thirty-six years it has been men like this, taking pride in performance, whether in shop or office, who have given life and vitality to the Saco-Lowell organization, and in whose continued pride the future of that organization rests. Could it be that the vast intricacies of economic and business evolution have some such absurdly simple common denominator as this?

APPENDICES

APPENDIX 1

LOCKS AND CANALS MACHINERY CONTRACTS, 1836–1839

A. Machinery Components, Prices, Costs, and Profits: Boott Mills Contracts, 1836–1837

Boott Mill #1			Boott Mill #2		Boott Mill #3	
	Cost[a]	Price[a]		Cost[a]		Cost[a]
2 Willows	$ 77.44	$100	2 Willows	$ 77.44	2 Willows	$ 77.44
2 Pickers	325.75	500	2 Pickers	325.75	12 Drawing Frames	108.14
12 Drawing Frames	108.14	150	12 Drawing Frames	108.14	2 Long Lap Winders	237.42
2 Lap Winders	165.40	225	2 Long Lap Winders	237.42	2 Grinders	43.32
2 Grinders	43.32	75	2 Grinders	43.32	20 Breaker Cards	207.20
56 Cards	200.79	300	20 Breaker Cards	207.20	24 Finisher Cards	194.48
6 Speeders	434.24	600	24 Finisher Cards	194.48	6 Speeders	434.24
10 Stretchers	606.99	950	6 Speeders	434.24	12 Stretchers	658.51
48 Throstle Frames	379.17	512	12 Stretchers	658.51	23 Warp Throstles	386.97
12 Dressing Frames	401.25	520	23 Warp Throstles	386.97	25 Filling Throstles	418.60
176 Looms	58.92	69	25 Filling Throstles	418.60	7 Dressing Frames	276.00
7 Warpers	104.29	130	8 Dressing Frames	276.00	250 Looms	53.57
			228 Looms	54.80	6 Warpers	104.29
			6 Warpers	104.29	Cost of Starting	955.30
			Cost of Starting	955.30		
Total cost	$56,558.03			$58,635.37		$58,480.72
Price charged	77,370.00			84,495.13		84,449.53
Profit	20,811.97 (27% of price)			25,859.76 (31% of price)		25,968.81 (31% of price)
Approximate price per spindle	$12.59			$11.00		$11.00

[a] Per machine.

Source: Locks and Canals Company records, Correspondence, vol. 25, folio 145.

B. Machinery Components and Prices
A Locks and Canals Mill and a Typical American Mill, 1839[a]

Locks and Canals Company Estimate for a 4,000 spindle mill[b]			A typical American mill: 4,992 spindles[c]		
2 Willows..........	@ $100	$ 200	1 Willow.........	@ $100	$ 100
2 Pickers...........	500	1,000	1 Scutcher.........	600	600
2 Lap winders......	210	420	1 Lapping Machine	250	250
20 Breaker Cards.....	270	5,400	40 Cards...........	210	8,400
2 Grinders.........	60	120			
20 Finisher Cards....	245	4,900			
5 Drawing Frames...	225	1,125	6 Drawing Frames..	200	1,200
4 Speeders..........	545	2,180	7 Extensors........	900	6,300
8 Stretchers........	760	6,080	4,992 Throstle Spindles.	4.50	22,464
2,048 Warp Spindles....	3.59	7,352	6 Spoolers.........	70	420
2,048 Filling Spindles...	3.86	7,905	6 Warpers.........	150	900
6 Warpers..........	130	780	9 Dressing Frames..	400	3,600
8 Dressing Frames...	510	4,080	128 Looms..........	75	9,600
120 Looms...........	70	8,400	6 Speeders.........	660	3,960
Total Price..........$12.20 per spindle			$11.58 per spindle		

[a] The variation in machinery components can be ascribed to differences in the types of cloth made in the two mills and, possibly, to the varying preferences of mill managers, no two of whom set up machinery in exactly the same way or in the same proportions. There actually was no such thing as a "typical" American mill.

[b] Locks and Canals Company records, Correspondence, vol. 24.

[c] Montgomery, *Cotton Manufacture of the U. S. A.*, pp. 114-117. Since Montgomery was employed in Saco, Maine, his figures probably reflect the situation there, and may not adequately recognize Rhode Island and Southern mill components and costs. For purposes of comparison, various miscellaneous costs have been omitted from Montgomery's tables, since they presumably are not included in the Locks and Canals figures.

C. Machinery Components and Prices
An 1814 and an 1836 Mill[a]

2,160 Spindle Mill, 1814[b]			Boott Mill #1 (6,144 spindles), 1836		
1 Picking Machine.	...	$ 300	2 Pickers..........	@ $500	$1,000
			2 Willows.........	100	200
			2 Grinders........	75	150
24 Cards............	@ $320	7,680	56 Cards...........	300	16,800
2 Drawing Frames.	240	480	12 Drawing Frames.	150	1,800
4 Roving Frames...	210	840	6 Speeders.........	600	3,600
			2 Lap Winders.....	225	450
4 Stretching Frames	600	2,400	10 Stretchers.......	950	9,500
2,160 Throstle Spindles.	5.00	10,800	6,144 Throstle Spindles.	4.00	24,576
Reels, Cans, etc........	...	1,500			
Total Price of Machinery........$11.11 per spindle			$9.45 per spindle		

[a] This comparison requires that only the preparatory machinery and not the weaving and finishing machinery of the 1836 mill be shown. The mills of the 1814 period and earlier, of course, were spinning mills only.

[b] Isaac Briggs manuscripts, Baker Library, Harvard Graduate School of Business Administration.

APPENDIX 2

CHARTER
SACO WATER POWER COMPANY
1837

March 24, 1837

State of Maine

In the year of our Lord One thousand Eight hundred and Thirty seven.

An Act to incorporate the Saco Water Power Company.

Be it enacted by the Senate and House of Representatives in Legislature assembled, that Samuel Fales, Charles Bradbury, Charles W. Cartwright, Samuel Batchelder and their associates and successors, be and they hereby are constituted and made a body politic and corporate by the name of the Saco Water Power Company, with all the powers and privileges, and subject to all the duties and liabilities, provided in the several laws of this State regulating manufacturing Corporations, and are authorized to purchase five hundred thousand dollars, and the same may improve, lease, sell and convey, as other proprietors and owners of real estate may lawfully do. And said Company are authorized to carry on at Saco Falls in the towns of Saco and Biddeford, the manufacture of Cotton, Wool, Iron and other metals & materials, and may erect and construct upon their own lands and privileges the necessary works, mills and machinery for that purpose, provided, that said works are so constructed as not to impede the navigation of Saco River, nor affect the rights of other individuals or corporations on said River.

In the House of Representatives, March 20, 1837. This Bill having had three several readings, passed to be enacted.

H. Hamlin, Speaker

In Senate, March 21, 1837, This bill having had two several readings, passed to be enacted.

J. C. Talbot, President

March 22, 1837. Approved. Robert P. Dunlap.

Secretary's Office
Augusta, March 24, 1837.

I hereby certify that the foregoing is a true copy of the original deposited in this office.

Attest A. R. Nichols
Secretary of State

Source: Pepperell Collection, Saco Water Power Company records, Baker Library, Harvard Graduate School of Business Administration.

APPENDIX 3

TOOLS IN USE IN EARLY MACHINE SHOPS

A. Schedule of Tools in the Machine Shop of Otis Pettee, Newton Upper Falls, 1834

Two large water wheels	$ 1,000
Drums, pulleys, and belts to drive lathes and other machinery	1,000
One high-pressure and one low-pressure steam engine of ten horse power with two boilers 20′ long and 24″ diameter	1,350
One punching machine and dies	200
Three small trip hammers	300
Three pair bellows	45
Five smiths anvils	25
One pair shears	20
One set of "swages"	50
Three heavy blocks cast iron	20
Five small swages	20
Thirty leading tools	30
Hammers, sledges, tongs, and other small tools in blacksmith shop	40
Forty hand lathes at $25 each	1,000
Two new double engine lathes, iron frames 14′ long	700
One large engine lathe, iron frame 12′ long	250
One single engine lathe, iron frame 12′ long	180
Four small engine lathes, iron frames	200
Four spindle engines, iron frames 8′ long	240
Two double engine lathes, wooden frames 16′ long	250
Two engine lathes for card cylinders	150
One machine to drill spindle rails	180
Two machines to drill double speeder rails	400
Two spiral engines	700
One bevel engine	200
One engine for cone gears	150
Four habbing engines with apparatus	400
One fluting engine	150

One dividing engine	$ 200
Two polishing benches with twenty arbors and wheels	100
Forty bench vises	160
Five grindstones with frames	50
Set of tools to finish double speeder flyers	200
Set of tools for making spinning flyers	75
Machine to bore speeder cones	50
Machine to polish rollers	25
Six circular saws	120
Three boring lathes with 100 bits	105
One tennon machine	50
Other tools belonging to workshops	50
Benches in workshops	100
Benches in iron shops	100
Set of patterns for looms	150
Set of patterns for double speeders	200
Other patterns	200
Four stoves and pipes	50
Furnaces for warming	50
One clock	10
Cutters, drills, "birs," runners, screwplates, taps, chisels, dogs, & other small tools belonging to the shop	450
Total Valuation	$11,745

Source: Middlesex County, Mass., Deeds, vol. 336, p. 46.

B. Schedule of Tools and Machines in the Shop of the Saco Water Power Company, January 31, 1850

1 Large Planing Machine 26′ long, will plane 3′5″ wide.
1 Planing Machine 20′6″ long, will plane 2′6″ wide.
2 Planing Machines 14′ long, will plane 2′3″ wide.
1 Planing Machine 10′ long, will plane 2′6″ wide.
1 Planing Machine 7′10″ long, will plane 2′2″ wide.
1 Planing Machine 5′ long, will plane 1′10″ wide.
3 Small Planing Machines 3′ long.
1 Vertical Drill.
1 Bolt Machine (large), 1 Small Bolt Machine.
1 Splining Machine, 1 Bench (medium size), 2 Gear-cutting Machines.
1 Slabbing Machine (iron frame 4′ long 2′ wide).
1 Slabbing Machine (partly wood) 6′ long 25″ wide.
2 Fluting Machines 6′4″ long, 11″ wide.

1 Machine for cutting Flyers, 3 Spindle Grinders.
1 Machine for Turning Pulleys.
3 Machines for Turning Card Cylinders.
1 Machine for Turning Spiders for Card Cylinders.
1 Engine for Turning Doffer Cylinders.
1 Machine for Straightening Shafting.
1 Squaring Machine for Large Work.
1 Rail Drilling Machine, will drill rail 7′6″ long.
1 Slabbing Engine (all iron) 4′ long, 21″ wide.
1 Machine for drilling hobs for Card sheets, all iron, new.
1 Machine for squaring Bolt Heads.
1 Machine for drilling Whirls (6 spindles).
1 Large Engine Lathe, 20′ long, swing 7′6″.
4 Engine Lathes (geared) 20′ long, swing 2′.
2 Engine Lathes, wooden stringer 16′ long.
2 Engine Lathes geared with two heads each, 14′ long, swing 1′.
1 Engine Lathe geared 18′ long. Swing 20″, iron sides.
12 Hand Lathes, 6′6″ long. 41 Engine Lathes, 8′ long each.
9 Engine Lathes, 4′10″ long, swing 6½″. 4 Hand Lathes, 6′ long, swing 20″.
4 Drilling Lathes. 2 Engine Lathes (geared) 12′ long, swing 19″.
1 Chucking Lathe, swing 2′. 6 Hand Lathes, 2 heads each, 16′ long.
4 Engine Lathes, 6′ long, swing 7″. 4 Engine Lathes, 2 heads each, 16′ long, swing 11″.
1 Engine Lathe, 16′ long, swing 13″. 1 Engine Lathe, 10′ long, swing 6″.
2 Hand Lathes, swing 36″. 4 Small Lathes, 4′4″ long, swing 9″.
16 Hand Lathes, swing 16″. 4 Small Lathes, 4′6″ long, swing 10″.
4 Bolt Machines (small). 1 Set Screw Machine.
2 Machines for planing wood. 2 Boring Machines.
150 Vises of various sizes.
6 Grindstones.
3 Circular Saws.

APPENDIX 4

CHARTER
LOWELL MACHINE SHOP
1845

Commonwealth of Massachusetts

In the year One thousand eight hundred and forty five.

An Act to incorporate the Lowell Machine Shop.

Be it enacted by the Senate and House of Representatives in General Court assembled and by authority of the same, as follows;

March 12, 1845

Section 1st. Abbott Lawrence, Nathan Appleton, and John A. Lowell, their associates and successors are hereby made a corporation by the name of the Lowell Machine Shop, for the purpose of making machinery and manufacturing cotton, iron and wool, in the city of Lowell, in the county of Middlesex, and for this purpose shall have all the power and privileges, and be subject to all the duties, restrictions, and liabilities set forth in the thirty eighth and forty fourth Chapter of the Revised Statutes.

Section 2d. The said corporation may hold, for the purposes aforesaid, real estate to the amount of two hundred thousand dollars, and the whole capital stock of the said corporation shall not exceed the amount of five hundred thousand dollars.

House of Representatives Jan. 25, 1845. Passed to be enacted.
Saml H. Walley Jr. Spkr.
In Senate Jan. 28th, 1845. Passed to be enacted.
Levi Lincoln Presdt.
January 29th, 1845. Approved.
Geo. M. Briggs.
a true copy
attest
John G. Palfrey
Secretary

Source: Lowell Machine Shop, Directors' and stockholders' minutes.

APPENDIX 5

ORIGINAL SUBSCRIBERS TO LOWELL MACHINE SHOP STOCK, DECEMBER 7, 1845

Abbott Lawrence	$ 30,000
N. Appleton	15,000
Eben Hobbs and others	10,000
Wm. Sturgis	15,000
Thomas B. Wales	5,000
N. H. Emmons	1,500
Wm. Appleton	20,000
Amos Lawrence	10,000
Daniel P. Parker	10,000
J. Huntington Wolcott	10,000
William G. Lambert	5,000
Charles H. Parker	5,000
Eben Chadwick	5,000
John Clark by Eben Chadwick	5,000
Homer Bartlett by Eben Chadwick	5,000
Henry Hall	4,000
John Aiken by Henry Hall	2,000
John Wright by Henry Hall	1,000
Thomas G. Cary	5,000
Charles S. Storrow	4,000
Ignatius Sargent	5,000
I. Thos. Stevenson	5,000
G. H. Kuhn	5,000
Wm. C. Appleton	2,000
B. F. French by J. A. Lowell	5,000
J. A. Lowell	25,000
James Lawrence	5,000
Samuel Lawrence by A. Lawrence	5,000
George T. Bigelow by A. Lawrence	1,500
T. B. Curtis by A. Lawrence	5,000
H. Lee	5,000
George W. Lyman	5,000
Samuel Cabot	3,000
Alex Wright by W. C. Appleton	1,000
Charles L. Tilden by A. Lawrence	4,000
Charles T. Appleton by A. Lawrence	2,000
J. J. Bowditch	3,000
J. Avery by T. G. Cary	5,000
G. Motley by T. G. Cary	3,000
H. Lee for others	2,000
J. Pickering Putnam	3,000
John Richards by order of J. Clarke	500
Phineas Adams by order of J. Clarke	500
Daniel Huzzy	500
Joseph Bedlow by order of J. Aiken	1,000
Samuel Appleton by A. Lawrence	5,000

Thomas Motley by A. Lawrence	$ 3,000	Charles P. Curtis by A. Lawrence	$ 2,000
W. A. Burke by J. T. Stevenson	10,000	J. T. Stevenson	3,500
A. H. Fiske by A. Lawrence	1,000	Wm. Brown	500
Caleb M. Marvel by A. Lawrence	3,000	Daniel D. Crombie	500
		John P. Bigelow	2,000
		Total	$300,000

Source: Lowell Machine Shop, Directors' and stockholders' minutes, 1845.

APPENDIX 6

DISTRIBUTION OF LOCOMOTIVES BUILT BY THE LOCKS AND CANALS COMPANY AND THE LOWELL MACHINE SHOP, 1835–1861

Railroad	Locks & Canals 1835–40	Locks & Canals 1841–45	Lowell Machine Shop 1845–50	Lowell Machine Shop 1851–55	Lowell Machine Shop 1864	Total Both Shops
Boston & Lowell	9	3	3	2	..	17
Boston & Providence	4	..	..	2	..	6
Boston & Worcester	2	..	..	..	..	2
Boston & Maine	2	2	..	..	..	4
Boston, Lowell & Nashua.	..	..	..	2	..	2
Andover & Haverhill	3	..	..	2	..	5
Taunton Branch	2	..	..	..	..	2
Providence & Stonington	6	..	..	..	..	6
New York & Boston	..	..	..	1	..	1
Eastern	6	..	..	..	..	6
Nashua & Lowell	1	..	1	..	..	2
Western	7	8	..	4	..	19
Fitchburg	..	..	1	..	..	1
Western Vermont	..	..	..	1	..	1
Penobscot & Kennebec	..	..	..	2	..	2
Amherst & Belchertown	..	..	..	1	..	1
Buffalo & Niagara Falls	1	..	..	..	..	1
Paterson & Hudson River	1	..	..	..	..	1
Long Island	1	..	..	..	..	1
Phila., Wilmington & Baltimore	1	..	..	..	..	1
Baltimore & Susquehanna	8	..	..	..	..	8
Baltimore & Ohio	..	..	..	..	5	5
Marietta & Cincinnati	2	..	..	..	..	2
Philadelphia & Reading	..	12	..	..	..	12
Hudson River	..	..	..	16	..	16
Syracuse & Utica	..	..	..	4	..	4
Great Western (Canada)	..	..	..	10	..	10
Galena & Chicago Union	..	..	..	2	..	2
Mad River & Lake Erie	..	..	..	4	..	4
Michigan Central	..	..	..	4	..	4
Total	56	25	5	57	5	148

Source: List of locomotives furnished by Charles E. Fisher, editor, Railway & Locomotive Historical Society *Bulletin*. Lowell Machine Shop records, Orders for Work, 1864.

APPENDIX 7

GEORGE RICHARDSON ON THE WITNESS STAND

[Superintendent of the Lowell Machine Shop]

July 12, 1878

Circuit Court of the United States, District of Massachusetts. No. 885.
Oliver Pearl et al. v. *The Appleton Company et al.*

Cross Int. 55: *Where were you born?*

Ans.: Said to be born in Rochester, Vt.

Cross Int. 56: *How long did you reside in Rochester, Vt.?*

Ans.: Until March, about the 10th, 1846.

Cross Int. 57: *Were you engaged in any employment there, and if so, what was it?*

Ans.: The majority of my time from memory up was play and work. Probably from ten to twelve years to seventeen, a majority of my time was spent in helping my father farm, making boots and shoes, repairing watches and clocks. During this time I made skates; I made one or two fiddles; I made jackknife blades, rainy days and incidentally.

Cross Int. 58: *How large a farm did your father have at that time?*

Ans.: The farm proper, I think, contained one hundred and twenty five acres.

Cross Int. 59: *What portion of your time from twelve years of age to seventeen was spent in working upon that farm as nearly as you can state?*

[*Counsel for defendants objects to this cross examination as frivolous, impertinent, irrelevant, inadmissible, incompetent and unworthy of the practice of a member of the bar of this court.*]

Ans.: I usually had three months' schooling in the winter. The fall of 1844 and 1845 I attended what was then called a fall school or high school. The rest of my time was devoted to farming and mechanical productions, as heretofore mentioned.

Cross Int. 60: *What portion of your time as nearly as you can state before you were seventeen did you employ in making skates, as you have mentioned?*

[Same objection.]

Ans.: I cannot say how much of my time, but sufficient to make a pair for myself and some of my school associates and three or four other pair besides.

Cross Int. 61: *Did you make those skates in a machine shop?*

[Same objection.]

Ans.: Not a machine shop proper. It was a shop, however, where we had vises, files, cold chisels, drills, augers, planes, squares, adzes, and general mechanical tools.

Cross Int. 62: *Where was that shop located?*

[Same objection.]

Ans.: In Rochester, Vt., on what was known as the Richardson River Farm on the opposite side of the road directly opposite of our horse barn, directly north and adjoining to what we then called our upper house. Its name was called and known as the corn barn.

Cross Int. 63: *To whom did that shop then belong?*

[Same objection.]

Ans.: The title of that shop and farm mentioned, I believe, existed in the name of my grandfather. My father in the meantime had an interest in all of this property, and about that time, or immediately after, it was transferred to him.

Cross Int. 64: *Did you have any mechanical power in that shop for operating any of the tools or machinery which you used there?*

[Same objection.]

Ans.: None other but human power.

Cross Int. 65: *Were those tools which you used in that shop all operated by hand or were any part of them used in a machine operated by human power?*

[Same objection.]

Ans.: The tools I used were all operated by hand excepting the drills. We had two kinds of drills, one was called a bit-stock drill and the other was a fiddle-bow drill. The fiddle-bow and the bit-stock was operated by hand.

Cross Int. 66: *What studies did you pursue in the High School which you attended, and were any of them of a mechanical nature? I mean the High School which you attended previous to your being seventeen years of age, as you have mentioned?*

[Same objection.]

Ans.: Mathematics and philosophy were the only two branches, I think, that were of a mechanical nature.

. . . .

Cross Int. 69: *When you left Rochester, Vt., about March 10, 1846, where did you next go?*

[Same objection.]

Ans.: Lowell, Mass., touching at all important places for lodging and food.

Cross Int. 70: *When you went to Lowell, Mass., as you have just stated, what, if anything, did you first do there?*

[Same objection.]

Ans.: The first thing I did, my uncle took me to a barber's shop and had me shaved. I think he loaned me his overcoat that I might make a better appearance. Then my uncle took me to the American House, where I partook of a luncheon, a dinner, after which he conducted me to the Lowell Machine Shop, and ascertained, or tried to procure a situation for me to learn the machinist's trade. The foreman was unwilling then to offer any encouragement. He said, however, if I would come in the next morning, he would give me something to do until there was an opening in the shop proper. I appeared the next morning, and he formally presented me with a pickaxe and shovel, conducted me down the back side of our works, and requested me to shovel a road through a pile of ashes which was about five feet deep, probably seventy five feet long, and I should think about fifty feet wide. That was my first work. My next work was cleaning and dressing brick and wheeling them from one locality to another. I was then made acquainted with a wheelbarrow. I was then put at handling lumber. I had probably worked, in all, at the ash pile, brick pile, and lumber pile, I think, six weeks, after which I was invited to go into the shop and go to work.

Cross Int. 71: *When you were invited to go into the shop and go to work, as just mentioned, what did you do about it?*

[Same objection.]

Ans.: I went in and commenced work. My first work was assisting mechanics in drilling, tapping and putting together several trip-hammers then in process of construction.

Cross Int. 72: *How long were you engaged in the work you have just mentioned, as nearly as you can state?*

[Same objection.]

Ans.: I think I worked six weeks, as before stated, outside of the shop and about eight weeks on trip-hammers and very similar work.

Cross Int. 73: *During the time you were doing the work last mentioned, about eight weeks, did you use any tools or operate any machinery in the shop? And, if so, what tools and what machinery, as nearly as you can state?*

[Same objection.]

Ans.: I used hammer, chisel, file, scotch drill, tap wrench, oil can, and I believe I used to steal out occasionally and go to some other vise and do some little fancy work for myself.

Cross Int. 74: *After you had done this work with these tools, as you have mentioned, what did you next do, and where, as nearly as you can state?*

[Same objection.]

Ans.: According to my best memory and knowledge, I became dissatisfied with the progress I was making and I took it upon myself to leave the shop. The first application I made for business after then was to Mr. Johnson, a jeweler, now living in Lowell. I failed to get a position, and I went to Keene, N. H., where I have relatives. There I also tried to get business in a jeweler's shop; met with poor encouragement. I went out to my uncle's, worked three or four days at haying. From there I went into what was called Keene Village, about two miles and a half in, and engaged to work at shoemaking for a short period. I worked about two weeks. From there I went to Winchester, N. H., about eighteen miles distant, an entire stranger. I found a firm there running eight or ten tin carts. I engaged to run a tin cart. I did run a tin cart until I run it into the ground. I fancied that peddling tin was not my business. From there I went to Whitehall, N. Y., afoot all the way, and there beheld the first steamboat ever presented to my view. I went on board this boat. I interviewed the captain. I told him I wanted to go to Crown Point but had no money to pay, and wanted to work my fare. He engaged me to work my fare to Crown Point. Before reaching Crown Point he engaged me to serve as chief fireman for a few days. I fired up about two weeks. I began to think that wasn't my business. I settled with the captain; I left the vessel at what was then called Chipman's Landing. I was still short of funds. I felt the necessity of walking; probably begged some. I walked to Orwell, about twelve miles distant. I engaged with a Mr. Root to work two weeks at haying. I made my engagement good, took my pay and footed it over the mountain about thirty miles to my father's, weak and humble. During all this time my parents knew not where I was. Like loving parents, they gave me a warm reception, after which they asked me what next, without any reproving. I told them I was going to Lowell to learn a trade,—machinist's trade. I arrived in Lowell early in September, 1846. I offered myself to Gay & Silver, of Chelmsford. They refused to hire me. I went from there to North Andover to seek a job in a machine shop. They refused to hire me. I went back to the old shop in Lowell again, and finally engaged with Bement & Hardy, job hands in that shop at that time. Shall I continue this?

[All of the answer from and including the words "The first application I made for business" down to and including the words "They refused to hire me" objected to by counsel as not responsive to the question.]

Cross Int. 75: *When you commenced work in the Lowell Machine Shop again, as you have stated, what work did you do, and with what mechanical tools, if any?*

[Same objection.]

Ans.: My first work was cleaning out and filling up the teeth of fine gears at the vise. Probably about a week I worked at this. My next work was chucking, reaming, tapping, vise fitting, in order, for about sixty days. This last work just mentioned was making fifty small engine lathes.

Cross Int. 76: *How long did you continue to work at the Lowell Machine Shop after you engaged with Bement & Hardy, as nearly as you can state?*

[Same objection.]

Ans.: I have worked for Lowell Machine Shop ever since that date, with exception of my California trip and my three years' sickness. My California trip was in 1849. My three years' sickness was 1857, '58 and '59. My California trip was the result of poor health.

Cross Int. 106: *Is the spindle before you, being the one you produced yesterday, the type of Sawyer spindle which was made and put in use in spinning up to the summer of 1872, or about that time?*

Ans.: My first observation of the Sawyer spinning frames was at a private interview with and by the solicitation of Mr. Sawyer. He consulted me as a mechanic at this time. I have two and distinct reasons for remembering about the time. I recollect answering his question in this wise: He asked my opinion and I told him. Says I, "Mr. Sawyer, I think you have a very nice thing. I fear you have overdone it in making it as small as you have." The spindle he had, I think, must have had a butt materially shorter than this. I never made spindles substantially like what he had. I recollect that this interview was previous to a meeting of the New England Manufacturers' Association. It must have been somewhat previous, because at that meeting he presented a very elaborate diagram showing the power required to drive the ordinary flyer spinning frame; he showed also the power required to drive a common ring frame with common spindles. He showed by this diagram the power required to drive the Sawyer spindle in comparison with the two just described. I know that it must have taken him a long time to make the diagram and the record shown by the diagram. According to my best memory and knowledge the period at which he exhibited this diagram was April 19, 1871. Records of the Manufacturing Association, I think, will go to confirm this statement. I know that at that time, that event and that circumstance aroused my incentives for making and modifying common spindles.

The spindle I hold before me, I think, is very similar

to spindles having elevated bolsters such as I put into the first Sawyer frames of my make.

Other reasons go or went to excite my incentives besides these given. They are the result of what I considered an absolute outrage on my feelings. I recollect that George Draper at that meeting, or the one following it, made very impertinent remarks. I think he did convey fully to that meeting that machine builders had not at that time made good spindles; I think he considered they were not competent to make good spindles. He asserted at that meeting that his spindles were made of a superior steel. He asserted that no machine builder should make those spindles for the present. I recollect George Draper's saying that he proposed to take care of his own babies, he wouldn't allow others to do so. I was greatly outraged at that time, or felt so at least. I am not entirely cured of this outrage at present. I believe the day is not distant when Mr. Draper will give his reasons for thus outraging machine builders. I do know that my passion was so aroused by that occasion that then, or about then, I commenced thinking of different ways spindles might be made.

APPENDIX 8

NUMBER AND TYPES OF COTTON MACHINES SOLD
LOWELL MACHINE SHOP
1855–1905

A. Numbers of Principal Cotton Machines Sold
1855–1904

	1855	1860	1863	1865	1870	1878	1881	1888	1894	1899	1904
Cards	193	274	204	192	365	512	1,738	591	275	667	635
Drawing Frames	18	23	12	8	33	40	118	119	120	308	210
Speeders	19	3	54	85	123	86	337	136	2	32	...
Twisters & Winders	...	4	...	12	6	17	54	50	21	46	162
Stretchers	32	8	62	26	...	...	...	...	...	...	...
Spoolers	...	...	12	4	18	14	70	81	63	92	66
Fly Frames	...	7	...	...	...	...	2	115	144	418	381
Dressers	27	19	42	26	...	...	...	...	...	...	...
Warpers	27	4	17	8	4	25	46	67	55	73	68
Slashers	...	...	...	...	...	14	42	27	36	68	52
Throstle Frames	112	185	40	56	...	...	...	...	...	...	...
Ring Frames	...	165	43	129	279	285	987	1,066	1,033	1,375	888
Mules	4	4	...	7	50	26	10	10	...	...	...
Looms	453	1,049	314	1,838	1,594	1,534	5,646	4,764	3,277	4,420	1,040

B. Types of Machinery Manufactured in 1880

Top Flat Cards
Underflat Cards (Foss & Pevey)
Card Grinders
Lap Winders
Railway Heads
Drawing Frames
Speeders
Fly Frames
Ring Spinning Frames
Platt Mules
Spoolers
Warpers
Cylinder Slashers
Hot Air Slashers
Looms
Twisters
Yarn Reels
Filling Winders
Shearing Machines
Brushing Machines
Sewing Machines
Folders
Warping Engines
Cloth Stamping Machines
Hydraulic Presses
Double Screw Presses
Size Kettles and Pumps

Source: Lowell Machine Shop records, Orders for work series.

APPENDIX 9

SOME STATISTICAL EVIDENCES OF IMPROVEMENTS IN COTTON MACHINERY, 1840–1885

No accurate measures of the trend in prices of cotton machinery from 1840 to 1885 exist. There are some indications that, although cyclical fluctuations were wide, there was no pronounced upward or downward long-term movement in machinery prices. In 1840, machinery for an American cotton mill was said to have cost approximately $12 per spindle (Montgomery, *Cotton Manufacture of the U.S.A.*, pp. 115–117). In 1848 the cost of a cotton factory was placed at $14 per spindle (*Scientific American,* June 24, 1848, vol. iii, no. 4, p. 317). In 1872 the treasurer of the Lowell Machine Shop stated that the cost of machinery for a cotton mill in New England was from $12 to $13 per spindle. In 1879 it was reported (*Transactions,* New England Cotton Manufacturers Association, no. 27, p. 102) that the cost was from $12 to $15 per spindle.

Even if the assumption is made that the cost of machinery had not generally decreased, however, textile-mill operatives and the consuming public had profited from progress in the textile machinery industry. In 1885 Edward Atkinson, who was intimate with the industry as a mill operator, an insurance authority, a special census agent, and a textile economist, made the following statements of progress over the 1840–85 period (*Transactions,* N. E. Cotton Mfrs. Assn., no. 38, pp. 72–78):

(1) A 208% increase in efficiency of labor due to machine improvements.
(2) A 122% increase in value of product per mill operative per year.
(3) An 89% increase in hourly money wages of operatives.
(4) A 54³⁄₁₀% increase in yearly money wages.
(5) A 17³⁄₁₀% decrease in hours of labor per day.
(6) A 28% decrease in cost of goods to consumer.

The average return on capital invested in textiles, however, was stated by Atkinson to have decreased from 10 to 13 per cent in 1840 to from 4 to 6 per cent in 1885.

Atkinson's conclusions were necessarily couched in broadest terms. A specific example of the trends he observed was reported in 1876 by William Burke, the treasurer of the Lowell Machine Shop (*Transactions,* N. E. Cotton Mfrs. Assn., no. 21, pp. 6–9). Burke compared statistics gathered in the Boott Mills in 1838 and 1876. He reported the following differences between the output and costs at the two dates:

	May, 1838	*May, 1876*	
Average count of yarn..............	13.64	13.93	
Yards woven on a loom in 60 hours..	245½	264	(7.6% increase)
Pounds of cloth per hour per operative	1.012	3.333	(229.3% increase)[a]
Cost of labor per pound			
Picking, carding, roving..........	$1.0291	$ .6674	(35.2% decrease)
Spinning, spooling...............	.7105	.1786	(74.9% decrease)
Weaving.........................	1.9371	1.2627	(34.8% decrease)
Total labor cost per pound......	$4.7935	$2.8533	(40.4% decrease)

[a] The difference between this figure and the increase in yards woven on a loom in 60 hours arises presumably from an increase in the number of looms tended by an operative, an increase made possible by increasing mechanization of the weaving process.

Weekly wages of male operatives increased 40% from 1838 to 1876; weekly wages of female operatives increased 47% in the same period. These increases were for 16 fewer hours of labor per week. Burke, too, made the observation that capital in 1876 earned less than formerly.

The restricted value of the figures given by Atkinson and Burke arises from the difficulty of properly appraising the influences other than technological which helped to produce the observed results. These competent authorities, however, stated that decreasing costs and increasing productivity were the result of machinery improvements. A conservative conclusion would be that technical advance was a major factor in the variations noted above.

APPENDIX 10

LARGEST CUSTOMERS OF THE LOWELL MACHINE SHOP 1879–1905

(Mills purchasing $50,000 or more of machinery annually)

1879	Merrimack Mfg. Co.	Massachusetts	$265,100
	Lawrence Mfg. Co.	"	55,400
	Amoskeag Mfg. Co.	New Hampshire	235,000
	Boott Mfg. Co.	Massachusetts	148,800
1880	Amoskeag Mfg. Co.	New Hampshire	85,800
	Great Falls Mfg. Co.	" "	70,900
	Tremont & Suffolk Mills	Massachusetts	65,700
	Bibb Mfg. Co.	Georgia	52,000
1881	Nashua Mfg. Co.	New Hampshire	140,600
	Border City Mfg. Co.	Massachusetts	148,700
	Hamilton Mfg. Co.	"	410,300
	Clifton Mfg. Co.	South Carolina	77,000
	Pelzer Mfg. Co.	" "	61,500
1882	T. P. King Mfg. Co.	Georgia	52,300
	Tremont & Suffolk Mills	Massachusetts	78,900
	Enterprise Mfg. Co.	Georgia	108,500
	Tennessee Mfg. Co.	Tennessee	110,900
	Lawrence Mfg. Co.	Massachusetts	106,400
1883	No data		
1884	(Nine months)		
	Sibley Mfg. Co.	Georgia	72,800
	Pacific Mills	Massachusetts	64,000
1885	No customers ordering over $50,000		
1886	No customers ordering over $50,000		
1887	Orswell Mills	Massachusetts	69,000
	Pelzer Mfg. Co.	South Carolina	82,000
1888	Enterprise Mfg. Co.	Georgia	67,800
	Dallas Cotton & Woolen Mills	North Carolina	56,300
	Pacific Mills	Massachusetts	57,600
1889	Amoskeag Mfg. Co.	New Hampshire	66,100
	Riverside Cotton Mills	Georgia	51,900
	Howland Mills	Massachusetts	77,500
	Stark Mills	New Hampshire	50,500
	Appleton Mfg. Co.	Massachusetts	61,400

1890	D. E. Converse Co.	South Carolina	$ 96,400
1891	Lancaster Mills	Massachusetts	63,500
1892	Hamilton Mfg. Co.	Massachusetts	50,400
	West Boylston Mfg. Co.	"	70,000
1893	Langley Mfg. Co.	Georgia	99,700
	Riverside Cotton Mills	"	201,000
	Nockege Mills	Massachusetts	86,100
	Exeter Mfg. Co.	New Hampshire	64,200
	Mass. Cotton Mills	Massachusetts	60,600
1894	Takata & Co.	New York	53,000
	Tremont & Suffolk Mills	Massachusetts	113,400
	Durfee Mills	"	110,600
	Pelzer Mfg. Co.	South Carolina	83,900
1895	Riverside Cotton Mills	Georgia	136,800
	Nockege Mills	Massachusetts	50,000
	Brower & Love Bros.	Indiana	66,300
	Boston Duck Co.	Massachusetts	55,700
	Mass. Mills in Georgia	Georgia	268,700
	Henderson Cotton Mills	Kentucky	97,600
	Langley Mfg. Co.	Georgia	167,000
	Mass. Cotton Mills	Massachusetts	57,600
	Pelzer Mfg. Co.	South Carolina	84,500
1896	Lancaster Mills	Massachusetts	55,900
	Clifton Mfg. Co.	South Carolina	276,300
	Steeles Mills	North Carolina	62,800
1897	No customers ordering over $50,000		
1898	Porterdale Mills	Georgia	66,500
	Mobile Cotton Mills	Alabama	50,000
	Crown Cotton Mills	Georgia	79,200
	Stonewall Mfg. Co.	Mississippi	94,800
1899	Merrimack Mfg. Co.	Massachusetts	146,300
	Planters Compress Co.	Georgia	163,200
	Tallassee Falls Mfg. Co.	Alabama	131,400
	Brower & Love Bros.	Indiana	96,600
	Mass. Mills in Georgia	Georgia	64,500
	Strickland Cotton Mills	"	91,200
	Nashua Mfg. Co.	New Hampshire	139,700
	Clifton Mfg. Co.	South Carolina	155,700
	Steeles Mills	North Carolina	58,000
	Pelham Mfg. Co.	Georgia	52,300
	Appleton Mfg. Co.	Massachusetts	86,800

1900	Tallassee Falls Mfg. Co.	Alabama	$124,400
	Bemis Bros. Bag Co.	Missouri	177,900
	Tupelo Cotton Mills	Mississippi	57,600
	Dublin Cotton Mills	Georgia	51,600
	Limestone Mills	South Carolina	66,000
	Winona Cotton Mills	Mississippi	57,900
	Moultrie Cotton Mills	Georgia	51,400
	W. A. Handley Mfg. Co.	Alabama	53,900
	Gate City Mfg. Co.	Georgia	57,800
	Covington Mills	"	57,000
	Mobile Cotton Mills	Alabama	53,900
	Coffee Cotton Mills	"	52,900
	Bonham Cotton Mills	Texas	53,000
	Columbus Power Co.	Georgia	201,100
	Stark Mills	New Hampshire	51,300
1901	Enterprise Cotton Mills	Alabama	80,500
	Great Falls Mfg. Co.	New Hampshire	57,000
	Social Circle Cotton Mills	Georgia	53,600
	Henderson Cotton Mills	Kentucky	89,400
1902	Mass. Mills in Georgia	Georgia	234,400
	Boyd-Mangham Mfg. Co.	"	86,300
	D. E. Converse Co.	South Carolina	137,800
	Roberdel Mfg. Co.	North Carolina	61,500
	American Woolen Co.	Massachusetts	89,400
	Amoskeag Mfg. Co.	New Hampshire	116,500
1903	Manchester Mills	New Hampshire	64,100
	Durfee Mills	Massachusetts	89,200
	Lily Mill & Power Co.	North Carolina	51,400
	Merrimack Mfg. Co.	Massachusetts	340,800
	W. A. Handley Mfg. Co.	Alabama	56,700
1904	Mass. Cotton Mills	Massachusetts	82,800
	American Pad & Textile Co.	Georgia	150,700
	American Woolen Co.	Massachusetts	51,700
	James E. Hooper	Maryland	70,400
1905	(Five Months)		
	American Woolen Co.	Massachusetts	65,900
	Bemis Bros. Bag Co.	Missouri	186,000
	Wiscassett Mills	North Carolina	66,400
	Bigelow Carpet Co.	Massachusetts	74,000

APPENDIX 11

OFFICERS AND DIRECTORS

A. Officers and Directors of the Lowell Machine Shop, 1845–1912

Presidents

John A. Lowell	1845–50
Homer Bartlett	1850–57
George H. Kuhn	1857–76
John A. Lowell	1876–77
J. Huntington Wolcott	1877–85
Richard D. Rogers	1885–86
Samuel G. Snelling	1886–86
T. Jefferson Coolidge	1886–87
Augustus Lowell	1887–1900
Arthur T. Lyman	1900–05
Albert M. Lyon	1905–05
Robert F. Herrick	1905–11
Wilmot R. Evans	1911–12

Vice President

James C. Howe	1912

Treasurers

J. Thomas Stevenson	1845–76
William A. Burke	1876–84
Robert H. Stevenson	1884–88
Charles L. Peirson	1888–91
Robert H. Stevenson	1891–1905
Robert F. Herrick	1905, 1911–12
Haven C. Perham	1905–11

Superintendents

William A. Burke	1845–62
W. C. Bryant	1862–62
Andrew Moody	1862–70
George Richardson	1870–79
Charles L. Hildreth	1879–1905
Albert H. Morton	1905–12

Directors

John A. Lowell	1845–50, 1853–79
Abbott Lawrence	1845–50, 1859–64
Nathan Appleton	1845–62
Eben Chadwick	1845–54
J. T. Stevenson	1845–77
John Clark	1845–51
Homer Bartlett	1845–59
B. F. French	1850–53
J. H. Wolcott	1850–91
John Wright	1851–69
George H. Kuhn	1854–76
T. J. Coolidge	1862–87
William A. Burke	1864–87
Richard D. Rogers	1869–92
Samuel G. Snelling	1876–86
R. H. Stevenson	1877–1905
Augustus Lowell	1879–1901
George P. Upham	1887–1901
Arthur T. Lyman	1887–1905
Charles L. Peirson	1887–1905
Roger Wolcott	1891–93, 1901–05
Charles W. Amory	1892–1905
Edward M. Hooper	1893–1902
A. Lawrence Lowell	1901–05
Robert H. Gardiner	1902–05
Robert F. Herrick	1905–12
Albert M. Lyon	1905–06
Alfred B. White	1905–12
Guy Cunningham	1905–11
James G. Forbes	1905–06
Jeremiah Mackin	1905–12
Joseph Warren	1905–06
Haven C. Perham	1905–11
Joseph O. Procter	1911–12
Wilmot R. Evans	1911–12
Wilmot R. Evans, Jr.	1912–12

B. Officers and Directors of the Pettee Machine Works, 1882–1897

Presidents

Henry Billings	1882–87
David Nevins	1887–97

Treasurer

Rodman Paul Snelling	1882–97

General Agent

Frank J. Hale	1889–97

Directors

Henry Billings	1882–87
Samuel G. Snelling	1882–86
Henry S. Shaw	1886–97
Harcourt Amory	1887–97
David Nevins	1888–97
Rodman P. Snelling	1893–97
Frederick E. Clarke	1893–97

Superintendents

Richard Daly	(?) –1885
George T. Francis	1885–89
Frederick A. Flather	1889–93
Charles E. Mills	1893–97

C. Officers and Directors of the Saco Water Power Company, 1839–1867

	1839	1849	1867
Presidents	Joseph Balch	Joseph Balch	Th. Wigglesworth, Jr.[a]
Treasurers	Enoch Baldwin	Wm. Dwight[a]	Wm. Dwight[a]
Directors	Joseph Balch	Joseph Balch	Edw. Austin[a]
	Enoch Baldwin	Wm. Dwight[a]	Wm. Dwight[a]
	Tasker Swett	M. P. Wilder[a]	Tm. Wigglesworth[a]
	Robert Hooper, Jr.	John Clark[a]	Wm. Parsons[a]
	Joseph Hall	C. H. Brown[a]	C. H. Brown[a]
	Jeremiah Briggs	A. Gilmore	W. P. Haines[a]
	Sm. Batchelder	Sm. Batchelder[a]	John Hooper
	Daniel Treadwell	Sm. Hooper[a]	
	Elijah Loring	Geo. W. Hallett	

Superintendents

Rufus Nichols	1839–47
Otis Holmes	1847–50
R. M. Chapman	1851
Sylvanus Wetherell	1851–54
William Thompson	1854–67

[a] Officer or director in the Pepperell Manufacturing Co.

D. Officers and Directors of the Saco Water Power Machine Shop, 1867–1897

Treasurers

William Dwight	1867–70
Spencer W. Richardson	1870–97

Agent

James McMullan	1867–97

Directors (various dates)

1867

William Dwight
Wm. P. Haines
A. D. Lockwood
Benjamin Bates
Josiah Bardwell

Superintendents		1888
Charles Haines	(Dates unknown)	Grant Walker
Gilman P. Littlefield	(" ")	J. W. Danielson
		Spencer W. Richardson
		James McMullan
		P. C. Lockwood

E. Officers and Directors of the Saco and Pettee Machine Shops, 1897–1912

Presidents

James McMullan	1897–98
Henry S. Shaw	1898–1912

Vice-Presidents

David Nevins	1897–98
Harcourt Amory	1898–99
J. W. Danielson	1899–1911
C. E. Rogerson	1911–12

Treasurer

Rodman Paul Snelling	1897–1912

General Agent

Frank J. Hale	1897–1912

Directors

James McMullan	1897–98
Frank J. Hale	1897–1912
Rodman P. Snelling	1897–1912
David Nevins	1897–98
Spencer W. Richardson	1897–1904
Henry S. Shaw	1897–1912
J. W. Danielson	1897–1912
Seth M. Milliken	1898–1912
Harcourt Amory	1898–1912
C. E. Rogerson	1904–12

Note: Officers and directors of Saco-Pettee Company, 1910–12, same as Saco and Pettee Machine Shops for corresponding years.

F. Officers and Directors, Saco-Lowell Shops, 1912–1949

Presidents

Henry S. Shaw	1912–23
R. F. Herrick, Sr.	1923–26
David F. Edwards	1926–to date

Vice-Presidents

James C. Howe	1912–17
Frank J. Hale	1923–32
R. P. Snelling	1923–32
C. E. Rogerson	1917–32
R. F. Herrick, Jr.	1926–28
W. F. Lowell	1932–to date
F. E. Banfield	1932–35
R. A. Kettley	1935–47
E. C. Gwaltney	1947–to date
W. W. Gayle	1947–49
John S. Chafee	1946–to date

Comptrollers

R. A. Kettley	1927–28
J. A. Kiely	1947–to date

Treasurers

R. P. Snelling	1912–23
P. D. Howe	1923–24
R. F. Herrick, Jr.	1924–26
D. W. Hunter	1926
H. B. W. Snelling	1926–28
R. A. Kettley	1928–35
D. F. Edwards	1935–46
M. D. Shaffner	1946–to date

General Agents

Frank J. Hale	1912–23
R. F. Herrick, Jr.	1923–28

Chairman of the Board

R. F. Herrick, Sr.	1927–42

Secretaries

P. D. Howe	1915–20
C. E. Cooke	1920–44
M. D. Shaffner	1944–to date

Directors[a]

R. H. Herrick, Sr.	1912–42	G. S. Armstrong	1927–33
Harcourt Amory	1912–23	C. L. Stevens	1928–37
W. R. Evans	1912–26	R. D. Hale	1933–to date
F. J. Hale	1912–to date	W. F. Merrill	1933
R. P. Snelling	1912–36	J. R. Morss	1933–37
S. M. Milliken	1912–16	W. F. Lowell	1935–to date
C. E. Rogerson	1912–32	David Howie	1937–to date
H. S. Shaw	1912–23	R. A. Kettley	1935–47
J. C. Howe	1912–23	C. F. Mills	1928–to date
G. H. Milliken	1916–28	Robert Cutler	1932–40
R. F. Herrick, Jr.	1923–41	W. H. Raye	1937–42
P. D. Howe	1923–24	W. O. Oliver	1940–43
G. O. Hunter	1924–26	O. K. Anderson	1941–to date
Robert Amory	1924–33	Ralph Hornblower	1942–to date
D. W. Hunter	1925–34	John T. Noonan	1943–to date
P. M. Tucker	1925–33	Edward S. French	1947–to date
W. R. Evans, Jr.	1926–35	Thorvald S. Ross	1947–to date
H. B. W. Snelling	1926–28	John S. Chafee	1949–to date
D. F. Edwards	1926–to date		

[a] Directors Massachusetts corporation, 1912–37; Maine corporation, 1937–49.

APPENDIX 12

MILL SECURITY HOLDINGS
1896–1912

A. Mill Stocks Held by the Pettee Machine Works
November 1, 1896

Pineville Cotton Mills, Pineville, S. C.	$17,300
Gaffney Mfg. Co., Gaffney, S. C.	20,200
Mills Mfg. Co., Greenville, S. C.	2,000
Dilling Cotton Mills, King Mountain, N. C.	3,000
Lockhart Mills, Lockhart, S. C.	10,000
Richland Cotton Mills, Columbia, S. C.	6,300
Brookside Mills, Knoxville, Tenn.	2,500
Laurens Cotton Mills, Laurens, S. C.	8,000
Poe Mfg. Co., Greenville, S. C.	6,700
Manchester Cotton Mills, Rock Hill, S. C.	3,500
Lancaster Cotton Mills, Lancaster, S. C.	6,000
Granby Cotton Mills, Columbia, S. C.	8,500
Lannett Cotton Mills, West Point, Ga.	1,000

B. Mill Stocks Held by the Saco Water Power Machine Shop
April–December, 1897

Darlington Mfg. Co., Darlington, S. C.	$ 2,425
Lynchburg Cotton Mills, Lynchburg, Va.	4,100
Matthews Cotton Mills, Ala.	20,063
Kearney Cotton Mills, Kearney, Neb.	30,000
Dallas Mfg. Co., Huntsville, Ala.	34,400
Lockhart Mills, Lockhart, S. C.	25,000
Sherman Seamless Bag Co., Sherman, Texas	1,546
Aldrich Mfg. Co., Moosup, Conn.	15,520
Abbeville Mfg. Co., Abbeville, S. C.	15,000

Source: Data for Table A from Pettee Machine Shop records, Memorandum book of Frank J. Hale; Table B, Saco Water Power Machine Shop records, Baker Library, Ledger.

C. Mill Securities Taken by the Saco and Pettee Machine Shops 1897–1912

(Par value)

Stocks Held April 29, 1905

Siluria Cotton Mfg. Co.	Massachusetts	$ 5,600
Walhalla Cotton Mills	South Carolina	2,000
Mollohon Mfg. Co.	" "	36,700
Capital City Mills	" "	10,000
Hoskins Mills, Inc.	North Carolina	22,000
Olympia Cotton Mills	South Carolina	56,000
Rhode Island Co.	North Carolina	2,500
Kilburn Mill	Massachusetts	17,000
Chicopee Mfg. Co.	"	5,000
Chiquola Mfg. Co.	South Carolina	26,800
Davis Mills	Massachusetts	14,900
Total		$198,500

Stocks Taken Twelve Months Ending April 30, 1906

Loray Mills	North Carolina	$ 32,700
Mollohon Mfg. Co.	South Carolina	4,900
Drayton Mills	" "	30,000
Kilburn Mill	Massachusetts	10,000
Ninety Six Cotton Mill	South Carolina	700
Union Cotton Mills	North Carolina	300
Buffalon Cotton Mills	" "	5,300
Nantucket Mills	" "	25,000
Olympia Cotton Mills	South Carolina	34,800
Gainsville Cotton Mills	Georgia	10,000
Total		$153,700

Stocks Taken Twelve Months Ending April 30, 1907

Ninety Six Cotton Mill	South Carolina	$ 2,000
LeRoy Cotton Mills	New York	10,000
Luther Mfg. Co.	Massachusetts	5,000
Total		$17,000

Stocks Taken Twelve Months Ending April 30, 1908

Jackson Mills	South Carolina	$ 40,000
Toxaway Mills	North Carolina	5,000
Taber Mills	Massachusetts	40,800
Pickens Mill	South Carolina	10,800
Drayton Mills	" "	119,000
Fitchburg Yarn Co.	Massachusetts	5,000
Lincoln Mfg. Co.	"	8,000
Total		$228,600

Stocks Taken Twelve Months Ending April 30, 1909

Taber Mills	Massachusetts	$ 44,200
Ware Shoals Mfg. Co.	South Carolina	50,000
Lincoln Mfg. Co.	Massachusetts	12,000
Pickens Mills	South Carolina	5,200
Cheswell Cotton Mills	Not located	10,000
Lincoln Mfg. Co.	Massachusetts	84,300
Fountain Inn Mfg. Co.	North Carolina	8,850
Liberty Cotton Mills	New York	3,000
Bay State Cotton Corp.	Massachusetts	40,000
Total		$257,550

Stocks Taken Twelve Months Ending April 30, 1910

New Bedford Cotton Mills	Massachusetts	$140,000
Ottaray Mills	South Carolina	3,900
Greers Mfg. Co.	" "	12,500
Greenwood Cotton Mills	" "	26,600
Oconee Mills	" "	2,500
Ottaray Cotton Mills	" "	1,300
Fairmont Mfg. Co.	" "	2,600
Lincoln Mfg. Co.	Massachusetts	17,400
Manchester Cotton Mills	North Carolina	10,000
Bay State Cotton Mills	Massachusetts	27,500
Total		$244,300

Stocks Taken Twelve Months Ending April 30, 1911

Quissett Mills	Massachusetts	$162,000
Grendel Mills	South Carolina	8,510
International Cotton Mills	New York	25,000
Alice Mills	South Carolina	15,700
Quissett Mills	Massachusetts	18,000
Albany Cotton Mills	Georgia	15,000
Grendel Mills	South Carolina	805
Quissett Mills	Massachusetts	45,000
Suncook Mills	New Hampshire	10,000
Harmony Mills	New York	80,000
New Bedford Cotton Mills	Massachusetts	18,600
Marion Mfg. Co.	South Carolina	18,500
Walhalla Cotton Mills	" "	1,700
Grendell Mills	" "	1,380
International Cotton Mills	New York	30,250
Jackson Mills	South Carolina	25,000
Toxaway Mills	" "	4,500
Total		$479,945

Stocks Taken Eighteen Months Ending September 30, 1912

Harmony Mills	New York	$610,000
Quissett Mills	Massachusetts	2,000
Grendell Mills	South Carolina	900
Marion Mfg. Co.	" "	500
Parker Cotton Mills	" "	33,900
Buck Creek Cotton Mill	Alabama	17,000
International Cotton Mills	New York	14,500
Dunean Mills	South Carolina	271,500
Katrine Mfg. Co.	Not located	1,800
Woodside Cotton Mill	South Carolina	11,000
Middleburg Mfg. Co.	" "	10,000
Total		$973,100

Bonds on Hand April 30, 1905

Olympia Cotton Mills	South Carolina	$ 29,000
Richland Cotton Mills	" "	1,000
Rhode Island Co.	North Carolina	18,500
Davis Mills	Massachusetts	113,000
Total		$161,500

Bonds Taken, 1905–12

New Century Cotton Mills	Virginia	$ 1,000
Lily Mills	North Carolina	8,500
Taber Mills	Massachusetts	25,000
Columbus Mfg. Co.	Georgia	80,000
Total		$114,500

Summary

Total Stocks on Hand and Taken, 1905–12	$2,552,695
Total Bonds on Hand and Taken, 1905–12	276,000
Total stocks and bonds	$2,828,695

Source: Table C, Saco and Pettee Machine Shops records, General ledger.

APPENDIX 13

FORMATION OF THE SACO-LOWELL SHOPS
NOVEMBER 1, 1912

On March 31, 1912, certain assets and liabilities of the Kitson Machine Shop (a wholly owned subsidiary) were purchased by the Lowell Machine Shop for $150,000. Plans were made to dissolve the Kitson Machine Shop, but these plans were changed and a nominal amount of new Kitson stock was issued ($1,000) to keep the corporation alive, though by March 31, 1913, all Kitson assets and liabilities had been transferred to the Saco-Lowell books. This transaction had no effect whatsoever on operations of either company, but it did have the effect of simplifying the corporation's accounting problems.

On November 1, 1912, The Lowell Machine Shop authorized $1,350,000 additional common stock (13,500 shares) to bring the total capitalization to $3,600,000, of which $1,000,000 (10,000 shares) represented outstanding common stock, $1,350,000 represented new common stock authorized, and $1,250,000 (12,500 shares) represented outstanding preferred stock. The $1,600,000 of stock (16,000 shares) exchanged for Saco-Pettee Company assets consisted of the 13,500 shares of new common stock authorized and 2,500 shares of outstanding common stock donated by Herrick and Evans.

The Lowell Machine Shop charter was amended to change the name of the company to the Saco-Lowell Shops, and expressly to permit the company to acquire, hold, or sell the stocks of other corporations.

The Lowell Machine Shop bylaws were amended to give effect to the above changes, to create the offices of General Agent and Chairman of the Board, and to increase the number of directors from five to nine.

The Saco-Pettee Company changed its name to the Textile Securities Company and issued $800,000 of Textile Securities Company stock, share for share, to holders of the Saco-Pettee Company stock.

The Textile Securities Company transferred all assets and liabilities except $1,124,000 of mill stocks and notes receivable to the Saco-Lowell Shops, in exchange for 16,000 shares of Saco-Lowell stock, which was distributed, share for share, to the Textile Securities Company (Saco-Pettee) stockholders.

A. Balance Sheets of the Lowell Machine Shop, the Kitson Machine Shop, and the Saco-Pettee Company before Consolidation, November 1, 1912

Assets	Lowell	Kitson	Saco-Pettee
Cash	$ 547.03	$ 1,296.93	$ 137,445.04
Accounts and Notes Receivable	413,101.28	152,820.30	1,509,878.42
Stock on Hand	547,559.67	121,194.85	275,631.29
Mill Securities and Investments	18,700.00	74,440.00	484,950.00
Plant, Tools, and Real Estate	1,073,195.28[a]	....	1,000,013.45
Kitson Machine Shop	293,401.20	....	....
R. F. Herrick, Treasurer	211,701.60	98,361.66	....
Miscellaneous	5,810.00	....	....
Total Assets	$2,564,016.06	$448,113.74	$3,407,918.20
Liabilities and Net Worth			
Accounts and Notes Payable	....	....	$1,008,152.94
Miscellaneous Liabilities	$ 5,000.00	....	2,973.95
Capital Stock			
Common	1,000,000.00	....	1,600,000.00
Preferred	1,250,000.00	....	....
Reserves	....	....	362,046.40
Treasurer's Account	....	$293,401.20	....
Profit and Loss	309,016.06	154,712.54	434,744.91
Total Liabilities and Net Worth	$2,564,016.06	$448,113.74	$3,407,918.20

[a] Includes Kitson plant, valued at $116,000; Lowell plant, at $784,560; and Lowell tenements, at $171,940.

Source: Lowell Machine Shop records, Baker Library, Harvard Graduate School of Business Administration, Ledgers and journals.

B. Schedule of Property Transferred from Saco-Pettee Company to the Saco-Lowell Shops, November 1, 1912

Assets	
Plant, Tools, and Real Estate	$ 767,600.00
Stock on Hand	275,631.29
Accounts Receivable	504,828.42
Ashworth Co. Stock	160,000.00
Cash	137,445.04
Mill Stocks	171,600.00
Total Assets	$2,017,104.75
Liabilities	
Notes Payable	$ 905,000.00
Accounts Payable	103,152.94
Total Liabilities	$1,008,152.94
Net Assets transferred	$1,008,951.81

Source: Lowell Machine Shop records, Ledgers and journals.

C. Balance Sheets of the Saco-Lowell Shops and the Textile Securities Company after Consolidation, November 1, 1912

SACO-LOWELL SHOPS

Assets		*Liabilities and Net Worth*	
Cash	$ 235,695.96	Notes and Accounts Payable	$1,514,215.13
Stock on Hand	1,598,499.00		
Accounts Receivable	1,303,417.90		
Notes Receivable	141,125.21	Capital Stock	
Investments	134,134.63	Common	2,350,000.00
Mill Stocks	370,450.00	Preferred	1,250,000.00
Mill Bonds	2,300.00		
A. T. Atherton Stock	25,000.00		
Ashworth Bros. Stock	160,000.00	Profit and Loss	1,375,267.18
Petty Cash	5,549.61		
Tariff Matters, Joint Account	5,810.00		
Miscellaneous	7,500.00		
Plant, Buildings, Land, and Equipment	2,500,000.00		
Total	$6,489,482.31		$6,489,482.31

TEXTILE SECURITIES COMPANY

Assets		*Liabilities and Net Worth*	
Notes Receivable.......	$ 993,721.80	Capital Stock..........	$ 800,000.00
Mill Stocks............	118,950.00	Profit and Loss........	324,000.00
Interest...............	11,328.20		
Total............	$1,124,000.00		$1,124,000.00

Source: Lowell Machine Shop and Textile Securities Company records, Ledgers and journals.

D. Sales Comparison with Whitin Machine Works before and after 1912 Consolidation

Year	Saco-Pettee	Lowell Machine Shop	Saco-Lowell Shops	Whitin Machine Works
1908.............	$3,036,000	$2,682,400	....	$2,977,600
1909.............	2,316,500	1,449,600	....	3,917,800
1910.............	3,871,400	2,315,500	....	4,645,300
1911.............	3,795,300	2,116,000	....	3,096,900
1912.............	2,618,800	1,039,900	....	3,281,700
1913.............	....	....	$ 3,854,500	2,623,600
1914.............	....	....	3,444,100	2,348,200
1915.............	....	....	3,857,500	2,857,100
1916.............	....	....	6,208,200	5,510,300
1917.............	....	....	9,019,500	6,500,400
1918.............	....	....	10,796,500	5,277,000

Source: Saco-Pettee, Lowell Machine Shop, and Saco-Lowell records, Ledgers; Navin, *Whitin Machine Works*.

APPENDIX 14

FOREIGN COTTON-TEXTILE MACHINES INSTALLED IN AMERICAN MILLS

(Expressed as percentage of total installations of each type of machine)

Machine	1910–14	1905–09	1900–04	1895–99	1890–94	1885–89	1880–84
Openers, Pickers & Lappers	5	2	11	4	5	4	16
Cards	4	6	8	9	43	55	15
Drawing (Heads)	6	5	11	12	42	58	49
Railway Heads	none	1	6	none	none	none	none
Roving (spindles)	9	9	19	24	31	27	42
Ring Spinning (spindles)	0.1	0.2	1	none	none	none	0.4
Mule Spinning (spindles)	77	74	81	70	82	80	61
Twisters (spindles)	0.3	0.4	1	0.7	none	0.5	none
Spoolers (spindles)	1	2	2	0.2	3	0.3	none
Warpers	0.07	0.2	0.1	none	1	none	none
Slashers	3	4	3	5	6	12	3
Looms	0.1	0.2	0.07	0.01	0.2	0.4	0.6

Note. The table above presents only certain machines, enough to indicate the relative importance of foreign imports. The source from which this table was compiled gives all types of machines and is expressed in absolute numbers rather than percentages. I feel that this material is of value as a general measure of comparison between domestic and foreign installations and that it should not be relied upon as a measure of the number of cards, spindles, looms, and so on, installed in the various periods, even though no other information of this scope and nature has ever, to my knowledge, been compiled. I feel that the statistics published in the original source for the years preceding 1880 are not sufficiently accurate to be summarized in any form.

Source: U. S. Department of Commerce, Bureau of Foreign and Domestic Commerce, *The Cotton Spinning Machinery Industry*, miscellaneous series No. 37 (Washington, D. C., 1916), Table 44, p. 77.

APPENDIX 15

OPERATING STATISTICS OF THE SACO-LOWELL SHOPS 1912–1948

A. Sales Summary 1913–1926

Year	Total Net Sales Foreign and Domestic[a] (In dollars)	Foreign Sales[a] (In dollars)	Per Cent of Foreign to Domestic	Total Net Sales Foreign and Domestic at 1913 Prices
1913	3,854,500	....	..	3,854,000
1914	3,444,100	....	..	3,513,000
1915	3,857,500	....	..	3,356,000
1916	6,208,200	....	..	4,435,000
1917	9,019,500	....	..	6,360,000
1918	10,797,100	4,570,400[b]	12[b]	6,866,000
1919	13,982,500	4,231,000	30	9,435,000
1920	21,352,500	6,770,700	32	15,341,000
1921	19,053,500	7,933,700	42	13,041,000
1922	11,159,700	4,513,600	40	6,727,000
1923	13,872,100	1,702,200	12	9,440,000
1924	7,250,900	547,800	8	3,320,000
1925	7,035,600	1,583,700	23	3,760,000
1926	5,927,800	965,800	16	2,922,000

[a] Shipments.
[b] From 1913 to 1918, inclusive.
Source: Saco-Lowell records, Totals notebooks.

B. Geographic Distribution of Sales 1919–1926

Year	(Percentage of Total Sales) Northern Mills	Southern Mills
1919	68	32
1920	55	45
1921	87	13
1922	44	56
1923	34	66
1924	32	68
1925	46	54
1926	34	66

Source: Saco-Lowell records, Totals notebooks.

C. Analysis of Sales
1913–1926
(Expressed as percentages of total dollar sales)

Year	Types of Machines			Repair	Breakdown by Plants			
	Cotton	Worsted	Silk	Sales	Biddeford	Kitson	Lowell	Newton
1913.....	96.7	3.3[a]	..	19	34.4	12.2	31.9	21.5
1914.....	95.4	4.6	..	19	39.4	8.1	30.9	21.6
1915.....	94.5	5.5[a]	..	21	35.4	8.1	30.9	25.6
1916.....	89.9	6.3	3.8	19	35.0	8.2	30.5	26.3
1917.....	89.4	6.1	4.5	18	31.7	8.2	34.6	25.5
1918.....	88.2	8.7	3.1	22	33.6	10.5	35.8	20.1
1919.....	90.8	7.6	1.6	20	34.7	10.3	29.1	25.9
1920.....	87.6	7.5	4.9	19	31.5	10.3	35.0	23.2
1921.....	92.0	6.5	1.5	13	35.4	8.6	30.3	25.7
1922.....	91.5	7.8	.7	15	36.3	11.5	25.8	26.4
1923.....	81.8	13.7	4.5	17	29.4	12.1	35.0	23.5
1924.....	87.4	12.3	.3	25	30.3	14.6	30.2	24.9
1925.....	94.6	4.8	.6	29	29.7	13.5	32.0	24.8
1926.....	90.5	7.9	1.6	36	30.9	17.1	32.2	19.0

[a] Estimated.

Source: Saco-Lowell records, Totals notebooks.

D. Unit Production of Representative Machines, 1912–1926

	1913	1920	Total 1913–1926
Cotton Machinery			
Bale Breakers	5	140	809
Lappers	328	536	4,277
Vertical Openers	none	160	1,216
Automatic Feeders	172	247	3,065
Condensers	60	169	1,355
Cards	1,167	2,309	22,596
Drawing Deliveries	2,016	5,070	41,291
Card Strippers	none	978	5,867
Roving Frames (number of machines)	710	1,388	12,011
Spoolers (" " ")	155	235	1,854
Spinning Frames (" " ")	1,343	2,010	20,052
Twisters	137	479	4,281
Warpers	107	169	1,261
Slashers	60	104	803
Worsted Machinery			
Gill Boxes	85	119	1,299
Drawing Frames	none	88	616
Roving Frames	30	205	1,439
Spinning Frames	34	223	1,718
Silk Machinery			
Intermediate Gill Boxes	none	172	371
Intermediate Gill Drawing	none	18	44
Rotary Drawing Frames	none	72	218
Roving Frames	none	53	196
Spinning Frames	none	106	422

Source: National City Bank Survey of Saco-Lowell Shops, 1926.

E. Analysis of Foreign Sales
1912–1926
(000 omitted)

	China		Japan		South America		Other	
Year	Dollars	Per Cent of Total Foreign	Dollars	Per Cent of Total Foreign	Dollars	Per Cent of Total Foreign	Dollars	Per Cent of Total Foreign
1912–18	1,608	35	2,360	52	354	8	252	5
1919	2,422	57	1,300	31	259	6	250	6
1920	4,012	59	2,535	38	132	2	92	1
1921	5,086	64	2,277	29	140	2	431	5
1922	2,628	58	1,640	36	127	3	119	3
1923	126	7	1,343	79	36	2	197	12
1924	178	33	69	13	70	13	231[a]	41
1925	256	16	56	4	106	7	1,166[a]	73
1926[b]	343	36	87	9	37	3	499[a]	52

[a] Includes sales in Continental Europe of $134,000 in 1924, $1,000,000 in 1925, and $360,000 in 1926.
[b] To November 1, 1926.
Source: Saco-Lowell records, Totals notebooks; National City Bank Survey of Saco-Lowell Shops, 1926.

F. The Saco-Lowell Plants in 1912

	Biddeford	Newton	Lowell	Kitson
Appraised Plant Value[a]...	$1,267,300	$1,181,100	$1,499,300	$193,500
Ratio Appraised Value to Replacement Cost....	65%	72%	49%	52%
Manufacturing Space in Use.................	532,300 sq. ft.	346,500 sq. ft.	663,100 sq. ft.	115,500 sq. ft.
Constructed before 1850.	33%	none	10%	none
Constructed 1851–1890..	18	11%	89	100%
Constructed 1891–1912..	49	89	1	none
Appraised Value per Square Foot of Manufacturing Space...........	$0.86	$1.13	$0.51	$0.42
Appraised Value of Machine Tools.........	$385,500	$294,000	$302,800	$54,800
Ratio Appraised Value to Replacement Cost....	76%	74%	63%	69%
Date of Acquisition of Machine Tools				
Prior to 1880..........	3%	1%	9%	1%
1880–90..............	17	16	33	19
1891–1900............	30	42	33	40
1900–12...............	50	31	25	40

[a] Replacement cost as at November 1, 1912, less depreciation accrued since acquisition. "Plant" includes Buildings, Building Equipment, Tenements, Machinery, Land Improvements, Equipment, Tenement and Shop Land.

Source: Lockwood, Greene & Co., Inc., *Appraisal of the Saco-Lowell Shops as of November 1, 1912.*

G. The Saco-Lowell Plants, 1912–1926
(000 omitted)

	Biddeford	Newton	Lowell	Kitson	Total
Appraised Value Nov. 1, 1912......	$1,267	$1,181	$1,499	$194	$4,141
Plant Additions, 1913–1925[a].......	2,283	2,874	2,855	588	8,600
Book Value after Depreciation					
1912..........................	.....	.....	.....	...	2,533
1926..........................	.....	.....	.....	...	7,196
Total Floor Area (square feet)					
1880..........................	307	43	416	97	862
1910..........................	536	410	661	116	1,722
1926..........................	731	568	915	263	2,478
Per Cent Increase 1926 over 1910	35%	39%	38%	127%	44%
Machine Tools in Use in 1926					
Acquired prior to 1880........	2%	...	4%	...	....
Acquired 1880–90.............	8	8%	10	10%	....
Acquired 1891–1900...........	16	23	16	22	....
Acquired 1900–12.............	27	26	14	23	....
Acquired 1913–26.............	47	43	56	45	....
Annual Plant Capacity in 1926					
Cards.........................	.....	2,700	.....	...	.....
Drawing Frames.............	.....	5,400	.....	...	.....
Roving Frames..............	1,590	.....	.....	...	.....
Spinning Frames.............	1,590	.....	.....	...	.....
Annual Foundry Capacity in 1926 (in tons)..................	18,000	30,000	27,000	...	75,000

[a] Excluding additions to valuation made for tax purposes. Plant additions include expenditures for land, buildings, machinery, and equipment.

Source: Saco-Lowell records, Totals notebooks; National City Bank Survey of Saco-Lowell Shops, 1926.

H. Sales and Comparative Costs
1913–26
(000 omitted)

	Net Sales after Shop Transfers				Operating Profit			
Year	Biddeford	Kitson	Lowell	Newton	Biddeford	Kitson	Lowell	Newton
1913	$1,326	$ 469	$1,232	$ 827	$ 145	$230	$368[a]	$ 63[a]
1914	1,356	278	1,065	744	95	101	99[a]	45
1915	1,364	314	1,192	988	151	118	8[a]	156
1916	2,173	512	1,890	1,634	523	184	38[a]	368
1917	2,858	737	3,121	2,304	579	230	219	499
1918	3,624	1,135	3,868	2,169	437	397	219	387
1919	4,853	1,441	4,075	3,613	972	762	169	1,120
1920	6,721	2,198	7,478	4,956	1,037	731	336	893
1921	6,743	1,637	5,772	4,901	1,480	554	170	1,112
1922	4,130	1,301	2,926	3,001	1,177	415	410[a]	752
1923	4,082	1,673	4,857	3,260	779[a]	544	871[a]	554
1924	2,199	1,060	2,186	1,805	251[a]	462	699[a]	20
1925	2,095	947	2,248	1,747	171[a]	320	333[a]	94[a]
1926	1,550	1,322	1,815	1,197	114[a]	434	351[a]	22

	Operating Profit as Percentage of Net Sales				Labor, Selling, and Administrative Expense as Per Cent of Net Sales			
Year	Biddeford	Kitson	Lowell	Newton	Biddeford	Kitson	Lowell	Newton
1913	11	49	30[a]	8[a]	41	21	69	38
1914	7	36	9[a]	6	44	32	59	40
1915	11	38	.7[a]	16	43	31	59	38
1916	24	37	2[a]	23	36	28	56	32
1917	20	31	7	22	37	27	45	29
1918	12	35	6	18	42	25	50	31
1919	20	53	4	31	39	23	53	29
1920	15	33	5	18	40	25	52	30
1921	22	34	3	23	38	27	47	32
1922	29	32	14[a]	25	42	35	70	29
1923	19[a]	33	18[a]	17	59	36	72	41
1924	11[a]	44	32[a]	1	60	41	84	45
1925	8[a]	34	15[a]	5[a]	63	35	68	44
1926	7[a]	33	19[a]	2	59	26	77	49

[a] Deficit.

Year	Material Costs as Percentage of Net Sales				Taxes and Insurance as Percentage of Net Sales			
	Biddeford	Kitson	Lowell	Newton	Biddeford	Kitson	Lowell	Newton
1913	37	24	57	54	4	3	4	4
1914	37	27	30	35	9	10	10	10
1915	45	28	37	51	3	4	5	3
1916	44	38	50	45	2	3	3	2
1917	45	52	54	48	1	1	1	1
1918	44	41	42	52	1	2	2	2
1919	36	25	40	39	1	2	2	1
1920	43	40	46	49	2	4	1	2
1921	32	21	30	36	2	4	2	4
1922	29	20	31	35	1	3	3	2
1923	62	36	44	44	4	3	3	3
1924	31	27	37	33	5	5	6	7
1925	36	23	34	37	4	7	4	6
1926	26	23	35	37	4	5	5	6

[a] Deficit.

Source: National City Bank Survey of Saco-Lowell Shops, 1926; Saco-Lowell records, Totals notebooks.

I. Comparative Balance Sheets, December 31, 1912–1926

(In thousands of dollars)

	1912	1913	1914	1915	1916	1917	1918	1919	1920	1921	1922	1923	1924	1925	1926[a]
Assets															
Cash and Call Loans	142	175	183	353	315	353	369	618	1,043	2,082	526	1,020	1,171	658	1,066
Accounts Receivable	1,783	1,434	1,320	1,282	1,750	2,061	1,491	1,824	3,544	2,571	2,882	2,730	2,051	1,893	1,109
Notes Receivable	189	169	501	300	300	568	707	778	638	918	1,101	760	252	517	729
Less Reserve for Bad Accounts	199	167	100	100	100	100	100	100	50	170	154	154	53	34	34
Marketable Securities	...	...	...	...	...	348	126	1,728	...	1,200	100	...	...	...	...
Prepaid Items	58	65	53	53	63	89	100	108	111	117	91	161	156	177	115
Inventory	1,562	1,344	1,146	1,341	1,772	2,391	2,780	2,942	3,554	1,982	1,799	3,488	3,343	3,073	2,774
Less Reserve for Inventory	312	269	229	240	300	300	300	600	25	200	200	600	...	...	...
Total Current Assets	3,222	2,751	2,874	3,044	3,799	5,411	5,173	7,298	8,815	8,499	6,145	7,405	6,920	6,285	5,759
Land	...	...	...	...	...	...	...	637	698	701	727	770	770	770	770
Buildings	...	...	...	...	...	...	...	2,356	5,674	5,713	5,789	6,436	6,523	6,523	6,523
Machinery and Equipment	...	...	...	...	...	...	...	3,710	4,347	5,064	5,295	4,863	5,081	5,124	5,137
Total Investment in Plant	2,533	2,760	2,797	5,094	5,260	5,762	6,146	6,703	10,719	11,477	11,811	12,070	12,374	12,418	12,431
Less Reserve for Depreciation	...	...	67	2,436	2,574	2,852	3,158	3,489	4,967	5,464	5,992	4,314	4,663	5,041	5,235
Investment in Subsidiaries	...	...	...	...	...	...	...	...	...	...	...	...	...	...	...
Other Investments	483	175	203	328	68	193	416	115	114	105	362	357	890	1,043	1,066
Long-term Accounts Receivable	...	...	...	...	...	...	...	...	...	...	...	...	...	...	379
Accounts Due from Officers	...	...	...	...	...	...	...	...	...	...	...	...	...	22	22
Other Assets	68	68	68	65	82	447	385	347	116	1	54	174	614	462	218
Total Fixed Assets	3,084	3,004	3,001	3,052	2,835	3,550	3,789	3,676	5,982	6,119	6,236	8,286	9,215	8,904	8,881
Total Assets	4,417	4,072	4,166	4,233	4,771	5,473	5,762	9,112	10,303	10,884	11,273	10,950	10,133	10,310	9,779

I. Comparative Balance Sheets, December 31, 1912–1926 (cont.)

(000 omitted)

	1912	1913	1914	1915	1916	1917	1918	1919	1920	1921	1922	1923	1924	1925	1926[a]
Liabilities															
Notes Payable to Banks	1,745	1,620	1,635	1,720	1,675	2,910	2,534	1,095	3,657	2,940	285	4,215	5,640	4,000	4,000
Other Notes Payable	...	...	...	...	...	...	...	...	...	...	...	...	...	...	...
Accounts Payable	136	63	75	142	189	328	315	267	638	184	314	280	233	281	202
Accrued Items	8	...	...	...	...	...	...	...	200	46	4	19	...	90	102
Reserve for Federal Taxes	...	...	...	...	...	250	350	500	...	564	505	227	129	507	557
Total Current Liabilities	1,889	1,683	1,710	1,862	1,864	3,488	3,200	1,862	4,495	3,734	1,108	4,741	6,002	4,879	4,861
Five-year 7% Notes	...	...	...	...	...	...	...	...	...	...	...	...	...	1,567	1,567
6% Preferred Stock	1,250	1,250	1,250	1,250	1,250	1,250	1,250	1,250	1,250	1,250	1,250	1,250	1,250	1,250	1,250
7% Preferred Stock	...	...	...	...	...	...	...	...	...	...	2,644	2,644	2,644	2,644	2,644
Common Stock	2,350	2,350	2,350	2,350	2,350	2,350	2,350	3,525	3,525	2,525	5,288	5,288	5,288	4,849	4,318
Surplus	817	472	566	633	1,171	1,873	2,162	4,337	5,528	6,109	2,091	1,769	951		
Total Liabilities and Net Worth	4,417	4,072	4,166	4,233	4,771	5,473	5,762	9,112	10,303	10,884	11,273	10,950	10,133	10,310	9,779

[a] As of June 30.

Source: National City Bank Survey of Saco-Lowell Shops, 1926, Figure 2.

J. Comparative Income Accounts, 1913–1926

(Expressed as Per Cent of Net Sales)

	1913	1914	1915	1916	1917	1918	1919	1920	1921	1922	1923	1924	1925	1926
Net Sales	100.0	100.0	100.0	100.0	100.0	100.0	100.0	100.0	100.0	100.0	100.0	100.0	100.0	100.0
Labor	46.5	46.6	45.8	40.3	36.7	41.0	39.0	40.4	38.0	45.0	56.5	60.8	56.1	51.0
Material	45.3	34.0	42.6	45.7	49.2	44.9	37.0	45.0	31.4	30.3	48.1	32.5	33.8	30.4
Overhead	4.0	9.6	3.7	2.0	.8	1.6	1.5	1.8	2.4	1.7	3.1	6.0	5.0	5.1
Increase in inventory	...	...	5.0	6.9	6.7	3.6	1.6	2.8	...	...	7.7	...	...	...
Decrease in inventory	5.7	5.7	...	...	...	...	...	...	8.3	1.5	...	2.1	3.7	9.9
Depreciation	...	...	2.1	2.2	3.1	2.8	2.3	1.6	2.5	4.5	4.0	5.1	5.4	6.3
Total cost of sales	101.5	95.9	89.2	83.3	83.1	86.7	78.4	86.0	82.6	83.0	104.0	106.5	104.0	102.7
Operating Profit	1.5[a]	4.1	10.8	16.7	16.9	13.3	21.6	14.0	17.4	17.0	4.0[a]	6.5[a]	4.0[a]	2.7[a]
Advertising & selling	(b)	(b)	1.8	1.3	1.1	2.1	1.7	1.1	1.6	2.6	2.7	4.0	4.4	5.8
General & administrative	(b)	(b)	3.0	1.8	1.3	1.4	1.8	1.0	1.3	2.1	1.8	3.0	2.8	3.0
Reserve for bad debts	.3	.1	.8	.1	...	...	...	...	...	.5	.2[a]	.3[a]	.1[a]	
Total	.3	.1	5.6	3.2	2.4	3.5	3.5	2.1	2.9	5.2	4.3	6.7	7.1	8.8
Net Profit	1.8[a]	4.0	5.2	13.5	14.5	9.8	18.1	11.9	14.5	11.8	8.3[a]	13.2[a]	11.1[a]	11.5[a]
Other income	2.1	2.7	2.6	1.4	1.5	1.4	.8	.8	.6	2.2	1.2	1.5	2.1	1.7
Gross Income	.3	6.7	7.8	14.9	16.0	11.2	18.9	12.7	15.1	14.0	7.1[a]	11.7[a]	9.0[a]	9.8[a]
Total Deductions	4.4	.1	1.0	1.7	.3	.4	.3[a]	.1	.4	.5[a]	.3	.3	...	...
Income Available for Interest & Federal Taxes	4.1[a]	6.6	6.8	13.2	15.7	10.8	19.2	12.6	14.7	14.5	6.8[a]	12.9[a]	9.0[a]	9.8[a]
Interest on current loans	2.9	2.9	2.8	1.8	1.8	1.9	.75	1.1	1.6	1.0	1.5	3.8	3.3	3.8
Interest on 7% notes	...	...	...	...	...	...	...	...	...	...	...	...	.9	1.8
Federal income taxes	...	...	...	...	.2	2.0	1.15	3.6	2.9	4.4	1.4	1.5	...	.1
Total taxes and interest	2.9	2.9	2.8	1.8	2.0	3.9	1.9	4.7	4.5	5.4	2.9	5.3	4.2	5.7
Net Income	7.0[a]	3.7	4.0	11.4	13.7	6.9	17.3	7.9	10.2	9.1	9.7[a]	17.2[a]	13.2[a]	15.5[a]

[a] Deficit.
[b] Included in overhead.

Source: National City Bank Survey of Saco-Lowell Shops, 1926, Figure 12.

K. Sales Summary
1927–1941
(000 omitted)

Year	Total Sales	Foreign Sales	Domestic Sales	Repair Sales
1927	$ 7,086	$ 755	$ 6,331	$2,456
1928	4,720	796	3,924	1,854
1929	8,777	1,109	7,668	2,643
1930	4,096	1,082	3,015	1,360
1931	3,700	459	3,241	1,234
1932	1,982	251	1,731	703
1933	3,717	454	3,263	1,077
1934	6,490	1,004	5,486	1,377
1935	3,967	665	3,302	1,215
1936	6,978	992	6,086	1,792
1937[a]	9,026	1,852	7,174	2,034
1938	5,262	1,227	4,035	1,260
1939	6,508	987	5,521	1,702
1940	9,279	2,119	7,159	1,999
1941	11,964	1,481	10,484	3,251

[a] Eleven months.

Source: Saco-Lowell records, Annual statements.

L. Analysis of Sales — Major Products
1912–1947

Year	Openers & Pickers	Cards	Drawing Deliveries	Combers	Roving Frames[a]	Long-draft Roving Frames[a]	Spinning Frames[a]	Long-draft Spinning Frames[a]	Twisters
1912–26[b]	...	1,537	2,810	...	807	...	1,341	....	315
1927	373	1,051	1,504	...	393	...	596	....	153
1928	152	400	1,630	...	295	...	316	....	284
1929	190	1,205	2,044	...	367	...	797	....	503
1930	129	294	844	...	145	...	481	1,073	90
1931	85	129	872	...	68	...	519	1,340	69
1932	28	23	924	...	9	...	326	753	13
1933	31	94	1,656	...	31	...	772	1,165	40
1934	51	252	436	3	54	...	972	2,075	27
1935	56	35	360	12	90	...	389	1,395	59
1936	44	120	1,364	94	153	...	934	2,061	113
1937	104	382	1,020	33	208	...	1,338	2,017	133
1938	25	141	586	9	109	...	390	1,644	70
1939	26	127	1,579	33	130	127	485	1,921	219
1940	103	360	1,723	17	314	126	883	1,119	246
1941	88	524	1,247	58	163	570	1,002	1,197	221
1942	65	437	1,186	47	86	90	517	73	115
1943	27	165	650	8	1	32	4	194	179
1944	19	48	148	13	19	155	108	22	685
1945	26	145	789	33	110	104	567	514	53
1946	81	794	1,108	54	269	237	838	1,036	127
1947	177	1,473	2,759	147	381	319	1,205	1,385	226

[a] Expressed in numbers of machines.
[b] Annual average.

Source: Saco-Lowell records.

M. COMPARATIVE BALANCE SHEETS
1926–1949
(000 omitted)

	12 31 26	11 30 28	11 30 32	12 31 40	12 31 48	12 31 49
Assets						
Cash	$ 1,018	$ 993	$ 532	$ 1,546	$ 2,469	$ 2,646
Notes & Accounts Receivable	2,237	1,918	839	1,454	7,877	2,585
Inventory	2,346	1,658	695	1,879	11,533	7,454
Securities	873	606	164	....	15	9,291
Other Current	....	1,236	48	405	1,540	....
Total Current	$ 6,474	$ 6,411	$ 2,278	$ 5,284	$23,434	$21,976
Real Estate, Machinery & Equipment						
Gross Value	(a)	$11,355	(a)	$ 8,793	(a)	....
Less Reserve	(a)	6,214	(a)	5,330	(a)	....
Net Value	$ 6,997	5,141	$ 4,534	3,463	$ 7,301	$ 6,862
Deferred Assets	....	62	28	15	166	84
Miscellaneous Assets	156	....	....	....	229	203
Total Assets	$13,627	$11,614	$6,840	$8,762	$31,130	$29,125
Liabilities, Capital, and Surplus						
Current and Miscellaneous Liabilities	$ 206	$ 857	$ 171	$ 893	$14,086	$ 7,935
Ten Year Loan	....	....	312	....	....	....
Five Year Serial Loan	....	....	....	350	....	....
Funded Debt	6,161	6,068	2,753	....	....	....
Reserve for Contingencies	....	88	54	250	1,850	2,150
6 Per Cent Preferred Stock	1,250	1,250	1,250	....	....	....
2nd Preferred Stock	2,644	2,644	2,644	....	....	....
Convertible Preferred Stock	....	....	....	840	....	....
Common Stock	3,366	(b)	(b)	967	1,500	1,500
Surplus	....	707	344[c]	5,462	13,694	17,540
Total Liabilities, Capital and Surplus	$13,627	$11,614	$6,840	$8,762	$31,130	$29,125

[a] No data. [b] No equity. [c] Deficit. Source: Saco-Lowell records, Annual reports and Annual statements.

N. Evolution of Capital Structure and Funded Debt
1928–1948
(000 omitted)

	1928	1929	1930	1931	1932	1933	1934	1935	1936	1937	1940	1948
3-year 5% Class A Notes	4,550	3,413	...	...	...	...	...	...	...	...	...	...
5-year 7% Gold Notes	122	...	...	...	...	...	...	...	...	...	...	...
5-year 7% Gold Notes	500	478	...	...	...	...	...	...	...	...	...	...
5-year 5% Class B Notes	895	895	895	895	895	...	...	...	...	...	...	...
6% Class A Notes	...	...	2,730	2,730	1,274	...	...	...	...	...	...	...
7% Convertible Gold Notes	...	...	478	478	478	...	...	...	...	...	..	...
5% Class A Notes	...	...	...	...	...	1,160	901	698	473	...	...	...
7% Class C Notes	...	...	...	...	...	62	62	47	46	...	...	...
7% Class D Notes	...	...	...	...	...	415	415	395	385	...	...	...
7% Class B Notes	...	...	...	...	...	895	895	895	895	...	...	...
6% Preferred Stock	1,250	1,250	1,250	1,250	1,250	1,250	1,250	1,250	1,250	...	...	...
Second Preferred Stock	2,644	2,644	2,644	2,644	2,644	2,643	2,643	2,643	2,643	...	...	...
Class A Preferred Stock	...	...	...	...	...	...	...	...	...	1,254	...	...
Class B Preferred Stock	...	...	...	...	...	...	...	...	...	546	...	...
Convertible Preferred Stock	...	...	...	...	...	...	...	...	...	...	839	...
Old Common Stock & Surplus	708	1,757	889	416	344[a]	115[a]	405	416	1,141	...	...	...
New Common Stock	...	...	...	...	...	...	...	...	...	710	1,036	1,500
Accrued Interest												
Class B Notes	...	...	71	89	107	174	246	321	400	...	...	...
Class C Notes	...	...	...	...	...	29	60	87	117	...	...	...
Class D Notes	...	...	...	...	...	...	...	...	9	...	...	...
Accumulated Unpaid Dividends												
6% Preferred Stock	...	...	413	488	563	638	713	788	863	...	...	...
Second Preferred Stock	...	...	1,064	1,249	1,434	1,619	1,804	1,990	2,175	...	...	...
Interest Charges	334	326	275	260	250	193	205	170	152	117	47	...

[a] Deficit.

Source: Saco-Lowell Records, Directors' minutes and annual reports to stockholders.

O. Operating Statements, 1927–1940

(In thousands of dollars)

	1927	1928	1929	1930	1931	1932	1933	1934	1935	1936	1937	1938	1939	1940
Net Sales	7,086	4,720	8,777	4,096	3,700	1,982	3,717	6,490	3,967	6,978	9,026	5,262	6,508	9,279
Cost of Sales														
Payroll	3,477	2,750	3,893	2,120	1,832	1,325	1,727	2,505	1,889	2,921	3,590	2,112	2,997	3,666
Purchases	2,335	1,674	3,390	1,217	1,133	864	1,877	2,383	1,431	2,970	3,783	1,572	2,780	3,707
Royalties	18	14	61	36	41	18	26	61	57	131	95	25	34	44
Insurance and Taxes	221	177	93	77	73	43	29	39	39	82	176	184	218	244
Depreciation	388	360	288	291	291	254	238	196	198	201	188	200	154	158
Decrease in Inventory	691[a]	...	...	902	352	144	...	263	...	...	...	786	..	...
Sundry Expenses	103	...	...	...	...	...	...	...	...	..	...	...	...	...
Less:														
Increase in Inventory	...	8	435	...	...	...	745	...	73	661	251	...	462	247
Sundry Credits	100	539	275	378	244	467	171	255	157	307	397	324	392	490
Net Cost of Sales	7,133	4,428	7,015	4,265	3,478	2,181	2,981	5,192	3,384	5,337	7,184	4,555	5,329	7,082
Gross Profit	47[b]	292	1,762	169[b]	222	199[b]	736	1,298	583	1,641	1,842	707	1,179	2,197
(Per cent of Net Sales)	.7	6.2	20.1	4.1	6.0	10.0	19.8	20.0	14.7	23.5	20.4	13.4	18.1	23.7
Selling, Administrative and Patent Expense	468	407	425	482	454	327	287	393	341	408	535	497	640	698
Net Operating Profit	515[b]	115[b]	1,337	651[b]	232[b]	526[b]	449	905	242	1,232	1,307	210	539	1,498
(Per cent of Net Sales)	7.3	2.4	15.2	15.9	6.3	26.5	12.1	13.9	6.1	17.7	14.5	3.9	8.3	16.2
Sundry Income	140	182	166	115	71	74	38	46	30	22	25	28	42	37
Sundry Expenses	364	960	499	354	325	310	259	337	261	259	227	173	164	154
Net Profit Before Federal Taxes	739[b]	893[b]	1,004	890[b]	486[b]	761[b]	228	614	11	995	1,105	65	417	1,381
(Per cent of Net Sales)	10.4	18.9	11.4	21.7	3.1	38.4	6.1	9.5	.3	14.3	12.2	1.2	6.4	14.9
Less:														
Federal Taxes	...	...	...	...	...	...	...	95	...	282	166	8	81	297
Provision for Contingencies	...	...	...	...	...	...	...	...	...	...	...	...	...	200
Net Profit to Surplus	739[b]	893[b]	1,004	890[b]	486[b]	761[b]	228	519	11	713	939	57	336	884
(Per cent of Sales)	10.4	18.9	11.4	21.7	3.1	38.4	6.1	8.0	.3	10.2	10.4	1.1	5.2	9.5

[a] Includes provision for depreciation reserve of $308,000.
[b] Deficit.
Source: Audited annual reports.

P. Summary of Consolidated Income
1941–1949
(000 omitted)

	1941	1942	1943	1944	1945	1946	1947	1948	1949
Net Operating Profit	$2,378	$3,257	$4,830	$4,693	$1,163[a]	$1,530	$6,802	$8,521	$8,824
Other Income	35	32	34	61	211	27	42	181	170
Gross Income	$2,413	$3,289	$4,864	$4,754	$1,374[a]	$1,557	$6,844	$8,702	$8,994
Other Expenses	332	351	634	573	64	329	508	702	498
Contingency Reserve	900	600	...	...	...	...	468	100	...
Provision for Federal Income Tax	231	1,430	3,525[b]	3,350[b]	8	450	2,500	3,300	3,300
Net Income	$ 950	$ 908	$ 705	$ 831	$1,318[a]	$ 778	$3,368	$4,600	$5,196
Less Income Appropriated for Excess of Replacement Cost over Original Cost of Plant Property	...	...	...	...	...	...	350	500	...
Balance to Surplus	$ 950	$ 908	$ 705	$ 831	$1,318[a]	$ 778	$3,018	$4,100	$5,196

[a] Deficit.
[b] Includes provision for refunds from re-negotiation of war contracts.
Source: Saco-Lowell Shops, Annual reports to stockholders.

APPENDIX 16

REPORT ON PLANT CONSOLIDATION BY DAVID F. EDWARDS, DECEMBER, 1927

Boston, Mass., December 15, 1927

To the Directors,
Gentlemen:

The report on consolidation of the properties of this Company has now been in your hands for almost a week and you are in a position to consider what action the Board should take at its meeting on Friday. It seems in order, therefore, that I should review the findings of the report and state my own opinions, for such value as they may have, as to the course I think we should follow.

In the first place, it seems unmistakably clear, from the careful study that has been made, that consolidation in some form is advisable. The cost will not be prohibitive considered in relation to the savings to be realized which will be large, even larger in my judgment than the figures given in the report. Mr. Kettley, working from an operating point of view, has reached the definite conclusion that Plans 4 and 7 offer the best method of consolidation and in the main I concur in his opinion with some reservations and modifications as to Plan 4.

At the outset, I should like to emphasize strongly the point that all calculations as to savings have been based on the volume of business actually done during the first nine months of this year and not on any expected volume later on. If we can assume, as seems reasonable, that the volume during the first nine months of this year has been abnormally small and that any moderate increase will bring increased savings, then the estimates as to the savings and advantages of consolidation are clearly conservative. Moreover, they do not include any intangible savings which always result from steadier work, in larger volume, in fewer plants, with consequent betterment in the tone and efficiency of operation.

Plan 7, which calls for the consolidation of the Springfield Plant of the Metallic Drawing Roll Company, into our Newton Plant, seems to require little discussion. The work of the Metallic Plant is very similar to that now done in Newton; the Newton Plant already takes approximately 75% of Metallic's output; the cost of this consolidation is moderate — about $11,000., and the annual estimated savings are considerable — about $19,000. It would seem, therefore, that this Plan should be approved and carried into effect as soon as possible.

The stock of the Metallic Drawing Roll Co. is carried on our books at $68,550. In the event of consolidation we can continue to maintain the corporate identity of Metallic and continue to carry its stock in our securities account, or we can liquidate the Company, add to our own asset accounts such values as seem justified and charge the difference between these values and the investment we now have in Metallic to Surplus or to Reserve against Securities. This is largely an accounting question and though somewhat awkward, does not seem of enough importance to stand in the way of the consolidation proposed when the operating advantages and economies are so clear and substantial.

It has sometimes been said also that our competitors and the trade, as a whole, would be more likely to buy Metallic's product from an independent company than from Saco-Lowell Shops. I believe it is pretty generally known that Saco-Lowell Shops owns Metallic Drawing Roll Company, and even where that is not the case, it is likely that purchasers desiring the product of the Metallic Company would buy as freely from Saco-Lowell Shops as from a separate company. Anyhow, as already stated, since we ourselves use approximately 75% of the production of the Springfield Plant, I do not think that we should be influenced greatly by this consideration.

The question of what to do with our worsted business is a puzzling one. The profit and loss record of the last thirty years furnishes little or no justification for continuing it, yet from the standpoint of general policy there are certain very real objections to giving it up. We are the only company in this country making a complete line of Worsted Machinery from Cards to Looms. We make good machinery that gives satisfaction, and the Trade knows it. A large amount of our machinery is installed in the mills today and we have an obligation which we must recognize to service it. Unless we do this, we shall unquestionably undermine in some degree the confidence, not only of the Worsted, but of the Cotton Mills as well, in our reliability as a permanent source of supply for textile machinery. If this should happen at this time, it would be most unfortunate.

Yet to continue the production and sale of repair parts as we are doing today will require almost as much expense and effort as to continue the production of new machinery. Then too, it seems reasonably certain that if we abandon the production of new machinery our business in repair parts will rapidly dwindle and we will be in the position of having made provision and reservation for it at some cost and a few years later will have little to show in the way of return for this cost. We have a large inventory of Bradford and French Worsted material amounting to about $244,000. which would have only slight value if we gave up the business. This inventory and that of Silk Machinery material amounting to another $24,000., must be considered and handled in such a way as to get the most out of it.

The new building in Lowell is a relatively small, compact manufacturing unit, modern in every detail (except for lack of sidetrack facilities) and is just about large enough to house economically a business of around $1,000,000. a year in Worsted and Silk Machinery. At the present time it contains a considerable amount of material for the manufacture of Refrigerator Cabinets, which business must be continued for another four or six months in order to liquidate it in an orderly way. It is probable, therefore, that we shall have to continue making some use of this building until next May or June. If Plan 4 is adopted we should, of course, proceed with all possible energy and dispatch to clear the old Lowell Plant and reach the point where we can close it up and stop as completely as possible all further operating expense. Yet this too must be done in an orderly way and will require perhaps six months for its completion.

It may be also that our undoubted obligation to service our machinery will not prove so difficult as we now think and perhaps can be met in other ways. We must study further our sales of repair parts, find out how many of them, like Caps, Tubes and Spindles, are made by other shops in this country, what ones are imported in considerable quantities, and perhaps work out to a conclusion that after all the job of servicing our machinery on those parts, which cannot be readily obtained from other sources, is simpler and smaller than we thought. Most of the parts in our machinery are interchangeable with parts in the English and French models from which they were copied. In any event, whatever we may do ultimately, it would seem to me unwise either to announce or admit at this time in a rather abrupt way that we had decided finally to go out of the Worsted Machinery business. Even though we should finally decide to do this there should be a tapering off period during which the Trade will gradually make the adjustment and change to other sources of supply on repairs without inconvenience.

Meanwhile, we must also inform ourselves more fully about the new Worsted Spinning Frame which Prince Smith & Sons, our most formidable competitor, has just announced and which embodies a considerable number of new patented features which may or may not be significant improvements and a distinct advance beyond what we, ourselves, are building today. This new "Primus" frame is attracting a good deal of attention and may, after all, be something that we would have to match with a redesign of our own frame in order to compete effectively when and if the business should come back. The cost of redesigning our frame in a rather thoroughgoing way would no doubt be considerable and would have to be very carefully considered before it was undertaken.

Without doubt the Worsted business of this country will some day get back on its feet, make money, and buy new machinery. There are already signs of slight improvement and this improvement may go far within the next few years. The question of the price at which we can sell, in moderate volume, is the "kernel" of the question and as yet we haven't found a way to extract it. We cannot go on indefinitely doing business at a loss, but there is also danger of going astray if we try to chart our course just when the Worsted fog is thickest as it is today. Perhaps we might decide next Spring to continue supplying such repair parts as are necessary to avoid injury to our reputation in the Trade and simply keep our patterns, tools and machinery intact against the day when we will know better what to do with them than we do now.

An investigation, made by Mr. Havey, seems to show that French Worsted can be sold at a profit and also that the outlook in the French Worsted line is more hopeful than for Bradford. We should be able to manufacture at lower cost in the new building than with the layout we now have. If depreciation on buildings, machinery, tools and patterns, which we already own, were ignored we might break even or make a little money at the prices now in effect. The all-important point which we must have a little more time to determine is whether or not we can sell machinery in any quantity at the prices now in effect. These prices, which are still too low, have not been in effect long enough to enable us to reach any conclusion on this point with certainty and I should assuredly not want to undertake to manufacture and sell at any lower prices.

Such being the case, I would suggest that we defer for the present our final decision on the Worsted and Silk business, go right ahead with the execution of the other provisions of Plan 4 as rapidly as possible and continue to supply Worsted repairs for the next four to six months from the old Lowell Plant without any change in the present arrangement of machinery. This will give us opportunity to analyze the Worsted and Silk inventory carefully at the end of the year when our closing inventory is taken and enable us to determine whether it is fairly well balanced or just a haphazard accumulation of materials of doubtful value for further production.

Reference is made in the report to the possibility that it may ultimately be advisable to consolidate Kitson into Newton. In my judgment this possibility deserves careful consideration later on. A long step toward it will be taken if the making of castings for Kitson is consolidated into Newton. When that is done and it must be done as a part of Plan 4, the successive steps toward complete consolidation might be taken easily and naturally, one at a time, making sure that the footing is firm before we put our weight on it and thus gradually and without disturbance of production, complete the absorption of the small but valuable business of Kitson into Newton. If this is done in the right way it should greatly benefit Newton and do no injury to the valuable Kitson business which must be jealously safeguarded.

Of course, I recognize also that the Kitson Machine Shop was set up as a separate corporation with a definite purpose in mind at the time of the reorganization and nothing should be done to disturb or defeat that purpose unless the reasons for so doing are clear and convincing. Even then, of course, it would be a matter of action by the Board and satisfactory adjustment of existing undertakings with the parties interested. Plan 4, however, contemplates doing nothing more at this time than changing Kitson's source of supply on castings from Lowell Foundry to Newton. At present the castings are made in the Lowell Foundry, loaded onto trucks and hauled to the Kitson Plant, a distance of about a quarter of a mile. The operation would be exactly the same in obtaining castings from Newton except for the much longer haul between Plants. The loading, unloading, and handling, however, would be exactly the same. The interlocking of operations and management under the proposed arrangement would be no greater than it is now. I can foresee a very strong likelihood that the reasons in favor of complete consolidation of Kitson into Newton ultimately, in order to give Newton a larger and steadier volume of business and effect substantial operating economies, may take on compelling force. However, I do not want the Board to get the impression from this statement that hasty or ill-considered action of any kind that might kill or even cripple slightly the Kitson goose that is laying our golden eggs today, is contemplated.

It seems clear from the report that to do a thoroughgoing job of consolidation, one that looks well ahead into the future, and will accomplish the maximum result in the way of savings, we must either move the Biddeford operations to Lowell and abandon the Biddeford Plant entirely, or close the old Lowell Plant (almost identical in floor area with the Biddeford Plant) and consolidate its operations into Biddeford, Newton and possibly into the new building in Lowell. For months, while the investigation was in progress, my opinion as to which of these two plans was the better was balanced on a knife edge. The way in which reasons for were matched and offset by reasons against each plan was most baffling until the returns were all in and the votes, that is the costs and savings, were finally counted and tabulated. Mr. Kettley had much the same experience and I refrained from trying to influence his conclusions, preferring that he should reach them in his own way. It is fair to say, also, I think that each of us approached the problem independently with absolutely impartial and unbiased minds.

Plan 4, as stated in the report, is as follows:

Close that part of Lowell Plant south of Dutton Street (including Foundry).

Transfer manufacture of Worsted and Silk Machinery and repair parts to new buildings north of Dutton Street, thus making a compact unit.

Continue manufacture of Flyers and Drop Forge parts in new buildings north of Dutton Street, as heretofore.

Transfer manufacture of Heavy Twisters, Spoolers, and past model Cotton repair parts to Biddeford.

Transfer manufacture of Warpers and Slashers to Newton.

Newton to furnish Kitson Plant and Worsted department remaining in Lowell with castings.

The estimated cost of Plan 4 is $384,000. and the estimated savings based on the actual business done in the first nine months of this year are $287,000. annually. Knowing something of the conservative methods used in calculating the savings, I think that chances are strongly in favor of the savings being $300,000. or more per year.

Plan 3 is stated in the report as follows:

Close the entire Biddeford Plant.

Transfer all Biddeford products to Lowell.

Lowell to supply Kitson with castings, as heretofore.

The cost of this plan is estimated at $200,000. and the annual saving at $184,000.

The estimated expenditure for Plan 4 is $184,000. greater and the annual saving is $103,000. greater than for Plan 3. The figure for savings includes nothing for tax-exemption. The estimated amount to be realized from liquidation of the surplus machine tools under Plan 3 is $45,000. greater than under Plan 4, but this figure is at best only a very rough guess and not much importance can be attached to it. These differences in costs and savings between the two plans call for comment.

I felt that the calculations with respect to the various plans should be carried through to a point where we were sure of having a thoroughly satisfactory, permanent and economical manufacturing setup. With this in mind, I asked Mr. Kettley to go to whatever length seemed reasonable and sensible in calculating the cost of desirable changes and improvements in existing plant layout and equipment. By following this method, I felt that we would know the worst as to costs and the best as to savings. This has been done for both Plans 3 and 4, but the detail of the cost of changes and improvements has been set up in such a way as to permit of review and separate consideration of each of the major items with the idea that all of the suggested changes and improvements need not be made at this time.

At first thought, it may seem unwise to advocate the adoption of the most costly of the several plans presented. It might be said that we are forgetting that we are trying to contract and not expand our manufacturing facilities. Moreover, in times like these it is particularly necessary to conserve liquid resources and maintain a strong war chest of cash in order to withstand the siege of abnormally depressed business and hold out successfully until relief comes. I appreciate fully the force of these arguments, but would like to go farther and see just how much force they really have as applied to our consideration of Plan 4 versus Plan 3.

Any worthwhile plan of consolidation necessitates a certain amount of taking apart and putting together again of our facilities. We can't "make an omelet without breaking some eggs" and we can't consolidate without spending some money. The real question is the value of the results obtained considered in relation to the expenditures to be made, the whole consideration being projected far enough ahead to give us a reasonably permanent and efficient operating arrangement in our plants, thus safeguarding our earning power for the future when better business, which we confidently expect, has come.

The Spinning, Roving and Twisters, made in our Biddeford Plant, and the large and valuable repair business that goes with them, will probably make up fully half of our total business during the next five or ten years. When the successful mills start making their long-deferred replacements of obsolete and worn-out machinery, Spinning will be by long odds the biggest single item they will buy. The machinery manufacturers, who expect to do a large volume of business during the next five or ten years and take full advantage of improved demand for machinery, must be in a position to build and sell a large amount of Spinning. This consideration must play an important part in all our planning for the future.

Plan 3 would move the production of this most important part of our business into the Lowell Plant, crowding it in more or less, without displacing to any great extent the considerable amount of equipment now set up in the Lowell Plant for the production of Worsted. The Lowell Plant is rather badly laid out for economical manufacture. This condition, however, is fundamental and little could be done to remedy it without excessive cost for rebuilding that would not be justified. The new building in itself is a splendid unit, its only drawback being the lack of a siding, but it is so separated and distinct from the rest of the Lowell Plant that its operation as a part of that plant with a flow of material back and forth is awkward and expensive. If we moved Biddeford to Lowell, we would have an arrangement that would work but it would be greatly inferior to what can be accomplished at Biddeford and would provide less margin of capacity for Spinning, Roving and Twisters, the sale of which in large volume, must ultimately be our salvation.

There is some opinion in our organization to support the idea that if Worsted is retained, it should be combined and intermingled with the manufacture of Cotton Machinery in the same plant. The argument of course is that it helps to carry the overhead and in periods when there is no Worsted business the organization will work on Cotton Machinery. Without going into a detailed discussion of this interesting operating question, I would simply point out that in my own opinion and in the opinion of others experienced in manufacturing operations, there is grave doubt as to whether the presence of Worsted in a plant intended primarily to build Cotton Machinery is advisable. The interference it causes and the cost of reserving and maintaining capacity and some specialized personnel to take care of Worsted probably adds to the total plant overhead and therefore to the cost of the Cotton Machinery, which is the bread and butter product, more burden expense than is absorbed on the small Worsted production turned out. Then too, if the Worsted product must be sold at a very low price in relation to costs, there is always the temptation to go even lower in price because we have the capacity reserved, and it seems superficially that overhead is saved and that the Cotton Machinery production will more or less carry the low price Worsted. This is the kind of a question that can be debated without end because it is not susceptible of accurate accounting determination from the very meagre cost records we possess and even if we had more complete cost records, it would still be very difficult to disentangle all of the considerations affecting the Worsted costs and set them apart clearly by themselves.

Having all this in mind, and also the fact that we may eventually decide to give up Worsted entirely, I am strongly of the opinion that if we finally decide to give Worsted another trial for a time, we should put it in the new building by itself, under the spotlight, so to speak; scale operating expenses to the irreducible minimum, make it stand on its own feet, keep it under very close scrutiny and control, and abide by the result. To throw Biddeford's large and valuable production into Lowell along with Worsted, as it is now set up, would involve, in my judgment, a real sacrifice in our ability to build good Spinning in large quantities at low cost and that is a sacrifice that I don't think we are justified in making for any advantage that the retention of Worsted seems to promise at this time. If we decided ultimately to abandon Worsted after we had mixed it up with Cotton Machinery production, that would mean another convulsion in our operating scheme, which would be unfortunate.

All the improvements to the Biddeford Plant indicated in Plan 4, are desirable and from an operating point of view only can be justified, but I am very sensitive to any large drain on our cash resources at this time and after checking through the detail of the improvement program, I believe that the cost of Plan 4 should be scaled down to $300,000. at least for the present. This would mean cutting out the foundry mono-rail, yard storage bins, and scale car, new sand shed, re-locating siding and air compressors, and changes in buildings No. 13 and No. 14. All other foundry improvements would be retained, together with the re-arrangement of the machine shops and storage space, the latter giving us, among other things, much better inventory control which is badly needed.

The omission of the changes and improvements enumerated will reduce somewhat the estimates of savings, but I am convinced that these would still be easily in excess of $250,000. per year, which would mean that the revised cost of Plan 4 would be amortized from operating savings alone within a period of fifteen months. Furthermore, the operating condition at Biddeford would be much improved, full advantage would be taken of the excellent manufacturing layout possible in the big building, only imperfectly used at present, and the most serious weaknesses in the foundry would be corrected. If we don't make these improvements now we will pay for them just the same in avoidable operating losses in the course of a few years and have nothing to show for the outlay. Before work on the proposed changes and improvements is started, each item would again be considered carefully, an appropriation set up for it, and every effort made to control the actual expenditure and keep it within the amount authorized.

The equipment moved from Lowell should be placed permanently to the best advantage in the new location and nothing should be done that would have to be undone later if we should decide to go ahead with the rest of the improvements. When the job was finished we would have a plant in Biddeford distinctly superior in point of economical operating efficiency to anything we could get in Lowell under Plan 3 and would have much greater capacity for building Spinning, Roving and Twisters of excellent quality in large volume, at low cost, and be in a position to take the fullest advantage of any considerable increase in business. Please bear in mind again, however, that all estimates of savings have been based on the actual volume of business done during the first nine months of this year and not on expectations and hopes of larger business later.

In the report reference is made to the action on tax abatement taken by the Board of Aldermen and Common Council of the City of Biddeford on November 14th. The order passed at that time gave us exemption from taxes for five years, but contained the qualifying clause, "or until such time within said five year period said corporation may be in a position to pay its tax."

Realizing that this order was not legally binding and that its force was further weakened by the qualification quoted, I went to Biddeford last week and had a very frank talk with a group of men, including the Mayor, City Treasurer, City Clerk, leading members of the Board of Aldermen and Common Council, the President of the Chamber of Commerce, President of the First National Bank, and other prominent citizens. The gist of my statements briefly, was that they, as well as we, knew that the order for tax abatement had no real legal validity and was weakened by the reservation regarding ability to pay. I told them that the decision we had to make was a close one, (at the time I had reached no final opinion on the matter myself), and that the case for Biddeford would be much stronger if the order could be amended so as to omit the qualification mentioned, and furthermore that I wanted to be sure that the whole matter was clearly understood by the people of Biddeford; that they were genuinely and wholeheartedly for it and that the order registered the overwhelming sentiment of the whole community and was a pledge behind which public opinion in every class of the population stood solidly.

I also made it very clear that we were making no commitments whatever as to the quantity of equipment that would be moved from Lowell or as to the effect this would have on the Biddeford payroll. These matters were to be governed entirely by our own operating requirements and nothing else. I suggested also that letters and resolutions from the Chamber of Commerce, other groups and from leading citizens, stating their belief in the certainty of the scrupulous observance of the order and pledging their support to its enforcement would be significant to us.

There has been a rather amazing response to these suggestions. The Board of Aldermen and Common Council at their regular meeting last Monday night voted unanimously the following amended order:

> Ordered, That the City of Biddeford grant an exemption of taxes to the Saco-Lowell Shops for a period of five years, said exemption to commence in 1928, provided however, that in working out its consolidation plans the said Saco-Lowell Shops shall move to Biddeford and operate such part of the equipment of its Lowell Plant as it may find advisable from the standpoint of its operating requirements.

In addition, I have a sheaf of about forty letters and resolutions from all sort of organizations, business houses, banks and individuals, pledging their support and stating their conviction that the order will be scrupulously lived up to. As a sample, I quote the resolution of the Chamber of Commerce, a very large, active and representative organization.

Moved by Mr. James P. Rundle, and seconded by Rev. J. A. Laflamme, that the Board of Directors of the Biddeford Chamber of Commerce, Inc. representing a membership of over 600, comprising local representative citizens, believing that the welfare of the city is largely dependent upon the retention of the Saco-Lowell Shops in the city and that this fact is recognized by all of the citizenship, therefore, it unanimously and most heartily endorses the action of the City Government in exempting the Saco-Lowell Shops from taxation for a term of five years without restriction, and further, *pledges the officials of said Company its individual and organized support in the fulfillment of this agreement* on the part of the City. Unanimously Carried.

In five other cases (though all of them were very small of course as compared with ours), the City of Biddeford has voted tax exemption for ten years and in each case the exemption has been fulfilled to the letter. One of these covered a new building in our own plant costing around $900,000., and the other additions to the plant of the Pepperell Co. The City's record on the matter to date, therefore, is perfectly clear.

For my own part, after very close personal contact with the situation and though I recognize clearly that the order for abatement, legally speaking, is only a "gentlemen's agreement," I am convinced that the observance of the exemption is a practical certainty and that we may safely rely on it in making our plans. It is without doubt a very real additional argument in favor of the move to Biddeford, involving as it does an average saving in taxes of $48,000. a year for a period of five years, or a total of $240,000., which is 80% of the total modified cost of Plan 4. In other words, the City of Biddeford would be paying 4/5s of the cost of consolidation under Plan 4, and when it is finished we will have a much better operating setup in Biddeford than we have today. Yet this saving from tax abatement has not been included in our estimate of operating savings of $250,000. per year. If it is included the total is increased to about $300,000. or the full amount of the modified cost of Plan 4.

This is a fair statement of the case, I think, because our taxes in Biddeford today are moderate and much lower than in our other locations. Lowell has offered to reduce our assessment on the old Lowell Plant at least for one year to an amount which would make our tax on that Plant no greater than we are now paying at Biddeford. The City Officials expressed the opinion that this reduced assessment would probably continue for some years, but were quite explicit in saying that they can offer no assurance beyond 1928. Of course the question will naturally be raised as to what will happen when the exemption in Biddeford expires. My attention has been called to the assessments levied in other cases where the exemptions have expired and they seem to be reasonable and moderate. It is my own belief that we need not be greatly concerned over what may happen at the end of five years.

Adoption of Plan 4 would also, in my judgment, be the safest course because it would involve less disturbance in our present operating scheme, less threat to the quality of our most complicated and important product, and greater assurance of lower costs for years to come, particularly on Spinning, Roving and Twisters, and their repairs, which should make up fully half our total volume. Labor rates in Biddeford are considerably lower than in Lowell, being 4% less on direct machine shop labor and 10% less on general foundry labor. This is a substantial differential in cost that will go on year after year and have a real effect on our earnings. Lowell is a larger labor market than Biddeford though Biddeford and Saco together have a population of 23,000, much more than a village. Labor in Biddeford also is very stable and the turnover in our payroll is very small. The following figures for the Biddeford Plant are of interest:

Percent of Employees on Payroll	5 years or longer,	72%
" " " " "	10 " " "	50%
" " " " "	15 " " "	32%
Percent of Employees living in their own homes or in homes owned by members of their families		40%

It would probably require a year or two at least to create and train a working force for building Biddeford's products in Lowell equal in point of specialized skill, experience, quality sense, and reliability to that we now have in Biddeford. Having once been through the experience of moving a metal working plant, building a complicated product, from one location to another and recruiting a new labor force, I have a very real appreciation of the importance of the labor consideration.

Another late development subsequent to the completion of Mr. Kettley's report was a message from Mr. Coolidge, Assistant Treasurer, of the Pepperell Mfg. Co., to the effect that we can, so far as they are concerned, fill in Jordan Creek, a short by-pass from one point in the Saco River to another, which runs through the heart of our property and on the flowage rights of which Pepperell has a lease, having nine years still to run. Mr. Coolidge said the matter was one on which his Trustees would have to act, but that he felt so confident of their favorable action that we can virtually consider the matter settled. To fill in this Creek was regarded some years ago as a very desirable thing to do.

Calculations made within the last few days indicate that filling this Creek would reclaim valuable land area amounting to about 23,500 square feet. The refuse from the foundry and boilers could be dumped in the Creek bed with a saving in hauling expense we now pay for the amount required to make the fill, of about $9,000. The cost for concrete retaining walls and for re-locating sewers would be about $2,600. showing a saving in operating expense of around $6,400. when the job was finished, in addition to which we would have the reclaimed land and greater freedom of general movement in the heart of the plant. This voluntary offer on the part of Pepperell was a cordial and friendly action and may yet be of considerable value to us.

Mr. Kettley has stated quite fully and impartially the arguments for and against the various plans and they need not be repeated here. This memorandum, already much longer than I intended, is meant simply to amplify and emphasize the reasons for adopting Plans 4 and 7 with modifications as suggested.

My recommendations are—

1—That Plan 4 be approved, with the understanding:

A. That Worsted and Silk production will not be moved

to the new building in Lowell until the other provisions of the plan have been executed and we are ready to close up the old Lowell Plant, thus giving ourselves more time in which to reach a final decision on Worsted and Silk production.

B. That nothing shall be done to disturb the operation of the Kitson Plant beyond shifting its source of supply on castings from Lowell to Newton, without further approving action by the Board.

C. That the cost of executing Plan 4 shall not exceed $300,000. and that the expenditure of this amount, besides effecting consolidation, will result in a much improved operating condition at Biddeford that will permit of making the further suggested improvements later if desired without disturbing or undoing any significant portion of the work covered by the $300,000. which expenditure it is expected, will show operating savings of at least $250,000. per year.

2 — That Plan 7, calling for the consolidation of the operations of Metallic Drawing Roll Co. into the Newton Plant be carried into effect as soon as practicable.

It is understood, of course, that the program of consolidation approved by the Board will be made effective in an orderly and well-planned way as rapidly as possible, having regard on the one hand for the need of avoiding undue disturbance to current operations and on the other for the importance of realizing quickly the large savings which should result from consolidation.

Yours very truly,

[signed] David F. Edwards

President.

APPENDIX 17

EXTRACTS FROM ANNUAL REPORTS TO THE STOCKHOLDERS BY DAVID F. EDWARDS, 1930–1948

March, 1930

The profit for 1929 was substantial, but in considering its significance for the future, certain fundamental characteristics of this business must be kept clearly in mind. The buying of textile machinery fluctuates very widely from one year to another. This is true to a considerable extent, even in periods when the cotton textile industry as a whole is not depressed, as it is today. It is not uncommon for the fluctuations in sales volume to range from 35% to 100% of capacity within any one year and also from one year to another.

These wide fluctuations are largely caused by the accidental grouping of occasional large orders. The very nature of the Company's business is such that it cannot be uniform and sustained in volume. Its market is definitely limited to cotton mills, and the average size of its orders is quite large in relation to its total sales volume. It is not unusual for a dozen large orders to make up half, or two-thirds, of its annual sales of new machinery.

. . . .

Moreover, it is not possible in this business to contract and expand expenditures for wages and salaries in as close conformity with the fluctuations in production and sales as is possible in many other lines of business. The range and variety of machines composing the Company's line presents a technical problem of large proportions and great complexity, and this in turn demands that the Company maintain a large group of thoroughly trained, experienced men in its selling, engineering and manufacturing organizations, who are specialists in handling this highly specialized technical business, with its frequent, sudden changes in volume. . . .

All this simply means that if a business of this character is to remain sound, develop and improve its product in a progressive way, and show a moderate profit over a period of years, the earnings of the occasional good years must be large enough to offset, with some margin to spare, the lack of profit or actual losses in the poor years, of which there are sure to be some. This explanation has been made at some length to aid the stockholders in forming a correct opinion as to the significance of the operating results for last year and to forestall any unduly optimistic conclusions that might be drawn from those results.

The cotton textile industry is still in a very demoralized and depressed condition. In fact, the condition today in certain respects, is perhaps worse than it has ever been. On the other hand, there is also a far more general understanding and conviction than ever before throughout the industry that permanent, sustained curtailment of excessive working hours will correct the evil of over-production and restore the industry to a normal condition. Price demoralization, resulting from over-production, caused by excessive working hours, has grown so bad that the instinct for self-preservation has been aroused as never before in the industry. The remedy for this condition, namely, effective permanent reduction of working hours to a sound basis, will be applied sooner or later, and when it is applied, the condition of the industry will steadily improve, and so will the demand for new machinery to make long overdue replacements of great quantities of worn-out and obsolete equipment.

March, 1931

For the year 1930 your Company showed a loss, after all charges, of $890,340.26. . . .

This large loss was caused by an unprecedented slump in the volume of sales which necessitated the most drastic curtailment of operations. During the first four months of the year production was at the rate of about 50% of capacity. During the last eight months of the year production averaged about 25% of capacity. With this savage curtailment in volume, it was inevitable that substantial operating losses should occur.

The market for your company's products is limited practically to cotton mills. The year 1930 marked the culmination of a period of about seven years of steadily declining earnings in the cotton mill industry. The acute and widespread depression in general business, which developed last year, was superimposed on an already deplorable condition of excessive over-production and price demoralization, which had prevailed in the cotton textile industry for years past, with ruinous consequences to earnings and to the ability of the mills to make necessary purchases of new machinery for replacement of worn-out equipment.

The disastrous conditions of last year were especially aggravated and intensified by the extreme and prolonged decline in the price of cotton which necessitated heavy write-downs in inventory values in addition to the losses resulting from greatly reduced volume of sales at excessively low prices. The combination of all these adverse factors in the cotton textile industry virtually paralyzed the buying of new machinery and reduced even the buying of repair parts, the most stable part of the machinery business, far below normal volume.

Many cotton mills have found their working capital so greatly reduced by the losses of the past year, more particularly the losses on cotton, that they feel they must wait until there is some real and sustained improvement in the cotton textile business and some restoration of earning power before they can commit themselves for purchases of new machinery. Improvement in the machinery business usually lags six months or more behind improvement in the cotton textile industry. It is not likely, therefore, that there will be any considerable improvement in the sale of new machinery before early Autumn and then only if there has developed, in the meantime, some improvement in the cotton textile business which gives promise of being sustained and permanent.

March, 1932

The sales volume for the year was only 31% of full capacity. In fact, both the physical and dollar volume of sales were the lowest since 1914.

. . . .

This brutal hammering down of our sales volume to pre-war levels has made it absolutely necessary to devise and enforce the most drastic operating economies, and to consolidate still further the company's manufacturing operations in order to realize the fullest measure of economy. In December, after thorough consideration of the plans and recommendations submitted by the management, the Directors voted unanimously to consolidate the operations of the plant in Newton Upper Falls into Biddeford and Saco, Maine.

. . . .

In connection with this final consolidation of the company's operations into one location, it is pertinent to review briefly the extent to which the plant capacity for manufacturing preparatory and spinning machinery of the kind made by this company has been liquidated and consolidated in recent years. In 1920 there were nine well-known establishments, each of which had started as an independent company, actively engaged in the production of the kinds of cotton machinery which this company makes. Today there are only three plants left. Liquidation and consolidation, made imperative by continued operating losses, have removed the other six. . . . The mortality in the cotton textile industry during the last decade has been great, but the mortality in the business of making preparatory and spinning machinery, which is wholly dependent on the cotton textile industry, has been greater still.

March, 1933

The annual report of last year contained the statement that the volume of sales in 1931 was the lowest, both in physical and dollar volume, since 1914. At the time this statement was made, it did not seem possible that a further heavy shrinkage in sales volume could occur. However, that is exactly what has happened. Our sales volume in 1932 was only about 54%, or a little more than one-half, of that in 1931, and yet the company was able to secure its share of such orders as were placed for the products that it makes.

. . . .

In view of the chaotic and catastrophic conditions existing today, it would be futile and foolish to attempt to define the outlook and predict results for the current year. At present the mills, with few exceptions, are buying practically no new machinery. Their purchases are limited largely to what they must have to keep their active machinery running. Repair parts are bought from hand to mouth and in quantities barely sufficient to meet the day-to-day needs and prevent break-downs in operating schedules. Under the conditions now prevailing, which have largely stopped forward-looking action for the future, the machinery builder gets only that negligible part of the mill's dollar which is left after all other acute current needs for working capital have been met. The steel industry, machine tool business, and in fact practically all companies making equipment the purchase price of which would be classified as capital expenditure, find their markets paralyzed for the time being and unresponsive to selling effort.

But these conditions, incredibly bad as they are, can change quickly if sustained constructive developments should occur. During the late Spring and early Summer of last year many mills were virtually shut down and most of the others were running on greatly reduced schedules. The buying of products, made by the machinery builders, was virtually non-existent as it is today. About mid-summer, however, the price of cotton began to advance. The demand for cotton textiles showed marked improvement and soon the volume of inquiry regarding new machinery and orders for repair parts swelled from a trickle to a steady stream. This spurt was short-lived because the price of cotton quickly slumped again and sagged down to its previous low levels. The response of our market to this temporary improvement, however, showed clearly and convincingly the strength of the pent-up demand and the acute need for new and better machinery and repair parts.

March, 1934

In the Annual Report of last year the statement was made that "many well-informed observers believe that the cotton textile industry will be one of the first to recover and regain some measure of earning power." This opinion seems to have been justified by subsequent developments to date. Inquiries regarding new machinery from our customers became active during June, and in July we began booking orders for substantial quantities of new machinery.

The Code for the cotton textile industry seems to have provided a specific and effective remedy for the ills of that industry which had been caused largely by chronic over-production and the consequent suicidal price-cutting which had kept the mills in a condition of ruinous demoralization for years past. This demoralization has been corrected to a large extent and there is much evidence to support the belief that the cotton textile industry, operating under its Code as now set up, is on a more solid foundation of orderly production and distribution which, if it proves permanent, should enable the well-equipped and ably-managed mills to continue profitable operations. . . .

The year 1923 was the last year in which the cotton mills took anything like their normal replacement requirements of new machinery. For ten years thereafter our customers, in the main, were compelled to defer much needed replacements of worn-out and obsolete machinery because of declining earnings, which in many cases eventuated in heavy losses. As a result, there is a large pent-up and long over-due demand for replacements. If a substantial proportion of the mills can continue to make moderate earnings, they should continue to be actively interested in the purchase of new machinery.

March, 1935

During the first half of the year buying of new machinery was active and the Company was able to operate in good volume and build up a substantial back-log of orders. After mid-Summer, however, the intake of new business began to decline, practically stopped during the general textile strike in September, and has been very small since then. The Company was able to operate in fair, but steadily diminishing volume during the second half of the year only because of the momentum and orders accumulated during the first half.

Just now the cotton textile industry is in a badly depressed condition. Over-production with its consequent demoralization of prices, is widespread in many sections of the industry. On numerous types of fabrics prices have been driven down to ruinously low levels. Japanese competition is causing increasing concern and discussion. The possibility of further labor disturbances is an unfavorable factor in the minds of some mill executives. There seems to be a strong and widely held conviction that the processing tax on cotton is exerting a harmful influence on cotton mill operations and should be repealed. The National Industrial Recovery Act expires on June 16th next and there is doubt and difference of opinion as to what may happen to the Code under which the industry is now operating. These factors, and others not so specifically related to the cotton textile industry but affecting economic conditions throughout the country as a whole, have created so much uncertainty and lack of confidence that buying of new cotton mill machinery has again fallen to very low levels.

In previous annual reports the statement has been made repeatedly that the industry's need for new machinery is acute and that the volume of new machinery that should be bought is tremendous. The force of this statement increases with each year that passes. More and more the standard of competitive performance essential to successful operation is being set by the well-equipped mills. Of the approximately 30,000,000 spindles in place in the cotton mills of the country (about 5,000,000 of which are now inactive) certainly one-half are obsolete in design, largely worn out, and the urgent need to replace them grows more imperative year by year.

March, 1936

The annual report of last year stated that at the time the report was issued the cotton textile industry was again in a badly depressed condition and gave some of the reasons therefor. This condition continued until late Summer of last year, at which time some signs of improvement began to appear. By early Autumn moderate improvement was under way and conditions today are somewhat better than they were a year ago. Notwithstanding this improvement, however, the cotton mills, with few exceptions, showed losses for the year. A good many mills that had been able to operate at some profit in previous bad years found their volume so fluctuating and their prices so low last year that they were unable to escape losses. As always happens, your company suffered along with its customers, the cotton mills.

Reference is made each year in these reports to the number and condition of the spindles active and in place in the cotton textile industry. This repetition is justified by the important bearing these figures have on the outlook for the sale of new cotton mill machinery. During 1935 the number of spindles in place was again reduced, this time by over 1,500,000, and stood on December 31st (the last month for which final figures are now available) at about 29,250,000, as compared with a peak in spindlage in place in 1925 of about 37,900,000, a reduction during the ten year period of 8,650,000 spindles. In appraising the significance of this reduction in spindles, however, it must be understood that today the industry is operating quite generally on two shifts of 40 hours each, whereas twenty years ago, or prior to the entrance of the United States into the World War, operation on a single shift was the prevailing practice throughout the industry.

March, 1937

As indicated by the earnings of almost a million dollars before Federal taxes applicable to income, your company's volume of business in 1936 showed marked improvement over the previous year. The value of shipments was 75% greater than in 1935 in which year the company just about broke even. This improvement has been sustained during the current year to date and at the time this statement is issued the volume of unfilled orders on the books is over 75% greater than at the corresponding time last year. The cotton mills which are the company's customers are in most instances operating in good volume and at a fair margin of profit. Accordingly, they are interested in the decisive advantages of new machinery and are able to purchase it. As has been stated repeatedly in previous annual reports there is a substantial accumulated volume of business long held back by the inability of the cotton mills generally to show sustained earnings. This pent-up demand for new machinery, if released at a moderate rate through continuation of improved earnings by the cotton mills, would provide a good volume of business for the textile machinery builders.

February, 1938

You are all familiar with the sharp decline in general business in this country, which began late last summer. This decline has been particularly acute in the cotton textile industry, which is the market for your Company's products. From a high point in August, 1937, your Company's volume of unfilled business has steadily diminished. At the present time only a negligible volume of new business is being booked. In consequence your Company has been forced to curtail its operations drastically. At the time this report is issued it is not possible to make a reliable forecast as to how soon improvement may be expected.

Notwithstanding the current stagnation of business, your Company is able to face the future with confidence and a feeling of security made possible by the completion of its Reorganization Plan, which greatly reduced its debt and strengthened its financial position.

February, 1939

For the fiscal period ended November 30, 1938, . . . the net profit, after all charges, was $634,433.09. This heavy shrinkage in earnings was due to the fact that the volume of sales in 1938 was only a little more than one-half of the sales volume in 1937. This experience is typical of the violent fluctuations in sales volume which are characteristic of this business and which follow closely the fluctuations in the earnings of the cotton mills, our customers.

The year 1938 was a very poor year indeed in the cotton mill business. The great majority of mills showed operating losses, which in many instances were quite large. During the first half of the year buying of cotton products was stagnant and at low ebb. In consequence, prices were at ruinous levels. About the middle of the Summer the volume of buying began to show some improvement, but because of large inventories, prices did not respond and move upward as they should have done. However, the improvement in volume has been sustained fairly well to date and a more hopeful outlook prevails in the cotton textile industry at the present time. Nevertheless, there must be additional and considerable improvement in prices of cotton products before the mills can recover the earning power necessary for a real and sustained improvement in the demand for textile machinery. Meanwhile your Company is operating about fifty percent of the capacity of its active plants.

The question is frequently asked as to whether or not the cotton textile industry, as a whole, is sloughing off its excess productive capacity and approaching a position where a reasonable balance between normal consuming demand and productive capacity may be expected. In his annual report to stockholders for the year ended June 30, 1938, Mr. Russell H. Leonard, President and Treasurer of the Pepperell Manufacturing Company, comments as follows on this question:

Study of the changes in productive equipment in the industry should encourage the patient shareholder in cotton textile mills. In spite of recent heavy losses, we think that the industry as a whole is fundamentally in a sounder condition than for many years. Conservatively, more than 10 million spindles have been junked in the past decade and the recent depression has given fresh impetus to this movement. Perhaps it may be necessary to discard a few millions more of spindles before productive capacity is reasonably in line with demand, but the period is approaching when this desirable result will have been accomplished. When that shall occur, cotton textiles should, once again, furnish a fairer return to the investor and steadier work to the employee.

When the cotton textile industry has achieved the condition of greater stabilization to which Mr. Leonard refers, the earning power of the cotton mills should be more consistent and sustained and it is reasonable to expect that the business of your company should be benefited.

February, 1940

During the first half of the fiscal year just ended conditions in the cotton textile industry . . . were not good. The number of spindle hours run was rather large, but stocks were also large, buying was on a short range basis, prices were at low levels, and operations generally were not profitable. By early Summer a slight tendency toward improvement began to manifest itself, but this tendency did not become really strong until, first the threat, and then the actual outbreak of war, caused a rise in prices for fabricated cotton products. This advance started a buying movement in cotton goods which quickly gathered momentum and reached very large proportions by the end of the first week in September. The wave of buying, however, began to subside during the latter part of September and by the middle of October current buying was again below the current rate of production for the industry as a whole. It has remained there ever since except for occasional flurries of increased buying which have not been sustained.

. . . .

The question is frequently asked as to what effect the widespread use of rayon is having on the cotton textile industry as a market for your Company's products. [Quotations from *Rayon Organon* and U. S. Census surveys given showing comparative rayon and cotton consumption and spindlage in the United States.]

The conclusion to be drawn from this very brief survey is that rayon has become an important fiber in the textile industry. But it does not appear to have reduced appreciably the quantity of cotton actually consumed before rayon became important . . . although undoubtedly the industry would have consumed even more cotton if rayon had not displaced cotton to some extent. Moreover, it should be noted that since 1920 there has been a noticeable tendency toward a somewhat lower (i.e. coarser) average count of yarn spun and a consequent larger quantity of cotton consumed per spindle hour run for the industry as a whole. Final figures for spindle hours run in the year 1939 are not available at the time this report goes to press, but the forecast (with only December's figures lacking) would indicate that these 1939 figures will be not far below the figures for 1937, which were the highest in the last ten years, though not as high as in some years prior to 1939.

In short, having regard only for the experience to date and avoiding any hint of prophecy for the future, the cotton textile industry seems to be consuming about as much cotton and running not far from as many spindle hours as it ever did, although cotton consumption and spindle hours run would unquestionably be somewhat greater if rayon had not been introduced as a competing fiber. As already stated, the use of continuous filament rayon, which is over three-quarters of the total poundage of rayon produced, does not require the use of preparatory and spinning machinery of the kind your Company makes. To the extent, however, that stapled or cut rayon is used, and the use of this stapled fiber has increased very rapidly in the last five years, as is indicated by the figures previously given, the market for the products of your Company has not been adversely affected to any significant extent.

February, 1941

Activity in the cotton textile industry of the United States . . . was in large volume during the year just ended. . . . Notwithstanding the large volume of productive activity indicated by these figures, however, there was during 1940 no general and widespread advance in prices or wages in the cotton textile industry.

. . . .

In other words, what this means is that the cotton textile industry, the market for your Company's products, is still sober, stable, and free from inflation in either prices or costs. When our customers buy machinery they buy for the same reasons and are governed by the same considerations as those which prevailed last year and the year before. They must buy at a fair price and show a return on their investment when they sell their own products in a competitive market. In short, there is no run-away demand for textile machinery at sharp advances in price and there is not likely to be. Rumors to this effect have circulated occasionally, but they were without foundation in fact.

The year just ended has been an excellent one judged by the standards of modest profits which prevail in this industry. It can also be said with a fair degree of certainty that the sales outlook for the current year is encouraging and the business on order and in immediate prospect would seem to give reasonable assurance of operations in satisfactory volume throughout the first half of the current year. Whenever your Company has an exceptionally good year, however, it is wise to emphasize the inescapable fact that this business is inherently one of widely fluctuating volume and correspondingly fluctuating profits.

February, 1942

The year just closed was one of exceptionally large volume. In fact, the volume was just about double that of 1938, which comparison illustrates one of the basic characteristics of this business that must never be lost sight of, namely, its highly fluctuating character. The stimulus of the rapidly developing Defense Program caused a steady expansion in the operations of the cotton textile industry and this, in turn, caused a steady increase in the demand for textile machinery during 1941. A marked increase in orders from South America also occurred.

Although your Company closed the year with a large volume of unfilled orders on its books, there is no certainty as to how many of these orders can be manufactured and shipped because of the acute shortage of critical materials, chiefly iron and steel, which are now strictly controlled by priorities. A considerable, but fluctuating, percentage of our orders carry priorities of some kind. There is ground for reasonable hope that materials can be obtained for these orders. With respect to the remainder that carry no priority, there is great uncertainty as to our ability to fill them because of the shortage of materials. The only new orders that can be accepted today are those which carry priorities high enough to provide a reasonable assurance of our ability to obtain the materials required to manufacture them. In short, the business of your Company today is dominated by the war effort and the controls over essential materials made necessary by that effort.

. . . .

By the end of the current year it is probable that your Company will be producing nothing except textile machinery required for the war effort and covered by allocations and priorities, repair parts for textile machinery, and war work of other kinds, chiefly, ordnance equipment. The manufacture of textile machinery for purely civilian needs is rapidly becoming impossible because of the shortage of materials.

. . . .

The difficulty of obtaining and holding an adequate supply of skilled labor during the past year has been very great and this situation is growing increasingly more difficult all the time. It has been necessary to employ large numbers of new and inexperienced people who must be trained for their jobs. This has added appreciably to our costs of operations, but all commercial metal working plants are having much the same experience. It is merely one of the inevitable and inescapable consequences of the widespread dislocation caused by the tremendous war effort and must be accepted cheerfully and ways and means contrived to deal with it.

During the year just closed two general advances of 10% each have been made in the wages paid to our employees. These advances have greatly increased our costs of production because wages make up so large a part of the total cost of our products. . . . The cost of materials has also advanced considerably during the past year. Notwithstanding these advancing costs of production, the textile machinery industry has been notified that a ceiling will soon be placed on the prices of its products as a part of the general effort now being made by the Office of Price Administration in Washington to stabilize prices and keep them from getting out of hand. This, of course, is something which must be done if the terrible consequences of inflation are to be avoided. It is mentioned because it points clearly to one of the many hazards of operating a manufacturing business in wartime.

February, 1943

The loss of the Company's regular Textile Machinery business has been offset by orders for war products. It is impossible, however, to predict with certainty what the experience with this new business may be. Cancellation, curtailment, or suspension of war orders may occur at any time because of the rapidly changing needs of the Armed Forces, and the displacement of one type of product by another of new and better design. These changes in design and shifts in emphasis on various types of products are inevitable in the war effort, are based on sound principles of strategic control, and must be recognized and accepted as such. They do, however, introduce elements of uncertainty in the future planning of Companies active in the War Program. One substantial contract, held by the Company, was cancelled last October because the product in question had been displaced by other products of new and better design.

The war products your Company is called upon to make are wholly new to our organization and completely different from anything we have made before. What the operating results and profit margins may be on these products only time and experience will tell. Moreover, profits on war contracts are subject to regular review and adjustment by the Price Adjustment Boards of the Armed Services. In spite of these uncertainties and hazards which of necessity must be a part of the all-out war effort, to which the Company is committed, your Directors believe that the Company's operating performance during the critical year of 1943 is likely to be a creditable one.

February, 1944

If the contracts for the particular war products we are making should be cancelled or drastically cut back before the war ends, it isn't likely that they can be replaced immediately by orders for our regular products because, in all likelihood, the production of textile machinery will still be governed and limited by the wartime controls on critical materials. . . . In any event a considerable period of time would elapse before the Company could retool, reorganize its facilities, and get into production in comparable volume on other types of war material. In the meantime, production would be drastically reduced and earnings would be reduced accordingly. . . .

Will wartime controls and restrictions on the manufacture of products for civilian use be continued after the war in Europe ends, and even after Japan is beaten? The best informed opinion seems to be that, with many modifications and progressive relaxation, these controls and restrictions will be continued for some period of time after the war ends. In other words, it is not likely that the Company will be completely free to buy all the material it wants, build up its inventories and expand its manufacture of textile machinery as rapidly as its orders permit when the war is over. . . .

There is every indication now that there will be a strong demand for textile machinery after the war. Many of our customers tell us that they want to buy substantial quantities of machinery as soon as we are able to make and deliver it. In this respect, the Company seems to be in a fortunate position as far as the post-war outlook is concerned, but this statement must be considered in connection with the problem of ceiling prices.

Right now this Company is experiencing no hardship under ceiling prices so far as its over-all operations are concerned. So long as the greater part of its business is on special war products, not subject to ceiling prices, the Company is not suffering and the problem is not immediate and acute. But when the contracts for special war products are cancelled or drastically reduced, this problem of ceiling prices on our regular textile machinery products will become very acute indeed and will remain so until prices can be adjusted to compensate for increased costs.

February, 1945

At the close of 1943 the Company had a large volume of unfilled orders for special war products on its books. Today, with negligible exceptions, these orders have been completed or cancelled. . . .

Civilian demand for textile machinery is very strong indeed. Our customers, both in the United States and in our foreign markets, tell us they want to buy large quantities of machinery as soon as we are able to make and deliver it. . . .

Ceiling prices on textile machinery, established as of October 1, 1941, also remain to be dealt with. Our manufacturing costs have risen steadily during the three years since the ceiling prices were established and today, in most instances, exceed the prices themselves. Profit margins have been wiped out and replaced by loss margins. For the Company to manufacture and sell a large volume of textile machinery, before its ceiling prices have been increased to compensate for increased costs, would have ruinous consequences. Last year the Company suffered no hardship under ceiling prices because large production of special war products, not under ceiling prices, made its over-all earnings satisfactory. Today, the situation is completely changed because the Company's production of special war products has almost entirely disappeared and it is dependent for earning power on its production of textile machinery.

February, 1946

Reference has already been made to the very heavy current demand for textile machinery. This demand comes not only from our customers in the United States, but from all over the world. It will last as long as the existing worldwide shortage of textile products, yarns and fabrics, continues. When the supply of yarns and fabrics in this country and throughout the world overtakes and balances the demand, then normal competitive conditions will gradually re-assert themselves among our customers and soon thereafter the textile machinery plants will also be back on a basis of normal competitive selling and moderate volume.

. . . .

No prediction can be made now as to what may happen to our ceiling prices during 1946. Our production volume is slowly, but steadily, increasing, and the efficiency of operation is beginning to show some improvement. However, long continued strikes in industries which supply us with essential materials would seriously retard or even completely wreck our operating program.

Operating results continue to be unsatisfactory, but are getting better. In short, the difficulties of reconversion will continue to affect our operations at least during the first half of the current year though in a diminishing degree. Earnings will continue unsatisfactory until a reasonable relationship between our greatly increased costs and our prices has been re-established.

February, 1947

As stated already, demand for the company's product is very heavy and it comes from all over the world. As yet, there are no significant indications of a lessening in this demand. The volume of unfilled orders on hand was large at the end of last year and has increased greatly during the year just ended. O.P.A. price controls on textile machinery were removed last April and it is legally possible now to re-establish a fair relationship between costs and prices. However, it should be noted that competition is becoming increasingly active again in the textile industry among our customers, and it is obvious that costs and prices of textile machinery cannot continue to advance as they have during the last few years without soon encountering sharp sales resistance.

Since payrolls take more than half of our sales dollar, it is clear that wages must be stabilized if volume of sales and production, and therefore of employment, is to be maintained. Certainly the company's profit during the last year, as reflected in this report, does not afford any cushion for absorbing increased costs without compensating increases in prices. Without adequate profit, no competitive business can remain strong and capable of providing steady employment at good wages for its employees and a product and service of high merit to its customers.

There is some evidence that new competition is coming into the textile machinery industry both in this country and abroad. The British are reported to have increased their capacity for making textile machinery by taking over, with the help of the Government, certain new war plants. They have also joined with a native group to establish a plant near Bombay, India. The British, whose level of wages today is less than half our own, already had the largest textile machinery building capacity in the world before the war. A new textile machinery plant has been established in Argentina. From other quarters come reports of new or increased capacity which may compensate for capacity in Europe destroyed or badly crippled by the war. It is quite possible that when demand returns to normal volume several years hence, there may be some competition from new sources. However, at the moment, the company's sales outlook appears to be excellent and from the evidence now available seems likely to continue so for some years to come.

February, 1948

The unfilled orders on hand at the end of the year were somewhat greater than at the beginning notwithstanding heavy shipments during the year. As yet, there is no immediate or significant indication of a slackening of the demand for textile machinery and the outlook for new business continues good. Our customers are making substantial earnings and are using them, in part, to replace worn out machinery and in some instances to expand capacity. The tremendous increase in wages in the textile industry during the last few years has enhanced and emphasized strongly the value of new machinery as a means of holding down costs. This emphasis on the value of modern machinery will continue and become even greater as volume begins to contract and competition in the textile industry again becomes keen and margins narrow.

On the other hand, it should be said that international tension, more stringent exchange restrictions and the worldwide dollar shortage are beginning to make themselves felt in many of our foreign markets and may before long have a retarding influence on our foreign shipments in spite of the high essentiality of our product.

February, 1949

The backlog of orders is still large particularly for certain types of machines, but during the latter part of the year shipments exceeded new orders, and there is no good reason to believe that this trend will be reversed during 1949. The volume of orders on hand at the end of the year was about 20% below what it was at the beginning. There is still a steady inflow of new orders, but the volume is growing steadily less than the current rate of shipments, and there is a growing lack of balance in the backlog of orders for various types of machines, which will soon cause a corresponding lack of balance in our production schedules and in our utilization of plant capacity.

Our business in foreign markets is more and more hampered and curtailed by multiplying exchange controls and import-export restrictions of all kinds. The dollar shortage is growing more stringent in practically all countries to which we export machinery, and it seems certain that our foreign business will feel the effect of the dollar shortage acutely as the year advances. There is still a real need for textile machinery not yet satisfied throughout the world. China alone desperately needs millions of new spindles to restore her textile industry, which was largely destroyed during the war.

APPENDIX 18

COMMENTARIES ON LABOR RELATIONS AT SACO-LOWELL SHOPS, 1941–1948

1. Grievance Procedures and Experience

Early grievance discussions were characterized by uncertainty on the part of the local union organization as to rights and procedures. There was uncertainty on the part of the company as well. While discussions were lengthy and animated, the local union officials' actions frequently were inconclusive and exhibited a reluctance to pursue differences to the point of arbitration.

For the first few months following the signing of the first union agreement (May 19, 1941) most of the grievances presented by the Textile Workers Union related to the foundry division of the plant. These included charges of discrimination in the allocation of work and overtime and in layoff and discharge; "influence and coercion;" questions on piece rates; and many other matters. Most of these early foundry grievances were found either to concern necessary practices or to be unjustified.

The first union agreement provided for successive steps in the handling of shop grievances, as follows:

(1) Conference between employee concerned and/or a union grievance committeeman and the foreman or second hand of the department.
(2) Conference between Shop Grievance Committee of union or the employee concerned or both and divisional foreman or plant superintendent.
(3) Conference between national representative of union or Shop Grievance Committee of union or employee concerned or any one or more of them and the representative of the company.
(4) Arbitration. Three arbitrators: one representing the employee,

one representing the company, and the third chosen by the other two.

"Union Presence"

Until 1945 the company had been successful, in each new labor agreement, in providing for the first presentation of a grievance to be made either directly by the aggrieved employee or through the union steward of his department. The union had invariably demanded that all grievances be initiated through the steward. The first union agreement, indeed, made it possible for the individual employee to pursue his own grievance to the point of arbitration without recourse to the union at any point. Later agreements required the union's presence at the second and subsequent stages of the procedure, and in 1945 the company capitulated on the point of union presence at the first stage. All grievances were then and thereafter required to be taken through the steward from the beginning.

Resurrection of Old Grievances

Adopting a policy which was later found to be pursued by many other employers, the company's Labor Relations Department did not press for a statement of settlement of each grievance. There is little doubt of the long-term wisdom of this course — as many grievances were permitted by the union to die a natural death after full investigation and discussion, without the embarrassment to the union of a tantamount admission of error such as would be implied in a written statement that the grievance had been withdrawn. Rather than give such a statement the union would, in most cases, have persisted in debate on the grievance. Nevertheless, a weakness in this policy was repeatedly encountered when the union resurrected grievances long believed to have been dropped and cited them as evidence of the company's dilatory tactics or refusal to bargain — for example, in September of 1944, when the union had filed notice of intention to strike and was charging the company with failure to settle a large number of grievances stemming from job evaluation. A number of grievances thought by the company to have been dropped by the union as much as fifteen months previously were resurrected and used as evidence of the company's remissness.

The great waste of time and the trouble caused by the resurrection of old, unsettled, but presumably abandoned grievances was ended in 1944. A schedule of time limits for each stage of grievance procedure was agreed upon; a grievance became outlawed if the union failed to take the next consecutive step within the prescribed time; and a grievance, once outlawed, could not be reopened. After a certain lapse of time, however, it might be presented as a new grievance. Action by the company was also held within the time limitations stated, and the arrangement did much to accelerate grievance procedure, in addition to correcting the troublesome resurrection of old grievances.

Pay for Time Spent in Grievance Procedure

The earlier union agreements provided for grievance procedure to take place, as far as was possible, outside the working hours of employees involved, and without payment by the company for any time spent in grievance procedure by the aggrieved or others acting in behalf of the union. Later, however, the company undertook to pay for time lost by the steward, members of the Union Grievance Committee, and the employee concerned. This offer was made as a trading point for the union's acceptance of the time-limit schedule referred to above. The provision for holding grievance procedures outside the working hours of those concerned was abandoned during World War II, when employees were working as much as 78 hours per week. Payment was only made for working time lost during the first two stages of the procedure. The union agreement of January, 1948, continued these provisions.

2. Union Negotiations and the Wage Incentive System

Demand for Copies of Incentive Rates

In some few cases the union's initial unfamiliarity with machine-shop practices worked in the company's favor. On no point was this more true than on that of the company's wage structure.

Year after year the union persistently demanded copies of all incentive rates. In principle this demand was not unreasonable, and many of the union's agreements with textile mills provided for such copies to be furnished the union by the employer. Union officers apparently were thinking in terms of textile mills when they made their requests of Saco-Lowell, for in the mills the complete list of incentive rates rarely exceeded 1,000 different values in total. At Saco-Lowell Shops the number of different incentive rates was variously estimated to lie somewhere between 200,000 and 500,000, and many hundreds of changes in rate took place each year, owing to constant redesign, retooling, improved methods, changes of materials, and changes in working conditions. The union would have had to enlarge its local offices to house the records (time-study copies also having been requested), and would have had to engage a sizable staff to keep the files in order and posted up to date. With all such data available to them on request in the company's files, this added burden could be avoided without prejudice to the union's bargaining position. Considerable time elapsed before the national and local officers of the union appeared to be fully satisfied that the demand was irrational and that the information requested would be of limited use.

Union Reaction to Wage Structure and Controls

The unscientific and loose application of the Bedaux system at Biddeford placed the company in a potentially weak bargaining position in matters having to do with wage rates and job classifications. Lacking experience in machine-shop practice, however, national officers of the union were not in a strong position to challenge or admit the company's points with regard to relative skills and wage rates. Beyond general expressions of dissatisfaction by the union, the wage structure, per se, was not subjected to intensive, analytical attack at any time. Had it been made the subject of arbitration the company's case would not have been strong. In August, 1944, a job evaluation plan and job rates were submitted to the War Labor Board for approval, over the joint signatures of the company and the union. Approval was obtained in October of that year, and in February, 1945, the first adjustments of hourly wages under the plan took place. The inequities and weaknesses of the Bedaux application at Biddeford, however, were not eliminated.

The company's incentive system was a fertile ground for complaint, but the number of serious grievances lodged is said to have been small in view of the potentiality of this field.

The union persistently demanded to be represented during the company's investigation of any incentive rate that was the subject of a grievance. The company's experience over a number of years, particularly in the machine shop, was that in most cases where an experienced worker questioned an incentive rate of some long standing, he was found to be justified because of some undetected change in the conditions of his job or because of the application of the wrong rate. In such cases, correction of the condition or the rate was freely made and restitution accorded the worker. Because of the huge potential variation in methods, materials, and standards such adjustments were a routine, daily procedure. The point, however, was pressed by the union year after year at the time of contract negotiations, and with particular insistence in 1945. At this time the company drafted a written procedure to be followed by the worker and/or the steward when an incentive rate was questioned, and this procedure was incorporated in the agreement. With the company's additional offer to notify the union of all cases of changes in incentive rates, this matter was at last settled to the union's satisfaction without requiring the presence of the steward at the first investigation of the challenged rate.

3. Arbitration

First Arbitration Case

The initial reluctance of the local union officers to push grievances to the point of arbitration has been already noted. The first case taken to arbitration was in January, 1942, eight months after the Textile Workers Union had been bargaining agent for the shop employees. This case involved a quite reasonable demand for information, arising from a fear that certain conditions existed, rather than from a heated attack against the company or any named official.

The case arose out of union suspicions of discrimination, on the part of different foremen, between union members and non-union employees in recommendations for periodic increases for individual workmen who were earning less than their job rates.

The union demanded notification of all particulars of each such increase. The company held that many employees regarded their wage rate as a confidential matter and would not wish the possible publicity which would result from having their rates become open knowledge through the union files.

Solomon Barkin, director of research for the Textile Workers Union of America, and David Edwards, president of the Saco-Lowell Shops, acted as arbitrators for the union and the employer, respectively. Professor Sumner Slichter, Lamont Professor at Harvard University Graduate School of Business Administration, served as the impartial arbitrator. The decision required the company to notify the union monthly, by departments, of the number of individual increases granted to union members and the number granted to nonmembers, with the amount of each increase. The company was not required to reveal the names of the workers receiving the increases.

Victor Beecroft, personnel manager of the company prior to 1947, states that of some twenty-five to thirty cases taken to arbitration during the 1941–47 period, only one (to the best of his knowledge) was lost by the company. In view of the particularly fertile ground for grievances constituted by the company's incentive systems and rates, the fact is of some interest that on only two occasions were differences concerning rates and applications of rates taken to arbitration. Both cases involved the same workman and both were decided, without compromise, in the company's favor.

A host of grievances arose out of the Job Evaluation Plan, chiefly on the point of classification of employees, but with a fair number of cases heard dealing with job rates themselves. Out of a total of 150 cases on these points presented at one time by the union, the number was reduced by different forms of settlement until, in 1946, the union requested arbitration on 23 cases. By agreement, these cases were distributed for hearing between three different impartial arbitrators. Of seven cases heard before one arbitrator, six decisions were made in the company's favor and one compromise decision was rendered. Of six cases heard before the second arbitrator, one was withdrawn by the union just before hearings commenced, four were decided in the company's favor, and the sixth was a compromise decision. Of the remaining ten cases, the company conceded two and the union withdrew the other eight.

The high proportion of decisions in the company's favor in its arbitration experience is indicative of the quality of managerial judgment brought to bear in settling the union's grievances. No case was allowed to proceed to arbitration if the company had any serious doubt of the validity of its own position in the matter. The union deserves equal credit because of its readiness to submit successive cases to the same arbitrator despite his frequent rulings in the company's favor.

4. Miscellaneous Aspects of Company-union Relations

Foundry Troubles

The very nature of foundry operations, with their ceaseless shift of urgency from one phase of operations to another, the unavoidable variation in materials handled, and the high physical demands imposed on the workers under exacting conditions, made this department of the company a prolific field for employee dissatisfaction. Feuds and factions which had their origins in the foundry strike in the early 1920's still smoldered beneath the surface. Moreover, an emphasis on foundry affairs grew naturally out of the fact that the enthusiastic president of a new union was employed there.

In early August, 1941, a union member accused a non-member of appropriating, under false pretenses, a petition he was circulating. There was a great deal of partisanship in the matter, and feeling among the employees ran high. The union member quit his work and left the premises during working hours, without leave. Another union man accompanied him, and both were discharged under the plant rules which were in force at that time. (There had been no negotiation with the union of plant rules at the time this incident occurred.)

The union took up the matter, and the company supported the action of the foundry superintendent. Despite the "no strike" provision of the recent labor agreement, many of the foundry workers on the night-shift walked out. Others followed in the next twenty-four hours.

The union's president (Renouf) and the field organizer (Daoust) maintained that the strike was unauthorized. They did not, however, order the men back to work. Many employees remained at work, and the plant did not close down. Three days later the matter was settled by George Baldanzi, later to become executive vice-president of the Textile Workers Union, who ordered the strikers back to work, and who, without reservation, laid the blame at the door of union officials in Biddeford.

Immediately preceding this incident the company had received notice from the national union of its intention to remove Field Organizer Daoust and replace him with one Anthony England. England was prompt in proving his capabilities.

In late August or early September, 1941, a troublesome practice indulged in by the foundry night crew came to the company's attention. This difficulty appears to have had its roots in the unauthorized strike which had occurred just previously.

The "buggy men" in the night crew would not permit their buggies to be filled with molten iron. The amount they allowed to be poured in was insufficient to prevent cooling before the buggies could be taken to the different molding stations preparatory to being emptied into the waiting molds by the pouring crews. A high proportion of this cooled iron from each buggy had to be poured into "pigs." This necessitated a higher gross melt, at considerable cost in materials and labor; interfered with analysis of the iron the succeeding day; delayed the pouring-off process to the point where it seriously interfered with the 24-hour cycle of foundry operation; inflated the percentage of bad castings; and increased the labor cost of pouring off and dumping.

The foundry schedule at this time was a very heavy one, and the matter was serious. The plant was engaged in the biggest year's program of textile-machinery building in many years, and the foundry was already behind in its work. The recent strike, originating in this same night shift, had left an aftermath of bad feeling and the men in the night crew were difficult to handle. England was a stranger in Biddeford and, apparently, *persona non grata,* as far as the night crew was concerned.

Company officials took England into the foundry during the pouring-off, and the half-empty buggies were pointed out to him. He expressed his regret, and called a meeting of the night crew in the union hall. What took place there is not recorded, but the company experienced no more trouble with partly filled buggies.

Check-Off Clause and Escape Provision in Union Contract

The company had granted the union's request for a check-off clause (company-made deduction of union dues from union members' pay) without demur in the first union contract, but had insisted upon an escape clause which permitted union members to withdraw from the union at a stated period, upon written notification to the company and to the union of their desire to do so.

Controversy over these notifications occurred, and a U. S. Labor Department conciliator was called in. He failed to get at the roots of the matter, which originated in the action of some unknown anti-union person, who distributed among the company employees a number of printed notifications of intent to withdraw from the union, with space for date and signature. This distribution was effected each year just before the period prescribed for such notification.

The union was naturally much disturbed at this organized anti-union act and rejected the printed notifications they received. The company, however, had no alternative but to accept them, on its part, as adequate notification legally fulfilling the requirements of the "escape" provision. Pending settlement of the disputed cases, union dues continued to be deducted from the pay of the employees involved and the money was held in escrow by the company. Settlement was troublesome and tedious, and the matter was highly embarrassing to both parties. The union officers did not charge the company with complicity in the affair.

In 1944 the company conceded a maintenance-of-membership clause without an "escape" provision. The workers had had three years in which to watch the union at work. Those who might have joined thoughtlessly at the outset, or who found the union not to their liking after joining, had been given ample opportunity to withdraw. In the company's judgment the union had shown itself to be a reasonably responsible organization in the treatment of its members, and not likely to abuse the powers conferred by an irrevocable maintenance-of-membership clause. As an additional safeguard to the members, the company conditioned this concession upon inclusion of an arbitration provision under which any worker who was ejected from the union (and thus, through the maintenance-of-membership clause, dismissed from his job with the company) could, if he so desired, arrange for his case to be taken to arbitration.

Seniority

From the outset, the union demanded a straight seniority clause to be written into each successive contract. The company subscribed to the principle of seniority in all sincerity, but the nature of operations and of the manufacturing organization was such as to defy all attempts to write an effective clause to which the company could undertake to adhere. From 1941 to 1946, therefore, the seniority clause in each contract was purposely worded vaguely, and the union was consistently and strongly dissatisfied.

The problem was aggravated by the multiplicity of jobs, and by the necessity for retaining versatile men and certain specialized skills even among skeleton crews, in order to permit all functions to be carried out, on a reduced scale, during times of business recession. At such times it was essential to retain certain men, using them mostly in jobs to which they had no seniority claim and in which they were not particularly skilled — frequently making work for them in departments other than their own in order that they might be on hand to perform certain infrequent but highly specialized jobs in which no other workers were skilled. Such men the company simply could not afford to lose.

Further, the company had experienced occasions when, in times of poor business, over a thousand of its workers were laid off at the same time. Many of these were qualified to do several different kinds of work and, from the point of view of ability, they could lay claim to several different jobs, any or all of which might be duplicated in several different departments. The problem of recalling these men, a few at a time, while satisfying at once the union, the individual, and the provisions of the seniority clause was felt by the company to be virtually impossible, except after interminable controversy and reshuffling of personnel.

Recognition of seniority principles in a manner satisfactory to the union was accomplished at times of major departmental layoff (such as that which resulted when the company changed from textile machinery to war work, or from one war contract to another) by consultation with the union before actual layoff took place. From 1942 on, there was a marked rarity of contested grievances on this matter, and it is probable that any certain, set procedure written into the union contract would have hindered rather than helped the solution of the many cases smoothly handled through union consultation. Flexibility of action was requisite to an extent that defied written prescription.

In 1946, and probably stemming from the national union's drive for consistently worded agreements with the different employers (mostly textile mills, where the problem was less acute), the union's stand on the seniority clause became inflexible. Two changes in the company's internal affairs had, in the meantime, tended somewhat toward simplification of the problems involved. These were:

(1) The Employment Department was in a better position to study seniority rights of individuals with regard to the different jobs. This resulted from the re-allocation of functions which accompanied the formation of the Industrial Relations Department. The employment manager was relieved of a number of time-consuming and burdensome responsibilities, such as the Medical Department, the Cafeteria, Employers' Liability, Wage Control, and Personnel Records.

(2) Job evaluation and employee reclassification had provided a somewhat clearer definition of skills required in the different jobs and in the skills exercised by the different employees.

Partly as a result of these factors and partly as a trading point in contract negotiations, the company conceded for the first time a definite seniority clause, which was written into the 1946 contract.

Time-Study Men, Checkers, Clerical Workers, and Pattern-Makers

In 1945 Alphonse Renouf, then business manager for Local 406, representing the company's production and maintenance workers, approached the company with a demand for the sole representation of its time-study men and checkers, both of which groups were then employed in the Standards Department.

The company took the position that the time-study men were representatives of management in their function of setting incentive rates, and that they acted in a supervisory capacity with regard to the checkers. Thus, the company claimed, the time-study men and the checkers did not constitute an appropriate bargaining unit.

This matter was submitted to the War Labor Board at a hearing in Biddeford, and the company's position was upheld. A consent election was duly held among the checkers alone. The union polled a majority, and a new Local — Number 799 — was formed.

In 1946 Renouf asked for sole representation of all clerical workers at the Biddeford plant, claiming to have enrolled a large number of them as union members. The company acceded to this request, allegedly, it has been stated, to forestall a unionization threat from a different, and much more radical, union. Clerical workers doing work of a supervisory or confidential nature were excluded from this agreement, no election was held, no separate union was formed, and Local 406 showed comparatively little concern over this new group of members.

In 1946 an American Federation of Labor affiliate demanded sole and exclusive bargaining rights for the company's pattern-makers (some 14 to 16 men), claiming that all but one or two of them had signed membership cards in this particular union. The company pointed out that these men were already represented by the Textile Workers Union of America, and maintained that their interests were not sufficiently distinct from those of other employees to warrant separate representation by another union.

The matter was submitted to the War Labor Board jointly by the American Federation of Labor affiliate, the Textile Workers Union, and the company. The Board's decision supported the company's contention, and the threat of a jurisdictional dispute was removed. This hearing was conducted in good spirit, and the American Federation of Labor representative, after pointing out that the company's wage scale for its pattern-makers was considerably below the national level, admitted in an aside to the company's representative that he wouldn't be able to get top wages for these men were they working elsewhere, because of the limited range of their experience.

Union Attitude toward Jamaican Labor

In 1944 the company's program for the manufacture of twisters was accorded extremely high priority by the War Production Board. For some time previously, the emphasis had been on other war materials and products, mostly of steel and non-ferrous metals, and the foundry operation had become reduced to almost skeleton proportions. The demand for twisters required a very large increase in foundry output, but the local labor market offered no men of the right physique for foundry work. The War Manpower Commission suggested the employment of Jamaicans, considerable numbers of whom had been granted entry into the country to do essential work in war plants.

The company found suitable accommodations in Portland for about sixty of these men and made arrangements for their transportation to and from Biddeford. The union was then approached for approval of the engagement of the Jamaican men, such a step being required under U. S. Department of Labor regulations. The union withheld its approval on the grounds that the company could induce local men, then working in the Portland shipyards, to enter its foundry employ if the wage scale was increased. Not being willing to arm the union with such a lever for a general wage increase over and above those already granted in the recent past, the company had to forego the employment of the Jamaicans and its war production suffered accordingly.

Use of Microphones and Recording Apparatus in Union Negotiations

During the 1946 union contract negotiations in Biddeford the conference room was equipped with microphones coupled to a remote recording station, the union having agreed to this experiment. Copies of all discussions were to be typed from these recordings. The chief value of the arrangement proved to be pyschological. Statements were more carefully phrased, there were fewer interruptions of speakers, idle comment and irrelevant discussion were held to a minimum, and the proceedings were accelerated. Unfortunately, as a result of electrical interference with the recording apparatus, most of the transcriptions were unintelligible.

Note: Most of the foregoing information was furnished by Victor Beecroft, former employment manager and director of the Industrial Relations Department. This information was checked by many talks with present members of the department, with employees, and with members of company management. Copies of union contracts and union correspondence in the Boston office files furnished supplementary and corroborative information.

NOTES AND REFERENCES

CHAPTER I

1. Address by F. C. Lowell, *Exercises at the 75th Anniversary of the Incorporation of the Town of Lowell* (Lowell, Mass., 1901), pp. 42 ff.

2. L. Vernon Briggs, *History and Genealogy of the Cabot Family, 1475–1927* (Boston, 1927), p. 514.

3. Kenneth Wiggins Porter, *The Jacksons and the Lees: Two Generations of Massachusetts Merchants, 1765–1844* (Cambridge, 1937), vol. i, p. 114.

4. *Ibid.*, vol. i, p. 113.

5. Tench Coxe, *Digest of Manufactures,* American State Papers, Finance (Washington, 1832), vol. ii, p. 690.

6. Nathan Appleton, *Introduction of the Power Loom and Origin of Lowell* (Lowell, 1858), p. 7.

7. J. Leander Bishop, *History of American Manufactures from 1608 to 1860* (Philadelphia, 1868), vol. ii, p. 13; Tench Coxe, *A View of the United States of America* (Dublin, 1795), p. 441.

8. U. S. Department of Commerce, Bureau of the Census, *Report on the Manufactures of the U. S. at the 10th Census* (Washington, 1883), p. 618.

9. Bezaleel Taft, Jr., in *Documents Relative to the Manufactures in the United States, 1832,* 22d Congress, 2d Session (Washington, 1833), vol. i, p. 80.

10. G. S. White, *Memoir of Samuel Slater* (Philadelphia, 1836), p. 106.

11. See Greville and Dorothy Bathe, *Jacob Perkins: His Inventions, His Times, and His Contemporaries* (Philadelphia: Historical Society of Pennsylvania, 1945), for an account of this important and talented mechanic.

12. J. D. Van Slyck, *Representatives of New England: Manufacturers* (Boston, 1879), pp. 338–340.

13. Boston Manufacturing Company manuscripts, Baker Library, Harvard Business School, vol. 25.

14. Bishop, *op. cit.,* vol. ii, p. 70.

15. Isaac Briggs manuscripts, Baker Library, Harvard Business School.

16. E. Everton Foster, editor, *Lamb's Textile Industries of the United States* (Boston, 1916), vol. i, p. 137.

17. Boston Mfg. Co. MSS, vol. 25.

18. Appleton, *op. cit.,* p. 9.

19. Information about Elliot comes from L. V. Briggs, *op. cit.,* pp. 337–339, 478.

20. Middlesex County, Mass., *Deeds,* vol. 80, pp. 26–27.

21. *Ibid.,* vol. 210, p. 34.

22. Bishop, *op. cit.,* vol. ii, pp. 268–270.

23. L. V. Briggs, *op. cit.,* pp. 279–280, 442; Porter, *op. cit.,* vol. i, p. 122;

Middlesex County, Mass., *Deeds,* vol. 302, p. 353; Reverend Abner Morse, *A Genealogical Register of the Descendants of Several Ancient Puritans* (Boston, 1859), pp. 143–163.

24. C. F. Ware, *The Early New England Cotton Manufacture* (Boston, 1931), p. 37.

25. Such as that of the Reverend Mr. Cogswell, who stated before the Massachusetts Historical Society in 1815, "It is no exaggeration to say, there is probably not a better place in the world for all kinds of mills and factories. . . . This town will one day be celebrated for its manufactures." Quoted in George Folsom, *History of Saco and Biddeford* (Saco, Maine, 1830), p. 307.

26. Folsom, *op. cit.,* p. 261. York County, Maine, *Deeds,* Thomas Cutts to Josiah Calef, Dec. 5, 1811.

27. *Loc. cit.*

28. *Ibid.,* May 6, 1822.

29. Folsom, *op. cit.,* p. 306.

30. York County, Maine, *Deeds,* Josiah Calef to Saco Iron Works Co., May 18, 1825.

CHAPTER II

1. Middlesex County, Mass., *Deeds,* vol. 200, p. 429; vol. 207, p. 3.

2. Boston Mfg. Co. MSS, vol. 25, p. 3.

3. *Ibid.,* pp. 9, 34.

4. Bathe, *Jacob Perkins,* pp. 44–45.

5. Boston Mfg. Co. MSS, vol. 25, p. 71.

6. William R. Bagnall, "Sketches of Manufacturing and Textile Establishments in New York City, and of Textile Establishments in the Eastern States" (3 vols. of unpublished materials edited by Victor S. Clark), vol. iii, p. 2000.

7. The first cloth consisted of 309¾ yards of sheeting at 30¢ per yard and 37½ yards of shirting at 24½¢ per yard. Boston Mfg. Co. MSS, vol. 25, p. 110.

8. Bagnall, *Sketches of Mfg. and Textile Establishments,* vol. iii, p. 2003.

9. Ware, *Early N. E. Cotton Manufacture,* pp. 66, 69–70; *Docs. Rel. to Manufs. in U. S.,* 1832; Boston Mfg. Co. MSS, vol. 25; Bagnall, *Sketches of Mfg. and Textile Establishments,* vol. iii, p. 2001.

10. Boston Mfg. Co. MSS, vols. 13–14, 27.

11. Dividends were paid on invested capital as follows:

1817 — 17 %	1821 — 20 %
1818 — 12½	1822 — 27½
1819 — 12½	1823 — 25
1820 — 15	1824 — 25

Boston Mfg. Co. MSS, Directors' records.

12. *Ibid.,* vol. 25, p. 34; vol. 2, entry of August 31, 1823.

13. See *Docs. Rel. to Manufs. in U. S.,* 1832.

14. These two inventions were the saw gin of Eli Whitney, patented in 1793, and the card-setting machines of Amos Whittemore, patented in 1797.

15. White, *Memoir of Samuel Slater*, p. 48.

16. *Docs. Rel. to Manufs. in U. S.*, p. 70.

17. White, *op. cit.*, p. 187; Victor Selden Clark, *History of Manufactures in the United States, 1607–1914* (New York, 1929), vol. i, pp. 422–429; Evan Leigh, *Science of Modern Cotton Spinning*, vol. i, pp. 54–55.

18. Leigh, *op. cit.*, vol. i, pp. 78–87; Sir Edward Baines, *History of the Cotton Manufacture in Great Britain* (London, 1835), pp. 171–179; New England Cotton Manufacturers Association, *Transactions*, no. 12, pp. 36–37 (1872).

19. Leigh, *op. cit.*, vol. ii, p. 177.

20. For a good description of the improvement and of the water frame and early throstle frames in general use see James Montgomery, *The Theory and Practice of Cotton Spinning . . .* (Glasgow, 1833), pp. 152–160; and *Dr. Ure's Dictionary of Arts, Manufactures and Mines* (London, 1867), vol. i, p. 943.

21. Briggs MSS, Harvard Business School.

22. Baines, *op. cit.*, p. 235.

23. In hand weaving, mechanisms to perform the three basic weaving motions (passing the shuttle through the warp, alternately raising and lowering the warp, and beating up the filling to form the cloth) were activated by the weaver. In the new power loom these motions were imparted either by steam or by water power. The full labor-saving potentialities of the power loom were not realized all at once, however, and close attention on the part of the operative was still required. In England as late as 1823 one operative could tend only two looms (Baines, *op. cit.*, p. 240), and this ratio existed in America as common practice in 1836 (James Montgomery, *A Practical Detail of the Cotton Manufacture of the United States of America*, Glasgow, 1840, p. 107). The saving in productivity was greater. In 1823 one relatively unskilled English steam-loom weaver tending two looms could turn out seven times as much work as the very best hand weaver on his single loom (Baines, *op. cit.*, pp. 239–240).

24. Appleton, *Introduction of the Power Loom and Origin of Lowell*, p. 9.

25. The best description of the differences between the Scotch and the Waltham looms is found in Bagnall, *Sketches of Mfg. and Textile Establishments*, vol. iii, pp. 1997–1998.

26. In 1817, patent rights for a temple were purchased from J. Stimpson (Boston Mfg. Co. MSS, vol. 192). In 1824, patent rights for a "self-acting temple" were purchased from Ira Draper (Boston Mfg. Co. MSS, Agreement between Ira Draper and the Boston Mfg. Co., Oct. 25, 1824).

27. Bagnall, *Sketches of Mfg. and Textile Establishments*, vol. iii, p. 2008.

28. Samuel Batchelder, *Introduction and Early Progress of the Cotton Manufacture in the United States* (Boston, 1863), p. 68.

29. Appleton, *op. cit.*, p. 9.

30. Edmund Burke, *List of Patents for Inventions and Designs, 1790–1847* (Washington, 1847).

31. Bagnall, *Sketches of Mfg. and Textile Establishments,* vol. iii, p. 1999.

32. The terms employed in the identification of roving frames have resulted in considerable historical confusion. Originally, roving frames which embodied the principle of winding the yarn on bobbins (in contrast to the revolving can frame) were referred to as "fly frames" — a name derived from the flyer arms of the machine which performed the winding-on action. This name was not widely used, however, and such machines were more commonly known in America as "speeders" or "double speeders." Much later in the 19th century an English improvement was labeled the "bobbin and fly frame" or simply the "fly frame." It is this later development to which technical writers of that day refer when setting forth the triumph of the "fly frame" over the "double speeder." Actually the double speeder was itself a fly frame.

33. Bagnall, *Sketches of Mfg. and Textile Establishments,* vol. iii, pp. 2090–2091; Batchelder, *op. cit.,* p. 67.

34. In the live-spindle throstle frame the spindle was made to revolve directly, carrying with it the bobbin and flyer. In the dead-spindle throstle frame power was applied to the flyer instead of to the spindle, and the flyer, revolving at high velocity, carried the bobbin with it. The dead-spindle frame was so named because the spindles in the earliest frames of this type were stationary, consisting of a peg upon which the flyer and bobbin took their bearing. In the dead-spindle frame the flyer was supported at top and bottom, instead of at the top only, as was the live-spindle flyer. Thus vibration was checked and higher speeds made possible. See Montgomery, *Theory and Practice of Cotton Spinning,* pp. 165–168.

35. Boston Mfg. Co. MSS, Letter from F. C. Lowell to David Greenough, June 9, 1816.

36. Jonathan T. Lincoln, "Beginnings of the Machine Age in New England: Document Relating to the Introduction of the Power Loom," *Bulletin of the Business Historical Society,* vol. vii, no. 5 (Oct., 1933), p. 12.

37. Boston Mfg. Co. MSS, vol. 10, p. 140, and vol. 34, p. 73. This sale of machinery appears to be the transaction referred to by Lowell in his letter to Greenough in June, 1816.

38. The bobbin machines, otherwise unidentified, may have been the winding frames, which soon after this time were made obsolete by Moody's invention of the filling frame. These two bobbin machines are the only ones sold by the company.

39. Bishop, *History of American Manufactures,* vol. ii, p. 309.

40. Batchelder, *op. cit.,* p. 72.

41. Briggs MSS, Harvard Business School.

42. Lincoln, *Beginnings of Machine Age in N. E.,* pp. 10–12; Boston Mfg. Co. MSS, Dover Factory Company agreement dated Oct. 12, 1821.

43. Boston Mfg. Co. MSS, Agreement with the Merrimack Mfg. Co., dated Feb. 28, 1822; Agreement with the Elliot Mfg. Co., dated Oct. 1, 1823.

44. Boston Mfg. Co. MSS, vols. 34–35.

45. Examples of early diversification in textile-machinery building are to be found in New York in the shop of John Daniel (Bagnall, *The Textile Industries of the United States,* pp. 185–186); in New Jersey in the activities of Daniel Dod (Briggs MSS, Baker Library, Harvard Business School); in Providence in the shop of David Wilkinson (Lincoln, "Beginnings of Machine Age in N. E.," pp. 6–13); in Philadelphia in the shop of Alfred Jenks (Joseph Wickham Roe, *English and American Tool Builders,* New Haven, 1916, p. 123); in North Carolina in the shop of Milton Schenk (*Lamb's Textile Industries of the United States,* vol. i, p. 217). See also *A Series of Tables of the Several Branches of American Manufactures,* U. S. Treasury Department, 1813.

46. The information presented in the company records is too fragmentary to warrant the construction of price indices. It is worth noting, however, that the few cases studied are consistent with the trend noted in the Warren and Pearson *Index of Wholesale Prices in the United States, 1786–1931* (G. F. Warren and F. A. Pearson, *Prices,* N. Y., 1933, Table 3, p. 25).

47. This central clearing account was labeled "P. T. Jackson, Treasurer," and its origins are to be found in the mercantile accounting practice of making all transactions ultimate charges or credits to the merchant in person. The account as used in manufacturing enterprise served as a "catch-all" — in essence, a profit and loss account (which in the 19th century was far more comprehensive in content than the profit and loss account of comparatively recent date). To the clearing account were made all charges which accounting practice had not yet found the means or the necessity for allocating more exactly. It became the familiar "Manufacturing" account of later 19th century practice, and it declined in importance in direct proportion to the increasing success of accountants in assigning costs to their proper place in business. It is highly significant that at so early a date the Boston Manufacturing Company charged so relatively few costs to the "catch-all" account.

48. John L. Hayes, *American Textile Machinery . . .* (Cambridge, 1879), p. 29, quoting William Burke, of the Lowell Machine Shop.

49. Boston Mfg. Co. MSS, vol. 25, pp. 103, 182.

50. White, in his *Memoir of Samuel Slater,* p. 340, gives some comparable wage statistics for the year 1825, at which time he says that the best machine-makers, forgers, etc., received $1.94 per day in England and $1.50 to $1.75 per day in America. Ordinary machinists received $1.10 per day in England and from $1.25 to $1.42 in America.

51. Boston Mfg. Co. MSS, vols. 80, 86. These computations do not include Paul Moody's salary of $1,500 per year, nor that of Faulkner.

52. *Ibid.,* vol. 192.

53. *Ibid.,* Directors' records, vol. 2.

54. See footnote 2, Chapter III.

55. Boston Mfg. Co. MSS, vols. 27, 35.

56. The $52,000 profit is computed from the Machinery account, Boston

Manufacturing Company records, vol. 35, and consists of the balance of that account at closing, less an adjustment of approximately $13,500 for credits to the account which were not charged to the Merrimack Manufacturing Company.

57. Boston Mfg. Co. MSS, vol. 2, Letter of P. T. Jackson dated Oct. 7, 1823, and dividend records.

58. The size and capitalization of the Boston Manufacturing Company was not unprecedented. In 1791 the Society for Establishing Useful Manufactures in New Jersey applied ambitious plans and $200,000 of capital to the exploitation of the falls of the Passaic. This endeavor was far in advance of its times, and mismanagement coupled with technical difficulties made the precedent an unfortunate one (White, *op. cit.*, pp. 236–237). In 1794 the "Proprietors of the Newburyport Woolen Manufactory" constructed a building 100 feet long, 40 feet wide, and 3 stories high to accommodate the business of the Scholfield brothers. Thirty local residents subscribed $300,000 of capital. English competition and competition from American hand weavers proved fatal to this enterprise in five years (Horace Nathaniel Stevens, *Nathaniel Stevens, 1786–1865: An Account of His Life and the Business He Founded,* N. Andover, Mass., 1946, pp. 14–15).

CHAPTER III

1. It is little short of miraculous that this site was not immediately chosen by Jackson. The area was well known to many as the terminus of the Middlesex Canal and the site of the Pawtucket Canal around the falls — both extensively used by back-country traders and lumbermen. There was an early farming community there, as well as a road, a public house, and a bridge. Both commercial and sport fishermen were intimately familiar with the falls and the great salmon, shad, and alewife pool below them. There is evidence that Jackson did know of the existence of this water-power site, but was furnished with misleading evidence that convinced him of the undesirability of the location for his purposes. The fact that the misapprehension was not immediately corrected is an evidence of the secrecy with which the search for a site was carried on. Bagnall, *Sketches of Mfg. and Textile Establishments,* vol. iii, pp. 2132–2134. See also *Correspondence between Nathan Appleton and John A. Lowell in Relation to the Early History of the City of Lowell* (Boston, 1848).

2. Control of the Merrimack Manufacturing Co. was vested in the stockholders of the Boston Manufacturing Co. These stockholders and the Boston Manufacturing Co. itself owned a large majority of the Merrimack stock. John Boott and Kirk Boott, sons of a successful Boston merchant, together owned 180 out of the 600 shares of the new company. Boston Mfg. Co. MSS, Directors' records; Ware, *Early N. E. Cotton Manufacture,* Appendix K, pp. 321–322.

3. To avoid speculation Jackson employed an agent to purchase the Locks and Canals stock and the farmlands. Great secrecy was maintained, and there

was much bitterness in later years when the former owners of stock and land witnessed the tremendous inflation of values. There seem to be no logical grounds for complaint against Jackson's methods, however. Fair current prices were paid, and the later increment in values came as a direct result of the efforts of the purchasers. Kirk Boott relates one example of the rise in value of the farm lands — in this case the Warren farm, occupying the site on which the Middlesex Manufacturing Company was later built. Boott related, "I purchased, in 1822, nine tenths, undivided, of a farm of 110 acres, for $1,800. The owner of the other tenth had agreed to convey it for $200, but dying, suddenly, insolvent, it was sold by order of the court, and I gave, for seven and a half tenths of his one tenth, upwards of $3,000. All his debts being satisfied the remainder was sold, a year afterwards, for the benefit of minor children for nearly $5,000." Letter of Kirk Boott to Matthew Carey, quoted in White, *Memoir of Samuel Slater,* pp. 252–255. See also Samuel Adams Drake, *History of Middlesex County* (Boston, 1880), 3 vols., vol. ii, p. 61, and "Address by the Reverend Thomas M. Clarke D.D.," published in the *Proceedings, Semi-Centennial Celebration of the City of Lowell* (1876), p. 59.

4. Proprietors of the Locks and Canals records, Correspondence, Holley to Boott, Dec. 17, 1821. This source will hereafter be described as "Locks and Canals records," and it is the source of all pertinent material in this chapter not otherwise identified. The Locks and Canals records are located in the Locks and Canals office in Lowell, Massachusetts.

5. *Merrimack Journal* (Lowell, Mass.), Mar. 10, 1826.

6. Bagnall, *Sketches of Mfg. and Textile Establishments,* vol. iii, p. 2157.

7. *Ibid.,* vol. iii, p. 2216.

8. The water power required for a 3,584-spindle mill was 25 cubic feet of water on a 30-foot fall (54.5 horse power), and the mill-power unit entitled the user to employ such water 24 hours per day (later changed to 15 hours per day).

9. The Hamilton Manufacturing Co., like the Merrimack Manufacturing Co., was predominantly a promotion of the Boston Manufacturing Co. stockholders.

10. Locks and Canals records, Directors' records.

11. Porter, *The Jacksons and the Lees,* vol. i, p. 770. Letter of P. T. Jackson dated Nov. 11, 1824.

12. The original 500 shares of Locks and Canals stock had been increased to 600 shares and, in 1824, were being held by trustees in the name of the Merrimack Manufacturing Co. stockholders in the ratio of one share of Locks and Canals stock for each share of Merrimack stock owned. In 1825, there were 600 new shares issued (at $500 par) to Merrimack stockholders in the same ratio. All were subscribed.

13. Bagnall, *Sketches of Mfg. and Textile Establishments,* vol. iii, pp. 2072–2073.

14. The size of this building was probably 142 feet long and 42 feet wide, with 5 stories above the basement. This was the standard size of the early

Lowell mills, and the machine shop was erected on the same plan as the other mills. *Proceedings, Semi-Centennial Celebration of the Incorporation of the Town of Lowell;* Charles Cowley, *Illustrated History of Lowell* (Boston, 1868), p. 46.

15. See the various issues of the *Contributions,* Old Residents Historical Association, Lowell, Massachusetts. One idealistic account of the town in 1825 read as follows:

> On the banks of the Merrimack are already three superb factories and two immense piles of brick buildings for calico printing. In front of these, on the banks of the factory canal which is fenced in and ornamented with a row of elms, are situated the houses of the people. They are handsomely and uniformly planted, with flower gardens in front, and separated by wide avenues. There is a beautiful Gothic stone church opposite the dwelling houses, and a parsonage of stone is erecting. There is a post office, fine taverns, one of which is a superb stone edifice with outbuildings of the same material, and perhaps two hundred houses all fresh from the hands of the workmen. The ground is intersected with fine roads and good bridges. The whole seems like enchantment.

16. Bagnall, *Sketches of Mfg. and Textile Establishments,* vol. iii, pp. 2240–2241.

17. Locks and Canals records, Directors' records, Feb. 23, 1829.

18. *Ibid.,* July 11, 1829.

19. On June 15, 1830, the Middlesex Manufacturing Co. was incorporated, and purchased two mill powers of the Locks and Canals Co. The Middlesex Company was established to manufacture woolens, broadcloths, and cassimeres, and may have purchased its machinery outside of Lowell. There is no conclusive evidence to indicate that the Locks and Canals Co. built machinery for Middlesex, although a contemporary source states that the Locks and Canals Company did build woolen machinery. White, *op. cit.,* p. 255.

20. Locks and Canals records, Directors' records, Mar. 4 and 20, 1831; Aug., 1833; Mar. 16, 1835.

21. Locks and Canals records, Correspondence, 1832–33.

22. Lawrence Mfg. Co. records, Baker Library, Harvard Business School, Ledger, vol. 62.

23. Locks and Canals records, Correspondence, A. Lawrence to Kirk Boott, Mar. 3, 1835.

24. George F. Kenngott, *The Record of a City: A Social Survey of Lowell, Mass.* (New York, 1912), p. 22.

25. *Ibid.,* quoting statistics of Lowell manufactures for the year 1836.

26. *Contributions,* Old Res. Hist. Assn., vol. i, pp. 258–259; vol. ii, p. 329.

27. Kenngott, *op. cit.,* p. 22.

28. Locks and Canals records, Directors' records, Jan. 22, 1830.

29. Bagnall, *Sketches of Mfg. and Textile Establishments,* vol. iii, p. 2305; Locks and Canals records, Correspondence, vol. 25, folio 145.

30. Massachusetts Cotton Mills records, Pepperell Mfg. Co. collection, Baker Library, Harvard Business School, Report of Stockholders' Committee (undated, but approximately 1845).

31. See Montgomery, *Theory and Practice of Cotton Spinning*, pp. 208–214, for a description of this invention.

32. U. S. Patent Office records, Boston Public Library, unnumbered specification drawing dated Sept. 16, 1833, entitled "W. B. Leonard, Drawing Frame for Spinning Mach." The railway drawing head was, in effect, a drawing frame attached to a series of carding machines. The cards delivered sliver into a trough, or railway, instead of into the old-style individual cans. In the trough the combined sliver from several cards traveled to the railway drawing head, where it was drawn. The principal advantage was in eliminating handling of individual cans and in providing a more or less automatic flow from the carding to the drawing process.

33. Locks and Canals records, Correspondence, letter Godwin Clarke & Co. to Kirk Boott, dated Oct. 31, 1832.

34. Two other leases of interest are those which brought the self-acting mule to Lowell. In 1842 the Locks and Canals Company began to negotiate with the Matteawan Machine Shop, of Fishkill, New York, for the right to build the Smith self-acting mule. This mule appears to have been American in origin and was a strong competitor of the Mason and the Sharpe & Roberts models. These three mules dominated the American market of the early 1840's. In December, 1843, an agreement was concluded by which the Locks and Canals Company agreed to build and sell the Smith mule, charging customers a patent fee of 24¢ per spindle. This fee was divided equally between the Locks and Canals Company, the Matteawan Machine Shop, and the inventor (Locks and Canals records, Correspondence, Jan., 1843). The first Mason mule in Lowell appears to have been installed in 1844 — probably in the mills of the Lawrence Manufacturing Co. The Locks and Canals Co. secured a model from Mason in February of 1844. Mason agreed to furnish castings, at cost, for the mules to be built at Lowell, and gave the Locks and Canals Co. information on prices paid for job work on the mule. Mason received a patent fee of 25¢ per spindle. The Locks and Canals Co. billed Lawrence at a price of $2.68 per spindle (Locks and Canals records, Correspondence, Feb., 1844).

35. Leather belting had been used in America to drive machinery from almost the beginning of colonization in the 17th century. In England, France, and elsewhere on the Continent it was in use for such purposes at much earlier dates. Artisans from the Middle Ages onward used foot-treadle machines driven by roping or belting.

36. See Montgomery, *Cotton Manufacture of the U. S. A.*, pp. 19–25, for the best discussion of English and American power-driven systems and for plans of typical belt-driven American factories of the 1830's.

37. Safford and Hamilton, "The American Mixed-flow Turbine and Its Setting," *Transactions*, American Society of Civil Engineers, vol. 85, paper

1503, pp. 1242–1251. This paper comprises an interesting and complete account of the development of the turbine wheel in America.

38. Jonathan J. Lincoln, "Material for a History of American Textile Machinery: The Kilburn-Lincoln Papers," *Journal of Economic and Business History*, vol. 4, no. 2 (Feb., 1932), pp. 268–269; Safford and Hamilton, *op. cit.*

39. Two outstanding fire-protection features had been incorporated in the mills designed by the Locks and Canals Co. After 1829 the picking process, the source of a high percentage of fires in textile mills, was relegated to a separate house, apart from the main buildings of the mills. By 1839 at the latest, and probably as early as 1827, the Lowell mills were equipped with forcing pumps by which water could be supplied to every part of the mills. A reservoir also was established for the joint protection of the mills. There were few serious fires in Lowell. Locks and Canals records, Correspondence, 1839; *Contributions,* Old Res. Hist. Assn., vol. ii, p. 467.

40. Samuel Webber, "Reminiscences of Early Machine Practices," *Transactions,* American Society of Mechanical Engineers, vol. xvi, pp. 742–761.

41. In 1842 the Locks and Canals Co. was purchasing its pig iron from the firm of Leonard & Hone, Pine Street, New York. This firm identified itself as a commision agency which sold cloth; dealt in cotton, woolen, and other machinery, machine parts, tools, and mechanics' articles in general; and made purchases of iron, steel, and cotton for machine shops and cotton mills.

42. Montgomery, *Cotton Manufacture in the U. S. A.,* p. 171. Montgomery states that in 1839 the Locks and Canals Co. used 1,225 tons of cast and wrought iron. Company records for that year show that the best Pennsylvania boiler iron cost as much as $160 a ton, $25 more than imported spring steel. Best American pig iron cost from $35 to $40 per ton, the approximate price range of Garthshire, the best Scotch pig. Inferior grades of American pig iron ranged from $27.50 to $40.00 per ton.

43. Atkinson, *Statistics of Lowell Manufactures,* Jan. 1, 1848; Locks and Canals records, Directors' records, Feb. 20, 1850.

44. Kenngott, *op. cit.,* pp. 8–11; *Contributions,* Old Res. Hist. Assn., vol. i, pp. 93–96; vol. iv, pp. 110–111; Harriet Jane Robinson, *Loom and Spindle* (New York, 1898), pp. 9–10; Bagnall, *Sketches of Mfg. and Textile Establishments,* vol. iii, pp. 2143–2148.

45. A particularly bitter controversy developed in 1834 between Kirk Boott and the Lawrence interests over the question of a proper price for additional mill powers. The Lawrence Manufacturing Co. offered to pay $2.50 per spindle for the additional power required for a change in their mills. This price had been charged by the Locks and Canals Co. in past instances. Boott demanded $6.00, and a settlement was finally made at a price of $5.00. The Lawrence interests were indignant, and charged Boott with discrimination against them in favor of the Merrimack Manufacturing Co., a competitor. Boott denied any selfish interest, and stated that he had acted in his capacity as agent of the Locks and Canals Company, for the best interests of that company alone and not in behalf of the Merrimack, with which he had long

been intimately associated. Locks and Canals records, Correspondence, Dec., 1834; Lawrence Manufacturing Company records, vol. 758, Letters, Dec., 1834.

46. In 1836 the foreign-born inhabitants of Lowell (mostly from the British Isles) numbered 2,661 out of a total population of 17,633 (Kenngott, *op. cit.,* p. 33). The great Irish influx had yet to come, but a steady trickle of English and Irish workmen, skilled and unskilled, had commenced. The labor unrest of the 1840's is difficult to appraise. One basic issue was a demand for a ten-hour workday. Another issue, seized upon by idealists and political vagrants alike, was general denunciation of the "aristocracy bound together by the iron bands of self-interest, or by the golden ones of wealth and power." This movement fed upon the lurid pictures of the condition of English textile operatives which appeared at frequent intervals in American periodicals. It would appear from election results in 1844, when the various agitating groups unsuccessfully sponsored candidates for public office, that the dissatisfaction had not become general, the hue and cry in the periodicals to the contrary notwithstanding (See Lowell *Journal,* Sept. 21, 1849, pp. 1–2, and Lowell *Patriot,* 1844, *passim*).

47. Locks and Canals records, Correspondence, letters dated Mar. 24, 1829, and May 6, 1839.

48. *Ibid.,* Letter of Mrs. Stuart to Paul Moody, Oct. 16, 1827.

49. The Middlesex Mechanics Association looked for its precedent to the Massachusetts Charitable Mechanics Association, formed in Boston in 1806. The preamble to the charter of the older organization was copied verbatim in the newer. The primary object of the Middlesex Mechanics Association appears to have been to control the evil of apprentice-stealing. This association gradually evolved into an educational and social institution. In 1828, overseers from the textile mills were made eligible for membership. By 1834 the organization had become dominated by the Lowell corporations and had lost its youthful vigor, though its usefulness as an educational institution was to continue for many years. *Contributions,* Old Res. Hist. Assn., vol. 6, no. 3, p. 279; Kenngott, *op. cit.,* p. 9.

50. In 1844 the Locks and Canals Company machine shop was turning out openers, pickers, cards, railway heads, drawing frames, speeders, mules, throstle spinning frames, warpers, dressers, and looms. A complete line of cotton machinery had been made, of course, since the early days of the Boston Manufacturing Company.

51. *Manufactures of the United States in 1860,* compiled from the original returns of the 8th Census (Washington, 1865), p. xix.

52. Railway and Locomotive Historical Society *Bulletin,* no. 4, p. 45.

53. George L. Vose, *A Sketch of the Life and Works of George W. Whistler, Civil Engineer* (Boston, 1886), gives a complete and interesting account of Whistler's career.

54. Letter of the Secretary of the Treasury on the subject of steam engines, quoted in the Railway and Locomotive Historical Society *Bulletin,* no. 6, pp. 23 ff.

55. Locks and Canals records, Account in correspondence file, July 31, 1838.

56. Letter of the Secretary of the Treasury on the subject of steam engines, cited in note 54.

57. See Appendix 6 for distribution of Locks and Canals locomotives.

58. Computed from a list of Locks and Canals locomotives compiled by Charles E. Fisher, editor of the Railway and Locomotive Historical Society *Bulletin,* and made available by him to the author. See also George S. Gibb, "Three Early Railroad Equipment Contracts," *Bulletin of the Business Historical Society,* vol. 31, no. 1 (Feb., 1947), pp. 10–17, for a description of specific contracts between the Locks and Canals Company and railroad customers.

59. Locks and Canals records, Correspondence, letter of Howard to Jackson, dated Feb. 2, 1839.

60. *Ibid.,* Correspondence, letter dated Mar. 11, 1842.

61. See Gibb, "Three Early R. R. Equipment Contracts," pp. 10–17.

62. Locks and Canals records, Directors' records, Sept. 20, 1842.

63. *Ibid.,* Account dated July 31, 1838, in correspondence file.

64. *Ibid.,* Correspondence file, letter of J. A. Lowell to K. Boott, Nov. 22, 1836.

65. *Ibid.,* Nov. 10, 1836.

66. Stock prices quoted are from Joseph Gregory Martin, *Boston Stock Market, 1835–1861* (Boston, 1862), p. 42. All other information in this section, unless otherwise indicated, is from the Locks and Canals Directors' records.

67. Locks and Canals Correspondence, 1843–44.

68. Bagnall, *Sketches of Mfg. and Textile Establishments,* vol. 3, p. 2123; Locks and Canals records, Directors' records, 1845.

69. Report of stockholders' committee, Mass. Cotton Mills, Pepperell manuscript collection.

CHAPTER IV

1. Very little has been known about the Saco Manufacturing Co., and there appeared to be no surviving business records of the firm. In searching through the early records of the York Manufacturing Co., however, I discovered two journals of the Saco Manufacturing Co. which reveal parts of the "lost" story of the first cotton factory at Saco Falls. These journals are the source of all information not otherwise documented. Even with this additional source material, however, the picture of this historic company is far from clear.

2. Tatterson, *Three Centuries of Biddeford.*

3. *A Chronicle of Textile Machinery* (Cambridge, Mass., 1824, privately printed history of the Saco-Lowell Shops), p. 54.

4. Pepperell MSS, Baker Library, Atlantic Bank Indenture Agreement, Dec. 30, 1829.

5. Lowell *Journal,* Feb. 24, 1830.

6. Pliny Cutler, holding 40 shares, was elected treasurer. Cutler had been a partner in the largest wholesale grocery firm in Boston and had entered the banking field. In 1832 he was president of the Atlantic Bank and was interested in the Tremont and the Trader banks. Other large stockholders were James Johnson (30 shares), a director of the Atlantic Bank; Edwin Munro (40 shares), who was interested in the Tremont, the Suffolk, and the National banks; Charles Cartwright (15 shares), a commission merchant active in banking and marine insurance; Samuel Fales (30 shares), dry-goods retailer and wholesaler and president (after 1834) of the Union Bank; and Samuel Batchelder (30 shares). The strong banking connections evidenced here are unquestionably more than coincidental with the prior interest of many of these same banks in the old Saco Manufacturing Company. However, because of the meager records of the period, the connection cannot be positively traced.

7. By the terms of this contract Batchelder was to receive $2,000 per annum in salary, a rent-free house, and the right to purchase a tenth-interest in the stock of the company at slightly more than 60% of par value. Funds to pay for this stock were to be advanced to Batchelder by the company. In addition, Batchelder was to receive 10% of the net profits earned and remaining after stockholders had received 6% in dividends. Batchelder was to allow the company the right to use any inventions he might make while in the company's employ, and was to share equally with the company any profits arising from the sale of such inventions. "Contract with Samuel Batchelder, Agent, August 16, 1831," York Mfg. Co. records.

8. See Justin Winsor, editor, *Memorial History of Boston* (Boston, 1880–81), vol. iv, pp. 164–166.

9. *Exec. Docs. Rel. to Manuf. in U.S.*, vol. i, p. 13.

10. *Ibid.*, p. 1, letter of Asa Clapp to Hon. Louis McLane, Secretary of the Treasury.

11. York Mfg. Co., Directors' records. Unless otherwise indicated, all information about the company presented hereafter was taken from this source, or from early York journals and ledgers.

12. In addition to hiring Batchelder as general agent, the York directors followed the example of several Lowell mills in sending to Great Britain for a mechanic versed in the latest developments there. In November, 1835, a contract was made with James Montgomery, of Glasgow, for his services and assistance at Saco. Montgomery became well known as the author of the two most famous treatises of the day on cotton machinery. These two works (*Theory and Practice of Cotton Spinning*, 1833; *Cotton Manufactures of the U. S. A.*, 1840) are prolific sources of historical information about English and American machines and techniques of the 1830's.

13. Saco Water Power Company records, Copy of Act of Incorporation. This charter is presented in Appendix 2.

14. Present at this meeting: Joseph Balch, Elijah Loring, Tasker Swett, Robert Hooper, Jr., Joseph Hall, Jr., and Enoch Baldwin. Saco Water Power

Co. records, Directors' records. Subsequent information about the company in this section, unless otherwise noted, is taken from this source.

15. At a lower level of management this factor is even more obvious. The superintendents of the two companies were hired men first and stockholders second. Their position and career demanded that they should advance the interest of their own company, even at the expense of companies in which they and their employers owned stock.

16. York Mfg. Co., Directors' records, July 13, 1840.

17. *Ibid.*, "Articles of Agreement, York Manufacturing Company and Saco Water Power Company, October 17, 1840."

18. Original statement summarized and condensed.

19. Saco Water Power Co. records; report of Saco Water Power committee chosen by the directors to build and furnish a machine shop, signed by Samuel Batchelder and accepted by the directors on Aug. 23, 1841. Little is known of Nichols' background. His name appears in the records of the old Saco Manufacturing Company, though there is no way of ascertaining whether he was an employee, the machinery superintendent, or an independent contractor. His connection with machinery building at the Falls definitely went back at least to 1828 (Saco Mfg. Co. records, Ledgers and accounts current).

20. Saco Water Power Co. records, Letterbook, vol. 71. All company material in this section not otherwise documented is taken from this source and from company journals, ledgers, and financial statements.

21. *York County Herald,* undated excerpt in York Mfg. Co. records.

22. Saco Water Power Co. records, Agreement with York Mfg. Co., dated Nov. 10, 1841. Cost information is taken from a memorandum slip attached to this agreement. According to a letter from Nichols to Baldwin the machinery for this 6,000-spindle mill required 22,500 pounds of steel, all of which was to be imported.

23. In view of the fact that as yet the Water Power Company had not acquired title from York to the Saco and Biddeford properties, the fact is strange that machine-shop operations were shown on the Water Power Company books and rents from the properties were being collected by the company. The most plausible explanation is that an agreement to this effect was in force between the companies pending the final settlement.

24. For the faithful performance of his financial duties the treasurer was required to post a bond of $8,000, with the stipulation that should funds in his custody exceed this amount, additional bond should be posted to cover the excess.

25. The seventh regulation promulgated by the directors' committee on accounts (in Nov., 1841) set forth the fundamental manufacturing accounting procedure adopted. This regulation reads:

> *Seventh* That all sums expended for the purchase of materials to be wrought into articles for sale as also the wages of the machinists and others employed in and about the Machine Shop and all expenses incident to that establishment be charged

to an account to be denominated Machine Factory — and that the proceeds of all articles manufactured in said Factory & sold, and all sales of articles which have been previously charged to the establishment be credited to same account as also all articles sold from the Blacksmiths Shop & receipts for work done in either establishment and so in any department of the Machine Factory.

26. It is of interest from an accounting viewpoint to note that even in 1843 there was a keen awareness of the elusiveness of the "book value" figure. The committee refrained from stating that each share of stock was positively worth $301.47. The report used the cautious wording that the book value per share was $301.47 "if worth cost." Any implied guarantee of the replacement or market value of the assets was carefully avoided.

27. Saco Water Power Company records, Stockholders' petition, dated May 23, 1843.

28. A comparison of this contract with that made for the fourth York mill reveals few significant differences in machinery components. Spoolers and spreaders are mentioned in the Laconia contract, and these machines had not been built for the York. In 1844, as in 1841, however, no picking or opening machinery was being built at Biddeford.

29. The actual cost, upon completion in October, 1845, totaled only $175,-042, much of the difference being accounted for by savings in the mill building and in the machinery ($8,232 and $16,150, respectively, less than estimated).

30. Five hundred shares of Laconia stock were issued, to be offered to the Water Power Company stockholders at the rate of one Laconia share for each two Water Power Company shares held. Only 33 of the 500 shares were not taken up as offered by the Water Power Company shareholders. In addition to a common treasurer, four of the Water Power Company directors were elected directors of Laconia. At this time 75% of the Water Power Company stock was still held by York shareholders. Thus, although the interest of York shareholders in the Water Power Company had declined some 20% in five years, ownership of the three companies was very closely interlocked. The principal stockholders in each of the three companies were almost identical. Of the holders of large blocks of stock only Benjamin Loring (holding 40 shares in York and 65 shares in the Water Power Company) failed to subscribe to his allotted share in Laconia. He took only 15 Laconia shares, and soon sold 9. "Abstract of Corporation Returns," 1844, Secretary of State, Maine; Saco Water Power Co. records, Memoranda and agreements.

31. There is considerable evidence at this time (1847) that no great future was being planned for the machine shop. One suggestion, made in 1847, was that eventually the existing shop would be converted to a cotton mill, and another small machine shop be erected up-river where a five-foot fall would be entirely sufficient for "a machine shop of any magnitude that would be necessary for our purposes at Biddeford." Saco Water Power Co. records, Committee of directors' report dated Mar. 8, 1847.

32. Evelyn H. Knowlton, *Pepperell's Progress: History of a Cotton Textile Company, 1844–1945* (Cambridge, 1948), Chap. 4. The reader should consult this source for additional information on manufacturing operations at Saco and Biddeford in this period.

33. The contract with the Lowell Machine Shop was signed after bids had been received from the Essex Co., in Lawrence, Massachusetts. This fact is significant, for it indicates that the new textile center on the Merrimack had already become a factor in the textile machinery industry. The Lowell Machine Shop agreed to undertake the task on a cost-plus-10% basis. "Cost" was defined in the contract as actual (direct) cost of labor and materials plus 10% for overhead; transportation costs extra.

34. Knowlton, *op. cit.,* Chap. 1.

35. Like the Laconia Company, the Pepperell Manufacturing Company had been chartered some time before there was any positive assurance that the Water Power Company would sell rather than operate the mills it was building. The Pepperell charter, for example, had been obtained in 1844. The Water Power Company's action in causing these charters to be secured indicates that separate ownership had been considered a very strong possibility from the beginning.

36. Knowlton, *op. cit.,* Chap. 1.

37. Saco Water Power Co. records, Committee report to the stockholders, July, 1855.

38. Construction work was not confined exclusively to machinery, mills, tenements, and dams. The Water Power Co. did much to develop the town of Biddeford. A hotel, a bank, a post office, and a depot were built by the company, and these activities served to bridge the gap between completion of the Laconia contracts and the commencement of the Pepperell mills. The Biddeford House (now the Thacher Hotel) was opened in July, 1847. The Biddeford Bank, the post office, and the depot were opened successively in January, February, and March, 1848. In addition to construction of the bank building, the Water Power Company had made the formation of the bank possible by subscribing to a large block of the bank's stock.

39. Saco Water Power Co. records, Treasurer's reports of profits and losses.

40. Bagnall, *Sketches of Mfg. and Textile Establishments,* vol. iii, p. 2405.

41. Saco Water Power Co. records, "Organization of the Machine Shop of the Saco Water Power Company," Jan. 31, 1850.

CHAPTER V

1. Background material for the Newton story and some specific information about Otis Pettee and his early efforts comes from Samuel Adams Drake, *History of Middlesex County* (Boston, 1880), 3 vols., vol. ii, pp. 235–237; Francis Jackson, *A History of the Early Settlement of Newton, 1639–1800, with a Genealogical Register of Its Inhabitants Prior to 1800* (Boston,

1854); *Wade's Fibre and Fabric,* Aug. 1, 1885, p. 173; Samuel Francis Smith, *History of Newton* (Boston, 1880), pp. 463–464, 473; in Duane Hamilton Hurd, editor, *History of Middlesex County, Massachusetts* (Philadelphia, 1890), see article on industries and manufactures, written by Otis Pettee, son of the founder of the machine shop, vol. iii, pp. 89 ff.

2. Middlesex County, Mass., *Deeds,* vol. 336, p. 46.

3. *Loc. cit.*

4. In *Docs. Rel. to Manufs. in U. S.,* see letters from various manufacturers giving reasons for unprofitable operations prior to 1832.

5. Middlesex County, *Deeds,* vol. 302, p. 353.

6. *Ibid.,* vol. 397, p. 241.

7. *Ibid.,* vol. 427, p. 458.

8. Abner Forbes, *Rich Men of Massachusetts, Containing a Statement of the Reputed Wealth of about Two Thousand Persons with Brief Sketches of Nearly Fifteen Hundred Characters* (Boston, 1852), 2d ed., p. 123.

9. Middlesex County, *Deeds,* vol. 316, p. 352; vol. 321, p. 40; vol. 342, p. 352.

10. *Ibid.,* vol. 342, p. 352.

11. Roe, *English and American Tool Builders,* p. 123. See this source for an excellent, though incomplete, account of the work of early American machinists.

12. Thomas R. Navin, *The Whitin Machine Works since 1831: A Textile Machinery Company in an Industrial Village* (Cambridge, 1950), Chap. 2, section entitled "A Diversified Product Line."

13. The pre-Civil War development of cotton factories in the South has been largely ignored by business and economic historians, possibly because of the overwhelming statistical importance of New England's position. Neither has the extent and importance of the pre-Civil War textile industry in New York and Pennsylvania been adequately recognized. In the 1830's and 1840's these areas were conceived to have great potentialities. The advantages of cheap labor and accessibility of raw material in the southern States were appreciated at an early date. See the issues of *Farmer and Mechanic* of 1848 for evidence of the interest in the southern movement of the textile industry in this period.

14. *Docs. Rel. to Manufs. in U. S.,* vol. i, has many examples of the rapid obsolescence of textile machinery in mills prior to 1832.

15. The marketing of textile machinery in this period has consciously been passed over as being a comparatively insignificant part of the total story. Insofar as can be determined, there were no salesmen employed as such by the machine shops. Then, as later, the solicitation of business was on a personal basis between owners of shops and owners of mills. The Matteawan Machine Shop had a branch office in New York and did some advertising in scientific periodicals, but these practices were not followed throughout the industry. Some shops exhibited their machines at fairs, but no instances where the Saco-Lowell parent companies exhibited prior to 1850 have been discovered.

16. Bishop, *History of American Manufactures,* vol. ii, p. 143.

17. N. S. B. Gras and Henrietta M. Larson, *Casebook in American Business History* (New York, 1939), pp. 667–668.

18. Warren and Pearson, *Prices,* Table I, p. 30.

19. Montgomery, *Cotton Manufacture of the U. S. A.,* pp. 24–25.

20. Hayes, *American Textile Machinery,* pp. 31–32.

21. *Farmer and Mechanic,* Dec. 21, 1848, p. 609.

22. Roe, *op. cit.,* p. 4.

23. Clark, *History of Manufs. in U. S.,* vol. i, p. 435, quoting British Parliamentary Papers, 1841, VII, 111–113, questions 1544–1556. Important American textile machines successfully introduced into England prior to 1853 included Whittemore's card-setting machinery, Arnold's compound gear, Batchelder's stop motion, the Taunton tube frame speeder, and Danforth's cap spinner. The Restrictive Acts operated far more effectively than any American tariff in protecting American machine shops from foreign competition, and the existence of these Acts appears to account for the lack of attention paid to machinery tariff rates in this period. This fact by no means implies that machinery manufacturers were not concerned with tariff questions. Their interest in tariff rates on textiles was intense. Whatever the actual effects of or the necessity for the generally protectionist tariffs which prevailed after 1816, textile and textile-machinery manufacturers alike conceived them to be a matter of primary concern. On at least two occasions in Saco-Lowell's history in this period the mere possibility that tariff rates might be lowered was enough to cause the cancellation or postponement of machinery orders. The support which candidates for federal office received from manufacturing districts in New England was determined largely by the extent of the candidates' sympathy for protection. Since the War of 1812 no other single political issue, including abolition of slavery and secession, could be calculated to stir the fervor of manufacturers to a pitch comparable to that inspired by matters of tariff policy. Tariff rates on textile machinery (included under "Manufactures of Iron" in the tariff acts) were as follows:

1790 — 7½%, gradually increased to 35% in 1816
1819 — 20 %
1825 — 25 %, gradually reduced to 21.5% in 1842
1842 — 30 %

24. Clark, *op. cit.,* p. 436.

25. See Montgomery, *Cotton Manufacture of the U. S. A.,* for a detailed comparison of the English and American textile machines and manufacturing methods about 1840.

26. The most notable exceptions, aside from Pettee, were William Mason, founder of the Mason Machine Works, and William A. Burke, superintendent and later treasurer of the Lowell Machine Shop.

27. Ware, *Early N. E. Cotton Manufacture,* pp. 149–151.

28. This is not to say that no mechanics in American machine shops were

foreign-born. To an increasing extent in the 1840's the Irish immigrants who first came to the manufacturing districts as laborers began to appear in the machine shops as semi-skilled or even skilled mechanics. The second generation shared with the sons of native Americans the opportunities for apprenticeship in skilled professions.

29. Zachariah Allen, *Science of Mechanics* (Providence, 1829), p. 349.

30. *Farmer and Mechanic,* Jan. 20, 1848, p. 31.

CHAPTER VI

1. Information about the Shop in this chapter, unless otherwise noted, comes from Lowell Machine Shop records, Minutes of directors' and stockholders' meetings.

2. See Appendix 4 for copy of the Lowell Machine Shop charter. The pattern of organization set forth in the bylaws closely followed that of the Locks and Canals Company and the other Lowell corporations. Officers consisted of a president, a treasurer, a clerk, and seven directors, of whom the president and the treasurer should be two. The president's duties were nominal, and the burden of managing company affairs rested upon the treasurer, who was designated as "General Agent" of the corporation. The specific powers and responsibilities of the treasurer were to receive and pay all monies, collect all debts and assessments, and have a general care of all the pecuniary concerns of the corporation; make purchases and sales of stock; superintend and regulate the concerns of the company, when so authorized by the directors; keep accounts; and at all times, when requested by the directors, provide statements of the condition of the corporation. The president of the corporation was to be elected by the stockholders; the treasurer by the directors. Vacancies in the directorate were to be filled by vote of the remaining directors. The only feature of the Lowell Machine Shop bylaws which warrants additional comment is that contained in Article 6. This article provided that, although each stockholder was entitled to one vote for each share or proxy held, no one stockholder should be entitled to cast more than 125 votes.

3. Lawrence in his youth shared the aversion of most Boston merchants to domestic manufactures. To him is ascribed a classic bit of bad advice which ranks with the Cabot brothers' predictions in 1814 of the failure of the Boston Manufacturing Company. In 1816 Lawrence advised Nathaniel Stevens, who was founding what was to become an outstandingly successful woolen firm, that he had best give up the manufacture, which had no future since such goods could be imported cheaper than they could be made. Lawrence fortunately changed his mind about domestic textile mills in time to participate in some of the most successful New England enterprises.

4. See Appendix 5 for the list of original subscribers and their holdings. An accurate accounting of the interests of Lowell Machine Shop stockholders in other companies in 1845 would be virtually impossible. Some hint of the extent of those interests and their importance to the new company may be

gained from the tabulation below. The companies and institutions listed herewith are those in which, in the 1840's, the seven Lowell Machine Shop directors and William Appleton, largest stockholder outside the directorate, were officers or principal stockholders. This list does not include the companies in which these men held stock, unless they were the largest stockholders. The list, in all probability, is far from complete.

Boston Mercantile Houses
J. W. Paige & Co., Wm. Appleton & Co., A. & A. Lawrence, John Clark & Co., Curtis & Stevenson.
Boston Banks
Old Boston National, New England, Columbian, Merchants National, Boston, Hamilton National, Provident Institute of Savings, Suffolk, Merchants (Eagle), Roxbury Institute of Savings.
Textile Mills
Amoskeag Mfg. Co., Manchester Mills, Stark Mills, Cocheco Mfg. Co., Laconia Co., Pepperell Mfg. Co., York Mfg. Co., Boston Mfg. Co., Merrimack Mfg. Co., Hamilton Mfg. Co., Appleton Mfg. Co., Tremont Mills, Suffolk Mills, Massachusetts Cotton Mills, Boott Mills, Middlesex Co., Prescott Mfg. Co., Essex Co., Lawrence Mfg. Co., Great Falls Mfg. Co., Atlantic Mills, Pacific Mills, Chicopee Mfg. Co., Dwight Mfg. Co., Perkins Mills, Ware Mfg. Co., Cabot Mfg. Co., Hadley Falls Co., Lancaster Mills.
Other Manufacturing Companies
Saco Water Power Co., Locks and Canals Co. (Lowell).
Insurance Companies
Merchants, Massachusetts Hospital Life, Boston.
Railroads
Nashua & Lowell, Western, Taunton Branch, Boston & Providence, Boston & Lowell, Salem & Lowell, Stony Brook.
Government
Lowell City government, Massachusetts House of Representatives, U. S. House of Representatives.

5. Only thirty-four years old, Burke, in 1845, had already been in charge of three machine shops. His career began at the age of fifteen in the machine shop of the Nashua Manufacturing Company. In 1826 he walked from Nashua to Lowell to obtain employment in the machine shop of the Locks and Canals Company, where he remained two years before returning to Nashua. In 1833 he helped to set up the machine shop of Ira Gay & Co., in North Chelmsford, Massachusetts. From 1836 to 1839 Burke served as master mechanic of the Boott Cotton Mills in Lowell, and in the latter year he went to Manchester, New Hampshire, to take charge of the repair shop of the Amoskeag Co., where he was employed until he took over his duties as superintendent at Lowell.

6. J. G. Martin, *A Century of Finance: Martin's History of the Boston*

Stock and Money Markets, One Hundred Years (Boston, 1898), pp. 128–129.

7. Sales figures for the years 1846–49 are computed from the shop ledger for those years. Sales from 1850 to 1860, inclusive, are estimates based on the number of various types of machines built, weighted and checked by changes in shop payroll. Unless otherwise noted, all information in this section comes from Lowell Machine Shop ledgers, journals, and miscellaneous records.

8. Warren and Pearson, *Prices,* Table I, pp. 10–13.

9. Lowell *Journal,* Dec. 24, 1847. See also Willard L. Thorp, *Business Annals* (New York, 1926), pp. 76–77. The files of the Boston *Traveler,* the Lowell *Journal,* and the Lowell *Advertiser* for the 1846–49 period are valuable in ascertaining the business psychology of the time. Care must be exercised, however, to study both Whig and Democratic papers.

10. Prices of Lowell Machine Shop stock are from Martin, *A Century of Finance,* pp. 126–127, 130.

11. The construction of the Prescott Manufacturing Co. mills resulted in an order for $191,600 of machinery in 1846. Expansion of the Hamilton Manufacturing Co. in the same year involved an order for $103,900 of machinery. In 1848 a tremendous order ($280,572) was placed by the Merrimack Manufacturing Co. for reëquipping four of its six mills.

12. Cowley, *History of Lowell,* p. 63.

13. The process of substituting ring for throstle spinning in American mills is reflected in the Lowell Machine Shop records as follows:

	1855	*1860*	*1865*	*1870*
Throstle Frame orders	100%	48%	25%	none
Ring Frame orders	none	52%	75%	100%

14. Wellman's self-stripper was designed to clean the top flats of the card, against which the main cylinder brushed to perform the carding action. Hitherto, these flats (which accumulated dirt and waste rapidly) had been removed from the card and cleaned by hand. Wellman's device performed the operation automatically, and represented a real contribution to the efficiency of the carding process. Wellman, who appears to have been an employee of one of the Lowell mills and who was not connected with the Machine Shop, offered the right to use his invention to these mills for the sum of $3,000. This offer, says a local historian (Cowley, *History of Lowell,* p. 146) was "stupidly refused." The average cost of stripping a card by hand was $300 yearly, all of which cost was saved by the invention, the application of which involved an expenditure of only $60 per card. The first recorded sale of Wellman's attachment by the Lowell Machine Shop was in July, 1857. Very few were sold until after 1860. For information on the famous patent suit attending the introduction of the "self-stripper" see Thomas R. Navin, Jr., "The Wellman-Woodman Patent Controversy in the Cotton Textile Industry," *Bulletin of the Business Historical Society,* vol. xxi, no. 5 (Nov., 1947), pp. 144–152.

15. Between 1850 and 1863 some 270 improvements in looms were recorded (Bishop, *Hist. of Amer. Manufs.*, vol. ii, p. 488). Some of these inventions appear to have been adaptations of the standard power loom to the production of various types of fancy goods. The perfection of the ingrain-carpet loom and the Brussels tapestry-carpet looms in 1846 and 1847, for example, affected a relatively small segment of the industry, and had no apparent effect on the Lowell Machine Shop, which did not build them. Many of these inventions, however, represented minor improvements in the basic loom types. The most important loom invention of the period appears to have been the Dutcher temple, patented in 1863.

16. The process of roving, in which the loose strand of fibers called a "sliver" which came from the drawing frame was drawn out into a finer, more cohesive roving, exhibits a complex development. The reader will recall from Chapter II that the so-called "fly frame" replaced the archaic revolving-can type of roving frame in the second and third decades of the 19th century. In America the early fly frame was called a speeder, of which there were several types: the Taunton or Tube Frame, the Double Speeder, the Plate Speeder, the Eclipse, etc. Not only did the speeder require intricate adjustments, but it failed to impart enough twist to the roving. On coarse work this latter deficiency was not important, because the roving was strong enough to be processed, even with little twist. On finer numbers twist had to be imparted to give the roving sufficient strength to hold together under subsequent processing. At the time the various speeders were being used in America, a new system was being evolved in England which grew out of improvements effected by Houldsworth in 1826. This system usually involved the use of three roving frames, designated the slubber, the intermediate, and the fine roving or jack frame, all of which incorporated Houldsworth's basic improvements. During the years in which the speeder had reigned supreme, the term "fly frame" had fallen into disuse in America. It was revived, however, and used to describe the new English slubbers, intermediates, and jack frames. The term "slubber" was used in early years to describe one variation of the old revolving-can type of roving frame, and this fact causes additional confusion, for the new type of slubber was, of course, a fly frame. The essence of the improved English roving process, which eventually displaced the American speeder, was the subdivision of that process — the use of three (sometimes four) machines, instead of one or two. (The speeder was often used in conjunction with the so-called stretcher, a machine of considerable antiquity, which refined the roving further than was possible on the speeder.) Builders of the old-type speeder did not concede defeat readily. Realizing that the system of working roving down to the requisite fineness on three or four highly specialized machines was superior to the existing practice of achieving that same fineness by repeated doublings through one machine, or even by processing through two machines (the speeder and the stretcher), these manufacturers (among them the Lowell Machine Shop) began to build three varieties of speeders. These were called coarse, intermediate, and fine speeders. This remedy postponed, but did not prevent, the triumph of the English fly

frames. The basic mechanical superiority of the latter over the speeder could not be overcome by this rather transparent modification of the American system.

For additional information on the evolution of the roving process see Andrew Ure, *The Cotton Manufacture of Great Britain* (London, 1861), vol. ii, pp. 40–55; Leigh, *Science of Modern Cotton Spinning,* vol. ii, pp. 174–181; Montgomery, *Cotton Manufacture of the U. S. A.,* pp. 60–67; R. H. Baird, *American Cotton Spinner* (Boston, 1854), pp. 125–135; D. W. Snell, *The Manager's Assistant* (Hartford, 1850), pp. 32–41; *Proceedings,* N. E. Cotton Mfrs. Assn., no. 3, pp. 16–18, no. 4, pp. 25–26, no. 37, p. 52, no. 71, pp. 258–265.

17. Between 1845 and 1851 Bement designed the following machines and tools, and possibly others for the Lowell Machine Shop: small chucking and reaming lathe, upright drill, engine lathe (two models), gear-cutting lather (two models), hydrostatic press, slotting and paring machine, and two models of power looms. The firm which Bement left Lowell to later form grew into the famous Niles, Bement & Pond.

18. List of locomotives supplied the author by Charles E. Fisher. See Appendix 6 for distribution of locomotive customers.

19. Railway & Locomotive Historical Society *Bulletin,* no. 8, pp. 24 ff.

20. Cowley, *History of Lowell,* pp. 48–58. See also the various issues of the Lowell *Journal,* 1861–65, for accounts of Lowell in the war years.

21. *Ibid.,* p. 58.

22. The extreme fluctuations in this table result from the very small number of Shop customers, and from the fact that in this period of restricted demand a single large order could obscure the general trend. Table 10 is misleading in that it does not show the high level of textile-machinery orders in 1865. In that year card and spinning-frame sales inexplicably lagged behind sales of other machines, which more than made up the deficiency. With these exceptions this table does, however, give a generally accurate picture of war demand.

23. Frederick W. Coburn, *History of Lowell and Its People* (New York, 1920), vol. i, p. 235.

24. Lowell Machine Shop records, *Orders For Work Series,* no. 4, p. 53. The terms of this interesting contract specified that the Shop was to receive "one hundred and ten percent above what we pay our men on all smithy work, and on all other labor of every description seventy five percent above what we pay our men." Materials were to be charged in "at such prices as we charge other parties."

25. Company tradition says that the Lowell Machine Shop turned the *Monitor* turrets on a huge lathe, which was built in the Locks and Canals shop in 1820. The *Monitor* was constructed, however, in 1861 by the Continental Iron Works, in Greenpoint, Long Island. Had the Lowell Machine Shop been a party to this contract, the fact would certainly have been recorded in some form in the unusually detailed manufacturing records which were kept and which have been preserved.

26. A clear view of business in the 1865–79 period can be obtained from Gras & Larson, *Casebook in American Business History*, pp. 706–725. For financial trends in New England see Martin, *Century of Finance*, pp. 34–40, 52–64. For financial and price background summary see Warren and Pearson, *op. cit.*, pp. 349–354, and Thorp, *op. cit.* For an excellent account of expansion in the textile industry see Samuel Webber, *Manual of Power for Machines, Shafts, and Belts* (New York, 1879), pp. 63–75.

27. U. S. Dept. of Commerce, *Manufactures of the U. S. in 1860*, p. xix; Webber, *Manual of Power*, p. 75; U. S. Dept. of Commerce, *Report on Manufacturing Industries in the U. S. at the 11th Census, 1890* (Washington, 1895), part iii, pp. 171-172.

28. Webber, *Manual of Power*, p. 75.

29. Navin, *Whitin Machine Works*, Chap. 5, section heading "Boom of the Early 'Seventies."

30. The best available statistical basis for comparing the record of the Lowell Machine Shop with that of its customers is that of dividends paid. This basis is far from satisfactory as a measure of prosperity, and is acceptable for use only over a considerable period of years. A comparison of Shop dividends with average dividends of most of the Shop's largest customers from 1865 to 1879 reveals a significant variation after 1873. In this comparison of data from Martin, *Century of Finance*, pp. 128–133, dividends of from 31 to 34 of the Lowell Machine Shop customers were averaged. The sampling includes most of the large northern New England mills and contains some of the most spectacularly successful and conspicuously unsuccessful mills. All dividends, cash and stock, regular and extra, are included in the average. Despite certain inconsistencies and possible errors in Martin's figures, I believe the summary below to be a useful one. The record of dividends from 1865 to 1879, expressed as a percentage of capital, reads as follows:

	Lowell Machine Shop Dividends	*Average Dividends 31 to 34 New England Textile Mills*
1865	8	13.0
1866	12	17.0
1867	12	10.9
1868	12	11.0
1869	12	12.5
1870	12	8.2
1871	12	12.7
1872	12	13.7
1873	20	11.1
1874	29	8.4
1875	12	5.8
1876	12	5.3
1877	40	6.6
1878	10	6.3
1879	30	7.3

Annual average for period: Lowell Machine Shop 16.3%; textile mills 10.0%.

31. This protest was registered frequently and in many different forms in the papers and discussions of the New England Cotton Manufacturers Association (founded in 1866), to the *Transactions* of which the reader is referred.

32. *Ibid.,* no. 2, pp. 5–6.

33. Lancaster Mills records, Directors' records and stock receipt books, Baker Library, Harvard University.

34. For an obviously biased but nonetheless interesting suggestion of these results see J. C. Ayer, *Some of the Usages and Abuses in the Management of Our Manufacturing Corporations* (Lowell, 1863). See also Vera Shlakman, *Economic History of a Factory Town,* Smith College Studies in History (Northampton, 1935), vol. xx, nos. 1–4, Oct., 1934–July, 1935, pp. 36–47.

35. J. Herbert Burgy, *The New England Cotton Textile Industry: A Study in Industrial Geography* (Baltimore, 1932), p. 30. Some large replacement orders were subsequently taken from Fall River customers, even though the Shop did not make the original installation.

36. These fairs grew out of American colonial custom, which, in turn, savored of the medieval practice of periodic gatherings at which the stock and produce of the countryside were exhibited for sale. The great stimulus to the custom, insofar as it related to manufactures, was the London Exhibition of 1851, which attracted worldwide recognition, and again in 1867, when the famous Paris Exhibition was held. At this latter exhibition some American manufactured goods, including looms and card clothing, attracted favorable comment. None of the largest American textile machine shops exhibited there, however.

37. *Scientific American,* vol. vi, p. 34, Oct. 19, 1850.

38. Coburn, *op. cit.,* vol. i, p. 351.

39. Navin, *Whitin Machine Works,* Chap. 5, section entitled "Effect of the Depression on Sales Policies."

40. These terms were arranged with the Atlantic Cotton Mills at Lawrence, Massachusetts, and the Provident Institute of Savings in Boston.

41. Further information about marketing practices of the day is extremely fragmentary. It is of some interest to note that machinery was shipped to Southern markets almost exclusively by water until about 1870. Thereafter, a rapid change was made possible by the extension of Southern rail networks, and by the mid-1870's almost all machinery went south by rail. The favored rail route out of Lowell to the south was not the Boston & Lowell Railroad and the Boston & Providence Railroad, but the western route via Springfield and Hartford. This route was made available for Lowell shippers by the Stony Brook connection, opened in 1848. Shipments north could go by way of the Nashua & Lowell line or by the Boston & Maine network, to which a cut-off was available via Lawrence after 1852.

42. The Matteawan Machine Works in Matteawan, New York, appears to have lost its early position in the industry, for reasons unknown. The Bridesburg Machine Works in Philadelphia was making a full line of cotton machinery in 1867, but was only slightly more than a third as large as the Lowell

Machine Shop and may have served only the regional and Southern markets. In the 1880's this shop lost its earlier prestige and importance, possibly through failure in the ring-spinning field. The machine shops at Lawrence and at Manchester, New Hampshire, formed to imitate the Lowell shop, soon abandoned the ambition. The former was converted to a cotton mill; the latter turned to locomotives, pumps, and fire engines. The Saco Water Power Machine Shop built a very complete line of machinery and appears to have been a strong competitor in a limited geographic area (Maine and New Hampshire), but was much smaller than the Lowell Machine Shop. Otis Pettee's machine shop was suffering reverses and was not a factor to be reckoned with in the market of 1879; it was, moreover, developing an increasingly specialized line.

43. Actually, there is evidence to indicate that the competitors of the Lowell Machine Shop were coöperating to some extent in filling orders for complete mills at a fairly early date. In 1863 Whitin and the Providence Machine Company agreed to furnish A. D. Lockwood with machinery for his Lewiston mill (Navin, *Whitin Machine Works,* Chap. 5, section entitled "Business Practices in a Sellers' Market"). It is perhaps significant that, although these competing shops were regularly exchanging price information, there is not one example of this practice in the Lowell Machine Shop treasurer's correspondence. The Shop played a solitary rôle.

44. A comparison of size and capacity can be made with Whitin, but not with Mason. In 1868 John C. Whitin said he produced five times as many railway heads as did Lowell, and in 1877 he stated that he made more ring frames than all other shops put together. These figures show how the Lowell Machine Shop was outsold in particular lines. Employment figures, however, gave a clue to over-all size. Whitin employment reached a peak of 630 men in 1873, at which time Lowell employees numbered between 1,000 and 1,200. Navin, *Whitin Machine Works, passim.*

45. The reader is referred to Navin, *Whitin Machine Works,* Appendix 7, for a chart of the principal machine-builders and their products in 1874.

46. *Manufactures of the U. S. in 1860,* pp. clxxxviii and 738. *A Compendium of the Ninth Census, June 1, 1870* (Washington, 1872), p. 806. House of Representatives Miscellaneous Documents 6, part i, *Report of the Tariff Commission, 1882* (Washington, 1882), vol. ii, pp. 2373–2374. Figures given by these sources for output of the industry are: in 1860, $4,902,704; in 1870, $13,311,118; in 1882, $20,000,000 to $25,000,000 — the last figure is an estimate only. The statement that the increase in number of establishments had been halted and reversed was made before the Tariff Commission in 1882 by Stockton Bates, of Philadelphia, and William A. Burke, treasurer of the Lowell Machine Shop (House Document 6, part i, vol. ii, pp. 2268–2270, 2373–2374).

47. Lowell Machine Shop records, Treasurer's correspondence, William A. Burke to G. W. Burke, Washington, D. C., dated Apr. 6, 1870; William A.

Burke to B. F. Nourse, Nov. 7, 1878; *Report of Tariff Commission, 1882,* House Doc. 6, part ii, vol. ii, pp. 2268–2270.

48. Lowell Machine Shop records, Treasurer's correspondence, William A. Burke to Edward Atkinson, Special Census Agent, Jan. 1, 1880.

49. In 1898 it was reported (N. E. Cotton Mfrs. Assn., *Transactions,* no. 64, pp. 18–24) that one dresser formerly supplied warp for 100 looms at a labor cost of $18 to $24 per week, while one slasher supplied warp for 500 to 700 looms at a labor cost of $9 to $12, and in addition gave more uniform results. Even allowing for improvements in the slasher between 1879 and 1898, the savings at the earlier date must have been large.

50. *Ibid.,* 1872, no. 12, pp. 36–37.

51. Boston *Journal of Commerce,* vol. 15, Feb. 28, 1880; N. E. Cotton Mfrs. Assn., *Transactions,* no. 29, pp. 8–61. The article by Channing Whitaker on page 19 of the last-named reference is recommended as an excellent exposition of the history of carding improvements. Whitaker, who was the patent expert of the Lowell Machine Shop, says that the card built by the Locks & Canals Company prior to 1845 had 12 top flats which occupied 23 per cent of the circumference of the cylinder. In 1845 the Lowell Machine Shop card had 14 flats, occupying 35 per cent of the circumference. The Foss & Pevey model as built in 1880 had 17 top and 17 under flats, which engaged 76 per cent of the cylinder's circumference.

52. The Lowell Machine Shop built the Platt Brothers' (English) mule. This machine was built under license from the English makers, and a royalty of 42 cents per spindle was paid, but the slasher apparently was not built under license. How the Shop was able to avoid licensing fees on one machine and not on another is not clear. Neither are the various ramifications of international patent law as applied to specific industries, an important field which awaits further study.

53. The principle underlying the improvement was a simple one which consisted of extending the bolster of the spindle to provide support at the spindle's center of gravity, thereby reducing the vibration which had hitherto been the limiting factor in spindle speed. The spindle revolution is well documented. A minute, though tedious and highly technical account is given in the famous suit of *Pearl* v. *Appleton,* Circuit Court of the United States, Massachusetts District, no. 885. For more condensed accounts, together with many comparisons of the performance of various types of new and old spindles, the reader is referred to the *Transactions* of the New England Cotton Manufacturers Association after 1870, and particularly to *Transactions,* no. 50, pp. 13–41, an article by George Draper on the history of the spindle. The most complete and readable distillation of the voluminous data on this subject, including much hitherto unpublished information, may be found in Navin, *Whitin Machine Works,* Chap. 10, entitled "The Spindle Controversy," to which source I am indebted for much material presented herewith.

54. It is not clear whether this was under license from Whitin or not.

55. The following information comes from George Richardson's own testimony in *Pearl* v. *Appleton,* vol. ii, pp. 918–1060.

56. Lowell Machine Shop records, Treasurer's correspondence, William A. Burke to George Richardson, Nov. 6, 1877.

57. The Pearl charges that Lowell's "Jackson" spindle was an infringement culminated in a suit in which the Jackson Company rather than the Lowell Machine Shop was named as defendant. The Lowell Shop, however, was directly involved as the maker of the spindles which the Jackson Company was using. As was often done in such circumstances, the Lowell Machine Shop assumed the burden of defending its customer, the Jackson Company, and agreed to be responsible for all costs and damages arising from the suit (Lowell Machine Shop records, Treasurer's correspondence, Wm. A. Burke to Frederick Amory, treasurer, Jackson Co., Dec. 5, 1877). As stated in the text, this suit appears not to have come to trial, yielding place to the more important Pearl-Appleton suit.

58. Navin, *Whitin Machine Works,* Chap. 9, section heading "Litigation." It is a matter of some interest to note that Judge Lowell subsequently was employed by the Lowell Machine Shop as a legal adviser on patent matters.

59. Lowell Machine Shop records confirm the popularity of the Sawyer spindle. In the year ending Mar. 31, 1879, the spinning frames produced were: Sawyer spindles, 43,842; Pearl spindles, 1,280; common (old-style) spindles, 3,652.

60. *Pearl* v. *Appleton,* Deposition of George Draper, Aug. 6, 1878, vol. ii, p. 1297. See also Appendix 7 for the reaction to these remarks by the superintendent of the Lowell Machine Shop.

61. Lowell Machine Shop records, Treasurer's correspondence, Wm. A. Burke to S. F. Gates, dated Sept. 17, 1879. For a tabulation of the cotton machinery built by the Shop see Appendix 8.

62. Navin, *Whitin Machine Works,* Chap. 4, section heading "Destiny of the Factory Village."

63. Kenngott, *Record of a City,* p. 147. Kenngott's book gives much information of value about labor conditions in Lowell. See also Cowley, *op. cit.,* and H. C. Meserve, *Lowell, An Industrial Dream Come True* (New York, 1923).

64. One of these was a branch of the Machinists and Blacksmiths Union established in 1859 in Lowell, but whether in the Lowell Machine Shop or not cannot be ascertained (Cowley, *op. cit.,* p. 199). Another was the Mule Spinners Association of the United States, which ordered strikes in 1867 and 1875 in Lowell factories. The effective organization of the mule spinners (largely English operatives) was certainly an important factor in hastening the triumph of the ring frames over mules for spinning filling.

65. Lowell Machine Shop records, Directors' minutes, report of Wm. A. Burke, June 7, 1845, and Feb. 12, 1847. These reports give full details of the changes contemplated. The most significant of these were: new machine-

shop and foundry addition in 1847 ($102,000); three new buildings in 1848 providing increased capacity for manufacturing and storage ($32,500); brick tenements for employees in 1847 ($59,000); locomotive and turbine shop in 1854 ($50,000); new storehouses in 1855 ($30,000); general alterations and enlargements authorized in 1870 ($100,000); and new countinghouse, authorized in 1879. Other improvements included new steam-heating system, better toilet facilities, and a lunchroom where employees who could not get home for the noon meal could eat lunches they brought. The last-named facility was far from usual at the time.

66. Boston *Herald,* Aug. 23, 1876.

67. Lowell Machine Shop records, Directors' minutes, Sept. 20, 1876.

68. The following men became directors in the 1845–79 period: B. F. French (1850), president of the Railroad Bank in Lowell; J. Huntington Wolcott (1850), partner in A. & A. Lawrence; John Wright (1851), agent of the Suffolk Mfg. Co.; George H. Kuhn (1854), a retired merchant with exceptionally wide interests in the textile industry and in Boston banks and insurance companies and a member of the State legislature; T. Jefferson Coolidge (1862), banker, diplomat, treasurer of the Boott Mills, and investor in many textile mills and railroads; Samuel G. Snelling (1876), partner in the firm of Appleton & Snelling, metal supply house.

69. Lowell Machine Shop records, Treasurer's correspondence, letter dated Nov. 23, 1877.

70. Ayer, *op. cit.,* p. 16.

71. Tax rates in Lowell were to play a part of increasing importance in the industrial history of the city. This subject is discussed in Chapter VII.

72. N. E. Cotton Mfrs. Assn., *Transactions,* no. 20, p. 29.

73. With the exception of the years from 1864 to 1868, when war excise taxes were levied on products sold.

CHAPTER VII

1. See Appendix 11, Table A, for a complete record of Shop officers and directors.

2. Lowell *Daily Courier,* Aug. 20, 1886.

3. Two defalcations occurring in 1886 profoundly shocked the Boston business world because they involved prominent companies and supposedly unimpeachable men. One involved the misuse of huge sums of Atlantic Mill funds, and ended in the suicide of the treasurer, William Gray. The other was a much smaller affair, but more significant to the present discussion because it involved Samuel G. Snelling, who was president of the Lowell Machine Shop at the time. Snelling had been a successful iron merchant and was intimately connected with the Pettee Machine Works. In his capacity as treasurer of the Lowell Bleachery, Snelling had made unauthorized advances of funds to a New York customer for the purchase of Bleachery goods.

Failure of this customer to pay forced Snelling into insolvency and apparently revealed other irregularities which, though not uncommon at the time, were nonetheless illegal. The Lowell Bleachery affair and the Gray defalcations created great uneasiness on State Street, and much excitement throughout Massachusetts. These events clearly marked an epoch in accounting practice; also, they inaugurated an era of increasingly effective financial controls; first, by business itself, and later, by State governments. The Lowell Bleachery defalcation is reported in the Boston *Daily Advertiser,* July 23, 24, 29, Aug. 5, 17, 20, 21, Sept. 2, 13, 21, 1886; in the Boston *Journal of Commerce,* July 24, Aug. 7, 14, 1886; and in the Lowell *Daily Courier,* July 22, Aug. 4, 19, 1886. See also Chapter IX for further information about Snelling.

4. Earned surplus of the Lowell Machine Shop from 1846 to 1897 was as follows:

1846	$ 38,400	1863	$ 85,100	1880	$355,600
1847	154,300	1864	97,100	1881	605,600
1848	105,000	1865	118,200	1882	449,500
1849	115,300	1866	no data	1883	378,800
1850	78,700	1867	129,600	1884	228,900
1851	68,500	1868	62,600	1885	156,200
1852	58,300	1869	195,600	1886	165,000
1853	78,400	1870	186,600	1887	196,200
1854	113,000	1871	231,400	1888	262,800
1855	35,300	1872	281,300	1889	341,100
1856	88,000	1873	337,300	1890	340,800
1857	52,100	1874	521,500	1891	302,100
1858	41,900	1875	403,200	1892	263,200
1859	47,900	1876	456,100	1893	278,500
1860	67,700	1877	230,500	1894	285,600
1861	90,000	1878	246,500	1895	303,300
1862	67,300	1879	248,700	1896	388,200
				1897	400,600

Source: Lowell Machine Shop records, Directors' minutes, treasurer's reports, Profit & Loss account balance. These reports show certain other balances which probably were special reserve accounts, but which are not included in the tabulation above.

5. The Civil War marked the end of an era in Lowell city government. Up to that time the corporations had virtually dominated civic affairs, though to a diminishing extent through the 1850's. After the war, civic control was permanently lost, primarily because the votes of the factory operatives could no longer be directed. A definite anti-corporation feeling, which had been fermenting since Kirk Boott's day and which the corporations had

chosen to ignore rather than combat, gathered momentum. Local indignation was easily stirred by reference to the one-sided argument that most of the profits from the great manufacturing establishments went to investors in Boston and elsewhere. The inevitable culmination of this civic-corporate strife was a strong "tax the corporations" movement. Added strength was imparted to the drive by the rise to political power of the Irish, who with much justice felt that as a laboring group they had been exploited by the corporations. The pendulum swung its full course. The excesses of one group provoked excesses in retaliation, and all parties to the struggle were destined to suffer. On both sides there was a minimum of tolerance and a total failure to grasp the serious long-range implications of the actions and counter-actions taken. Lowell taxes, stated in terms of rate per thousand on assessed valuations, did not compare unfavorably with similar communities, such as Fall River, Lawrence, and New Bedford. The actual tax paid, however, depended more on the valuations assigned than on the rate. Valuations as between various communities are almost impossible to compare. Lowell valuations appear to have been excessive. In 1872 the Lowell Machine Shop plant was carried on the company books at $450,000. The valuation assigned for tax purposes was $521,795, on which a tax of $13 per thousand, or $6,783, was paid. In 1886 the company carried plant at $410,000, while the city fathers assessed it at $910,465. From 1870 to 1885 the valuation for tax purposes was increased 97% by the Lowell assessors, while the company books showed a decrease in value of the same property of 9%. The assessed value of land in the factory yard was raised 33 1/3% in one year (1885); in 15 years (1870–1885) the assessed value was increased 124%. The assessed value of land in the foundry yard was raised 230% over this same 15-year period. The dangerous implications of heavy taxation in Massachusetts cities were becoming apparent by 1897, though the textile mills were more affected than the machine shops. The city fathers of half a score of Massachusetts textile centers were oblivious to a change in the competitive situation which their tax policies were aggravating — the rise of the Southern mills. Mill valuations in Massachusetts recognized only the number of buildings, the number of machines, and the quantity of other tangible property, with little or no attempt to appraise the market value of such property in a changing industry. This was a serious mistake, but it cannot truthfully be said that Massachusetts learned her lesson. Even though taxes actually constituted a small part of total costs of manufacture, business men placed a heavy emphasis upon this cost factor. A rise in material or labor costs of 1% might escape note or comment, but a rise in taxes of this amount would inevitably stir up the most bitter protests. It seems clear that any study of the effect of Massachusetts municipal taxes upon industry which neglects the psychological effect of tax policies on the business man must inevitably be inadequate and misleading.

6. Profit and loss figures are available only after 1868.

7. Lowell *Journal,* June 29, 1849; *Scientific American,* June 24, 1848.

8. The net increase in spindles in States south of the District of Columbia between 1860 and 1870 was 29,320 (Broadus Mitchell, *Rise of Cotton Mills in the South,* Baltimore, 1921). Between 1865 and 1870 the Lowell Machine Shop sold 18,074 spindles in these States. Lowell's share in this market appears larger than it actually was because the 29,320 spindle increase was made despite a probable large decline in spindles in war years. The total number of new spindles installed was obviously much larger than the net increase of 29,320. Even so, Lowell's share of the market must have been large.

9. *Textile World,* Jan., 1896. Navin, *Whitin Machine Works,* computed from Appendices 29 and 36.

10. All information about Whitin comes from the Navin history.

11. Lowell Machine Shop records, Treasurer's letters, Stevenson to Enterprise Manufacturing Co., Dec. 1, 1884.

12. Navin, *op. cit.,* Chap. 11, section entitled "Common Stocks for Cotton Machinery."

13. All information about the ACF affair comes from two record books in the Lowell Machine Shop collection, in which was copied all correspondence relating to the Atlanta Cotton Factory contracts. The principal machinery ordered was as follows:

54 Breaker cards
54 Finisher cards
1 Lap head
6 Railway heads
12 Apron troughs
8 Drawing frames
14 Speeders
1 Slasher
24 Filling ring frames, 224 spindles each, Pearl spindles
22 Warp ring frames, 224 spindles each, Pearl spindles
4 Spoolers
3 Warpers
250 Web looms, 32- to 40-inch
Finishing machines and parts

The opening and picking machinery was furnished by the Kitson Machine Co.

14. See N. E. Cotton Mfrs. Assn., *Transactions,* 1885, no. 39, p. 34; Boston *Journal of Commerce,* Jan. 9, 1886.

15. *Annual Reports,* Chief of Bureau of Statistics on Foreign Commerce and Navigation, imports listed under "Iron and Manufactures of Iron," subhead "Other," sub-division "Machinery." Note that this classification must have included much other machinery besides textile machinery.

16. Lowell Machine Shop records, Treasurer's correspondence, vol. 412, letter dated Mar. 11, 1872; vol. 415, letter dated Mar. 2, 1880. Navin, *op. cit.,* Chap. 12, section entitled "Formation of a Trade Association." The necessity for concerted action in tariff matters gave rise to another organization in which textile-machinery manufacturers were active. This was the Home Market Club. The membership in this club included the most prominent business men in New England, and its activities appear to have been greatest

in the 1880's and 1890's. Unfortunately, little information has survived about the club. It certainly was an effective medium for the exchange of ideas and a unifying element in New England Republican business circles. I have been unable to discover the extent of the club's lobbying activities, if any. T. Jefferson Coolidge notes in his autobiography under the year 1891 the usual dinner of the Home Market Club at the Hotel Vendome in Boston, 485 guests at the tables, General Draper presiding.

17. Lowell Machine Shop records, Treasurer's correspondence, vol. 417, letter dated May 11, 1880.

18. *Ibid.*, letters dated Feb. 9 and Mar. 4, 1882.

19. *Report of the Tariff Commission*, 47th Congress, 2d session, House Misc. Doc. 6 (Washington, 1882), part 1, vol. ii, pp. 2268–2270.

20. The extreme example of the strength of proximity is afforded by the cotton mills at Lowell, which, according to William A. Burke's statements before the Tariff Commission in 1882, had purchased little or no English machinery.

21. In Chapter VIII the history of the revolving flat card and the evolution of American carding techniques are discussed in detail in connection with the history of the Pettee Machine Works.

22. Boston *Journal of Commerce*, Aug. 15, 1885.

23. Lowell Machine Shop records, Superintendent's correspondence, letters of Hildreth to Hill, Apr. 1 and Dec. 9, 1904; interview with Frederick A. Flather, Oct. 23, 1944. It is perhaps more amusing than significant that as late as 1904 Superintendent Hildreth was doggedly insisting that the Lowell speeder was better than the fly frame for coarse work.

24. In 1870 the number of ring and mule spindles in use in America was approximately equal: 3,694,477 ring spindles and 3,437,938 mule spindles. In 1890 there were 8,824,617 ring spindles and 5,363,486 mule spindles. From 1890 to 1900, ring spindles increased by nearly 2,000,000, while mule spindles increased less than 100,000. *Report on Manufacturing Industries at the 11th Census, 1890*, Part III, *Selected Industries*, p. 168: Department of Commerce and Labor, Bureau of the Census, *Manufactures*, Part III: *Special Reports on Selected Industries* (1900), p. 47.

25. Navin, *op. cit.*, Chap. 9, section entitled "The Whitin Gravity Spindle."

26. Terms of this agreement are incorporated in the Lowell Machine Shop directors' minutes, Aug. 1, 1887.

27. The details of this suit are to be found in Navin, *op. cit.*, Chap. 10, section entitled "Whitin Machine vs. The Sawyer Spindle Company."

28. Lowell Machine Shop records, Treasurer's correspondence, Stevenson to Draper, Feb. 13, 1894.

29. It is said that the Lowell Machine Shop, upon being offered the rights to build a Draper loom (possibly the Northrop), felt obliged to refuse the opportunity when confronted with the attendant necessity of assigning to Draper all subsequent improvements which the Shop might make (interview

with Frederick A. Flather, Oct. 23, 1944). This, however, was by no means an unusual arrangement between licensor and licensee at that time or later.

30. Interview with Arthur B. Silcox, June, 1948.

31. Molding machines were designed to replace the hand process of ramming or packing the sand. The origins of machine molding are probably to be found in English practice of the late 1860's. The first molding machines ordered by the Lowell Machine Shop were double-plate machines from Reynolds & Company. These were shortly superseded by the single-plate machines of Henry Pridmore. *Transactions of the American Society of Mechanical Engineers,* 1892, vol. xiii, pp. 537 ff.; interviews with Frederick A. Flather, Oct. 23, 1944, and Jan. 30, 1948; interview with Arthur B. Silcox, Dec. 15, 1947.

CHAPTER VIII

1. This paragraph quotes and paraphrases T. Jefferson Coolidge's comments in his *Autobiography* (Boston, 1923). See also Stevens, *Nathaniel Stevens, 1756–1865; Wade's Fibre and Fabric,* 1890–97; Lowell *Journal,* 1890–97.

2. Charlotte, North Carolina, *City Directory,* 1893.

3. Navin, *Whitin Machine Works,* Chap. 12, section entitled "Informal Marketing Groups;" see this history for a more detailed account of the various Southern agencies. The Charlotte Machine Co. is considered in detail in my Chapter X.

4. The use of the manufacturer's agent and full-time salesmen by the textile machinery industry came remarkably late in the evolution of American marketing techniques. The textile machinery industry was at least half a century behind consumer goods industries in utilizing marketing specialists, and did not begin to use them until long after other producer goods industries had started to do so. The concentrated market areas served previously to 1880 and the small number of customers probably explain the retarded marketing development.

5. *150 Jahre Joh. Jacob Rieter & Cie.* See this history for a most interesting account of the Rieter firm in particular, and the Continental industry in general. References to international competition are abundant, and it is of some interest to note that even the progressive and skillful Swiss shops feared the English. This volume was privately printed in Switzerland in 1947.

6. Lowell Machine Shop records, Superintendent's correspondence, C. A. Hildreth to Henry A. Allen, Mexico City, Feb. 13, 1900.

7. U. S. Bureau of the Census, *Mfg. Industries in U. S. at 11th Census,* part III, *Selected Industries,* pp. 171–172; *ibid., Manufactures, Special Reports on Selected Industries,* p. 45.

8. Kenngott, *Record of a City,* pp. 160–169.

9. Knowlton, *Pepperell's Progress,* Chap. 13.

10. Kenngott, *op. cit.,* p. 169.

11. Lowell Machine Shop records, Treasurer's correspondence, letter dated May 2, 1894.

12. Navin, *op. cit.,* Chap. 12, section entitled "Price Agreements."

13. In 1885, for example, Southern mill managers passed a resolution suspending production for thirty days in order to raise the price of cloth goods. *Wade's Fibre and Fabric,* no. 22, Aug. 1, 1885.

14. Pepperell Mfg. Co. records, Saco Water Power Machine Shop correspondence, Draper letters to James H. McMullan, dated Feb. 12, June 14, June 26, July 3, Sept. 27, and Oct. 2, 1895.

15. Navin, *op. cit.,* Chap. 12, section entitled "Price Agreements."

16. Clipping in a scrapbook kept by the Pettee Machine Works and now a part of the Saco-Lowell collection, Baker Library. This clipping appears to be from the *Manufacturers Record,* Aug. 14, 1896, and quotes the *Industrial Record,* of Boston.

17. Navin, *op. cit.,* Chap. 12, section entitled "Price Agreements."

18. My analysis of the competitive situation in the South from 1894 to 1905 is based in part on talks with A. K. Landau, advertising manager, Saco-Lowell Shops, who commenced his career in the office of A. H. Washburn, assistant manager of the Charlotte Machine Company and Southern agent of the Pettee Machine Works and the Saco and Pettee Machine Shops; Frank J. Hale, general agent of the Pettee Machine Works, the Saco and Pettee Machine Shops, and the Saco-Lowell Shops, successively; Frank Nagel, editor for many years of the *Textile World;* and information received from Minnie Cranford, who worked with Washburn in Charlotte and was intimately acquainted with competitive conditions. Facts provided by these extremely competent observers were augmented by frequent references, hitherto acknowledged, to Navin's study of the same problem as it was faced by the Whitin Machine Works. Some of the most valuable information known to exist lies in the Whitin records, and the reader interested in this phase of the industry's history is urged to consult Navin's synthesis of this material. The Hildreth letters in the Lowell Machine Shop collection were indispensable both as a source of original material and as a means of checking information received from other sources.

19. Interview with A. K. Landau, May, 1948.

20. Information on evasion of price agreements comes from Hildreth's letters; from talks with A. K. Landau, Frank J. Hale, and others; and from Navin, *op. cit.,* Chap. 12, section entitled "Price Agreements."

21. Navin, *op. cit.,* Chap. 13, section entitled "Whitin Makes Pickers Again."

22. Interview with Joseph Marshall, Sept. 1, 1948.

23. In 1898 the Lowell Machine Shop was building the following worsted machines: double-can gill boxes; 2-spindle gill boxes; 6- and 8-spindle drawing boxes; 8-spindle finishing boxes; 24-spindle reducer frames; 24-spindle roving frames; 152- and 160-spindle cap spinning frames; 152- and 160-spindle trap twisters; 36-spindle reels. By 1904 all types and sizes of worsted

drawing and spinning machinery except combs, cards, and jack spools were being built. Lowell Machine Shop records, Letters, Worsted Department, 1899–1904.

24. *Ibid.*, Flather to Gilbert, Sept. 2, 1899.

25. *Ibid.*, Shaw to Ontario Mfg. Co., Nov. 23, 1904.

26. In 1905 a corporate change brought new men to Lowell. Hildreth, with whom Shaw had been a favorite, retired. Shaw himself, foreseeing his discharge, had taken the precaution of having copies surreptitiously made of the Shop's worsted-machinery designs, and he at once formed the Shaw Machine Company, the existence of which was predicated upon an order which Shaw had obtained from the American Woolen Company. Shaw had persuaded several Shop men to join him, and Hildreth was a director of the company. Some financial backing may have been extended by officers of the American Woolen Co., and the son of the manager of one of the largest units in the American Woolen group of mills became an executive of the Shaw Machine Co. This company, of course, had the immediate favor of the American Woolen Co., but was so grossly mismanaged that in a few months it was in bankruptcy. The actual output was about 17 spinning frames sold to the American Woolen Co., and these had to be completed by the Lowell Machine Shop. An ironic result of this venture was the enmity of the American Woolen Co. officers involved in the affair toward the Lowell Machine Shop. After this time no business of any importance came to the Lowell Machine Shop from the American Woolen Co., and for many years an unfriendly feeling persisted in that organization toward the Lowell Shop. (Saco-Lowell records, report of F. C. Havey on the Worsted Department; interviews between the author and Frederick A. Flather, C. C. Hedrick, Joseph Marshall, and Arthur B. Silcox.)

27. Of the broad movements exerting influence on American manufacturing techniques in the late 19th century, perhaps the most significant was the alliance of science and practice. This occurred in America much later than in England, where the work of scientists and scholars had materially speeded the Industrial Revolution. In America the traditional trial-and-error methods prevailed until long after the Civil War, though exceptions such as theoretician Francis Cabot Lowell should be pointed out. The founding of the Massachusetts Institute of Technology in 1865 must be considered as an event of great importance to the textile industry and the textile machinery industry. Interest in education for trade reached a high point in New England shortly thereafter. The Commonwealth of Massachusetts exhibited an exceptionally progressive attitude in education which contrasted sharply with, and helped to combat, the exceptionally short-sighted taxation policies of Massachusetts municipalities. Perhaps this contrast grew out of the fact that business leaders, though often impotent in municipal politics, were able to exert considerable influence in the Massachusetts legislature. In 1870 a legislative act introduced drawing into the school curriculum. An act in 1872 permitted cities and towns to establish industrial schools. In 1895 an act was passed requiring

manual training in high schools of cities with 20,000 or more population. In this same year a Massachusetts law was passed which permitted and encouraged by State grants the formation of textile trade schools. Fear of the Southern textile development probably was a factor in securing passage of this important law. The result was the formation of textile schools in Lowell, Lawrence, Fall River, and New Bedford. The Lowell Textile School, the first of these to organize, was considered of sufficient promise to attract contributions of machines from the Lowell Machine Shop, Davis & Furber, Whitin, Draper, Crompton & Knowles, and other shops. Charles C. Hedrick, chief engineer of the Lowell Machine Shop, played an important part in the administration of the school and taught a class of 30 pupils, many of whom were Shop employees, the principles of mechanical drawing and machine design. These schools and, on a different level, the Massachusetts Institute of Technology fed a steadily increasing stream of young men into the mills and machine shops of the entire country. Looked down upon by the old-fashioned mechanics, these men often contributed more and went further than the bench-trained machinists. The schools did not destroy the existing apprentice system; rather, they augmented it and made it more effective. When the apprentice system began to break down of its own weight, trade schools, though obviously lacking some of the merits of apprentice training, helped to fill the breach.

28. My information about the internal organization of the Lowell Machine Shop comes from interviews with Frederick A. Flather, Arthur Silcox, and Joseph Marshall, each of whom not only knew the organization as it existed at the turn of the century, but was acquainted with men whose careers reached well back into the 19th century. O. E. Nutter, who was associated with the Pettee Machine Works at that time, provided informative comments based on an outsider's viewpoint. The Lowell Machine Shop records provide only fragmentary glimpses of shop organization.

29. Navin, *op. cit.*, Chap. 12, section entitled "Price Agreements."

CHAPTER IX

1. Navin, *Whitin Machine Works,* Chap. 13, section entitled "Whitin Makes Pickers Again."

2. See *Wade's Fibre and Fabric,* 1898–1904; Gras and Larson, *Casebook in American Business History,* pp. 730–735.

3. *Wade's Fibre and Fabric,* Mar. 25, May 27, June 3, 1905; *Textile Manufacturers Journal,* June 17, 1905.

4. Lowell Machine Shop records, Directors' minutes, Mar. 8, 1905.

5. Saco and Pettee Machine Shop ledger; Navin, *op. cit.,* Chap. 13, Section heading "Whitin Makes Pickers Again;" interview with Frank J. Hale, Mar. 12, 1946.

6. The best exposition of this argument that I have found is contained in an article in the *Textile Manufacturers Journal,* June 17, 1905.

7. Interview with Frank J. Hale, Oct. 15, 1948. Source material for the ensuing paragraphs on Herrick and his affiliations comes from interviews by the author with Frank J. Hale; Edward Taft, administrator of the Herrick estate and Herrick's brother-in-law; John T. Noonan, member of the Herrick law firm; Charles E. Cooke, former secretary and clerk of the Saco-Lowell Shops; Wallace B. Donham, vice-president of the Old Colony Trust before becoming dean of the Harvard Graduate School of Business Administration. Other sources include Herrick's own testimony and that of other witnesses in *Willett* v. *Herrick*, Massachusetts Superior Court, Jan., 1924; *Director of Directors for the City of Boston; Directory of Directors for the City of New York;* Lowell Machine Shop records, Directors' and stockholders' minutes; and various Harvard Alumni Class Books. Information about Wing and the First National group comes from Gras and Larson, *op. cit.*, and Gras, *The Massachusetts First National Bank of Boston, 1784–1934* (Cambridge, 1937).

8. F. L. Higginson in his preface to *Red Top, Reminiscences of Harvard Rowing,* compiled by Robert F. Herrick (Cambridge, 1948), to which work the reader is referred for an account of Herrick's rowing interests and achievements.

9. This last-named transition is clearly discernible, but the reasons for it require further study. A logical surmise would be that the selling houses were unable to meet the financial needs of a rapidly expanding industry and in curtailing their financial assistance, they relinquished their control as well.

10. Lowell Machine Shop records, Directors' minutes.

11. Until 1905 Whitin and the Lowell Machine Shop supplied Kitson machinery on orders from their customers calling for picking and opening equipment. Saco and Pettee Machine Shop customers who wished to purchase Kitson machinery, however, could not obtain it through Saco-Pettee, which had a marketing arrangement with Atherton rather than Kitson. Since the Atherton line was regarded in many mill circles as inferior to the Kitson line, Saco-Pettee was at a disadvantage in competing for complete mill orders. Thus, the acquisition of the Kitson Shop by the Lowell Machine Shop (in which Saco-Pettee held a one-fifth interest) was of principal benefit to Saco-Pettee, enabling that company to secure access to the Kitson line on terms comparable to those hitherto enjoyed only by Lowell and Whitin.

12. The early history of Abel T. Atherton, Charles T. Atherton, and their partners, James C. Potter and Allen Whitehead, is obscure. The firm of Whitehead and Atherton was established in Lowell shortly after the Civil War to manufacture picking and opening equipment, doubtless in an effort to emulate the Kitson shop and capture a share of Richard Kitson's profitable business. In 1888 the Potter and Atherton Machine Co. was formed in Pawtucket by the Athertons, Allen Whitehead, James Potter, and others. At about the same time, the Atherton Machine Co. was formed at Lowell. The original firm of Whitehead and Atherton appears to have remained in existence, for in 1902 the Kitson Machine Co. purchased the Whitehead and Atherton patterns, and

J. H. Estes & Son purchased the manufacturing plant. There is no information that explains the formation of the Atherton Machine Co., but this firm, like the Pawtucket plant, actually commenced manufacturing operations. The Potter and Atherton Machine Co. at Pawtucket paid very large dividends for six years (50% of invested capital in 1889; 75% in 1890; 30% in 1891; 15% in 1892; 60% in 1893; and 15% in 1894). In 1893 the name of the firm was changed to the A. T. Atherton Machine Co. In 1896 the firm inexplicably and suddenly changed hands, the Athertons having surrendered or sold a large part of their holdings. The affairs of the company by this time were in desperate condition, as a result of internal struggles, increasing debt, certain unfavorable lawsuit decisions, and extremely depressed trade. For the next eight years the firm struggled on under a handicap of limited working capital, and Herrick's offer in 1905 of $75,000 for net assets amounting to $189,800, book value, was accepted. The Atherton Machine Co. at Lowell, in the meantime, had remained in existence until 1900, when it was sold, presumably to the Kitson shop. Thus, between 1869 and 1905 Abel T. Atherton had formed four companies and sold them all, but this was not the end of his career. In 1910 the Atherton Picking Machinery Co. was formed in Providence, and was purchased three years later by the Whitin Machine Works. Superficial evidence suggests that Atherton capitalized on his nuisance value and formed firms for the purpose of harassing the trade. One story has it that the terms of one of these "sell-outs" specified that Atherton turn over to the purchaser all patterns which were in the shop. Atherton, however, concealed certain machinery plans under a stone slab in the floor and used these as the basis for founding a new company. Obviously, efforts to remove Atherton from the competitive scene were thwarted in each case by his versatility in turning up with new machine patterns and a new company. There is evidence that either A. T. Atherton himself or some one of his business associates was a highly competent machinist and designer, and there is no doubt but that at times the various Atherton companies produced enough machinery to constitute a genuine competitive threat.

Sources of information on the Atherton story include directors' minutes of the Potter and Atherton Machine Co. and the A. T. Atherton Machine Co., which are part of the Lowell Machine Shop records collection at Baker Library; letters from C. L. Hildreth to John Hill dated May 18, 1900, and Apr. 14, 1902 (Lowell Machine Shops records, Superintendent's letters); and Navin, *op. cit.*, Chap. 12, Section heading "The Saco-Lowell Merger."

13. Boston *Journal of Commerce,* July 18, 1885.

14. Interview with William Shaw, former Kitson and present-time Saco-Lowell engineer, Apr., 1946.

15. Technical details of the Kitson history come from Robert S. Curley and William Shaw, who came to Saco-Lowell from the Kitson Shop; from various Kitson catalogues in Shaw's possession; and from patents in the Saco-Lowell manuscript collection.

16. In 1876 the company was advertising that laps finished by the Kitson Patent Evener varied only a quarter of an ounce to the yard. This machine yielded to the so-called Clarke & Perham three-roll sectional evener in 1880, which, in turn, gave way in 1890 to the Perham & Davis evener. Before 1890 it had been customary to feed cotton by hand on the apron of the machines, with resultant unevenness of the lap formed and with high labor cost. In 1892 Albert H. Morton adapted the so-called Bramwell Feed, which had been used to feed wool on the apron of woolen cards for use on the cotton machines built by Kitson, and this automatic feed system quickly became standard equipment. (Unpublished article on Kitson's technological history, written in 1923 by Robert S. Curley.)

17. Agreement dated June 18, 1879, between William T. Emmott and the Kitson Machine Co., Saco-Lowell manuscript collection, Baker Library, Harvard Graduate School of Business Administration.

18. Robert S. Curley, unpublished article, Saco-Lowell manuscripts.

19. *Textile Manufacturers Journal,* June 17, 1905, p. 29; Boston *Herald,* May 22, 1905.

20. *Textile Manufacturers Journal,* June 17, 1905.

21. Navin, *op. cit.,* Chap. 13, section entitled "Whitin Makes Pickers Again."

22. Interview with Joseph Marshall, who served under Perham in the Lowell shop, Sept., 1948.

23. *Ibid.*

24. Lowell Machine Shop records, Superintendent's letters, vol. 139, p. 225, Morton to Hill, Dec. 4, 1905.

25. *Ibid.,* pp. 410–411, Morton to Whiteknact, Dec. 18, 1905.

26. *Ibid.,* pp. 642–644, Morton to American Mutual Liability Insurance Co., Jan. 9, 1906.

27. *Ibid.,* vol. 140, p. 445, Morton to F. W. Hutchins, Secretary, National Founders Association, Feb. 15, 1906.

28. Interview with John K. Whittier, Oct., 1948.

29. Information about the 1911 purchase comes from ledgers, journals, and stockholders' and directors' minutes of the Lowell Machine Shop, the Kitson Machine Shop, and the Saco-Pettee Co., and from conversations with Frank J. Hale, Charles E. Cooke, and others.

CHAPTER X

1. The liquidation of Pettee's estate in 1853 effectively broke up the industrial village economy which Pettee had founded and fostered at Newton Upper Falls. Otis Pettee & Co. retained some residential properties, but most of these holdings were dispersed. Henceforth none of Saco-Lowell's parent companies was to become extensively involved in community affairs, though the shop at Newton continued to own more real estate than either the Biddeford or the Lowell shop. At Whitinsville, as in many other industrial villages, company interest extended into homes and civic institutions and facilities. In 1853 the

beginnings may be found of what was destined to become a major difference in policy between the Saco-Lowell Shops and the Whitin Machine Works.

2. Interview with Frank J. Hale, Apr. 26, 1946.

3. Frank J. Hale, interview with author, Apr. 26, 1946, and with Professor N. S. B. Gras, Oct. 9, 1944.

4. Boston *Journal of Commerce,* Mar. 27, 1880.

5. Massachusetts Corporation Reports, vol. 89, p. 538.

6. Statements of Condition, Massachusetts Corporations, Pettee Machine Works, June 6, 1883. These statements are the source of all asset and liability figures quoted hereafter, unless otherwise noted.

7. David Nevins and his associates (other than Samuel Snelling) owned most of the 690 shares of Pettee stock not held by the Snelling and Billings families in 1883.

8. *Harvard College Class of 1881, Class Report, 1884.* Rodman Paul Snelling was born in Forest Hills, Mass., Apr. 26, 1861. After attending St. Paul's School at Concord, N. H., Snelling entered Harvard, where he became a member of the cricket team, the Glee Club, the Hasty Pudding Club, the Institute of 1770, and the Porcellian Club, 1791. Following graduation in 1881 Snelling was employed for a short time in the commission iron business of his father.

9. Boston *Journal of Commerce,* Jan. 24, Mar. 7, 21, May 9, July 1, 1885, Aug. 14, 1886. The Pettee combination card was particularly popular, being in use in some of the best mills in the country. The chief feature of this card was a patent doffer reversing movement, invented by Philip T. Bagley, assistant superintendent of the company, which appears to have been a great improvement over existing methods of automatically and continuously removing the lap, or fleece, from the main cylinder. The Boston *Journal of Commerce* reported (Aug. 15, 1885) that this card was attracting attention from Europe, and that an order had been received from Switzerland.

10. Real estate owned by the Pettee Machine Works in 1886 totaled $59,754; machinery, $77,991; cash and receivables, $20,244; inventory, $99,658; debts, $75,000; capital stock, $200,000.

11. Lowell *Daily Courier,* July 22, Aug. 4, 19, 20, 1886. So generous and kind a friend to the Snellings was Henry Billings that Paul Snelling never knew that the stock which he inherited from his father had been paid for, in effect, by Billings himself.

12. A payroll book has survived which covers the period of Frank J. Hale's early employment. His name first appears on the rolls in Mar., 1880, at which time he was plugging cylinders at the rate of 20 cents per cylinder and earning $8.00 per month, working part time. In Sept., 1880, Hale appears as a full-time employee, earning, as office boy, the rather large pay (for that time and position) of six shillings ($1.00) per day.

13. Information about the early career of these men comes from the men themselves, in interviews as follows: Frank J. Hale with Professor N. S. B. Gras, Oct. 9, 1944, and many subsequent interviews with the author; Oscar E. Nutter with Professor Gras, Oct. 19, 1944, and with the author, Apr. 3, 1946;

Frederick A. Flather with Professor Gras, Oct. 23, 1944, and with the author, Jan. 30, 1948.

14. *Transactions* of the New England Cotton Manufacturers Association for the 1880–90 period contain excellent information about the introduction of the revolving flat card, and valuable commentaries on American carding techniques.

15. The revolving flat card differed from the conventional stationary flat card in that the wire-covered flats against which the main cylinder brushed to perform the carding action were fixed on an endless-chain device which kept them constantly in motion into, across, and out of the carding area. The basic improvements were that clean wire was constantly coming into the carding area, for the flats were automatically cleaned during the interval in which they were traveling out of contact with the main cylinder. Flats did not have to be set so often, and only six points required setting adjustments, as compared with 136 points on the Wellman card. The cylinder and doffer could be stripped and ground on the machine. There was less waste, for the flats did not have to be lifted from the cylinder to be stripped, a process which on the old-style card left a space through which the cotton escaped. These and many other improvements can be summarized by stating that much lower labor costs, better work, and less waste were implicit in the new type of machine, and productivity was double that of the old-style card. Moreover, single carding, which the revolving flat card made possible, resulted in tremendous savings in floor space as compared with double carding, and resulted in a simplification of the process, with attendant savings in repairs and maintenance. These advantages far outweighed the high initial cost of the new card.

In a thesis written at the Massachusetts Institute of Technology in 1887, Oscar E. Nutter, later to become superintendent and agent of the Newton shop, reported a comparison between the Platt revolving flat card (single carding) and double carding as practised in several American mills. The following table, taken from his thesis, has considerable historical interest:

Figures for a Mill Producing 18,000 Pounds of Carded Cotton per Day

	Single Carding	*Double Carding*
Production of 1 card per day of 10 hours	140 pounds	55.72 pounds
Number of cards necessary	130	646
Horsepower to run cards	95.68	102.32
Cost of 1 card	$ 720	$ 175.30
Total cost of cards	$93,600	$113,243
Space occupied by cards, drawing, frames and slubbers	24,517 sq. ft.	48,449 sq. ft.
Cost of room @ 75 cents per square foot	$17,138	$ 36,337
Number of drawing frame deliveries	384	220
Per cent of waste made by cards	6.38	10.98

A further comparison between the new card and the old is found in one of Nutter's notebooks, the entry apparently having been made about the turn of the century:

Cost of Help in Card Room at Dwight Mfg. Co.

(Labor cost per week)

Old System with Double Carding	
2 card strippers	$11.60
1 front boy	4.64
½ lap man	2.61
1 winder boy	4.64
1 stripper on finishers	5.80
1 front boy on finishers	4.64
1 railway boy	4.64
2 drawing hands	7.54
2 grinders	18.32
Total labor cost	$64.43

After 40" Revolving Flat Cards Had Been Put In	
2 card strippers	$11.60
1 can boy	4.64
2 drawing hands	11.60
1 grinder	9.16
½ lap man	2.61
	$39.61

The origin of the revolving flat card is obscure, but it appears to have been used much earlier than has commonly been supposed. The machine is an interesting example of the lag so frequently found between conception of a new idea and widespread commercial adaptation. Evan Arthur Leigh was popularly believed to have invented the revolving flat card, with basic patents issued in England in 1850, 1852, and 1857 (*Transactions,* N. E. Cotton Mfrs. Assn., no. 39, p. 18). Actually, the machine appears to have come from the Continent. *Spon's Encyclopaedia* (London, 1882, 4 vols., vol. ii, p. 747) states that it was invented by M. Heilman, of Mulhausen, and became familiar to the English after a demonstration at the London Exhibition of 1851. A group of Manchester spinners purchased the patent rights for £30,000, and eventually leased the patents out on a royalty basis. In a report included in the U. S. Census of 1900, Edward Stanwood reported that the revolving flat-card principle had been devised in 1834 (*12th Census of the U. S.,* vol. 60, *Manufactures,* Part M, *Special Reports on Selected Industries,* p. 43). The Swiss firm of Rieter developed a revolving flat card in 1846 (*150 Jahre Joh. Jacob Rieter & Cie., 1795–1945,* pp. 226–228). The revolving flat cards in England before the late 1870's, however, were inferior in capacity to existing cards. The stationary flat cards then in use were 50 inches in diameter and 40 or 50 inches wide. Large carding capacity was in favor, and the 40-inch width and 40-inch diameter size of the revolving flat cards introduced at the time attracted little favor. In the late 1870's the new card was enlarged to 50 inches in diameter, and widespread adoption followed. By 1885 this card was in universal use in England, but only experimental installations had been made in America.

16. The earliest instance I have been able to find of revolving flat cards in use in America is the installation of some of these cards by the Harmony

Mills, New York, in 1859. These are supposed to have been the first ever imported (*Transactions,* N. E. Cotton Mfrs. Assn., no. 39, p. 21). It was not until 1883 that a formal notice was made by the association of the new card as improved by Leigh and others (*ibid.,* no. 35, p. 43).

17. R. P. Snelling testimony before the U. S. Tariff Commission, *Report of the U. S. Tariff Commission,* 1890, vol. i, p. 490.

18. Frederick A. Flather, interview with author, Jan. 30, 1948.

19. Pressure from influential stockholders to get the machine into production was certainly a natural product of the anxieties which were rife. An earlier and more famous analogy was the concern of the Boston Manufacturing Company stockholders over the efforts of Francis Cabot Lowell and Paul Moody to start the power loom in 1814. This was not the only pressure, however, that was brought to bear on Superintendent Francis in this trying period. There was a strong demand on the part of certain stockholders who were financially interested in American card-clothing concerns to adopt the inferior domestic cylinder clothing. To Francis' everlasting credit, he stood firm and insisted upon incorporating the unsurpassed steel-wire clothing from Sykes, in England. I mention this incident as one of the few specific cases known where the corporate interrelationships in the textile and textile machinery industries, mentioned at several points in the text, exerted an immediate and strong influence upon business policy — in this case, an unhealthful influence.

20. The Pettee revolving flat card was a very close copy of the Platt Brothers card. The specifications were as follows: 84 flats, 1⅜ inches wide; cylinder 50 inches in diameter, 41 inches wide; screens by Hill Mfg. Co.; clothing by T. K. Earle; coiler, English pattern, by E. A. Leigh & Co.; can dimension 10 inches by 36 inches (Saco-Lowell Shops, Specifications Book, 1886–1893). Subsequent improvements included increase in the number of flats from 84 to 100 in 1892, and to 110 flats in 1894. Several other improvements were incorporated to facilitate the accurate and economical production of parts (C. E. Mills, "Some Detail Developments in the History of the Revolving Flat Card," a talk given before a group of Saco-Lowell salesmen at Newton on Dec. 29, 1922).

21. Interview with Frank J. Hale, Mar. 12, 1946. Nevins later confessed that Hale had made the stock so valuable that he hoped he would not be held to this rash promise! Instead, Nevins offered Hale and Snelling financial assistance in purchasing stock of their own.

22. See Chapter VII for an account of Flather's work at Lowell. Flather himself tells of one embarrassing aspect of his change in positions. Until 1893 he had been active in convincing various mill men of the unsurpassed quality of the Pettee card. After this time the requirements of his new position demanded that he approach the same mill men with a view to convincing them of the supremacy of the Lowell card (Frederick A. Flather, interview with author, Jan. 30, 1948).

23. Frank J. Hale, interview with author, Mar. 12, 1946.

24. These general explanations of the true significance of the figures in Table 21 must be amended by the addition of one further point. There is justification for a reasonable suspicion that the Pettee Machine Works was more prosperous than the official Statements of Condition, furnished annually by the company to the Commonwealth, indicated. The evidence in support of this suspicion lies in the differences between the figures contained in Table 21 (the figures given in the Statements of Condition) and the actual ledger balances contained in company records. These differences appear to have their origin in the fact that the laws of the Commonwealth relative to statements of condition from corporations could be complied with completely without complete disclosure of a company's true condition. The figures furnished below are further evidence, if any is needed, of the care with which published corporate records in this period must be used by students of business. In the two statements below there is a discrepancy in dates of one month. The statements, however, cover the same accounting period.

Pettee Machine Works Ledger Balances, May 1, 1895

Real Estate and Machinery	$154,766.13	Capital Stock	$200,000.00
New Tools and Additions	328,638.09	Bills Payable	193,400.00
Stock on Hand	67,168.21	Accounts Payable	76,078.93
Cash	6,363.93	Reserve	253,469.15
Bills Receivable	32,646.68	Profit and Loss	51,320.98
Mill Stocks	30,630.00		
Accounts Receivable	154,056.02		
Total	$774,269.06		$774,269.06

Pettee Machine Works
Statement of Condition, Massachusetts Corporation Records
June 5, 1895

Real Estate	$134,934.47	Capital Stock	$200,000.00
Cash and Receivables	193,066.63	Cash Borrowed	193,400.00
Inventory	67,168.21	Book Accounts	76,078.93
Machinery	95,000.00	Profit and Loss	51,320.38
Miscellaneous	30,630.00		
Total	$520,799.31		$520,799.31

In 1897 total assets of $433,500 were reported to the Commonwealth, while ledger balances showed actual assets, after write-downs of inventory and mill stocks, of $871,529.96.

25. My information about the early career of Frank J. Hale comes from the best possible source — the men who worked with and under him. These include Frederick A. Flather, Oscar E. Nutter, Alexander Rankeillor, and A. K.

Landau. Many of the facts of his early career and much information about Paul Snelling come from Hale himself.

26. Frank J. Hale, interview with author, Mar. 12, 1946. Another weapon employed against the Pettee Machine Works was the technique later to be known as the "tie-in" sale. Until 1898, when pickers were covered by price agreements, these machines were often included in large orders at a very low price, or even given away. This practice was particularly effective in the years before the Pettee Machine Works was able to retaliate in kind with the Atherton line carried by the Charlotte Machine Co.

27. In 1896 the Charlotte Machine Co., under the direction of H. S. Chadwick, represented the following companies in the South: A. T. Atherton Machine Co. (openers, feeders, and lappers); Pettee Machine Works (cards, railway heads, drawing frames); Providence Machine Co. (roving frames); Fales & Jenks Machine Co. (spinning and twisting frames); Easton & Burnham Machine Co. (slashers, size kettles, and sizing machinery); Knowles Loom Works (looms); Curtis & Marble Machine Co. (finishing machinery); B. F. Sturtevant Co. (heating and ventilating systems, forges, steam engines); General Electric Company (electrical apparatus of all kinds); U. S. Aerophor Air-Moistening and Ventilating Co. (factory humidifiers); Jones & Laughlin (steel shafting, couplings, hangers, pulleys); Corliss Steam Engine Co. (boilers, heaters, pumps).

28. Memorandum book of Frank J. Hale. See also Navin, *op. cit.*, Chap. 12, section entitled "Price Agreements."

29. *Loc. cit.*

30. This conclusion was also reached by Navin in his study of the Whitin Machine Works records. See my Appendix 12 for a list of the mill stocks held by the Pettee Machine Works in 1896. The details surrounding the acquisition and disposal of these stocks up to 1897 are not known. Only one contract involving the acceptance of stock in payment for machinery appears to have survived. This contract is dated June 30, 1896, and was made between the Charlotte Machine Co. and the Arkwright Mill, of Spartanburg, South Carolina. The contract stated the following terms:

Machinery ordered, $8,500 net value.

Terms of payment:

50% of order in capital stock of Arkwright Mill. Stock valued at par ($100 per share).

25% of order in cash, New York exchange, 30 days from average date of Bills of Lading.

25% of order by 6-month note, renewable, if necessary, for a period of 8 months, interest 6% per annum.

The attempt, in 1896, of the Northern machine shops to curb the practice of accepting stock (Chapter VIII) appears to have been inspired by liberal terms like those quoted above. A more usual arrangement was to accept 25% of the payment in stock, the remainder in cash and notes.

31. These ten largest mills were:

Pelzer Mfg. Co. (S. C.)	107,026 spindles.
Clifton Mfg. Co. (S. C.)	86,000 "
Spartan Mills (S. C.)	72,160 "
Riverside Mills (Va.)	65,500 "
Piedmont Mfg. Co. (S. C.)	58,000 "
Pacolet Mfg. Co. (S. C.)	55,924 "
Union Cotton Mills (S. C.)	52,762 "
Gaffney Mfg. Co. (S. C.)	52,000 "
Eagle & Phenix Mills (Ga.)	50,000 "
Henderson Mills (Ky.)	50,000 "

Of these, only the Clifton Mfg. Co., the Riverside Mills, and the Henderson Mills were not using Pettee cards in 1896. All three of these had been Lowell Machine Shop customers in the past, and may have been using Lowell cards.

32. Memorandum book of Frank J. Hale, p. 118; Boston *Journal of Commerce,* June 29, 1895.

33. The Pettee Machine Works was paying royalties to an English firm for the exclusive right to build this grinder in America. The Lowell Machine Shop, however, purchased the English patent outright, so that royalties were henceforth payable to Lowell.

34. Most of the information about the Newton plant was furnished me by Oscar E. Nutter, who modestly omitted mention of his own contributions, of which I learned from talks with his contemporaries. It has been claimed that the Newton foundry was the first among all textile-machine-shop foundries to adopt machine molding. As will be seen in Chapter XI, which deals with the Saco Water Power Machine Shop, this claim cannot be sustained. The Newton foundry, however, adopted this method and other advanced techniques well ahead of the industry. The cost advantage of machine over hand molding is illustrated by the following figures, dated about 1904, taken from a notebook belonging to Nutter:

Name of Piece	Labor Cost per Piece: Machine Molding	Labor Cost per Piece: Hand Molding	Number of Pieces Which must be Made before Savings Pay for Cost of Machine Pattern
Card Side	$.78	$1.16	1,618
Cylinder Spider	.31	.56¼	790
Arch	.33	.56¼	1,400
Card Side Panel	.03½	.08	673
Doffer Shroud	.14	.37½	713
Feed Apron	.20⅛	.45	602
Tube Gear	.08	.20½	no data
Main Card Pulleys	.13	.37½	no data
Doffer Spider	.11	.17	no data

35. Oscar E. Nutter, interview with author, Mar. 31, 1948; Memorandum book of Frank J. Hale, p. 82. At this time molders averaged $2.09 per day, coremakers $1.25, and lumpers $1.19. The average rate of daily pay in the carpenter shop was $1.72; in the paint shop, $1.19; in the smith shop, $2.10; in the tool room, $1.88; for drawing-frame erecting, $1.75; and for card erecting, $1.81.

36. Frank J. Hale, interview with author, Mar. 12, 1946.

37. See Appendix 11, Table B, for list of officers and directors of the Pettee Machine Works, 1882–97. The board of directors was never larger than five men. Henry S. Shaw, who served from 1887 to 1897, was Nevins' assistant and associate. Frederick E. Clarke, who served from 1889 to 1897, was agent of the Pemberton and Methuen companies, two of Nevins' mills. Harcourt Amory, who served from 1887 to 1897, was closely allied with the Lancaster Company, the Indian Head Mills of Alabama, and the Nashua and Jackson Companies, already mentioned as being closely linked with Nevins and the Pettee Machine Works.

38. Memorandum book of Frank J. Hale, pp. 52–53, 78.

CHAPTER XI

1. See Appendix 11, Table C, for list of the officers and directors of the Saco Water Power Company, 1839–67.

2. Unless otherwise indicated, all information about the Saco Water Power Company comes from company records on deposit at Baker Library, Harvard Graduate School of Business Administration. These include correspondence between the treasurer and the superintendent of the company and many summary financial statements, but no ledgers or journals.

3. The Sharpe and Roberts mule which Wetherell brought back from England was discarded in favor of a Hibbert, Platt & Sons mule secured from the shop of Hawes, Marvel & Davol, of Phoenix, Rhode Island. Knowlton, *Pepperell's Progress,* p. 55.

4. Prominent among the pre-Civil War customers were the Hill Mfg. Co. and the Bates Mfg. Co., in Maine; the Exeter Mfg. Co. and the New Market Mfg. Co., in New Hampshire; and the Pacific Mills, in Massachusetts. In 1855 and 1856, orders from Pepperell for mules, drawing frames, roving frames, and spinning frames for Mill Number 3 totaled $200,000. *Ibid.,* p. 57.

5. *The Union,* Saco, Maine, July 27, 1852, p. 2, col. 3.

6. Navin, *Whitin Machine Works,* Chap. 5, section entitled "Business Practices in a Sellers' Market."

7. These prices were as follows:

72-spindle	slubber,	bobbin	9½ x 5	—$13.25	per spindle
80-"	intermediate,	"	9 x 4½	— 12.50	" "
120-"	"	"	7 x 3½	— 9.00	" "
152-"	jack	"	6 x 3	— 8.00	" "

8. The terms of one of Thompson's contracts were as follows:

Base salary, $1,800.
Plus one-half of proceeds from year's sales, minus:
(1) Expenditures, including those for tools and patterns.
(2) One-half expenses of treasurer's office in Boston.
(3) Insurance, taxes, interest, and general expenses.
(4) $6,000 for rent of property.

If this residual sum amounts to more than $8,200, then the balance is to be divided one-third to Thompson and two-thirds to the company.

9. Considerable information exists concerning land operations of the Saco Water Power Company which I have purposely passed over. This department was headed by Thomas Quinby, and was charged with responsibility for regulating the water power rented to local mills and for buying and selling property. In 1850 real estate, exclusive of machine-shop buildings, owned by the company totaled $496,700. A year later $5,000 was appropriated to purchase additional lands, and in 1854 the Water Power Company, Pepperell, and Laconia divided expenses of $13,500 incurred in acquiring the outlet of Ossipee Lake and land and privileges at Hiram Falls. By 1862 the real estate account stood at $527,600. A substantial part of the income received from land operations (shown in Table 28 of text) consisted of rentals of a wide variety of property which ranged from the Biddeford House (the local hostelry built and owned by the company) to mill powers and tenements. Rental income usually was about $30,000 a year, and additional income was provided by land sales of up to $30,000 a year.

10. My information is based on figures taken from the treasurer's report of May 31, 1866, the latest complete figures available. The purchase price was $489,803 less than the book value of the Water Power Company stock. Since so many Water Power shareholders were not Pepperell or Laconia shareholders, it is of some interest to examine the financial returns involved in ownership of Water Power Company stock alone, from 1839 to 1866. The following figures were computed from company records on a per-share basis:

Paid in per share, 1839		$500
Dividends received, 1839–1866	$330	
Liquidation dividends, 1867	$220	$550
Net Gain Per Share in 23 Years		$ 50 (.4% per year)

11. Amos D. Lockwood had purchased a substantial interest in the Quinebaug Mfg. Co. in 1851; reorganized the Pacific Mills in 1860; built the Hill Mill Number Six in 1861; organized the Wauregan Mills in 1863; and purchased the Lewiston Foundry and converted it to a machine shop. He had been active in a managerial capacity in mills in Lewiston and Waterville, Maine, and at the Quinebaug mill. His talents were so extensive on the technical side

that he gradually worked into the consulting field, and was certainly one of the first and most famous mill engineers in the country.

12. *The Union and Journal,* Biddeford, Maine, Dec. 28, 1866, p. 2.

13. Information relating to the character of James McMullan comes from his daughter, Mrs. John W. Gulick, from Roderic Tarr, and from Alexander Rankeillor.

14. Saco Water Power Machine Shop records, Treasurer's correspondence. All information hereafter is taken from company records, unless otherwise indicated.

15. Mrs. Gulick, interview with author, May 9, 1946.

16. See Appendix 11, Table D, for list of Saco Water Power Machine Shop officers and directors.

17. These rights were challenged by other shops and, by 1869, others in America appear to have been building this mule.

18. Alexander Rankeillor, interview with Professor N. S. B. Gras, Mar. 5, 1945.

19. *Ibid.,* Nov. 17, 1944. McMullan had previously (1880) declined to take an interest in the Pearl spindle patents.

20. Dane Yorke, "Introduction to Biddeford's History" (mimeographed). Yorke states that this information comes from reminiscences of one of the old-time workmen.

21. Boston *Journal of Commerce,* Apr. 24, 1886, p. 18.

22. Interview with Mrs. Gulick, May 9, 1946.

23. Alexander Rankeillor, interview with Professor Gras, Nov. 17, 1944.

24. McMullan's experience with the Atlanta Cotton Factory would certainly seem to justify the decisive action taken previously by the Lowell Machine Shop. Less than a year after accepting the Atlanta contract McMullan was telegraphing William Burke, treasurer of the Lowell shop, to ask the name of Lowell's Atlanta counsel. McMullan appears to have met with as little success as had Burke before him in obtaining a settlement of any kind. McMullan, too, complained of lack of good faith among the promoters. In 1894, fourteen years after taking the order, McMullan was telling Spencer W. Richardson, "I send you herewith letter from Atlanta Cotton Mills which I have not answered — as you have the notes leave it to you, and suppose there is nothing for us to do but accept their proposition, and hope for the future." The outcome of McMullan's dealings with the Atlanta Factory is not known.

25. Saco Water Power Machine Shop records, Letter dated Dec. 25, 1886.

26. Between 1880 and 1885 the Saco Water Power Machine Shop extended notes for, or otherwise accommodated, the Piedmont Mfg. Co., the Clifton Mfg. Co., the Newberry Cotton Mills, and the Pacolet Mfg. Co., in South Carolina; the John P. King Mfg. Co., in Georgia; and the Matthews Cotton Mills in Alabama. All these mills, which included some of the most prosperous in the South, became good customers for Biddeford machinery.

27. Navin, *op. cit.,* footnote 12 to Chap. 12.

28. Frank J. Hale, interview with author, Mar. 12, 1946.

CHAPTER XII

1. Information about the terms of the merger of 1897 comes from ledgers and journals of the two companies, stockholders' and directors' minutes of the Pettee Machine Works, and conversations with Frank J. Hale. Figures upon which the terms of the merger were predicated were those standing on the books of the two companies on Apr. 30, 1897.

2. I consider the fairly complete figures which record the transactions on the books of both companies as almost meaningless insofar as actual values involved in the merger are concerned. The use of book values of stock, representing stockholders' equity in the business, as a yardstick for the transaction yields the following results:

	Book Value Per Share	*Exchanged for*
Pettee Machine Works stock	$351	$70 in cash and $225 (par value) in shares of new company stock.
Saco Water Power Machine Shop stock (estimated)	$106	$100 in cash and $58.33 (par value) in shares of new company stock.

The higher cash returns received by the Saco Water Power Machine Shop stockholders were a result of a more complete liquidation of Biddeford assets. Only plant, stock, and some cash were turned over to the new company, as follows:

Plant (after being depreciated 13% from book value)	$260,000.00
Stock (at full book value)	52,368.55
Cash	37,631.45
Total assets exchanged for stock	$350,000.00

Receivables, payables, mill stocks, and other assets and liabilities were liquidated, the proceeds accounting for the estimated $100 in cash received by the Biddeford stockholders.

3. Frank J. Hale, interview with author, Mar. 12, 1946.

4. Biddeford *Record,* June 7, 1901, article and editorial.

5. In this table figures for the Saco and Pettee Machine Shops are carried through in unbroken series under that designation from 1898 to 1912, despite the fact that in 1910 the operating company became the Saco-Pettee Company, and the Saco and Pettee Machine Shops commenced liquidation.

6. U. S. Department of Commerce, Bureau of Foreign and Domestic Commerce, Miscellaneous Series No. 37, *The Cotton-Spinning Machinery Industry*

(Washington, 1916), Chap. 2. The classification "preparatory machinery" includes all machinery up to, but not including, the weaving process.

7. In 1908 the *Textile World* (vol. xxxiv, p. 337) reported inquiries from India for American textile machinery and the opinion of the American consul there that, since English makers were quoting eighteen-months delivery, American shops might gain an entry there. To this the *Textile World* made the significant and familiar reply that American shops were still unable to meet English prices and that they had all the business they wanted at home, at their own prices. The U. S. Department of Commerce report on the cotton-spinning machinery industry also noted the fact that, for the years 1906–14, virtually no American preparatory cotton machinery was exported (Department of Commerce, *op. cit.*, Chap. 8).

8. A. K. Landau, interview with author.

9. Minnie G. Cranford, letter to author, Feb. 18, 1948.

10. Boston *Journal of Commerce,* Jan. 3, 1885. In 1897 Deering, Milliken & Co. were selling agents for the Darlington, Lockhart, Pacolet, Spartan, and Whitney mills in South Carolina; the Barker and Lockwood mills in Maine; the Dallas mill in Alabama; and the Quinebaug mill in Connecticut.

11. Navin, *Whitin Machine Works,* Chap. 11, section entitled "Common Stocks for Cotton Machinery."

12. *Ibid.*

13. *Directory of Directors for the City of Boston,* 1912; *Directory of Directors for the City of New York,* 1912.

14. *Lamb's Textile Industries,* vol. i, pp. 279 ff. The contact with Myron C. Taylor was formed when Taylor came to Hale and Snelling to secure machinery for mills which he had acquired. Hale and Snelling were greatly impressed by Taylor, and extended liberal credits on the machinery ordered. The first of the Taylor mills was purchased with the intent to manufacture fabric for mail bags which Taylor's father had contracted to supply to the United States Government. In 1907 a selling agency, the Boston Yarn Co., was organized to handle the products of the two mills then controlled by Taylor and others (the LeRoy Cotton Mills in LeRoy, New York, and the Warner Cotton Mills in Newburyport, Massachusetts). Hale participated in the affairs of the selling agency, which in 1910 was sold to the J. Spencer Turner Co., of New York. The Bay State Cotton Corporation, in which both Hale and Snelling were interested, was a holding company for stock of the Lowell Weaving Co., the Warner Cotton Mills, and the LeRoy Cotton Mills. The International Cotton Mills was a holding company for the shares of the Consolidated Cotton Corporation, J. Spencer Turner Company, the Boston Yarn Co., and the Bay State Cotton Corporation (Lamb, *op. cit.*, pp. 279 ff.; Frank J. Hale, conversation with author, Sept. 21, 1948).

15. Saco and Pettee Machine Shop records, Stock transfer ledger.

16. From June 1, 1898, to Nov. 1, 1912, fifty-seven directors' meetings were held. Attendance was as follows:

Henry S. Shaw	57	meetings
John W. Danielson	11	"
Rodman P. Snelling	57	"
Frank W. Hale	54	"
Harcourt Amory	42	"
Seth Milliken	10	"
Charles E. Rogerson	37	meetings out of 41 held during his term of office (1904–12)

17. The minutes of the directors' meetings and other formal records of the company tell little about how the company was actually run. My information comes largely from talks with Hale.

18. The legal side of business history has been neglected, apparently because few business historians have been lawyers, and few lawyers have been business historians. With reference to the vital changes occurring in corporation law at the turn of the century the reader is referred to Walter C. Noyes, *A Treatise of Law on Inter-Corporate Relations* (Boston, 1909) for technical information, and to the Commonwealth of Massachusetts, *Report of the Committee on Corporation Laws,* created by Acts of 1902, Chapter 335, Jan., 1903 (Boston, 1903), for a most valuable and readable account of contemporary trends.

19. This figure differs from that given in Appendix 12 because it includes all securities held or accepted, whereas Appendix 12 lists only textile securities.

20. The principal exceptions were stock of the Lowell Machine Shop ($335,509.57) and Ashworth Bros., Inc. ($90,000) retained on the books of the Saco and Pettee Machine Shops, and $171,600 of mill stocks transferred in 1912 to the Saco-Lowell Shops.

21. Navin, *op. cit.,* footnote 24 to Chap. 21.

22. U. S. Department of Commerce, Bur. of For. and Dom. Com., *op. cit.,* Chap. 5.

23. Oscar E. Nutter, conversation with author, Sept., 1948.

24. The mechanics of obtaining net profits for the Newton and Biddeford shops were as follows: The recorded semiannual net profits were corrected for write-downs in inventory values of as high as two-thirds of the cost value of the inventory. Some of this charged-off value undoubtedly represented genuine losses on inventory, but in the absence of any serious or prolonged downward movement in metal prices most of the depreciation was obviously artificial. The resulting profit figure was then further corrected for large write-downs in mill securities, which in certain years were charged off against operating expense. In some instances income from stock dividends was credited to operations, and this, too, was removed. No depreciation expense was regularly charged to operations on company books. Instead, large reserves for depreciation were periodically set up out of earned surplus. I was unable to make any allocation

of depreciation expense, and the reserves set aside for depreciation actually appear to have been far in excess of needs. Such reserves probably constituted one means of concealing accumulated profits. My profit figures, therefore, reflect no depreciation charges as such, but the distortion should not be serious. Charges which today would be made against accumulated depreciation reserves were, in the period under consideration, customarily included in repairs or other operating expense accounts.

25. U. S. Department of Commerce, *op. cit.,* Chap. 2. I found the figures in this very useful report, in the case of the Saco and Pettee Machine Shops at least, to be misleading and tending to understate actual profits by a considerable amount. However, if (as seems likely) all shops were similarly conservative in reporting, the statistics have value as measures of comparative performance. In the published report no shops were designated by name. Thomas R. Navin and I, working from records at our disposal, were able to identify the six shops reported on and referred to by number in the report.

26. Since the preferred stock represented additional paid-in capital, the return on that stock has not been included in these computations, but is shown separately in Table 37.

27. Oscar E. Nutter and Alexander Rankeillor, interviews with author.

28. U. S. Department of Commerce, *op. cit.,* Chap. 7, Table 34. This report does not indicate whether foremen's earnings are included in the averages. Since such earnings are included in the wage figures given for the Newton and Biddeford shops in the 1870's and 1880's, there is a possibility that a small margin of error exists in the comparisons, though scarcely enough to invalidate the conclusions drawn.

29. Much of my information about the Biddeford shop comes from Roderic Tarr, who in this period was employed in the drafting room of the shop, and from Alexander Rankeillor, who was assistant superintendent. Oscar E. Nutter provided information about E. E. Blake.

30. Biddeford *Weekly Journal,* Mar. 4, 26, 1904, Nov. 17, 1922; Pepperell manuscripts, Baker Library, Harvard Business School, Correspondence book, vol. 604, letter from Robert McArthur to Philip DeNormandie, dated Apr. 7, 1904.

CHAPTER XIII

1. Source material for this section, unless otherwise indicated, consists of directors' and stockholders' minutes of the Lowell Machine Shop, the Saco-Pettee Company, the Textile Securities Company, the Kitson Machine Shop, and the Saco-Lowell Shops; ledgers and journals of the Saco-Lowell Shops; and a series of notebooks (referred to hereafter as "Totals notebooks") containing summary figures and other information of great value which were prepared as reports to the directors.

2. Frank J. Hale, interview with author, Oct. 18, 1948. Morton's managerial methods were so far from normal that it seems almost inevitable that he would

have been dismissed immediately by anyone who had not observed his results over a period of years. So successful was he in delegating responsibility and so keen was he in sensing trouble spots in the organization that Morton actually had leisure time during the day. He spent hours in the shop which an administrator of more usual ability could scarcely have spared from the office, and he occasionally forsook the shop entirely for an afternoon of golf. As far as the new management was concerned, however, Morton's fatal mistake was in baiting the dignified Paul Snelling. At this time Morton was receiving large royalties on his automatic distributor. Since it was quite unusual for an inventor employed by a machine shop to receive any royalties whatsoever (both by contract and long-established precedent shop employees assigned all patents on inventions made during their employment period to the employer), Snelling was chronically irritated by the size of the checks he was forced to sign for Morton. Instead of waiting for these checks to arrive by mail, Morton took keen delight in going to the treasurer's office and asking for them in person. "A day's use of that money is as good to me as it is to you, Mr. Snelling," he blandly observed on one occasion.

3. Records of Saco-Lowell stock ownership in the 1912–26 period are extremely fragmentary. In Oct., 1916, there were (as in 1912) 36,000 shares of voting stock outstanding: 23,500 of common stock and 12,500 of preferred stock. The common stock was divided among 212 shareholders, of whom the following are of particular interest:

Harcourt Amory	224 shares	Seth Milliken	484 shares
Nevins Estate	800 "	R. I. Hospital Trust Co. for	
Harriet Nevins	370 "	A. D. Lockwood	530 "
Sarah Danielson	522 "	C. E. Rogerson	500 "
W. R. Evans	3,920 "	Shaw family	1,323 "
F. J. Hale	500 "	R. P. Snelling	365 "
Herrick family	3,621 "		

Herrick and Evans held little, if any, of the preferred stock.

4. Information in this section comes from directors' and stockholders' minutes of the Saco-Lowell Shops, and from interviews with Frank J. Hale; Charles E. Cooke, secretary of the Shops in this period; Parkman D. Howe, treasurer of the company, 1923–24; Frank Lowell, present vice-president in charge of sales; Edward T. Taft, Herrick's brother-in-law and partner in the law firm of Herrick, Smith, Donald, Farley & Ketchum; John T. Noonan, member of the same firm and present Saco-Lowell counsel; Robert Cutler, president of the Old Colony Trust Co., former partner in the Herrick law firm, and a classmate of Robert Herrick, Jr., and others.

5. Robert F. Herrick, Jr., was born in 1893, attended Milton Academy and Harvard College (Class of 1916). Herrick went to work for the Saco-Lowell Shops after college and war service, starting as a molder in the foundry. He attended the Lowell Textile School, was graduated from the two-year course

in cotton spinning, and in 1920 left the Lowell shop to enter the Boston office (Robert Herrick, Jr., in Harvard Class Reports).

6. Parkman D. Howe, interview with author, Oct. 7, 1948. James C. Howe left the company to enter upon a banking career with the Old Colony Trust Co.

7. A possible exception may have been the Draper Corporation, which had the automatic loom. It is not definitely known whether the replacement of old looms with new had been substantially completed by 1921. There is some evidence that the replacement process was still going on; if so, Draper probably suffered less than the other shops.

8. Oscar E. Nutter, interview with author, Sept., 1948.

9. See Appendix 14 for trend of foreign textile-machinery imports to 1914.

10. Saco-Lowell records, National City Bank, "Report on Saco-Lowell Shops, September 20, 1926." This report presents the following statistics:

5-Year Period Ending	*Annual Average, Total Spindles Sold in U. S.*	*Annual Average Saco-Lowell Domestic Spindle Sales*	*Per Cent of Total*
1915	1,250,000	326,000	26.1
1920	875,000	255,000	29.2
1925	825,000	201,000	24.3

11. The Mason Machine Works had been a sporadic competitor, withdrawing from the textile-machinery market at times to manufacture printing presses, then coming back into the competitive picture again. With the retirement of its capable treasurer, William Bent, the company appears to have entered into a period of internal strife. The depression of the early 1920's found the company with inadequate working capital, and the manufacture of textile machinery appears to have ceased about 1925 or 1926. The manufacture of parts for Mason machines, however, was continued. The firm apparently passed out of the hands of William Mason's descendants in the early 1940's. Today (1949) the lineal descendant of the Mason Machine Works may be found in one wing of a brick building standing amid several acres of crumbling structures which housed this once powerful and famous company. Here the manufacture of textile-machinery parts is still carried on, though on a limited scale and under a different name.

12. The Metallic Drawing Roll Co. had its origins in the transition from leather-covered to metallic drawing rolls which was going on in the closing decades of the 19th century. The purchase of this company appears to have been actuated by Saco-Lowell's desire to acquire exclusive rights to the skills, patents, and equipment of the Drawing Roll Co., which was closed down in 1928 after five years of unbroken operating deficits. The Pawtucket Spinning Ring Co., on the contrary, was allowed to continue in operation at Central Falls, R. I. This company traced its history back to 1882, when John Booth left the

shop of Fales & Jenks to set up a small establishment of his own to manufacture spinning rings and travelers. Later the traveler department of the business was sold, and Booth concentrated on spinning rings alone. The business passed in family line to J. Arthur MacAllen, and in 1909 a new brick shop was constructed. Saco-Lowell's offer to buy the establishment was actuated by a desire to assure itself of a steady supply of this vital part at preferential prices. MacAllen appears to have had little choice but to sell, since Saco-Lowell was his largest customer and both Draper and Whitin either built these parts themselves or had already established contacts with ring suppliers. Some new equipment was added following the purchase, but few other changes were made, and MacAllen continued to manage this shop until 1938, when he was replaced by Harold E. Robbins, who was sent to Pawtucket from the Biddeford shop.

13. In 1918 the Whitin loom patents were distributed to Whitin stockholders as a dividend, and turned over by those stockholders to the Draper firm. Navin, *Whitin Machine Works,* Chap. 13, section entitled "Competition from the Draper Automatic Loom."

14. Navin, *op. cit.,* Chap. 16, section entitled "The Textile Machinery Industry Retrenches."

15. See Navin, *op. cit.,* Table 12.

16. Saco-Lowell records, National City Bank Survey, 1926, p. 34.

17. So dependent upon personal effort and influence was the sale of textile machinery that in this period, as in earlier years, advertising expenditures were very modest. From 1914 to 1918, the only years for which advertising expense figures can be separated from general selling expense, expenditures on advertising were never larger than .2 per cent of sales.

18. H. E. Michl, *The Textile Industries* (Washington, 1938), pp. 144–146; Warren F. Doane, *The Flight of Capital and Industry from Massachusetts* (Philadelphia, 1935), pp. 8–25.

19. Over the period from 1897 to 1926 the Lowell shop sold approximately 800,000 Bradford-system worsted spindles. The Bradford system of worsted spinning was best adapted to hard fabric for men's clothing. In 1923 the Lowell shop began to build machinery for the so-called "French system," which was better adapted to softer fabrics for women's wear. For both systems the machinery market in America was limited (2,800,000 worsted spindles, in 1926, as compared with 38,800,000 cotton spindles), and more than three-quarters of the worsted machinery in place in American mills was foreign-built. Worsted machinery sales over the 1913–26 period totaled approximately $10,000,000. The spun silk machinery enjoyed an even narrower market. This machinery was for spinning waste silk and filaments from the broken cocoons, in contrast to the reeled or thrown silk which was processed on different machines to make the true silk yarn. In 1926 there were fewer than 225,000 spun-silk spindles in America, in comparison with more than 2,000,000 thrown-silk spindles. Saco-Lowell's chief market for this machinery, however, was in the Orient. Between 1916 and 1925, inclusive, 153,000 spun-

silk spindles were sold by Saco-Lowell, as compared with 420,000 worsted spindles. Dollar sales of silk machinery from 1912 to 1926 totaled $3,340,000.

20. *Textile World,* vol. xxxvii, Oct., 1908–Mar., 1909, p. 636.

21. National City Bank Survey, pp. 12–13.

22. Much of the information about foreign sales comes from talks with W. F. Lowell, present vice-president in charge of sales and former foreign salesman, and from C. C. Hedrick, who traveled extensively for the company in China and Japan in the period under consideration.

23. An effort was made to build up the European market through an export company, which was formed to perform there the same services that Andersen, Meyer & Company was providing in the Orient. Edward Farnham Greene, of Lockwood, Greene & Company, was in Europe shortly after the end of the first World War. Greene, a man of great enthusiasms and promotional ability, thought he saw an opportunity for American machine shops to participate in the rebuilding of the French textile industry. This idea he carried back to America. Saco-Lowell, Whitin, and Draper jointly backed the American Textile Machinery Corporation, formed in 1919 to effect the invasion of the European market. A Paris office was opened, and an agreement was concluded for the sharing of orders on preparatory machinery between Whitin and Saco-Lowell. At one point J. F. Havey, Saco-Lowell's foreign sales manager, served as president of the company.

This venture was not a success. Saco-Lowell received through the new firm orders for machinery for only one complete mill in France and one in Germany. Small orders were received, but the wholesale rebuilding of the French textile industry which Edward Farnham Greene felt would grow out of the European armistice agreements did not immediately materialize, and the price differential in Europe between American machines and those of the English, Swiss, and Alsatian shops inevitably excluded Whitin and Saco-Lowell from this market. In 1922 the American Textile Machinery Corporation was abandoned. The only tangible benefit which Saco-Lowell realized from the venture was a contact with LeBlan & Cie., which was the seed of Saco-Lowell's long-draft spinning development (W. F. Lowell, interview with author, Dec., 1948).

24. U. S. Department of Commerce, Bureau of Foreign and Domestic Commerce, *Foreign Commerce and Navigation of the United States,* Exports of Domestic Merchandise.

25. Navin, *op. cit.,* Chap. 15, section entitled "Foreign Sales."

26. Saco-Lowell subscribed to $100,000 of Andersen, Meyer preferred stock. This holding was increased in 1925 by the addition of $183,700 of preferred stock accepted in settlement of a claim against the Yu Foong Cotton Mills which Saco-Lowell had assumed.

27. National City Bank Survey, p. 16.

28. Material in this section, unless otherwise noted, comes from "Appraisal of the Saco-Lowell Shops as of November 1, 1912," Lockwood, Greene & Co., Inc., Engineers, Boston, Massachusetts.

29. Many vestiges of the old shop-owned tenement system remained, although, as noted in an earlier chapter, neither the Newton, the Biddeford, nor the Lowell company had built so many tenements as had Whitin, Draper, or many of the cotton mills. In 1912 the company owned 21 houses accommodating 39 families at Biddeford. In Lowell there were 25 tenements accommodating about 60 families. At Newton, where the shop had been forced by inadequate community accommodations to maintain many homes, 35 houses accommodating 51 families were owned by the company. The word "tenement" does not accurately describe these dwellings, most of which were one- and two-family houses. Only at Lowell were "tenements" in the present-day sense of the word maintained. Here, on Dutton Street, stood four three-story brick structures which appear to have accommodated ten families each.

By 1926 all the Lowell tenements and most of the Biddeford houses had been sold or torn down to make room for plant additions. At Newton, however, the trend was in the opposite direction. After 1912 the influx of workers forced the company to acquire 20 additional houses with room for 23 families. To further ease the impact of business boom upon the primarily residential community at Newton Upper Falls, the Pettee Inn was constructed in 1912, and a hotel, a clubhouse, and a boathouse with bowling alleys were acquired thereafter. The record indicates that no residential properties were disposed of at Newton between 1912 and 1926.

30. The oldest machine tool in use at Biddeford in 1912 was a double-column metal slotter, with countershaft and ten-inch stroke, built in 1845 in the shop. The oldest machine in use at Lowell was a lathe with eight-foot swing and twelve-foot bed, built by the Union Works of S. Wilmarth and possibly acquired by the Boston Manufacturing Company in 1820. If the date assigned this lathe by the Lockwood, Greene survey is accurate, this machine, it should be noted, antedated the first machine shop at Lowell and may have been used in the early shop at Waltham. Company tradition, however, says that it was built in 1825. Presumably this was the lathe which turned the turret rings of the *Quinsigamond* in 1864. The subsequent history of the *Quinsigamond* lathe is almost as interesting as its early history. About 1928, when the Lowell plant was dismantled, the lathe was sold as scrap, and subsequently was seen no more. During World War II a former superintendent of the Lowell shop was astonished to discover, on a trip through a large New England metal-working plant, the old lathe standing on the shop floor. Its bed was cracked and makeshift gears had been fitted, but the ancient relic had operated through its fifth war. Inquiring into the circumstances surrounding the acquisition of the lathe, the former superintendent was told that it had been purchased at the start of the war for several thousand dollars.

The oldest machines in use at Newton in 1912 were youthful in comparison with this hoary survivor of more than a century of textile-machinery building. At Newton was still to be found in operation a special turning lathe built in the shop of Otis Pettee in 1850. Kitson's oldest was an eight-foot turning lathe built by the Putnam Machine Co. and acquired in 1870.

31. National City Bank Survey, p. 58.

32. Herrick's expenditures at Lowell included many new tools, a pattern storehouse (actually used for manufacturing, rather than storage), and a large concrete shop building on Dutton Street to house the new French worsted department.

33. National City Bank Survey, pp. 12–13.

34. H. B. Drury, *Scientific Management, A History and Criticism,* Columbia University Studies in History, Economics, and Public Law, vol. lxv, no. 2.

35. Navin, *op. cit.,* Chap. 15, section entitled "Scientific Management."

36. My information about production controls and efficiency engineering at the various shops in the 1912–26 period comes from talks with many of the men who were superintendents then, with others who were in a position in the various offices to observe these systems, and with a few men who worked in the shops. Much material was provided by A. V. Stuart, who served as plant accountant at Biddeford from 1928 to 1945, and whose keen historical interest in this usually neglected field has preserved many more details than can possibly be presented here.

37. A. V. Stuart, letter to author, Nov. 17, 1948.

38. *Ibid.*

39. There seems no way to measure fairly the relative success and efficiency of the Bedaux installation at each of the four shops. The best installation unquestionably was at Newton, where a modern and already highly efficient plant was engaged in the production in large volume of a standardized product. When the Newton organization became integrated into the Biddeford plant, the looseness of the Biddeford standards made it necessary to re-study most of the Newton operations and loosen them in order to eliminate inequalities in earnings which otherwise would have existed. The Kitson installation probably ranked second to that at Newton in effectiveness, the problems here being minimized by the small size of the operation. The Lowell installation was complicated by the diversity of operations performed there, many of which were new in the shop. Standards were set with great rapidity there (in order to minimize installation fees), and were generally set too tight. Nevertheless, Bedaux principles were closely followed and many aspects of the installation were commendable. The Biddeford installation was the least effective of any. Here standards were loosely set, there was much duplication in the standards setup, and checking on piece counts and on operation setups was inadequate.

40. National City Bank Survey, pp. 27, 39.

41. From Jan. 1, 1920, to June 30, 1926, the Pawtucket Spinning Ring Company reported sales of $950,300 and net profits of $240,800. Dividends paid to Saco-Lowell from 1922 to 1926 totaled $85,000, and an additional $85,000 was allowed the parent company in quantity discounts. Between June 30, 1923, and June 30, 1926, the Metallic Drawing Roll Co. showed total sales of $215,500 and a total loss of $23,700.

42. After 1912 terminology crystallized along lines followed at Newton

before this time. The operating head of each shop was called the "agent." This was a minor but confusing variation from earlier practice at Lowell and Biddeford, where the head of the shop was often or usually referred to as the "superintendent."

43. Information about the 1922 strike comes from conversations with many of the men who were directly involved and from the files of the Biddeford *Weekly Journal.*

44. National City Bank Survey, p. 5.

45. Saco-Lowell gained from the Biddeford foundry strike a highly competent foundry boss — a man whose strike-breaking experience in many foundries had acquainted him with the best foundry practices. This man did much in subsequent years to modernize the obsolete Biddeford foundry, over which he ruled with undisputed authority for two decades. His presence there served as a perpetual reminder of the violence of 1923, and his removal became a primary, if unofficial, objective of later union protagonists.

46. For particularly interesting comparisons of labor policy see Charles W. Moore, *Timing a Century: History of the Waltham Watch Company* (Cambridge, Mass., 1945), Chap. xi; and Gras and Larson, *Casebook in American Business History,* case xxviii, Dennison Manufacturing Company, 1844–1938.

47. Financial information in this and succeeding paragraphs comes from Saco-Lowell records, Totals notebooks, ledgers, journals, and the National City Bank Survey of 1926.

48. Navin, *op. cit.,* Table 12.

49. Security acquisitions by the Textile Securities Co. included $1,500,000 of stock in the Harmony Mills, purchased from Saco-Lowell in 1916. This stock had been taken by Saco-Lowell to reduce the debts of the mill and "to bring nearer the time when dividends can safely be paid" (Textile Securities Co., Directors' and stockholders' minutes). A transaction of similar size was effected in 1917, when $1,500,000 of stock in the Winnboro Cotton Mills was purchased from Saco-Lowell. These two acquisitions appear to have been the largest made by Saco-Lowell and the Textile Securities Co. Security holdings of the latter, however, were not confined to mill stocks. In 1922, for example, the Textile Securities Co. held stock in the Old Colony Trust Co., The Universal Winding Co., the Greelock Co. (a holding company for Pacific Mill stock, promoted by Lockwood, Greene & Co.), the North American Edison Co., and several others. As had been the case with the Eastern Machinery Co. and the Saco and Pettee Machine Shops, securities were not permitted to accumulate. The greatest value of securities shown on the books of the Textile Securities Co. on semi-annual closing dates was $607,000, in Dec., 1926. Regular dividends were paid from 1913 to 1928 totaling $2,192,000, or an annual average return of about 13% on invested capital. The fact should be recalled, however, that the Saco-Pettee stockholders had actually paid nothing for this stock in 1912, receiving it somewhat in the nature of a stock dividend in the 1912 merger. Following the sale to Jackson & Curtis in 1928, liquidation dividends were paid totaling $1,609,362. After deducting the original paid-in capital valuation

of $800,000, this left a liquidation profit equivalent to 112% of that valuation.

50. Navin, *op. cit.,* Chap. 15, section entitled "Scientific Management."

51. A man who was a witness to these events of 1922 says that conservative Paul Snelling balked at the $2,643,800 preferred stock dividend, and yielded only when told that this increase in capitalization would invalidate Whitin's claim of being the "largest" textile-machine shop in America.

52. The H & B American Machine Company, faced with a similar problem, invested its surplus funds in the stock market and lost heavily in the 1929–32 stock-market crash. Thus, even this alternative solution was by no means free of hazard, quite aside from the vulnerability of such liquid assets to demands from stockholders for dividends. In the late 1920's, however, close to five million dollars of Whitin's liquid capital was invested outside the company. Losses in the early 1930's were small, owing to the financial acumen of E. Kent Swift, and this capital remained available for use when required by subsequent expansion in operations (Navin, *op. cit.,* Chap. 16, section entitled "Whitin Weathers the Depression").

53. Executive and supervisory salaries best reflect the burden of overhead which the company was carrying. Individual salaries were not excessive for a company of Saco-Lowell's size. The number of high-salaried positions, however, was relatively large. In 1922 salaries of $37,500 were paid to the general agent; $37,500 to the treasurer; $9,000 to the assistant general agent; $12,000 to the assistant treasurer; and $10,000 to the chairman of the board of directors. The functions of these offices were performed at Whitin by two men only (E. Kent Swift and L. P. Keeler). The general agent and the treasurer of Saco-Lowell received, in addition, a salary of $7,500 for filling similar offices in the Textile Securities Company. Saco-Lowell's Southern sales agent received $18,000, the Northern sales agent $9,000, and the foreign sales agent $12,000. The two shop agents and three superintendents received a total in salaries of $39,500. These salaries remained virtually unchanged in the depressed years following 1922.

The subject of executive salaries has received scant attention, for information is not available for much of Saco-Lowell's earlier history. A few comparisons between salaries in the 1920's and those paid in earlier years are possible. The general agent and the treasurer of the Saco and Pettee Machine Shops (1897–1910) received salaries of $7,500 each in 1897, a rate which was gradually increased until it stood at $18,000 in 1908 and following years. In addition, salaries of unknown size were received for similar positions held in the Eastern Machinery Co. The position of president of the Lowell Machine Shop paid $10,000 from 1905 to 1912, and the salary of the treasurer was $6,000. The treasurer received an additional salary of $14,000 for holding that office in the Kitson Machine Shop.

54. Frank J. Hale offered to purchase all of Saco-Lowell's paper from the Newton Trust Company, his "home" bank. When told that this paper could be had at a substantial discount, Hale insisted on paying the bank the face value of the notes.

55. These notes were to come due on Apr. 15, 1930, and were convertible into common stock at the rate of three shares of stock for each $100 note. Stockholders were given the right to subscribe for $50 of gold notes for each share held. Common stock of the company was changed from a par value of $100 a share to no par stock in order to conform with the terms of the indenture agreement.

56. The investigations were made by George S. Armstrong and Harding C. Woodall.

57. Assets carried on the balance sheets at $14,640,000 on June 30, 1926, were estimated in the National City Bank Survey to be worth $9,236,000 in gradual liquidation and $5,316,000 in drastic liquidation. In gradual liquidation the sum left after settling current trade and tax liabilities was sufficient to pay off the bank notes and the gold notes outstanding, leaving enough to redeem most of the preferred stock but still leaving nothing for the common stockholders.

58. *George F. Willett et al.* v. *Robert F. Herrick, et al.*, Massachusetts Superior Court, Dedham, Mass. Stenographer's transcript of trial proceedings, *Charge to Jury*, vol. i, pp. 19 ff., Baker Library, Harvard Graduate School of Business Administration.

CHAPTER XIV

1. The conditions of Edwards' contract with the company were as follows:

(1) Term of office for three years, beginning January 14, 1927.
(2) Salary of $40,000 the first year; $42,000 the second year; $45,000 the third year.
(3) 3,000 shares of Saco-Lowell common stock to be transferred to Edwards immediately; 1,500 shares more in one year; 1,500 shares more in two years; and option given to purchase 1,000 additional shares at $10 per share.

2. Edwards' work as industrial secretary of the Boston Chamber of Commerce included an effort to clear the Chamber of the political charge that it represented only the interests of big banks and big business. Edwards instituted an industrial survey of Greater Boston, and on the basis of this survey proposed the foundation of the Industrial Development Co., organized in 1911 to assist in financing small business enterprises in the area. This was Edwards' first real experience in industrial organization.

3. David F. Edwards, interview with N. S. B. Gras, Nov. 11, 1944.

4. *Ibid.*, Nov. 10, 1944.

5. According to the so-called "New Plan" of refinancing adopted on Nov. 1, 1926, Herrick, Hale, and Snelling agreed to subordinate the $895,000 of gold notes which they had taken in 1925 to the new three-year notes which were to be issued to the banks in 1926. The New Plan effected the following changes

in the liability accounts, the capital structure, and the funded debt of the company. Saco-Lowell records, Directors' minutes and Totals notebooks.

Sept. 30, 1926	*Dec. 31, 1926*
$4,000,000 Notes payable held by banks.	$4,550,000 3-year 5% Class A notes.
$ 550,000 7% 5-year gold notes taken by Boston banks in 1925.	
$ 122,500 7% 5-year gold notes taken by stockholders in 1925.	$ 122,500 7% 5-year gold notes.
$ 895,000 7% 5-year gold notes taken by Herrick, Hale and Snelling in 1925.	$ 895,000 7% 5-year gold notes (Class B notes).
$ 550,000 7% 5-year gold notes underwritten but not subscribed by Boston banks in 1925.	$ 550,000 3-year 5% notes (underwritten but not subscribed).
	$ 500,170 5-year 7% unsecured convertible notes, subscribed by officers and stockholders.
$1,250,000 Preferred stock.	$1,250,000 Preferred stock.
$2,643,800 Second preferred stock.	$2,643,800 Second preferred stock.
$4,132,742 Common stock (52,875 shares).	$3,365,672 Common stock (55,875 shares).

6. Information in this section comes from Kettley's survey, which is incorporated in the Saco-Lowell collection at Baker Library, Harvard Graduate School of Business Administration.

7. Planned capacity after consolidation compared with past output was as follows:

	Planned Output after 1928 Consolidation	*Annual Average Output 1912–1926*	*Annual Average Output 1917–1923*
Cards	1,500	1,527	1,882
Drawing Deliveries	3,000	2,810	3,616
Spinning Frames	1,500	1,341	1,612
Roving Frames	700	807	1,096
Twisters	300	314	437
Spoolers	100	124	142
Warpers	100	85	106
Slashers	100	55	54

8. Wilmot R. Evans, one of the most active of the Saco-Lowell directors, summarized the tax situation in these words:

> The tax rate is not important. The gross amount paid in taxes is the essential feature. Local taxes in Newton are high, and for the year 1927 were $55,717.00. The tax rate for 1927 is $27.40 per $1,000.00. The tendency in Newton is to assess well up to the value of the plant. The tax situation in general in Massachusetts is unsatisfactory. If we concentrate at Newton, we shall have a considerable portion of

our plant taxed at a high rate. It is therefore to the advantage of the company that part of the plant can be in some other state or community, where taxes are less severe. The taxes in Biddeford for 1927 were $42,671.00. The tax rate in Biddeford is high, but apparently the assessment is not excessive, and the gross tax is apparently less in proportion than in the other plants. I suppose that in the figure given in the report, the tax on inventory, which is levied in Maine, is included. This therefore increases the gross tax. Nevertheless, the advantage, from the standpoint of taxation, is all in favor of Biddeford. . . . In Lowell, the 1927 tax was $67,023.00. The tax on the Kitson plant was $12,073.00, and on the Kitson foundry, $3,841.00. These three items make a total tax paid to the City of Lowell of $87,937.00. Even with a reduction of $25,000.00 on the Lowell tax, which may or may not come, the amount to be paid in taxes in Lowell for the coming year would be $62,937.00, which is much higher than the gross tax paid either in Newton or in Biddeford.

Saco-Lowell records, Evans, "Saco-Lowell Machine Shops, Reorganization."

9. These figures are not strictly comparable, for some consolidation expense was absorbed in Newton and Biddeford operating costs, and the costs and savings arising from abandonment of the worsted business are not included in the estimated figures. The comparison between actual and estimated costs is useful only as a general measure of accomplishment. Estimates were taken from Kettley's survey and from the Directors' minutes (Mar. 13, 1928). Actual costs came from Saco-Lowell financial statements.

10. The absurdly low figure at which this land was sold is explicable in terms of the heavy tax liability which was attached to the land and to a contractual responsibility for maintaining the side walls of the two canals. Saco-Lowell's loss on this sale was largely offset by tax savings made possible by the transaction.

11. Michl, *The Textile Industries,* pp. 144–146. Spindles in place in New England declined from 18,856,000 in 1921–22 to 13,478,000 in 1929–30. Over the same period spindles in place in cotton-growing States increased from 16,074,000 to 19,122,000. Active spindles in New England declined from 17,-928,000 to 11,351,000, and in the cotton-growing States increased from 15,-906,000 to 18,585,000.

12. Saco-Lowell Shops, *Annual Report to Stockholders,* Dec. 31, 1928.

13. These annual commentaries by Saco-Lowell's president provide a graphic and valuable insight into the dynamic business situation of the depression years. Selected excerpts are presented in Appendix 17.

14. David F. Edwards, interview with N. S. B. Gras, Dec. 15, 1944.

15. This bonus plan was on a relatively small scale. Stock distributed to employees under this plan in 1933, 1934, 1935, and 1936 totaled $2,750.

16. The Biddeford shop was paying the Cumberland Power & Light Company $65,000 per year for power in 1932. It was estimated at this time that on the same scale of activity as was then prevailing Saco-Lowell would buy $125,000 of electricity if Newton operations were moved to Biddeford.

17. Saco-Lowell Shops, Minutes of directors' meetings, Oct. 20, 1931.

18. The need for subordination of such claims was scarcely questioned, and on only one occasion was there any substantial protest by stockholders against the terms of the various refunding operations. This protest was lodged by Roger W. Babson against the 1932 refinancing plan. The Babson Park Co., holding 16,820 shares of convertible notes, refused to exchange these notes for the extended notes specified in the plan. Rather than incur the risk of a lawsuit at a time when new working-capital loans were being negotiated, a settlement with Babson was effected. Saco-Lowell issued new notes to the Babson Park Co., and these notes were then immediately purchased by Saco-Lowell officers. Hale purchased $5,000; Robert Herrick, Sr., purchased $8,400 (through the Manufacturers Co., his personal holding company); and Wilmot Evans purchased $1,250 of the Babson notes. This incident, trivial though it was, well illustrates the support given the company throughout this trying period by the various officers.

19. Navin, *Whitin Machine Works,* Chap. 16, section entitled "The Textile Machinery Industry Retrenches."

20. *Ibid.,* Table 12.

21. Shortly after the first World War a decided change in cotton fibers began to be noticed. These changes were brought about by the adoption of early and rapidly maturing varieties of cotton, intensive cultivation, and heavy fertilization. All these factors tended to produce a crop in which the staple in any given lot of cotton varied between wide limits, with a large proportion of the staple much shorter than the nominal length. For example, tests revealed that in a lot of cotton with nominally one-inch staple, as much as 85% might be under specified length.

22. The clearest and most complete account of long-draft spinning that I have seen is to be found in "Long Draft Spinning, Its History, Present Status and Future Possibilities" (*Saco-Lowell Bulletin,* Apr., 1942, p. 22), by Robert M. Jones, executive engineer, Saco-Lowell Shops. Much of the information in this section has been taken from that source.

23. A. K. Landau memorandum to David F. Edwards, July 15, 1949, Saco-Lowell manuscript collection, Baker Library.

24. Jones, *op. cit.,* pp. 9–10.

25. Unless otherwise noted, information about the development of the long-draft roving frame comes from *W. G. Reynolds, E. A. Terrell, and The Terrell Machine Company* v. *Saco-Lowell Shops,* District Court of the United States, Middle District, North Carolina, *Defendants Brief,* Jan. 1, 1943; *Reply Brief for Defendants* (undated); Depositions of C. Wendell Hill, R. A. Kettley, R. M. Jones, Carl Webber, William G. Reynolds, and others; *Opinion, Judgment and Decree,* Judge Johnson J. Hayes, United States District Judge.

26. The difficulty in applying a long draft to the roving process lay in the looseness of the strand at the roving stage. This characteristic seriously hampered efforts to apply methods of fiber control which had made long drafts possible in the spinning process, at which stage, of course, the yarn was much

better formed and more cohesive. Reynolds had the idea of performing two drafting operations (instead of one) on one machine. To do this he interposed between the two drafting elements a device which condensed or folded the loose strand of fiber and gave it sufficient strength to withstand the additional drafting. The folding device consisted of a revolving tongue and groove arrangement which formed the sliver. The difficulty with this arrangement was that the movable parts clogged, and the tongue and groove frame was not self-threading, thereby increasing the necessity for attention to the machine by the operative.

27. Jones substituted a stationary forming trumpet for Reynolds' movable tongue and groove device. The "J1" frame was the original version of Jones' invention. The "J2" frame (first sold in 1938) adapted the long-draft roving process to long-staple rayons. The "J3" frame (first sold in 1940) was an improvement on the "J1" machine, which had shown a tendency to clog up with lint and dirt.

28. *Reynolds* v. *Saco-Lowell, Defendants Brief,* p. 79.

29. Because of tax savings the Reynolds judgment actually cost Saco-Lowell only about $25,000 (David F. Edwards interview with author, June 17, 1949).

30. Reynolds charged that Frederick E. Banfield, who resigned from Saco-Lowell and went to Whitin as Works Manager in 1935, had taken his knowledge of Reynolds' work with him and had used it in developing the new Whitin long-draft roving element. Banfield vigorously denied this charge and stated that he had no influence upon the work at the Whitin Works. Judge Hayes stated in the Whitin case opinion, "This is a very complicated case and the most skillfully contested patent case which has ever confronted the court. . . . It presents a striking example of a branch of federal court jurisdiction which should be set aside exclusively for determination by a court of competent patent experts instead of leaving it to judges who like myself are entirely devoid of mechanical skill and therefore unable to bring to the solution of the case the skill essential to the broader and better decision." As in the Saco-Lowell case, Judge Hayes appears to have based his decision upon the moral rather than the legal-technical issues and adopted the position that he was acting as a protector of an individual set upon by an unscrupulous combination of Northern machinery manufacturers (Navin, *op. cit.,* Appendix 15).

31. The Saco-Lowell advertising department made certain that these developments were not ignored. The "New Deal" inspired this editorial comment in the January–February, 1934, issue of the *Saco-Lowell Bulletin:*

> We firmly believe that the principles of the new deal having to do with wages and working conditions have practically prohibited the further use of much obsolete machinery and have made the question of mechanical efficiency one of the most important confronting mill executives at this time.

32. This was a high compliment to R. A. Kettley, who came to be known as a sheet-metal man and who was instrumental in furthering the conversion

process at Saco-Lowell. Works Manager Tarr, despite a lifetime of training in textile-machinery building traditions, also favored replacement of iron with steel whenever possible. One basic objection to the use of steel in textile machinery was that in using it the large shops laid themselves open to competition (particularly in opening and picking machinery) from smaller shops which were springing up in the South. These small shops could machine steel parts where they could not, for lack of the tremendously expensive foundry installations of Whitin and Saco-Lowell, reproduce cast-iron parts and machines.

33. Moore, *Timing A Century,* Chap. vii.

CHAPTER XV

1. David F. Edwards, *Annual Report,* Saco-Lowell Shops, Nov. 30, 1940. Unless otherwise noted, the information for this section is taken from the various annual reports.

2. Unless otherwise noted, information about Saco-Lowell's war contracts has been gathered from talks with men in the shop and from various departmental reports covering specific phases of the war effort.

3. Early in 1942 the first of the so-called Ordnance Industry Integrating Committees was formed. These committees were conceived by Lieutenant General L. H. Campbell, Jr., Chief of Ordnance, in order to facilitate exchange of engineering information, manufacturing experience, critical materials, machine tools, and machine capacity among the many sub-contracting firms who were working on parts for certain types of ordnance items. On May 1, 1942, the formation of the Remote Control Systems Committee was authorized, and this committee was divided into eight sub-committees. Saco-Lowell became a member of the Large Cable System Sub-Committee, which served to coördinate the activities of the four principal sub-contractors for this particular ordnance item.

4. Information in this section and in Appendix 18 about labor relations and union affairs comes from reminiscences of Victor Beecroft, former assistant works manager and personnel manager of the company, who was intimately connected with union negotiations. These reminiscences, which were very kindly forwarded to me in manuscript form, proved to be invaluable in reconstructing the events of the 1941–47 period. Additional and corroborative information was obtained in talks with David F. Edwards, with several men in the Biddeford office and the Industrial Relations Department, and with men in the shop. Other material came from A. V. Stuart, former plant accountant. The company placed at my disposal all files of executive correspondence in the Boston office.

5. In summary, the 1948 labor agreement contained the following principal provisions, exclusive of wage increases. Some of these provisions, of course, had been established by earlier contracts, and some had been made compulsory by federal legislation.

(1) Modified union shop.
(2) Check-off of union dues.
(3) Replacement of existing wage incentive system.
(4) Promise of union coöperation in establishing new wage incentive system.
(5) 10 cent per hour premium for night-shift work.
(6) Guarantee of 4 hours of work and pay to employees ordered to report to work at regular hours. Guarantee of full-shift work and pay for employees ordered to report on night shift.
(7) Equality of pay for women employees with men performing comparable jobs.
(8) Company to furnish union with occupational job rates and changes thereto.
(9) Time-and-one-half pay for work in excess of 8 hours per day and 40 hours per week.
(10) Double pay for Sunday shifts.
(11) Time-and-one-half pay for work on New Year's Day, Patriots' Day (April 19), Memorial Day (May 30), Independence Day (July 4), Labor Day, Armistice Day (November 11), Thanksgiving Day, and Christmas.
(12) New Year's Day, Patriots' Day, Memorial Day, Labor Day, Thanksgiving Day, and Christmas to be paid holidays, even though they fall on unscheduled workdays.
(13) Guarantee against strikes and lockouts. Provision for arbitration of disputes.
(14) Effective recognition of seniority principle (in contrast to the vague provisions of the 1941 agreement).
(15) Paid vacations.
(16) $500 company-paid life insurance for employees; $1,000 life insurance if death is due to accident not already covered by Workmen's Compensation.
(17) Dismemberment benefits up to $500.
(18) Company-paid hospitalization benefits up to 31 days for accidents; 14 days for maternity cases.
(19) Company-paid sickness and accident benefits; maximum $20 per week, 13 weeks.
(20) Company-paid doctor visits up to $150 per year.
(21) Instruction in time-study procedure outside working hours, class members to be paid at regular hourly rates.
(22) Safety equipment provided by company.

6. Information in this section is taken from Victor Beecroft's sketch of the background and development of the Industrial Relations Department, with some additional information provided by men in the present department. Conclusions advanced are my own.

7. The Personnel Department in 1944 administered the following activities: grievance procedure and investigation; employment and employment advertising; standards and piece rates (certain aspects, only); job analysis and evaluation; employee classification; absentee and attendance reports; safety; medical; welfare; plant hygiene; employee counseling; veteran placement and counseling; employee transportation; gas rationing; cafeteria; plant matron; medical department; plant physician; janitress service.

At this time a suitable building (Number 17), affording 9,000 square feet of floor space, was provided to house the new department. By June of 1945 the offices had been set up and were functioning. For a time the Employment Department and the Medical Section were geographically separated from the Personnel Department, necessitating the duplication of many wage records.

In August, 1945, A. A. Alden came to work for the company to revive the apprentice training program (see text) and later that same year Glen R. Cheney, then Deputy Area Director of the War Manpower Commission, joined the company and began the task of preparing a policy manual. At this same time the Personnel Department took over the internal administration of the company's Retirement Annuity Plan for salaried employees, and home visitation of sick and absent employees was begun. The Employees' Activities Association was formed under a manager (C. Parslow) elected by the employees, with E. F. Lewis, assistant personnel manager, representing the company. In January, 1946, the Personnel Department moved into its new premises on the ground floor of Building 17, to which floor the Employment Department and the Medical Department were moved in April of that year. The title of the Personnel Department, now entirely housed under one roof (except for the Cafeteria) was changed to the "Industrial Relations Department."

Wage control was transferred from the Employment Department to the Job Evaluation and Wage Department, and all records were consolidated under a new filing section. Routine divisional functions and divisional stenography and typing, together with a divisional reference library, divisional files, and mailing, were placed under an office manager, and a receptionist was installed in the main entry to help stem the previous disturbance caused by visitors wandering through the various sections and engaging their members in conversation while looking for someone who was absent at the time. The office manager was also made responsible for a properly operated bulletin-board service throughout the plant.

In the preparation of the new quarters for the Medical Department, full advantage had been taken of the opportunity for installing new and modern equipment. Registered nurses were engaged for the first time and given laboratory training in Boston, under the direction of the Liberty Mutual Life Insurance Co. A plant medical laboratory was equipped and put into operation in October, 1946, where tests were given to prospective employees and, periodically, to older employees. Appropriate follow-up, in coöperation with the State Department of Health, or with the employee's family physician, was pursued. Anti-influenza inoculation was offered free to all employees in the winter of 1946–47. At the same time a shop safety program was instituted. In February, 1947, a meeting of employees interested in forming an employees' credit union was called and officers elected. Initial steps toward an Employee Indoctrination program were taken early in 1947.

Other activities, both within and outside the framework of the Industrial Relations Department, contemplated raising the educational standards of the company employees. At the present time (1949) the company is sponsoring evening instruction classes in textile machinery, blueprint reading, foundry practice, business-letter writing, office practice, mathematics, mechanical drawing, manufacturing methods, applied pyschology, metallurgy, slide-rule reading, stenography, English, and economics.

8. The reader is urged to consult Navin, *Whitin Machine Works,* Chap. 17, entitled "New Product Developments, 1927–1949," for a detailed account of technical developments in the field of non-cotton fibers, and for an excellent assessment of the charge of technological stagnation in the field of textile machinery.

9. This comparison contains a distortion. Dollar sales in 1947 include long-draft change-overs, lattice openers, and combers, none of which were being sold in 1920. This element of inconsistency, however, in no way detracts from the comparison of machine units sold nor does it appear to distort the picture of relative dollar sales to a significant degree.

10. The machinery price index was compiled by myself from actual prices of Saco-Lowell machines. The metal prices were taken from a company report on foundry costs dated July 23, 1946. The wage index was prepared by the company. The wage and machinery price index annually was as follows, with 1941 as the base year:

	Machinery prices	*Wages*
1941	100	100
1942	115	133
1943	115	140
1944	115	145
1945	152	154
1946	184	190
1947	188	210
1948	201	245

11. David F. Edwards, interview with author, June 17, 1949.

12. My sources of information about the reorganization have been too diverse for detailed enumeration. I talked with scores of people in Biddeford and in Boston. The scope of these interviews ranged from the top to the bottom of the organization. In addition to these firsthand accounts I also spent considerable time examining executive correspondence in the Boston office, in order to cross check on information received by word of mouth.

INDEX

Bei Fragen zur Produktsicherheit wenden Sie sich bitte an:
If you have any questions regarding product safety,
please contact:

Walter de Gruyter GmbH
Genthiner Straße 13
10785 Berlin
productsafety@degruyterbrill.com